Frommer's®

Provence & the Riviera

5th Edition

by Darwin Porter & Danforth Prince

Here's what the critics say about Frommer's:

"Amazingly easy to use. Very portable, very complete."

—Booklist

"Detailed, accurate, and easy-to-read information for all price ranges."
—Glamour Magazine

"Hotel information is close to encyclopedic."

—Des Moines Sunday Register

"Frommer's Guides have a way of giving you a real feel for a place."
—Knight Ridder Newspapers

Wiley Publishing, Inc.

About the Authors

As a team of veteran travel writers, **Darwin Porter** and **Danforth Prince** have produced numerous titles for Frommer's, including best-selling guides to Italy, France, the Caribbean, England, and Germany. Porter, a former bureau chief of the *Miami Herald*, is also a Hollywood biographer. His most recent releases are *The Secret Life of Humphrey Bogart* and *Katherine the Great*, the latter a close-up of the private life of the late Katherine Hepburn. Prince was formerly employed by the Paris bureau of the *New York Times* and is today the president of Blood Moon Productions and other media-related firms.

Published by:

Wiley Publishing, Inc.

111 River St.
Hoboken, NJ 07030-5774

ISBN-13: 978-0-7645-9824-1
ISBN-10: 0-7645-9824-4

Editor: Marc Nadeau
Production Editors: Jana M. Stefanciosa
Cartographer: Liz Puhl
Photo Editor: Richard Fox
Production by Wiley Indianapolis Composition Services

Front cover photo: Sunflower fields in the Vaucluse, Provence.
Back cover photo: Menton's scenic harbor.

For information on our other products and services or to obtain technical support, please contact our Customer Care Department within the U.S. at 800/762-2974, outside the U.S. at 317/572-3993 or fax 317/572-4002.

Wiley also publishes its books in a variety of electronic formats. Some content that appears in print may not be available in electronic formats.

Manufactured in the United States of America

5 4 3 2 1

Contents

⑦ The Eastern Riviera: From Biot to Monaco to Menton   282

Appendix: Glossary of Useful Terms   358

Index   365

List of Maps

An Invitation to the Reader

In researching this book, we discovered many wonderful places—hotels, restaurants, shops, and more. We're sure you'll find others. Please tell us about them, so we can share the information with your fellow travelers in upcoming editions. If you were disappointed with a recommendation, we'd love to know that, too. Please write to:

Frommer's Provence & the Riviera, 5th Edition
Wiley Publishing, Inc. • 111 River St. • Hoboken, NJ 07030-5774

An Additional Note

Please be advised that travel information is subject to change at any time—and this is especially true of prices. We therefore suggest that you write or call ahead for confirmation when making your travel plans. The authors, editors, and publisher cannot be held responsible for the experiences of readers while traveling. Your safety is important to us, however, so we encourage you to stay alert and be aware of your surroundings. Keep a close eye on cameras, purses, and wallets, all favorite targets of thieves and pickpockets.

Other Great Guides for Your Trip:

Frommer's Paris
Frommer's France
Frommer's Europe
Frommer's Irreverant Guide to Paris
Frommer's Memorable Walks in Paris
Suzy Gershman's Born to Shop Paris
Frommer's Gay & Lesbian Europe

Frommer's Star Ratings, Icons & Abbreviations

Every hotel, restaurant, and attraction listing in this guide has been ranked for quality, value, service, amenities, and special features using a **star-rating system.** In country, state, and regional guides, we also rate towns and regions to help you narrow down your choices and budget your time accordingly. Hotels and restaurants are rated on a scale of zero (recommended) to three stars (exceptional). Attractions, shopping, nightlife, towns, and regions are rated according to the following scale: zero stars (recommended), one star (highly recommended), two stars (very highly recommended), and three stars (must-see).

In addition to the star-rating system, we also use **seven feature icons** that point you to the great deals, in-the-know advice, and unique experiences that separate travelers from tourists. Throughout the book, look for:

Finds	Special finds—those places only insiders know about
Fun Fact	Fun facts—details that make travelers more informed and their trips more fun
Kids	Best bets for kids and advice for the whole family
Moments	Special moments—those experiences that memories are made of
Overrated	Places or experiences not worth your time or money
Tips	Insider tips—great ways to save time and money
Value	Great values—where to get the best deals

The following **abbreviations** are used for credit cards:

AE	American Express	DISC	Discover	V	Visa
DC	Diners Club	MC	MasterCard		

Frommers.com

Now that you have the guidebook to a great trip, visit our website at **www.frommers.com** for travel information on more than 3,000 destinations. With features updated regularly, we give you instant access to the most current trip-planning information available. At Frommers.com, you'll also find the best prices on airfares, accommodations, and car rentals—and you can even book travel online through our travel booking partners. At Frommers.com, you'll also find the following:

- Online updates to our most popular guidebooks
- Vacation sweepstakes and contest giveaways
- Newsletter highlighting the hottest travel trends
- Online travel message boards with featured travel discussions

What's New in Provence & the Riviera

The area from the Languedoc-Roussillon region in western France to the string of Riviera towns in eastern France is the most dynamic part of the country. It is also the most fashionable, and trends change rapidly. Here is a preview of some of the major changes occurring in this sunny region.

TOULOUSE After a complete renovation, **Hôtel de la Garonne,** 22 Descente de la Halle aux Poissons (℃ **05-34-31-94-80**), has emerged as the most charming and tranquil boutique hotel in the city. It's a snug retreat in the heart of Toulouse. See p. 79.

Among restaurants, **Le Bon Vivre,** 15 bis Place Wilson (℃ **05-61-23-07-17**), has become the most cost-conscious bistro serving the hearty regional cuisine of the Southwest. Occupying a historic 18th-century mansion, its chefs turn out Toulouse's best cassoulet. See p. 82.

MONTPELLIER This university city's most fabled attraction, **Musée Fabre,** 2 rue Montpellieret (℃ **04-67-14-83-00**), is scheduled to reopen in 2006 following renovations. Visitors will be able to visit one of the great provincial art museums in France, occupying the former Hotel Massilian where Molière played for a season. See p. 116.

ARLES An expat Québeçoise, Madame Gigi Boucher, has opened **Chez Gigi,** 49 rue des Arènes (℃ **04-90-96-68-59**), serving an unusual menu in that it offers both a savory Mediterranean cuisine and a list of regional specialties from Mexico. She's credited with waking up the sleepy taste buds of Arles in her distinctive new restaurant. See p. 158.

APT Although it opened months earlier, **Domaine des Andéols,** Les Andeois, Saint-Saturnin-les-Apt (℃ **04-90-75-50-63**), only began to be discovered by the French critics of gastronomy in 2004 and early in 2005. An upmarket country inn, it was created by the world's most famous chef, Alain Ducasse. The location is in a tranquil setting 40km (24 miles) southeast of Avignon, surrounded by lakes, gardens, and orchards. See p. 181.

AIX-EN-PROVENCE The leading woman chef of this ancient city, Reine Sammut, has transformed a former candy factory into **Le Passage,** 6 bis rue Mazarine (℃ **04-42-37-09-00**). It is now a showcase for her Mediterranean cuisine in a contemporary brasserie setting. Just wait until you try her deep-fried stuffed vegetables. See p. 190.

ST-TROPEZ This chic resort continues to take antique buildings and turn them into hotels of charm and grace. **Hôtel La Maison Blanche,** place des Lices (℃ **04-94-97-52-66**), was converted from a private 19th-century villa into a government-rated four-star hotel in the center of town. A 3-minute walk from the beach, it's been much expanded and altered since its original construction. See p. 225. In another development, a 19th-century town house has been turned into **Hôtel La Mistralée,** 1 av. du Général Leclerc (© **04-98-12-91-12**), lying only a 2-minute walk from the old port. Each room is individually and beautifully designed. See p. 226.

The latest restaurant of consequence is **Colors,** 3 rue du Temple (© **04-94-97-00-15**), serving the best grills in town from a wood-burning oven. Fresh meats and fresh fish are slowly cooked to perfection. See p. 228.

CANNES Two boutique hotels have opened here that are among the most tranquil at the resort. **California's Hôtel,** 8 Traverse Alexandre-III (© **04-93-94-12-21**), is set in a scented garden of citrus and olive trees with an outdoor pool. Rooms are furnished with handmade furniture and original artwork. See p. 256. Equal in charm is **Le Cavenish,** 11 bd. Carnot (© **04-97-06-26-00**), converted into a charming boutique hotel from a late-19th-century residence. Rooms were completely modernized in a massive renovation, but many of the old-fashioned architectural details were left intact. See p. 258.

But the big resort news is a 32km (20-mile) drive north of Cannes. **Four Seasons Provence at Terre Blanche,** Tourrettes (© **04-94-39-36-00**) has become one of the grandest and most deluxe hotels along the Côte d'Azur since opening. With two 18-hole golf courses, it is awash with amenities, luxuries, and superb accommodations that come in many shapes or sizes. From its spa to its array of first-class restaurants and facilities, this resort represents Riviera-style living on a grand scale. See p. 259.

CAGNES-SUR-MER The modern hilltop hotel of **Domaine Cocagne,** 30 Chemin du Pain de Sucre (© **04-92-13-57-77**), is now the finest at this resort set in a 4.8 hectare (12 acre) park. A swimming pool, savory Mediterranean cuisine, and well-furnished bedrooms make this one a winner. See p. 297.

NICE Once hailed as the Queen of the Nice Riviera, **Palais de la Méditerranée,** 13–15 promenade des Anglais (© **04-92-14-77-00**), has made a spectacular comeback. Shuttered since 1978, this glittering seaside palace, once the rendezvous point for celebrities, has undergone a massive restoration. Its Art Deco facade remains, although everything is state of the art with such new facilities as a casino and a fitness center. See p. 308.

In another development, **Hotel Hi,** 3 av. des Fleurs (© **04-97-07-26-26**), has been created out of a boardinghouse. The hotel actually opened in 2003, but did not come into its own until the winter of 2004 and 2005 when it was discovered by the French press. It's the most avant-garde place to stay in Nice. See p. 309.

MONACO This principality forges ahead with new developments in the wake of Prince Rainier's death. Loews is gone, having turned over management to Fairmont. This modern palace is now the **Fairmont Hôtel Monte Carlo,** 12 av. des Spélugues (© **93-50-65-00**). It's the same hotel as we go to press, although improvements might be made during the life of this edition. See p. 344.

Even bigger news has been generated by the opening of **Hôtel Port Palace,** 7 av. John F. Kennedy (© **97-97-90-00**), Monte Carlo's first boutique hotel. It overlooks Monte Carlo Marina and is the last word in opulence. Each of the *luxe* accommodations is a suite, and some units contain a steam room. See p. 344.

The Societé des Bains de Mer has opened its first hotel in 75 years: **Monte-Carlo Bay Hotel & Resort,** 40 av. Princess Grace (© **92-16-28-32**). It's a sumptuous new address, set in a lush 4-hectare (10-acre) Mediterranean garden. From its lavish casino to its pools and spa treatments, it attracts a well-heeled client seeking the pampered life.

The Best of Provence & the Riviera

Provence is one of the world's most evocative regions—both the western area, known simply as Provence, whose landscapes and magical light have seduced innumerable artists, and the eastern coastal area, known as the Riviera, whose beach resorts have seduced innumerable hedonists. Provence and the Riviera are beautiful, diverse, and culturally rich, offering everything from fabulous beaches to amazing art museums, to white-hot nightlife, to a distinctive cuisine that blends the best of the mountains and the sea.

As you're heading to the south of France to luxuriate in life along the sunny Mediterranean—not to exhaust yourself making difficult decisions—we've searched out the best deals and once-in-a-lifetime experiences for this book. What follows in this chapter is our roster of the best of the best, the kind of discoveries we'd share with our closest friends.

1 The Best Travel Experiences

- **Partying in the Land of Festivals:** Provence is called the Land of Festivals with good reason: It hosts some 500 with an astonishing 4,000 events. Of course, the ultimate example is the you-won't-believe-it-until-you've-seen-it Cannes Film Festival in May. July and August are the busiest months, as Aix-en-Provence, Toulon, and Nice host jazz festivals and Nîmes and Arles stage theater and dance performances. On May 16, St-Tropez's riotous *bravades* honor the saint in theory but are really just an excuse for revelry. Many festivals have deep roots in Provençal folklore, honoring the bounty of earth and sea: the wine harvest in numerous villages, the rice harvest in Languedoc's Camargue, and the apple harvest in Peyruis. Everything seems to end in a feast where the wine and pastis flow.

Contact any tourist office for the free booklet *Provence—Terre de Festivals.* See "When to Go" in chapter 2.

- **Absorbing a Unique Lifestyle:** Provence and Languedoc share a uniquely Mediterranean lifestyle. Compared to the rest of France, the air here is drier, the sun beats down more strongly, and the light beloved by so many painters appears clearer. Nothing could be more typical than a game of boules played under shade trees on a hot afternoon in a Provençal village. This is a place that respects time-honored crafts; Picasso might have arrived here a painter, but he left a potter. And nothing is finer in life than to be invited into a Provençal kitchen—the heart of family life—and smell the aroma of herbs and wines cooking with the catch of the day. To walk in the gardens filled with vegetables, flowers, and fruit trees is reason enough to visit. Attend a harvest, not just of grapes, but perhaps of linden blossoms. The dramatic landscape somehow seems at its most romantic when hit with the dreaded mistral winds. Discovering this land of ingrained traditions and making it your own is one of the great rewards of all European travel, especially if you go in the best months: May and September. See chapters 4 and 5.

- **Dining and Drinking Provence Style:** Many people flock to the south of France specifically to enjoy *cuisine Provençale,* a Mediterranean mix of bold flavors with an emphasis on garlic, olive oil, and aromatic local herbs like thyme and basil. The world's greatest bouillabaisse is made here, especially in Marseille; Provençal lamb is among the best in France; and the vegetables (such as asparagus, eggplant, tomatoes, and artichokes) will make you realize that this is France's market garden. The regional wines, though not equaling those of Bordeaux and Burgundy, are the perfect accompaniment, ranging from the warm, full-bodied Châteauneuf-du-Pape to the rare, choice Bellet, produced on Nice's hill slopes.

- **Spending a Day in St-Rémy-de-Provence:** Our favorite town in Provence is St-Rémy. To wander St-Rémy's streets is to recapture Provence's essence, especially its Vieille Ville (Old Town). After exploring its alleys, pause on one of its immaculate leafy squares. Then go in search of an art gallery or two and perhaps reward yourself with a painting and a memory. See "St-Rémy-de-Provence" in chapter 5.

- **Following in the Footsteps of the Great Artists:** Modern art wasn't born in Provence, but artists from all over came here to paint its "glaring

festive light." The good news is that most of them left behind fabulous legacies. Perhaps it all began when Monet arrived with Renoir in 1883. In time, they were followed by a host of others, including Bonnard, who took a villa in St-Tropez. Van Gogh arrived in Arles in 1888, and Gauguin showed up a few months later. Even the Fauves sought out this region, notably Matisse, whose masterpiece is his chapel at Vence. Not long afterward, Picasso arrived at Antibes. Deeply jealous of Picasso and Matisse, Chagall moved to Vence and was later infuriated that the street on which he lived was renamed avenue Henri-Matisse. He got over it and lived and painted on the Riviera until he died at 97. See chapters 5, 6, and 7.

- **Sunning and Swimming on the Riviera Beaches:** There are greater beaches but none more fabled, overcrowded though they are. Most of them are sandy, except those stretching from Antibes to the Italian frontier, including Nice's. These are shingled (covered with gravel or pebbles), but that doesn't stop the world from flocking to them. A beach mattress fits just fine on the shingles, and umbrellas are for rent when you want to escape the relentless sun. Along the Riviera, topless sunbathing is *de rigeur.* Legend has it that it began with Brigitte Bardot, who pulled off her bra and said, "Let's wake up sleepy St-Trop." Nudist beaches also exist, notably at Cap d'Agde and Port Cros. If you decide not to go topless or bottomless, you can still wear your most daring bikini or thong. See chapters 6 and 7. Also see "The Best Beaches," below.

- **Having Fun Day and Night:** If nothing else, the Riviera is about the art of entertainment, both high and low.

The Côte d'Azur offers not only beaches and racecars and yachts, but also fêtes and festivals and even bullfights, real Spanish-style ones where the animals are killed, in the old Roman arenas at Arles and Nîmes. Glittering casinos are seemingly everywhere—Monte Carlo, Cannes, Cassis, and Beaulieu, to name a few. Many cities have elegant restaurants and opera houses with resident companies. But mainly the Riviera offers white-hot nightclubs and dance clubs for all sexes and sexual orientations, especially in Cannes, Nice, Monte Carlo, and St-Tropez. See chapters 6 and 7.

- **Breaking the Bank at Monte Carlo:** Few other casinos can match the excitement generated at the Monte Carlo Casino. The world's wealthy flocked to Monaco when the casino was opened by Charles Garnier in 1878. But since 1891 much of the nonwealthy world has followed—even those who can't afford losses. During a 3-day gambling spree that year, Charles Deville Wells, an American, turned $400 into $40,000, an astonishing amount back then. His feat was immortalized in the song "The Man Who Broke the Bank at Monte Carlo." Even if you do no more today than play the slot machines, a visit to this casino will be a highlight of your trip as you bask amid the extravagant decor and under the gilded rococo ceilings. (Some not as lucky as Wells have leaped to their deaths from the casino windows or the "Suicide Terrace.") See "Monaco" in chapter 7.

2 The Best Romantic Getaways

- **Les Baux** (Provence): Les Baux stands in a spectacular position on a promontory of sheer rock ravines. In the distance across the plain, you can view the Val d'Enfer (Valley of Hell). After a turbulent history, the town today is one of the great escapes for the savvy French who can gaze from their windows on the thousands of olive trees (many planted by the Greeks) that produce the best oil in France. A pocket of posh, it has some of the country's grandest inns and finest cuisine. The most notable is **L'Oustau de Beaumanière,** Maussanel-les-Alpilles (© **04-90-54-33-07**)—after you and your loved one sample the ravioli with truffles, you'll understand why. See "Les Baux" in chapter 5.

- **Iles d'Hyères** (Provence): If an off-the-record weekend is what you have in mind, there's no better spot than what were known during the Renaissance as the "Iles d'Or" because of the golden glow of the island rocks in the sun. This string of enchanting little islands is 39km (24 miles) east-southeast of the port of Toulon. The largest and westernmost island is Ile de Porquerolles, thickly covered with heather, eucalyptus, and exotic shrubs. Ile de Port-Cros is hilly and mysterious, with spring-fed lush vegetation. The best spot for a romantic retreat is on this island—**Le Manoir** (© **04-94-05-90-52**), an 18th-century colonial-style mansion set in a park. See "Iles d'Hyères" in chapter 5.

- **Mougins** (Western Riviera): Only 8.1km (5 miles) north of Cannes, the once-fortified town of Mougins is a thousand years old, but never in its history has it been so popular as a place to enjoy the good life. Picasso, who could afford to live anywhere, chose a place nearby, Notre-Dame-de-Vie, to spend his last years. The wonderful old town is known for its cuisine, and Roger Vergé reigns supreme at his elegant **Le Moulin de Mougins** (© **04-93-75-78-24**). However, you can live for less at more secluded and less publicized oases. See "Mougins" in chapter 6.

- **Peillon** (Eastern Riviera): Of all the "perched" villages *(villages perchés)* along the Côte d'Azur, this fortified medieval town on a craggy mountaintop 19km (12 miles) northeast of Nice is our favorite. Peillon is the least spoiled of the perched villages and still boasts its medieval look, with covered alleys and extremely narrow streets. Tour buses avoid the place, but artists and writers flock there (we once spotted Françoise Sagan) to escape the mad carnival of the Riviera. For a cozy hideaway with your significant other, try the **Auberge de la Madone** (© **04-93-79-91-17**). Dinner for two on the terrace set among olive trees is the best way to start a romantic evening. See "Peillon" in chapter 7.

- **Roquebrune and Cap-Martin** (Eastern Riviera): Along the Grande Corniche, Roquebrune is one of the most charming of the Côte d'Azur's villages, and its satellite resort of Cap-Martin occupies a lovely wooded peninsula. Between Monaco and Menton, these two have long been romantic retreats. The best choice for hiding away with that certain someone is the **Hôtel Vista Palace,** Grande Corniche (© **04-92-10-40-00**), a modern luxury hotel clinging giddily to a cliff side over Monte Carlo. See "Roquebrune & Cap-Martin" in chapter 7.

3 The Most Dramatic Countryside Drives

- **From Carcassonne to Albi** (Languedoc-Roussillon): From the walled city of Carcassonne, D118 takes you north into the Montagne Noire (Black Mountains), which are both arid and lush in parts, marking the southeastern extension of the Massif Central. You can spend a full day here exploring the Parc Régional du Haut-Languedoc, crowned by the 1,110m (3,700-ft.) Pic de Noire. You can base yourself in the old wool town of Mazamet and have lunch here before continuing northwest on N112 to Castres, with its Goya Museum. Then you can continue exploring the surrounding area or head for Albi, 40km (25 miles) away, the hometown of Toulouse-Lautrec. See chapter 4.

- **From St-Rémy-de-Provence to Eygalières** (Provence): A 64km (40-mile) drive northeast of Arles takes you into some of the most dramatic and forlorn countryside in Provence, even to the Val d'Enfer (Valley of Hell). At the beginning of the tour, you pass Roman monuments before climbing into the hills, with their distant views of the Parc Naturel Régional de la Camargue and Mont Ventoux. The tour also takes you to Les Baux, the most dramatically situated town in Provence and today a gourmet citadel. After many turns and twists, you eventually reach the ancient village of Eygalières, with its medieval castle and church. See chapter 5.

- **Along the Ours Peak Road** (Western Riviera): The best driving tour in the area starts in St-Raphaël and lasts for only 56km (35 miles), but because the terrain is so rough and torturous, allow at least 3 hours. The views are among the most dramatic along the Côte d'Azur, as you traverse a backdrop of the red porphyry slopes of Rastel d'Agay. Along the way, you'll go through the passes of Evèque and Lentisques. Eventually, hairpin bends in the road lead to the summit of Ours Peak (Pic de l'Ours), at 488m (1,627 ft.), and you're rewarded with a superb panorama. See chapter 6.

- **From Vence to Grasse** (Western and Eastern Riviera): After calling on the Matisse chapel in Vence, you can take D2210 through some of the most luxuriant countryside along the French Riviera, with views of the Gorges du Loup, and a stopover in the artisans' village of Tourrettes-sur-Loup, where the main street is filled with the ateliers of craftspeople. As you continue, follow the signs to Point-du-Loup and you'll be rewarded with a panorama of waterfalls; later you will pass fields of flowers that eventually lead to the perfume center of Grasse. See chapter 7.

- **From Nice to Mont Chauve** (Eastern Riviera): The hilltops surrounding Nice have long been known for their colorful villages and rural scenery. In our view, the best countryside and the best panoramas unfold by driving to Mont Chauve (Bald Mountain) across a circuit that traverses 53km (33 miles). You can stop at several villages along the way, including Aspremont and Tourette-Levens. You'll even pass the Gorges du Gabres, with its sheer walls of limestone, before reaching the enchanting village of Falicon. Eventually you'll come to Mont Chauve. Allow at least 30 minutes to hike to the summit. See chapter 7.

4 The Best Beaches

Read below to discover the best beaches throughout Provence and the Riviera. See the chapters indicated to find out more about lodging, dining, and other activities in the general vicinity of these great strips of sand.

- **La Côte Vermeille** (Languedoc-Roussillon): In contrast to the eastern Riviera's pebbly beaches, the Côte Vermeille is filled with sand stretching toward Spain's Costa Brava. The best place for fun in the sun is the 11km (6-mile) beach between the resorts of Leucate-Plage and Le Barcarès in the Pyrénées-Orientales district near Perpignan. The "Vermilion Coast" takes its name from the red-clay soil studded with the ubiquitous olive groves. Henri Matisse was so taken with the light on this coast that he painted it. See chapter 4.

- **Beaches of Ile de Porquerolles** (Provence): These beaches lie 15 minutes by ferry from the Giens peninsula east of Toulon. One of the Iles d'Hyères, Porquerolles is only 8.1km (5 miles) long and some 2.4km (1½ miles) across and enjoys national park status. Its beaches, along the northern coast facing the mainland, get 275 days of sunshine annually. There are several white-sand beaches; the best are **Plage d'Argent, Plage de la Courtade,** and **Plage de Notre-Dame.** See "Iles d'Hyères" in chapter 5.

- **Plage de Tahiti** (St Tropez, Western Riviera): And God created woman and man and all the other critters found on this sizzling sandy beach outside St-Tropez. Tahiti is France's most infamous beach, mainly because of all the topless or bottomless action going on. Ever since the days of Brigitte Bardot, this beach has been a favorite of movie stars. It's very cruisy and animated, with a French nonchalance about nudity. If you bother to wear a bikini, it should be only the most daring. See "St-Tropez" in chapter 6.

- **Plage Port Grimaud** (St-Tropez, Western Riviera): This long golden-sand beach is set against the backdrop of the urban architect François Spoerry's *cité lacustre,* facing St-Tropez. Spoerry created this 98-hectare (247-acre) marine village inspired by an ancient fishing village. The world has since flocked to Port Grimaud and its beach; homeowner Joan Collins comes here to hide from the paparazzi. Some of the Riviera's most expensive yachts are tied up in the harbor. This beach isn't as decadent as those at St-Trop, but it does pick up the "overflow" on the see-and-be-seen circuit. See "St-Tropez" in chapter 6.

• **The Beaches at Cannes** (Western Riviera): From the Palais des Festivals and west to Mandelieu, the beach at Cannes has real sand, not pebbles as at Nice. This beach resort offers a movable feast of high-fashion swimsuits. Ever since the 1920s, the word on the beach here has been: "Menton's dowdy. Monte's brass. Nice rowdy. Cannes is class!" Along the fabled promenade, La Croisette, the white sands are littered with sun beds and parasols rented at the beach concessions. The beach is actually divided into 32 sections, our favorites being **Plages Gazagnaire, Le Zénith,** and **Waikiki.** Some of the beaches are privately run, but the best public beach is in front of the Palais des Festivals. See "Cannes" in chapter 6.

• **Monte-Carlo Beach** (at the Monaco border, Eastern Riviera): This beach, once frequented by Princess Grace, is actually on French soil. Of all the Riviera's beaches, this is the most fashionable, even though its sands are imported. The property adjoins the ultrachic **Monte-Carlo Beach Hotel,** 22 av. Princesse-Grace (✆ **92-16-25-25**). The great months to be here are July and August, when you never know who's likely to be sharing the sands with you—perhaps Luciano Pavarotti or Claudia Schiffer. The main topic on the beach? Both legal and funny money. See "Monaco" in chapter 7.

5 The Best Offbeat Experiences

• **Spending a Night in Aigues-Mortes** (Languedoc-Roussillon): St. Louis sailed from this port to fight in the Crusades to the east. He died in Tunis in 1270, but his successor, Philip III, held this port, the only stretch of the Mediterranean in French hands at the time. Great walls were built around the town, and ships all the way from Antioch used to anchor here. But beginning around the mid–14th century, Aigues-Mortes began to live up to its name of "dead waters," as the harbor filled with silt and the waters receded. Today it sits marooned in time and space right in the muck of the advancing Rhône delta. Nothing along the coast is as evocative of the Middle Ages as this town, where you can walk along its walls and slumber in one of its inns. See "Aigues-Mortes" in chapter 4.

• **Checking In and Stripping Down** (Cap d'Agde, Languedoc-Roussillon): Except in foul weather, it's compulsory to walk around nude in the holiday town on the outskirts of Cap d'Agde. You'll have to check your apparel at the gate. Along the Languedoc coast, between the Rhône delta and Béziers, Cap d'Agde was constructed like a pastiche of a local fishing village, similar to Port Grimaud near St-Tropez. At its outskirts is a town with supermarkets, nightclubs, a casino, and rooms for 20,000 bodies—nude bodies. See "Liberté, Egalité, Fraternité . . . Nudité" in chapter 4.

• **Exploring Massif des Calanques** (between Marseille and Cassis, Provence): At the old fishing port of

Cassis, with its white cliffs and beaches that were a favorite of Fauve painters, you can rent a boat and explore the Calanques, small fjords along the rugged coast. Covered with gorse and heather, the white cliffs form a backdrop for this adventure. By car from Cassis, you can drive to the creek of Port Miou, with its rock quarries. To reach the Port Pin and En Vau creeks farther west, you must travel on foot (trails are well signposted). You can, however, take one of the boat excursions that leave regularly from Cassis. If you go on your own (not on the boat), you can take a picnic and spend the day skinny-dipping in these cool crystal waters. See "Exploring the Massif des Calanques" in chapter 5.

6 The Best Small Towns

- **Cordes-sur-Ciel** (Languedoc-Roussillon): Perched like an eagle's nest on a hilltop, Cordes is an arts-and-crafts town, its ancient houses on narrow streets filled with artisans plying their trades. Once fabled in France for the brilliance of its silks, today it's a sleepy town 25km (16 miles) northwest of Albi, the city of Toulouse-Lautrec. Ideally, you should visit Cordes as a side trip from Albi, but you might become enchanted with the place and decide to stop over in this town of a hundred Gothic arches. See "Cordes-sur-Ciel" in chapter 4.
- **Uzès** (Provence): Uzès is a gem, a bit of a time capsule with lofty towers and narrow streets. Racine once lived here and was inspired by the town to write his only comedy, *Les Plaideurs*. André Gide also found a home in this "dream of the Middle Ages." Once Louis XIII called Uzès "the premier duchy of France." You can see why by staying at the stately 18th-century **Château d'Arpaillargues.** See "Uzès" in chapter 5.
- **Gordes** (Provence): One of the best known of Provence's hill villages, Gordes, east of Avignon, is deservedly called *le plus beau village de France*. Today an escape for in-the-know Parisians, it's a town of silk painters, weavers, and potters. The setting is bucolic, between the Coulon valley and the Vaucluse plateau. Houses built of golden stone rise to the Renaissance château crowning the top. The late artist Victor Vasarély lived here in a fortified château that has been turned into a museum displaying much of his work. See "Gordes" in chapter 5.
- **Roussillon** (Provence): Northeast of Gordes, Roussillon stands on a hilltop in the heart of "ocher country," where the earth is a bright red (*roussillon* means "russet"). This ancient village boasts houses in every shade of burnt orange, dusty pink, and russet red—they take on a particular brilliance at sunset. Roussillon, however, is no longer the sleepy village described in Laurence Wylie's *A Village in the Vaucluse*. Artists, writers, and trendy Parisians have discovered its charms, and today many use it as their second home. See "Roussillon & Bonnieux" in chapter 5.
- **Roquebrune** (Eastern Riviera): This medieval hill village southwest of Menton is the finest along the Côte d'Azur. It has been extensively restored, and not even the souvenir shops can spoil its charm. Steep stairways and alleys lead up to its feudal castle crowning the village. But before heading here, take in rue Moncollet, flanked by houses from

the Middle Ages. This castle, dating from the 10th century, is the oldest in France—in fact, it's the only Carolingian castle left standing. See "Roquebrune & Cap-Martin" in chapter 7.

7 The Best Châteaux & Palaces

• **Château d'If** (off Marseille, Provence): One of France's most notorious fortresses, this was the famous state prison whose mysterious guest was the Man in the Iron Mask. Alexandre Dumas père's *Count of Monte Cristo* made the legend famous around the world. It doesn't really matter that the story was apocryphal: People flock here because they believe it, just as they go to Verona to see where Romeo and Juliet lived and loved and died. The château was built by François I in 1524 as part of the defenses of Marseille. To reach it, you take a boat in the harbor to the islet 3.2km (2 miles) offshore. See "Marseille" in chapter 5.

• **Palais des Papes** (Avignon, Provence): This was the seat of Avignon's brief golden age as the capital of Christendom. From 1352 to 1377, seven popes—all French—ruled here, a period called "the Babylonian Captivity." And they lived with pomp and circumstance, knowing "fleshly weaknesses." The Italian poet Petrarch denounced the palace as "the shame of mankind, a sink of vice." Even after Gregory XI was persuaded to return to Rome, some cardinals remained, electing their own pope or "anti-pope," who was finally expelled by force in 1403. See p. 139.

• **Château de la Napoule** (La Napoule, Western Riviera): The Riviera's most eccentric château is also the most fascinating. This great medieval castle was purchased in 1917 by American sculptor Henry Clews, heir to a banking fortune. He lived, worked, and was buried here in 1937. In this castle, Clews created his own grotesque menagerie—scorpions, pelicans, gnomes, monkeys, lizards, whatever came to his tortured mind. His view of feminism? A distorted suffragette depicted in his *Cat Woman*. He likened himself to Don Quixote. See p. 243.

• **Les Grands Appartements du Palais** (Monte Carlo, Monaco, Eastern Riviera): The world has known greater palaces, but this Italianate one on "The Rock" houses the man who presides over the tiny but incredibly rich principality of Monaco, Europe's second-smallest state. In 2005, Prince Rainier III, Europe's longest-reigning monarch, passed away, leaving the throne to Prince Albert. When the prince is here, a flag flies. You can watch the changing of the guard every day at 11:55am. The throne room is decorated with paintings by Holbein, Brueghel, and others, and in one wing of the palace is a museum devoted to souvenirs of Napoleon. See p. 338.

• **Villa Kérylos** (Beaulieu, Eastern Riviera): This villa is a faithful reconstruction of an ancient Greek palace, built between 1902 and 1908 by the archaeologist Théodore Reinach. Reinach, a bit of an eccentric, lived here for 20 years, preferring to take baths and eat and dress with his male friends (who pretended to be Athenian citizens), while segregating the women to separate suites. Designated a historic monument of France, with its white, yellow, and lavender Italian marble and its ivory and bronze copies of vases and mosaics, Kérylos is a visual knockout. The parties that went on here are legendary. See "Beaulieu" in chapter 7.

8 The Best Museums

- **Musée Toulouse-Lautrec** (Albi, Languedoc-Roussillon): This museum displays the world's greatest collection from this crippled genius, who immortalized cancan dancers, cafe demimonde, and prostitutes. In the brooding 13th-century Palais de la Berbie in the artist's hometown, the "red city" of Albi, this museum takes you into the special but tortured world of Toulouse-Lautrec. Particularly memorable are the posters that marked the beginning of an entirely new art form. When he died, his family donated the works remaining in his studio. See p. 89.

- **Musée Picasso** (Antibes, Western Riviera): After the bleak war years in Paris, Picasso returned to the Mediterranean in 1945. He didn't have a studio, so the curator of this museum offered him space. Picasso labored here for several months—it was one of his most creative periods. At the end of his stay, he astonished the curator by leaving his entire output on permanent loan to the museum, along with some 200 ceramics he produced at Vallauris. This museum reveals Picasso in an exuberant mood, as evoked by his fauns and goats in cubist style, his still lifes of sea urchins, and his masterful *Ulysses et ses Sirènes.* A much-reproduced photograph displayed here shows him holding a sunshade for his lover, Françoise Gilot. See p. 278.

- **Musée National Fernand-Léger** (Biot, Eastern Riviera): Ridiculed as a Tubist, Léger survived many of his most outspoken critics and went on to win great fame. This museum was built by Léger's widow, Nadia, after his death in 1955, and it became one of the first in France dedicated to a single artist. It owns some 300 of Léger's highly original works. You wander into a dazzling array of robot-like figures, girders, machines, cogs, and cubes. The museum allows you to witness how he changed over the years, dabbling first in Impressionism, as shown by his 1905 *Portrait de l'oncle.* Our favorite here—and one of our favorite artworks along the Riviera— is Léger's *Mona Lisa,* contemplating a set of keys with a wide-mouthed fish dangling at an angle over her head. See p. 284.

- **Fondation Maeght** (St-Paul-de-Vence, Eastern Riviera): One of Europe's greatest modern art museums, this foundation is remarkable for both its setting and its art. Built in 1964, the avant-garde building boasts a touch of fantasy, topped by two inverted domes. The colorful canvases radiate with the joy of life. All your favorites are likely to be here: Bonnard, Braque, Soulages, Chagall, Kandinsky, and more. Stunningly designed is a terraced garden that's a setting for Calder murals, Hepworth sculptures, and the fanciful fountains and colorful mosaics of Miró. A courtyard is peopled with Giacometti figures that look like gigantic emaciated chessmen. See p. 287.

- **Musée des Beaux-Arts** (Nice, Eastern Riviera): In the former home of the Ukrainian Princess Kotchubey, the collection comes as an unexpected delight, with not only many Belle Epoque paintings but also modern works, including an impressive number by Sisley, Braque, Degas, and Monet, plus Picasso ceramics. There's whimsy, too, especially in the sugar-sweet canvases by Jules Chéret, who died in Nice in 1932. Well represented also are the Van Loo family, a clan of Dutch descent whose members worked in Nice. The gallery of sculptors honors Rude, Rodin, and J. B. Carpeaux. See p. 303.

- **Musée Ile-de-France** (St-Jean-Cap-Ferrat, Eastern Riviera): Baronne Ephrussi de Rothschild left a treasure trove of art and artifacts to the Institut de France on her death in 1934. The Villa Ephrussi, the 1912 palace that contains these pieces, reveals what a woman with unlimited wealth and highly eclectic tastes can collect. It's all here: paintings by Carpaccio and other masters of the Venetian Renaissance; canvases by Sisley, Renoir, and Monet; Ming vases; Dresden porcelain; and more. An eccentric, she named her house after the ocean liner *Ile de France* and insisted that her 35 gardeners dress as sailors. See p. 324.

9 The Best Cathedrals & Churches

- **Basilique St-Sernin** (Toulouse, Languedoc-Roussillon): Consecrated in 1096, this is the largest and finest Romanesque church extant. It was built to honor the memory of a Gaulish martyr, St. Sernin, and was for a long time a major stop on the pilgrimage route to Santiago de Compostela in Spain. The octagonal bell tower is particularly evocative, with five levels of twin brick arches. Unusual for a Romanesque church, St-Sernin has five naves. The crypt, where the saint is buried, is a treasure trove of ecclesiastical artifacts, some from the days of Charlemagne. See p. 74.

- **Cathédrale St-Jean** (Perpignan, Languedoc-Roussillon): In 1324, Sancho of Aragón began this cathedral, but the consecration didn't come until its completion in 1509. Despite the different builders and architects over the decades, it emerged as one of Languedoc's most evocative cathedrals. The bell tower contains a great bell that dates from the 1400s. The single nave is typical of church construction in the Middle Ages and is enhanced by the altarpieces of the north chapels and the high altar, the work of the 1400s and the 1500s. See p. 100.

- **Cathédrale St-Just** (Narbonne, Languedoc-Roussillon): Though construction on this cathedral, begun in 1272, was never completed, it's an enduring landmark. Construction had to be halted 82 years later to prevent breaching the city's ancient ramparts to make room for the nave. In High Gothic style, the vaulting in the choir soars to 130 feet. Battlements and loopholes crown the towering arches of the apse. The cathedral's greatest treasure is the evocative *Tapestry of the Creation*, woven in silk and gold thread. See p. 109.

- **Cathédrale Notre-Dame des Doms** (Avignon, Provence): Next to the Palais des Papes, this was a luminous Romanesque structure before baroque artists took over. It was partially reconstructed from the 14th through the 17th century. In 1859, it was topped by a tall gilded statue of the Virgin, which earned it harsh criticism from many architectural critics. The cathedral houses the tombs of two popes, John XXII and Benedict XII. You'd think this cathedral would be more impressive because of its role in papal history, but it appears that far more time and money went into the construction of the papal palace. Nevertheless, the cathedral reigned during the heyday of Avignon. See p. 141.

- **Basilique St-Victor** (Marseille, Provence): This is one of France's most ancient churches, first built in the 5th century by St. Cassianus to honor St. Victor, a 3rd-century martyr. The saint's church was destroyed by the Saracens, except for the crypt. In the 11th and 12th centuries, a fortified Gothic church was erected. In the crypt are both pagan and early Christian sarcophagi; those depicting the convening of the Apostles and the Companions of St. Maurice are justly renowned. See p. 195.

10 The Best Vineyards

Southern France is home to thousands of vineyards, many of which are somewhat anonymous agrarian bureaucracies known as *cooperatives*. Employees at these cooperatives tend to be less enthusiastic about showing off their product than those who work at true vineyards, where the person pouring your *dégustation des vins* might be the son or daughter of one of the owners. At least in southern France, don't assume that just because the word *Château* appears in the name that there'll be a magnificent historic residence associated with the property. In some cases, the crenellated battlement you're looking for might be nothing more than a feudal ruin.

We selected the vineyards below because of the emotional involvement of their (private) owners, their degree of prestige, and, in many cases, their architectural interest. We've provided you with all of the information you need to visit the vineyards below, but see "A Taste of Provence" in the appendix for more information about the wines produced in these areas.

- **Château de Simone,** 13590 Meyreuil (✆ 04-42-66-92-58; www.chateausimone.fr): This well-respected vintner lies less than .5km (⅓ mile) north of Aix-en-Provence. The vineyards surround a small 18th-century palace that might have been transported unchanged from *La Belle du bois dormant*. You can't visit the interior, but you can buy bottles of the recent crops of reds, rosés, and whites for between 25€ ($33) and 28€ ($36) each. Because production at this vineyard is relatively small, you're limited to purchases of between 3 and 12 bottles, depending on the vintage. Advance notification is important. From Aix, take N7 toward Nice and then follow the signs to Trois Sautets.

- **Château Virant,** R.D. 10, 13680 Lançon-de-Provence (✆ 04-90-42-44-47; www.chateauvirant.com): Set 23km (14 miles) west of Aix-en-Provence and 35km (22 miles) north of Marseille, and named after a nearby rock whose ruined feudal fortress is barely standing, this vineyard produces Appellation d'Origine Contrôlée–designated Côteaux d'Aix-en-Provence, as well as a translucent brand of olive oil from fruit grown on the property. The English-speaking Cheylan family showcases a labyrinth of cellars dating from 1630 and 1890. Tours and tastings can be arranged. The most expensive bottle here costs 14€ ($18). Ask for an explanation of their trademark *vin cuit* (cooked wine) *de Virant,* which is popular around these parts as a beverage at Christmastime. Notification in advance of your visit is wise.

- **Château de Calissanne,** R.D. 10, 13680 Lançon-de-Provence (✆ 04-90-42-63-03; www.calissanne.fr): On the premises is a substantial 18th-century white-stone manor house sporting very old terra-cotta tiles and a sense of the *ancien régime.* Even older is the Gallo-Roman *oppidum Constantine,* a sprawling ruined fortress that you can visit if you obtain a special pass from the sales staff. Set amid the vineyards, it evokes old Provence. The white, rosé, and red Côteaux d'Aix-en-Provence and the two grades of olive oil produced by the property are sold in an outbuilding. Wine sells for less than 18€ ($23) per bottle. Advance reservations are vital. You'll find this place clearly signposted in Lançon-de-Provence, nearly adjacent to the above-mentioned Château Virant.

- **Château d'Aqueria,** Route de Roquemaure, 30126 Tavel (© **04-66-50-04-56;** www.aqueria.com): Wines produced near the Provençal town of Tavel are considered some of the finest rosés in the world, and vintners here are expert at the fermentation of a brand that's sought after by wine lovers from as far away as Paris. An 18th-century château on the premises can be viewed only from the outside, and cellars and wine shops sell bottles of the famous pink wine at prices that rarely exceed 11€ ($14) a bottle. To reach it, drive 6km (4 miles) northwest of Avignon along the Route de Bagnols, following the signs to Tavel.

- **Château de Fonscolombe** (© **04-42-61-70-01)** and **Château de La-Coste** (© **04-42-61-89-98)**, 13610 Le Puy Ste-Réparade: These vineyards are adjacent to each other, 20km (13 miles) north of Aix-en-Provence. Fonscolombe has an exterior-only view of an 18th-century manor house and its garden, and offers tours of a modern facility of interest to wine-industry professionals. LaCoste is smaller and less state of the art, but it offers an exterior view of a stone-sided villa that was built for a cardinal during the reign of the popes in Avignon. At either of these outfits, you can buy their red, white, and rosé wines, the most expensive of which sells for only 12€ ($16). Advance notification is required. From Aix, take the A51 in

the direction of Sisteron, exiting at exit 12 toward Le Puy Ste-Réparade.

- **Domaine de Fontavin,** 1468 route de la Plaine, 84350 Courthézon (© **04-90-70-72-14;** www.fontavin. com): Set 10km (6 miles) north of Carpentras, this is one of the leading producers of the heady, sweet dessert wine known as Muscat des Baumes de Venise. Because the organization here dates only from 1989, there's nothing particularly noteworthy in terms of architecture on-site. But oenophiles who come to this place appreciate its proximity to some of the most legendary grapevines in the French-speaking world. Bottles of the sweet elixir are sold at a price that rarely exceeds 15€ ($20) each. Follow the N7 from Carpentras in the direction of Orange and Courthézon.

- **Château de Coussin,** 1468 route de la Plain, 13530 Trets (© **04-90-70-72-14;** www.sumeire.com): This property, 16km (10 miles) east of Aix-en-Provence, is centered on a 16th-century manor whose stone facade bears geometric reliefs associated with Renaissance-era construction in Provence. The vineyards are scattered over three neighboring regions and have been owned by the same family for nearly a century. The château's interior (it contains a vaulted cloister) can be visited only with the hard-to-obtain permission of the owners, but the overview of the winemaking industry as seen within its bottling facility is worth the trip. Bottles sell for a maximum of 36€ ($47) each, and in some cases for much less.

- On a property that's almost immediately adjacent, an amiable competitor also offers wine tours to those who phone in advance: **Château de Grand'Boise,** 13530 Trets (© **04-42-29-22-95)**, whose venerable 19th-century château is the centerpiece of vineyards, olive groves, forests, and hunting preserves. The château itself, as well as the organization's cellars, can be visited if you phone in advance for an appointment. Bottles of red, white, and rosé sell for less than 12€ ($16) each.

- **Château de Capitoul,** Route de Gruissan, 1100 Narbonne (© 04-68-49-23-30; www.chateau-capitoul.com): Set farther to the west than most of the other vineyards mentioned within this survey, Château de Capitoul produces reds ("La Clape des Rocailles"), whites, and rosés that usually sell for 5.40€ to 8.50€ ($7–$11) a bottle but, in some rare instances, go as high as 36€ ($47). Nestled amid its vineyards is a 19th-century manor house that can be visited if special permission is granted in advance from the owners. More easily accessible are the cellars, which lie within a nearby annex. Call in advance of your arrival. From Narbonne, drive 5km (3 miles) east, following the D32 (Route de Gruissan).

11 The Best Luxury Hotels

- **InterContinental Carlton Cannes** (Western Riviera; © 04-93-06-40-06): A World War II Allied commander issued orders to bombers to avoid hitting the Carlton "because it's such a good hotel." The 1912 hotel survived the attack and today is at its most frenzied during the annual film festival. Taste and subtlety aren't what the Carlton is about—it's all glitter, glitterati, and glamour, the most splendid of the area's architectural "wedding cakes." The white-turreted doyenne presides over La Croisette like some permanent sand castle. See p. 254.
- **Hôtel du Cap–Eden Roc** (Cap d'Antibes, Western Riviera; © 04-93-61-39-01): Looming large in F. Scott Fitzgerald's *Tender Is the Night,* this is the most stylish of the Côte's luxury palaces, standing at the tip of the Cap d'Antibes peninsula in its own manicured garden. The hotel reflects the opulence of a bygone era and has catered to the rich and famous since it opened in 1870. See p. 278.
- **Hôtel Negresco** (Nice, Eastern Riviera; © 04-93-16-64-00): An aging Lillie Langtry sitting alone in the lobby, her once-great beauty camouflaged by a black veil, is but one of the many memories of this nostalgic favorite. Self-made millionaires and wannabes rub shoulders at this 1906 landmark. We could write a book about the Négresco, but here we'll give only two interesting facts: The carpet in the lobby is the largest ever made by the Savonnerie factory (the cost was about one-tenth the cost of the hotel), and the main chandelier was commissioned from Baccarat by Tsar Nicholas II. See p. 306.
- **Grand Hôtel du Cap-Ferrat** (St-Jean-Cap-Ferrat, Eastern Riviera; © 04-93-76-50-52): The Grand Hôtel, built in 1908, competes with the Hôtel du Cap–Eden Roc as the Riviera's most opulent. Set in a well-manicured garden, it was once a winter haven for royalty. This pocket of posh has it all, including a private beach club with a heated seawater pool and a Michelin-starred restaurant utilizing market-fresh ingredients. See p. 324.
- **Hostellerie du Château de la Chèvre d'Or** (Eze, Eastern Riviera; © 04-92-10-66-66): In striking contrast to the palaces above, this gem of an inn lies in a medieval village 396m (1,300 ft.) above sea level. Following in the footsteps of former guests like Roger

Moore and Elizabeth Taylor, you can stay in this artistically converted medieval château. All its elegant rooms open onto vistas of the Mediterranean. Everything here has a refreshingly rustic appeal rather than false glitter. As the paparazzi catch you sipping a champagne cocktail by the pool, you'll know you've achieved Côte d'Azur chic. See p. 332.

- **Hôtel de Paris** (Monte Carlo, Monaco, Eastern Riviera; ℂ **92-16-30-00**): The 19th-century aristocracy flocked here, and though the hotel isn't quite that fashionable anymore, it's still going strong. Onassis, Sinatra, and Churchill long ago checked out, but today's movers and shakers still pull up in limousines with tons of luggage. This luxury palace boasts two Michelin-starred restaurants, the more celebrated of which is Le Louis XV, offering the sublime specialties of Alain Ducasse. Le Grill boasts Ligurian-Niçois cooking, a retractable roof, and a wraparound view of the sea. See p. 343.

12 The Best Hotel Bargains

- **La Réserve** (Albi, Languedoc-Roussillon; ℂ **05-63-60-80-80**): La Réserve's design approximates a *mas provençal,* the kind of severely dignified farmhouse usually surrounded by scrublands, vineyards, olive groves, and cypresses. It's less expensive than many of the luxurious hideaways along the nearby Côte d'Azur and has the added benefit of lying just outside the center of one of our favorite fortified sites in Europe, the medieval town of Albi. See p. 90.

- **Hôtel Renaissance** (Castres, Languedoc-Roussillon; ℂ **05-63-59-30-42**): In the quaint town of Castres, with its celebrated Musée Goya, this hotel is a good introduction to the bargains awaiting you in provincial France. Built in the 1600s as a courthouse, it was long ago converted from a dilapidated site into a hotel of discretion and charm—all at an affordable price, even if you opt for a suite. Some rooms have exposed timbers, and you'll sleep in grand but rustic comfort. See p. 92.

- **Le Donjon et Les Remparts** (Carcassonne, Languedoc-Roussillon; ℂ **800/528-1234** in the U.S. and Canada, or 04-68-11-23-00): Built into the solid bulwarks of Carcassonne, one of France's most perfectly preserved medieval towns, is this small-scale hotel whose well-appointed furnishings provide a vivid contrast to the crude stone shell that contains them. A stay here truly allows you personal contact with a site that provoked bloody battles between medieval armies. See p. 96.

- **Hôtel du Palais** (Montpellier, Languedoc-Roussillon; ℂ **04-67-60-47-38**): In the old town, in a labyrinth of narrow streets, this hotel dates from the late 18th century but has been successfully modernized to receive guests today at prices that are within the range of most travelers' budgets. The rooms are cozily arranged, and the hotel has a special French charm. It's one of the most historic hotels in town, and the bedrooms are relatively large, ideal for a short or even a long visit. See p. 119.

- **Hôtel Danieli** (Avignon, Provence; ℂ **04-90-86-46-82**): Built during the reign of Napoleon, this 29-room gem is classified a historic monument. Small and informal, it has Italian flair but Provençal furnishings. The tile floors, chiseled stone, and baronial stone staircase add style in a town where too many budget hotels are bleak. See p. 146.

- **Hôtel d'Arlatan** (Arles, Provence; ✆ **04-90-93-56-66**): At reasonable rates, you can stay in one of Provence's most charming cities at the former residence of the comtes d'Arlatan de Beaumont, built in the 15th century on the ruins of an old palace. Near the historic place du Forum, this small hotel has been run by the same family since 1920. The rooms are furnished with Provençal antiques, and the antique tapestries are grace notes. See p. 157.

- **Hôtel Clair Logis** (St-Jean-Cap-Ferrat, Eastern Riviera; ✆ **04-93-76-51-81**): The real estate surrounding this converted 19th-century villa is among Europe's most expensive; nonetheless, the hotel manages to keep its prices under levels that really hurt. If you opt for one of the pleasant rooms (each named after a flower that thrives in the garden), you'll be among prestigious predecessors: Even General de Gaulle, who knew the value of a *centime* and *sou,* selected it for his retreats. See p. 325.

13 The Best Luxury Restaurants

- **Le Languedoc** (Carcassonne, Languedoc-Roussillon; ✆ **04-68-25-22-17**): Acclaimed chef Didier Faugeras is the creative force behind this century-old dining room that serves some of the finest regional specialties in the area. Its most famous dish is *cassoulet au confit de canard,* a casserole with the duck meat cooked in its own fat. See p. 98.

- **Le Jardin des Sens** (Montpellier, Languedoc-Roussillon; ✆ **04-99-58-38-38**): Twins Laurent and Jacques Pourcel have set off a culinary storm in Montpellier. Michelin has bestowed two stars on them, the same rating it gives to Ducasse at his Monaco citadel. Postnouvelle reigns supreme, and both men know how to turn the bounty of Languedoc into meals sublime in flavor and texture. Though inspired by other chefs, they now feel free to let their imaginations roam. The results are often stunning, like the fricassée of langoustines and lamb sweetbreads. See p. 120.

- **Christian Etienne** (Avignon, Provence; ✆ **04-90-86-16-50**): In a house as old as the nearby papal palace, Etienne reigns as Avignon's culinary star. A chef of imagination and discretion, he has a magical hand, reinterpreting and improving French cuisine. He keeps a short menu so that he can give special care and attention to each dish. His menu is often themed—one might be devoted to the tomato. Save room for his chocolate/pine-nut cake, something of a local legend. See p. 147.

- **Oustaù de Beaumanière** (Les Baux, Provence; ✆ **04-90-54-33-07**): This Relais & Châteaux occupies an old Provençal farmhouse. Founded in 1945 by the late Raymond Thuilier, the hotel's restaurant was once touted as France's greatest. It might long ago have lost that lofty position, but it continues to tantalize today's palates. Thuilier's heirs carry on admirably as they reinvent and reinterpret some of the great Provençal recipes. At the foot of a cliff, you dine in Renaissance charm, enjoying often flawless meals from the bounty of Provence. See p. 161.

- **Chantecler** (Nice, Eastern Riviera; ✆ **04-93-16-64-00**): The most prestigious restaurant in Nice, and the most intensely cultivated, Chantecler is currently in the hands of Alain Llorca, who's attracting the area's demanding gourmets and gourmands. You dine in a monument to turn-of-the-20th-century extravagance, and the menu is attuned to the seasons and to quality ingredients. A true taste of the country is evident in the fresh asparagus, black truffles, sun-dried tomatoes, and beignets of fresh vegetables—all deftly handled by a chef on the rise. See p. 316.

• **Le Louis XV** (Monte Carlo, Monaco; ℭ **92-16-29-76**): Maybe because he was spending too much time at his

other restaurants in New York or Paris, the 2001 Michelin guide lowered chef Alain Ducasse's rating here from three stars to two stars. The good news is that even without Michelin's wholehearted approval, this restaurant is just as good as it's always been, whether Ducasse shows up or not. The kitchen specializes in the ultimate blending of the flavors of Liguria with the tastes and aromas of Provence and Tuscany. Yes, Ducasse dares grace the local macaroni gratin with truffles. See p. 346.

14 The Best Deals on Dining

• **Emile** (Toulouse, Languedoc-Roussillon; ℭ **05-61-21-05-56**): On one of the most beautiful old squares of Toulouse, this restaurant serves one of the finest regional cuisines in the area, all at an affordable price. The cassoulet Toulousain is hailed as the town's best. The flower-filled terrace is a magnet in the summer. See p. 81.

• **Le Bistro Latin** (Aix-en-Provence, Provence; ℭ **04-42-38-22-88**): The economic virtue of this Provençal restaurant lies in its fixed-price menus, whose composition is something of an art form. The prices are low, the flavors are sensational, and hints of Italian zest pop up frequently in such dishes as risotto with scampi. See p. 191.

• **La Fourchette** (Avignon, Provence; ℭ **04-90-85-20-93**): Creative cookery

at modern prices is offered at this authentically French bistro in the center of town. Long known for its value and good food, the airy dining rooms here tempt you with platter after platter, everything from monkfish stew with endive to fresh sardines flavored with citrus. See p. 147.

• **Le Safari** (Nice, Eastern Riviera; ℭ **04-93-80-18-44**): This ever-popular, ever-crowded brasserie overlooking the cours Saleya market soaks up every ray of Riviera sun. Dressed in jeans, waiters hurry back and forth, serving the habitués and visitors alike on the sprawling terrace. This place makes one of the best salad Niçoise concoctions in town, as well as a drop-dead spring lamb roasted in a wood-fired oven. See p. 319.

15 The Best Shopping Bets

• **Centre Sant-Vicens** (Perpignan, Languedoc-Roussillon; ℭ **04-68-50-02-18**): This region of France is next door to Catalonia, whose capital is Barcelona. Catalan style, as long ago evoked by Antoni Gaudí, is modern and up-to-date here—at affordable prices. Textiles, pottery, and furnish-

ings in forceful geometric patterns are displayed at this showcase. See "Perpignan" in chapter 4.

• **Mistral-Les Indiens de Nîmes** (Avignon, Provence; ℭ **04-90-86-32-05**): Provence has long been celebrated for its fabrics, and one of the best, most original, and affordable selections is

THE BEST SHOPPING BETS

found here. Open since the early 1980s, this outlet went back into the attic to rediscover old Provençal fabrics and to duplicate them in a wide assortment. The fabric is sold by the meter and can be shaped into everything from clothing to tableware. See "Avignon" in chapter 5.

- **Les Olivades Factory Store** (St-Etienne-du-Grès, Provence; © 04-90-49-19-19): About 12km (7½ miles) north of Arles on the road leading to Tarascon, this store features the region's most fully stocked showroom of art objects and fabrics inspired by the traditions of Provence. You'll find fabrics, dresses, shirts for men and women, table linen, and fabric by the yard. Part of the Olivades chain, this store has the widest selection and the best prices. See "Arles" in chapter 5.

- **Santons Fouque** (Aix-en-Provence, Provence; © 04-42-26-33-38): Collectors from all over Europe and North America purchase *santons* (figures of saints) in Provence. You'll find the best ones here, cast in terra cotta, finished by hand, and decorated with an oil-based paint. The figures are from models made in the 1700s. See "Aix-en-Provence" in chapter 5.

- **Verreries de Biot** (Biot, Eastern Riviera; © 04-93-65-03-00): Biot has long been known for its unique pottery, *verre rustique*. Since the 1940s, artisan glassmakers here have been creating this bubble-flecked glass in brilliant colors like cobalt and emerald. They're collector's items but sold at affordable prices on home turf. The Verreries de Biot is the oldest, most famous, and most frequently visited outlet. A half-dozen others are within a short distance of the town. If you arrive at this shop on any day except Sunday, you can actually see the glassmakers creating this unique product. See "Biot" in chapter 7.

2

Planning Your Trip to the South of France

In the pages that follow, we've compiled everything you need to know about the practical details of planning your trip: what documents you'll need, how to use French currency, how to find the best airfare, when to go, and more.

1 The Regions in Brief

LANGUEDOC-ROUSSILLON Languedoc might be a less popular destination than Provence, but it's compelling all the same and is also less frenetic and more affordable. Much of its landscape, cuisine, and lifestyle is similar to that of its neighbor, Provence. **Roussillon** is the rock-strewn arid French answer to ancient Catalonia, just across the Spanish border, linked more to Barcelona than to Paris. The **Camargue** is the name given to the steaming marshy delta formed by two arms of the Rhône River. Rich in bird life, it's famous for its flat expanses of tough grasses and for such fortified medieval sites as **Aigues-Mortes.** Also appealing are **Toulouse,** the bustling pink capital of Languedoc; and the "red city" of **Albi,** birthplace of Toulouse-Lautrec. **Carcassonne,** a marvelously preserved walled city with fortifications begun around A.D. 500, is the region's highlight.

PROVENCE This legendary region flanks the Alps and the Italian border along its eastern end and incorporates a host of sites that have long been frequented by the rich and reclusive. It's a land of gnarled olive trees, cypresses, umbrella pines, almond groves, lavender fields, and countless vineyards. The western section is more like Italy, its Mediterranean neighbor, than like France. Premier destinations are **Aix-en-Provence,** associated with Cézanne; **Arles,** "the soul of Provence," captured so brilliantly by van Gogh; **Avignon,** once the capital of Christendom during the 14th century; and **Marseille,** a port city established by the ancient Phoenicians (in some ways more North African than French). Special Provence gems are the small villages, like **Les Baux, Gordes,** and **St-Rémy-de-Provence,** birthplace of Nostradamus.

THE COTE D'AZUR (FRENCH RIVIERA) The strip of glittering coastal towns along Provence's southern edge is known as the Azure Coast. Long a playground of the rich and famous, the Riviera has become hideously overbuilt and spoiled by tourism. Even so, the names of its resorts still ring with excitement and evoke glamour: **Cannes, St-Tropez, Cap d'Antibes, St-Jean-Cap-Ferrat.** July and August are the most crowded times, but spring and fall can be a delight. **Nice** is the most affordable base for exploring the area. The principality of **Monaco,** the fabled piece of the Côte d'Azur, occupies less than a square mile. Don't expect sandy beaches—most are rocky. Topless

The South of France

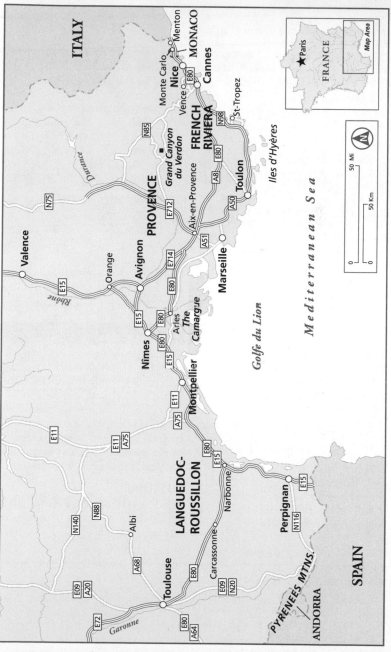

ITALY

MONACO

Menton

Monte Carlo

Nice

Vence

E80

Cannes

St-Tropez

FRENCH RIVIERA

N98

N85

Grand Canyon du Verdon

E80

A8

Toulon

Iles d'Hyères

PROVENCE

Aix-en-Provence

A50

E712

N75

A51

Durance

E714

Marseille

Valence

Orange

Avignon

E80

Mediterranean Sea

E15

Rhône

E15

E80

Arles

The Camargue

E80

Nîmes

E15

Golfe du Lion

Montpellier

E11

E11

A75

E11

A75

E80

E15

N140

N88

Albi

LANGUEDOC-ROUSSILLON

Narbonne

Perpignan

E15

N116

A68

Carcassonne

E09

A20

E80

Toulouse

E09

N20

SPAIN

E72

Garonne

E80

A64

PYRENEES MTNS.

ANDORRA

50 Mi

50 Km

★ Paris

FRANCE

Map Area

bathing is common, especially in St-Tropez. Glitterati and eccentrics have always been attracted to this narrow strip of real estate, but so have dozens of artists and their patrons, who have left behind a landscape of world-class galleries and art museums.

2 Visitor Information

REGIONAL INFORMATION

Your best source of information before you go is the **French Government Tourist Office;** visit its website at www.franceguide.com. In the United States, you can also call ℂ **410/286-8310** to request information. In Canada, call ℂ **514/876-9881;** in the United Kingdom, ℂ/fax **020/7493-6594;** in Ireland, call ℂ **015/60-235-235;** and in Australia, call ℂ **02/9231-5244.** There's no representative in New Zealand, so you can call the Australian office.

INFORMATION ON MONACO

Information on travel to Monaco is available from the **Monaco Government Tourist and Convention Office** at www.visitmonaco.com. Most of its facilities (along with its consulate) are in New York at 565 Fifth Ave., 23rd Floor (ℂ **800/753-9696** or 212/286-3330). In London, the office is at 3/18 Chelsea Garden Market, The Chambers, Chelsea Harbour, SW10 0XF (ℂ **020/7352-9962**).

MORE INFORMATION ONLINE

Other helpful websites include Beyond the French Riviera (**www.provence beyond.com**), Guide Web Provence (**www.provence.guideweb.com**), Relais & Châteaux (**www.relaischateaux.com**), and FranceScape (**www.france.com/francescape**).

3 Entry Requirements & Customs

For an up-to-date country-by-country listing of passport requirements around the world, go to the "Foreign Entry Requirement" Web page of the U.S. State Department at www.travel.state.gov.

The French government no longer requires visas for **U.S. citizens,** as long as they're staying in France for less than 90 days. For longer stays, U.S. visitors must apply for a long-term visa, residence card, or temporary-stay visa. Each requires proof of income or a viable means of support in France and a legitimate purpose for remaining in the country. Applications are available from the Consulat-Général de France; check **www.france-consulat.org** for the location of the nearest office.

Document requirements for travel to Monaco are exactly the same as those for travel to France, and there are virtually no border patrols or passport formalities at the Monégasque frontier.

CUSTOMS

WHAT YOU CAN BRING INTO FRANCE Customs restrictions for visitors entering France differ for citizens of

---

Tips **Museum Passes**

Carte Musée Côte d'Azur gives you entry to more than 60 museums and other attractions along the Riviera. A 1-day pass costs 10€ ($13), a 3-day pass costs 17€ ($22), and a 7-day pass costs 27€ ($35). For details, call ℂ **04-97-03-82-20** or visit www.crt-riviera.fr.

the European Union and for citizens of non-E.U. countries. **Non-E.U. nationals** can bring in duty-free 200 cigarettes, 100 cigarillos, 50 cigars, or 250 grams of smoking tobacco. You can also bring in 2 liters of wine, 1 liter of alcohol over 22 proof, and 2 liters of wine 22 proof or under; 50 grams of perfume; a quarter liter of eau de toilette; 500 grams of coffee; and 200 grams of tea. Visitors 15 and over can bring in other goods totaling 75€; for those 14 and under, the limit is 90€. (Customs officials tend to be lenient about general merchandise, realizing that the limits are unrealistically low.) **Citizens of E.U. countries** can bring in any amount of goods as long as these goods are intended for their personal use and not for resale.

WHAT YOU CAN BRING HOME

Returning U.S. citizens who have been away for 48 hours or more are allowed to bring back, once every 30 days, $800 worth of merchandise duty-free. You'll be charged a flat rate of 4% duty on the next $1,000 worth of purchases. Be sure to have your receipts handy. On mailed gifts, the duty-free limit is $200. With some exceptions, you cannot bring fresh fruits and vegetables into the United States. For specifics on what you can bring back, download the invaluable free pamphlet *Know Before You Go* online at **www.customs.gov**, or contact the **U.S. Customs Border Protection (CBP)**, 1300 Pennsylvania Ave. NW, Washington, DC 20229 (© **877/287-8867**), and request the pamphlet.

For a clear summary of **Canadian** rules, write for the booklet *I Declare,* issued by the **Canada Customs and Revenue Agency** (© **800/461-9999** in Canada, or 204/983-3500; www.cbsa-asfc.gc.ca). Canada allows its citizens a C$750 exemption once a year and only after an absence of 7 days, and you're allowed to bring back duty-free 1 carton of cigarettes, 1 can of tobacco, 40 imperial ounces of liquor, and 50 cigars. In addition, you're allowed to mail gifts to Canada valued at less than C$60 a day, provided that they're unsolicited and don't contain alcohol or tobacco (write on the package "Unsolicited gift, under $60 value"). All valuables should be declared on the Y-38 form before departure from Canada, including serial numbers of valuables you already own, such as expensive foreign cameras.

Citizens of the United Kingdom who are returning from a European Union country will go through a separate Customs Exit (called the "Blue Exit") especially for E.U. travelers. In essence, there is no limit on what you can bring back as long as the items are for personal use (this includes gifts) and you have already paid the necessary duty and tax. However, Customs law sets out guidance levels. If you bring in more than these levels, you might be asked to prove that the goods are for your own use. Guidance levels on goods bought in the E.U. for your own use are 3,200 cigarettes, 200 cigars, 400 cigarillos, 3 kilograms of smoking tobacco, 10 liters of spirits, 90 liters of wine, 20 liters of fortified wine (such as port or sherry), and 110 liters of beer. For more information, contact HM Customs & Excise at © **0845/010-9000** (from outside the United Kingdom, 020/8929-0152), or consult the website www.hmce.gov.uk.

The duty-free allowance in **Australia** is A$400 or, for those under 18, A$200. Citizens can bring in 250 cigarettes or 250 grams of loose tobacco, and 1,125 milliliters of alcohol. If you're returning with valuables you already own, such as foreign-made cameras, you should file form B263. A helpful brochure available from Australian consulates or Customs offices is *Know Before You Go*. For more information, call the **Australian Customs Service** at © **1300/363-263,** or log on to www.customs.gov.au.

The duty-free allowance for **New Zealand** is NZ$700. Citizens over 17 can bring in 200 cigarettes, 50 cigars, or 250 grams of tobacco (or a mixture of all three if their combined weight doesn't exceed 250g), plus 4.5 liters of wine and beer or 1.125 liters of liquor. New Zealand currency does not carry import or export restrictions. Fill out a certificate of export listing the valuables you are taking out of the country; that way, you can bring them back without paying duty. Request the free pamphlet *New Zealand Customs Guide for Travellers, Notice no. 4* from **New Zealand Customs,** The Customhouse, 17–21 Whitmore St., Box 2218, Wellington (© **04/473-6099** or 0800/ 428-786; www.customs.govt.nz).

4 Money

France, and especially the Riviera, is one of the world's most expensive destinations. But, to compensate, it often offers top-value food and lodging. Part of the problem is the value-added tax (VAT—called TVA in France), which tacks between 6% and 33% onto everything.

It's expensive to rent and drive a car in France (gasoline is costly, too), and flying within France generally costs more than flying within the United States. Train travel is relatively inexpensive, however, especially if you purchase a rail pass.

It's a good idea to exchange some money—enough to cover airport incidentals and transportation to your hotel—before you leave so you can avoid the less favorable rates at airport currency exchange desks. You can exchange money at your local **American Express** (© **800/807-6233;** www.americanexpress.com), or **Thomas Cook** (© **800/223-7373;** www. thomascook.com) office or your bank.

It's best to exchange currency or traveler's checks at a bank, not a currency exchange desk, hotel, or shop.

CURRENCY

The **euro,** the single European currency, became the official currency of France and 11 other participating countries on January 1, 1999. The old currency, the French franc, disappeared into history on March 1, 2002, replaced by the euro, whose official abbreviation is EUR. Exchange rates of participating countries are locked into a common currency fluctuating against the dollar.

ATMs

ATMs are linked to a national network that most likely includes your bank at home. **Cirrus** (© **800/424-7787;** www. mastercard.com) and **Plus** (© **800/843-7587;** www.visa.com) are the two most popular networks.

Note: Find out your daily withdrawal limit before you depart. Also keep in mind that many banks impose a fee every time a card is used at a different bank's ATM, and that fee can be quite high for international transactions (up to $5 or more).

TRAVELER'S CHECKS

Traveler's checks, though they have become less important since the advent of the ATM, still offer security to many travelers. If they are lost or stolen and you have a record of their serial numbers, they are easily replaced.

American Express offers traveler's checks in denominations of $10, $20, $50, $100, $500, and $1,000. You'll pay a service charge ranging from 1% to 4%. You can also get American Express traveler's checks over the phone by calling © **800/221-7282.** By using this number, Amex gold and platinum cardholders are exempt from the fee.

Visa offers traveler's checks at Citibank locations nationwide, as well as at

Foreign Currencies vs. the U.S. Dollar

Conversion ratios between the U.S. dollar and other currencies fluctuate, and their differences could affect the relative costs of your trip. The figures reflected in the currency chart below were valid at the time of this writing, but they might not be valid by the time of your departure. This chart would be useful for conversions of relatively small amounts of money, but if you're planning on any major transactions, check for updated rates prior to making any serious commitments.

The U.S. Dollar and the Euro. One U.S. dollar was worth approximately 0.76€ at the time of this writing. (Inversely stated, that means that 1€ was worth approximately 1.30 U.S. cents.)

The British Pound, the U.S. Dollar, and the Euro. At presstime, £1 equaled approximately 1.90 U.S. or approximately 1.45€.

The Canadian Dollar, the U.S. Dollar, and the Euro. At presstime, 1 Canadian dollar equaled approximately 84 U.S. cents or approximately 63 eurocents.

Euro €	US$	UK £	C$	Euro €	US$	UK £	C$
1.00	1.30	0.68	1.58	75.00	97.50	51.00	118.50
2.00	2.60	1.36	3.16	100.00	130.00	68.00	158.00
3.00	3.90	2.04	4.74	125.00	162.50	85.00	197.50
4.00	5.20	2.72	6.32	150.00	195.00	102.00	237.00
5.00	6.50	3.40	7.90	175.00	227.50	119.00	276.50
6.00	7.80	4.08	9.48	200.00	260.00	136.00	316.00
7.00	9.10	4.76	11.06	225.00	292.50	153.00	355.50
8.00	10.40	5.44	12.64	250.00	325.00	170.00	395.00
9.00	11.70	6.12	14.22	275.00	357.50	187.00	434.50
10.00	13.00	6.80	15.80	300.00	390.00	204.00	474.00
15.00	19.50	10.20	23.70	350.00	455.00	238.00	553.00
20.00	26.00	13.60	31.60	400.00	520.00	272.00	632.00
25.00	32.50	17.00	39.50	500.00	650.00	340.00	790.00
50.00	65.00	34.00	79.00	1000.00	1300.00	680.00	1580.00

several other banks. The service charge ranges between 1.5% and 2%; checks come in denominations of $20, $50, $100, $500, and $1,000. Call ℂ **800/732-1322** for information. AAA members can obtain Visa checks without a fee at most AAA offices or by calling ℂ **866/339-3378. MasterCard** also offers traveler's checks. Call ℂ **800/223-9920** for a location near you.

CREDIT CARDS

Credit cards are a safe way to carry money and also provide a convenient record of all your expenses. You can also withdraw cash advances from your credit cards at any bank (though you'll start paying hefty interest on the advance the moment you receive the cash). At most banks, you don't even need to go to a teller; you can get a cash advance at the ATM if you

Tips   How to Get Your VAT Refund

French sales tax, or **VAT (value-added tax)**, is now a hefty 19.6%, but you can get most of that back if you spend 175€ ($228) or more at any participating retailer. The name of the refund is *détaxe*, meaning exactly what it says. You never really get the full 19.6% back, but you can come close.

After you spend the required minimum amount, ask for your détaxe papers; fill out the forms before you arrive at the airport and allow at least half an hour for standing in line. All refunds are processed at the final point of departure from the E.U., so if you're going to another E.U. country, apply for the refund there.

If you're considering a major purchase, especially one that falls between 175€ ($228) and 304€ ($395), ask the store policy before you get too involved—or be willing to waive your right to the refund.

know your PIN. (If you've forgotten your PIN or didn't even know you had one, call the phone number on the back of your credit card and ask the bank to send it to you.) Keep in mind that credit card companies try to protect themselves from theft by limiting the funds someone can withdraw outside their home country, so notify your credit card company before you leave home.

If your wallet has been lost or stolen, notify your credit card companies immediately and file a report at the nearest police precinct. Your credit card company or insurer might require a police report number or record of the loss.

For tips and telephone numbers to call if your wallet is stolen or lost, see "Lost & Found" in the "Fast Facts: The South of France" section, later in this chapter.

5 When to Go

In terms of weather, the most idyllic months for visiting the south of France are May and June. Though the sun is intense, it's not uncomfortable. Coastal waters have warmed up by then, so swimming is possible, and all the resorts have come alive after a winter slumber but aren't yet overrun. The flowers and herbs in the countryside are at their peak, and driving conditions are ideal. In June, it remains light until around 10:30pm.

The most overcrowded times—also the hottest, in more ways than one—are July and August, when seemingly half of Paris shows up in the briefest of bikinis. Reservations are difficult to make, discos are blasting, and space is tight on the popular beaches. The worst traffic jams on the coast occur all the way from St-Tropez to Menton.

Aside from May and June, our favorite time is September and even early October, when the sun is still hot and the great hordes have headed back north. This is also a good time for seeing the art museums along the Côte d'Azur and the cultural attractions in Avignon and other Provençal cities.

In November, the weather is often pleasant, especially at midday, though some of the restaurants and inns you'll want to visit might take a sudden vacation. It's the month that many chefs and hoteliers elect to go on their own vacations after a summer of hard work.

Winter hasn't been the fashionable season since the 1930s. In the early days of tourism, when Queen Victoria came to visit, all the fashionable people showed up in winter, deserting the Côte by April. Today it's just the reverse. However, winter on the Riviera is being rediscovered, and many visitors (particularly retired people or those with leisure time) elect to visit then. If you don't mind the absence of sunbathing and beach life, this could be a good time to show up. However, some resorts, like St-Tropez, become ghost towns when the cold weather comes, though Cannes, Nice, Monaco, and Menton remain active year-round.

WEATHER

The Mediterranean coast has the driest climate in France. Most rain falls in spring and autumn. Summers are comfortably dry—beneficial to humans but deadly to much of the vegetation, which (unless it's irrigated) often dries and burns up in the parched months.

Provence dreads le mistral (a cold, violent wind from the French and Swiss Alps that roars south down the Rhône Valley). It most often blows in winter, sometimes for a few days, but sometimes for up to 2 weeks.

Average Temperature & Rainfall in Provence & the Riviera

	Jan	Feb	Mar	Apr	May	June	July	Aug	Sept	Oct	Nov	Dec
Marseille												
Temp. (°F)	44	46	50	55	62	70	75	74	69	60	51	46
Temp. (°C)	6.7	7.8	10	13	17	21	24	23	21	16	11	7.8
Rainfall (in.)	1.9	1.6	1.8	1.8	1.8	1.0	0.6	1.0	2.5	3.7	3.0	2.3
Nice												
Temp. (°F)	48	49	52	55	62	68	74	74	70	62	54	50
Temp. (°C)	8.9	9.4	11	13	17	20	23	23	21	17	12	10
Rainfall (in.)	3.0	2.9	2.9	2.5	1.9	1.5	0.7	1.2	2.6	4.4	4.6	3.5

HOLIDAYS (JOURS FERIES)

In France, holidays are known as jours feriés. Shops and many businesses (banks and some museums and restaurants) close on holidays, but hotels and emergency services remain open.

The main holidays—a mix of secular and religious—include New Year's Day (Jan 1), Easter Sunday and Monday (early Apr), Labor Day (May 1), V-E Day in Europe (May 8), Whit Monday (mid-May), Ascension Thursday (40 days after Easter), Bastille Day (July 14), Assumption of the Blessed Virgin (Aug 15), All Saints' Day (Nov 1), Armistice Day (Nov 11), and Christmas (Dec 25).

PROVENCE CALENDAR OF EVENTS

January

Monte Carlo Motor Rally. The world's most venerable car race. For more information, call ℂ **377-92-16-61-66.** Usually mid-January.

February

Fête de la Chandeleur (Candlemas), Basilique St-Victor, Marseille. A celebration in honor of the arrival in Marseille of the three Marys. A procession brings the Black Virgin up from the crypt of the abbey. For more information, call ℂ **04-91-13-89-00.** Early February.

Carnival of Nice. Float processions, parades, confetti battles, boat races, street music and food, masked balls, and fireworks are part of this ancient celebration. The climax follows a 113-year-old tradition in which King Carnival is burned in effigy, an event preceded by Les Batailles des Fleurs (Battles of the Flowers), during which members of opposing teams pelt one another with flowers. Come with proof of a hotel reservation. For information or reservations, contact the **Nice Convention and Visitors Bureau,** at ✆ **08-92-70-74-07,** or visit www.nice tourism.com. Mid-February to early March.

April

Féria Pascale (Easter Bullfighting Festival), Arles. This is a major bullfighting event that includes not only appearances by the greatest matadors, but also *abrivados* and *bodegas* (wine stalls). For more information, call ✆ **04-90-18-41-20.** Easter.

Procession des Pénitents (Procession of the Penitants). These marches are conducted in both **Arles** ✆ **04-90-18-41-20** and **Collioure** ✆ **04-68-82-15-47.** Good Friday.

Procession du Christ Mort (Procession of the Dead Christ). On the French Riviera, one of the most fascinating religious processions is in **Roquebrune-Cap Martin** ✆ **04-93-35-62-87.** Good Friday.

May

La Fête des Gardians (Camargue Cowboys' Festival), Arles. This event features a procession of Camargue cowboys through the streets of town. Activities feature various games involving bulls, including Courses Camarguaises, in which competitors have to snatch a rosette from between the horns of a bull. For information, call ✆ **04-90-18-41-20.** May.

Cannes Film Festival. Movie madness transforms this city into the kingdom of the media-related deal, with daily melodramas acted out in cafes, on sidewalks, and in hotel lobbies. It's great for voyeurs. Reserve early and make a deposit. Getting a table on the Carlton terrace is even more difficult than procuring a room. Admission to some of the prestigious films is by invitation only. There are box-office tickets for the less important films, which play 24 hours. For information, contact the Palais des Festivals, esplanade Georges-Pompidou, 06400 Cannes ✆ **04-93-99-86-35;** www.festival-cannes.org. Mid-May.

Festival des Musiques d'Aujourd'hui, Marseille. This festival presents the works of young French and European composers in music and dance. For more information, call **Experimental Music Groups of Marseille** at ✆ **04-91-39-29-00.** Mid-May.

Monaco Grand Prix de Formule. Hundreds of cars race through the narrow streets and winding corniche roads in a surreal blend of high-tech machinery and medieval architecture. For more information, call ✆ **377-93-15-26-00;** www.acm.mc. Mid-May.

Fête de la Transhumance (Move to Summer Grazing), St-Rémy. This event celebrates the now-abandoned custom of shepherds presenting their flocks to the public before moving them to higher ground for summer. In this mock event, the flocks move off as if really going up to the mountains. For more information, call ✆ **04-90-92-05-22.** Mid- to late May.

Le Pélerinage des Gitans (Gypsies' Pilgrimage), Stes-Maries-de-la-Mer. This festival is in memory of the two Marys for whom the town is named (Mary, the mother of James the lesser, and Mary Salome, the mother of James the greater and John). A model boat containing statues of the saints and a statue of St. Sarah, patron saint of Gypsies, is taken to the seashore and blessed by the bishop. For more information, call ℂ **04-90-97-82-55;** www.saintesmaries.com. Last week of May.

June

Festival de la St-Eloi, Maussane-les-Alpilles. For this festival, wagons are decorated and raced in the Carreto Ramado, followed by Mass, a procession in traditional dress, and a benediction. Special events are held and local produce and handicrafts are sold. For more information, call ℂ **04-90-54-52-04.** Mid-June.

Festival Aix en Musique, Aix-en-Provence. Concerts of classical music and choral singing are held in historic buildings, such as the Cloisters of the Cathédrale St-Sauveur and the Hôtel Maynier d'Oppède. For more information, call ℂ **04-42-16-11 61.** Throughout June and July.

Festival d'Expression Provençale, Abbaye St-Michel de Frigolet, Tarascon. At this festival, homage is paid to the region's language with works by Provençal writers that are acted in French and Provençal. For more information, call ℂ **04-90-91-03-52.** Late June to early July.

Fête de la Tarasque, Tarascon. The town relives St. Martha's victory over the dragon known as the Tarasque, which was believed to live in the Rhône in the 1st century. There's a procession of horsemen, an archery competition, historical events, a medieval tournament, a Tarasque procession, Novilladas (young bull-fighters), and an orchestral concert with fireworks. For more information, call ℂ **04-90-91-03-52.** Late June.

Feu de la St-Jean (St. John's Fire), Fontvieille. This event features folk troupes and Camargue cowboys who gather in front of the Château de Montauban. For more information, call ℂ **04-90-54-67-49.** June 25.

Reconstitution Historique, Salon-de-Provence. This pageant held in honor of Nostradamus includes a cast of 700 in historical costume and is followed by a son-et-lumière at the Château d'Empéri. For more information, call ℂ **04-90-56-27-60.** Late June to early July.

Festival de Marseille Méditerranée. This festival features concerts and recitals of music and song from the entire Mediterranean region. Theater and dance are also presented, along with special exhibitions in the city's main museums. For more information, call ℂ **04-91-13-89-00** or fax 04-91-13-89-20. Late June to late July.

July

St-Guilhem Music Season, St-Guilhem le Désert, Languedoc. This festival of baroque organ and choral music is held in a medieval monastery. For information, call ℂ **04-67-57-44-33;** www.saint-guilhem-le-desert.com. Month of July.

La Fête des Pêcheurs (Fishermen's Festival), Cassis. The local "Prud'hommes" (members of the elected industrial tribunal) walk in procession wearing traditional dress, and a Mass is held in honor of St. Peter, followed by a benediction. For more information, call ℂ **04-42-01-71-17.** Early July.

Bastille Day. Celebrating the birth of modern-day France, the festivities in the south reach their peak in Nice with street fairs, pageants, fireworks, and feasts. The day begins with a parade down the promenade des Anglais and ends with fireworks in the Vieille Ville. No matter where you are, by the end of the day you'll hear Piaf warbling "La Foule" (The Crowd), the song that celebrated her passion for the stranger she met and later lost in a crowd on Bastille Day. Similar celebrations also take place in Cannes, Arles, Aix, Marseille, and Avignon. July 14.

Nuit Taurine (Nocturnal Bull Festival), St-Rémy-de-Provence. At this festival, the focus is on the age-old allure of bulls and their primeval appeal to roaring crowds. *Abrivados* involve bulls in the town square as "chaperoned" by trained herders on horseback; *encierros* highlight a Pamplona-style stampeding of bulls through the streets. Music from local guitarists and flaming torches add drama. For more information, call © **04-90-92-05-22.** Mid-July.

Nice Jazz Festival. This is the biggest, flashiest, and most prestigious jazz festival in Europe, with world-class entertainers. Concerts begin in early afternoon and go on until late at night (sometimes all night in the clubs) on the Arènes de Cimiez, a picturesque hill above the city. Reserve hotel rooms way in advance. For information, contact the Grand Parade du Jazz, c/o the tourist office of Nice © **04-92-14-46-46;** www.nicejazzfest.com. Mid-July.

Festival d'Aix-en-Provence. This musical event par excellence features everything from Gregorian chant to melodies composed on computerized synthesizers. The audience sits on the sloping lawns of the 14th-century papal palace for operas and concertos. Local recitals are performed in the medieval cloister of the Cathédrale St-Sauveur. Make advance hotel reservations and take a written confirmation with you when you arrive. Expect heat, crowds, and traffic. For more information, contact the **Festival International d'Art Lyrique et de Musique,** Palais de l'Ancien Archévêche, 13100 Aix-en-Provence © **04-42-17-34-00;** www.festival-aix.com. Throughout July.

Les Chorégies d'Orange, Orange. One of southern France's most important lyric festivals presents oratorios and choral works by master performers whose voices are amplified by the ancient acoustics of France's best-preserved Roman amphitheater. For more information, call © **04-90-34-24-24;** www.choregies.asso.fr. Mid-July to early August.

Festival d'Avignon. One of France's most prestigious theater events, this world-class festival has a reputation for exposing new talent to critical acclaim. The focus is usually on avant-garde works in theater, dance, and music by groups from around the world. Make hotel reservations early. For information, call © **04-90-14-14-14;** www.festival-avignon.com. Last 3 weeks of July.

Fête de la St-Eloi (Feast of St. Eloi), Gémenos. Some hundred draft horses draw a procession of traditional flower-decked wagons. Folk troupes also perform. For more information, call © **04-42-32-18-44.** Late July.

August

Fêtes Daudet (Daudet Festival), Fontvieille. At this festival, Mass said in Provençal is held on the Avenue of Pine Trees. There's folk dancing outside Daudet's mill and a torchlight procession through the streets of town to the mill. For more information, call © **04-90-54-67-49.** Mid-August.

Féria de St-Rémy, St-Rémy-de-Provence. This event features a 4-day celebration of bulls with *abrivado* and *encierro* (see the Nuit Taurine entry, above), branding, and Portuguese bull fighting (matadors on horseback). For more information, call © **04-90-92-05-22.** Mid-August.

September

Féria des Prémices du Riz (Rice Harvest Festival), Arles. Bullfights are held in the amphitheater with leading matadors, and a procession of floats makes its way along boulevard des Lices; there are also traditional events with cowboys and women in regional costume. For more information, call ℂ **04-90-18-41-20.** Early September.

Fête des Olives, Mouriès. A Mass is held in honor of the green olive. There's a procession of groups in traditional costume, an olive tasting, and sales of regional produce. For more information, call ℂ **04-90-47-56-58.** Mid-September.

Journée de l'Olivier en Provence, Salon-de-Provence. Another celebration of the olive, this event is attended by producers of olive oil, Marseille soap, olive-wood articles, booksellers, and pottery and earthenware makers. Special events are held in the history center. For more information, call ℂ **04-90-56-27-60.** Late September.

October

Perpignan Jazz Festival. Musicians from everywhere jam in what many visitors consider Languedoc's most appealing season. For more information, call ℂ **04-68-51-13-41;** www.jazzebre.com. Month of October.

November

Marché aux Santons, Tarascon. Craftspersons from throughout Provence congregate in this medieval village to sell their *santons* (carved representations of saints). For more information, call ℂ **04-90-91-03-52.** Four days in late November. This event is supplemented, sometimes with the same sellers, who move to the **Foire aux Santons** in Marseille, held between late November and Christmas. For more information, call ℂ **04-91-13-89-00** or fax 04-91-13-89-20.

December

Fête des Bergers (Shepherds Festival), Istres. This festival features a procession of herds on their way to winter pastures. There are cowboys, a Carreto Ramado, a blessing of the horses, an all-night Provençal party with shepherds and Provençal storytellers, and folk troupes. For more information, call ℂ **04-42-55-51-15.** First weekend in December.

Foire de Noël, Mougins. Hundreds of merchants, selling all manner of Christmas ornaments and gifts, descend on Mougins in Provence, to herald in the Christmas spirit. For more information, call ℂ **04-93-75-87-67.** Mid- to late December.

Midnight Mass, Fontvieille. A traditional midnight Mass, including the *pastrage* ceremony, the presentation of a newborn lamb. There's a procession of folk troupes, Camargue cowboys, and women in traditional costume from Daudet's mill to the church, followed by the presentation of the lamb. For more information, call ℂ **04-90-54-67-49.** December 24.

Noël Provençal, Eglise St-Vincent, Les Baux. The procession of shepherds is followed by a traditional midnight Mass, including the *pastrage* ceremony, traditional songs, and performance of a nativity play. For more information, call ℂ **04-90-54-34-39.** December 24.

Fête de St-Sylvestre (New Year's Eve), nationwide. Along the Riviera, it's most boisterously celebrated in Nice's Vieille Ville around place Garibaldi. At midnight, the city explodes. Strangers kiss strangers, and place Masséna and the promenade des Anglais become virtual pedestrian malls. December 31.

6 Travel Insurance

Check your existing policies before you buy travel insurance for trip cancellation, lost luggage, medical expenses, or car rental insurance. You might have partial or complete coverage. But if you need more, ask your travel agent about a package. The cost of insurance varies, depending on the cost and length of your trip, your age and health, and the type of trip you're taking. Insurance for sports or adventure travel costs more than coverage for a European cruise. Some insurers provide packages for specialty vacations like skiing or backpacking. More dangerous activities might be excluded from basic policies.

TRIP-CANCELLATION INSURANCE Trip-cancellation insurance helps you get your money back if you have to back out of a trip, if you have to go home early, or if your travel supplier goes bankrupt. Allowed reasons for cancellation can range from sickness to natural disasters to the State Department declaring your destination unsafe for travel. (Insurers usually won't cover vague fears, though, as many travelers discovered when they tried to cancel their trips in Oct 2001 because they were wary of flying.) In this unstable world, trip-cancellation insurance is a good buy if you're getting tickets well in advance. Insurance policy details vary, so read the fine print—and especially make sure that your airline or cruise line is on the list of carriers covered in case of bankruptcy. For information, contact one of the following insurers: **Access America** (© 866/807-3982; www.accessamerica.com); **Travel Guard International** (© 800/826-4919; www.travelguard.com); **Travel Insured International** (© 800/243-3174; www.travelinsured.com); and **Travelex Insurance Services** (© 888/457-4602; www.travelex-insurance.com).

MEDICAL INSURANCE Most health insurance policies cover you if you get sick away from home—but check, particularly if you're insured by an HMO. With the exception of certain HMOs and Medicare/Medicaid, your medical insurance should cover medical treatment—even hospital care—overseas. However, most out-of-country hospitals make you pay your bills upfront and send you a refund after you've returned home and filed the necessary paperwork. And in a worst-case scenario, there's the high cost of emergency evacuation. If you require additional medical insurance, try **MEDEX Assistance** (© 410/453-6300; www.medexassist.com) or **Travel Assistance International** (© 800/821-2828; www.travelassistance.com; for general information on services, call the company's Worldwide Assistance Services, Inc., at © **800/777-8710**).

LOST-LUGGAGE INSURANCE On international flights (including U.S. portions of international trips), baggage is limited to approximately $9.07 per pound, up to approximately $635 per checked bag. If you plan to check items more valuable than the standard liability, see if your valuables are covered by your homeowner's policy, get baggage insurance as part of your comprehensive travel-insurance package, or buy Travel Guard's BagTrak product. Don't buy insurance at the airport; it's usually overpriced. Be sure to take any valuables or irreplaceable items with you in your carry-on luggage because many valuables (including books, money, and electronics) aren't covered by airline policies.

If your luggage is lost, immediately file a lost-luggage claim at the airport detailing the luggage contents. For most airlines, you must report delayed, damaged, or lost baggage within 4 hours of arrival. The airlines are required to deliver luggage, once found, directly to your house or destination free of charge.

7 Health & Safety

STAYING HEALTHY

In general, France is viewed as a "safe" destination. You don't need to get shots, most food is safe, and the water in France is potable. It is easy to get a prescription filled in French towns and cities; Provence and the Riviera have some of the best medical facilities in Europe, and finding an English-speaking doctor is generally no problem in most of the top resorts of the Riviera or major cities in Provence such as Avignon.

If you get sick, consider asking your hotel concierge to recommend a local doctor—even his or her own. You can also try the emergency room at a local hospital; many have walk-in clinics for emergency cases that are not life-threatening. You might not get immediate attention, but you won't pay the high price of an emergency room visit.

STAYING SAFE

Criminals frequent tourist attractions such as museums, monuments, restaurants, hotels, beaches, trains, train stations, airports, and subways. Purse snatching and pickpocketing occur throughout the south of France. Americans in Provence and Monaco should be particularly alert to pickpockets in train stations and on public transportation. Passports should be carried on the body when necessary, and over-the-shoulder bags should not be used.

Crimes involving vehicles with nonlocal license plates are common. Thefts from cars stopped at red lights are also common, particularly in the Nice-Antibes-Cannes area and in Marseille. Car doors should be kept locked at all times while traveling to prevent incidents of "snatch and grab" thefts. In this type of scenario, the thief is usually a passenger on a motorcycle. Similar incidents have also occurred at tollbooths and rest areas. Special caution is advised when entering and exiting the car because that offers opportunity for purse-snatchings. There have also been a number of thefts at Nice Airport, particularly at car-rental parking lots where bags have been snatched as drivers have been loading luggage into rental cars.

Traveling with Minors

It's always wise to have plenty of documentation when traveling in today's world with children. For changing details on entry requirements for children traveling abroad, keep up to date by going to the U.S. State Department website: www.travel.state.gov.

To prevent international child abduction, E.U. governments have initiated procedures at entry and exit points. These often (but not always) include requiring documentary evidence of relationship and permission for the child's travel from the parent or legal guardian not present. Having such documentation on hand, even if not required, facilitates entries and exits. All children must have their own passport. To obtain a passport, the child **must** be present—that is, in person—at the center issuing the passport. Both parents must be present as well. If not, then a notarized statement from the parents is required.

Any questions parents or guardians might have can be answered by calling the **National Passport Information Center** at © 877/487-2778 Monday to Friday 8am to 8pm Eastern Standard Time.

Break-ins of parked cars are also frequent. Locking valuables in the trunk is not a safeguard. Valuables should not be left unattended in a car.

The loss or theft of a passport should be reported immediately to local police and your nearest embassy or consulate, where you can obtain information about passport replacement.

8 Specialized Travel Resources

TRAVELERS WITH DISABILITIES

Facilities for travelers with disabilities are above average in France, and nearly all modern hotels in the south of France now provide rooms designed for persons with disabilities. However, older hotels (unless they've been renovated) might not have elevators, special toilet facilities, or ramps for wheelchair access.

The new high-speed **TGV trains** are wheelchair accessible; older trains have special compartments for wheelchair boarding. Guide dogs ride free. Be aware that some older stations don't have escalators or elevators.

Association des Paralysés de France, 17 bd. Auguste-Blanqui, 75013 Paris (© 01-40-78-69-52; www.apf.asso.fr), is a privately funded organization that provides wheelchair-bound individuals with documentation, moral support, and travel ideas. In addition to the central Paris office, it maintains an office in each of the 90 *départements* of France and can help you find accessible hotels, transportation, sightseeing, house rentals, and (in some cases) companionship for paralyzed or partially paralyzed travelers. It's not, however, a travel agency.

Many travel agencies offer customized tours and itineraries for travelers with disabilities. **Flying Wheels Travel** (© 507/451-5005; www.flyingwheelstravel.com) offers escorted tours and cruises that emphasize sports and private tours in minivans with lifts. **Access-Able Travel Source** (© 303/232-2979; www.access-able.com) offers extensive access information and advice for traveling around the world with disabilities. **Accessible Journeys** (© 800/846-4537 or 610/521-0339; www.disabilitytravel.com) caters specifically to slow walkers and wheelchair travelers and their families and friends.

Organizations that offer assistance to travelers with disabilities include the **Moss Rehab Hospital** (www.mossresourcenet.org), which provides a library of accessible-travel resources online; the **Society for Accessible Travel and Hospitality** (© 212/447-7284; www.sath.org; annual membership fees $45 adults, $30 seniors and students), which offers a wealth of travel resources for all types of disabilities and informed recommendations on destinations, access guides, travel agents, tour operators, vehicle rentals, and companion services; and the **American Foundation for the Blind** (© 800/232-5463; www.afb.org), which provides information on traveling with Seeing Eye dogs.

In the United Kingdom, **RADAR** (Royal Association for Disability and Rehabilitation), Unit 12, City Forum, 250 City Rd., London ECIV 8AF (© 020/7250-3222; www.radar.org.uk), publishes holiday "fact packs," which sell for £2 each or £5 for a set of all three. The first one provides general information, including planning and booking a holiday, insurance, finances, and useful organization and holiday providers. The second outlines transport and equipment, transportation available when going abroad, and equipment for rent. The third deals with specialized accommodations.

Another good resource is the **Holiday Care Service,** Sunley House, 7th Floor, 4 Bedford Park, Croydon, Surrey CR0 2AP, UK (© **0845/124-9971;** fax 01293/784-647; www.holidaycare.org.uk), a national charity that advises on accessible accommodations for the elderly and persons with disabilities. Once a member, you can receive a newsletter and access to a free reservations network for hotels throughout Britain and, to a lesser degree, Europe and the rest of the world.

FOR GAY & LESBIAN TRAVELERS

France is one of the world's most tolerant countries toward gays and lesbians, and no special laws discriminate against them. "The Gay Riviera" boasts a large gay population, with dozens of gay clubs and restaurants.

Gay Provence, 42 rue du Coq, Marseille (© **04-91-84-08-96;** www.gay-provence.org), is operated by a group of gays and lesbians, each native to Provence, who offer tours to American and European gays and lesbians. Various interests can be either preplanned or customized, and tours range from 1 day to 1 week. Participants are welcomed into the private homes of gay or gay-friendly locals—perhaps a cheese brunch at a goat farm or an evening in a private 18th-century castle. Attractions include such outdoor excursions as hiking, biking, or horseback riding, or cultural activities such as Mediterranean cooking lessons or meetings with artists and artisans.

The International Gay & Lesbian Travel Association (IGLTA) (© **800/448-8550** or 954/776-2626; www.iglta.org) is the trade association for the gay and lesbian travel industry, and offers an online directory of gay- and lesbian-friendly travel businesses.

Many agencies offer tours and travel itineraries specifically for gay and lesbian travelers. **Above and Beyond Tours** (© **800/397-2681;** www.abovebeyond

tours.com) is the exclusive gay and lesbian tour operator for United Airlines. **Now, Voyager** (© **800/255-6951;** www.nowvoyager.com) is a well-known San Francisco–based gay-owned and -operated travel service. **Olivia Cruises & Resorts** (© **800-631-6277;** www.olivia.com) charters entire resorts and ships for exclusive lesbian vacations and offers smaller group experiences for both gay and lesbian travelers.

The following travel guides are available at most travel bookstores and gay and lesbian bookstores, or you can order them from **Giovanni's Room** bookstore in Philadelphia (© **215/923-2960;** www.giovannisroom.com): *Out and About* (© **800/929-2268;** www.outandabout.com), which offers guidebooks and a newsletter 10 times a year packed with solid information on the global gay and lesbian scene; *Spartacus International Gay Guide* and *Odysseus,* both good, annual English-language guidebooks focused on gay men, but many of the addresses featured can be out of date—the curse of writing a gay publication; the *Damron* guides, with separate annual books for gay men and lesbians; and, of course, *Frommer's Gay & Lesbian Europe.*

FOR SENIORS

Many discounts are available for seniors—men and women of the "third age," as the French say. Contact the French Government Tourist Office (see "Visitor Information," earlier in this chapter).

At any rail station in France, seniors 60 and over (with proof of age) can get **A La Carte Senior.** The pass costs 50€ ($65) and is good for a 50% discount on unlimited rail travel throughout the year. The *carte* also offers reduced prices on some regional bus lines and half-price admission at state-owned museums. There are some restrictions—for example, you can't use it between 3pm Sunday and noon Monday and from noon Friday to noon Saturday.

Air France offers seniors a 10% reduction on its regular nonexcursion tariffs on travel within France. Some restrictions apply. Discounts of around 10% are offered to passengers 62 and over on selected Air France international flights. Be sure to ask for the discount when booking.

Members of **AARP** (© 888/687-2277; www.aarp.org) get discounts on hotels, airfares, and car rentals. AARP offers members a wide range of benefits, including *AARP The Magazine* and a monthly newsletter. Anyone over 50 can join.

Many reliable agencies and organizations target the 50-plus market. **Elderhostel** (© 877/426-8056; www.elderhostel.org) arranges study programs for those 55 and over (and a spouse or companion of any age). Most courses last 5 to 7 days in the United States and 2 to 4 weeks abroad, and many include airfare, accommodations in university dormitories or modest inns, meals, and tuition. **ElderTreks** (© 800/741-7956; www.eldertreks.com) offers small-group tours to off-the-beaten-path or adventure travel locations, restricted to travelers 50 and older.

Recommended publications offering travel resources and discounts for seniors include the quarterly magazine *Travel 50 & Beyond* (www.travel50andbeyond.com); *Travel Unlimited: Uncommon Adventures for the Mature Traveler* (Avalon); *101 Tips for Mature Travelers,* available from Grand Circle Travel (© 800/221-2610 or 617/350-7500; www.gct.com); *The 50+ Traveler's Guidebook* (St. Martin's Press); and *Unbelievably Good Deals and Great Adventures That You Absolutely Can't Get Unless You're Over 50* (McGraw-Hill).

FOR STUDENTS

If you're planning to travel outside the United States, you'd be wise to arm yourself with an **International Student Identity Card (ISIC),** which offers substantial savings on rail passes, plane tickets, and entrance fees. It also provides you with basic health and life insurance and a 24-hour help line. The card is available for $22 from **STA Travel** (© 800/781-4040,** and if you're not in North America, there's probably a local number in your country; www.statravel.com). If you're no longer a student but are still under 26, you can get an **International Youth Travel Card (IYTC)** for the same price from the same people, which entitles you to some discounts. (*Note:* In 2002, STA Travel bought competitors **Council Travel** and **USIT Campus** after they went bankrupt. It's still operating some offices under the Council name, but it's owned by STA.) **Travel CUTS** (© 800/667-2887 or 416/614-2887; www.travelcuts.com) offers similar services for both Canadians and U.S. residents. Irish students should turn to **USIT** (© 01/602-1600; www.usitnow.ie).

If you'd like to travel with other like-minded souls, check out the menu of trips offered by **Contiki** (© 866/CONTIKI; www.contiki.com), the world's largest travel company for 18- to 35-year-olds. Popular tours include "The Best of France" and "Mediterranean Highlights."

SURFING FOR AIRFARES

The "big three" online travel agencies, **Expedia.com, Travelocity.com,** and **Orbitz.com,** sell most of the air tickets bought on the Internet. (Canadian travelers should try **Expedia.ca** and **Travelocity.ca**; U.K. residents can go to **Expedia.**co.uk and **Opodo.co.uk.**) Each has different business deals with the airlines and might offer different fares on the same flights, so it's wise to shop around. Of the smaller travel agency websites, **SideStep** (www.sidestep.com) has received the best reviews from Frommer's authors. It's a

Frommers.com: The Complete Travel Resource

For an excellent travel-planning resource, we highly recommend **Frommers.com** (www.frommers.com). We're a little biased, of course, but we guarantee that you'll find the travel tips, reviews, monthly vacation giveaways, and online-booking capabilities thoroughly indispensable. Among the special features are our popular **Message Boards,** where Frommer's readers post queries and share advice (sometimes even our authors show up to answer questions); **Frommers.com Newsletter,** for the latest travel bargains and insider travel secrets; and **Frommer's Destinations Section,** where you'll get expert travel tips, hotel and dining recommendations, and advice on the sights to see for more than 3,000 destinations around the globe. When your research is done, the **Online Reservations System** (www.frommers.com/book_a_trip) takes you to Frommer's preferred online partners for booking your vacation at affordable prices.

browser add-on that purports to "search 140 sites at once," but in reality it beats competitors' fares only as often as other sites do.

Also remember to check **airline websites.** Even with major airlines, you can often shave a few bucks from a fare by booking directly through the airline and avoiding a travel agency's transaction fee. But you'll get these discounts only by **booking online.** For the websites of airlines that fly to and from your destination, go to "Getting to the South of France," below.

If you're willing to give up some control over your flight details, use an **opaque fare service** like **Priceline** (www.priceline.com or www.priceline.co.uk) or **Hotwire** (www.hotwire.com). Both offer rock-bottom prices in exchange for travel on a "mystery airline" at a mysterious time of day, often with a mysterious change of planes en route. The mystery airlines are all major, well-known carriers, and the airlines' routing computers have gotten a lot better than they used to be. Your chances of getting a flight from New York to Nice via Chicago are low, but your chances of getting a 6am or 11pm

flight are pretty high. Hotwire tells you flight prices before you buy; Priceline usually has better deals than Hotwire, but you have to play its "name our price" game. If you're new at this, the helpful folks at **BiddingForTravel** (www.biddingfortravel.com) do a good job of demystifying Priceline's prices. Priceline and Hotwire are great for flights within North America and between the United States and Europe.

For much more about airfares and savvy air-travel tips and advice, pick up a copy of *Frommer's Fly Safe, Fly Smart* (Wiley Publishing, Inc.).

SURFING FOR HOTELS

Shopping online for hotels is much easier in the United States, Canada, and certain parts of Europe, including Provence, than it is in the rest of the world. Of the "big three" sites, **Expedia** might be the best choice, thanks to its long list of special deals. **Travelocity** runs a close second. Hotel specialist sites **hotels.com** and **hoteldiscounts.com** are also reliable. An excellent free program, **TravelAxe** (www.travelaxe.net), can help you search multiple hotel sites at once, even ones you might never have heard of.

Priceline and Hotwire are even better for hotels than for airfares; with both, you're allowed to pick the neighborhood and quality level of your hotel before offering up your money. Priceline's hotel product covers Europe and Asia, though it's much better at getting luxury lodging for bargain prices than at finding anything at the bottom of the scale. *Note:* Hotwire overrates its hotels by one star.

SURFING FOR RENTAL CARS

For booking rental cars online, the best deals are usually found at rental-car company websites, although all the major online travel agencies also offer rental-car reservations services. Priceline and Hotwire work well for rental cars, too; the only "mystery" is which major rental company you get, and for most travelers, the difference among Hertz, Avis, and Budget is negligible.

10 The 21st-Century Traveler

INTERNET ACCESS AWAY FROM HOME

Travelers have any number of ways to check their e-mail and access the Internet on the road. Of course, using your own laptop—or even a PDA or electronic organizer with a modem—gives you the most flexibility. But if you don't have a computer, you can still access your e-mail and even your office computer from cybercafes.

WITHOUT YOUR OWN COMPUTER

It's hard nowadays to find a city that *doesn't* have a few cybercafes. Although there's no definitive directory for cybercafes—these are independent businesses, after all—three places to start looking are at **www.cybercaptive.com**, **www.netcafeguide.com**, and **www.cybercafe.com**.

To retrieve your e-mail, ask your **Internet service provider (ISP)** if it has a Web-based interface tied to your existing e-mail account. If your ISP doesn't have such an interface, you can use the free **mail2web** service (www.mail2web.com) to view and reply to your home e-mail. For more flexibility, you might want to open a free, Web-based e-mail account with **Yahoo! Mail** (http://mail.yahoo.com) or **Fastmail** (www.fastmail.fm). (Microsoft's Hotmail is another popular option, but it has severe spam problems.) Your home ISP might be able to forward your e-mail to the Web-based account automatically.

If you need to access files on your office computer, look into a service called **GoToMyPC** (www.gotomypc.com). The service provides a Web-based interface for you to access and manipulate a distant PC from anywhere—even a cybercafe—provided that your "target" PC is on and has an always-on connection to the Internet (such as with Road Runner cable). The service offers top-quality security, but if you're worried about hackers, use your own laptop rather than a cybercafe to access the GoToMyPC system.

WITH YOUR OWN COMPUTER

Wi-fi (wireless fidelity) is the buzzword in computer access, and more and more hotels, cafes, and retailers are signing on as wireless "hotspots" from where you can get high-speed connection without cable wires, networking hardware, or a phone line (see below). You can get wi-fi connection on in several ways. Many laptops old in the last year have built-in wi-fi capability (an 802.11b wireless Ethernet connection). Mac owners have their own networking technology, Apple AirPort. For those with older computers, an 802.11b/**Wi-fi card** (around $50) can be plugged into your laptop. You sign up for wireless access service much as you do cellphone service, through a plan offered by one of several commercial companies that have made wireless service available in airports, hotel lobbies, and coffee shops, primarily in the U.S. (followed by the U.K. and Japan). **Boingo** (www.boingo.com) and **Wayport** (www.wayport.com) have set up networks in airports and high-class hotel lobbies. IPass providers (www.ipass.com) also give you access to a few hundred wireless hotel lobby setups. Best of all, you don't need to be staying at the Four Seasons to use the hotel's network; just set yourself up on a nice couch in the lobby. The companies' pricing policies can be byzantine, with a variety of monthly, per-connection, and per-minute plans, but in general you pay around $30 a month for limited access—and as more and more companies jump on the wireless bandwagon, prices are likely to get even more competitive.

There are also places that provide **free wireless networks** in cities around the world. To locate these free hotspots, go to www.personaltelco.net/index.cgi/Wireless Communities.

If wi-fi is not available at your destination, most business-class hotels throughout the world offer dataports for laptop modems, and a few thousand hotels in the U.K. and Europe now offer free high-speed Internet access using an Ethernet network cable. You can bring your own cables, but most hotels rent them for around $10. **Call your hotel in advance** to see what your options are.

USING A CELLPHONE

The three letters that define much of the world's **wireless capabilities** are GSM (Global System for Mobiles), a big seamless network that makes for easy cross-border cellphone use throughout Europe and dozens of other countries worldwide. In the United States, T-Mobile, AT&T Wireless, and Cingular use this quasi-universal system; in Canada, Microcell and some Rogers customers are GSM; and all Europeans and most Australians use GSM.

If your cellphone is on a GSM system and you have a world-capable phone, such as many (but not all) Sony Ericsson, Motorola, Nokia, or Samsung models, you can make and receive calls across much of the globe. Just call your wireless operator and ask for "international roaming" to be activated on your account. Unfortunately, per-minute charges can be high—usually $1 to $1.50 in western Europe.

That's why it's important to buy an "unlocked" world phone from the get-go. Many cellphone operators sell "locked" phones that restrict you from using any other removable computer memory phone chip (called a **SIM card**) card other than the ones they supply. Having an unlocked phone allows you to install a cheap, pre-paid SIM card (found at a local retailer) in your destination country. (Show your phone to the salesperson; not all phones work on all networks.) You'll get a local phone number—and much, much lower calling rates. Getting an already locked phone unlocked can be a complicated process, but it can be done; just call your cellular operator and say you'll be going abroad for several months and want to use the phone with a local provider.

For many, **renting** a phone is a good idea, but it doesn't come cheap. You'll usually pay $40 to $50 per week, plus airtime fees of at least a dollar a minute. If you're traveling to England, though, local rental companies often offer free incoming calls within their home country, which can save you big bucks. The bottom line: Shop around.

Two good wireless rental companies are **InTouch USA** (© 800/872-7626; www.intouchglobal.com) and **RoadPost** (© 888-290-1606 or 905/272-5665; www.roadpost.com). Give them your itinerary, and they'll tell you what wireless products you need. InTouch will also advise you on whether your existing phone will work overseas for free; simply call © 703/222-7161 between 9am and 4pm EST, or go to www.intouchglobal.com/travel.htm.

11 Getting to the South of France

FROM NORTH AMERICA
BY PLANE

Most airlines divide their year roughly into seasonal slots, with the lowest fares between November 1 and March 13. Shoulder season, between the high and low seasons, is only slightly more expensive and includes mid-March to mid-June and all of October. These can be ideal times to visit southern France.

THE MAJOR U.S. CARRIERS All major airlines fly to Paris from the U.S. cities listed below. Once you fly into Orly or Charles de Gaulle, you must take **Air France** (✆ 800/237-2747; www.air france.com), to reach your destination in Languedoc, Provence, or the Riviera. From Orly and Charles de Gaulle, there are 20 flights per day to Marseille and to Nice, 16 to Toulouse, and 4 from Monday to Friday and 2 Saturday and Sunday to Avignon.

American Airlines (✆ 800/433-7300; www.aa.com) offers daily flights to Paris from Dallas–Fort Worth, Chicago, Miami, Boston, and New York. **Delta Airlines** (✆ 800/241-4141; www.delta.com) flies nonstop to Paris from Atlanta. Delta also operates daily nonstop flights from both Cincinnati and New York. All these flights depart late enough in the day to permit transfers from much of Delta's vast North American network. Note that Delta is the only American airline offering nonstop service from New York to Nice.

Continental Airlines (✆ 800/525-0280; www.continental.com) provides nonstop flights to Paris from Newark and Houston. Flights from Newark depart daily, while flights from Houston depart four to seven times a week, depending on the season. **US Airways** (✆ 800/428-4322; www.usairways.com) offers daily nonstop service from Philadelphia to Paris.

THE FRENCH NATIONAL CARRIER **Air France** (✆ 800/237-2747; www.airfrance.com) was formed from a merger combining three of France's largest airlines. The airline offers a daily nonstop flight between New York and Nice and also offers regular flights between Paris and such North American cities as Newark; Washington, D.C.; Miami; Atlanta; Boston; Cincinnati; Chicago; New York; Houston; San Francisco; Los Angeles; Montréal; Toronto; and Mexico City.

THE MAJOR CANADIAN CARRIER Canadians usually choose the **Air Canada** (✆ 888/247-2262 in the U.S. and Canada; www.aircanada.ca) flights to Paris from Toronto and Montréal that depart every evening. Two of Air Canada's flights from Toronto are shared with Air France and feature Air France aircraft.

GETTING THROUGH THE AIRPORT

Bring a **current, government-issued photo ID** such as a driver's license or passport. Keep your ID ready to show at check-in, the security checkpoint, and sometimes even the gate. Children under 18 do not need government-issued photo IDs for domestic flights, but they do for international flights to most countries.

Federalization has stabilized **what you can carry on** and **what you can't.** The general rule is that sharp things are out, nail clippers are okay, and food and beverages must be passed through the X-ray machine—but security screeners can't make you drink from your coffee cup. Bring food in your carry-on rather than checking it because explosive-detection machines used on checked luggage have been known to mistake food (especially chocolate, for some reason) for bombs. The Transportation Security Administration (TSA) has issued a list of restricted items; check its website at **www.tsa.gov** for details.

FLYING FOR LESS: TIPS FOR GETTING THE BEST AIRFARE

Passengers sharing the same airplane cabin rarely pay the same fare. Travelers who need to purchase tickets at the last minute, change their itinerary at a moment's notice, or fly one-way often get stuck paying the premium rate. Here are some ways to keep your airfare costs down.

* Passengers who can book their ticket **long in advance,** who can **stay over Saturday night,** or who **fly midweek** or **at less-trafficked hours** will pay a fraction of the full fare. If your schedule is flexible, say so, and ask if you can secure a cheaper fare by changing your flight plans.

* You can also save on airfares by keeping an eye out in local newspapers for **promotional specials** or **fare wars,** when airlines lower prices on their most popular routes. You rarely see fare wars offered for peak travel times, but if you can travel in the off-months, you might snag a bargain.

* Search **the Internet** for cheap fares (see "Planning Your Trip Online," earlier in this chapter).

* **Consolidators,** also known as bucket shops, are great sources for international tickets. Start by looking in Sunday newspaper travel sections; U.S. travelers should focus on the *New York Times, Los Angeles Times,* and *Miami Herald.* For less-developed destinations, small travel agents who cater to immigrant communities often have the best deals. *Beware:* Bucket shop tickets are usually nonrefundable or have stiff cancellation penalties, often as high as 50% to 75% of the ticket price, and some put you on charter airlines, which may leave at inconvenient times and experience delays. Several

reliable consolidators are worldwide and available on the Net. **STA Travel** is now the world's leader in student travel, thanks to its purchase of Council Travel. It also offers good fares for travelers of all ages. **ELTExpress (Flights.com) (© 800/TRAV-800;** www.eltexpress.com) started in Europe and has excellent fares worldwide, particularly to that continent. It also has "local" websites in 12 countries. **FlyCheap (© 800/FLY-CHEAP;** www.1800flycheap.com) is owned by package-holiday megalith MyTravel and has especially good fares to sunny destinations. **Air Tickets Direct (© 800/778-3447;** www.airtickets direct.com) is based in Montréal and leverages the currently weak Canadian dollar for low fares; it'll also book trips to places that U.S. travel agents won't touch, such as Cuba.

* Join **frequent-flier clubs.** Accrue enough miles, and you'll be rewarded with free flights and elite status. It's free, and you'll get the best choice of seats, faster response to phone inquiries, and prompter service if your luggage is stolen, if your flight is canceled or delayed, or if you want to change your seat. You don't need to fly to build frequent-flier miles—frequent-flier credit cards can provide thousands of miles for doing your everyday shopping.

FROM PARIS
BY PLANE

From Paris, if you're heading for the French Riviera, your connecting flight will probably land you in Nice's international airport, Aéroport Nice–Côte d'Azur. There are also airports at Avignon, Marseille, Montpellier, Nîmes, and Toulouse.

BY TRAIN

With some 50 cities in France, including Marseille and Nice, linked by the world's fastest trains, you can reach the south of

France in just a few hours. With 24,000 miles of track and about 3,000 stations, **SNCF** (French National Railroads) is fabled throughout the world for its on-time performance. You can travel first- or second-class by day as well as in a couchette or sleeper by night. Many trains carry dining facilities, which range from cafeteria-style meals to formal dinners.

The **TGV Méditerranée High-Speed Rail Line** (or TGV Med), which opened in June 2001, brought the south of France closer to Paris. Trip time between Paris and Marseille takes only 3 hours now instead of the usual 5. The high-speed track has been extended from the Provençal city of Avignon, where the track splits to go in one direction to Marseille and in the other direction to Nîmes. The link cost $3.25 billion and took 12 years to complete. Five hundred bridges and 20 viaducts were built between Valence and Marseille for the new tracks, with 1 million trees planted to meet environmental standards. New double-decker carriages on the trains, giving visitors a bird's-eye view of the lavender fields and vineyards of Provence, are being added.

INFORMATION   If you plan much travel on European railroads, get the latest copy of the *Thomas Cook European Timetable of Railroads.* It's available online at www.thomascooktimetables.com.

For more information in the United States and to purchase rail passes (see below) before you leave, contact **Rail Europe** at ✆ **800/848-7245** or www.rail europe.com. In Canada, Rail Europe offices are at 2087 Dundas St. East, Suite 105, Mississauga, ON L4X 1M2 (✆ **800/ 361-7245**). In London, SNCF maintains offices at Rail Europe, 179 Piccadilly, London W1V OBA (✆ **0870/584-8848**).

For train information or to make reservations in Paris, call **SNCF** at ✆ **08-36-35-35-39** or check www.sncf.com. You can also go to any local travel agency, of course, and book tickets. A simpler way to book tickets is to take advantage of the *Billetterie* or ticket machines in every train station.

FRANCE RAIL PASSES   Working cooperatively with SNCF, Air Inter Europe, and Avis, Rail Europe offers three flexible rail passes that can reduce travel costs considerably.

The **France Railpass** provides unlimited rail transport in France for any 4 days within 1 month, at $263 in first class and $229 in second. You can purchase up to 6 more days for an extra $34 per person per day. Children 4 to 11 travel for half price.

The **France Rail 'n' Drive Pass,** available only in North America, combines good value on both rail travel and Avis car rentals, and is best used by arriving at a major rail depot and then striking out to explore the countryside by car. It includes the France Railpass (see above) and use of a rental car. A 4-day rail pass (first class) and 2 days' use of the cheapest rental car (with unlimited mileage) is $225 per person (assuming two people traveling together).

The best deal if you're traveling in France with a friend—or even 3 or 4 friends—is the **France Saverpass,** granting 4 days of unlimited travel in a 1-month period. The cost is $225 per person first class or $195 second class. There's also a **France Youthpass** for travelers 25 or under, granting 4 days of unlimited train travel within a month. The cost is $195 in first class or $172 in second class. Prices for solo travelers start at $285 for first class.

EURAILPASSES   In-the-know travelers take advantage of one of Europe's greatest travel bargains, the **Eurailpass,** which permits unlimited first-class rail travel in any country in western Europe except the British Isles (good in Ireland). Passes are sold only in North America and are nontransferable. A Eurailpass costs $588 for 15 days, $762 for 21 days, $946 for 1 month, $1,338 for 2 months, and $1,654 for 3 months. Children 3 and under travel free if they don't occupy a seat (otherwise they're charged half fare); children 4 to 11 are charged half fare.

If you're under 26, you can purchase a **Eurail Youthpass,** entitling you to unlimited second-class travel for $382 for 15 days, $495 for 21 days, $615 for 1 month, $870 for 2 months, and $1,075 for 3 months. Regardless of the pass, you'll have to pay a supplement for the high-speed TGV train anywhere in France.

Reservations are required on some trains (and cost an additional 10€/$13 per person). Many trains have *couchettes* (sleeping cars), which also cost extra. Obviously, the 2- or 3-month traveler gets the greatest economic advantages; the Eurailpass is ideal for extensive trips. You can visit all of France's major sights, from Normandy to the Alps, then end your vacation in Norway, for example. Eurailpass holders are entitled to discounts on certain buses and ferries as well.

Travel agents and railway agents in such cities as New York, Montréal, and Los Angeles sell Eurailpasses. You can purchase them at the North American offices of CIT Travel Service, the French National Railroads, the German Federal Railroads, and the Swiss Federal Railways.

The **EurailDrive Pass** offers 4 days of train travel and 2 days of Avis or Hertz car rental. You have 2 months to complete your travel. The cost of a package is $858 for two adults with first-class train travel and a compact car rental. The **Eurailpass** offers 5 consecutive days of unlimited travel, with various time slots featured—for example, $498 per person for 15 days of first-class rail travel.

Eurail Flexipass allows you to visit Europe with more flexibility. It's valid in first class and offers the same privileges as the Eurailpass. However, it provides a number of individual travel days you can use over a longer period of consecutive days. That makes it possible to stay in one city for a while without losing days of rail travel. There are two passes: 10 days of travel in 2 months for $694, and 15 days of travel in 2 months for $914.

The Eurail Youth Flexipass has many of the same qualifications and restrictions as the Flexipass. Sold only to travelers under 26, it allows 10 days of travel within 2 months for $451, and 15 days of travel within 2 months for $594.

FROM ELSEWHERE IN EUROPE
BY PLANE

From London, **Air France** (© 0845/ 084-5111; www.airfrance.com) and **British Airways** (© 0845/773-3377; www.ba.com) fly frequently to Paris, with a trip time of 1 hour. These airlines operate up to 17 flights daily from Heathrow. Many commercial travelers also use flights originating from the London City Airport in the Docklands. A ballpark figure for rates is London to Paris £29 ($42) one-way.

Direct flights to Paris also exist from other U.K. cities such as Manchester, Edinburgh, and Southampton. Contact Air France, British Airways, or **British Midland** (© 0870/607-0555; www.fly bmi.com). Daily papers often carry ads for cheap flights. The highly recommended **Trailfinders** (© 020/7937-5400; www.trailfinders.com) sells discounted fares.

You can reach Paris from any major European capital. Your best bet is to fly on the national carrier, Air France, with more connections into Paris from European capitals than any other airline. From Dublin, try **Aer Lingus** (© 866/IRISH-FLY; www.aerlingus.com), with the most flights to Paris from Ireland. From Amsterdam, the convenient choice is **KLM** (© 800/374-7747; www.klm.com).

If you don't want to go to Paris before flying to the south of France, you'll find a number of British flights going directly to the Nice–Côte d'Azur Airport, the Marseille-Provence Airport, and the Toulouse Airport. Daily flights are offered by British Airways, Air France, British Midland, and easyJet.

BY TRAIN

From the United Kingdom, most passengers arrive in Paris before going the rest of the way by train to Provence. Passengers can take the **TGV Med** from the Gare de Lyon. The TGV Med zips from Paris to Avignon in 2½ hours, to Marseille in 3 hours, and to Nice in 5½ hours. From the United Kingdom check www.raileurope.co.uk.

BY FERRY FROM ENGLAND

Ferries and hydrofoils operate day and night in all seasons, with the exception of last-minute cancellations during storms. Many crossings are timed to coincide with the arrival and departure of trains (especially those between London and Paris). Trains let you off a short walk from the piers. Most ferries carry cars, trucks, and freight, but some hydrofoils take passengers only. The major routes include at

Under the Channel

Queen Elizabeth and the late French president François Mitterrand opened the Channel Tunnel in 1994, and the *Eurostar Express* has daily passenger service from London to Paris and Brussels. The $15-billion tunnel, one of the great engineering feats of our time, is the first link between Britain and the Continent since the Ice Age. The 50km (31-mile) journey takes 35 minutes, with actual time spent in the Chunnel 19 minutes.

Eurostar tickets are available through **Rail Europe** (© 800/848-7245; www.raileurope.com). In London, make reservations for Eurostar (or any other train in Europe) at © 0870/584-8848. In Paris, call © 01-70-70-60-88. Chunnel train traffic is competitive with air travel, if you calculate door-to-door travel time. Trains leave from London's Waterloo Station and arrive in Paris at Gare du Nord. London-Paris one-way passenger fare is $225 for second class and $315 for first class.

Fares are complicated and depend on a number of factors. The cheapest one-way fare is Leisure RT, requiring a purchase at least 14 business days before the date of travel and a minimum 2-night stay. A return ticket must be booked to receive this discounted fare. The most expensive passage is a one-way fare of $400 in first class.

The Chunnel accommodates not only trains, but also passenger cars, buses, taxis, and motorcycles, from $145 each way for a small car. **Le Shuttle**, a train carrying vehicles under the Channel (© 0870/535-3535 in the U.K.; www.eurotunnel.com), connects Calais, France, with Folkestone, England. It operates 24 hours a day, 365 days a year, running every 15 minutes during peak travel times and at least once an hour at night. Before boarding Le Shuttle, you stop at a toll booth to pay and then pass through Immigration for both countries at one time. During the ride, you travel in air-conditioned carriages, remaining in your car or stepping outside to stretch your legs. An hour later, in France, you simply drive off.

least 12 trips a day between Dover or Folkestone and Calais or Boulogne.

Hovercraft and hydrofoils make the trip from Dover to Calais, the shortest distance across the Channel, in just 40 minutes during good weather, while the ferries might take several hours, depending on the weather and tides. If you're bringing a car, it's important to make reservations because space below decks is usually crowded. Timetables can vary depending on weather conditions and many other factors.

The leading operator of ferries across the channel is **P&O Ferries** (© **0870/ 520-2020;** www.poferries.com). It operates car and passenger ferries between Portsmouth, England, and Cherbourg, France (three departures a day; 4¼ hr. each way during daylight hours, 7 hr. each way at night); between Portsmouth and Le Havre, France (three a day; 5½ hr. each way). Most popular is the route between Dover, England, and Calais, France (25 sailings a day; 75 min. each way), costing £10 ($19) one-way; children under 4 go free.

The shortest and most popular route across the Channel is between Calais and Dover. **Hoverspeed** runs at least 12 hovercraft crossings daily; the trip takes 35 minutes. It also runs a SeaCat (a catamaran propelled by jet engines) that takes just under 1 hour between Dover and Calais; the SeaCats depart about four times a day on the 55-minute voyage. For reservations and information, call Hoverspeed (© **800/677-8585** in North America, or 0870/240-8070 in the U.K.; www. hoverspeed.com). Typical one-way fares are £28 ($53) per person.

If you plan to transport a rental car between England and France, check with the company about license and insurance requirements and drop-off charges. Many forbid transport of their vehicles over the water between England and France. Transport begins at £95 ($181) each way. A better idea is to ask about a car exchange program (Hertz's is called "Le Swap"), in which you drop off a right-drive car and pick up a left-drive vehicle at Calais.

12 Package Deals & Escorted Tours

For package tours that offer adventure and activity, see "Special-Interest Trips," below.

Before you start your search for the lowest airfare, you might want to consider booking your flight as part of a travel package such as an escorted tour or a package tour. What you lose in adventure, you'll gain in time and money saved when you book accommodations, and maybe even food and entertainment, along with your flight.

PACKAGE VACATIONS

Packages are not the same thing as escorted tours. They are simply a way to buy airfare and accommodations at the same time. For popular destinations like the south of France, they are a smart way to go because they save you a lot of money. In many

cases, a package that includes airfare, hotel, and transportation to and from the airport will cost you less than just the hotel alone would have, had you booked it yourself. That's because packages are sold in bulk to tour operators—who resell them to the public at a cost that drastically undercuts standard rates.

Packages, however, vary widely. Some offer flights on scheduled airlines, while others book charters. In some packages, your choice of accommodations and travel days might be limited. Some packages let you choose between escorted vacations and independent vacations; others allow you to add on just a few excursions or escorted day trips (also at lower prices than you could locate on your own) without booking an entirely escorted tour. Each destination usually has one or two packagers that are usually cheaper than the rest because they buy in even greater bulk. If you spend the time to shop around, you will save in the long run.

FINDING A PACKAGE DEAL The best place to start your search is the travel section of your local Sunday newspaper. Also check the ads in the back of national travel magazines like *Travel & Leisure, National Geographic Traveler,* and *Condé Nast Traveler.*

Liberty Travel (© 888/271-1584 to be connected with the agent closest to you; www.libertytravel.com), one of the biggest packagers in the Northeast, often runs a full-page ad in the Sunday papers. **American Express Travel** (© 800/335-3342; www.americanexpress.com) is another option. Check out its **Last Minute Travel Bargains** (www.last minute.com) site, offered in conjunction with **Continental Airlines,** with discounted vacation packages and reduced fares that differ from the E-savers bargains Continental e-mails weekly to subscribers.

Another good resource is the airlines themselves, which often package their flights with accommodations. Check the offerings from **American Airlines Vacations** (© 800/321-2121; www.aavacations. com) and **US Airways Vacations** (© 800/455-0123; www.usairwaysvacations.com).

The **French Experience** (© 800/283-7262 or 212/986-3800; www.french experience.com) offers inexpensive tickets to Paris on most scheduled airlines and arranges tours and stays in country inns, hotels, private châteaux, and B&Bs. In addition, it takes reservations for small hotels in Avignon, Aix-en-Provence, Cannes, and Nice.

ESCORTED TOURS

Escorted tours are structured group tours, with a group leader. The price usually includes everything from airfare to hotels, meals, tours, admission costs, and local transportation.

Many people derive a certain ease and security from escorted trips. Escorted tours let travelers sit back and enjoy their trip without having to spend lots of time behind the wheel. All the little details are taken care of, you know your costs upfront, and there are few surprises. Escorted tours are particularly convenient for people with limited mobility.

Before you invest in an escorted tour, ask about the **cancellation policy:** Is a deposit required? Can the company cancel the trip if it doesn't get enough people? Do you get a refund if the trip is canceled? If *you* cancel it? How late can you cancel if you are unable to go? When do you pay in full? *Note:* If you choose an escorted tour, think strongly about purchasing trip-cancellation insurance, especially if the tour operator asks you to pay upfront.

BOOKING AN ESCORTED TOUR The two largest tour operators conducting escorted tours of France and Europe are **Globus + Cosmos Tours** (© 800/276-1241; www.globusandcosmos.com) and **Trafalgar** (© 866/544-4434; www. trafalgartours.com). Both companies have first-class tours that run about $130 a day and budget tours for about $90 a day. The differences are mainly in hotel location and the number of activities. There's little difference in the companies' services, so choose your tour based on the itinerary and preferred date of departure. Brochures are available at travel agencies, and all tours must be booked through travel agents.

Tauck World Discovery (© 800/788-7885; www.tauck.com) provides first-class, escorted coach grand tours of France as well as 1-week general tours of regions within France. Its 14-day tour of France covering the Normandy landing beaches, the Bayeux Tapestry, and Mont-St-Michel costs $3,790 per person, double occupancy (land only), while a 13-day trip beginning in Nice and ending in Paris costs $4,490 to $4,900 per person.

13 Special-Interest Trips

Provence and the Côte d'Azur are especially well organized for visitors looking for sports pursuits. Most clubs will accept temporary members, and activities are wide-ranging, from biking through the countryside to golfing on the pine-fringed fairways of Provence, to swinging a tennis racquet close to Mediterranean waters. If you like your activities offbeat, you can even go barging along the lowlands of the Camargue.

Of course, if you want to go really local, you'll take up boules and its local variant, *pétanque.* The game is relatively simple to learn—any local can teach you—and it's played with small metal balls on earth courts in every dusty village square.

BARGING

Before the advent of the railways, many of the crops, building supplies, raw materials, and other products that sustained France were barged through a series of rivers, canals, and estuaries. Many of these are still graced with their old-fashioned locks and pumps, allowing shallow-draft barges easy passage through idyllic countryside.

Le Boat, 45 Whitney Road, Suite C-5, Mahwah, NJ 07430 (© **800/992-0291** or 201/560-1941; www.leboat.com), focuses on regions of France not covered by many other barge operators. The company's trio of barges are luxury craft of a size and shape that fit through the relatively narrow canals and locks of the Camargue, Languedoc, and Provence. Each 6-night tour accommodates no more than 10 passengers in five cabins outfitted with mahogany and brass, plus meals prepared by a Cordon Bleu chef. Prices depend on many factors and are highly variable, but call for information.

BICYCLING

A well-recommended company since 1979 is the California-based **Backroads,** 801 Cedar St., Berkeley, CA 94710 (© **800/462-2848** or 510/527-1555; www.backroads.com). Its well-organized tours of Provence last between 6 and 8 days and include stays in everything from Relais & Châteaux hotels to campgrounds where staff members prepare meals featuring local cuisine. All tours include an accompanying vehicle that provides liquid refreshments and assists in the event of breakdowns. A 7-day tour costs $3,898 per person.

Euro-Bike & Walking Tours, P.O. Box 990, DeKalb, IL 60115 (© **800/321-6060** or 815/758-8851; www.eurobike.com), offers 11-day tours in Provence ($2,645–$3,795 per person), and 7-day tours of Provence ($2,095–$2,795 per person). All are escorted and include room, breakfast, and dinner.

If you're interested in bicycling through selected regions of the south of France, the local tourist offices of each of the towns covered in this guide are, to an increasing degree, able to provide addresses, maps, and contacts for whatever a cyclist might need. In many cases, bikes can be rented within railway stations of any given town. For general advice on biking in France, contact the **Fédération Française du Cyclotourisme,** 12 rue Louis Bertrand, 74207 Paris (© **01-56-20-88-88;** www.ffct.org).

FISHING

The Mediterranean provides a variety of fish and fishing methods. You can line fish from the rocks along the coast or from small boats known as *pointu.* Local fishers often take visitors along when fishing in the sea for tuna. The rivers provide sea trout, speckled trout, and silver eel, and the sandy shores of the Camargue offer the *tellina,* or sunset shell, which are small shellfish. For more information on regulations and access to fishing areas, contact the **Comité Régional PACA de**

la Fédération des Pêcheurs en Mer
(© 04-91-72-63-96).

GOLF

The area around Bouches-du-Rhône has many fine golf courses, with seven 18-hole courses, five 9-hole courses, and several practice courses in the Provence area. One excellent 18-hole course is **Golf de la Salette**, impasse des Vaudrans, 13011 Marseille (© **04-91-27-12-16;** www.opengolfclub.com). One of the finest courses is **Golf de Valcros,** La Londe-Les Maures, 37km (23 miles) east of Toulouse off N98. Call © **04-94-66-81-02** for more information.

Golf International, Inc., 14 East 38th St., New York, NY 10016 (© **800/833-1389** or 212/986-9176; www.golfinternational.com), offers the Golfing Epicurean package: a weeklong trip based in the historic hilltop village of Mougins, a 10-minute drive from Cannes. Mougins is the golfing capital of the south of France and provides a wealth of fine dining opportunities. As part of this package, you spend 6 nights at the luxurious Les Mas Candille, a 200-year-old converted farmhouse in the village. The price includes golf on four of the best courses in the area: Royal Mougins, Cannes-Mougins, Valbonne, and Cannes-Mandelieu. Also included is a car rental with collision-damage waiver insurance and unlimited mileage. The cost is $2,685 to $3,285. You can request a copy of Golf International's *Complete Golfing Vacation Guide* by calling the number above.

For more information on the options available, contact the **Fédération Française de Golf,** 69 av. Victor-Hugo, 75116 Paris (© **01-41-40-77-00;** www.ffg.org).

GOURMET TOURS

Cuisine International, P.O. Box 25228, Dallas, TX 75225 (© **214/373-1161;** www.cuisineinternational.com), offers a 6-day culinary experience in Provence. Accommodations are in hotels and private homes, such as the one overlooking a lake in Provence that houses the school. Classes are arranged to allow time for sightseeing, and meals are eaten in restaurants and private homes. Rates are inclusive, except for airfare: The price is $2,600 to $3,250. **The French Kitchen,** 5 Ledgewood Way, no. 6, Peabody, MA 01960 (© **800/852-2625;** www.thefrenchkitchen.com), touts culinary vacations during which you stay in an 18th-century farmhouse (also the school) between Bordeaux and Toulouse. The price of a 6-day/5-night tour is $3,250 per person, including lodging, cooking classes, most meals, touring, and local transportation. In addition, four people can charter a 26m (85-ft.) barge for a week of cooking, dining, and touring.

HIKING

The Bouches-du-Rhône area is a walker's heaven, whether you enjoy a stroll or a strenuous long-distance hike or even mountain climbing. Walking challenges include the wetlands of the Camargue, the semiarid desert of La Crau, and the mountainous hills to the wild rocky inlets of Les Calanques. Long-distance hiking paths, **Sentiers de Grande Randonnée** (GRs), join the area's major places of interest. GR6 starts in Tarascon, runs along the foot of the Lubéron Hills, and crosses the Alpilles Hills. GR9 goes down the Lubéron, passes Mont Ste-Victoire, and ends in Ste-Baume. GR98 is an alternative path linking Ste-Baume with Les Calanques and ends in Marseille. GR51 links Marseille and Arles via La Crau. GR99A links GR9 to the highlands of the Var département.

Spring and autumn are the best for hiking; many of the paths are closed in summer because of forest fires. Be sure to check with the département before you begin your walk. For information, call © 02-38-58-49-64; or **Comité Départmental Mont-Alp-Escalade (Bouches-du-Rhône Mountaineering & Climbing**

Committee), Daniel Gorgeon, 5 impasse du Figuier, 13114 Puyloubier (© **04-42-66-35-05**).

Adventure Center, 1311 63rd St., Suite 200, Emeryville, CA 94608 (© **800/228-8747** or 510/654-1879; www.adventurecenter.com), sponsors 8-day hiking/camping trips in Provence, beginning and ending in Nice. The cost of an outing, exclusive of airfare and other travel-related expenses, is $790 to $820 per person, 160€ ($208) of which is a local fee added in France. Included are 4 nights of campground accommodations. Eight evening meals are provided; the other seven lunches are usually purchased in Provençal restaurants along the way. Campers are also expected to purchase three lunches. The company offers 16 trips per year, and though dates might vary, these include departures from May to September.

HORSEBACK RIDING

One of the best ways to see the wildlife, salt swamps, and marshlands of the Camargue or the wooded hills around Alpilles, Ste-Baume, and Mont Ste-Victoire is on horseback. For more information, contact **Manade Saliérène,** 13123 Arles (© **04-66-87-45-57**; www.manadesalierene.com) or the **Association Camarguaise de Tourisme Equestre (Camargue Equestrian Tourism Association),** Centre de Ginès-Pont de Gau, 13460 Stes-Maries-de-la-Mer (© **04-90-97-86-32**).

A clearinghouse for at least eight French stables is **Equitours** (The Soul of Provence), P.O. Box 807, Dubois, WY 82513 (© **800/545-0019** or 307/455-3363; www.ridingtours.com). It can arrange 8-day cross-country treks through Provence and the Camargue regions, with prices starting from $1,685 per person.

LANGUAGE SCHOOLS

A clearinghouse for information on French-language schools is **Lingua Service Worldwide,** 75 Prospect St., Suite 4, Huntington, NY 11743 (© **800/394-5327**; www.linguaserviceworldwide.com). Its programs cover Antibes, Aix-en-Provence, Avignon, Cannes, Juan-les-Pins, Montpellier, and Nice. Courses can be long- or short-term, the latter with 20 lessons per week. They range from $792 to $1,911 for 2 weeks, depending on the city, the school, and the accommodations.

14 Getting Around the South of France

The most charming Provençal villages and best country hotels always seem to lie away from the main cities and train stations. You'll find that renting a car is usually the best way to travel once you get to the south of France, especially if you plan to explore in depth and not stick to the standard route along the coast.

If you're not driving, you'll find that the south of France has one of the most reliable bus and rail transportation systems in Europe. Trains connect all the major cities and towns, such as Nice and Avignon. Where the train leaves off, you can most often rely on local bus service.

BY CAR

Driving time in Europe is largely a matter of conjecture, urgency, and how much sightseeing you do along the way. The driving time from Marseille to Paris is a matter of national pride, and tall tales abound about how rapidly the French can do it. With the accelerator pressed to the floor, you might conceivably make it in 7 hours, but we always make a 2-day journey of it.

CAR RENTALS To rent a car, you'll need to present a passport, a driver's license, and a credit card. You'll also have to meet the minimum-age requirement of the company. (For the least expensive cars, this is 21 at Hertz, 23 at Avis, and 25 at Budget. More expensive cars might require that you be at least 25.) It usually isn't obligatory within France, but certain companies have at times asked for the presentation of an International Driver's License, even though this is becoming increasingly superfluous in western Europe.

Note: The best deal is usually a weekly rental with unlimited mileage. All car-rental bills in France are subject to a 19.6% government tax. The rental company won't usually mind if you drive your car into, say, Germany, Switzerland, Italy, or Spain.

Unless it's factored into the rental agreement, an optional **collision-damage waiver (CDW)** carries an extra charge of 13€ to 21€ ($17–$27) per day for the least expensive car. Buying this usually eliminates all but $250 of your responsibility in the event of accidental damage to the car. Because most newcomers aren't familiar with local driving customs and conditions, we recommend you buy the CDW, though you should check with your credit card company first to see if it will cover this automatically when you rent with its card. (It might cover damage but not liability, so make sure you understand this clearly.) At some companies, the CDW won't protect you against theft, so if this is the case, ask about buying extra theft protection. This cost is 9€ ($12) extra per day.

Automatic transmission is considered a luxury in Europe, so if you want it, you'll have to pay dearly.

For rentals of more than 7 days, in most cases cars can be picked up in one French city and dropped off in another, but there are additional charges. Still, Budget's rates are among the most competitive, and its cars are well maintained. **Budget** (www.budget.com) has numerous locations in southern France, including

those in **Avignon** at the railway station (C) 04-90-82-97-92; in **Marseille** at the airport (C) 04-42-14-24-55, at 40 bd. De Plombières ((C) 04-91-64-40-03); in **Montpellier** at the airport (C) 04-67-20-07-34; in **Nice** at the airport ((C) 04-93-21-42-51); at 23 rue de Belgique, opposite the rail station ((C) 04-93-87-45-37); and in **Toulouse** at the airport ((C) 05-61-71-85-80).

Hertz (www.hertz.com) is also well represented, with offices in **Avignon** at the airport ((C) 04-90-84-19-50) and at the train station ((C) 04-32-74-62-80); in **Marseille** at the airport ((C) 08-25-09-13-13) and at 15 bd. Maurice-Bourdet ((C) 04-91-14-04-24); in **Montpellier** at the airport ((C) 04-67-20-04-64); in **Nice** at the airport ((C) 08-25-34-23-43); and in **Toulouse** at the airport ((C) 05-61-71-27-09) and at the rail station ((C) 05-62-73-39-47). When making inquiries, be sure to ask about promotional discounts.

Avis (www.avis.com) has offices in **Avignon** at the airport ((C) 04-90-87-17-75) and at the railway station ((C) 04-90-27-96-10); in **Marseille** at the airport ((C) 04-42-14-21-67) and at 267 bd. National ((C) 04-91-50-70-11); in **Montpellier** at the airport ((C) 04-67-20-14-95) and at 900 av. des Prés d'Arènes ((C) 04-67-92-51-92); in **Nice** at the airport ((C) 04-93-21-36-33) and at place Massena, 2 av. des Phocéens ((C) 04-93-80-63-52); and in **Toulouse** at the airport ((C) 05-34-60-46-50) and at the train station ((C) 05-61-62-50-40).

National (www.nationalcar.com) is represented in France by Europcar, with locations in **Avignon** at the train station ((C) 04-90-27-30-07); in **Marseille** at the airport ((C) 04-42-14-24-90) and the St-Charles train station, 96 blvd. Rabatau ((C) 04-91-83-05-05); in **Montpellier** at the airport ((C) 04-67-15-13-47); in **Nice** at the airport ((C) 04-93-21-80-90); and in **Toulouse** at the airport ((C) 05-61-30-00-01). You can rent a car on the spot at any of these offices, but lower rates are available by making advance reservations from North America.

Two United States–based agencies that don't have France offices but act as booking agents for France-based agencies are **Kemwel Holiday Auto** (© 800/678-0678; www.kemwel.com) and **Auto Europe** (© 800/223-5555; www.autoeurope.com). These can make bookings in the United States only, so call before your trip.

GASOLINE   Known in France as *essence,* gas is expensive for those accustomed to North American prices. All but the least expensive cars usually require an octane rating that the French classify as *essence super,* the most expensive variety. Depending on your car, you'll need either leaded *(avec plomb)* or unleaded *(sans plomb).*

Beware the mixture of gasoline and oil called *mélange* or *gasoil* sold in some rural communities; this mixture is for very old two-cycle engines.

Note: Sometimes you can drive for miles in rural France without encountering a gas station, so don't let your tank get dangerously low.

DRIVING RULES   Everyone in the car, in both the front and the back seats, must wear seat belts. Children under 12 must ride in the back seat. Drivers are supposed to yield to the car on their right, except where signs indicate otherwise, as at traffic circles.

If you violate the speed limit, expect a big fine. Those limits are about 130kmph (80 mph) on expressways, about 100kmph (60 mph) on major national highways, and 90kmph (56 mph) on country roads. In towns, don't exceed 60kmph (37 mph).

MAPS   For France as a whole, most motorists opt for Michelin map 989. For regions, Michelin publishes a series of yellow maps that are quite good. Big travel-book stores in North America carry these maps, and they're commonly available in France (at lower prices). In this age of congested traffic, one useful feature of the Michelin map is its designations of alternative *routes de dégagement,* which let you skirt big cities and avoid traffic-clogged highways. They also highlight routes in green, which are recommended for tourists.

Another recommended option is *Frommer's Road Atlas Europe.*

BREAKDOWNS/ASSISTANCE   A breakdown is called *une panne* in France. Call the police at © **17** anywhere in France to be put in touch with the nearest garage. If the breakdown occurs on an expressway, find the nearest roadside emergency phone box, pick up the phone, and put a call through. You'll be connected to the nearest breakdown service facility.

BY PLANE

Regrettably, there are few competitors in the world of domestic air travel within France. **Air France** (© 800/237-2747) serves about eight cities in France. Airfares tend to be much higher than for comparable distances in the United States, and discounts are few. Sample round-trip fares from Paris are $146 to Nice and $137 to Toulouse. Air travel time from Paris to most anywhere in France is about an hour.

BY TRAIN

Rail services between the large cities of Languedoc-Roussillon and Provence and the French Riviera are excellent. If you don't have a car, you can tour all the major hot spots by train. Of course, with a car you can also explore the hidden villages, such as the little Riviera hill towns, but for short visits with only major stopovers on your itinerary, such as Nice and Avignon, the train should suffice. Service is fast and frequent.

The major train hub for Languedoc is the city of Toulouse in southwestern France, which has frequent service from Paris and Lyon. Toulouse is also linked to Marseille by 11 trains running every day. Montpellier is another major transportation hub for the Languedoc-Roussillon area. Eleven high-speed TGVs arrive daily from Paris, taking just 3½ hours. Montpellier also has good rail connections to Avignon. The ancient city of Nîmes, one of the most visited in the area, also is a major transportation rail terminus, a stop on the rail link between Bordeaux and Marseille.

Marseille, the largest city in the south of France, has rail connections with all major towns on the Riviera as well as with the rest of France. Seventeen high-speed TGVs arrive from Paris daily (trip time: 3 hr. 15 min.).

The major rail transportation hub along the French Riviera is Nice, although Cannes also enjoys good train connections. Nice and Monaco are linked by frequent service, and in summer about eight trains per day connect Nice with the rapid TGV train from Paris to Marseille. In winter, the schedule is curtailed depending on demand.

The most visited Riviera destination in the east, Monaco also has excellent rail links along the Riviera.

BY BUS

While the trains are faster and more efficient if you are traveling between major cities, both the towns and villages of Languedoc and Provence, including the French Riviera, are linked by frequent bus service. You can use the network of buses that link the villages and hamlets with each other and the major cities to get off the beaten path.

Historic towns like Castres and Albi (of Toulouse-Lautrec fame) can be reached by bus from Toulouse; St-Paul-de-Vence from Nice; and Grasse, the perfume center, from Cannes.

Plan to take advantage of the bus services from Monday to Saturday when they run frequently; very few buses run on Sunday.

15 Tips on Accommodations

The French government rates hotels on a one- to four-star system. One-star hotels are budget accommodations, two-star lodgings are quality tourist hotels, three stars go to first-class hotels, and four stars are reserved for deluxe accommodations. In some of the lower categories, the rooms might not have private bathrooms; instead, many have what the French call a *cabinet de toilette* (hot and cold running water and maybe a bidet). In such hotels, bathrooms are down the hall. Not all private bathrooms have a tub/shower combination; ask in advance if it matters to you. Nearly all hotels in France have central heating, but, in some cases, you might wish the owners would turn it up a little on a cold night.

RELAIS & CHATEAUX Known worldwide, this organization of deluxe and first-class hostelries began in France for visitors seeking the ultimate in hotel living and dining in a traditional atmosphere. Relais & Châteaux establishments (there are about 150 in France) are former castles, abbeys, manor houses, and town houses converted into hostelries or inns and elegant hotels. All have a limited number of rooms, so reservations are imperative. Sometimes these owner-run establishments have pools and tennis courts. The Relais part of the organization refers to inns called *relais*, meaning "post house." These tend to be less luxurious than the châteaux but are often charming. Top-quality restaurants are *relais gourmands*. Throughout this guide, we've listed our favorite Relais & Châteaux, but there are many more.

For a catalog of member establishments, send 9€ ($11) to **Relais & Châteaux,** 11 E. 44th St., Suite 707, New York, NY 10017 or download it free of charge on their website. For information and reservations, call ✆ **800/735-2478** or 212/856-0115, or check out the website www.relaischateaux.com.

BED-AND-BREAKFASTS   Called *gîtes-chambres d'hôte* in France, these might be one or several bedrooms on a farm or in a village home. Many offer one main meal of the day as well (lunch or dinner).

There are at least 6,000 of these listed with **La Maison des Gîtes de France et du Tourisme Vert,** 59 rue St-Lazare, 75439 Paris (✆ 01-49-70-75-75; www.gites-de-france.fr). Sometimes these B&Bs aren't as simple as you might think: Instead of a bare-bones farm room, you might be in a mansion in the French countryside.

In the United States, a good source for this type of accommodation is **The French Experience,** 370 Lexington Ave., Room 511, New York, NY 10017 (✆ **800/283-7262** or 212/986-3800; www.frenchexperience.com), which also rents furnished houses for as short a period as 1 week.

Many Provence-bound visitors prefer to deal directly with a stateside agency. The best is **Provence West,** P.O. Box 3146, Evergreen, CO 80439 (✆ **303/674-3726;** www.provencewest.com). They have connections with some 120 of the best accommodations in the region, including such nuggets as a farmhouse 16km (10 miles) south of Avignon with three bedrooms. A 14-page booklet that describes the *gîte* experience is provided upon booking, with valuable tips including how to secure inexpensive car rentals. Another source is **France: Homestyle** (✆ **206/325-0132;** www.francehomestyle.com), run by Claudette Hunt. These lodgings are a bit fancier than a typical

bare-bones *gîte*. Her repertoire in Provence includes more than 300 properties.

CONDOS, VILLAS, HOUSES & APARTMENTS   If you can stay for at least a week and don't mind doing your own cooking and cleaning, you might want to rent long-term accommodations. The local French Tourist Board might help you obtain a list of agencies that offer this type of rental (which is popular at ski resorts). In France, one of the best groups of estate agents is the **Fédération Nationale des Agents Immobiliers,** 106 rue de l'Université, 75007 Paris (✆ 01-47-05-44-36; www.fnpc.fr).

In the United States, **At Home Abroad, Inc.,** 163 Third Ave., Box 319, New York, NY 10003 (✆ 212/421-9165; www.athomeabroadinc.com), specializes in villas on the French Riviera and in the Dordogne as well as places in the Provençal hill towns. Rentals are usually for 2 weeks. For a $10 registration fee (applicable to any rental), you'll receive photographs of the properties and a newsletter.

A worthwhile competitor is **Vacances en Campagne,** British Travel International, P.O. Box 299, Elkton, VA 22827 (✆ **800/327-6097;** www.britishtravel.com). Its $5 directory contains information on more than 700 potential rentals across Europe, including France.

Barclay International Group, 3 School St., Glen Cove, NY 11542 (✆ **800/845-6636** or 516/759-5100; www.barclayweb.com), can give you access to about 3,000 apartments and villas throughout Languedoc, Provence, and the Riviera, ranging from modest modern units to those among the most stylish. Units rent from 1 night up to 6 months; all have color TVs and kitchenettes, and many have concierge staffs and lobby-level security. The least-expensive units cost $100 per night, double occupancy. Incremental discounts are granted for a stay of 1 week or 3 weeks. Rentals must be prepaid in U.S. dollars or by a major U.S. credit or charge card.

Hometours International, Inc., 1108 Scottie Lane, Knoxville, TN 37919 (© **866/690-8484**), offers beautiful Riviera villas, all with pools, at reasonable rates.

HOTEL ASSOCIATIONS

For budget travelers, **Hometours International, Inc.** (see above) offers a prepaid voucher program for the Campanile hotels, a chain of about 350 two-star family-run hotels throughout France. Rates begin as low as $90 per night double. This is an excellent alternative to B&B hotels because all chain members provide a buffet breakfast for only 6.50€ ($8.45) per person. B&B catalogs for $9 or apartment brochures for free are available from the address above.

Others wanting to trim costs might want to check out the **Mercure** chain, an organization of simple but clean and modern hotels offering attractive values throughout France. Even at the peak of the tourist season, a room at a Mercure in Provence rents for $111 to $185 per night. For more information on Mercure hotels and a copy of a 100-page directory, call **ACCOR** at © **800/MERCURE** in the United States.

Formule 1 hotels are bare bones and basic though clean and safe, offering rooms for up to three at around $30 per night. Built from prefabricated units, these air-conditioned, soundproof hotels are shipped to a site and assembled. (Formule 1, a member of the French hotel giant Accor, also owns the Motel 6 chain

in the United States, to which Formule 1 bears a resemblance.)

While you can make a reservation at any member of the Accor group through the RESINTER number (© 914/472-0370 in the United States), the chain finds that the low cost of Formule 1 makes it unprofitable and impractical to pre-reserve (from the United States) rooms in the Formule chain. So, you'll have to reserve your Formule 1 room on arrival in France. Be warned that Formule 1 properties have almost none of the Gallic charm for which some country inns are famous, but you can save money by planning your itinerary at Formule 1 properties. For a directory, contact **Formule 1/ETAP Hotels,** 6–8 rue du Bois Bernard, 91021 Evry CEDEX (© **01-69-36-75-00**).

Other worthwhile economy bets, sometimes with a bit more charm, are the hotels and restaurants belonging to the **Fédération Nationale des Logis de France,** 83 av. d'Italie, 75013 Paris (© **01-45-84-83-84;** www.logis-de-france. fr). This is a marketing association of 3,828 hotels, usually simple country inns especially convenient for motorists, most rated one or two stars. The association publishes an annual directory. Copies are available for $25 from the **French Government Tourist Office,** 444 Madison Ave., 16th Floor, New York, NY 10022 (© 212/838-7800).

At the most inexpensive end, **Hostelling International USA,** 8401 Colesville Rd., Silver Springs, MD 20910 (© **301/495-1240;** www.hiayh.org), offers a directory of low-cost accommodations around the country.

16 Recommended Reading

GENERAL INTEREST

One obvious place to start is *A Year in Provence,* by Peter Mayle (Vintage Books, 1991). With its wit, warmth, and wicked

candor, this foray into Provençal domesticity became an international best seller. It was called "part memoir, part homeowner's manual, and part travelogue." If you become addicted to Mayle, you can also read his *Hotel Pastis: A Novel of Provence* and *Toujours Provence.*

Artists and writers flocked to the Riviera in the 1920s and early 1930s, and this "hunt for happiness" is marvelously evoked by art critic and historian Xavier Girard in *French Riviera: Living Well Is the Best Revenge* (Assouline, 2002). You can witness first hand the lifestyles of the Riviera's most celebrated couple, Gerald and Sara Murphy, and all the "gang" that included everybody from Chanel to F. Scott Fitzgerald (whose *Tender Is the Night* is set on the Riviera). Edith Wharton's love affair with the Riviera, launched in 1919, is brilliantly glimpsed in *Edith Wharton on the Riviera* (Flammarion, 2002). She found the Riviera both a haven for writing and a "terrifying superficial world."

The Most Beautiful Villages of Provence (Thames & Hudson, 1994) proves successfully that Provence—"a land apart"— is best evoked by its villages. Brilliantly illustrated, the book includes more than 30 special villages to visit, many off the beaten track.

Robert Kanigel's *High Season: How One French Riviera Town Has Seduced Travelers for Two Thousand Years* (Viking Press, 2002) is a love letter to Nice. The impressions of Yankee GI's to Russian royalty are combined to paint a memorable and ever-changing portrait of the French Riviera's capital city.

ART

Barbara Freed and Alan Halpern's *Artists and Their Museums on the Riviera* (Harry N. Abrams, 1998) is an intriguing book that follows the footsteps of celebrated artists who have lived and found inspiration on the Riviera, including Renoir, Picasso, Jean Cocteau, Chagall, and Matisse. From the private homes of the artists to museums or chapels they decorated, this book shows that the Riviera is a mecca for devotees of contemporary art.

Nina Athanassoglou-Kallmyer explores how Provence became a defining cultural force that shaped all aspects of the Cézanne's work, even his self-portraits, in *Cézanne and Provence: The Painter in His Culture* (University of Chicago Press, 2003). Lavishly illustrated, the book claims that Cézanne reconstructed a "modern French Arcadia."

CUISINE

Provence is celebrated for its cuisine, and Peter Johnson's *Provence: The Beautiful Cookbook* (Collins, 1993) is a beautifully illustrated book that sets a good table. Johnson takes us to the region where Georges Auguste Escoffier, the patron saint of French cooking, was born, and we learn much about how to make the most evocative dishes of the region. You'll even learn what specific herbs make up the celebrated Herbes de Provence. It's also a walk down memory lane.

FAST FACTS: The South of France

Auto Club An organization designed to help motorists navigate their way through breakdowns and motoring problems is **Club Automobile de Provence,** 149 bd. Rabatau, 13010 Marseille (© **04-91-78-83-00**).

Business Hours Business hours here are erratic, as befits a nation of individualists. Most banks are open Monday to Friday from 9:30am to 4:30pm. Many, particularly in smaller towns or villages, take a lunch break at varying times. Hours are usually posted on the door. Most museums close 1 day a week (often Tues), and they're generally closed on national holidays. Usual hours are from

9:30am to 5pm. Some museums, particularly the smaller and less-staffed ones, close for lunch from noon to 2pm. Most French museums are open on Saturday; many are closed Sunday morning but open Sunday afternoon. Again, refer to the individual museum listings.

Generally, offices are open Monday to Friday from 9am to 5pm, but always call first. In larger cities, stores are open from 9 or 9:30am (often 10am) to 6 or 7pm without a break for lunch. Some shops, particularly those operated by foreigners, open at 8am and close at 8 or 9pm. In some small stores, the lunch break can last 3 hours, beginning at 1pm.

Drugstores In France they are called *pharmacie*. Pharmacies take turns staying open at night and on Sunday; the local Commissariat de Police will tell you the location of the nearest one.

Electricity In general, expect 200 volts, 50 cycles, though you'll encounter 110 and 115 volts in some older hotels. Adapters are needed to fit sockets.

Embassies & Consulates All embassies are in Paris. The **Embassy and Consulate of the United States** are at 2 av. Gabriel (© **01-43-12-22-22**; Métro: Concorde), open Monday through Friday from 9am to 6pm. Passports are issued at the consulate; getting a passport replaced costs about $55. The United States also maintains a consulate in Marseille at Place Varian Fry, 13286 Marseille (© **04-91-54-92-00**).

The **Embassy of Canada** is at 35 av. Montaigne (© **01-44-43-29-00**; Métro: Franklin-D-Roosevelt), open Monday through Friday from 9am to noon and 2 to 5pm; the Canadian Consulate is at the same address. The **Embassy of the United Kingdom** is at 35 rue du Faubourg St-Honoré (© **01-44-51-31-00**; Métro: Concorde), open Monday through Friday from 9:30am to 1pm and 2:30 to 5pm; the U.K. consulate, 18 bis rue d'Anjou (© **01-44-51-31-02**; Métro: Concorde), is open Monday through Friday from 9am to noon and 2 to 5pm.

The **Embassy of Australia** is at 4 rue Jean-Rey, 15e (© **01-40-59-33-00**; Métro: Bir-Hakeim), open Monday through Friday from 9:15am to noon and 2:30 to 4:30pm. The **Embassy of New Zealand** is at 7 ter rue Léonard-de-Vinci (© **01-45-01-43-43**; Métro: Victor-Hugo), open Monday through Friday from 9am to 1pm and 2:30 to 6pm. The **Embassy of Ireland** is at 4 rue Rude, 75116 Paris (© **01-44-17-67-00**; Métro: Etoile). Hours are Monday through Friday from 9:30am to noon and 2:30 to 5:30pm.

Emergencies In an emergency while at a hotel, contact the front desk to summon an ambulance or do whatever is necessary. But for something like a stolen wallet, go to the police station in person. Otherwise, you can get help anywhere in France by calling © **17** for the **police** or © **18** for the **fire department** *(pompiers)*. For roadside emergencies, see "Getting Around the South of France," earlier in this chapter.

Legal Aid The French government advises foreigners to consult their embassy or consulate (see above) in case of an arrest or similar problem. The staff can generally offer advice on how you can obtain help locally and can furnish you with a list of local attorneys. If you are arrested for illegal possession of drugs, the U.S. embassy and consular officials cannot interfere with the French judicial system. A consulate can advise you only of your rights.

Lost & Found To speed the process of replacing your personal documents if they're lost or stolen, make a photocopy of the first few pages of your passport and write down your credit card numbers (and the serial numbers of your traveler's checks, if you're using them). Leave this information with someone at home—to be faxed to you in an emergency—and swap it with your traveling companion. Be sure to tell all of your credit card companies the minute you discover your wallet has been lost or stolen, and file a report at the nearest police precinct. Your credit card company or insurer may require a police report number or record of the loss.

Use the following numbers in France to report your lost or stolen credit card: **American Express** (call collect) *C* 336/393-1111; **MasterCard** *C* 08-00-90-13-87; www.mastercard.com; **Visa** *C* 08-00-90-11-79; www.visaeurope.com. Your credit card company may be able to wire you a cash advance immediately or deliver an emergency card in a day or two.

If you need emergency cash over the weekend when all banks and American Express offices are closed, you can have money wired to you through **Western Union** ((*C* 800/325-6000; www.westernunion.com).

Identity theft and fraud are potential complications of losing your wallet, especially if you've lost your driver's license along with your cash and credit cards. Notify the major credit-reporting bureaus immediately; placing a fraud alert on your records may protect you against liability for criminal activity. The three major U.S. credit-reporting agencies are **Equifax** (*C* 800/766-0008; www.equifax.com), **Experian** (*C* 888/397-3742; www.experian.com), and **Trans-Union** (*C* 800/680-7289; www.transunion.com).

Mail Most post offices in France are open Monday through Friday from 8am to 7pm, and Saturday from 8am to noon. Allow 5 to 8 days to send or receive mail from your home. Airmail letters to North America cost .65€ (85¢) for 20 grams. Letters to the U.K. cost .45€ (65¢) for up to 20 grams. An airmail postcard to North America or Europe (outside France) costs .65€ (85¢).

You can exchange money at post offices. Many hotels sell stamps, as do local post offices and cafes displaying a red TABAC sign outside.

Police Call *C* 17 anywhere in France.

Restrooms If you're in dire need, duck into a cafe or brasserie. It's customary to make some small purchase if you do so. France still has many "hole-in-the-ground" toilets, so be forewarned.

Safety Those intending to visit the south of France, especially the Riviera, should exercise extreme caution—robberies and muggings here are commonplace. It's best to check your baggage into a hotel and then go sightseeing instead of leaving it unguarded in the trunk of a car, which can easily be broken into. Marseille is among the most dangerous cities.

Taxes Watch it: You could get burned. As a member of the European Union, France imposes a value-added tax (VAT) on many goods and services. The standard VAT on merchandise is 19.6%. Refunds are made for the tax on certain goods, but not on services. The minimum purchase is 175€ ($228) for nationals or residents of countries outside the E.U. See "How to Get Your VAT Refund," on p. 26, for more details.

Telephone The French use a **télécarte,** a phone debit card, which you can pur-chase at rail stations, post offices, and other places. Sold in two versions, it allows you to use either 50 or 120 charge units by inserting the card into the slot of most public phones. Depending on the type of card you buy, the cost is 7.45€ to 15€ ($9.70–$20).

If possible, avoid making calls from your hotel; some French establishments double or triple the charges.

For tips on calling Monaco, which has its own phone system, see "Number, Please: Monaco's Telephone System," on p. 336.

Time The French equivalent of daylight saving time lasts from around April to September, which puts it 1 hour ahead of French winter time. Depending on the time of year, France is 6 or 7 hours ahead of U.S. Eastern Standard Time.

Tipping All bills, as required by law, are supposed to say *service compris,* which means that the tip has been included. Here are some general guidelines: For **hotel staff,** tip 1.05€ to 1.50€ ($1.35–$1.95) for every item of baggage the porter carries on arrival and departure, and 1.50€ ($1.95) per day for the chambermaid. You're not obligated to tip the concierge, doorperson, or any-one else—unless you use his or her services. In cafes, **waiter** service is usually included. For **porters,** there's no real need to tip extra after their bill is pre-sented, unless they've performed some special service. Tip **taxi drivers** 10% to 15% of the amount on the meter. In theaters and restaurants, give **cloakroom attendants** at least .75€ ($1) per item. Give **restroom attendants** about .30€ (45¢) in nightclubs and such places. Give **cinema and theater ushers** about .30€ (45¢). Tip the **hairdresser** about 15%, and don't forget to tip the person who gives you a shampoo or manicure 2€ ($2.60). For **guides** of group visits to sights, .75€ to 1.50€ ($1–$1.95) per person is reasonable.

3

Suggested Itineraries

If you have unlimited time, one of Europe's greatest pleasures is getting "lost" in Provence and the Riviera, wandering about at random, making new discoveries every day off the beaten path, finding charming towns you may never have heard of, like Gordes and Uzès.

But few of us have a generous amount of time. Vacations are getting shorter, and a "lean-and-mean" schedule is called for if you want to experience the best of any country in a short amount of time.

If you're a time-pressed traveler, you may find "Provence in 1 Week" or "The Riviera in 2 Weeks" most helpful. If you've been to the Riviera before, you might want to explore a different area of Southern France this time, notably Languedoc and the Roussillon.

The south of France ranks with Germany in offering Europe's fastest and best-maintained superhighways. But part of the fun is to wander the secondary roads that take you into the hill towns overlooking the Riviera.

Provence also has one of the fastest and most efficient public transportation systems in the world, especially the national train system. You can, for example, travel by rail from Paris to Nice on the Riviera in just 6½ hours—or fly much quicker, of course.

The itineraries that follow take you to some major attractions such as the museums and beaches of Nice but also direct you to quaint hill towns such as St-Paul-de-Vence. The pace may be a bit brisk for some visitors, so skip a town or sight occasionally to have some chill-out-time—after all, you're on vacation.

1 Provence in 1 Week

The very title of this tour is a misnomer. There is no way you can see all of Provence in 1 week, merely a few of the highlights. But you can have a memorable vacation in Provence in 1 week if you budget your time carefully.

You can use the following itinerary to make the most out of a week in Provence, but feel free to drop a place or two to save a day to relax.

One week provides just enough time, although barely, to introduce yourself to the attractions of **Avignon** and its papal palace, with extra days spent in such towns as **Arles** to see its famous Roman monuments, and at **Les Baux,** the most dramatically situated town in Provence.

Still, in only a week, visits are also possible at **St-Rémy-de-Provence,** former retreat of Vincent van Gogh, and **Aix-en-Provence,** with its many memories and associations with Cézanne. Finally, you can cap the visit with a stopover in **Marseille,** the largest and most vital city in Provence.

Days ❶ & ❷: Avignon: ⭑⭑⭑
"Gateway to Provence"

At the Gare de Lyon in Paris, you can hop aboard a TGV that will put you in Avignon in just 2 hours and 38 minutes. You can arrive in town for a late lunch.

In the capital of Provence, wander about that afternoon leisurely, getting the lay of the land in the Old Town. Perhaps you'll buy some colorful Provençal fabrics and see one of the sights as the **pont St-Bénézet** (p. 140, also known as the Bridge of Avignon). Before 6pm, duck into the **Cathédrale Notre-Dame des Doms** (p. 141) to see some of the Gothic tombs of the apostate popes. Order predinner drinks at **Le Grand Café** (p. 149), our favorite watering hole in Avignon, before enjoying a meal of typical Provençal specialties that night. Plan to stay here for 2 nights.

The following morning on **Day 2,** spend 2 hours touring the **Palais de Papes** (p. 139), which in the 14th century was the capital of Christendom in that period in history when the popes lived here during the so-called "Babylonian Captivity."

Before lunch, take a walk through **Quartier de La Balance** (p. 140), where local Gypsies lived in the 19th century. After a Provençal lunch, try to catch some of the minor sights in the afternoon, notably **La Fondation Angladon-Dubrujeaud** (p. 142), with its splendid art collections, or the **Musée Calvet** (p. 142), with its collection of ancient silver displayed in an 18th-century town house. If you can make it here before 6pm, you can also see the **Musée Lapidaire** (p. 142), with some of the most intriguing Gallo-Roman sculptures in Provence.

Day ❸: Arles: ⭑⭑⭑
"The Soul of Provence"

On **Day 3,** in a rented car, leave Avignon and drive for 89km (55 miles) to Arles on

the Rhône River. Plan to overnight here. You should arrive in time for a long walk through its Old Town that so enchanted van Gogh. Head for a cafe on **place du Forum,** site of the former Café de Nuit, immortalized in a painting by van Gogh.

After lunch in a local restaurant, visit the town's two major sights in the afternoon. These include **Musée de l'Arles Antique** (p. 154), with one of the world's best collections of Roman and Christian sarcophagi, and the **Théâtre Antique/ Amphitheatre** or **Les Arènes** (p. 155), the ruins of a Roman theater begun by Augustus in the 1st century. If you have time before its 7pm summer closing, also visit **Les Alyscamps** (p. 154), one of the world's most famous necropolises. This is a burial ground of legend and lore, and was even mentioned in Dante's *Inferno.*

Day ❹: Les Baux: ⭑⭑⭑ **"Nesting Place for Eagles"**

Leave Arles on **Day 4,** driving 19km (12 miles) to the mysterious little town of Les Baux in the southern Alpilles. It's known for its shadowy rock formations. After checking into a hotel, spend the day exploring the medieval village and its evocative ruins. If time remains, drive through the jagged and bleak **Val d'Enfer (Valley of Hell;** see p. 160), stopping en route at the **Cathédrale d'Images** (p. 160).

Day ❺: St.-Rémy-de-Provence

From Les Baux on **Day 5,** drive 25km (16 miles) northeast to the little city of St.-Rémy-de-Provence, the former home of the famous French astrologer Nostradamus. This town of considerable charm—our favorite in Provence—was also a favorite retreat of van Gogh who painted several notable works here including *Cypresses.* Before lunch you'll have time to spend 2 hours exploring its Old Town.

After lunch and in the afternoon, you can also visit the town's major attractions, including the **Glanum** (p. 166), with its

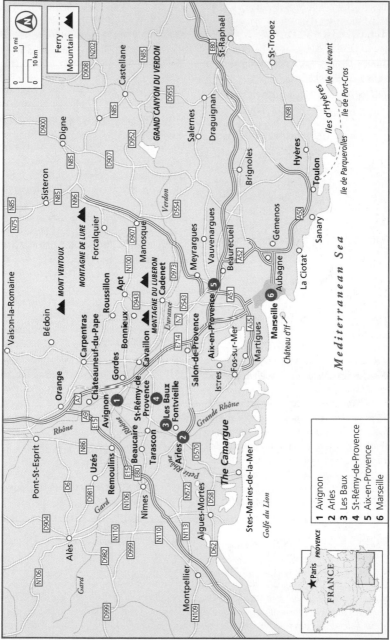

ancient ruins; the **Musée Archéologique** (p. 180), with its Roman artifacts, and **Monastère-de-St-Paul-de-Mausolée** (p. 164), a 12th-century asylum made famous by van Gogh's paintings. Overnight in St-Rémy.

Day ⑥: Aix-en-Provence

On the morning of **Day 6,** leave St-Rémy and continue southeast 75km (47 miles) to this university city. As you approach Aix, you may recognize some of the landscapes from the paintings of Cézanne. After checking into a hotel, head immediately to **cours Mirabeau** (p. 186), the most beautiful main street in Europe. Have lunch in one of the sidewalk cafes lining the street. After lunch, visit the main attractions, including the **Atelier de Cézanne** (p. 186), the studio of the painter who founded Cubism. Other attractions worth a look include **Cathédrale St-Sauveur** (p. 186) and the **Musée des Tapisseries** (p. 186) in a former archbishop's palace.

Day ⑦: Marseille: ⟨★★★⟩ Capital of Provence

For your final day in Provence, head to bustling Marseille, the second-largest city in France. It's a 31km (19-mile) drive south of Aix-en-Provence. After checking into a hotel, preferably one along the waterfront, spend 2 hours wandering the Vieux Port (p. 195), or Old Port, ducking in and out of its narrow streets. After lunch, enjoy your coffee at **La Canebière,** the main street of town (World War II GIs pronounced it "can of beer").

In the afternoon take a boat to the **Château d'If** (p. 197), an island that Alexandre Dumas used as a setting for his novel, *The Count of Monte Cristo.* If you return to Marseille in time, visit its **Musée des Beaux-Arts** (p. 187) and the **Basilique St-Victor** (p. 195), exploring its early medieval crypt. You must arrive, however, by 7pm. Overnight in Marseille, one of France's great transportation hubs, with numerous rail and plane connections.

2 The Riviera in 2 Weeks

With 2 weeks to explore the Riviera, you aren't as rushed as you might have been with only a week for Provence. With more breathing time, you can traverse the Côte d'Azur beginning in the west at **St-Tropez,** hitting the high spots as you eventually make your way to **Menton** in the east on the border with Italy. Highlights include not only St-Tropez, but the chic resort of **Cannes,** bustling **Nice** (the capital of the Riviera), and even elegant **Monaco.**

You can take in the best of the beaches, but you may want to save some time to explore some of the world's best galleries and museums of contemporary art. The Riviera has both in abundance.

Days ❶ & ❷: St-Tropez: ⟨★★⟩ Gateway to the Riviera

Following in the footsteps of blonde goddess, actress Brigitte Bardot, you can arrive at the nearest rail station in St-Raphaël, making the rest of the journey to **St-Tropez** by boat or bus. For details, see "Getting There," under St-Tropez (p. 220).

St-Tropez is all about beaches, the best of which include the amusingly named Plage de la Bouillabaisse or Plage des Graniers. Following a day at the beach, drop into **Café de Paris** (p. 230) for a pre-dinner drink and a look at the locals, the most colorful set of characters on the Riviera. Enjoy a long, lingering dinner and take a stroll along the harborfront at night, inspecting the fleet of yachts from all over the world.

On **Day 2,** before heading for another day at the beach—perhaps a different one

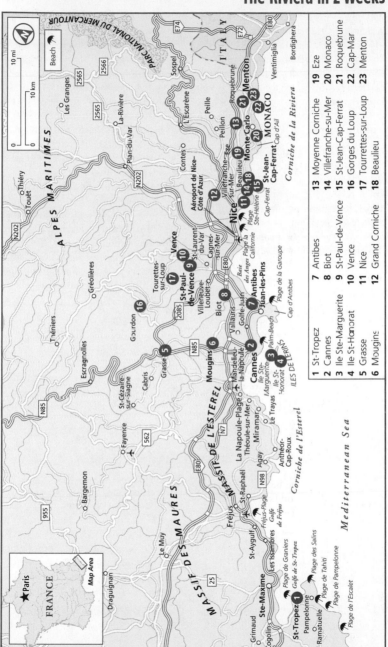

1	St-Tropez	7	Antibes	13	Moyenne Corniche	19	Eze
2	Cannes	8	Biot	14	Villefranche-su-Mer	20	Monaco
3	Ile Ste-Marguerite	9	St-Paul-de-Vence	15	St-Jean-Cap-Ferrat	21	Roquebrune
4	Ile St-Honorat	10	Vence	16	Gorges du Loup	22	Cap-Mar
5	Grasse	11	Nice	17	Tourrettes-sur-Loup	23	Menton
6	Mougins	12	Grand Corniche	18	Beaulieu		

this time—inspect the **Musée de l'Annonciade** (p. 223), the first of the modern art collections that opened on the Riviera in 1955. Do some boutique hopping before your descent on Plage de Tahiti, a favorite of exhibitionists. If you dare, wear next to nothing. Head to the harborfront in the center of town for your final night in St-Tropez.

Days ❸ & ❹: Cannes ⚹⚹⚹

On **Day 3,** drive east 86km (53 miles) along the coast to the Riviera's most fabled resort, chic, sophisticated Cannes, site of the famous International Film Festival. After checking into your hotel, take a long walk along the **promenade de la Croisette** (p. 247) to see what the excitement is all about. Find a waterfront restaurant for lunch and head for the beach in the afternoon. The best one is **Plage de la Croisette,** extending between Vieux Port (Old Port) and Port Canto.

On the morning of **Day 4,** take a ferryboat trip to **Ile Ste-Marguerite** (p. 251), the most famous of the Lérins Islands where the mysterious "Man in the Iron Mask" was held prisoner. You can spend all morning exploring the island and have lunch here. You can also visit the second major island, **Ile St-Honorat** (p. 251), with its Abbaye de St-Honorat, or else you can return to Cannes for another afternoon at the beach. If you're a gambler, you can patronize one of the resort's glittering casinos. See recommendations beginning on p. 264.

Day ❺: Grasse ⚹⚹, Mougins ⚹ & Antibes ⚹⚹

Leaving Cannes by rented car on the morning of **Day 5,** drive north 14km (9 miles) along N85 to Grasse, reached in only 20 minutes. This is the perfume capital of France, and you can visit its factories, called *parfumerie* in French. The best are **Fragonard** (p. 266) and **Molinard** (p. 266). Instead of lunching in Grasse, head back 8km (5 miles) on the road to

Cannes but stopping off in the village of **Mougins,** which was a favorite spot for Picasso. The main reason for coming here is to order lunch, as Mougins has some of the best restaurants on the Riviera. Our recommendations begin on p. 270.

Heading back to the coast, follow the route into Antibes where you can spend the night. Picasso also lived here, as evidenced by the array of paintings he left to the **Musée Picasso** (p. 278), one of the greatest collections of his work.

After seeing the museum, drive along the chic **Cap d'Antibes** (p. 277) to see how the very rich live and have done so ever since F. Scott Fitzgerald dramatized the resort strip in his novel, *Tender Is the Night*. Overnight in Antibes and promenade along its port at night, finding a typical bistro serving seafood.

Day ❻: Biot ⚹ & St-Paul-de-Vence ⚹⚹

Leaving Antibes in the morning, drive north 12km (8 miles) to the town of Biot, which is celebrated for its beautiful pottery (our shopping recommendations begin on p. 284). While here, you can also visit the **Musée National Fernand-Léger** (p. 284), with the greatest collection of Léger's work in the world.

After a lunch in the town, head northeast 10km (6 miles) for a night to the most famous hill town along the Riviera: **St-Paul-de-Vence.** After checking into your hotel, visit the **Fondation Maeght** (p. 287), the most famous—and the best—gallery of modern art on the Riviera, and actually one of Europe's finest such museums. Spend the late afternoon or early evening wandering the town's cobblestone streets.

Days ❼ & ❽: Vence ⚹ & Nice ⚹⚹⚹

On the morning of **Day 7,** drive 6km (4 miles) over to the neighboring hill town of Vence to see **Chapelle du Rosaire** (p. 291), the chapel that Henri Matisse designed and decorated between

1947 and 1951. He viewed it as his masterpiece. After an hour's visit, drive southeast 40km (25 miles) to Nice for a 3-night visit, part of which will be devoted to excursions.

After checking into a hotel, stroll through **Vieille Ville** (p. 302), the Old Town beginning at the foot of "the Rock." Enjoy a snack of *socca,* a round crepe made with chickpea flour that's sold steaming hot by street vendors. Then head for the **promenade des Anglais** (p. 300), the wide boulevard along the waterfront. You can spend at least an hour strolling along, perhaps stopping at one of the grand cafes bordering the water for a Niçoise lunch. In the afternoon, head for one of the beaches. Back in the Old Town for dinner that night, visit a typical bistro.

On **Day 8,** work in some, but try to hit some of the major sights of Nice as well. These include the two most important museums: **Musée d'Art Moderne et d'Art Contemporain** (p. 302), one of the best modern art museums in the region, and the **Musée des Beaux-Arts** (p. 303), the latter devoted to the masters of the Second Empire and the belle époque era. For the remainder of the afternoon, head for the satellite village of **Cimiez** and try to visit the **Musée Matisse** (p. 304), seeing works by the master himself. Return to Nice for the night, taking in an opera, some casino action, or some live music at one of Vieux Ville's many bars.

Day ❾: Grande Corniche 👁👁👁 & Moyenne Corniche 👁👁

On **Day 9,** while still based in Nice, head out for the grandest drive in the south of France, the **Grande Corniche** built by Napoleon in 1806. The trip of 32km (20 miles) takes about 3 hours of straight driving, although many motorists stop for a series of grand views, stretching the trip out to at least 5 hours.

From Nice, head east along avenue des Diables-Bleus. From points along the way, you can look down 450m (1,400 ft.) to Monaco. Highlights along the drive are panoramic views at **Vistaëro**—it's signposted—which lies 300m (1,000 ft.) above the sea. Another grand view can be seen at Eze Belvedere. The highest point along the Grande Corniche is **Trophée des Alps** (p. 331), a rock formation at 450m (1,500 ft.).

You can have lunch at Menton before returning to Nice along the **Moyenne Corniche** or Middle Corniche, stretching 31km (19 miles). This superhighway, built "between the wars," also runs from Nice to Menton and goes in and out of tunnels cut through mountains. Panoramic views, including some of Monaco, are possible to enjoy at many points along this grand highway. Return to Nice for the night.

Day ❿: Villefranche-sur-Mer 👁 & St-Jean-Cap Ferrat 👁

To save money because of its affordable hotels, you can still use Nice as your home base as you set out to see such highlights along the Riviera as Villefranche and St-Jean-Cap-Ferrat on **Day 10.** You can arrive at **Villefranche** after a 6km (4-mile) drive east of Nice. You can walk its vaulted **rue Obscure** (p. 321) and visit its 14th-century Romanesque **Chapelle St-Pierre** (p. 321) with frescoes painted by Jean Cocteau.

By late morning after an hour or two in Villefranche, you can drive over to posh **St-Jean-Cap-Ferrat,** a 15km (9-mile) promontory that lies 10km (6 miles) east of Nice.

Here you will find one of the Côte d'Azur's most legendary villas, today the home of the art-stuffed **Musée Ile-de-France** (p. 324). Budget 2 hours for a visit and get in some beach time, perhaps at **Plage de Paloma,** before returning to Nice for the night.

Day ⓫: Exploring the Gorges du Loup

Again, with Nice as your hotel base, set out on **Day 11** to see some of the most dramatic scenery in the mountains above the Côte d'Azur by visiting **Gorges du Loup** (coverage begins on p. 292, where you'll also find driving directions from Nice.)

You can take a 13km (8-mile) drive filled with dramatic scenery such as waterfalls, rock spurs, and decaying castles.

For lunch, aim for the town of **Tourrettes-sur-Loup** (coverage begins on p. 285), which lies 29km (18 miles) west of Nice. You can spend the afternoon here wandering its ancient streets and exploring more crafts studios than any other town its size in Provence. The best of these are showcased along the **Grand'Rue**. Return to Nice in the afternoon, hopefully in time for the beach. Overnight in Nice before checking out the following day to head east.

Days ⓬ & ⓭:Beaulieu 𝒜, Eze & Monaco 𝒜𝒜𝒜

Leave Nice on **Day 12,** heading east along the Lower Corniche or Corniche Inférieure. First stop: the posh resort of **Beaulieu** at a distance of only 10km (6 miles) east of Nice (coverage begins on p. 326). The town opens onto the tranquil Baie des Fourmis, and you can walk its Boulevard Alsace-Lorraine lined with beautiful gardens. The seafront promenade is another idyllic place to stroll. The highlight of your visit will be **Villa Kérylos** (p. 327), a replica of an ancient Greek residence filled with art.

After a visit, continue along the coast to the village of **Eze,** lying 11km (7 miles) northeast of Nice. Here you can have lunch and explore the medieval core of this old town, which is filled with shops, artisan studios, and art galleries. Visit the **Jardin d'Eze** (p. 331), which features cacti and offers panoramic views of the eastern Riviera.

After a visit, continue east to the principality of **Monaco,** for a stopover of 2 nights. The location is 18km (11 miles) east of Nice. After checking into a hotel, head for **Le Café de Paris** (p. 348), the heart of local life. Perhaps you'll have dinner here.

On **Day 13,** set out to explore the attractions of this principality, perhaps witnessing the changing of the guard and visiting **Les Grands Appartements du Palais,** where Prince Albert now rules the Monégasques following the death of Prince Rainier in 2005. Allow 45 minutes or so to see the **Jardin Exotique** (p. 331), filled with exotic plants. The other most visited attraction is the **Musée de l'Oceanographie** (p. 338) whose name says it all. If time remains, take in **Prince Rainier III's Collection des Voitures Anciennes** (old automobiles; p. 337). Spend yet another night in the principality, walking its seafront promenades before dinner.

Day ⓮: Roquebrune 𝒜𝒜, Cap-Martin 𝒜𝒜 & Menton 𝒜𝒜

On **Day 14,** your final day on the Riviera, continue along the Lower Corniche until you come to the twin attractions of **Roquebrune** and **Cap-Martin.** Roquebrune is a hill village that you can explore in 1½ hours. Stroll its covered streets, which are filled with craft studios, art galleries, and souvenir shops. The most evocative street is **rue Moncollet** (p. 351), dating from the 10th century. Head for a stopover at Cap-Martin, which lies 2km (1½ miles) west of Roquebrune. After lunch here, we suggest you take one of the great walks along the Riviera, a 3-hour trek along a coastal path, **Sentier Touristique** (p. 352).

After that, make your way to **Menton** for the night, a distance of 8km (5 miles) east of Monaco. After checking into a hotel, wander its old fishing town, selecting a local bistro.

The following morning, drive back to Nice, the transportation hub of the Riviera.

3 Provence & the Riviera for Families

Provence and the Riviera offer many attractions that kids enjoy. Perhaps your main concern with having children along is pacing yourself with some museum time. Our suggestion is to spend 2 days in Provence, exploring the two towns with the most appeal to families, **Avignon** and **Les Beaux,** before tackling the three big resorts of the Riviera: **St-Tropez, Cannes,** and **Nice.** Because its hotels are the most affordable on the Riviera, you can spend 3 nights in Nice, using the resort as a base for exploring the two most highly rated hilltowns, **St-Paul-de-Vence** and **Vence,** with a final day reserved for the **Principality of Monaco.**

Day ❶: Avignon: ⟨★★★⟩
Gateway to Provence

The TVG (high-speed train) from Paris delivers you to the ancient papal city of Avignon in just 2 hours and 38 minutes. If you leave Paris early enough in the morning, you'll have a full day of sightseeing. First, head for the **pont St-Bénézet** (p. 140), the ancient bridge of Avignon, which inspired the nursery-room ditty, "*Sur le pont d'Avignon, l'on y danse, l'on y danse.*" After a visit, take your family for a stroll through the Old Town of Avignon, followed by a 2-hour visit to the **Palais des Papes** (p.139), the papal residence during the so-called period of "Babylonian Captivity," when there was a pope ruling in Avignon, plus a rival pope in Rome.

After a lunch in the Old Town, take the kids to the **Musée Requien** (p. 144) for a visit to its herbarium with some 200,000 specimens gathered by botanists from around the globe. Spend the rest of the afternoon wandering around the village of **Villeneuve-Lèz-Avignon** (p. 149) across the Rhône.

Day ❷: Les Baux

On **Day 2,** in a rented car from Avignon, drive southwest to Les Baux where you can check into a hotel for the night. This bare rock spur, with ravines on each side, is fascinating to explore. You can wander at leisure, visiting the ruins of a fortified castle, even exploring the "ghost village" (often called "the dead village"). After

lunch you can drive into the surrounding area, exploring the gorge called **Val d'Enfer** or "Valley of Hell" (p. 160). Plan a stop at the **Cathédrale d'Images** (p. 160), which always fascinates kids. Return to Les Baux for the evening.

Day ❸: St-Tropez: ⟨★★★⟩
Gateway to the Riviera

From Les Baux drive southeast to the chic resort of St-Tropez. Although the world image of St-Tropez is that of a decadent adult retreat, many French parents with children also vacation here. After checking into a hotel, head for the beach. The best sandy strips for families are those near town, including **Plage de la Bouillabaisse** and **Plage des Graniers.** You needn't return to town until later as you can enjoy lunch on the beach. After mid-afternoon you can head back to the resort for a stroll along the yacht-clogged harbor and the waterfront. Overnight here.

Day ❹: Cannes

After driving east from St-Tropez to Cannes on **Day 4,** check into a hotel and go for a stroll along the **promenade de la Croisette,** bordering the harbor. This is one of the grandest walks on the Riviera. After lunch, take one of the ferryboats leaving from the harbor for an afternoon visit to **Ile Ste-Marguerite** (p. 251) where the famous prisoner in the iron mask was held. You can return to Cannes for some beach life at the **Plage de la Croisette** before heading back to your hotel and making dinner plans.

Day ❺: Nice: ✦✦✦ Capital of the Riviera

On **Day 5,** drive east from Cannes to this larger city, which has more of interest than any other town on the Riviera. It also makes the best place for exploring the hilltowns or the resorts to its immediate east, including Monaco. After checking into a hotel for 3 nights, take the kids on the **Train Touristique de Nice,** which will get them acquainted with the town. After a ride, take a long stroll along the **promenade de Anglais** (p. 300), that wide boulevard bordering the water, before heading into **Vieille Ville** (p. 302), or Old Town, for a lengthy stroll and a lunch at a typical Niçoise tavern. In the afternoon most kids will go along with you to visit Nice's two most important museums: **Musée d'Art Moderne et d'Art Contemporain** (p. 302) and the **Musée des Beaux-Arts** (p. 303). If they absolutely refuse, then head for the beach.

Day ❻: St-Paul-de-Vence ✦✦ & Vence ✦

While still based in Nice, on **Day 6,** head for the Riviera's most beautiful hilltown, **St-Paul-de-Vence,** 31km (19 miles) to the north. Kids will delight in spending the morning walking the streets of this historic hilltown, especially **rue Grande** (p. 287). After lunch, take the kids to **Fondation Maeght** (p. 287). Even if your child isn't an art lover, this museum is so daringly avant-garde that there will be something to intrigue here.

In the afternoon, drive to Vence to visit the **Chapelle du Rosaire** (p. 291), the chapel that Henri Matisse viewed as his masterpiece. Spend the remaining part of the afternoon exploring the old streets of Vence before returning to Nice.

Day ❼: The Principality of Monaco ✦✦✦

While still based in Nice, on **Day 7,** your final day for the Riviera, head east for a distance of only 18km (11 miles). This tiny little country was largely put on the map when Grace Kelly married Prince Rainier and went to live in this fairy-tale kingdom by the sea. Kids delight in watching the **changing of the guard** at **Les Grands Appartements du Palais** (p. 338) where Prince Albert lives. After a visit, take them for a walk through the **Jardin Exotique** (p. 337), known for its cactus collection, before ordering lunch, perhaps at the **Café de Paris** (p. 348).

After lunch, there will still be time to visit the fascinating **Musée de l'Oceanographie** (p. 338), filled with exotic creatures of the sea, as well as the **Collection des Voitures Anciennes** (p. 337), an antique-car collection.

Return to Nice for the night. Because it's the transportation hub of the Riviera, it will be relatively easy from here to get to where you are going next.

4 Languedoc/Roussillon & the Camargue in 1 Week

This guide not only explores the highlights of Provence and major resorts along the strips of both the Western and Eastern Riviera, but takes in the history-rich sections of **Languedoc, Roussillon,** and the **Camargue,** some of the most fascinating terrain in all of France. This region has not only world-class tourist meccas, including the walled city of **Carcassonne** and the ancient capital of **Toulouse,** but the ancient university city of **Montpellier,** the capital of Mediterranean Languedoc, and the Roman city of **Nîmes,** with one of the best preserved Roman amphitheaters in the world. Moving with a certain speed, you can take in the chief glories of these provinces in a week, with time enough to dip into the "cowboy country" of France, the Camargue.

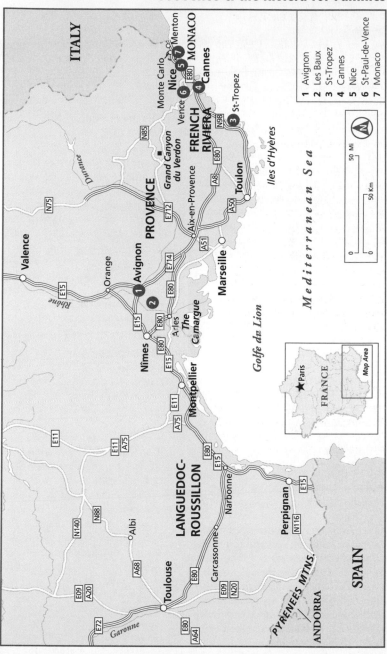

ITALY

Menton

Monte Carlo

Nice

MONACO

Cannes

Vence

St-Paul-de-Vence

St-Tropez

FRENCH RIVIERA

N85

Grand Canyon du Verdon

Aix-en-Provence

A8

Toulon

A50

Iles d'Hyères

Durance

PROVENCE

E712

A51

Marseille

Mediterranean Sea

N75

Valence

Orange

E15

1 Avignon

2

Rhône

E15 E80

Arles

The Camargue

E80

Golfe du Lion

Nîmes

E15

Montpellier

E11

A75

E11 A75

E80

E15

Narbonne

E11

LANGUEDOC-ROUSSILLON

N88

Albi

N140

A68

Carcassonne

E09 N20

Perpignan

N116

E15

E09 A20

Toulouse

E80

E72

Garonne

A64 E80

PYRENEES MTNS.

ANDORRA

SPAIN

1 Avignon
2 Les Baux
3 St-Tropez
4 Cannes
5 Nice
6 St-Paul-de-Vence
7 Monaco

N

50 Mi

50 Km

0

0

Paris

FRANCE

Map Area

Day ❶: Toulouse: ✸✸✸
Gateway to Languedoc

The fourth-largest city in France and the old capital of Languedoc, the cosmopolitan city of Toulouse can be reached by air, although most visitors from Paris take the high-speed TGV train, which arrives in Toulouse after only 5 hours.

After checking into a hotel for the night, you can spend 1½ hours exploring the **Basilique St-Sernin** (p. 74), the largest and best Romanesque church extant in Europe. Before lunch, you can also take in the **Cathédrale St-Etienne** (p. 76), Toulouse's other major ecclesiastical monument. After a lunch of some of the specialties of Southwest France, visit the best museum of Toulouse in the afternoon: **Musée des Augustins** (p. 77), a former monastery that today is the repository of some splendid art, including some of the best works of old masters long associated with the southwest, including the incomparable Toulouse-Lautrec and Ingres. Allow at least 1½ hours for a visit. Other attractions you might fit into a comfortable afternoon include **Eglise des Jacobins** (p. 77), a restored convent. Wind down in the afternoon by heading for **Place Wilson,** a fabulous 19th-century square known for its fashionable cafes.

Day ❷: Albi: City of
Toulouse-Lautrec

In a rented car from Toulouse on **Day 2,** head 76km (47 miles) to the "red city" of Albi on the banks of the River Tarn to see the world's greatest collection of the paintings of hometown boy Toulouse-Lautrec. After checking into a hotel, visit the **Musée Toulouse-Lautrec** (p. 89), allowing 1½ to 2 hours for a visit. Before lunch, you can also visit the town's towering monument, **Cathédrale Ste-Cécile** (p. 88), a cathedral from the 13th century that is fortified with ramparts and parapets.

In the afternoon, you can visit the family seat of Toulouse-Lautrec, the **Château de Bosc** (p. 89) in Camjac, 46km (29 miles) from Toulouse. Getting there and back, as well as visiting the château, will eat up the rest of your afternoon. Overnight in Albi.

Day ❸: Carcassonne: ✸✸✸
The Walled City

You can leave Albi early in the morning of **Day 3,** making the 105km (65-mile) drive south to Carcassonne, the most heavily visited city in the southwest of France. It is the picture postcard of the Middle Ages. After checking into a hotel, set out to explore the walled city, walking its ramparts. This will occupy the rest of your morning and part of your afternoon. After lunch, you can visit the **Basilique St-Nazaire** (p. 94), the **Musée des Memoires du Moyen Age** (p. 95), and **Château Comtal** (p. 95). Overnight in Carcassonne.

Day ❹: Narbonne ✸
& Perpignan ✸✸

On **Day 4,** a busy two-city tour, you can drive 96km (38 miles) east of Carcassonne to medieval Narbonne, whose port rivaled Marseille in the days of the Romans. You can arrive early enough in the morning for a walk around its Old Town and a visit to its major monument, **Cathédrale St-Just** (p. 109). Before lunch you can also spend an hour wandering around the **Palais des Archevêques.** Of the three museums in this complex, the one that merits attention is the **Musée Archéologique** (p. 109).

After lunch in Narbonne, continue to the ancient Catalonian city of Perpignan, 64km (40 miles) south of Narbonne. Check into a hotel here for the night. In the afternoon, you can walk around its historic core, visiting **Castillet/Musée des Arts et Traditions Populaires Catalans** (p. 100) and the **Cathédrale St-Jean** (p. 100) from the late Middle Ages.

Day ❺: Montpellier: 👁👁 Capital of Mediterranean Languedoc

On **Day 5,** you'll need to backtrack from Perpignan to Narbonne, taking the E15 autoroute and bypassing Narbonne to arrive in the ancient university city of Montpellier, 96km (59 miles) east of Narbonne. Check into a hotel for the night.

In what remains of the morning, wander through the **Jardin des Plantes** (p. 116) and pay a visit to the **Cathédrale St-Pierre** (p. 117), spending 1½ to 2 hours taking in one of France's greatest provincial art galleries. Allow time for a long stroll along the 17th-century **promenade de Peyrou** 👁👁, one of the great terraced parks of southwest France, opening onto the Mediterranean. If time remains, stroll **Place de la Comédie,** where you'll find some 120 boutiques selling unusual merchandise.

Day ❻: Nîmes: 👁👁👁 Roman Monuments

On **Day 6,** from Montpellier drive 88km (55 miles) northeast to the ancient city of Nîmes where you can check into a hotel for the night. Set out for a busy day of sightseeing, heading first for **Maison Carrée** (p. 123), one of the world's greatest Roman temples. You can also head for the **Amphithéâtre Romain** (p. 122), taking in the Roman amphitheater and doing so before lunch in a typical Nîmes restaurant.

In the afternoon, visit the **Carrée d'Art/Musée d'Art Contemporain** (p. 122), to see both its permanent and temporary art exhibitions. Walk through its beautiful gardens, **Jardin de la Fontaine** (p. 124), taking in views of its Roman ruins. Try also to visit the city's largest museum, **Musée des Beaux-Arts** (p. 124), with its mammoth collection of French painting and sculpture from the 17th century to modern times.

Day ❼: Arles 👁👁👁 & the Camargue

On your final day, **Day 7,** set out in the morning to drive 32km (20 miles) southwest of Nîmes for a morning visit to Arles. Worthy of the trip are: **Les Alyscamps** (p. 154), one of the world's most famous necropolises; **Théâtre Antique/Amphithéâtre** (p. 155), a Roman theater founded by Augustus in the 1st century and an ancient amphitheater. Have lunch in Arles.

In the afternoon, continue south to the Camargue, heading for the capital of the Camargue, **Aigues-Mortes,** a distance of 48km (30 miles) southwest of Nîmes. Called "the city of dead waters," Aigues-Mortes is France's most preserved walled town and makes a good hotel base for the night. Spend what remains of the afternoon exploring its ancient streets and touring its **ramparts** (p. 112). In the morning, journey to Marseille where you can make rail or plane connections to anywhere in Europe.

Languedoc-Roussillon & the Camargue

Languedoc, one of southern France's great old provinces, is a loosely defined area encompassing such cities as Nîmes, Toulouse, and Carcassonne. It's one of France's leading wine-producing areas and is fabled for its art treasures.

The coast of Languedoc—from Montpellier to the Spanish frontier—might be called France's "second Mediterranean," with first place naturally going to the Côte d'Azur. A land of ancient cities and a generous sea, it's less spoiled than the Côte d'Azur. An almost-continuous strip of sand stretches west from the Rhône and curves snakelike toward the Pyrenees. Back in the days of de Gaulle, the government began an ambitious project to develop the Languedoc-Roussillon coastline that has since become a booming success, as the miles of sun-baking bodies in July and August testify.

Ancient **Roussillon** is a small region of greater Languedoc, forming the Pyrenees-Orientales *département*. It includes the towns of Perpignan and Collioure within its borders. This is the French Catalonia, inspired more by Barcelona in neighboring Spain than by remote Paris. Over its long and colorful history, it has known many rulers. Legally part of the French kingdom until 1258, it was surrendered to James I of Aragón, and until 1344 it was part of the ephemeral kingdom of Majorca, with Perpignan as the capital. By 1463, Roussillon was annexed to France again. Then Ferdinand of Aragón won it back, but by 1659 France had it once again. In spite of some local sentiment for reunion with the Catalans of Spain, France still firmly controls the land.

The **Camargue** encompasses a marshy delta between two arms of the Rhône. Arles serves as the area's northern border, and the village Sète functions as a gateway to the region. South of Arles is cattle country, and here strong wild black bulls are bred for the arenas of Arles and Nîmes. Cattle are herded by *gardiens,* French cowboys, who wear wide-brimmed black hats and ride amazingly graceful small white horses, said to have been brought here by the Saracens. The whitewashed houses of the Camargue, plaited-straw roofs, pink flamingos that inhabit the muddy marshes, vast plains, endless stretches of sandbars—all this qualifies as "exotic" France.

1 Toulouse ✶✶✶

705km (438 miles) SW of Paris; 245km (152 miles) SE of Bordeaux; 97km (60 miles) W of Carcassonne

The old capital of Languedoc and France's fourth-largest city, Toulouse (known as *la ville en rose,* or the city in pink) today is cosmopolitan in flavor. The major city of the southwest, it's the gateway to the Pyrenees mountain range. Toulouse might be a city with a distinguished historical past, but it is also a city of the future and the high-tech

Languedoc-Roussillon & the Camargue

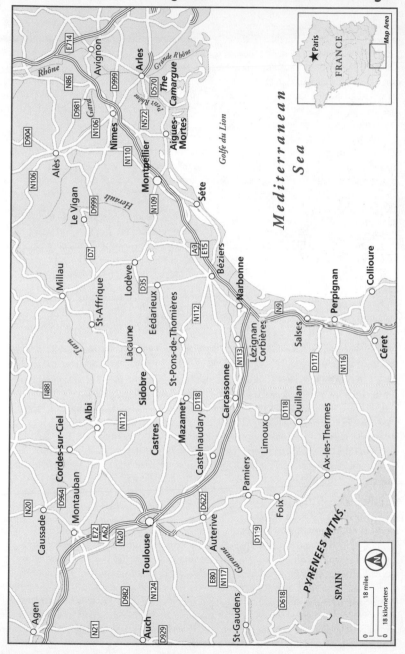

center of the aerospace industry in France. It is home to two huge aircraft makers—Airbus and Aérospatiale—and the National Center for Space Research has been headquartered here for more than 3 decades. The first regularly scheduled airline flights from France took off from the local airport in the 1920s. Today long-range passenger planes of the Airbus consortium, the most important rivals in the world to Boeing, are assembled in a gargantuan hangar in the suburb of Colombiers. In 1997, Toulouse launched an air and space museum (see the entry below for **La Cité de l'Espace**). Also making the city tick is its extraordinarily high population of students: some 110,000 in all, out of a population of 800,000.

An ancient city filled with gardens and squares, Toulouse has a stormy history. It has played many roles: Once it was the capital of the Visigoths and later the center of the *comtes de Toulouse* (counts of Toulouse). The city has 20 historic pipe organs, more than any other city in France, and hosts an annual international organ festival.

ESSENTIALS

GETTING THERE   The Toulouse-Blagnac international **airport** lies in the city's northwestern suburbs, 11km (7 miles) from the center; for flight information, call **𝄞 08-25-38-00-00. Air France** (**𝄞 08-20-82-08-20**) has about 25 flights a day from Paris. **British Airways** (**𝄞 08-25-82-54-00**) flies to Toulouse from London.

Some nine high-speed TGV **trains** per day arrive from Paris (trip time: 5 hr.; one-way fare: 80€/$104), eight from Bordeaux (trip time: 1 hr., 50 min.), and 11 from Marseille (trip time: 3½ hr.). For information, call **𝄞 08-92-35-35-35.** The **drive** from Paris takes 6 to 7 hours. Take A10 south to Bordeaux, connecting to A62 to Toulouse. The Canal du Midi links many of the region's cities with Toulouse by waterway.

VISITOR INFORMATION   The **Office de Tourisme** is in the Donjon du Capitole in the Square de Gaule (**𝄞 05-61-11-02-22;** www.ot-toulouse.fr).

GETTING AROUND   Toulouse has the most efficient public transportation system of any city in southwestern France. The heart of the city, the historic core of most interest to visitors, is served by a modern and efficient Métro (subway to Americans) system administered by SEMVAT, 49 rue de Gironis (**𝄞 05-61-41-70-70**). The service operates daily from 5am to midnight, and tickets and maps are available at the ticket booths. The average Métro fare is 1.30€ ($1.70) per ticket. The most useful stops, which are within walking distance of all the main attractions, are Capitole, Jean Jaurès, and Esquirole.

SEEING THE SIGHTS
THE TOP ATTRACTIONS

Basilique St-Sernin 𝄞𝄞𝄞   The city's major monument, consecrated in 1096, is the largest and finest Romanesque church extant in Europe; try to avoid touring it during Sunday morning Mass. An outstanding feature is the Porte Miègeville, opening onto the south aisle and decorated with 12th-century sculptures. The door to the south transept is the Porte des Comtes. Look for the Romanesque capitals surmounting the church's columns; the ones here depict the story of Lazarus. Nearby are the tombs of the comtes de Toulouse. Entering by the main west door, you can see the double side aisles that give the church five naves, an unusual feature in Romanesque architecture. An upper cloister forms a passageway around the interior.

In the axis of the basilica, 11th-century bas-reliefs depict *Christ in His Majesty.* The ambulatory leads to the crypt (ask the custodian for permission to enter), containing the relics of 128 saints, plus a thorn said to be from the Crown of Thorns. In the

Toulouse

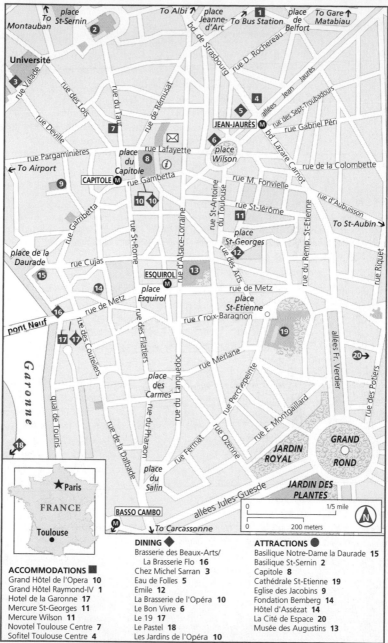

ACCOMMODATIONS ■
Grand Hôtel de l'Opera **10**
Grand Hôtel Raymond-IV **1**
Hotel de la Garonne **17**
Mercure St-Georges **11**
Mercure Wilson **11**
Novotel Toulouse Centre **7**
Sofitel Toulouse Centre **4**

DINING ◆
Brasserie des Beaux-Arts/
  La Brasserie Flo **16**
Chez Michel Sarran **3**
Eau de Folles **5**
Emile **12**
La Brasserie de l'Opéra **10**
Le Bon Vivre **6**
Le 19 **17**
Le Pastel **18**
Les Jardins de l'Opéra **10**

ATTRACTIONS ●
Basilique Notre-Dame la Daurade **15**
Basilique St-Sernin **2**
Capitole **8**
Cathédrale St-Etienne **19**
Eglise des Jacobins **9**
Fondation Bemberg **14**
Hôtel d'Assézat **14**
La Cité de Espace **20**
Musée des Augustins **13**

Fun Fact **La Ville en Rose**

Toulouse is a brick-built city, whereas most cities of the Middle Ages were constructed of stone. In Toulouse, the nearest stone quarries were some 50 miles away. Instead of stone, the builders of Toulouse learned to fashion red bricks from readily available Garonne clays. They were cheap, robust, and rosy, earning the city the nickname of *la ville en rose*, or "the city in pink." Because of the clay, these rose-colored bricks were lighter in tone than those in other cities such as Albi. For extra grandeur, the builders of Toulouse trimmed their bricks in white marble, giving the city an architectural touch of elegance and splendor.

---

ambulatory, the old baroque altar shelves and shrine have been reset; the relics here are those of the Apostles and the first bishops of Toulouse.

Place St-Sernin. ℭ **05-61-21-80-45.** Free admission to church; combined admission to the crypt and ambulatory 2€ ($2.60). Church summer daily 8:30am–5:45pm, off season daily 8:30–11:45am and 2–5:45pm; no sightseeing during Sun-morning Masses. Crypt and ambulatory summer daily 8:30am–5:45pm; off season Mon–Sat 10–11:30am, daily 2:30–5pm.

Cathédrale St-Etienne ⚐ This is the city's other major ecclesiastical building. Because of the time required to build it (it was designed and constructed between the 11th c. and the 17th c.), some critics scorn it for its mishmash of styles, yet it nonetheless conveys a solemn dignity. The rectangular bell tower is from the 16th century. It has a unique ogival nave to which a Gothic choir has been added.

Place St-Etienne, at the eastern end of rue de Metz. ℭ **05-61-52-03-82.** Daily 8am–7pm.

Fondation Bemberg Opened in 1995, this quickly became one of the city's most important museums. Housed in the magnificent Hôtel Assézat (built in 1555, with a 16th-c. courtyard), the museum offers an overview of 5 centuries of European art, with world-class paintings from the Renaissance to the late 19th century. The nucleus of the collection represents the lifelong work of collector extraordinaire Georges Bemberg, of a German-French family, who donated 331 works. The largest bequest was 28 paintings by Pierre Bonnard, including his *Moulin Rouge.* Bemberg also donated works by Pissarro, Matisse *(Vue d'Antibes),* and Monet, plus the Fauves. The foundation owns Canaletto's much-reproduced *Vue de Mestre* as well. The mansion also houses the **Académie des Jeux-Floraux,** which since 1323 has presented flowers made of wrought metal to poets.

Place d'Assézat, rue de Metz. ℭ **05-61-12-06-89.** Admission 4.60€ ($6), 2.75€ ($3.60) students and persons 8–18, free to children 7 and under. Tues–Wed and Fri–Sun 10am–12:30pm and 1:30–6pm; Thurs 10am–9pm.

La Cité de l'Espace ⚐ Some half a million visitors a year come here to learn what it's like to program a satellite's launch into orbit or how to maneuver one in space. Both an interactive teaching tool and a fun place to visit, here life-size structural models abound, including one of an astronaut riding an exercise bike in zero gravity. On the grounds outside you can walk through the Mir orbital station constructed by the Russians. The top floor focuses on exploration of the universe, with close-up shots of the moons of Jupiter taken by fly-by satellites.

Av. Jean Gonord. ℭ **05-62-71-48-71.** www.cite-espace.com. Admission 14€ ($18) adults, 12€ ($15) ages 13–25, 11€ ($14) children 6–12, free for children under 6; family tickets (2 adults, 2 children) 42€ ($55). July–Aug daily

9am–7pm; Sept–June Tues–Sun 9:30am–5pm (until 6pm Sat–Sun). Closed Jan 3–25. Follow N126 from the center of town to the E. Peripheral Rte. and take Exit 17. Bus: 37 (Sat–Sun only).

Musée des Augustins 🔯🔯   The museum was established in this convent in 1793, shortly after the French Revolution, when revolutionary acts closed this institution— then one of the city's most important monasteries—and adapted it for public use. In addition to the fabulous paintings, a stroll through this place gives you the chance to view a 14th-century monastery in all its mystical splendor. This museum's 14th-century cloisters contain the world's largest and most valuable collection of Romanesque capitals. The sculptures and carvings are magnificent, and the collection includes some fine examples of early Christian sarcophagi. On the upper floors is a large painting collection, with works by Toulouse-Lautrec, Gérard, Delacroix, and Ingres. The museum also contains several portraits by Antoine Rivalz, a local artist and major talent.

21 rue de Metz. ℃ 05-61-22-21-82. Admission 2.40€ ($3.10), free for children under 12. Wed 10am–9pm; Thurs–Mon 10am–6pm. Closed Jan 1, May 1, and Dec 25.

MORE SIGHTS

The Gothic brick **Eglise des Jacobins** 🔯🔯, parvis des Jacobins (℃ 05-61-22-21-92), in Old Toulouse, is west of place du Capitole along rue Lakanal. The church and the restored convent, daring in its architecture and its use of "palm tree"–shaped vaults, form the largest extant monastery complex in France. It's open daily from 10am to 7pm. Admission to most of the complex is free, but a visit to the cloisters costs 2.50€ ($3.25).

Small, charming, and dating mostly from the 18th century, the **Basilique Notre-Dame La Daurade,** 1 place de la Daurade (℃ 05-61-21-38-32), gets its name from the gilding that covers its partially baroque exterior. Its prize possession is a statue of the Black Virgin, about 1m (3 ft.) tall, to which some locals attribute quasi-mystical powers. The one you'll see today was crafted in 1807 as a replacement for a much older statue that was burnt during the French Revolution. Admission is free, but opening times are inconsistent.

In civic architecture, **Le Capitole** 🔯, place du Capitole (℃ 05-61-22-34-12), is an outstanding achievement and one of the most potent symbols of Toulouse. Built in a baroque style in 1753, it houses the **Hôtel de Ville** (city hall) as well as the **Théâtre National du Capitole** (℃ 05-61-22-31-31), which presents concerts, ballets, and operas. Renovated in 1996, it's outfitted in an Italian-inspired 18th-century style with shades of scarlet and gold. In the Hôtel de Ville, the only area that can be visited is the richly ornate **Salle des Illustres,** where you can see portraits of personalities who influenced the politics or culture of the city. Entrance is free. The Capitole complex is open Monday through Saturday 9am to noon, Monday through Friday 2 to 6pm.

The city has a number of fine old mansions, most of them dating from the Renaissance when Toulouse was one of the richest cities in Europe. The finest is the **Hôtel d'Assézat,** on rue de Metz. Built in 1555, it has an unaltered 16th-century courtyard. It houses the Académie des Jeux-Floraux (Academy of the Floral Games), whose purpose is to uphold the highest literary traditions of the region. Since 1323, it has presented to poets awards of flowers made of wrought metal. The mansion is also the headquarters of the above-mentioned Fondation Bemberg.

After all that sightseeing, head for the oval **place Wilson,** a showcase 19th-century square boasting fashionable cafes.

SHOPPING

Head for **rue d'Alsace-Lorraine,** which is rich in clothing and housewares. At the well-stocked shopping mall, the **Centre Commercial St-Georges,** rue du Rempart St-Etienne, you can fill your suitcases with all kinds of glittery loot. For upscale boutiques, head to **rue Croix-Baragnon, rue des Arts,** and **rue St-Antoine du T.** The pearly gates of antiques heaven are on **rue Fermat.** More down-market antiques spread out each Sunday from 8am to noon during the weekly **flea market** adjacent to the Basilique St-Sernin. In addition to that, in the same spot, a *brocante* (knickknack) sale takes place on the first weekend (Fri–Sun) of each month from 8am to 1pm.

Violets grow in abundance in meadows on the outskirts of Toulouse. Two shops that sell everything imaginable connected with violets include **Violettes & Pastels,** 10 rue St-Pantaléon (© 05-61-22-14-22), and **Péniche Maison de la Violette,** Canal du Midi, just in front of the rail station (© 05-61-90-01-30). Inventories include violet-scented perfume, and clothing—especially scarves—patterned with the dainty purple flower.

WHERE TO STAY
EXPENSIVE

Grand Hôtel de l'Opéra *⊘⊘⊘*   This is the most elegant oasis in Toulouse, and the owners have won several prestigious awards for transforming a 17th-century convent into a sophisticated hotel. The public rooms contain early-19th-century antiques and Napoleonic-inspired tenting over the bars. Some of the spacious and stylish guest rooms have urn-shaped balustrades overlooking formal squares, and all have high ceilings and modern amenities. The beds are elegantly attired in tasteful fabrics, with soft pillows, most richly refurbished in the early millennium. Each well-maintained tiled bathroom has a tub/shower combination. The hotel restaurant is the town's most prestigious.

1 place du Capitole, 31000 Toulouse. © **05-61-21-82-66.** Fax 05-61-23-41-04. www.grand-hotel-opera.com. 57 units. 161€–323€ ($209–$420) double; 328€ ($426) suite. AE, DC, MC, V. Parking 14€ ($18). Métro: Capitole. **Amenities:** Restaurant (see "Where to Dine," below); brasserie; bar; gym; sauna; steam room; limited room service; laundry service/dry cleaning; nonsmoking rooms; limited-mobility rooms. *In room:* A/C, TV, dataport, minibar, hair dryer, safe.

Sofitel Toulouse Centre *⊘⊘* *(Kids*   Business travelers deem this hotel, built in 1989, as the best in town (though we prefer the Grand Hôtel de l'Opéra as the most tranquil retreat). Adjacent to place Wilson, this Sofitel employs a charming bilingual staff and offers suites big enough to fit an entire family or serve as an office away from the office. The rooms are furnished in chain format, and each comes with a bathroom with a tub/shower combination.

84 allée Jean-Jaurès, 31000 Toulouse. © **05-61-10-23-10.** Fax 05-61-10-23-20. www.sofitel.com. 119 units. 228€–248€ ($296–$322) double; 265€–345€ ($345–$449) suite. AE, DC, MC, V. Parking 5.50€ ($7.15). Métro: Jean-Jaurès. **Amenities:** Restaurant; bar; health club; business center; 24-hr. room service; babysitting; laundry service/dry cleaning; nonsmoking rooms; limited-mobility rooms. *In room:* A/C, TV, dataport, minibar, hair dryer, safe.

MODERATE

Grand Hôtel Raymond-IV   On a quiet street close to the town center and the train station, this 19th-century redbrick building contains pleasant rooms with bland but comfortable furniture and restful beds. All of the individually decorated accommodations are different—some small, others rather grand—with a vaguely Art Deco motif. Some rooms have air-conditioning. The compact bathrooms have showers. Although breakfast is the only meal served, the English-speaking staff will direct you to nearby restaurants.

16 rue Raymond-IV, 31000 Toulouse. ⓒ **05-61-62-89-41.** Fax 05-61-62-38-01. www.hotelraymond4-toulouse.com. 38 units. 70€–145€ ($91–$189) double. AE, MC, V. Parking 10€ ($13). Métro: Jean-Jaurès or Capitole. **Amenities:** Bar; limited room service; laundry service/dry cleaning; nonsmoking rooms. *In room:* TV, dataport, minibar, hair dryer.

Hôtel de la Garonne ★★ *Finds* One of the most delightful hotels of Toulouse—certainly the most tranquil—is this little charmer connected with Le 19, a well-recommended restaurant (see below). Midsize bedrooms are snug and cozy, renovated in 2004 and outfitted in a dignified style, often incorporating tones of deep red and beige. Each comes with a well-equipped private bathroom with tub and shower. If you stay here, you get not only one of the finest rooms in Toulouse, but can also enjoy one of the best meals in town. The restaurant itself lies directly opposite the hotel in a 16th century vaulted ceiling of red brick. You get elegance, charm, an affordable price, and a retreat right in the heart of the city.

22 Descente de la Halle aux Poissons, 31000 Toulouse. ⓒ **05-34-31-94-80.** Fax 05-34-31-94-81. www.hotel garonne.com. 14 units. 150€–175€ ($195–$228) double; 259€ ($337) suite. Rates include breakfast. AE, DC, MC, V. Métro: Esquirol. Parking 12€ ($16). **Amenities:** Restaurant; bar; limited room service. *In room:* A/C, TV, dataport.

Mercure St-Georges   Just a few paces from the Mercure Wilson (see below; the two share staff and management), this seven-story hotel is the less historic twin of the older and cozier-looking hotel. Decor here is rigidly standardized—bedrooms are identical, though comfortably modern, with small, clean bathrooms. Business travelers are the primary clientele at this location.

Rue St.-Jérome (place Occitaine), 31000 Toulouse. ⓒ **05-62-27-79-79.** Fax 05-62-27-79-00. 148 units. 80€–125€ ($104–$163) double; 160€–230€ ($208–$299) suite. AE, DC, MC, V. Parking 13€ ($17). Métro: Capitole. **Amenities:** Restaurant; bar; limited room service; laundry service/dry cleaning. *In room:* A/C, TV, minibar, hair dryer, safe (in some).

Mercure Wilson ★   This is the more appealing of the two Mercure hotels that stand almost adjacent to each other in the heart of Toulouse's historic central zone. Built around 1850, it's constructed of the distinctive pink-toned bricks cherished by local preservationists. In 1999, Mercure radically upgraded the hotel's interior, transforming it into one of the most up-to-date middle-bracket places in town. Most bedrooms are a comfortable size, and in spite of their chain format, furnishings are agreeable. Bathrooms have tub/shower combos. There's no restaurant on the premises, but guests can easily migrate a few steps to the premises of the Mercure St-Georges (see above).

7 rue Labéda, 31000 Toulouse. ⓒ **05-34-45-40-60.** Fax 05-34-45-40-61. 95 units. 128€–158€ ($166–$205) double; 178€ ($231) suite. AE, DC, MC, V. Parking 11€ ($14). Métro: Capitole. **Amenities:** Bar; lounge; limited room service; babysitting; laundry service/dry cleaning; limited-mobility rooms. *In room:* A/C, TV, minibar, hair dryer, dataport.

Novotel Toulouse Centre   Set in the most verdant part of Toulouse's center, this modern and efficient hotel is a few paces from the city's Japanese gardens. The Matabiau train station is within a 5-minute walk, and the nerve center of the old city, place St-Sernin, is less than half a mile away. All rooms are alike, each with a single bed (which can be converted into a couch), a double bed, a long writing desk, and a roomy, fully equipped bathroom. In spite of the chain-style format, this is one of the best Novotel hotels, with larger than usual bedrooms. Bathrooms have tub/shower combos.

5 place Alfonse-Jourdain, 31000 Toulouse. ⓒ **05-61-21-74-74.** Fax 05-61-22-81-22. 131 units. 124€–146€ ($161–$190) double; 165€–175€ ($215–$228) suite. AE, DC, MC, V. Parking 7€ ($9.10). Bus: 1 or 2. **Amenities:** Restaurant; bar; pool; limited room service; babysitting; laundry service/dry cleaning, nonsmoking rooms; limited-mobility rooms. *In room:* A/C, TV, hair dryer, dataport.

WHERE TO DINE
EXPENSIVE

Chez Michel Sarran ✿✿✿ MODERN FRENCH   At the most stylish restaurant in Toulouse, you can enjoy the cuisine of master chef Michel Sarran. Sarran's wife, Françoise, oversees the three red, green, or violet dining rooms, in the heart of town on separate floors of a building near the Novotel Centre. The creative dishes have attracted diners as diverse as the prime minister of France and show-biz types like Sophie Marceau and Gilbert Becaud. The food brings out the flavors of southern and southwestern France. Start with a warm soup of foie gras and oysters, or perhaps a cup of organic yogurt studded with black truffles from the Périgord. Move on to a succulent version of poached sea bass served with a creamy polenta and lobster sauce; or perhaps a portion of roasted wild black boar from the underpopulated Bigorre region of France, served in a stewpot with thyme and wine-roasted potatoes. Dessert might include ravioli stuffed with creamed oranges and served with an aspic of sweet white Gaillac wine.

21 bd. Armand du Portal. © **05-61-12-32-32.** www.michel-sarran.com. Reservations recommended. Main courses 30€–60€ ($39–$78); fixed-price menu lunch 45€–140€ ($59–$182), dinner 75€–140€ ($98–$182). AE, MC, V. Mon–Fri noon–2pm and 8–9:45pm (closed Wed for lunch). Closed Aug, 1 week around Christmas. Métro: Capitole.

Le 19 ✿ MODERN FRENCH   One of the city's finest restaurants is a high-profile, cellar restaurant whose wood panels and carpeting contrast with its terra-cotta bricks. It's 19 steps down from the street, in the high-ceilinged cellar of a medieval building once used for the storage of fish and the salts to preserve them. The delicate, creative menu items change with the seasons. Among delectable dishes are a terrine of deliberately undercooked foie gras, served with figs; cream of watercress soup with warm oysters; magret of duckling served with ginger and crushed apples; roasted shoulder of rabbit served in a stewpot, with polenta and baby vegetables; filet of baked red snapper with spider-crab sauce, and filet of curried duck breast with Asian-style vegetables. To end your meal, try a stir-fry of mandarin oranges flavored with balsamic vinegar, or saffron-flavored sabayon with ice cream made from unpasteurized milk.

The restaurant is part of the **Hôtel de la Garonne** (see above).

19 Descente de la Halle aux Poissons. © **05-34-31-94-84.** Reservations recommended. Main courses 19€–35€ ($22–$40); fixed-price lunch 29€–55€ ($33–$63). AE, DC, MC, V. Tues–Fri noon–2pm; Mon–Sat 8–10:30pm. Métro: Esquirol.

Le Pastel ✿✿ FRENCH   One of the best restaurants in the area occupies a stone-sided manor house built around 1850. It lies 7 minutes southwest of the center by car, within the city limits. Today it's the domain of Paris-trained chef and entrepreneur Gérard Garrigues. The setting is as restful as the cuisine is superb: Terraces ringed with flowers near an outdoor pergola and dining rooms accented with paintings by local artists contribute to the placidity. Menu items change every week. During our visit, the menu featured such dishes as scallops "jubilatoire," roasted at very high temperatures (300°C/570°F) with beef marrow, garlic, and balsamic vinegar; deliberately undercooked foie gras with a confit of quince and cornmeal brioche; roebuck with wine sauce and old-fashioned vegetables; and steak of sea bass with hearts of artichoke and truffled vinegar. Wine choices are as sophisticated as anything else you're likely to find in Toulouse.

237 rte. de St-Simon. © **05-62-87-84-30.** Reservations required. Main courses 30€–42€ ($39–$55); fixed-price menus 38€–98€ ($49–$127). AE, DC, MC, V. Tues–Sat noon–2pm and 8–9:30pm. Métro: Basso-Cambo.

Toulousy-Les Jardins de l'Opéra ✿✿✿ FRENCH   The entrance to the city's best restaurant is in the 18th-century Florentine courtyard of the Grand Hôtel. The dining area is a series of salons, several of which face a winter garden and a reflecting pool. The gracious Maryse Toulousy, whose husband, Dominique, prepares modern and old-fashioned French cuisine, will greet you. A long-standing staple, developed by the owner and praised by gastronomes, is ravioli stuffed with foie gras of duckling and served with essence of truffles. Equally appealing are carpaccio of lobster served with foie gras; tartare of sturgeon, mushrooms, and oysters; sautéed pikeperch with a gratinated crust of shredded coconut, vanilla-flavored citrus sauce, and a chiffonade of fruits, vegetables, and truffles; and spicy breast of pigeon with a "surprise" preparation of the bird's organs decorated with rosettes of zucchini. One of the most appealing desserts is figs poached in red Banyuls wine, stuffed with homemade vanilla ice cream.

In the Grand Hôtel de l'Opéra, 1 place du Capitole. ⓒ **05-61-23-07-76.** Reservations required. Main courses 32€–85€ ($42–$111); fixed-price menu 40€–92€ ($52–$120) lunch, 52€–105€ ($68–$137) dinner. AE, DC, MC, V. Tues–Sat noon–2pm and 8–10pm. Closed Jan 1–8 and July 28–Aug 29. Métro: Capitole.

MODERATE

Brasserie des Beaux-Arts/La Brasserie Flo TRADITIONAL FRENCH   This early-1900s brasserie has an authentic Art Nouveau interior that's been enhanced because of its connection with the Jean Bucher chain (the most successful director of Art Nouveau French brasseries in the world, some of which are classified as national historic monuments). The carefully restored decor features walnut paneling and mirrors. The cuisine emphasizes well-prepared seafood and all the typical local dishes, including cassoulet, magret of duckling, lightly smoked salmon with lentils and mussels, and confit of duckling. Try foie gras or country-style sauerkraut, accompanied by the house Riesling, served in an earthenware pitcher. During warm weather, eat on the terrace. The staff is likely to be hysterical and less than suave during peak times.

In the Hôtel des Beaux-Arts, 1 quai de la Daurade. ⓒ **05-61-21-12-12.** Reservations recommended. Main courses 14€–25€ ($18–$33); fixed-price menu 23€–32€ ($30–$42). AE, DC, MC, V. Daily noon–2:30pm and 7:30pm–2am. Métro: Esquirol.

Emile 👉 *Finds* TOULOUSIEN   In an old-fashioned house on one of Toulouse's most beautiful squares, this restaurant offers the specialties of chef Christophe Fasan. In winter, meals are served upstairs overlooking the square; in summer, seating moves to the street-level dining room and flower-filled terrace. Menu choices include cassoulet Toulousian (cooked in goose fat), magret of duckling in traditional style, a medley of Catalonian fish, and a very fresh *parillade* (mixed grill) of fish with a pungently aromatic cold sauce of sweet peppers and olive oil. The wine list is filled with intriguing surprises.

13 place St-Georges. ⓒ **05-61-21-05-56.** Reservations recommended. Main courses 20€–28€ ($26–$36); fixed-price menu 17€–48€ ($22–$62) lunch, 36€–45€ ($41–$52) dinner. AE, DC, MC, V. Tues–Sat noon–2pm and 7:30–10:30pm (mid-May to Sept, also Mon 7–10:30pm). Métro: Capitole or Esquirol.

Le Brasserie de l'Opéra FRENCH   Le Brasserie, in the most prestigious hotel in the city, evokes memories of the old Brasserie Lipp in Paris. It is warmly decorated with rich cove moldings, lots of burnished hardwood, shimmering glass, and cut flowers. Fresh shellfish is featured. Other specialties include filet of braised red snapper, duck stew, "butterfly oysters," and an array of *plats du jour,* or dishes of the day, based on traditional brasserie cuisine. Seasonal ingredients are used "with respect," in the words of one food critic.

In the Grand Hôtel de l'Opéra, 1 place du Capitole. ⓒ **05-61-21-37-03.** Reservations recommended. Main courses 11€–22€ ($14–$28); fixed-price lunch 16€ ($21); fixed-price dinner 26€ ($34). AE, DC, MC, V. Mon–Fri noon–11pm. Closed Aug 1–15. Métro: Capitole.

INEXPENSIVE

Eau de Folles *(Value* TRADITIONAL FRENCH   This restaurant's low prices and the variety of its menu promise to make it a long-term contender. Within a mostly white, *fin-de-siècle* setting that includes lots of mirrors, you'll be offered a fixed-price menu with a choice of 10 starters, 10 main courses, and 10 desserts. Menu items vary according to the inspiration of the chef, the availability of fresh ingredients, and whatever happens to be in stock on the day of your visit. You might begin with a marinade of fish, followed with strips of duck meat with green-pepper sauce, and end it all with a homemade pastry such as a *tarte tatin* or a cup of rice pudding. Everything is very simple, served within a cramped but convivial setting.

14 allée du President Roosevelt. ℭ **05-61-23-45-50.** Reservations recommended. Fixed-price menu 23€ ($30). MC, V. Mon–Sat noon–1:30pm and 7–11pm. Métro: Wilson.

Le Bon Vivre ℛ SOUTHWESTERN FRENCH   One of downtown Toulouse's most appealing cost-conscious bistros occupies the street level of a historic 18th-century mansion immediately adjacent to Town Hall (Hôtel de Ville). Established in 2004, it provides cost-conscious dining within an environment ringed with the pink-colored bricks of antique Toulouse, beneath a ceiling supported by equivalent vaultings. Menu items feature contemporary twists upon time-tested French specialties, many of them heralded by workaday diners who appreciate the attractive ratios of value-to-quality. The best examples include an unusual version of macaroni studded with flap mushrooms, truffles, and foie gras; and a version of cassoulet (the specialty of France's southwest) that's made with both duck and pork. An appropriate starter is a braised slice of foie gras with peaches and grapes.

15 bis Place Wilson. ℭ **05-61-23-07-17.** Reservations recommended. Main courses 12€–22€ ($16–$29); set-price lunch 12€–18€ ($16–$23); set-price dinners 15€–18€ ($20–$23). DC, MC, V. Daily 11:30am–3pm and 7–11:30pm.

WHERE TO STAY & DINE NEARBY

La Flanerie   Within a large garden that slopes down to the edge of the Garonne, about 8km (5 miles) south of Toulouse, stands this dignified-looking manor house, originally built in 1799 for a local landowner. Part of its allure derives from the early 1970s, when it was the site of a hotel favored by French celebrities and international rock stars, whose names fill the guestbook that the Irish born owners, the Moloney family, present since their acquisition of the place late in 2004. You might be happiest interpreting this place as an informal bed-and-breakfast, where the rooms just happen to be country-elegant and the welcome particularly warm. An oddity associated with the place involves the fact that there's a free-standing garage for each of the establishment's 12 bedrooms, a quirk deriving from one of the auto-obsessed former owners. Accommodations are stylish and midsize, and although there's no restaurant on-site, the owners are well-informed about dining options nearby.

Rte. de Lacroix-Falgarde, 31320 Vieille-Toulouse. ℭ **05-61-73-39-12.** Fax 05-61-73-18-56. 12 units. 85€–110€ ($111–$143) double. AE, MC, V. Free parking. Bus: R. Take D4 south of Toulouse for 8km (5 miles). **Amenities:** Bar; outdoor pool; limited-mobility rooms. *In room:* A/C, TV, dataport, minibar, hair dryer.

TOULOUSE AFTER DARK

The theater, dance, and opera in Toulouse are often on a par with that found in Paris. The best way to stay on top of the city's arts scene is to pick up a copy of the free monthly magazine *Toulouse Culture* from the Office de Tourisme.

The city's most notable theaters are the **Théâtre du Capitole,** place du Capitole (ℭ **05-61-22-31-31**), which specializes in operas, operettas, and often works from the classical French repertoire; the **Théâtre de la Digue,** 3 rue de la Digue ((C) **05-61-42-97-79**), for ballets and works by local theater companies; and the **Halle aux Grains,** place Dupuy ((C) **05-61-62-02-70**). The home of the Orchestre du Capitole, the Halle aux Grains is the venue for mostly classical concerts. The **Théâtre Garonne,** 1 av. du Château d'Eau ((C) **05-62-48-56-56**), stages everything from works by Molière to current dramas. Another important venue is the **Théâtre Zenith,** 11 av. Raymond-Badiou ((C) **05-62-74-49-49**), which has a large stage and seating capacity. It usually schedules rock concerts, variety acts, and musical comedies from other European cities. A smaller competitor, with a roughly equivalent mix of music, theater, and entertainment, is the **Théâtre de la Cité,** 1 rue Pierre Baudis ((C) **05-34-45-05-00**).

The liveliest squares to wander after dark are **place du Capitole, place St-Georges, place St-Pierre,** and **place Wilson.**

For bars and pubs, **La Tantina de Bourgos,** 27 rue de la Garonette ((C) **05-61-55-59-29**), has a Latin flair that's popular with students, and the rowdier **Chez Tonton,** 16 place St-Pierre ((C) **05-61-21-89-54**), has an *après-match* atmosphere, complete with the winning teams boozing it up. A popular bar that schedules both live and recorded music is **Monsieur Carnaval,** 34 rue Bayard ((C) **05-61-99-14-56**), where there's lots of rocking and rolling *a la française* for the under 35 crowd.

The town's trendiest and most widely sought-after disco for persons under 35 is **Le Purple,** 2 rue Castellane. Set close to the also-recommended Sofitel, it's the disco that, at least at presstime, had the longest lines, generated the most interest within the counterculture press, and elicited the highest level of passion within the city's A-list wannabe junkies. The busiest English-style pub in town, woodsy and Celtic-looking, and often very crowded with the city's English-speaking community, is **Le Fog & Le Roast Beef,** rue de l'Industrie ((C) **05-61-99-28-57**). **Pelouse Interdit,** avenue des Etats-Unis, offers a charming restaurant and bar behind a simple, discreetly marked green door within a venue that incorporates a garden, a restaurant, a bar, and lots of charm where you wouldn't expect it. And if you have a car and don't mind driving about 20 minutes out of town (follow the signs pointing to Albi), a hip and sought-after rendezvous point is **Le Lounge 233,** 233 route d'Albi (no phone) where a fussy and complicated list of cocktails, something many young French clubbers are just getting used to, are available for from around 9€ ($12) each. A somewhat less cutting-edge, but very popular disco is **Cockpit,** 1 rue du Puits-Vert ((C) **05-61-21-87-53**). Near Le Capitol and the nocturnally animated place Wilson, it's been around longer that Le Purple, and is a bit less modish, but it still has a strong appeal to a danceaholic clientele that incorporates, as any good disco does, a mixed clientele of males, females, gays (who in recent years seem, at least here, to be increasing in their visibility), straight people, and in-betweens.

You'll find dozens of bars in the 18th-century neighborhood around the place Wilson, near Le Capitole. A bar with a higher-than-usual percentage of gays and lesbians is the shadowy and intimate **Le Ritmo-Bar,** 6 rue de la Colombette ((C) **05-61-99-61-87**), where a hip roster of recorded music accompanies the drinking and flirting.

Mostly heterosexuals migrate to **Disco Le Maximo,** 4 rue Gabrielle-Peri ((C) **05-34-41-15-65**), which starts hopping Wednesday through Saturday after 11pm, and which serves tapas with a distinctly French flair (foie gras on toast, perhaps). There's also a vaguely Iberian-looking establishment, **Bar La Bodega,** 1 rue Gabrielle-Peri ((C) **05-61-63-03-63**), that's about as beer-soaked and raucous as anything else in town. It's particularly interesting in the wake of one of the region's football (soccer) games, especially if the home team has won.

The oldest and most deeply entrenched gay bar in Toulouse is **Le New Shanghai,** 12 rue de la Pomme (© **05-61-23-37-80**), a man's dance domain playing the latest in techno; farther inside, it gives way to a darker and at its best, sexy cruise-bar environment with lots of hot men on the prowl. Entrance is free and it's open every night.

2 Auch (★

726km (451 miles) SW of Paris; 203km (126 miles) SE of Bordeaux; 64km (40 miles) W of Toulouse

The lively market town of Auch is on the west bank of the Gers in the heart of the ancient Duchy of Gascony, of which it was once the capital.

ESSENTIALS

GETTING THERE   Five to 10 SNCF **trains** or **buses** per day run between Toulouse and Auch (trip time: 1½ hr.); 6 to 13 SNCF buses (© **05-62-05-73-76**) arrive in Auch daily from Agen (trip time: 1½ hr.). The one-way train fare from Toulouse is 12€ ($16). For info, call © **08-92-35-35-35.** If you're **driving** to Auch, take N124 west from Toulouse.

VISITOR INFORMATION   The **Office de Tourisme** is at 1 rue Dessoles, at place de la Cathédrale (© **05-62-05-22-89;** www.tourisme.fr/office-de-tourisme/auch.htm).

EXPLORING THE TOWN

The town is divided into an upper and a lower quarter, connected by several flights of steps. In the old part of town in the upper quarter, the narrow streets, called *pousterles,* center on **place Salinis,** from which there's a good view of the Pyrenees. Branching off from here, the **Escalier Monumental** leads down to the Le Gers River and the lower quarter of town, a descent of 232 steps.

North of the square is the **Cathédrale Ste-Marie** (★★, place de la Cathédrale (© **05-62-05-72-71**). Built from the 15th to the 17th centuries, this is one of the handsomest Gothic churches in the south of France. It has 113 Renaissance **choir stalls** (★★★ made of carved oak. The impressive stained-glass windows crafted by Arnaud de Moles in the 16th century, are also from the Renaissance. The cathedral is open daily from 9:30am to noon and 2 to 6pm (until 5pm in winter). Entrance to the church is free; admission to the choir is 1.50€ ($1.95).

Next to the cathedral stands an 18th-century **archbishop's palace** with a 14th-century bell tower, the **Tour d'Armagnac,** which was once a prison. Both are closed to the public.

For shops and boutiques, walk down **rue Dessoles, rue de Pouille,** and **avenue de l'Alsace.** Here you'll find everything from confectionery shops to clothing stores. For a town of its relatively small size, Auch produces more wines, more fine Armagnacs, more foie gras, more cheese, more cured ham, and greater numbers of regional delicacies than a casual visitor might have expected. They'll virtually leap out of store windows as you promenade down the commercial streets of downtown Auch (the rue Dessoles is reserved only for pedestrian traffic, and especially dense with food outlets.) Three of the busiest and most respected outlets for regional foodstuffs, liqueurs (especially Armagnacs), and wines are **La Cave aux Gourmands,** 15 rue Dessoles (© **05-62-61-81-33**); **La Cave d'Artagnan,** 3 rue de la République (© **06-78-85-05-74**), and **Camin Dret,** 27 rue Dessoles (© **05-62-05-58-38**). *Bon appétit!*

WHERE TO STAY

Hôtel de France (Restaurant Jardin des Saveurs) ⚘ This is no longer a mandatory stop in southern France for serious foodies. The hotel is now a solid and reliable choice, even if its Michelin stars are long lost. It was built around the much-modernized 16th-century core of an old inn. The rooms are comfortable, conservative, and furnished with traditional but somewhat nondescript pieces. Some are a bit dowdy. The cuisine somewhat slavishly follows many of the culinary trends established by the since-retired founder, André Daguin, but with less panache. Today, with kitchens directed by Roland Garreau, the cuisine is "innovative within traditional boundaries." Lovers of foie gras sometimes look forward to something approaching an inundation of the velvety substance at this restaurant that lies smack in the heart of foie-gras production country. Start off, for example, with a platter featuring four different preparations of the stuff (each prepared with different herbs, spices, and flavorings), or perhaps some marinated Scottish salmon; followed with a main course with an entire lobe (meaning a big portion) of foie gras prepared, house-style, with Provençal herbs and wine. If you're not in the mood for so much foie gras, consider a truffled platter of crayfish instead. Set-price menus for both lunch and dinner are priced from 25€ to 48€ ($33–$62); main courses 21€ to 29€ ($27–$38). The restaurant is open daily noon to 2pm and Monday to Saturday 7:30 to 9:45pm. During July and August, its also open on Sunday night.

Place de la Libération, 32003 Auch. ℂ **05-62-61-71-84.** Fax 05-62-61-71-81. 29 units. 113€–126€ ($147–$164) double; 195€–298€ ($254–$387) suite. AE, DC, MC, V. Parking 12€ ($16). **Amenities:** Restaurant; bar; nonsmoking rooms. *In room:* A/C, TV, dataport, minibar.

WHERE TO DINE

Most people still head for the **Hôtel de France** (see above), if only for the memories. But gone are the days when this housed one of the great restaurants in the south of France.

Le Daroles TRADITIONAL FRENCH Despite its much, much lower prices, this Parisian-style brasserie attracts many of the former clients of the Hôtel de France. Within an old-fashioned setting that includes mirrors, polished copper, mahogany paneling, and leather banquettes, you can enjoy a bustling, no-nonsense cuisine. Examples include strips of duckling with seasonal berries, scallops with herb and wine sauce, sauerkraut, foie gras, and pepper steak.

Place de la Liberation. ℂ **05-62-05-00-51.** Fixed-price lunch or dinner 16€ ($21). DC, MC, V. Daily 7am–10pm (bar until 2am).

3 Cordes-sur-Ciel ✶✶

678km (421 miles) SW of Paris; 25km (16 miles) NW of Albi

This site is remarkable—it's like an eagle's nest on a hilltop, above the Cérou valley. In days gone by, many celebrities, such as Jean-Paul Sartre and Albert Camus, considered this town a favorite hideaway.

The name Cordes is derived from the textile and leather industries that thrived here during the 13th and 14th centuries. Artisans working with linen and leather prospered, and the town also became known throughout France for its brilliantly colored silks. In the 16th century, however, plagues and religious wars reduced the city to a minor role. A brief renaissance occurred in the 19th century, when automatic weaving machines were introduced.

Today Cordes is an arts-and-crafts city, and many of the ancient houses on the narrow streets contain artisans plying their skills—blacksmiths, enamelers, graphic artists, weavers, engravers, sculptors, and painters.

You must park outside the city and then walk through an arch leading to the old town.

ESSENTIALS

GETTING THERE If you're **driving,** take N88 northwest from Toulouse to Gaillac, turning north on D922 into Cordes-sur-Ciel. If you're coming by **train,** get off in Cordes-Vindrac and walk, rent a bicycle, or take a taxi the remaining 3km (2 miles) west of Cordes. For train information, call ⓒ **08-92-35-35-35.** For a **taxi,** call Taxi Barrois (ⓒ **05-63-56-14-80**). Taxis cost 10€ ($13) each way. There's no bus.

VISITOR INFORMATION The **Office de Tourisme** is in the Maison Fonpeyrouse, Grand-Rue Raymond VII (ⓒ **05-63-56-00-52;** www.cordes-sur-ciel.org).

EXPLORING THE TOWN

Often called "the city of a hundred Gothic arches," Cordes contains numerous **maisons Gothiques** ⭐⭐, old houses built of pink sandstone. Many of the doors and windows are fashioned of pointed (broken) arches that still retain their 13th- and 14th-century grace. Some of the best preserved line **Grand'Rue,** also called **"rue Droite."**

Musée d'Art et d'Histoire le Portail-Peint (Musée Charles-Portal), Grand'Rue (ⓒ **05-63-56-06-11**), is named after the archivist of the Tarn region who was also an avid historian of Cordes. The museum is in a medieval house, the foundations of which date from the Gallo-Roman era. It contains everyday artifacts of the textile industry of long ago, farming measures, samples of local embroidery, a reconstructed peasant home interior, and other medieval memorabilia. Official visiting hours are limited to the busiest seasons: In July and August, it's open daily from 11am to 1pm and 3:30 to 7:30pm; April through June and September and October, it's officially open only on Sunday and public holidays from 3 to 6pm. If you happen to arrive when the museum is closed, ask someone at the tourist office (see above) to accompany you for your visit; if they're not busy, they often will. Barring that, try to make an appointment for a visit later in the day. Admission is 2.30€ ($3) adults, 1.10€ ($1.45) students and ages 12 to 25, free for children under 12.

Maison du Grand-Fauconnier (House of the Falcon Master), Grand'Rue, is named for the falcons carved into the stonework of the wall. A grandly proportioned staircase in the building leads to the **Musée Yves-Brayer** (ⓒ **05-63-56-14-79**). Yves Brayer moved to Cordes in 1940 and became one of its most ardent civic boosters. After watching Cordes fall gradually into decay, he renewed interest in its restoration. The museum contains minor artifacts relating to the town's history; the most interesting exhibits are rather fanciful scale models of the town itself. The museum is open February to December daily from 10:30am to 12:30pm and 2 to 6pm. Admission costs 3€ ($3.90) adults, 1.50€ ($1.95) children under 12.

Eglise St-Michel, Grand'Rue, dates from the 13th century, but many alterations have been made since. From the top of the tower you can view the surrounding area. Much of the lateral design of the side chapels was likely influenced by the cathedral at Albi. Before being shipped here, the organ (dating from 1830) was in Notre-Dame de Paris. The church can be visited only as part of guided visits arranged through the tourist office. With many exceptions, they're usually organized every day at 11am and 3pm, last for about an hour, and admission is free.

WHERE TO STAY & DINE

Bistrot Tonin'ty *Value* FRENCH   This is the least expensive, and the least fussy, of the several restaurants in Cordes that are owned and operated by Yves Thuriès, a celebrity chef whose recipes have been publicized, and praised, throughout France. (The most upscale of the restaurants in the group is Maison du Grand Ecuyer; see below.) During clement weather, you'll dine on aluminum furniture beneath a majestically gnarled 300-year-old wisteria vine whose blue-violet blossoms perfume the courtyard every spring. Otherwise, there's a mostly scarlet-toned dining room, with massive ceiling beams and smallish tables with immaculate napery. Menu items focus on the time-tested, the flavorful, and the traditional and include, among others, cassoulet, a croustade of magret of duckling layered with apples; foie gras that's redolent with spices; roasted salmon in the style of the chef; and a tempting array of sophisticated salads. Prices here are kept deliberately low, with all but a few of the main courses priced 8€ ($10) each.

The restaurant is the centerpiece of L'Hostellerie du Vieux Cordes; see the review below for more details.

Rue St-Michel, 81170 Cordes. © **05-63-53-79-20.** www.thuries.fr. Reservations recommended. Main courses 8€–12€ ($10–$16); fixed-price menu (5 courses) 35€ ($46). AE, DC, MC, V. May–Oct daily noon–2:30pm and 7:30–9:30pm; Nov–Mar Tues–Sat 7:30–9:30pm, Wed–Sun noon–2:30pm. Closed Jan.

Hostellerie du Parc *Value* TRADITIONAL FRENCH   This inn originated in the 18th century as a landowner's thick-walled home. Today, in a verdant park, the stone house holds this charming getaway *restaurant avec chambres*. It serves generous meals in a garden or paneled dining room. Specialties include homemade foie gras, duckling, *poularde* (chicken) *occitaine*, rabbit with cabbage leaves, ballotine of duck with foie gras, and confit of roasted rabbit with pink garlic from the nearby town of Lautrec.

The hotel offers 13 well-furnished rooms; a double costs 60€ to 90€ ($78–$117).

Les Cabannes, 81170 Cordes. © **05-63-56-02-59.** Fax 05-63-56-18-03. www.hostellerie-du-parc.com. Reservations recommended. Main courses 9€–25€ ($12–$33); fixed-price menu 22€–44€ ($29–$57). AE, DC, MC, V. June–Oct daily noon–2pm and 7–10pm; off season Thurs–Sun noon–2pm, Thurs–Sat 7–10pm. Closed Nov 15–Dec 15. From the town center, take rte. de St-Antonin (D600) for about 1km (¾ mile) west.

L'Hostellerie du Vieux Cordes   This stylish and sophisticated inn is set midway along the length of the walled-in medieval city, within what was originally built in the 1200s as the monastery associated with the Eglise St-Michel, which sits immediately next door. Its centerpiece is its restaurant, a glamorous yet intimate affair (see Bistrot Tonin'ty, above). Public areas, including the scarlet-colored dining room, are more richly furnished than the bedrooms, which are outfitted with ceiling beams and massive wooden furniture that includes, in most cases, a bulky armoire. None of them is air-conditioned, but thanks to windows whose views sometimes sweep out over the valley, and ceiling fans, they're on the receiving end of welcome breezes. Each is accessed via a winding stone staircase that passes such atmosphere-inducing accessories as full suits of armor. Each room was renovated in the late 1990s or later, and each has a contemporary-looking tile-sheathed bathroom.

Rue St-Michel, 81170 Cordes. © **05-63-53-79-20.** Fax 05-63-56-02-47. www.thuries.fr. 18 units. 49€–79€ ($64–$95) double. AE, DC, MC, V. Free parking. Closed Jan. **Amenities:** Restaurant; bar; limited room service; babysitting; laundry service. *In room:* TV, dataport (in some), hair dryer.

Maison du Grand Ecuyer *★★★* MODERN FRENCH   The medieval monument that contains this restaurant (the 15th-c. hunting lodge of Raymond VII, comte de Toulouse) is a national historic treasure. Despite its glamour and undeniable charm, the restaurant remains intimate and unstuffy, although guests in recent years have included King Juan Carlos of Spain, the Emperor of Japan, and even Queen Elizabeth. Chef Yves Thuriès's platters have made his dining room an almost mandatory stop for the rich and famous. Specialties include three confits of lobster, red mullet salad with fondue of vegetables, confit of pigeon with olive oil and rosemary, and noisette of lamb in chicory sauce. The dessert selection is nearly overwhelming.

The hotel contains 12 rooms and one suite, all with antiques and modern comforts. Doubles cost 90€ to 150€ ($117–$195); the suite is 230€ ($299). The most popular room, honoring former guest Albert Camus, has a four-poster bed and a fireplace. During its annual closing, a twin hotel, **L'Hostellerie du Vieux Cordes** lies nearby. It's under the management of Thuriès, the region's grandest and most entrepreneurial chef. It's the **Hotel du Vieux Cordes,** 21 rue St-Michel, ✆ **05-63-53-79-20.** On the premises is a terrace that's shaded with an arbor and a 300-year-old wisteria vine. The house that contains this immediately abuts the Eglise St-Michel.

Grand-Rue Raymond VIII, Haute de la Cité, 81170 Cordes. ✆ **05-63-53-79-50.** Fax 05-63-53-79-51. www.thuries.fr. Reservations required. Main courses 29€–40€ ($38–$52); fixed-price menu 59€–73€ ($77–$95). AE, DC, MC, V. July–Aug daily noon–1:30pm and 7–9:30pm; mid-Apr to June and Sept to mid-Oct Tues–Sun 7–9:30pm. Closed mid-Oct to mid-Mar.

4 Albi

697km (433 miles) SW of Paris; 76km (47 miles) NE of Toulouse

The "red city" of Albi straddles both banks of the Tarn River. The cathedral and the bridges spanning the river are made of brick, as are most of the town's buildings, earning Albi its title—in the rosy glow of a setting sun, Albi often looks as if it were in flames, a spectacular sight.

The town is the birthplace of the famous painter Toulouse-Lautrec and contains an important museum of his works. The town's history has been stormy. The fortified cathedral that broods over the medieval center is a reminder of the bloody struggle between the Roman Catholic Church and the Cathars, a religious group the Church considered heretical. They were also called Albigenses after the town, which was an important center of their movement.

ESSENTIALS

GETTING THERE Fifteen **trains** per day link Toulouse with Albi (trip time: 1 hr.); the one-way fare is 13€ ($16). There's also a Paris-Albi night train. For rail information, call ✆ **08-92-35-35-35.** If you're **driving** from Toulouse, take N88 northeast.

VISITOR INFORMATION The **Office de Tourisme** is in the Palais de la Berbie, place Ste-Cécile (✆ **05-63-49-48-80;** www.albi-tourisme.fr).

SEEING THE SIGHTS

Cathédrale Ste-Cécile ⭐⭐⭐ Fortified with ramparts and parapets and containing frescoes and paintings, this 13th-century cathedral was built by a local lord-bishop after a religious struggle with the comte de Toulouse (the crusade against the Cathars). Note the exceptional 16th-century rood screen with a unique suit of polychromatic statues from the Old and New Testaments. Free classical concerts take place in July and August on Wednesday at 5pm and Sunday at 4pm.

Near place du Vigan, in the medieval center of town. ℂ **05-63-43-23-43.** Cathédrale: free admission. Treasury: 3€ ($3.90) adults, 2€ ($2.60) ages 12–25, free for children under 12. June–Sept daily 9am–6:30pm; Oct–May daily 9am–noon and 2–6:30pm.

Musée de la Pérouse   Set on the opposite bank of the Tarn from the bulk of Albi's medieval core (take the Pont-Vieux to reach it), within what was originally built in the 18th century as a factory for pasta, this museum honors the achievements of Albi's native son, Jean-François de la Pérouse. Commissioned as an explorer by Louis XVI in the late 1600s, he mapped and charted the coastlines of Alaska, California, and China, bringing the French up to speed against England in its rush for colonies outside of Europe. The museum contains maps, charts, navigational instructions and memorabilia that illustrate the progress and achievements of not only the explorer himself, but France's self-image during a period of some of its greatest glory.

Square Botany Bay. ℂ **05-63-46-01-87.** Entrance 2.50€ ($3.25) adults, 1.50€ ($1.95) students and persons 12–25, free for persons under 12. Apr–Sept Tues–Fri 9am–noon and 2–6pm, Sat–Sun 10am–noon and 2–7pm; Oct–Mar Tues–Fri 10am–noon and 2–5pm, Sat–Sun 2–6pm.

Musée Toulouse-Lautrec ★★   The Palais de la Berbie (Archbishop's Palace) is a fortified structure dating from the 13th century. This museum contains the world's most important collection of the artist's paintings, more than 600 in all. His family bequeathed the works remaining in his studio. The museum also owns paintings by Degas, Bonnard, Matisse, Utrillo, and Rouault. Late in 2005, the museum enlarged its premises with three additional display rooms, each of them a brick-lined refuge within the premises of a neighboring historic building. Within you'll see, gathered together, some of Toulouse-Lautrec's earliest works, formulated during his earliest creative years.

Opposite the north side of the cathedral. ℂ **05-63-49-48-70.** Admission 5€ ($6.50) adults, 2.50€ ($3.25) students, free for children under 14. July–Aug daily 9am–6pm; June and Sept daily 9am–noon and 2–6pm; Apr–May daily 10am–noon and 2–6pm; Mar and Oct Wed–Mon 10am–noon and 2–5:30pm; Nov–Feb Wed–Mon 10am–noon and 2–5pm. Closed Jan 1, May 1, Nov 1, and Dec 25.

WHERE TO STAY

Hostellerie St-Antoine ★★   Some historians say this is one of the oldest continuously operated hotels in France. Originally a monastery, then a medieval hospital, the

---

Toulouse-Lautrec: Little Big Man

Although he spent most of his life in Paris, Toulouse-Lautrec is closely connected with Albi. He was born in Albi in the **Hôtel Bosc;** it's still a private home and cannot be toured, but there's a plaque on the wall of the building at 14 rue Toulouse-Lautrec in the historic town core.

You can visit the family's **Château de Bosc,** Camjac, 12800 Naucelle (ℂ **05-65-69-20-83**), 29 miles (47km) from Toulouse. It was built in 1180 and renovated in the 1400s. The present owner, Mademoiselle de Céleran, and her team welcome visitors interested in Toulouse-Lautrec, but it's best to call ahead because tours are guided. It is usually open daily from 9am to 7pm. Admission is 5€ ($6.50) for adults, 2€ ($2.60) for children 8 to 14, and free for children 7 and under.

property became an inn in 1734 (when the present building was constructed). The same family has owned it for five generations; today the father-son team of Jacques and Jean-François Rieux manages it. Jacques's mother focused on Toulouse-Lautrec when designing the hotel, because her grandfather was a friend of the painter and was given a few of his paintings, sketches, and prints. Several are in the lounge, which opens onto a rear garden. The rooms have been delightfully decorated, with a sophisticated use of color, reproductions, and occasional antiques. They're generally spacious, furnished with French Provincial pieces. Most of the midsize bathrooms have tub/shower combinations. Even if you're not staying, visit the dining room. The Rieux culinary tradition is revealed in their traditional yet creative cuisine.

17 rue St-Antoine, 81000 Albi. ℂ **05-63-54-04-04.** Fax 05-63-47-10-47. www.saint-antoine-albi.com. 44 units. 70€–145€ ($91–$189) double; 165€–220€ ($215–$286) suite. AE, DC, MC, V. Parking 6.50€ ($8.45). **Amenities:** Restaurant; bar; limited room service; babysitting; dry cleaning; nonsmoking rooms; limited-mobility rooms. *In room:* A/C, TV, dataport, minibar, hair dryer.

Hôtel Chiffre (Value)

This hotel in the city center was built as a lodging for passengers on the mail coaches that hauled letters and people across France. The renovated building retains the original porch that sheltered carriages from the rain and sun. The rooms are artfully cozy, with upholstered walls in floral patterns; some have views of the inner courtyard. The midsize bathrooms come with tub/shower combinations or showers only. The hotel restaurant, **Bateau Ivre,** is popular among locals because of its good-value fixed-price menus. The menu, priced at 27€ ($35) per person, consists of choices that were compiled after Toulouse-Lautrec's death by his friends, who remembered the way he'd often prepare the dishes himself during his dinner parties, such as radishes stuffed with braised foie gras, suprême of *sander* (fish), and duckling roasted with garlic.

50 rue Séré-de-Rivières, 81000 Albi. ℂ **05-63-48-58-48.** Fax 05-63-47-20-61. www.hotelchiffre.com. 37 units. 84€ ($109) double. AE, MC, V. Parking 7€ ($9.10). **Amenities:** Restaurant; bar; limited room service. *In room:* A/C, TV, dataport, hair dryer.

Hôtel George V

This hotel offers a dignified kind of charm and a spartan, pleasingly old-fashioned setting at prices that are fair and reasonable. It was built around 1900 and is about a quarter-mile from the town center. Bedrooms are high-ceilinged and generally spacious; bathrooms are small. They are simply decorated, in some cases with a bit of whimsy, with efficient furniture. Request ahead if you prefer a shower or tub. Breakfast is the only meal served.

29 av. Maréchal-Joffre, 81000 Albi. ℂ **05-63-54-24-16.** Fax 05-63-49-90-78. www.hotelgeorgev.com. 9 units. 33€–44€ ($43–$57) double. MC, V. Free parking. *In room:* TV.

La Réserve ⭐⭐⭐

This country-club villa in a 1.6-hectare (4-acre) park on the northern outskirts of Albi is managed by the Rieux family, who also run the Hostellerie St-Antoine. The Mediterranean-style villa has a pool and a fine garden in which you can dine. The rooms, well furnished and color-coordinated, contain imaginative decorations (but avoid the rooms over the kitchen, which are noisy at mealtimes). The upper-story rooms have sun terraces and French doors. The modern tiled bathrooms come with deluxe toiletries and showers.

Rte. de Cordes à Fonvialane, 81000 Albi. ℂ **05-63-60-80-80.** Fax 05-63-47-63-60. www.relaischateaux.fr/lareserve albi. 23 units. 130€–255€ ($169–$331) double; 380€ ($494) suite. AE, DC, MC, V. Closed Nov–Apr. From the center of town, follow signs to Carmaux-Rodez until you cross the Tarn; then follow signs to Cordes. The hotel is adjacent to the main road leading to Cordes, 2km (1¼ miles) from Albi. **Amenities:** Restaurant; bar; outdoor pool; limited room service; babysitting; laundry service/dry cleaning; nonsmoking rooms; limited-mobility rooms. *In room:* A/C, TV, dataport, minibar, hair dryer, safe.

WHERE TO DINE

La Réserve (see "Where to Stay," above) boasts a wonderful restaurant.

Jardin des Quatre Saisons *★★* MODERN FRENCH   The best food in Albi is served by Georges Bermond, who believes that menus, like life, should change with the seasons—and that's how the restaurant got its name. The setting is a modern, deceptively simple pair of dining rooms where the lighting has been subtly arranged to make everyone look as attractive as possible. Service is always competent and polite. Menu items have been fine-tuned and include delicious versions of a fricassée of snails garnished with strips of the famous hams produced in the nearby hamlet of Lacaune, ravioli stuffed with pulverized shrimp and served with a truffled cream sauce, and a gratinée of mussels in a compote of fish. Most delectable of all—an excuse for returning a second time—is a pot-au-feu of the sea that contains three or four species of fish garnished with a crayfish-flavored cream sauce. The wine selection is the finest in Albi.

19 bd. de Strasbourg. ℂ 05-63-60-77-76. Reservations recommended. Main courses 13€–20€ ($17–$26); fixed-price menu 18€–32€ ($23–$42). AE, DC, MC, V. Tues–Sun noon–2:30pm; Tues–Sat 7:30–10pm.

Le Lautrec TRADITIONAL FRENCH   Part of its charm derives from its associations with Toulouse-Lautrec—it lies across the street from his birthplace and is decorated with paintings by local artists. Also appealing is the rich patina of its interior brickwork. The skillfully prepared food items include a salad of fried scallops that come with rose oil and essence of shrimp, sweetbreads with morels, and roasted rack of lamb marinated in a brewed infusion of Provençal thyme.

13 rue Toulouse-Lautrec. ℂ 05-63-54-86-55. Reservations recommended. Main courses 16€–23€ ($21 $30); fixed-price lunch Tues–Fri 15€ ($20); other fixed-price meals 28€–40€ ($36–$52). DC, MC, V. Tues–Sun noon–2pm; Tues–Sat 7–9:30pm.

5 Castres ★

727km (452 miles) SW of Paris; 42km (26 miles) S of Albi

Built on the bank of the Agout River, Castres is the point of origin for trips to the Sidobre, the mountains of Lacaune, and the Black Mountains. Today the wool industry here, whose origins go back to the 14th century, has made Castres one of France's two most important wool-producing areas. The town was formerly a Roman military installation. A Benedictine monastery was founded here in the 9th century, and the town fell under the comtes d'Albi in the 10th century. With its acquisition of a number of 1st-century relics of St. Vincent, and its role as a stopover for pilgrimages to the tomb of St. James in Spain, Castres also held some religious significance. During the 16th-century Wars of Religion, the Protestant town was invaded by religious fanatics, who stole relics from the basilica and dumped them into the river.

ESSENTIALS

GETTING THERE   From Toulouse, there are seven or eight **trains** per day (trip time: 1 hr., 15 min.); the one-way fare from Toulouse is 13€ ($16). For information, call ℂ 08-92-35-35-35. If you're **driving**, Castres is on N126 east of Toulouse and N112 south of Albi.

VISITOR INFORMATION   The **Office de Tourisme** is at 3 rue Milhau Ducommun (ℂ 05-63-62-62-62; www.ville-castres.fr).

THE TOP ATTRACTIONS

Eglise St-Benoît   The town's most visible and important church is Castres's outstanding example of French baroque architecture. The architect Caillau began construction of the church in 1677, on the site of a 9th-century Benedictine abbey. The baroque structure was never completed according to its original plans. The painting at the church's far end, above the altar, was executed by Gabriel Briard in the 18th century.

Place du 8-Mai-1945. © 05-63-59-05-19. Free admission. Mon–Sat 9am–noon and 2–6:30pm; Sun 8:30am–noon. Closed to casual visitors Sun Oct–May, except for religious services.

Le Centre National et Musée Jean-Jaurès   This museum is dedicated to the workers' movements of the late 19th and early 20th centuries. Its collection contains printed material from the various Socialist movements in France during that period, as well as paintings, sculptures, films, and slides. See, in particular, an issue of *L'Aurore* containing Zola's famous *"J'accuse"* article about the Dreyfus case.

2 place Pélisson. © 05-63-72-01-01. Admission 1.50€ ($1.95) adults, .75€ ($1) students and children under 14. Apr–Sept daily 10am–noon and 2–6pm; Oct–Mar Tues–Sun 10am–noon and 2–5pm.

Musée Goya ⊕   The museum is in the town hall, an archbishop's palace designed by Mansart in 1669. The paintings of Francisco Goya y Lucientes were donated to the town in 1894 by Pierre Briguiboul, son of the Castres-born artist Marcel Briguiboul. *Les Caprices,* created in 1799 after the illness that left Goya deaf, fills nearly an entire room. A satire on Spanish society, the work is composed of symbolic images of demons and monsters. The museum collection also includes 16th-century tapestries and Spanish paintings from the 15th to the 20th centuries.

In the Jardin de l'Evêché. © 05-63-71-59-30. Admission 2.30€ ($3) adults, free for children under 18. Apr–Sept daily 10am–noon and 2–6pm; Oct–Mar Tues–Sun 10am–noon and 2–5pm.

WHERE TO STAY

Hôtel de l'Europe ⊕ *Finds*   This hotel exudes charm, especially in the bedrooms capped with ceiling beams, where the pinkish-gray masonry from the building's original construction during the 18th century still remains. Plus, each room has a view over the oldest part of the historic town. The hotel has great style, and its accommodations offer a certain glamour, some boasting canopy-draped beds. A number of the bathrooms are quite luxurious and all have tub/shower combos.

5 rue Victor-Hugo, 81100 Castres. © 05-63-59-00-33. Fax 05-63-59-21-38. 38 units. 60€ ($78) double. AE, DC, MC, V. Parking 5€ ($6.50). **Amenities:** Restaurant; bar. *In room:* TV, minibar, hair dryer.

Hôtel Renaissance ⊕⊕   The Renaissance is the best hotel in Castres. It was built in the 17th century as the courthouse, and then functioned as a colorful but run-down hotel throughout most of the 20th century—until 1993, when it was opened in its present incarnation. Today you'll see a severely dignified building composed of *colombages*-style half-timbering, with a mixture of chiseled stone blocks and bricks. Some rooms have exposed timbers; all are clean and comfortable, evoking the crafts of yesteryear.

17 rue Victor-Hugo, 81100 Castres. © 05-63-59-30-42. Fax 05-63-72-11-57. www.hotel-renaissance.fr. 20 units. 60€ ($78) double; 70€ ($91) suite. AE, DC, MC, V. **Amenities:** Restaurant; bar; limited room service; laundry service/dry cleaning; nonsmoking rooms; limited-mobility rooms. *In room:* A/C, TV, dataport, hair dryer, minibar.

WHERE TO DINE

In addition to those below, another worthy choice is **Le Victoria,** 24 place du 8-Mai-1945 (© **05-63-59-14-68**), where meals cost 18€ to 40€ ($23–$52). A superb French cuisine is served, with regional products used whenever available.

Brasserie des Jacobins *(Value* FRENCH/PROVENÇAL   This modern brasserie is a good bet for solid cuisine. The decor features English-inspired furnishings with lots of well-oiled wood paneling. The menu includes a selection of regional platters as well as pizzas. Menu items include blanquettes of veal, cassoulets, and caramelized pork filets with Provençal herbs, as well as regional sausages served with purée of apples and cheese from the foothills of the Pyrenees. The decor is rustic; the service is polite, but pressed for time. Many visitors find it especially suitable for a simple noontime meal.

1 place Jean-Jaurès. (℃ 05-63-59-01-44. Reservations recommended. Main courses 7€–13€ ($9.10–$17); fixed-price menu 10€–19€ ($13–$25) lunch, 19€ ($25) dinner. AE, MC, V. Mon–Sat noon–2:30pm and 7–10:30pm.

La Mandragore *(⋆* LANGUEDOCIENNE   On an easily overlooked narrow street, this restaurant which is named after a legendary plant with magic powers, occupies a small section of one of the many wings of the medieval château-fort of Castres. The decor is simple, with stone walls and tones of autumn colors. The regional cuisine is among the best in town, and it's served with a smile. Among the best dishes are ravioli stuffed with braised snails and flavored with basil, rack of suckling veal with exotic mushrooms, and magret of duckling with natural Canadian maple syrup.

1 rue Malpas. (℃ 05-63-59-51-27. Reservations recommended. Main courses 15€–20€ ($20–$26); fixed-price menu 12€–30€ ($16–$39). DC, V. Tues–Sat noon–2pm and 7–10pm. Closed 2 weeks in Sept and 2 weeks in Feb.

6 Carcassonne *(⋆(⋆(⋆*

797km (495 miles) SW of Paris; 92km (57 miles) SE of Toulouse; 105km (65 miles) S of Albi

Evoking bold knights, fair damsels, and troubadours, the greatest fortress city of Europe rises against a background of the snow-capped Pyrenees. Floodlit at night, it captures a fairy-tale magic, but back in its heyday in the Middle Ages it was the target of assault by battering rams, grapnels, a mobile tower (inspired by the Trojan horse), catapults, flaming arrows, and the mangonel.

Today, the city is overrun with hordes of visitors and tacky gift shops. The elusive charm of Carcassonne comes out in the evening, when day-trippers depart and floodlights bathe the ancient monuments.

ESSENTIALS

GETTING THERE   Carcassonne is a major stop for **trains** between Toulouse and destinations south and east. There are 24 trains per day from Toulouse (trip time: 50 min.; one-way fare: 14€/$18), 14 per day from Montpellier (trip time: 2 hr.; 22€/$29 one-way), and 12 trains per day from Nîmes (trip time: 2½ hr.; 28€/$36 one-way). For rail information, call (℃ 08-92-35-35-35. If you're **driving,** Carcassonne is on A61 south of Toulouse.

VISITOR INFORMATION   The **Office de Tourisme** has locations at 28 rue de Verdun (℃ 04-68-10-24-30; www.carcassonne-tourisme.com) and in the medieval town at Porte Narbonnaise (℃ 04-68-10-24-36).

SPECIAL EVENTS   The town's nightlife sparkles during its summer festivals. During the **Festival de Carcassonne** in July, concerts, modern and classical dance, operas, and theater fill the city. Tickets run 20€ to 50€ ($26–$65) and can be purchased by calling (℃ 04-68-11-59-15. For more information, contact the **Théâtre Municipal** (℃ 04-68-25-33-13). On July 14, **Bastille Day,** one of the best fireworks spectacles in France lights up the skies at 10:30pm. Over 6 weeks in July and August, the merriment and raucousness of the Middle Ages overtake the city during the **Spectacles**

Medievaux, in the form of jousts, parades, food fairs, and street festivals. For information, contact the **Office de Tourisme** (© **04-68-10-24-30**).

EXPLORING LA CITE

Carcassonne consists of two towns: **La Bastide St-Louis** (also known as **La Ville Basse,** or Lower City), and the older, more evocative medieval **Cité.** The former has little interest, but the latter is a major attraction, the goal of many a pilgrim. The fortifications of La Cité consist of a double line of **ramparts,** with inner and outer walls. The inner rampart was built by the Visigoths in the 5th century. Clovis, king of the Franks, attacked in 506 but failed. The Saracens overcame the city in 728 and held it until 752, when Pepin the Short (father of Charlemagne) drove them out. During a long siege by Charlemagne, when the populace of the walled city was starving and near surrender, Dame Carcas came up with an idea. According to legend, she gathered up the last remaining bit of grain, fed it to a sow, and then tossed the pig over the ramparts. It's said to have burst, scattering the grain. The Franks concluded that Carcassonne must have unlimited food supplies and ended their siege.

Carcassonne's walls were further fortified by the vicomtes de Trencavel in the 12th century and by Louis IX and Philip the Bold in the 13th century. However, by the mid–17th century, its importance as a strategic frontier fort ended and the ramparts were left to decay. In the 19th century, the builders of the Lower Town began to remove the stone for use in new construction. But a revival of interest in the Middle Ages led the government to order Viollet-le-Duc (who restored Notre-Dame in Paris) to repair and, where necessary, rebuild the walls. Reconstruction continued until very recently.

Walks along the outer ramparts are free and are possible year-round without restriction. (Frankly, this is what we recommend for anyone with limited time in Carcassonne.) If you have more time on your hands, and really want to revel in the town's medievalism, you can pay for a guided tour of the city's innermost fortifications. (These inner rooms are known locally as "Le Château," but they're less spectacular than what "château" usually implies.) They incorporate visits to the Musée Lapidaire which is devoted to the collection of archaeological stones and carvings unearthed during the previous century of historical restorations and excavations. Tours also include a view of exhibits that honor the late-19th-century archaeologist Violet-le-Duc for the reconstruction he inspired and directed of Carcassonne. Tours also include a guided promenade along the top of some of the inner ramparts. The above-described tours depart daily, usually at intervals of between 30 and 60 minutes, depending on the season, every day at 10am, with tickets on sale beginning at 9:30am. They continue till 5pm between November and March, and until 6pm between April and October. Each lasts about an hour. They begin at 1 rue Viollet-le-Duc, on the Cité's western end, and cost 6.10€ ($7.95) for adults and 4.10€ ($5.35) for persons ages 18 to 25. Persons under 18 enter free. For more information, contact Carcassonne's local branch of the Caisse Nationale des Monuments Nationaux at © **04-68-11-70-77.** Another important monument in the fortifications is the **Basilique St-Nazaire** ☆, La Cité (© **04-68-25-27-65**), dating from the 11th to the 14th centuries and containing some beautiful stained-glass windows and a pair of rose medallions. The nave is in the Romanesque style, and the choir and transept are Gothic. The 16th-century organ is one of the oldest in southwestern France. The 1266 tomb of Bishop Radulphe is well preserved. The cathedral is open in July and August daily from 9am to 6pm, September through June daily from 9am to noon and 2 to 5pm. Mass is celebrated on Sunday at 11am. Admission is free.

Musée des Memoires du Moyen Age, Immeuble du Pont-Levis, Chemin des Anglais (© 04-68-71-08-65), is set within the stone bulwarks that used to contain the drawbridge. This museum documents the traumatic battles, sieges, and feuds that marked life in Carcassonne during the Middle Ages. You'll be shown a video depicting a thousand years of medieval life in the town, and exhibitions that showcase the values and lifestyles of long ago. Entrance is 5€ ($6.50) for adults and 3€ ($3.90) for children and students. It is open year-round daily from 10am to 7pm. In the highest elevation of the Cité, at the uppermost terminus of rue Principale (rue Cros Mayrevielle), you'll find the **Château Comtal,** place du Château (© 04-68-11-70-73), a restored 12th-century fortress that's open April to September daily from 9:30am to 6pm, October to March daily 9:30am to 5pm. Entrance includes an obligatory 40-minute guided tour, in French and broken English. It's also the only way to climb onto the city's inner ramparts. The cost is 6.50€ ($8.45) for adults, 4.50€ ($5.85) for students and ages 18 to 25, free for children under 18. The tour includes access to expositions that display the archaeological remnants discovered on-site, plus an explanation of the 19th-century restorations.

SHOPPING

Carcassonne has two distinct shopping areas. In the modern lower city, the major streets for shopping, particularly if you're in the market for clothing, are **rue Clemenceau** and **rue de Verdun.** In the walled medieval city, the streets are chock-full of tiny stores and boutiques; most sell gift items like antiques and local arts and crafts.

Stores worth visiting, all in the Cité, include **Cellier des Vigneronnes,** 13 rue du Grand Puits (© 04-68-25-31-00), where you'll find a wide selection of regional wines ranging from simple table wines to those awarded the distinction of Appellation d'Origine Controlée. Some antiques stores of merit are **Mme Faye-Nunez,** 4 place du Château (© 04-68-25-65-71), for antique furniture; **Antiquités Safi,** 54 rue de Verdun (© 04-68-25-60-51), for paintings and art objects; and **Dominique Sarraute,** 13 porte d'Aude (© 04-68-72-42-90), for antique firearms.

WHERE TO STAY
IN THE CITE

Hôtel de la Cité ★★★   Originally a palace for whatever bishop or prelate happened to be in power at the time, this has been the most desirable hotel in town since 1909. It's in the actual walls of the city, adjoining the cathedral. The Orient-Express Hotel group acquired the hotel in the '90s and fluffed it up to the tune of $3 million. You enter a long Gothic corridor-gallery leading to the lounge. Many rooms open onto the ramparts and a garden, and feature antiques or reproductions. A few accommodations contain wooden headboards and four-posters. The ideal unit is no. 308, which opens onto the most panoramic view of the city. Modern equipment has been discreetly installed throughout, including bathrooms of generous size with tub/shower combinations. The hotel is renowned for its restaurant.

Place de l'Eglise, 11000 Carcassonne. © 04-68-71-98-71. Fax 04-68-71-50-15. www.hoteldelacite.com. 61 units. 250€–400€ ($325–$520) double; 400€–1,200€ ($520–$1,560) suite. AE, DC, MC, V. Parking 15€ ($20). Closed late Nov to late Dec and Feb to early Mar. **Amenities:** 3 restaurants (including La Barbacane; see "Where to Dine," below); bar; outdoor pool; limited room service; babysitting; laundry service; nonsmoking rooms; limited-mobility rooms. *In room:* A/C, TV, minibar, hair dryer, safe.

Hôtel des Remparts   An abbey in the 12th century, this building at the edge of a stone square lies in the town center. It was converted into a charming hotel in 1983 after major repairs to the masonry and roof. The rooms contain no-frills furniture and acceptably comfortable mattresses. Most were renovated, or at least repainted, in the late 1990s. Bathrooms are just large enough. The owners are proud of the massive stone staircase that twists around itself. Make reservations at least a couple of months ahead if you plan to stay here during summer.

2 rue du Comte-Roger, 11000 Carcassonne. ⓒ **04-68-11-23-00.** Fax 04-68-25-06-60. 64 units. 125€–145€ ($163–$189) double. AE, DC, MC, V. Parking 10€ ($13). **Amenities:** Restaurant; bar; 2 tennis courts; limited room service; laundry service/dry cleaning; nonsmoking rooms. *In room:* A/C, TV, dataport, minibar, beverage maker, hair dryer, iron, safe.

AT THE ENTRANCE OF THE CITE

Le Donjon et Les Remparts 🌟🌟 *(Value)*   This little hotel is big on charm and is the best value in the moderate price range. Built in the style of the old Cité, it has a honey-colored stone exterior with iron bars on the windows. The interior is a jewel. Elaborate Louis XIII–style furniture graces the reception lounges. A newer wing contains additional rooms in medieval architectural style. Their furnishings are in a severe style that's consistent with the medieval look of the nearby ramparts. Each unit comes with a compact tiled bathroom, most with tub/shower combos. The hotel also runs the nearby Brasserie Le Donjon. In summer, the garden is the perfect breakfast spot.

2 rue du Comte-Roger, 11000 Carcassonne. ⓒ **800/528-1234** in the U.S. and Canada, or 04-68-11-23-00. Fax 04-68-25-06-60. www.hotel-donjon.fr. 62 units. 93€–145€ ($121–$189) double; 155€–214€ ($202–$278) suite. AE, DC, MC, V. Parking 10€ ($13). **Amenities:** Restaurant; bar; limited room service; laundry service/dry cleaning; nonsmoking rooms; limited-mobility rooms. *In room:* A/C, TV, minibar, hair dryer.

LA BASTIDE ST-LOUIS

Hôtel du Soleil le Terminus   Originally built in 1913, with frequent renovations ever since, and a historical role as the headquarters of the local Nazi regiments during World War II, this hotel re-opened in late April 2005 after a change in ownership and its transformation from a grand but rather dowdy family-owned monument into a streamlined and glossy-looking member of a big-time nationwide chain. Bedrooms are high-ceilinged and each of a different shape, layout, and size, some of them quite spacious, others a bit cramped. Touches of old-fashioned charm remain, thanks to the presence in many of the rooms of Art Deco pieces originally brought into the hotel during the late 1920s. The hotel lies in the heart of *La Ville Basse*, adjacent to the railway station and the Canal du Midi, about 3.2km (2 miles) from the medieval Cité.

2 av. Du Maréchal-Joffre, 11001 Carcassonne. ⓒ **04-68-25-25-00.** Fax 04-68-72-53-09. www.hotels-du-soleil.com. 110 units. 78€–218€ ($101–$283) double. MC, V. Parking 10€ ($13). Bus: 4. **Amenities:** Restaurant; bar; access to tennis courts; sauna. *In room:* A/C, TV, dataport, minibar, hair dryer.

Hôtel Montségur 🌟 *(Value)*   This stately town house with a mansard roof and dormers was built in 1887. Trees and a high wrought-iron fence screen the front garden from the street. Didier and Isabelle Faugeras have furnished the hotel with antiques, lending it a residential feel. Guest rooms vary in size, from small to spacious. Most of the small tiled bathrooms contain tub/shower combinations, the rest with shower. Continental breakfast is available; Didier is the chef at the highly recommended Le Languedoc, across the street.

27 allée d'Iéna, 11000 Carcassonne. ⓒ **04-68-25-31-41.** Fax 04-68-47-13-22. www.hotelmontsegur.com. 21 units. 70€–92€ ($91–$120) double. AE, DC, MC, V. Free parking. **Amenities:** Restaurant (see "Where to Dine," below); bar; 24-hr. room service; laundry service; nonsmoking rooms. *In room:* A/C, TV, dataport, hair dryer.

Trois Couronnes ⚐☆☆   Reliable and dependable, though not exciting, this service-able favorite is the best choice in Ville-Basse. It lies south of the landmark Square Gambetta, immediately west of the bridge, pont Vieux. Built in 1992, the hotel rises five stories. Rooms open onto views of the Aude River and the ramparts of the old city. A government-rated three-star hotel, "Three Crowns" has some of the best facil-ities in town, including an indoor pool. The rooms are functionally comfortable with tasteful furnishings. Service is top rate, and maintenance is good. A good regional cui-sine is served in the on-site restaurant.

2 rue des Trois Couronnes, 11000 Carcassonne. ℂ **04-68-25-36-10.** Fax 04-68-25-92-92. www.hotel-destrois couronnes.com. 68 units. 87€–101€ ($113–$131) double. AE, DC, MC, V. Parking 8€ ($10). **Amenities:** Restaurant; bar; indoor pool; fitness room; sauna; car rental; 24-hr. room service; limited-mobility rooms. In room: A/C, TV, mini-bar, hair dryer.

STAYING NEARBY

Domaine d'Auriac ⚐☆☆☆   Carcassonne's premier address for both food and lodg-ing is this moss-covered 19th-century manor house located about 2.5km (1½ miles) west of the Cité. It was built around 1880 as a cube-shape building, with about a half-dozen stone-sided annexes (site of many of the bedrooms) on the ruins of a medieval monastery, some of whose ceiling vaults are still visible within the cellars. Each bed-room has a photo-magazine aura, with lots of flowered fabrics, a range of decorative styles, and, in many cases, massive and sometimes sculpted ceiling beams. The tiled bathrooms are first-rate. Bernard and Anne-Marie Rigaudis are the experienced own-ers, assisted by their grown children Marie-Hélène and Pierre. Part of the allure of this Relais & Châteaux member is in the well-crafted and well-conceived meals that, dur-ing clement weather, are served beside the pool on flowering terraces. Fixed-price menus, priced from 40€ to 64€ ($52–$83) each, change several times each season but always demonstrate a sophisticated twist, making local recipes more glamorous and interesting. The hotel is one of the few in the region with its own golf course, from which sweeping panoramas are available over the surrounding countryside.

Rte. St-Hilaire, 11009 Carcassonne. ℂ **04-68-25-72-22.** Fax 04-68-47-35-54. www.relaischateaux.fr/auriac. 26 units. 140€–320€ ($182–$416) double; 420€–450€ ($546–$585) suite. AE, DC, MC, V. Free parking. Closed Closed Jan 3–Feb 7, Apr 25–May 2, and Nov 14–21. Take D104 W 2.5km (1½ miles) from Carcassonne. Pets 15€ ($20) extra. **Amenities:** Restaurant; bar; outdoor pool; 18-hole golf course; tennis court; secretarial service; 24-hr. room service; babysitting; laundry service/dry cleaning. In room: A/C, TV, dataport, minibar, hair dryer, safe.

WHERE TO DINE

Au Jardin de la Tour TRADITIONAL FRENCH   Part of the charm of this restau-rant derives from the location of its verdant garden adjacent to the western founda-tion of the château, providing a green space that's very much appreciated in the midst of the city's closely built-up medieval core. The building dates from the early 1800s, although wide-ranging renovations have brought it up-to-date. The decor features rus-tic finds from local antique fairs. You can order from a large selection of salads, filet of beef with morels, cassoulet, terrines of foie gras, and all kinds of grilled fish. The cookery is consistently good, relying on fresh ingredients deftly handled by a talented kitchen staff.

11 rue Porte-d'Aude. ℂ **04-68-25-71-24.** Reservations recommended in summer. Main courses 10€–22€ ($13–$29); fixed-price menu 22€–28€ ($29–$36). MC, V. Tues–Sat 7:30–10pm. Closed Nov 1–Dec 15.

La Barbacane ⚐☆ FRENCH   Sharing the name of the medieval neighborhood where it sits, this restaurant enjoys equal billing with the celebrated Hôtel de la Cité, which contains it. The soothing-looking dining room, with walls upholstered in fabric with gold fleur-de-lis on a cerulean blue background, features the cuisine of the noted chef Franck Putelat. Menu items are based on seasonal ingredients, with just enough zest. Examples are green ravioli perfumed with *seiche* (a species of octopus) in its own ink, a fraîcheur of Breton lobster with artichoke hearts and caviar, and organically fed free-range chicken stuffed with truffles. A particularly succulent dessert is chestnut parfait with malt-flavored cream sauce and date-flavored ice cream.

In the Hôtel de la Cité, place de l'Eglise. (C) **04-68-71-98-71.** Reservations recommended. Main courses 25€–55€ ($33–$72); fixed-price menu 60€–120€ ($78–$156). AE, DC, MC, V. Daily 7:30–10pm. Closed Dec–Mar.

Le Languedoc 👯 TRADITIONAL FRENCH   Acclaimed chef Didier Faugeras is the creative force behind the inspired cuisine here. The high-ceilinged century-old dining room is filled with antiques; a brick fireplace contributes to the warm Languedoc atmosphere. The specialty is *cassoulet au confit de canard* (the famous stew made with duck cooked in its own fat). It has been celebrated as a much-perfected staple here since the early 1960s. The *pièce de résistance* is tournedos Rossini, with foie gras truffles and Madeira sauce. A smooth dessert is flambéed crepes Languedoc. In summer you can dine on a pleasant patio or in the air-conditioned restaurant. (Faugeras and his wife, Isabelle, are the owners of the worthy Hôtel Montségur, just across the street.)

32 allée d'Iéna. (C) **04-68-25-22-17.** Reservations recommended. Main courses 16€–24€ ($21–$31); fixed-price menu 24€–44€ ($31–$57). AE, DC, MC, V. July–Aug daily noon–1:30pm and 7:30–9:30pm; Sept–June Tues–Sun noon–2pm, Tues–Sat 7:30–9:30pm. Closed last week of June and Dec 20–Jan 20.

DINING NEARBY

Château St-Martin 👯 FRENCH   One of Languedoc's most successful chefs operates out of this 16th-century château at Montredon, 4km (2½ miles) northeast of Carcassonne. Ringed by a wooded park, the restaurant serves the superb cuisine of co-owners Jean-Claude and Jacqueline Rodriguez. Dine inside or on the terrace. Recommended dishes are fish (according to the daily catch) with fondue of baby vegetables, sea bass with scallop mousseline, sole in tarragon, and *confit de canard carcassonnaise* (duck meat cooked in its own fat and kept in earthenware pots). Two other specialties are *cassoulet languedocienne* (made with pork, mutton, and goose or duck) and *boullinade nouvelloise* (made with different sorts of seafood that include scallops, sole, and turbot). On the premises are 15 simple, but comfortable hotel rooms. Doubles rent for 90€ ($117). The château is closed November 15 to the end of February.

Montredon, 11090 Carcassonne. (C) **04-68-71-09-53.** Fax 04-68-25-46-55. Reservations required. Main courses 17€–25€ ($22–$33); fixed-price menu 30€–53€ ($39–$69). AE, DC, MC, V. Thurs–Tues noon–1:30pm and 7:30–9:30pm (closed Sun night). From La Cité, follow signs pointing to Stade Albert Domec 4km (2½ miles) northeast.

CARCASSONNE AFTER DARK

Carcassonne nightlife centers on **rue Omer-Sarraut** in La Bastide and **place Marcou** in La Cité. **La Bulle,** 115 rue Barbacane ((C) **04-68-72-47-70**), explodes with techno and rock dance tunes for an under-30 crowd that keeps the place hopping till 4am Wednesday through Sunday. The cover charge begins at 10€ ($13) per person. Another enduringly popular disco, 4km (2½ miles) southwest of town, is **Le Black Bottom,** route de Limoux ((C) **04-68-47-37-11**), which plays every conceivable kind of dance music Thursday through Sunday beginning at 11pm. Entrance costs 10€ ($13) per person.

7 Perpignan ★★

904km (562 miles) SW of Paris; 369km (229 miles) NW of Marseille; 64km (40 miles) S of Narbonne

At Perpignan you might think you've crossed the border into Spain, for it was once Catalonia's second city after Barcelona. Even earlier it was the capital of the kingdom of Majorca. But when the Roussillon—the French part of Catalonia—was finally partitioned off, Perpignan became permanently French by the Treaty of the Pyrenees in 1659. However, Catalan is still spoken here, especially among the country people.

Legend has it that Perpignan derives its name from Père Pinya, a plowman who followed the Tèt River down the Pyrenees mountains to the site of the town today, where he cultivated the fertile soil while the river kept its promise to water the fields.

Today Perpignan is content to rest on its former glory. Its 120,000 residents enjoy the closeness of the Côte Catalane (the coastline of Catalonia, in neighboring Spain) and the mountains to the north. The pace is relaxed. You'll have time to smell the flowers that grow here in great abundance.

This is one of the sunniest places in France, but during summer afternoons in July and August, it's a cauldron. That's when many locals catch the 9.5km (6-mile) ride to the beach resort of Canet. Take bus no. 1 from the center of Perpignan costing 4€ ($5.20) every 15 minutes in summer. A young scene brings energy to Perpignan, especially along the quays of the Basse River, site of impromptu nighttime concerts, beer drinking, and the devouring of tapas, a tradition adopted from nearby Barcelona.

ESSENTIALS

GETTING THERE   Four trains per day arrive from Paris from both the Gare St. Lazare and the Gare de Nord (trip time: 6–10 hr.) after stopping at Montpellier; the one-way fare is 80€ ($104). There are also eight conventional trains from Marseille via Narbonne (trip time: 5 hr.; one-way fare: 35€/$46). For rail information and schedules, call ✆ **08-92-35-35-35.** If you're **driving** from the French Riviera, drive west along A9 to Perpignan.

VISITOR INFORMATION   The **Office Municipal du Tourisme** is in the Palais des Congrès, place Armand-Lanoux (✆ **04-68-66-30-30;** www.perpignantourisme.com).

SPECIAL EVENTS   In the heat of July during a 4-week cultural binge, **Les Estivales** (✆ **04-68-35-01-77;** www.estivales.com) causes the city to explode with music, expositions, and theater. Our favorite time to visit this area is during the **grape harvest** in September after the temperatures have dropped. If you visit then, you may want to drive through vineyards of the Rivesaltes district bordering the city to the west and north.

Perpignan is host to one of the most widely discussed celebrations of photojournalism in the industry, the **Festival International de Photo-Journalisme** (www.visa pourlimage.com). Established in the late 1980s, it's also called **Le Visa pour l'Image.** From late August until mid-September, at least 10 sites of historic (usually medieval) interest are devoted to photojournalistic expositions from around the world. Entrance to the shows is free, and an international committee awards prizes. For more information, call ✆ **04-68-66-18-00.**

SEEING THE SIGHTS

A 3-hour guided **walking tour** is a good way to see the attractions in the town's historic core. Some tour leaders even lace their commentary with English. Tours begin at 3pm daily from mid-June to mid-September, and for 2 weeks around Christmas. The rest of the year, they start at 2:30pm on Wednesday and Saturday only. They depart from in front of the tourist office and cost 4€ ($5.20) per person. For more details, contact the tourist office (see above).

Castillet/Musée des Arts et Traditions Populaires Catalans ✦   The Castillet is one of the chief sights of Perpignan. The machicolated and crenellated redbrick building from the 14th century is a combination gateway and fortress. It houses the museum, also known as La Casa Païral, which contains exhibitions of Catalan regional artifacts and folkloric items, including typical dress. Part of the charm of the Castillet derives from its bulky-looking tower, which you can climb for a good view of the town.

Place de Verdun. ℂ 04-68-35-42-05. Admission 4€ ($5.20) adults, 2€ ($2.60) students and children under 18. May–Sept Wed–Mon 10am–6:30pm; Oct–Apr Wed–Mon 11am–5:30pm.

Cathédrale St-Jean ✦   The cathedral dates from the 14th and 15th centuries and has an admirable nave and interesting 17th-century retables (altarpieces). Leaving through the south door, you'll find on the left a chapel with the *Devost-Christ* (Devout Christ), a magnificent wood carving depicting Jesus contorted with pain and suffering, his head, crowned with thorns, drooping on his chest. Sightseeing visits are discouraged during Sunday Mass. On Good Friday, the *Devost-Christ* is promenaded through the town center.

Place Gambetta/rue de l'Horloge. ℂ 04-68-51-33-72. Free admission. Daily 9am–noon and 3–7pm.

Palais des Rois de Majorque (Palace of the Kings of Majorca) ✦   At the top of the town, the Spanish citadel encloses the Palace of the Kings of Majorca. The government has restored this structure, built in the 13th and 14th centuries, around a court encircled by arcades. You can see the old throne room, with its large fireplaces, and a square tower with a double gallery; the tower has a fine view of the Pyrenees. A free guided tour, in French only, departs four times a day if demand warrants it.

Rue des Archers. ℂ 04-68-34-48-29. Admission 4€ ($5.20) adults, 2€ ($2.60) students, free for children under 8. June–Sept daily 10am–6pm; Oct–May daily 9am–5pm.

A MAJOR HISTORIC SITE NEARBY

Château de Salses ✦   This important historic site is in the hamlet of Salses, 25km (15 miles) north of the city center. Since the days of the Romans, this fort has guarded the main road linking Spain and France. Ferdinand of Aragón erected a fort here in 1497 to protect the northern frontier of his kingdom. Even today, Salses marks the language-barrier point between Catalonia in Spain and Languedoc in France. This Spanish-style fort, designed by Ferdinand himself, is a curious example of an Iberian structure in France. In the 17th century, it was modified by the French military engineer Vauban to look more like a château. After many changes of ownership, Salses fell to the forces of Louis XIII in September 1642, and its Spanish garrison left forever. Less than 2 decades later, Roussillon was incorporated into France. There's a small-scale gift shop dispensing film and cold drinks on the premises.

Salses, 16km (11 miles) north of the center of Perpignan. ℂ 04-68-38-60-13. Admission 6.10€ ($7.95) adults, 5.10€ ($6.65) ages 17–25, free for children under 17. Oct–May daily 10am–noon and 2–5pm; June–Sept daily 9:30am–7pm. From Perpignan, follow signs to Narbonne and RN9.

SHOPPING

With its inviting storefronts and pedestrian streets, Perpignan is a good town for shopping. Catalan is the style indigenous to the area, and it's reflected in textiles and pottery

Finds   **Céret: Birthplace of Cubism**

Driving 31km (19 miles) southwest of Perpignan, you reach this enchanting little town, long a mecca for artists. A group of avant-garde artists was drawn here when Manolo (1873–1945), the Catalonian sculptor, let fellow artists in on a secret: **Céret** is a little gem. In time, Picasso and Braque arrived, making Céret the capital of cubism.

In the center of town, you can visit **Musée d'Art Moderne** 〈★★〉, 8 bd. Maréchal-Joffre (℃ **04-68-87-27-76**), with one of the finest collections of art in the southwest. The museum is dedicated to the painters who have lived in and around Céret, if only briefly. Of course, most visitors come here to see works by Picasso, which include paintings, sculptures, and sketches. Also displayed are works by Chagall, Braque, Matisse, Maillol, and Miró, plus four paintings by Pierre Brune, founder of the museum. On the second floor, space is devoted to floating exhibits by contemporary French artists. July through September, museum hours are daily from 10am to 7pm; May through June and in October, hours are daily from 10am to 6pm; and November through April, hours are Wednesday through Monday from 10am to 6pm. Admission is 8€ ($10) for adults, 6€ ($7.80) for students, and free for ages 18 and under.

Information about the town is found at the **Office de Tourisme**, 1 av. Clemenceau (℃ **04-68-87-00-53**). Transports Vaills (℃ **04-68-87-10-70**) runs one bus per hour (trip time: 45 min.) from Perpignan to Céret during the day; one-way fare costs 8.50€ ($11).

in strong geometric patterns and sturdily structured furniture. For one of the best selections of Catalan pottery, furniture, and carpets, and even a small inventory of antiques, visit the **Centre Sant-Vicens,** rue Sant-Vicens (℃ **04-68-50-02-18**), site of about a dozen independent merchants. You'll find it 4km (2½ miles) south of the town center, following the signs pointing to Enne and Collioures. In the town center, **La Maison Quinta,** 3 rue des Grands-des-Fabriques (℃ **04-68-34-41-62**), offers Catalan-inspired items for home decorating.

WHERE TO STAY

Hôtel de la Loge   This beguiling little place dates from the 16th century but has been renovated into a modern hotel. It's located right in the heart of town, near Loge de Mer, the town hall, from which it takes its name, and the Castillet. The cozy rooms are attractively furnished, all with a sense of warmth and hospitality. The tiled bathrooms are small but offer adequate shelf space. Call ahead to request either a tub or shower.

1 rue des Fabriques d'en-Nabot, 66000 Perpignan. ℃ **04-68-34-41-02.** Fax 04-68-34-25-13. www.hoteldelaloge.fr. 22 units. 40€–57€ ($52–$74) double. AE, DC, MC, V. **Amenities:** Bar. *In room:* A/C, TV, minibar, hair dryer.

La Villa Duflot 〈★★★〉   This is the area's greatest hotel, yet its prices are reasonable for the luxury offered. Tranquillity, style, and refinement reign supreme. When this hotel opened, the mayor proclaimed, "Now we have some class in Perpignan."

Located in a suburb, La Villa Duflot is a Mediterranean-style dwelling surrounded by a large park of pine, palm, and eucalyptus. The hotel has an appealing, almost familial touch to it and isn't the least bit intimidating. You can sunbathe in the gardens surrounding the pool and order drinks at any hour at the outdoor bar. The guest rooms are situated around a patio planted with century-old olive trees. All rooms are spacious and soundproof, with marble bathrooms and Art Deco interiors.

Rond-Point Albert Donnezan, 66000 Perpignan. © **04-68-56-67-67**. Fax 04-68-56-54-05. www.villa-duflot.com. 24 units. 120€–160€ ($156–$208) double. Half board 108€–128€ ($140–$166) per person double occupancy. AE, DC, MC, V. From the center of Perpignan, follow signs to Perthus–Le Belou and A9, and travel 3km (2 miles) south. Just before you reach A9, you'll see the hotel. **Amenities:** Restaurant (see "Where to Dine," below); 2 bars; outdoor pool; limited room service; babysitting; laundry service; nonsmoking rooms; limited-mobility rooms. *In room:* A/C, TV, dataport, minibar, hair dryer, safe.

Park Hotel ✸   This four-story hotel facing the Jardins de la Ville offers well-furnished, soundproof rooms. Although the Park is solid and reliable, it is the town's second choice, having none of the glamour of Villa Duflot. Midsize to spacious bedrooms are comfortably furnished with taste but not much flair; each comes with an average-size bathroom.

The restaurant, Le Chapon Fin, serves up first-class Mediterranean cuisine. The food, made from prime regional produce, is some of the finest in the area. Post-nouvelle choices include roast sea scallops flavored with succulent sea urchin velouté (white sauce thickened with white roux), various lobster dishes, and penne with truffles. As an accompaniment, try one of the local wines—perhaps a Collioure or Côtes du Roussillon. The restaurant is open for lunch Monday through Saturday and for dinner Monday through Friday. The hotel also houses Le Bistrot du Park, a less expensive eatery specializing in seafood.

18 bd. Jean-Bourrat, 66000 Perpignan. © **04-68-35-14-14**. Fax 04-68-35-48-18. www.parkhotel-fr.com. 69 units. 70€–100€ ($91–$130) double; 180€–280€ ($234–$364) suite. AE, DC, MC, V. Parking 10€ ($13). **Amenities:** Restaurant; bar; limited room service; laundry service; nonsmoking rooms; limited-mobility rooms. *In room:* A/C, TV, dataport, minibar, hair dryer, iron, safe.

WHERE TO DINE

L'Assiette Catalane *Value* FRENCH/SPANISH/CATALAN   Known to virtually every resident of Perpignan for its well-prepared cuisine, this restaurant resembles something you'd expect across the Pyrenees in Spain. Hand-painted ceramic plates, rugby and flamenco posters, and antique farm implements cover the thick stone walls. Even the long, lively bar is inlaid with Iberian mosaics, and copies of artworks by Salvador Dalí and Picasso seem to stare back at you as you dine. Menu items include four kinds of *parrilladas* (mixed grills); one of the most appealing consists entirely of fish served on a hot slab of iron that's brought directly to your table; and Zarzuelas, paella, and tapas, prepared in the Spanish style, but served as an appetizer at table. Chicken with crayfish is another regional specialty. It seems appropriate to follow up with a portion of flan.

9 rue de la République. © **04-68-34-77-62**. Reservations recommended. Main courses 6.50€–15€ ($8.45–$20); fixed-price lunch 11€ ($14); fixed-price menu 15€–25€ ($20–$33). MC, V. Mon–Sat noon–2pm and Wed–Mon 7–11pm.

Le Clos des Lys ✸ *Value* FRENCH   This well-recommended restaurant, in a stately building that sits apart from its neighbors, has a terrace overlooking a copse of cypresses and bubbling fountains. It's supervised by Jean-Claude Vila and Frank

Sequret, respected chefs who have been finalists in several culinary competitions. The set-price menus vary widely in selection and cost. Dishes might include goat cheese in puff pastry, garnished with sesame seeds and a reduction of Banyuls dessert wine; terrine of three kinds of liver accompanied with a salad of wild greens and walnuts; foie gras of duck with passion fruit and mango chutney sauce; filets of sea wolf fried with sesame seeds and served with eggplant mousse and tomato-flavored risotto; and tournedos of beef with a layer of foie gras, creamed morels, and soufflé potatoes. The restaurant incorporates a thriving catering business that books conventions and weddings.

660 chemin de la Fauceille. ℂ 04-68-56-79-00. Reservations recommended. Set-price menu 14€–62€ ($18–$81) lunch, 20€–62€ ($26–$81) dinner. AE, DC, MC, V. Tues–Sun noon–2pm; Tues and Thurs–Sat 7–9:30pm. Closed 3 weeks in Feb. From the center of Perpignan, drive 2.5km (1½ miles) west, following the Rte. d'Espagne.

La Villa Duflot 𝑹𝑹   Slightly removed from the city center, this *restaurant avec chambres* is the most tranquil oasis in the area (see hotel review above). André Duflot, the owner, employs top-notch chefs who turn out dish after dish with remarkable skill and professionalism. Try, for example, a salad of warm squid, a platter of fresh anchovies marinated in vinegar, excellent foie gras of duckling, or lasagna of foie gras with asparagus points. A wonderful dessert is chocolate cake with saffron-flavored cream sauce. On the premises is an American-style bar.

Rond-Point Albert Donnezan, 66000 Perpignan. ℂ 04-68-56-67-67. Fax 04-68-56-54-05. Reservations required. Main courses 17€–23€ ($22–$30); Sat–Sun fixed-price menu 30€ ($39). Daily noon–2:30pm and 8–11pm. AE, DC, MC, V. From the center of Perpignan, follow signs to Perthus–Le Belou and A9, and travel 3km (2 miles) south. Just before you reach A9, you'll see the hotel.

PERPIGNAN AFTER DARK

Perpignan shows its Spanish and Catalan side at night, when a round of tapas and late-night promenades are among the activities. The streets radiating from **place de la Loge** offer a higher concentration of bars and clubs than any other part of town.

Hot and sometimes overheated Perpignan offers lots of diversions to amuse visitors during the cool of the night. An evening on the town involves a drink and a chat in one of the *bars de nuit,* followed by a visit to a disco. You might begin at **Le Habana-Club,** 5 rue Grande-des-Fabriques (ℂ **04-68-34-11-00**), where salsa and merengue play and sunset-colored cocktails flow. Suds with an Irish accent are the attraction at **Le Shannon Bar,** 3 rue de l'Incendie (ℂ **04-68-35-12-48**), where a small community of Irish expats (and Celtic wannabes) wax nostalgic.

Discos in Perpignan open around 11pm. **Le Napoli,** 3 rue place de Catalogne (ℂ **04-68-35-55-88**), a modern, mirror-sheathed space, might remind you of an airport waiting area without the chairs. (Yes, you'll have to stand up and mingle or dance, because there's almost nowhere to sit.) Another option for dancing is the **Uba-Club,** 5 bd. Mercader (ℂ **04-68-34-06-70**), which has a smallish dance floor and, thankfully, some sofas and chairs. One of the largest discos in town is **Le Milord,** 20 rue Jules-Verne (ℂ **04-68-55-40-77**), where a convivial crowd ages 30 to 50 gathers on the two floors for dancing, billiards, flirting, and reminiscing.

During summer, the beachfront strip at the nearby resort of **Canet-Plage,** 12km (7½ miles) east of Perpignan's historic core, abounds with seasonal bars and dance clubs that come and go with the tourist tides.

8 Collioure ★★

929km (577 miles) SW of Paris; 27km (17 miles) SE of Perpignan

You might recognize this port and its sailboats from the Fauve paintings of Lhote and Derain. It's said to resemble St-Tropez before it was spoiled. In the past, it attracted Matisse, Picasso, and Dalí. Collioure is the most authentic and alluring port of Roussillon, a gem with a vivid Spanish/Catalan image and flavor. Some visitors believe it's the most charming village on the Côte Vermeille.

ESSENTIALS

GETTING THERE Collioure has frequent **train** and bus service, especially from Perpignan (trip time: 20 min.). For train information and schedules, call ℂ **08-92-35-35-35.** Many visitors **drive** along the coastal road (RN114) leading to the Spanish border.

VISITOR INFORMATION The **Office de Tourisme** is on place du 18-Juin (ℂ **04-68-82-15-47).**

SPECIAL EVENTS The annual **Salon des Antiquaires** takes place on a 3-day weekend around November 1. Antiques dealers from throughout southern France set up shop for wholesalers and retailers. For more information, contact the tourist office.

EXPLORING THE TOWN

The town's sloping, narrow streets; charming semifortified church; antique lighthouse; and eerily introverted culture make it worth an afternoon stopover. This is the ideal small-town antidote to the condo-choked Riviera, and out of season, things around here are relatively calm.

The two curving ports sit on either side of the heavy masonry of the 13th-century **Château Royal,** place de 8-Mai-1945 (ℂ **04-68-82-06-43).** It's of interest in its own right for its medieval fortifications and overall bulk, but between the months of May and September, it's also the home to a changing series of special (temporary) exhibitions, each of which come and go at regular intervals. (Throughout the summer of 2005, it housed a comprehensive exhibit on the Fauvist painters, especially Matisse, their lives in Collioure, and their influence on modern art.) The château charges the same entrance charge regardless of whether a temporary exhibition is on display or not on the day of your visit: 4€ ($5.20) for adults, 2€ ($2.60) students and children ages 12 to 16, free for children 11 and under. From June to September, the château is open daily 10am to 6pm; October to May, daily 9am to 5pm. Also try to visit the **Musée Jean-Peské,** route de Port-Vendres (ℂ **04-68-82-10-19),** home to a collection of works by artists who painted here. It's open in July and August daily 10am to noon and 2 to 7pm, September through June Wednesday through Monday 10am to noon and 2 to 6pm. Admission is 2€ ($2.60) for adults, 1.50€ ($1.95) for children 12 to 16, free for children under 12.

WHERE TO STAY

Casa Païral ★ This is a small-scale, family-operated place, not too businesslike, but sort of charming. On sunny days, the most alluring part of this 150-year-old house is a swimming pool in the shadow of century-old trees. The small to medium-size bedrooms are comfortable and filled with charming old antiques alongside more modern pieces; bathrooms are small. The best doubles have a petit salon plus a small balcony.

Only breakfast is served, but many restaurants are nearby. The hotel lies 150m (492 ft.) from the port and the beach.

Impasse des Palmiers, 66190 Collioure. © **04-68-82-05-81.** Fax 04-68-82-52-10. www.hotel-casa-pairal.com. 28 units. 76€–145€ ($99–$189) double; 162€–180€ ($210–$234) suite. AE, MC, V. Parking 8€ ($10). Closed Nov–Mar. **Amenities:** Outdoor pool; limited room service; laundry service; limited-mobility rooms. *In room:* A/C, TV, dataport, minibar, hair dryer.

Hôtel Princes de Catalogne   This is a relatively modern hotel of little architectural interest, but its position is in the town center and it has a hardworking and cooperative staff. Bedrooms contain simple, angular furniture with touches of traditional Provençal upholsteries, writing tables, and comfortable beds; they are a bit more spacious than you might have expected. The tidy bathrooms are tiled and small.

Rue des Palmiers, 66190 Collioure. © **04-68-98-30-00.** Fax 04-68-98-30-31. www.hotel-princescatalogne.com. 36 units. 60€–73€ ($78–$95) double; 94€–110€ ($122–$143) suite. AE, MC, V. Free parking. **Amenities:** Bar; limited room service. *In room:* A/C, TV, minibar, hair dryer, safe.

Le Bon Port   Built during the 1940s, this stucco-sided hotel perches beside the port, across the water from the town center, which lies within a 5-minute walk. It offers comfortable, appealingly simple bedrooms with summery furniture, tile floors, and flowered upholsteries. Accommodations are scattered among three separate buildings, the smallest of which is a two-unit cabana set beside the swimming pool. Staff is soft-spoken and charming, and knows what's going on within Collioure.

12 rte. de Port-Vendres, 66190 Collioure. © **04-68-82-06-08.** Fax 04-68-82-54-97. www.bon-port.com. 22 units. 65€–85€ ($85–$111) double. MC, V. **Amenities:** Bar; pool; babysitting. *In room:* TV.

Les Caranques *(Value*   Constructed around the core of a private villa built after World War II and enlarged twice since then, this hotel is comfortably furnished, personalized, and one of the best bargains in town. The rooms are a bit small but neatly maintained. Set on the perimeter of Collioure, away from the crush (and the charm) of the center, the hotel features a terrace that opens onto a view of the old port. The terrace stretches from the hotel to the sea, where guests can swim directly from the rocks.

Rte. de Port-Vendres, 66190 Collioure. © **04-68-82-06-68.** Fax 04-68-82-00-92. www.les-caranques.com. 22 units. 65€–75€ ($85–$98) double. AE, MC, V. Free parking. Closed Oct 15–Mar. **Amenities:** Limited room service. *In room:* TV, dataport, minibar.

Les Templiers *(★ (Finds*   The most charming and atmospheric hotel in the town center maintains its headquarters about 15m (50 ft.) inland from the port, in a *fin-de-siècle* house whose ground floor is devoted to a recommended bar and restaurant (see "Where to Dine," below). Part of the charm of the place derives from the clusters of mature local men playing cards (and, in some cases, according to the staff, "cheating") at tables in the bar and conversing in Catalan. The hotel consists of four separate buildings, each within a short walk from one another. The most atmospheric, most comfortable, and most lavishly decorated of the four is the hotel's headquarters and site of registration for the annexes, which do not employ receptionists or check-in staffs of their own. In the main building, expect at least 2,000 paintings—so many that most of the wall surfaces are completely covered with them—and a bar that's artfully sculpted to resemble a boat, complete with a sculpture at one end of a mermaid comforting (or seducing) a much smaller depiction of a sailor. Bedrooms in the main building have polychrome (that is, painted) Catalan-style furniture and views of the town's château and, in some cases, the sea; those in the annexes have traditional but less-lavish decors and less-inspiring views.

12 Quai de l'Amirauté, 66190 Collioure. © **04-68-98-31-10.** Fax 04-68-98-01-24. www.hotel-templiers.com. 55 units. 41€–78€ ($53–$101) double. AE, DC, MC, V. Closed Jan to mid-Feb. **Amenities:** Restaurant; bar; limited room service; laundry service. *In room:* A/C, TV.

Relais des Trois Mas et Restaurant La Balette ★★   This is the town's premier hotel, and the restaurant of choice. This hotel was established more than 20 years ago by connecting a trio of older Provençal farmhouses. In the decor of its beautiful rooms, the hotel honors the famous artists who lived at Collioure. The rooms, which have spacious bathrooms with Jacuzzis, open onto water views. Even if you aren't a guest, you may want to take a meal in the dining room and enjoy its vistas of the harbor. Jose Vidal is the best chef in town. His cooking is inventive—often simple, but always refined. Set menus cost 32€ to 73€ ($42–$95) and are served daily at lunch and dinner.

Rte. de Port-Vendres, 66190 Collioure. © **04-68-82-05-07.** Fax 04-68-82-38-08. 23 units. 144€–280€ ($187–$364) double; 242€–450€ ($315–$585) suite. Half board 71€ ($92) per person. MC, V. Parking 12€ ($16). Closed Jan and Nov 15–Dec 20. **Amenities:** Restaurant; outdoor pool; sauna; limited room service; babysitting; laundry service; non-smoking rooms. *In room:* A/C, TV, dataport, minibar, hair dryer, safe.

WHERE TO DINE

Note that the **Restaurant La Balette** (see above) is the best dining room in town.

Le Puits CATALAN   Named after its kitchen's now-sealed-off well *(le puits)* that used to provide water for some of the houses nearby, this is a small-scale and charming restaurant that makes special efforts in its preparation of some time-honored Catalan specialties. Its dining room is accented with exposed beams and soft tones of red and orange, with an additional dozen seats lined up beside the all-pedestrian street in front. The well-intentioned family that owns this place is especially proud of the dining room's critically acclaimed fresco that was painted in 1950 by a local (and at presstime, still living) artist named Bernardi (first name unused and mostly unknown) A depiction of the grape harvest and fishers of Collioure, it's often cited as a good early example of this artist's work. Come here for, among other dishes, calamari stew prepared with local Banyuls wine; stuffed mussels; grilled pork jowls *(les galtes)* prepared either with local Banyuls wine or with herbs; and tuna steak in catalan (tomatoes, onions, and peppers) sauce.

2 rue Arago. © **04-68-82-06-24.** Reservations recommended. Main courses 12€–24€ ($16–$31). MC, V. Daily noon–3pm and 6:30–10:30pm. Closed Thurs Oct–May.

Les Templiers CATALAN   Part of its charm derives from a bar whose every inch of wall surface is covered with paintings, and a well-established role as the town's most popular card-playing venues for retired Catalan-speaking local gents. After an aperitif in the bar, you'll be prepared for a meal in the dining room, where stone vaults, more paintings, and the possibility of sitting at a table on the pavement in front add to the allure. Menu items are entirely based on old-fashioned Catalan traditions. An excellent starter is a circular platter of grilled anchovies, artfully arranged like spokes on a wheel, drizzled with olive oil and sprinkled with parsley and other herbs. Other options include a platter of fried fish that incorporates whatever was hauled in from the Mediterranean that day, a savory bouillabaisse, fresh codfish served with a "caviar" of mashed eggplant, shoulder of Pyrenean lamb with a spicy onion jam, and seafood paella. Dessert might include a time-tested crème Catalane or an unusual form of ice cream: Flavored with steamed and pulverized fennel, it's served with spice bread and saffron sauce.

12 Quai de l'Amirauté, 66190 Collioure. ℂ **04-68-98-31-10.** Reservations recommended in midsummer. Main courses 20€–30€ ($26–$39). AE, DC, MC, V. Daily 12:30–2pm and 7:30–10pm. Closed Jan to mid-Feb.

Le Trémail CATALAN/SEAFOOD   Set on a narrow, cobble-covered alleyway in the oldest part of Collioure, this is a rustic and authentically Catalan restaurant. It functioned for many generations as the family home of the owner, Jean-Paul Fabre. Le Trémail is local dialect that refers to the small nets used to catch fish in rocky shallow waters. Surrounded by stone walls, hand-painted Spanish tiles, and dangling fish nets, less than 18m (60 ft.) from the edge of the sea, it specializes in grilled fish *(à la plancha),* invariably served with olive oil and herb-enriched vinaigrette. Examples include marinated anchovies with braised onions and peppers, a succulent version of whatever the day's catch from the local fishing fleet might be, and desserts like *crème Catalán* or a homemade pastry. A limited number of "noble fish"—sole and turbot—might be on hand, along with a limited roster of meat. Particularly succulent are *rondelles* of calamari with red wine.

16 bis rue Mailly. ℂ **04-68-82-16-10.** Reservations recommended. Main courses 15€–27€ ($20–$35); set menu 15€–34€ ($20–$44). AE, DC, MC, V. Tues–Sun noon–2:15pm and 7–10:30pm; June–Oct also Mon. Closed Jan.

Neptune ✪✪✪ FRENCH/CATALAN   This is the best restaurant in Collioure, but much to the credit of its owners and staff, it is easygoing and remarkably unpretentious. You'll find it on the southeastern edge of town in a salmon-toned *mas Provençal* (farmhouse). The establishment has been the domain for many years of the talented, hardworking Mourlane family. Menu items are noteworthy for their top-quality ingredients and the respect and care with which they're handled. Our favorite starter is a platter of local anchovies marinated in herbs; you might opt for a salad of fresh wild greens garnished with chunks of lobster. Main courses change with the seasons but might include grilled Mediterranean sea wolf with oyster-flavored butter sauce; several versions of lobster; or rack of suckling lamb from the nearby salt marshes, served in orange sauce or an herb-flavored pastry crust. Equally appealing are lightly braised scallops in delicate butter, herb, and garlic sauce, and simple but succulent sole meunière.

9 rte. de Porte-Vendres. ℂ **04-68-82-02-27.** Reservations recommended. Main courses 26€–36€ ($34–$47); set-price menu 30€–70€ ($39–$91) lunch, 49€–70€ ($63–$91). AE, MC, V. Thurs–Mon noon–2pm and 7:30–9pm (closed Mon July–Aug). Closed Dec 7–24 and Jan.

9 Narbonne ⭐

845km (525 miles) SW of Paris; 61km (38 miles) E of Carcassonne; 93km (58 miles) S of Montpellier

Medieval Narbonne was a port to rival Marseille in Roman days, with its "galleys laden with riches." It was the first town outside Italy to be colonized by the Romans, but the Mediterranean, now 8km (5 miles) away, left it high and dry. It's an intriguing place, steeped in antiquity.

After Lyon, Narbonne was the largest town in Gaul. Even today, one can see evidence of the town's former wealth. Too far from the sea to be a beach town, it attracts history buffs to its memories of a glorious past. Some 50,000 Narbonnais live in what is really a sleepy backwater. However, many locals are trying to make a go with their vineyards. Caves are open to visitors in the surrounding area (the tourist office will advise). If you want to go to the beach, you'll have to head to the nearby sands at the village of **Gruisson** and the beach (Gruisson-Plage) that adjoins it, or to the suburb of **St-Pierre la Mer** and its adjoining beach (Narbonne-Plage). Both lie 14km (9 miles) south of Narbonne. Buses from the town center are frequent, marked with their respective destinations.

ESSENTIALS

GETTING THERE   Narbonne has rail, bus, and highway connections with other cities on the Mediterranean coast and with Toulouse. Rail travel is the most popular way to get here, with 14 **trains** per day arriving from Perpignan (trip time: 50 min.), 13 per day from Toulouse (trip time: 1½ hr.), and 12 per day from Montpellier (trip time: 1 hr.). Most rail passengers arriving from Paris take the TGV directly to Narbonne.

Finds **Liberté, Egalité, Fraternité . . . Nudité**

The municipality known as **Agde,** 40km (25 miles) northeast of Narbonne and 50km (31 miles) southwest of Montpellier, operates like every other *commune* in France, with one startling exception: its flourishing nudist colony. In the 1970s, the community's founder/matriarch, Mademoiselle Geneviève Oltha, had the idea of promoting a simple pine grove beside the sea as a place for an escape from the stresses of urban life. Within less than 25 years, the site burgeoned into the largest nudist colony in Europe, with a roster of about 100 midwinter residents and a midsummer population usually approaching 30,000.

Don't expect everyone in Agde to be nude, since the town's four major subdivisions (Cité d'Agde, Cap d'Agde, Grau d'Agde, and La Tamarissière) offer options for the clothed as well. However, in the clearly signposted and, for the most part, fenced-in **Quartier Naturiste Cap d'Agde** 𝄞 (℗ 04-67-26-00-26), nudity is required on the beaches and encouraged elsewhere. Stores, restaurants, and shops (most selling everything except—you guessed it—clothing) are part of the setup. Those who arrive on foot at the compound's gate pay 5€ ($6.50) for entrance; motorists with as many passengers as can be crammed into their cars pay 9€. The **Agde Office de Tourisme,** Espace Molière, Centre Ville (℗ 04-67-94-29-68), or its satellite branch, the **Office Municipal de Tourism,** Cap d'Agde, Les Plages (℗ 04-67-01-04-04), long ago became accustomed to answering questions for the clothed, the unclothed, and the clothing indecisive.

Conveniently close to but not within the nudist zone are two museums. The **Musée Agathois,** rue de la Fraternité (℗ 04-67-94-82-51), is noted for the homage it pays to (clothed) cultural models of the city's 19th-century fishing tradition and the region's handicrafts. The **Musée Ethèbe,** Mas de la Clape, Cap d'Agde (℗ 04-67-94-69-60), showcases the artifacts dredged up by marine explorations of the nearby sea bottom. Its star exhibit and namesake is the nearly life-size **l'Ethèbe,** a graceful-looking Greek statue from the 6th century B.C. Admission to each museum costs 4€ ($5.20).

The one-way fare from Paris is 92€ ($120); from Montpellier, 12€ to 17€ ($16–$22). For rail information, call ✆ **08-92-35-35-35.** If you're **driving,** Narbonne is at the junction of A61 and A9, easily accessible from either Toulouse or the Riviera.

VISITOR INFORMATION   The **Office de Tourisme** is on place Roger-Salengro (✆ **04-68-65-15-60;** www.mairie-narbonne.fr).

EXPLORING THE TOWN

The town's sights are concentrated in the medieval Vielle Ville (Old City), a massive central labyrinth of religious and civic buildings.

THE CENTRAL COMPLEX

A combination ticket (5.20€/$6.75 adults, 3.70€/$4.80 students and children under 18) admits you to all of these attractions. If you don't visit the palace, you can pay for those attractions separately.

The neo-Gothic **Hôtel de Ville** (town hall) in the complex was reconstructed by Viollet-le-Duc, the 19th-century architect who refurbished Notre-Dame in Paris between 1845 and 1850.

Cathédrale St-Just 🐾🐾   The cathedral's construction began in 1272, but it was never finished. Only the transept and a choir were completed. The choir is 39m (130 ft.) high, built in the bold Gothic style of northern France. At each end of the transept are 58m (194-ft.) towers from 1480. There's an impressive collection of Flemish tapestries. The cathedral is connected to the archbishop's palace by 14th- and 15th-century cloisters.

Place de l'Hôtel-de-Ville (enter on rue Gauthier). ✆ **04-68-32-09-52.** Free admission. June–Sept daily 10am–7pm; Oct–May daily 9am–noon and 2–6pm.

Donjon Gilles-Aycelin   If you happen to visit between mid-June and mid-September, you might want to participate in one of the occasional hikes up the steep steps of the watchtower. A watchtower and prison in the late 13th century, it has a lofty observation platform with a view of the cathedral, the surrounding plain, and the Pyrenees.

Place de l'Hôtel-de-Ville. ✆ **04-68-90-30-30.** 2.20€ ($2.85) for adults, 1€ ($1.30) for students and children 11–18. Daily 9am–noon and 2–6pm.

Palais des Archevêques (Archbishop's Palace, or Vieux-Palais)   The palace was conceived as part fortress, part pleasure residence. It has three military-style towers from the 13th and 14th centuries. The Old Palace on the right dates from the 12th century, and the so-called "New Palace" on the left dates from the 14th. It's said that the old, arthritic, and sometimes very overweight archbishops used to be hauled up the interior's monumental Louis XIII-style stairs on mules.

Today the once-private apartments of the former bishops contain three museums. The **Musée Archéologique** 🐾 contains prehistoric artifacts, Bronze Age tools, 14th-century frescoes, and Greco-Roman amphorae. Several of the sarcophagi date from the 3rd century, and some of the mosaics are of pagan origin. The **Musée d'Art et d'Histoire de Narbonne** is located three floors above street level in the archbishop's once-private apartments (the rooms where Louis XII resided during his siege of Perpignan). Their coffered ceilings are enhanced with panels depicting the nine Muses. A Roman mosaic floor and 17th-century portraits are on display. There's also a collection of antique porcelain, enamels, and a portrait bust of Louis XIV. In the **Horreum**

Romain, you'll find a labyrinth of underground passageways, similar to catacombs but without burial functions, dug by the Gallo-Romans and their successors for storage of food and supplies during times of siege.

Place de l'Hôtel-de-Ville. (© **04-68-90-30-30,** or 04-68-90-30-54 for museum information. Billet global or 5.20€ ($6.75). Apr–Sept daily 9:30am–12:15pm and 2–6pm; Oct–Mar Tues–Sun 10am–noon and 2–5pm.

MORE SIGHTS
Basilique St-Paul-Serge   This early Gothic church was built on the site of a 4th-century necropolis. It has an elegant choir with fine Renaissance woodcarvings and some ancient Christian sarcophagi. The chancel, from 1229, is admirable. The north door leads to the Paleo-Christian Cemetery, part of an early Christian burial ground.

Rue de l'Hôtel-Dieu. (© **04-68-32-68-98.** Free admission. Apr–Sept daily 9am–7pm; Oct–Mar daily 9am–noon, Mon–Sat 2–6pm.

Musée Lapidaire   Located in the 13th-century Notre-Dame de Lamourguier, this museum contains an important collection of Roman artifacts—broken sculptures and Latin inscriptions—as well as relics of medieval buildings. While it has no major exhibits, it does offer a vast array of classical busts, Roman lintels, and ancient sarcophagi that will satisfy all but the most feverish archaeologist. It takes less than an hour to see it all. You can enter with your general admission ticket to the museums of the archbishop's palace.

Most visitors buy a *pass-billet, or billet global,* allowing entrance to four of the town's museums (including the Musée Lapidaire), plus the *donjon,* and the *trésor* of the cathedral. The billet global costs 7.50€ ($9.75) for adults, 5.50€ ($7.15) for children. Entrance to any of the four museums is free for children under 10.

Place Lamourguier. (© **04-68-65-53-58.** Billet global or 3.70€ ($4.80) adults and students, free for children under 10. Oct–Mar Tues–Sun 9:30am–12:15pm and 2–6pm; Apr–Sept also open Mon.

WHERE TO STAY
Hôtel du Languedoc   Although it competes with a cookie-cutter chain hotel in town, the Novotel, and a motel on the outskirts, the Languedoc remains the traditional favorite because of its old-fashioned ambience and nostalgic feel of the province. It bravely keeps up with the times, however, and has a welcoming atmosphere because of a very helpful staff. It offers well-equipped rooms with acceptably comfortable mattresses. As is typical of an old hotel of this era, rooms come in various shapes and sizes.

Even if not a guest, consider a visit to its well-respected restaurant, which features an array of regionally inspired dishes. Try such specialties as grilled salmon served with anchovy butter or tender lamb from the hills cooked with broad beans. Fresh oysters are often on the menu. Also on site is the town's best wine bar, Le Bacchus, specializing in the many esoteric vintages grown nearby and willing to serve wine by the glass.

22 bd. Gambetta, 11100 Narbonne. (© **04-68-65-14-74.** Fax 04-68-65-81-48. www.hoteldulanguedoc.com. 40 units. 50€–68€ ($65–$88) double; 89€ ($116) suite. AE, DC, MC, V. Parking 7€ ($9.10). **Amenities:** Restaurant; bar/Breton-style crêperie; limited room service; laundry service. *In room:* TV.

La Résidence ⊕   Our favorite hotel in Narbonne is near the Cathédrale St-Just. The 19th-century La Résidence, converted from the premises of a once-stately villa, is decorated with antiques. Bedrooms are fitted with double or twin beds and fine linen. Bathrooms are small but neat. The hotel doesn't have a restaurant but offers breakfast and a gracious welcome.

6 rue du 1er-Mai, 11100 Narbonne. ℂ **04-68-32-19-41.** Fax 04-68-65-51-82. 25 units. 68€–96€ ($88–$125) double. AE, DC, MC, V. Parking 6.80€ ($8.85). Closed Jan 20–Feb 20. **Amenities:** Nonsmoking rooms. *In room:* A/C, TV, dataport, minibar, hair dryer.

WHERE TO DINE

L'Alsace FRENCH/ALSATIAN   Across from the train station, L'Alsace is the most reliable restaurant within Narbonne. The comfortable dining room is done in English style, with wood paneling and a glass-enclosed patio. In spite of the restaurant's name, the cuisine isn't from Alsace-Lorraine, but is typical of southwestern France, with a focus on seafood. The Sinfreus, who own the place, offer a fry of red mullet, a savory kettle of bourride, and magret of duck with flap mushrooms. Especially delectable is this restaurant's specialty: sea wolf or other whole fish baked in a salt crust, a method that usually produces a delightfully pungent and flaky product.

2 av. Pierre-Sémard. ℂ **04-68-65-10-24.** Reservations recommended. Main courses 20€–23€ ($26–$30); fixed-price menus 17€–29€ ($22–$38). AE, DC, MC, V. Wed–Mon noon–2:30pm and 7:30–10pm.

La Table St-Crescent 🛧🛧🛧 FRENCH/LANGUEDOCIENNE   This is one of the region's best-respected restaurants. It's just east of town, beside the road leading to Perpignan, in a complex of wine-tasting boutiques established by a local syndicate of growers. The foundations date, it's said, from the 8th century, when it functioned as an oratory (small chapel) and prayer site. Today it's outfitted with modern furniture that's little more than a foil for the cuisine. The chef delivers refined, brilliantly realized dishes, with sublime sauces and sophisticated herbs and seasonings. Menu items change four times a year based on the availability of seasonal ingredients and the inspiration of the owners. Main courses include sea bass marinated with olives, beef filet with foie gras and truffles, and lobster ravioli with oil of pistou. Especially succulent are roasted scallops floating on a bed of cream of celery soup; filet of red snapper with shellfish and almonds; ravioli stuffed with cheese-laced potatoes; and supreme of duckling with braised cabbage. Wine steward Sabrine Giraud (the chef's wife), and her assistant, Barbara, will help you select the perfect accompaniment.

In the Palais des Vins, 68 av. Général Leclerc, rte. de Perpignan. ℂ **04-68-41-37-37.** Reservations recommended. Main courses 22€–42€ ($29–$55); fixed-price menu 18€ ($23) Mon–Fri lunch, 32€–95€ ($42–$124) lunch and dinner. AE, DC, MC, V. Tues–Fri and Sun noon–1:30pm; Mon–Sat 8–9:30pm.

NARBONNE AFTER DARK

The city has some routine dance clubs—nothing special. Check out the action, if any, at **Dancing GM Palace,** Centre Commercial Forum Sud, Route de Perpignan (ℂ **04-68-41-59-71**).

10 Aigues-Mortes 🛧🛧

750km (466 miles) SW of Paris; 63km (39 miles) NE of Sète; 40km (25 miles) E of Nîmes; 48km (30 miles) SW of Arles

South of Nîmes, you can explore much of the Camargue by car, mainly on the roads of the **Parc Regional de Camargue.** The most rewarding target is Aigues-Mortes, the city of the "dead waters." It is France's most perfectly preserved walled town. In the middle of dismal swamps and melancholy lagoons, Aigues-Mortes stands on four navigable canals. Although it is now 6km (4 miles) from the sea, it was once a thriving port. Louis IX and his crusaders set forth from here on the Ninth Crusade.

The Legacy of Roman Blood & Gore

Bullfighting is alive and well in the Camargue. Bullfighters usually come in from Spain, but these high-energy odes to hi-jinks and high testosterone are conducted in ways that aren't completely *espagnol*. Sometimes the bull is killed and sometimes it will mangle a local youth during a bullring celebration. Most *gardiens* are too shrewd to participate in a head-on confrontation with a bull, though there are likely to be at least one or two on horseback in or near the ring during the contest.

Although some minor bullfights occur in July and August in small arenas in the Camargue, the best ones are staged in Arles at the **Amphitheater (Les Arénes; p. 155).** Tickets range in price from 10€ to 80€ ($13–$104). In modern times, the most avid aficionado of the bullfights in Arles was Picasso, who, in gratitude for the blood and gore, donated 70 of his drawings to the city of Arles. The corridas staged here Easter through September have been called "as bloody as anything presented to the Romans."

ESSENTIALS

GETTING THERE   Five **trains** and four **buses** per day connect Aigues-Mortes and Nîmes; the one-way fare is 7€ ($9.10). Trip time is about an hour. For information and schedules, call © **08-92-35-35-35.** If you're **driving** to Aigues-Mortes, take D979 south from Gallargues, or A9 from Montpellier or Nîmes.

VISITOR INFORMATION   The **Office de Tourisme** is at place St. Louis (© **04-66-53-73-00;** www.ot-aiguesmortes.fr).

EXPLORING THE TOWN

The main allure in Aigues-Mortes is the city itself. A sense of medievalism still permeates virtually every building, every rampart, and every cobbled street, and the town is still enclosed by **Ramparts** ✿✿ that were constructed between 1272 and 1300. The **Tour de Constance** ✿✿ (© **04-66-53-61-55**), which looks out on the marshes, is a model castle of the Middle Ages. At the top, which you can reach by elevator, a panoramic view unfolds. Admission is 6.10€ ($7.95) for adults, 4.10€ ($5.35) for ages 18 to 25, and free for children under 18. The monument is open May to August daily 10am to 7pm, September to April daily 10am to 5pm.

The city's religious centerpiece is the **Eglise Notre-Dame des Sablons,** rue Jean-Jaurès (no phone). Constructed of wood in 1183, it was rebuilt in stone in 1246 in the ogival style. Its modern stained-glass windows were installed in 1980 as replacements for the badly damaged originals. The church is open May to September daily from 8:30am to 6pm, October to April 9am to 5pm.

WHERE TO STAY

Note that the **Restaurant Les Arcades** (see below) also rents rooms.

Hostellerie des Remparts   Opened about 300 years ago, this weather-worn inn lies at the foot of the Tour de Constance, adjacent to the medieval fortifications. Popular and often fully booked (especially in summer), it evokes the defensive atmosphere of the Middle Ages, albeit with charm and a sense of nostalgia. Narrow stone staircases lead to the small, simply furnished rooms, each renovated in 2004. The living here is rather plain and basic. Each well-maintained unit has a small bathroom, 12 with tub and shower, the rest with showers. Breakfast is the only meal served.

6 place Anatole-France, 30220 Aigues-Mortes. (☎ 04-66-53-82-77. Fax 04-66-53-73-77. www.hoteldesremparts.com. 19 units. 60€–110€ ($78–$143) double. AE, V. **Amenities:** Restaurant; bar; limited room service; nonsmoking rooms; limited-mobility rooms. *In room:* A/C, TV.

Hôtel Les Templiers 🅐   The leading inn in town is a gem of peace and tranquillity. Protected by the ramparts built by St-Louis, king of France, this 17th-century residence has small- to medium-size rooms decorated in Provençal style, with just enough decorative objects to lend a homelike aura. Most of the midsize bathrooms have tub/shower combinations (three have showers only). You can relax in the courtyard, where you can also enjoy breakfast. The establishment contains two restaurants, each featuring competent and traditional, if not terribly experimental food: The less formal is open for both lunch and dinner every Thursday to Monday; the somewhat more formal restaurant is open only for dinner, every Thursday to Sunday.

23 rue de la République, 30220 Aigues-Mortes. (☎ 04-66-53-66-56. Fax 04-66-53-69-61. 13 units. 100€–130€ ($130–$169) double; 150€–190€ ($195–$247) suite. AE, DC, MC, V. **Amenities:** 2 restaurants; bar; outdoor pool; limited room service; limited-mobility rooms. *In room:* A/C, TV, dataport, hair dryer.

Hôtel St-Louis   Though not grand in any way or as fine as Hôtel Les Templiers, this is the town's second-place choice for lodgings. An inn near place St-Louis, it offers small but comfortably furnished bedrooms, each with a tiled and compact bathroom.

Many locals come here to enjoy the regional meals served in the hotel's restaurant, L'Archére, your best bet for steak and fresh fish. The area, of course, is known for its beef, and this dining room (open to nonresidents) serves some of the most tender and juicy steaks in the area. It also has a good bounty of seafood brought in daily from the nearby coast. Chefs are skilled in the kitchen, turning out an array of the local favorites along with homemade desserts prepared fresh every day.

10 rue de l'Amiral-Courbet, 30220 Aigues-Mortes. (☎ 04-66-53-72-68. Fax 04-66-53-75-92. 22 units. 85€–110€ ($111–$143) double. AE, MC, V. Parking 12€ ($16). Closed Jan–Mar 7. **Amenities:** Restaurant; bar; limited room service; laundry service/dry cleaning; nonsmoking rooms. *In room:* TV, minibar.

WHERE TO DINE

Restaurant Les Arcades 🅐🅐 TRADITIONAL FRENCH   There's no contest: This is the area's finest dining choice. This restaurant has several formal sections with beamed ceilings or stone vaults. Almost as old as the nearby fortifications, the place is especially charming on sultry days, when the thick masonry keeps the interior cool. The good, reasonably priced food is likely to include warm oysters, fish soup, fried stuffed zucchini flowers, grilled beef steak from the Camargue, roasted monkfish in red-wine sauce, and grilled duckling. A typical local dish is minced bull steak from the local salt marshes, served with regional herb sauce.

The owner also rents nine large, comfortable rooms with air-conditioning and TVs. The double rate of 90€ to 110€ ($117–$143) includes breakfast.

⌒ *Fun Fact* **Birth of the American Cowboy**

Many historians believe that the first real cowboys of North America were *gardiens,* imported from the Camargue to Louisiana to tend the flocks of the New World.

Moments   A Day in the Life of a Camargue Cowboy

The Camargue, where the cowboys of France ride the range, is an alluvial plain inhabited by wild horses, fighting black bulls, roaming Gypsies, pink flamingos, lagoons, salt marshes, wetlands, and gluttonous mosquitoes. Explore the rugged terrain by boat, bike, horse, or jeep.

With the most fragile ecosystem in France, the Camargue has been a national park since 1970. It's known for its small white horses, whose ancestors were brought here by the Arabs long ago. They roam wild in the national park, guarded by cowboys, or *gardiens,* who wear large felt hats and carry long three-pronged sticks to prod the cattle. The cowboys live in thatched huts called *cabanes.* Ancestors of the *gardiens* may have been the first American cowboys, who sailed on French ships to the port of New Orleans, where they rode the bayous of Louisiana and East Texas, rounding up cattle—in French, no less.

There's no more evocative sight than the proud snow-white horses running at liberty through the marshlands, with hoofs so tough that they don't need shoes. It is said that their long manes and busy tails evolved over the centuries to slap those pesky mosquitoes.

Exotic flora and fauna abound where the delta of the Rhône River empties into the Mediterranean. The bird life is the most luxuriant in Europe. The area, which resembles the Florida Everglades, is known for its colonies of pink flamingos *(flamants roses).* They share living quarters with some 400 other bird species, including ibises, egrets, kingfishers, owls, wild ducks, swans, and ferocious birds of prey. The best place to see flamingo colonies is the area around Ginès, a hamlet on N570, 5km (3 miles) north of Camargue's capital, Stes-Maries-de-la-Mer.

Exploring the Camargue is best undertaken on the back of a *camarguais* horse. The steeds can take you into the interior, which you couldn't see otherwise, fording waters to places where the black bulls graze and wild birds nest. You'll find two to three dozen stables (depending on the time of year) along the highway from Arles to Stes-Maries. Virtually all of them charge the same daily rate, 80€ ($104) or 12€ ($16) per hour, including a picnic lunch. The rides are aimed at the neophyte, not the champion equestrian. They're so easy that they're recommended even for those who have never been on a horse before.

23 bd. Gambetta, 30220 Aigues-Mortes. © **04-66-53-81-13.** Reservations recommended. Main courses 8€–28€ ($10–$36); fixed-price menu 32€–42€ ($42–$55). AE, DC, MC, V. Wed–Sun noon–2pm; Tues–Sun 7:30–10pm. Closed 2 weeks in Mar and 2 weeks in Oct.

A SIDE TRIP FROM AIGUES-MORTES
LES GARDIENS OF THE CAMARGUE 𝄞

Steamy, sweaty, and as flat as the plains of Nebraska, the marshy delta of the Rhône has been called a less fertile version of the Nile delta. The waterlogged flatlands encompassing the Grand and Petit Rhône were scorned by conventional farmers throughout the centuries because of their high salt content and root-rotting murk.

However, the area was considered a fit grazing ground for the local black-pelted longhorn cattle, so a breed of cowpokes and cowboys evolved on these surreal flat-lands, whose traditions will make you think of Dodge City combined with primal hints of ancient Celtic lore. These French cowboys, caretakers of the cattle that survive amid the flamingos, ticks, hawks, snakes, and mosquitoes of the hot, salty wet-lands, are known and loved by schoolchildren as *les gardiens.*

The tradition of *les gardiens* originated in the 1600s, when local monasteries began to disintegrate and large tracts of cheap land were bought by private owners. Wearing their traditional garb of leather pants and wide-rimmed black hats, the *gardiens* present a fascinating picture as they ride through the marshlands on their sturdy horses. Their terrain isn't the romantic wide, open space of America's West, but consists instead of monotonous stretches whose highest point might be a mound of debris left from a medieval salt flat. The *gardiens* tend not to be overly communicative to out-siders; in speaking to one another, they use a clipped, telegraphic form of Provençal whose syntax would make members of the Académie Française shudder. Motor homes and caravans are beginning to appear in the area today, but once *les gardiens* lived in distinctive, single-story *cabanes* with thatched roofs and without windows. Bull's horns were positioned above each building's entrance as a means of driving away evil spirits.

An ally in the business of tending cattle is the strong, heavy-tailed Camargue horse, probably a descendant of Arabian stallions brought here by Moorish invaders after the collapse of the Roman Empire. Brown or black at birth, these horses develop a white coat, usually after their fourth year. Traditionally, they had no sheltered sta-bles but were left to fend for themselves during the stifling summers and bone-chill-ing winters.

Today, in the world of modern tourism, the *gardiens* have become living symbols of an antique tradition that hasn't changed much—the cattle still run semiwild, identi-fied by the brand of their *manadier,* or owner. However, today you can expect to see fewer *gardiens* than in the past. They seem willing to participate in tourism only up to a point. Many reminders of their traditions remain in the form of felt-sided cowboy hats as well as commemorative saddles and boots whose style resembles that of cowherds on the faraway plains of Spain.

11 Montpellier ★★

758km (471 miles) SW of Paris; 161km (100 miles) NW of Marseille; 50km (31 miles) SW of Nîmes

The capital of Mediterranean (or Lower) Languedoc, the ancient university city of Montpellier is renowned for its medical school, founded in the 13th century. Nos-tradamus qualified as a doctor here, and Rabelais studied at the school. Petrarch came to Montpellier in 1317 and stayed for 7 years.

Today Montpellier is a bustling metropolis with a population of 380,000, one of southern France's fastest-growing cities, thanks to an influx of new immigrants. Although some suburbs are dreary, the city has a handsome core, with tree-flanked promenades, broad avenues, and historic monuments. Students make up a quarter of the population, giving the city a lively feel. In recent years, many high-tech corpora-tions, including IBM, have opened offices in Montpellier.

ESSENTIALS

GETTING THERE   Some 20 **trains** per day arrive from Avignon (trip time: 1 hr.), eight from Marseille (trip time: 45 min.), every 2 hours from Toulouse (trip time: 2 hr.), and 10 per day from Perpignan (trip time: 1½ hr.). Trains arrive hourly from Paris's Gare de Lyon, taking 8 to 10 hours, depending on the train, and usually requiring a change of equipment in Lyon. One TGV (high speed train) arrives daily from Paris, taking less than 4 hours. The one-way fare is 86€ ($112). For rail information, call ℭ **08-92-35-35-35.** Two **buses** a day arrive from Nîmes (trip time: 1¾ hr.; one-way fare: 14€/$18).

If you're **driving,** Montpellier lies off A9.

VISITOR INFORMATION   The **Office de Tourisme** is at 13 rue de la République (ℭ **04-67-60-60-60;** www.ot-montpellier.fr).

SPECIAL EVENTS   From late June to early July, classical and modern dancers leap into town for the **Festival International Montpellier Danse.** Tickets for performances cost 10€ to 55€ ($13–$72) and can be purchased through the box office, **Montpellierdanse,** 18 rue Ste-Ursule (ℭ **08-00-60-07-40** or 04-67-60-83-60). In late July, the **Festival de Radio France et de Montpellier** presents orchestral music, jazz, and opera. Tickets run 9€ to 38€ ($12–$49); call ℭ **04-67-02-02-01** or contact the **Théâtre Le Corum,** esplanade Charles de Gaulle (ℭ **04-67-61-67-61**).

EXPLORING THE TOWN

Called the Oxford of France because of its academic community, Montpellier is a city of young people, as you'll notice if you sit at one of the cafes on the heartbeat **place de la Comédie,** with its 18th-century Fountain of the Three Graces. It's the living room of Montpellier, the ideal place to chat, people-watch, or cruise.

Paul Valéry met André Gide in the **Jardin des Plantes,** 163 rue Auguste Broussonnet (ℭ **04-67-63-43-22**), and you might begin here, as it's the oldest such garden in France. It's reached from boulevard Henri-IV. This botanical garden, filled with exotic plants and a handful of greenhouses, was opened in 1593. Admission is free. It's open April through September, Tuesday through Sunday from noon to 8pm, and October through March, Tuesday to Sunday from noon to 5pm.

The town's greatest attraction is **Musée Fabre** 🟊🟊, 2 rue Montpellieret (ℭ **04-67-14-83-00**), which was closed for 2005 for extensive renovations and enlargements,

---

⟮*Moments* Oenophilia

If bending an elbow while holding a glass of wine is, in your opinion, a sport, consider a wine-lover's tour of one of the architectural oddities of Montpellier's wine district. Take a half-day exploration of the cellars and vineyards of the 18th-century **Château de Flaugergues,** in the hamlet of Flaugergues (ℭ **04-99-52-66-37;** www.flaugergues.com). Positioned within a 10-minute drive east of Montpellier, on the road leading to the seacoast, it accepts visitors who appreciate the nuances of the region's rough-and-ready reds, rosés, and whites. Appointments should be made in advance for visits that are usually scheduled any afternoon between 2:30 and 6:30pm. The castle's elaborate architecture is viewed by locals as one of the local *folies* (follies) of the region.

with a reopening announced for the summer of 2006. One of France's great provincial art galleries, it occupies the former Hôtel Massilian, where Molière once played for a season. The collection originated when Napoleon sent Montpellier an exhibition of the Royal Academy in 1803. François Fabre, a Montpellier painter, contributed its most important works in 1825. After Fabre's death, other paintings from his collection were donated to the gallery. Several were his own creations, but the more significant works were ones he had acquired—including Poussin's *Venus and Adonis,* plus Italian paintings like *The Mystical Marriage of Saint Catherine.* The museum continued to grow through other donations, notably in 1836 with a collection of Rubens, Gérard Dou, and Téniers. Admission is 5.50€ ($7.15) for adults and 2.50€ ($3.25) for students and youths ages 7 to 20. Free for children 6 and under. Open Tuesday to Friday 9:30am to 5:30pm, Saturday and Sunday 9:30am to 5pm.

Nearby is the town's spiritual centerpiece, the **Cathédrale St-Pierre,** on place St-Pierre (© **04-67-66-04-12**), founded in 1364. This is hardly one of the grand cathedrals of France, and it suffered badly in centuries of religious wars and revolutions. For a long time after 1795, it wasn't a cathedral at all, but was occupied by a medical school. Today the cathedral lacks pretension; its greatest architectural achievement is its unusual canopied porch, supported by two conical turrets. The best artworks inside are 17th-century canvasses in the transepts—notably the work of a Huguenot, Montpellier-born Sébastien Bourdon, who painted himself among the "heathen" in *The Fall of Simon Magnus.* Also moving is Jean Troy's *Healing of the Paralytic.* The church can be visited daily from 9am to noon and 2 to 7pm.

Before leaving town, take a stroll along the 17th-century **promenade du Peyrou** ★★, a terraced park with views of the Cévennes and the Mediterranean. This is a broad esplanade constructed at the loftiest point of Montpellier. Opposite the entrance is an Arc de Triomphe, erected in 1691 to celebrate the victories of Louis XIV. In the center of the promenade is an equestrian statue of Louis XIV and, at the end, the **Château d'Eau,** a pavilion with Corinthian columns that serves as a monument to 18th-century classicism. Water is brought here by a conduit, nearly 14km (9 miles long), and an aqueduct.

SHOPPING

Stroll down **place de la Comédie,** with its ultramodern Polygone shopping center, site of more than 120 independent boutiques, and **rue Jean-Moulin.** This town has a plethora of name-brand boutiques and department stores. For traditional regional delicacies, visit **Au Gourmets,** 2 rue Clos-René (© **04-67-58-57-04**), or visit **Pâtissier Schoeller,** 121 av. de l'Odàve (© **04-67-75-71-55**), for a plentiful supply of Ecusson de Montpellier (a chocolate praline with Grand Marnier wrapped in chocolate).

WHERE TO STAY

Note that **Le Jardin des Sens** (see "Where to Dine," below) also rents rooms.

IN MONTPELLIER
Expensive
Holiday Inn Montpellier ★   In the heart of Montpellier, this 1898 monument adjacent to the town's railway station stands behind an entrance with a soaring portal set into a dignified stone facade. It has undergone a radical renovation that retained the charming interior garden and the original detailing. The well-furnished, contemporary-looking bedrooms range in size from medium to spacious and are fitted with fine linens; the marble-sheathed bathrooms are roomy.

Finds **Exploring the Port Town of Séte**

Séte, reached after a 34km (21-mile) drive southwest of Montpellier, boasts the largest fishing port on the Mediterranean and was once the principal link to France's colonies in North Africa. Even today a car-ferry transports passengers to and from the coasts of North Africa. You can almost picture Marlene Dietrich leaving the port bound for Morocco in a 1930s movie.

In an architectural blend of Art Deco and Second Empire, Séte was built on a limestone rock on the slopes of Mont Saint-Clair and is connected to the mainland by two sand pits. This city of canals sprawls across two islands and a network of estuaries connected and crisscrossed by bridges. These canals evoke comparison with Venice.

If you're staying over and want to dine, your best bet is **Le Grand Hôtel,** 17 quai Maréchal de Lattre de Tassigny (© **04-67-74-71-77;** fax 04-67-74-29-27), at the center of the port, near the intersection of the two canals. Try for a front bedroom with its view of the moored boats. The limestone facade of the hotel is accented with elaborate corbels and bas-reliefs, some of which are designed like the prows of boats. The hotel's grandeur dates from the 1880s, with potted palms, a skylit atrium, and wickered armchairs. Today the place still retains much of its original beaux arts charm, and the bedrooms are generally roomy, well furnished, and modernized. Rooms are air-conditioned, containing minibars, and TVs. Doubles rent for 125€ ($163).

At the same address is the restaurant **La Quai 17** (© **04-67-74-71-77**), which takes up two impressive ground-floor rooms of the hotel and is under separate management. The chef specializes in seafood, as would be predicted, and dishes are fresh and full of flavor. The restaurant is open for lunch Monday, Tuesday, Thursday, and Friday from noon to 2pm, and dinner Monday through Saturday from 7:30 to 10pm. Full meals range in price from 27€ to 58€ ($35–$75); reservations are recommended.

For information about Séte and the area, stop in at the **Office de Tourisme,** 60 Grand'Rue (© **04-67-74-71**). Trains arrive every hour during the day from Montpellier (trip time: 20 min.), at a one-way fare of 5.50€ ($7.15).

3 rue Clos-Rene, 34000 Montpellier. © **04-67-12-32-32.** Fax 04-67-92-13-02. www.holiday-inn.com. 80 units. 170€ ($221) double; 230€ ($299) suite. AE, DC, MC, V. Parking 8€ ($10). **Amenities:** Restaurant; bar; fitness center; limited room service; laundry service/dry cleaning. *In room:* A/C, TV, fridge, coffeemaker, hair dryer, iron, trouser press.

Sofitel Antigone ⓡ In the heart of Montpellier, this angular, modern, glass-sheathed hotel is the number-one hotel for comfort and first-class amenities. In summer, it does quite a trade with visitors. A particularly appealing feature is the pool which, along with a bar and breakfast room, occupies most of the top floor. The rooms are chain format but first class. The Antigone is a winning choice, with the most efficient staff in the city. The bar is one of the coziest hideaways in town.

1 rue des Pertuisanes, 3400 Montpellier. © **04-67-99-72-72.** Fax 04-67-65-17-50. www.sofitel.com. 89 units. 190€–230€ ($247–$299) double; 420€ ($546) suite. AE, DC, MC, V. Parking 3€–7€ ($3.90–$9.10). **Amenities:** Restaurant; bar; outdoor pool; fitness center; Jacuzzi; sauna; limited room service; laundry service; dry cleaning; non-smoking rooms; limited-mobility rooms. *In room:* A/C, TV, dataport, hair dryer, safe.

Moderate

Hôtel du Palais ⟨⋆⟩ ⟨Value⟩   This hotel in the heart of a neighborhood loaded with antique dealers is one of the best bargains in town. Built in the late 18th century, Hôtel du Palais is in the center of Montpellier, amid a labyrinth of narrow streets and monumental plazas and parks. Much of the decor dates from around 1983, when the hotel was richly restored in a style that uses lots of fabrics, big curtains, and faux marble finishes on walls of public areas. Subsequent renovations, including most of the bathrooms in 2004 and 2005, have kept the property up-to-date. The guest rooms are relatively large and appealing, thanks to thoughtful placement of antique reproductions and good maintenance. Each has a neatly tiled bathroom with shower. Breakfast is the only meal served.

3 rue du Palais, 34000 Montpellier. ⟨℃⟩ **04-67-60-47-38.** Fax 04-67-60-40-23. 26 units. 61€–84€ ($79–$109) double. MC, V. Parking 5.50€ ($7.15). **Amenities:** Limited room service. *In room:* A/C, TV, dataport, minibar, hair dryer.

Hôtel du Parc ⟨⋆⟩ ⟨Finds⟩   One of the town's more charming moderately priced hostelries, this cozy hotel lies in the heart of the city near the Palais des Congrès. It was a Languedocian residence in the 18th century but has been turned into a hotel with a lot of grace notes and French provincial charm. Rooms have been carefully decorated and are accompanied by streamlined bathrooms. A garden and flowering terrace are available for breakfast outside. Numerous restaurants surround the hotel.

8 rue Achille-Bégé, 34090 Montpellier. ⟨℃⟩ **04-67-41-16-49.** Fax 04-67-54-10-05. www.hotelduparc-montpellier. com. 19 units. 45€–69€ ($59–$90) double. AE, MC, V. Free parking. **Amenities:** Breakfast room; lounge; limited room service. *In room:* A/C, TV, minibar, hair dryer.

La Maison Blanche ⟨⋆⋆⟩   This hotel seems to have worked hard to create a French Creole ambience: It's set in a modern clapboard motel whose balconies drip with ornate gingerbread and whose verdant gardens are bordered with lattices. The rooms are stylishly furnished in rattan and wicker and offer comfortable beds. Parts of the interior, especially the dining room, might remind you more of the France of Louis XIII than Old Louisiana, but overall the place is charming and unusual. The hotel is a 5-minute drive northeast of Montpellier's center.

1796 av. de la Pompignane, 34000 Montpellier. ⟨℃⟩ **04-99-58-20-70.** Fax 04-67-79-53-39. www.hotel-maison-blanche. com. 38 units. 81€ ($105) double; 138€ ($179) suite. AE, DC, MC, V. Free parking. Take bd. d'Antigone east until you reach the intersection with av. de la Pompignane, and head north until you see the hotel on your right. **Amenities:** Restaurant; bar; outdoor pool; limited room service. *In room:* A/C, TV, dataport, hair dryer.

Le Guilhem   Contained within a pair of interconnected stone-fronted 16th-century town houses, which needed to be almost completely rebuilt when the hotel was established in the 1950s, this is a well-managed hideaway with lots of southern (French) charm. Guests enjoy the tastefully antique-looking lobby area, a polite staff, and conservatively contemporary bedrooms outfitted in monochromatic tones of mostly yellow or blue or, to a lesser degree, pink. Many overlook the well-established trees of a substantial garden, and many contain the quirky angles and idiosyncratic dimensions of the building's original designs. Bathrooms have tub/shower combos. Other than breakfast, no meals are served, but considering the hotel's location near l'Arc de Triomphe, in Montpellier's historic core, there are many dining options nearby.

18 rue Jean-Jacques Rousseau, 34000 Montpellier. ⟨℃⟩ **04-67-52-90-90.** Fax 04-67-60-67-67. www.leguilhem.com. 36 units. 82€–152€ ($107–$198) double. AE, DC, MC, V. Parking 5€ ($6.50). **Amenities:** 24-hr. room service (drinks and snacks only); babysitting; laundry service. *In room:* A/C, TV, dataport, minibar, hair dryer.

Inexpensive

Hôtel Ulysse ✦ *Value*   One of the city's better bargains, and built in 1993, Ulysse delivers a lot of bang for your euro. The owners have worked hard to make the simple hotel as stylish as possible. Each room is uniquely decorated. The furnishings are in an original wrought-iron design, functional but with flair. The comfortable rooms have fully equipped tub/shower bathrooms. The hotel lies within a 15-minute walk south of Montpellier's center, close to the edge of the sea.

338 av. de St-Maur, 34000 Montpellier. © **04-67-02-02-30.** Fax 04-67-02-16-50. www.hotelulysse.com. 23 units. 61€ ($79) double. AE, DC, MC, V. Free parking. Tram: 1 (Le Mosson line) to Corum. From bd. d'Antigone, go north on av. Jean-Mermoz to rue de la Pépinière; continue right and make a left at the 1st intersection, which leads to av. de St-Maur or bus 8 direction Mas de Rochet. **Amenities:** Limited room service; limited-mobility rooms. *In room:* TV, dataport, minibar, hair dryer.

Les Arceaux   It's basic but still most acceptable, and the price is right. A hotel has stood at this prime location, right off the promenade du Peyrou, since the late 1800s. The smallish rooms are simply but pleasantly furnished, each renovated in 2005, each in a different color, and each compact bathroom has a shower unit. At the on-site bar, simple platters are served, overflowing into a summer garden. What you get is a "bar-bistro platter," but this is not a full-fledged restaurant. A shaded terrace adjoins the hotel.

33–35 bd. des Arceaux, 34000 Montpellier. © **04-67-92-03-03.** Fax 04-67-92-05-09. www.hoteldesarceaux.com. 18 units. 75€–90€ ($98–$117) double. AE, MC, V. Parking 3€ ($3.90) in nearby lot. **Amenities:** Bar; limited room service; nonsmoking rooms. *In room:* A/C in some, TV, dataport, minibar.

NEAR MONTPELLIER

Demeure des Brousses ✦✦ *Finds*   This 18th-century country house stands in a large, impressive park. The house was built by Monsieur and Madame Brousse, who made their fortune as *épiciers*, or spice merchants. A tranquil choice, it has been skillfully converted for guests. Rooms range from medium-size to spacious, each individually decorated in such 19th-century styles as French Empire. Public rooms are decorated like those of a gracious French country house, including loads of antiques, making this an intimate retreat. It's about a 10-minute drive from the heart of Montpellier.

Route de Vauguières, 34000 Montpellier. © **04-67-65-77-66.** Fax 04-67-22-22-17. www.demeure-des-brousses.com. 17 units. 85€–115€ ($111–$150) double. AE, DC, MC, V. Free parking. Take D-172E 2 miles east of the town center. **Amenities:** Restaurant; bar; limited room service; laundry service/dry cleaning. *In room:* AC, TV, hair dryer.

WHERE TO DINE
EXPENSIVE

Le Jardin des Sens ✦✦✦ FRENCH   This is one of the great restaurants of southern France, with three Michelin stars. The chefs, twins Laurent and Jacques Pourcel, have taken Montpellier by storm, and their cuisine could involve almost anything, depending on where their imaginations roam. The rich bounty of Languedoc goes through a process designed to enhance its natural flavor. A starter might be ravioli stuffed with foie gras of duckling and flap mushrooms, floating in chicken bouillon fortified with truffles, broad beans, and crispy potatoes. Main courses of note are shelled lobster, pressed flat and served with duck meat and vanilla oil; filet of dorado grilled with sesame and served with a marmalade of tomatoes, olives, and caramelized balsamic vinegar; and filet of pigeon stuffed with pistachios. A dessert specialty is gratin of limes with slices of pineapple *en confit*.

My, what an inefficient way to fish.

Ring toss, good. Horseshoes, bad.

Faster! Faster! Faster!

We take care of the fiddly bits, from providing over 43,000 customer reviews of hotels, to helping you find our best fares, to giving you 24/7 customer service. So you can focus on the only thing that matters. Goofing off.

travelocity
You'll never roam alone.

Frommers.com

So many places,
so little time?

TOKYO 7766 miles
LONDON 3818 miles
TORONTO 4682 miles
SYDNEY 5087 miles
NEW YORK 4947 miles
LOS ANGELES 2556 miles
HONG KONG 5638 miles

Frommers.com makes the going fast and easy.
Find a destination. ✓ Buy a guidebook. ✓ Book a trip. ✓ Get hot travel deals.
Enter to win vacations. ✓ Check out the latest travel news.
Share trip photos and memories. ✓ And much more.

Frommers.com
Rated #1 Travel Web Site by PC Magazine®

Le Jardin des Sens also rents 12 guest rooms, plus two suites, each designed in cutting-edge style by Bruno Borrione, a colleague of Philippe Starck. They cost 160€ to 225€ ($208–$293) for a double, 270€ to 400€ ($351–$520) for a suite.

11 av. St-Lazare. ℂ 04-99-58-38-38. Fax 04-99-58-38-39. www.jardindessens.com. Reservations required. Main courses 39€–51€ ($45–$59); fixed-price menu 46€ ($53) lunch Thurs–Fri, 110€–170€ ($127–$196) dinner. AE, MC, V. Thurs–Sat noon–2pm; Tues–Sat 7:30–10pm.

MODERATE

Compagnie des Comptoirs INTERNATIONAL   Set within a 5-minute walk east of the town center, and lodged behind a set of massive doors that were intricately sculpted by artisans in Morocco, this restaurant manages to evoke the aesthetic and the sense of internationalism of the late 19th-century French colonies in, say, India, North Africa, or Indochina. There's room inside for about 130 diners; a big outdoor terrace with flowering shrubs and a splashing fountain; and an ongoing emphasis on the kind of sunny, flavorful, and pungent cuisine you're likely to find around the edges of the Mediterranean. The best examples include a succulent version of tempura of crayfish; accras (beignets) of crab; grilled calamari with a confit of lemon; grilled steak from bulls of the Camargue, served with red-wine sauce; and a winning collection of desserts.

51 av. François Delmas. ℂ 04-99-58-39-29. Reservations recommended. Main courses 10€–25€ ($13–$33). AE, DC, MC, V. Daily noon–2:30pm and 8–11:30pm.

L'Olivier ⭐⭐ *Finds* MODERN FRENCH   This charming restaurant's cuisine is so satisfying that we consider it the finest in Montpellier outside the luxe Jardin des Sens. Chef Michel Breton, assisted by his charming wife, Yvette, cooks to perfection. The establishment seats only 20, in a subdued and rather bland modern space accented only by contemporary paintings. But you don't come to L'Olivier to look at the walls. You come for Breton's salmon with a tartare of oysters, warm monkfish terrine, roasted filet of lamb with sweetbread-studded macaroni, and haunch of rabbit stuffed with wild mushrooms. The welcome is warm and sincere.

12 rue Aristide-Olivier. ℂ 04-67-92-86-28. Reservations required. Main courses 25€–32€ ($33–$42); fixed-price menu 30€–45€ ($39–$59). AE, MC, V. Tues–Sat noon–2pm and 7:30–9:30pm. Closed Aug and holidays.

MONTPELLIER AFTER DARK

After the sun sets, head for **place Jean-Jaurès, rue de Verdun,** and **rue des Ecoles Laïques,** or walk down **rue de la Loge** and soak up its carnival atmosphere, watching talented jugglers, mimes, and musicians.

Rockstore, 20 rue de Verdun (ℂ 04-67-06-80-00), draws lots of students with 1950s rock memorabilia and live concerts. Up a flight of stairs is its disco, which pounds out techno and rock. There is no cover. For the best jazz and blues in town, check out **JAM,** 100 rue Ferdinand-de-Lesseps (ℂ 04-67-58-30-30). In a noisy, smoky, and even gritty space, its regular concerts attract jazz enthusiasts from miles around. Concert tickets average 15€ to 20€ ($20–$26).

A modern, noisy, convivial disco, known throughout the region, is **Le Pacha,** route de Carnon, in the hamlet of Lattes (ℂ 04-99-52-97-06) 4km (2½ miles) south of Montpellier. It attracts drinkers and dancers aged 23 to 40. Le Pacha is open Thursday through Sunday beginning around 10:30pm; on Friday and Saturday it charges a 10€ ($13) cover, which includes one drink. Gays and lesbians gather at the town's most animated bar and disco, **La Villa Rouge,** route de Palavas (ℂ 04-67-06-50-54), also in Lattes. **Le Corum** (ℂ 04-67-61-67-61), the most up-to-date theater in town, books many plays, dance recitals, operas, and symphonic presentations. It's in the Palais des Congrès, esplanade Charles-de-Gaulle. For ticket information and schedules, contact the Corum or the **Opéra Comédie,** place de la Comédie (℃ **04-67-60-19-99**).

12 Nîmes ★★★

708km (440 miles) S of Paris; 43km (27 miles) W of Avignon

Nîmes, the ancient Nemausus, is a great place to view some of the world's finest Roman remains. The city grew to prominence during the reign of Caesar Augustus (27 B.C.–A.D. 14). Today it possesses one of the best preserved Roman amphitheaters in the world and a near-perfect Roman temple. The city of 135,000 is more like Provence than Languedoc, and there's a touch of Pamplona (Spain) here in the festivals of the *corridas* (bullfights) at the arena. The Spanish image is even stronger at night, when the bodegas fill, usually with students drinking sangria and listening to the sounds of flamenco.

ESSENTIALS

GETTING THERE   Nîmes has bus and train service from the rest of France and is near several autoroutes. It lies on the main **rail** line between Marseille and Bordeaux. Nine TGV trains arrive daily from Paris's Gare de Lyon; the one-way fare is 82€ ($107). For train information and schedules, call ℃ **08-92-35-35-35**. If you're **driving,** take A7 south from Lyon to the town of Orange and connect to A9 into Nîmes.

VISITOR INFORMATION   The **Office de Tourisme** is at 6 rue Auguste (℃ **04-66-58-38-00;** www.ot-nimes.fr).

EXPLORING THE CITY
THE TOP SIGHTS
Amphithéâtre Romain ★★★   The elliptically shaped amphitheater is a better-preserved twin of the one at Arles and is far more complete than the Colosseum of Rome. It's two stories high, each floor having 60 arches, and was built of huge stones painstakingly fitted together without mortar. One of the best preserved arenas from ancient times, it once held more than 20,000 spectators, who came to see gladiatorial combats and wolf or boar hunts. Today it's used for everything from ballet recitals to bullfights.

Place des Arènes. ℃ **04-66-76-72-77.** Admission 4.45€ adults, 3.20€ students and children 15 and under. Apr–Oct daily 9am–6:30pm; Nov–Mar daily 9am–5:30pm.

Carrée d'Art/Musée d'Art Contemporain   Across the square stands the modern-day twin of the Maison Carrée, a sophisticated research center and exhibition space that contains a library, a newspaper kiosk, and an art museum. Its understated design

---

Fun Fact Denim de Nîmes

By 1860, the togas of Nîmes's citizenry had given way to denim, the cloth de Nîmes. An Austrian immigrant, Leví-Strauss, started to export this heavy fabric to California for use as material to make work pants for gold diggers in those boomtown years. The rest, as they say, is history.

Nîmes

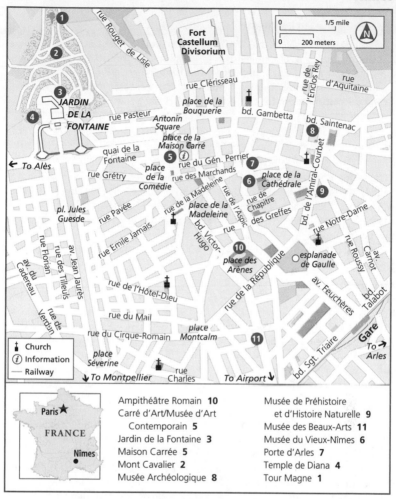

Ampithéâtre Romain **10**
Carré d'Art/Musée d'Art
   Contemporain **5**
Jardin de la Fontaine **3**
Maison Carrée **5**
Mont Cavalier **2**
Musée Archéologique **8**

Musée de Préhistoire
   et d'Histoire Naturelle **9**
Musée des Beaux-Arts **11**
Musée du Vieux-Nîmes **6**
Porte d'Arles **7**
Temple de Diana **4**
Tour Magne **1**

from 1993 was inspired by (but doesn't overpower) the ancient monument nearby. The museum's permanent expositions are often supplemented with temporary exhibits of contemporary art. ***Note:*** The view from this modern building's terrace allows you to rise above the roaring traffic and presents a panorama of ancient monuments and medieval churches.

Place de la Maison Carrée. ℭ **04-66-76-35-35.** Admission 4.65€ ($6.05) adults, 3.40€ ($4.40) students and children under 15. Free the 1st Sun of each month. Tues–Sun 10am–6pm.

Maison Carrée ✹✹✹   The pride of Nîmes, this is one of the most beautiful, and certainly one of the best preserved, Roman temples of Europe. It was built during the reign of Caesar Augustus. Set on a raised platform with tall Corinthian columns, it inspired Thomas Jefferson as well as the builders of La Madeleine in Paris. A changing roster of cultural and art exhibits is presented.

Tips   Your Lucky Ticket

If you want to see all of the city's monuments and museums, consider buying a **billet global** (Forfait Monuments & Musées), sold at the ticket counter of any of the local attractions. It provides access for a 3-day period to all the cultural sites described below. The fee is 10€ ($13) for adults, 5€ ($6.50) for students and children 10 to 15, free for children under 10.

Place de la Comédie. ℂ **04-66-36-26-76.** Free admission. Mid-Oct to mid-Mar daily 10am–5pm; mid-Mar to mid-Oct daily 9am–7pm.

Musée des Beaux-Arts   The city's largest museum contains French paintings and sculptures from the 17th to the 20th centuries, as well as Flemish, Dutch, and Italian works from the 15th to the 18th centuries. Seek out in particular one of G. B. Moroni's masterpieces, *La Calomnie d'Apelle,* and a well-preserved Gallo-Roman mosaic.

Rue Cité-Foulc. ℂ **04-66-67-38-21.** Admission 4.65€ ($6.05) adults, 3.40€ ($4.40) students and children under 17. Tues–Sun 10am–6pm.

MORE SIGHTS

One of the most beautiful gardens in France, **Jardin de la Fontaine** ⚜⚜, at the end of quai de la Fontaine, was laid out in the 18th century, using the ruins of a Roman shrine as a centerpiece. It was planted with rows of chestnuts and elms, adorned with statuary and urns, and intersected by grottoes and canals. The garden is open from April to mid-September daily from 7am to 10pm; from mid-September to March, daily from 7am to 6:30pm. Within the garden are the ruined **Temple of Diane** ⚜ and the remains of some Roman baths. Over the park, within a 10-minute walk north of the town center, is **Mont Cavalier,** a low, rocky hill on top of which rises the sturdy bulk of the **Tour Magne** ⚜, the city's oldest Roman monument. You can climb it for 2.50€ ($3.25) for adults, 2€ ($2.60) for students and children under 15. From April to October it is open daily from 10am to 7pm; November through March, daily from 10am to 5pm. It offers a panoramic view over Nîmes and its environs.

Nîmes is home to a great number of museums. If time allows, visit the **Musée du Vieux-Nîmes,** place aux Herbes (ℂ **04-66-76-73-70**), housed in an Episcopal palace from the 1700s. It's rich in antiques and antique porcelain and workday objects from the 18th and 19th century. Admission is free. Hours are Tuesday to Sunday from 10am to 6pm.

One of the city's busiest thoroughfares, **boulevard de l'Amiral-Courbet,** leads to the **Porte d'Auguste** (Porte d'Arles)—the remains of a gate built by the Romans during the reign of Augustus. About 45m (150 ft.) to the south are the **Musée de Préhistoire et d'Histoire Naturelle** (ℂ **04-66-76-73-45**) and the **Musée Archéologique** ⚜ (ℂ **04-66-76-74-80**), in the same building at 13 bis bd. l'Amiral-Courbet. Admission is free. Hours are Tuesday through Sunday from 10am to 6pm.

A FAMOUS ROMAN BRIDGE

Outside the city, 23km (14 miles) northeast, the **pont du Gard** ⚜ spans the Gard River; its huge stones, fitted together without mortar, stand as one of the region's most vivid reminders of ancient glory. Consisting of three tiers of arches arranged into graceful symmetrical patterns, it dates from about 19 B.C. Frédéric Mistral, national poet of Provence and Languedoc, recorded a legend alleging that the devil constructed the bridge with the promise that he could claim the soul of the first person to cross it. To visit it, take highway N86 from Nîmes to a point 3km (2 miles) from the village of Remoulins, where signs are posted.

The pont du Gard has a museum, **La Grande Expo du Pont du Gard,** B.P. 7, 30210 Vers Pont du Gard (© **04-66-37-50-99**). Four exhibits detail the bridge's construction, its function throughout the Middle Ages, and insights into its role as a symbol of the architectural savvy of ancient Rome. There's also a restaurant, cafe, and gift shop. It's open daily from May to September 9:30am to 7pm (until 6pm Feb–Apr and Oct; until 5:30pm Nov–Jan). The exposition opens every Monday at 1:30pm and closes at the hours noted, according to the season. It is closed the first three weeks in January. Admission is 10€ ($13) for adults, 9€ ($12) for persons under 25 and students.

SHOPPING

Head to the center of town and **rue du Général-Perrier, rue des Marchands, rue du Chapître,** and the pedestrian **rue de l'Aspic** and **rue de la Madeleine.** A Sunday market runs from 8am to around 1pm in the parking lot of the **Stade des Costières,** site of most of the town's football (soccer) matches, adjacent to the southern edge of the boulevard périphérique that encircles Nîmes.

To appease your sweet tooth, go to just about any pastry shop in town and ask for the regional almond-based cookies called *croquants villaret* and *caladons*. They're great for a burst of energy or for souvenirs. One of the best purchases you can make, especially if you're not continuing east into Provence, is a *santon*. These wood or clay figurines are sculpted into characters from Provençal country life and can be collected to create a unique country-French nativity scene. For a selection of *santons* in various sizes, visit the **Boutique Provençale,** 10 place de la Maison Carrée (© **04-66-67-81-71**).

WHERE TO STAY

EXPENSIVE

Imperator Concorde ★★   This chain hotel, the largest and finest in town, is adjacent to Les Jardins de la Fontaine—it's the one with the pale pink Italianate facade. In 2005, it underwent a major renovation that left it much improved. The artful and cozy good-size rooms have traditional or French furniture, with fluted or cabriole legs in one or another of the Louis styles. Each unit comes with a first-rate private bathroom with a tub/shower combination. You can order a meal in the hotel's verdant rear gardens or in a high-ceilinged dining room, L'Enclos de la Fontaine.

Quai de la Fontaine, 30900 Nîmes. © **04-66-21-90-30.** Fax 04-66-67-70-25. www.hotel-imperator.com. 62 units. 113€–207€ ($147–$269) double; 270€–326€ ($351–$424) suite. AE, DC, MC, V. Parking 13€ ($17). **Amenities:** Restaurant; bar; limited room service; babysitting; nonsmoking rooms. *In room:* A/C, TV, dataport, minibar, hair dryer, safe.

MODERATE

Hôtel Vatel ★   Built around 1990, the hotel lies 3km (2 miles) north of the town center, in a cluster of buildings that includes a university and a hospital. It's efficiently staffed with students from the local hotel school, who work here as part of their on-the-job training. The rooms are streamlined, tasteful, and modern, with terraces. Each comes with a midsize bathroom with a tub/shower combination. The modern establishment provides a level of comfort that older hotels, in more historic but limited settings, can't provide.

140 rue Vatel, B.P. 7128, 30913 Nîmes. ℂ **04-66-62-57-57.** Fax 04-66-62-57-50. 46 units. 97€ ($126) double; 185€ ($241) suite. AE, DC, MC, V. Free parking. From the A4 autoroute, exit at NÎMES OUEST. **Amenities:** 2 restaurants; bar; indoor pool; health club; sauna; limited room service; nonsmoking rooms; limited-mobility rooms. *In room:* A/C, TV, dataport, minibar, hair dryer, safe.

La Maison de Sophie

The big draw to "Sophie's House" is the on-site presence, like a kindly matriarch in charge of a house party, of Sophie Rigon and her husband, Yves. Another strong draw is its location in the heart of Nîmes, within a 5-minute proximity to the Arenas, where *"Olé!"* resounds as toreadors taunt bulls. The building is viewed by historians as an architectural gem: Built in 1901, and with public areas and bedrooms outfitted in furniture crafted in most cases between 1900 and 1930, it resembles a small but choice Venetian *palazzo,* replete with stained-glass and sometimes leaded windows and a scattering, in the entrance area, of marble columns. A lovely garden in back is loaded with old-species roses and irises, and an open-air swimming pool. The rooms aren't particularly luxurious, but each has a balcony and contains such basics as small bathrooms with showers. There's no restaurant on-site, but the Rigon family maintains a simple restaurant within a 10-minute walk from the hotel, Casa Bella, which is separately recommended in "Where to Dine," immediately below.

31 av. Carnot, 30000 Nîmes. ℂ **04-66-70-96-10.** Fax 04-66-36-00-47. www.hotel-lamaisondesophie.com. 5 units. 105€–290€ ($137–$377) double. AE, MC, V. **Amenities:** Breakfast room; outdoor pool; garden. *In room:* A/C, TV.

New Hôtel La Baume 🏵🏵

One of our favorite nests in Nîmes sits behind a facade of chiseled stone in the heart of the city's oldest section, within a 10-minute walk from the Roman arena and within a 5-minute walk from the Maison Carrée. Built in the 17th century as a private home, it's constructed around a spacious interior courtyard studded with flowering plants and accented with small tables and a magnificent stone staircase that's an architectural treasure in its own right. (Access to any bedroom is possible via elevator from the reception area, but frankly, it's a lot more glamorous to ascend the staircase instead.) Overall, the setting represents a winning combination of modern and traditional, with great attention paid to the preservation of the building's original architectural heritage. Each of the bedrooms is outfitted in a nostalgic Provençal style, each with a unique monochromatic color scheme (blues, greens, ochers, or soft oranges). Whereas the toilets within each unit are set within private enclosures (with doors), the tub/shower combination within each is partially open to view, allowing for stylish displays of nudity, which you, in a style that's very French, can enjoy with a companion.

21 rue Nationale, 30000 Nîmes. ℂ **04-66-76-28-42.** Fax 04-66-76-28-45. www.new-hotel.com. 34 units. 125€ ($163) double; 145€ ($189) junior suite. AE, DC, MC, V. Parking 7.60€ ($9.90). **Amenities:** Bar; limited room service; laundry service/dry cleaning; nonsmoking rooms; limited-mobility rooms. *In room:* A/C, TV, minibar, hair dryer, safe.

Novotel Atria Nîmes Centre

Opened in mid-1995, this cost-conscious member of a nationwide chain occupies a desirable site in the heart of Nîmes, adjacent to the ancient arena. Its six floors wrap around a carefully landscaped inner courtyard. Each room contains a double bed, a single bed (which converts into a sofa), a well-equipped bathroom, and a wide writing desk. All the rooms are renovated, although still in a rather sterile chain format.

5 bd. de Prague, 3000 Nîmes. ℂ **04-66-76-56-56.** Fax 04-66-76-56-59. www.accor-hotels.com. 119 units. 108€ ($140) double; 145€ ($189) suite. AE, DC, MC, V. Parking 8€ ($10). **Amenities:** Restaurant; bar; limited room service; laundry service/dry cleaning. *In room:* A/C, TV, minibar, dataport.

INEXPENSIVE

Hôtel de Milan   The three-story Hôtel de Milan is just across the street from the railway station and is especially convenient for Eurailpass holders on a tight budget. All rooms were just completely renovated in a basic Provençal style. They are a bit small but reasonably comfortable and a good value for the price; bathrooms, however, are cramped. The only meal served on the premises is breakfast, but the staff will direct you to several restaurants in the neighborhood.

17 av. Feuchères, 30000 Nîmes. ⓒ **04-66-29-29-90.** Fax 04-66-29-05-31. 33 units. 63€ ($82) double; 76€ ($99) triple. DC, MC, V. **Amenities:** Lounge; limited room service. *In room:* TV.

Hôtel l'Amphithéâtre *Value*   The core of this hotel dates from the 18th century, when it was built as a private home. A stay here involves trekking to your room up steep flights of creaking stairs and navigating a labyrinth of corridors. The small rooms are deliberately old-fashioned, usually containing antiques or antique reproductions and creaky, yet comfortable, beds. Most of the compact tiled bathrooms come with tub/shower combinations (four have shower only). The staff long ago grew jaded to the fact that the hotel is less than perfect, but at these prices, who's complaining?

4 rue des Arènes, 30000 Nîmes. ⓒ **04-66-67-28-51.** Fax 04-66-67-07-79. hotel-amphitheatre@wanadoo.fr. 15 units. 41€–51€ ($53–$66) double. MC, V. Parking 10€ ($13). Closed Jan 2–20. **Amenities:** Nonsmoking rooms. *In room:* TV.

WHERE TO DINE

The dining room at the **New Hôtel La Baume** (see above) is also a good choice.

EXPENSIVE

Alexandre (Michael Kayser) 🟆🟆🟆 TRADITIONAL FRENCH   The most charming restaurant around is on the outskirts of Nîmes, 8km (5 miles) south of the center. It's the elegantly rustic domain of Michel Kayser, who adheres to classic tradition, with subtle improvements. His wife, Monique, assists him in the ultra-modern dining room outfitted in tones of soft reds, ochers, and with gilded highlights. Menu items are designed to amuse as well as delight the palate: *île flottante*—a playful update of old-fashioned floating island, with truffles and velouté of cèpe mushrooms— roasted pigeon stuffed with vegetable purée and foie gras, tartare of oysters and shellfish with cardamom seeds, *"brandade de Nîmes"* (a regional version of brandade of codfish, elevated here to gourmet standards), and a filet of bull from the Camargue in red-wine sauce with Camarguais herbs. Especially appealing is the selection of goat cheeses from the region and worthy cheeses from other parts of France. The dessert trolley is incredibly hard to resist.

Rte. de l'Aéroport de Garons. ⓒ **04-66-70-08-99.** Reservations recommended. Main courses 28€–54€ ($36–$70); fixed-price menu 38€ ($49) lunch, 54€–87€ ($70–$113) dinner. AE, DC, MC, V. July–Aug Tues–Sat noon–1:30pm and 8–9:30pm; Sept–June Tues–Sun noon–1:30pm, Tues and Thurs–Sat 8–9:30pm. Closed 2 weeks in Feb. From town center, take rue de la République southwest to av. Jean-Jaurès; then head south and follow signs to the airport (toward Garons).

MODERATE

Casa Bella PROVENÇAL   It's less lavish and less stylish than the hotel (La Maison de Sophie, recommended separately in "Where to Stay," above) with which it is associated. But in spite of that, many locals, as well as many residents of the hotel, opt to dine here. The decor is simple and nostalgic, with a color scheme of pale pink and blue, and a gruff but friendly kind of charm. Cuisine is completely based on olive oil and traditional, time-tested dishes such as roasted shoulder of lamb cooked in a wood-burning oven and served with broad beans; various preparations of fish, including cod; and fresh salads.

6 place de la Révolution. ℂ **04-66-67-64-68.** Reservations recommended. Main courses 18€–22€ ($23–$29). AE, DC, MC, V. Tues–Sat 7–11pm.

Chez Jacotte PROVENÇAL   At least some of the charm of this restaurant derives from its setting on a narrow, traffic-free street in the old town, with outdoor tables overlooking a small, shaded, medieval-looking square. During harsher weather, opt for a table inside the ocher and russet-colored dining room, beneath crisscrossed ceiling vaults that were built, according to the charming owner, "in stages between the Middle Ages and the 18th century." Cuisine here is redolent with the flavors and perfumes of France's "Deep South" and is entirely based on very fresh ingredients and produce. Examples include several different variations of local lamb, usually roasted in its own juices and served with fresh vegetables; a rich and pungent version of *aïoli de morue* (codfish and garlic stew); crisp-skinned mullet in basil-flavored olive oil; goat cheese and fig gratin; and an old-fashioned version of *brandade de morue* (codfish) prepared in a style that many local residents remember from their childhoods.

15 rue Fresque (impasse). ℂ **04-66-21-64-59.** Reservations recommended. Fixed-price lunch menu 15€ ($20); main courses 13€–21€ ($17–$27). MC, V. Mon–Sat noon–2pm and 7–10pm.

Restaurant au Chapon Fin ALSATIAN/LANGUEDOCIENNE   This tavern-restaurant stands on a little square behind St. Paul's. It has beamed ceilings, small lamps, and a black-and-white stone floor. You'll have a choice of Alsatian and Langue-docienne specialties. From the a la carte menu you can order foie gras with truffles, casserole of roasted lamb and eggplant, beefsteak *péllardon* (with goat-cheese sauce), and brandade of codfish. New menu items include several kinds of Charolais beef-steak; a platter piled high with grilled sweetbreads and grilled veal kidneys; and several different variations of savory sauerkraut.

3 rue du Château-Fadaise. ℂ **04-66-67-34-73.** Reservations required. Main courses 16€ ($21); fixed-price menu 30€–45€ ($39–$59). MC, V. Mon–Fri noon–2pm; Mon–Sat 7:30–10pm (until 11pm on Fri and Sat).

Wine Bar Chez Michel *Value* TRADITIONAL FRENCH   This mahogany-pan-eled place has leather banquettes evocative of an early-1900s California saloon. Choices include an array of salads and platters. At lunch you can order a quick menu, including an appetizer, a garnished main course, and two glasses of wine. Typical dishes are magret of duckling and top-notch beefsteaks and fresh fish, usually grilled. You can also enjoy lunch on the terrace in the courtyard. A restaurateur extraordinaire, Michel Hermet makes his own wine at vineyards that have been associated with his family for many generations. More than 300 other varieties of wine are in stock, 15 of which are available by the glass or by the pitcher.

11 place de la Couronne. ℂ **04-66-76-19-59.** Main courses 8.50€–25€ ($10–$29); fixed-price menu 12€–21€ ($16–$27) lunch, 18€–22€ ($21–$25) dinner. AE, MC, V. Tues–Fri noon–2pm; Mon–Sat 7pm–midnight.

NIMES AFTER DARK

Once warm weather hits, all sorts of activities take place at the arena, including concerts and theater under the stars. The Office de Tourisme has a complete listing. For popular events like football (soccer), bullfights, and rock concerts, you can contact the **Bureau de Location des Arènes,** 4 rue de la Violette (ℂ **04-91-70-14-01**). Tickets for higher-brow events, such as symphonic or chamber-music concerts, theater, and opera performances, are sold through **Le Théâtre Municipal (Le Théâtre de Nîmes)**, 1 place de la Calade ((C) **04-66-36-65-00**).

If you like hanging out with students and soldiers, head to **Café Le Napoléon,** 46 bd. Victor-Hugo ((C) **04-66-67-20-23**). Popular with the intelligentsia is the **Haddock Cafe,** 13 rue de l'Agau ((C) **04-66-67-86-57**), which books weekly rock concerts.

The premier jazz venue in Nîmes is **Bar le Diagonale,** 41 bis rue Emile-Jamais ((C) **04-66-21-70-01**). Open nightly except Monday from 5:30pm till at least 2am, it offers a boozy, smoky, permissive environment where the live musicians derive from just about anywhere. Entrance is free.

Sexy, hip **La Comédie,** 28 rue Jean-Reboul ((C) **04-66-76-13-66**), is the hands-down best for dancing and attracts a pretty crowd of youthful danceaholics. A little less flashy but a lot more fun, **Lulu Club,** 10 impasse de la Curaterie ((C) **04-66-36-28-20**), is the gay and lesbian stronghold in Nîmes, but is a magnet for hip straight folk as well.

A youth-oriented contender is **Le C-Cafe,** 20 rue de l'Etoile ((C) **04-66-21-59-22**). Open Wednesday through Saturday at 11pm, it rocks and rolls to music from L.A. to London, with a youthful clientele.

Streets to explore on virtually any night of the week include **place de la Maison Carrée** and **boulevard Victor-Hugo.** From June to September, locals flock to the beach to patronize the shanty restaurants and bars. Bus no. 6 will take you to the **Plage de la Corniche** for nighttime partying.

5

Provence

Provence has been called a bridge between the past and the present, where yesterday blends with today in a quiet, often melancholy way. Peter Mayle's best-selling *A Year in Provence, Toujours Provence,* and *Encore Provence* have played no small part in the burgeoning popularity this sunny corner of southern France has enjoyed during recent years.

The Greeks and Romans filled the landscape with cities boasting Hellenic theaters, Roman baths, amphitheaters, and triumphal arches. These were followed in medieval times by Romanesque fortresses and Gothic cathedrals. In the 19th century,

Provence's light and landscapes attracted illustrious painters like Cézanne and van Gogh. Despite the changes over the years, the howling mistral, the legendary bone-chilling wind that blows through each winter, will forever be heard through the broad-leaved plane trees.

Provence has its own language and its own customs. The region is bounded on the north by the Dauphine, on the west by the Rhône, on the east by the Alps, and on the south by the Mediterranean. We'll focus in the next chapters on the part of Provence known as the glittering French Riviera or Côte d'Azur.

1 Orange ★★

658km (409 miles) S of Paris; 55km (34 miles) NE of Nîmes; 26km (16 miles) S of Avignon

Orange gets its name from the days when it was a dependency of the Dutch House of Orange-Nassau, not because it's set in a citrus belt. Actually, the last orange grove departed 2,000 years ago. The juice that flows in Orange today comes from its fabled vineyards, which turn out a Côtes du Rhône vintage. Many *caves* (vineyards) are spread throughout the district, some of which offer *dégustations* (wine tastings) to paying customers. The tourist office (see "Essentials," below) will provide you with a list.

Overlooking the Valley of the Rhône, today's Orange, with a somewhat sleepy population of about 30,000, tempts visitors with Europe's third-largest extant triumphal arch and best-preserved Roman theater. Louis XIV, who toyed with the idea of moving the theater to Versailles, said, "It is the finest wall in my kingdom." UNESCO has placed the arch on its World Cultural and Natural Heritage List in the hopes that it can be preserved "forever."

ESSENTIALS
GETTING THERE   Orange sits on major rail and highway arteries. Some 20 **trains** per day arrive from Avignon (trip time: 20 min.); the one-way fare is around 6€ ($7.80). From Marseille, there are five trains per day (trip time: 1¼ hr.), for 20€ ($26) one-way. From Paris, you can catch an SNCF or TGV train to Orange; the one-way fare is 80€ ($104), and the trip takes 4 to 8 hours. For rail information, call ⓒ **08-92-35-35-35** or 04-90-11-88-00. For information on bus routes, contact the **Gare**

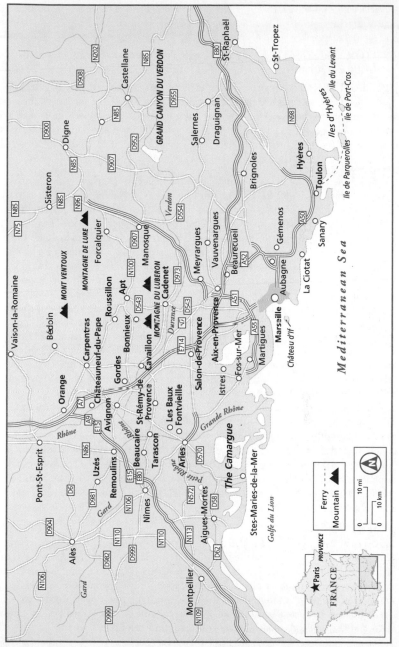

Routière (© **04-90-34-15-59**), place Pourtoules, behind the Théâtre Antique. If you're **driving** from Paris, take A6 south to Lyon, then A7 to Orange. The 684km (425-mile) drive takes 5½ to 6½ hours.

VISITOR INFORMATION   The **Office de Tourisme** is at 5 cours Aristide-Briand (© **04-90-34-70-88**).

SPECIAL EVENTS   From early July to early August, a drama, dance, and music festival called **Les Chorégies d'Orange** takes place at the Théâtre Antique, one of the most evocative ancient theaters in Europe. For information or tickets, visit or contact the office, 18 place Sylvain, adjacent to the theater (© **04-90-34-24-24;** www.choregies. asso.fr).

SEEING THE SIGHTS

In the southern part of town, the carefully restored **Théâtre Antique** 🟊🟊🟊, place des Frères-Mounet (© **04-90-51-17-60**), dates from the days of Augustus. Built into the side of a hill, it once held 8,000 spectators in tiered seats. The theater is nearly 105m (350 ft.) long, 38m (125 ft.) high, and noted for its acoustics. It's open April through September daily from 9am to 7pm, October through March daily 9am to 6pm. Admission is 7.50€ ($9.75) for adults, 4.50€ ($5.85) for students and children under 18.

West of the theater stood a huge temple which, along with a gymnasium, formed one of the greatest buildings in the empire. Across the street, the **Musée Municipal d'Orange,** place du Théâtre-Antique (© **04-90-51-17-60**), displays fragments of the temple. Your ticket to the theater also admits you to the museum, which is open April to September daily from 9am to 6pm, October to March daily from 9am to 5pm.

Even older than the theater is the **Arc de Triomphe** 🟊🟊, on avenue de l'Arc-de-Triomphe. It has decayed a bit, but its decorations and other elements are fairly well preserved. Built to honor the conquering legions of Caesar, it rises 22m (72 ft.) and is nearly 21m (70 ft.) wide. Composed of a trio of arches held up by Corinthian columns, it was used as a dungeon in the Middle Ages.

Before leaving Orange, head for the park **Colline St-Eutrope,** adjacent to the Théâtre Antique, for a view of the valley and its mulberry plantations.

After exploring the town, drive south for 13km (8 miles) along A9 to **Châteauneuf-du-Pape,** where you can have lunch (Tues–Sun) at the **Hostellerie du Château des Fines-Roches,** route d'Avignon (© **04-90-83-70-23**). Although the hostellerie was built in the 19th century, its medieval features make it look feudal. If you're pressing on to Avignon, it's only another 13km (8 miles) south along any of three highways (each marked AVIGNON).

WHERE TO STAY

Hôtel Arène 🟊 *(Finds)*   On a pedestrian street in the shade of century-old plane trees, this hotel sits in the center of the historic district. The bull's-eye location is a compelling reason to stay here. Try to get a room with a balcony opening onto the old square in front; it's more nostalgic. A series of four antique town houses woven into a seamless whole make up this complex. Guest rooms are traditionally furnished with French decor. Each unit has a private bathroom with shower. Amenities are up-to-date, and the staff is among the more courteous and helpful in town.

Place de Langes, 84100 Orange. © **04-90-11-40-40.** Fax 04-90-11-40-45. www.provenceguide.com/arene/index.html. 30 units. 59€–122€ ($77–$159) double; 122€–184€ ($159–$239) triple. AE, DC, MC, V. Parking 8€ ($10). **Amenities:** Limited room service; nonsmoking rooms; limited-mobility rooms. *In room:* TV, dataport, minibar, hair dryer, safe.

Hôtel Le Louvre et Terminus *Value*   Surrounded by a garden terrace, this conservatively decorated Logis de France offers a good value, housed in a much-renovated building begun around 1900. Don't expect grandeur: Everything is simple, efficient, and rather brusque. Bedrooms, ranging from small to medium in size have all the basic necessities and either double or twin beds; the tiled bathrooms are small, each with shower.

89 av. Frédéric-Mistral, 84100 Orange. © **04-90-34-10-08.** Fax 04-90-34-68-71. www.hotel-louvre-orange.com. 32 units. 70€–100€ ($91–$130) double; 105€–120€ ($137–$156) suite. AE, DC, MC, V. Parking 8€ ($10) in garage. **Amenities:** Restaurant; bar; outdoor pool. *In room:* A/C, TV, minibar, hair dryer.

Park Inn Orange   This comfortable modern hotel lies about a kilometer (half-mile) west of the city, in a 20-year-old building whose wings curve around a landscaped courtyard. Its well-furnished rooms are arranged around a series of gardens. This is your best bet for general overnight comfort far from the crowds. It is completely renovated, with an upgrade of the bedrooms. Bathrooms are small but neat with tub/shower combos.

80 rte. de Caderousse, 84100 Orange. © **04-90-34-24-10.** Fax 04-90-34-85-48. www.orange.parkinn.fr. 99 units. 135€ ($175) double. AE, DC, MC, V. Free parking. Drive about a kilometer (half-mile) west of the city center, following directions to Caderousse. **Amenities:** Restaurant; bar; outdoor pool; limited room service; laundry service/dry cleaning. *In room:* A/C, TV, dataport, minibar.

Driving Les Routes de la Lavande

As characteristic of Provence as heather is of the Yorkshire moors, lavender has played a major role here for hundreds of years. When it was part of the Roman Empire, Provence produced the flowers to scent the public baths. In the Middle Ages, villages burnt piles of the plant in the streets, the prevalent medical theory being that disease was spread by vapors in the air. But it was during the Renaissance that the current industry took root, linked to the Médicis, who padded their wealth with a brisk trade in the distillation of the flower's essential oils. Today lavender production and distillation are more than just trades—they're a way of life for many families.

The heart of lavender production lies in Provençal fields stretching from the foothills of the Vercors mountains to the Verdon canyons and from Buech to the Luberon range. Plants grown and distilled in this area are sold under the Haute-Provence label, renowned for its quality. A drive through the region is most scenic just before the midsummer harvest, when the countryside is a purplish hue from the blossoms of the lavender plants, spread out in seemingly endless rows to the horizon. Not only can you take in the sight and scent of the flowers, but you can also tour the distilleries and farms. Some of these facilities are open only during summer, when the year's harvest is undergoing distillation. Those that are open year-round offer tours. They also sell the plants themselves, as well as the essential oils and dried flowers of the plant (used in Provençal cooking), perfumes, honey, and herbal teas.

One of the best places to visit lavender farms and distilleries is Nyons, 42km (26 miles) northeast of Orange. From Orange, take A7 northwest for 3km (1¾ miles) to Route 976 and drive northeast for 13km (8 miles) to St-Cécile-les-Vignes, where the road becomes Route 576. Continue northeast for 6km (3¾ miles) to Tulette, turn right onto Route 94, and go 22km (14 miles) northeast to Nyons. Stop at the **Office de Tourisme,** place Libération (℃ **04-75-26-10-35**), to pick up the brochure *Les Routes de la Lavande,* offering a brief explanation and history of lavender production and a map of the region and its production facilities, with addresses, phone numbers, and hours.

WHERE TO DINE

Le Parvis 🄺ids TRADITIONAL FRENCH   Jean-Michel Berengier sets the best table in Orange, albeit in a rather austere dining room. He bases his cuisine on prime vegetables and the best ingredients from "mountain or sea." Try escalope of braised sea bass with fennel or asparagus, or lamb with garlic cream sauce. A can't-miss dish is foie gras. Fresh and flavorful seafood is prepared in different ways according to the season, and the staff prides itself on its dozens of preparations. The service is efficient and polite, and there's a children's menu.

55 cours Pourtoules. ℃ **04-90-34-82-00.** Reservations required. Main courses 14€–21€ ($18–$27); fixed-price menu 18€–42€ ($23–$55); children's menu 12€ ($16). AE, MC, V. Tues–Sun noon–2:30pm; Tues–Sat 7:30–9:15pm. Closed Nov 7–Dec 3 and Jan 16–Feb 3.

On the outskirts of Nyons, start out at the **Jardin des Arômes (Garden of Scents)**, promenade de la Digue (© 04-75-26-20-51), with its collection of aromatic plants and lavenders; it's open around the clock throughout the year and charges no admission. To reach it from Nyons, follow the road signs pointing to Gap. After viewing and enjoying the scent of the living plants close by, go to **Bleu Provence,** 58 promenade de la Digue (© **04-75-26-10-42)**, a family-owned distillery founded in 1926, for thyme, rosemary, lavender, and "every other spice that's Provençal." There's a shop on the premises where you can find the essential oils, soaps, and unguents, as well as staff that will take you on a guided English or French-language tour. If you walk around the premises on your own, the visit is free; to participate in the 45-minute guided tours, the cost is 2.50€ ($3.25) per person. You must call in advance for an appointment. There's also a perfume workshop, creating a lavender eau de toilette at 15€ ($20) per person.

In St-Nazaire-le-Desert, northeast of Nyons, you can visit **Gérard Blache,** in the village center next to the Auberge du Desert (© 04-75-27-51-08), place de la Fontaine, a shop that sells all things lavender in July and August daily from 9:30am to 7:30pm. From here, head southeast to **Rosans,** where the distillery of the Cooperative des Producteurs de Lavande des Alpes (Lavender Cooperative of the Alps), on D94 west of Rosans (© **04-75-26-95-00),** offers short guided tours and sales of essential oils from mid-June to August daily from 10am to noon and 2 to 6pm. Southwest of here is **Buis-les-Baronnies,** where the Shop Bernard Laget, in the village center on place aux Herbes (© **04-75-28-12-01),** includes lavender products among its medicinal and aromatic plants; it's open Tuesday through Sunday from 9:30am to noon and 3:30 to 7pm. Finally, head southeast of Buis to **Savoillan,** where the Ferme St-Agricole (St. Agricol Farm) (© **04-92-75-98-90)** boasts botanical paths leading through an experimental garden, a species preservation garden, and a greenhouse. The farm is open daily from June 15 to September 15 from 10:30am to 1pm, and from September 16 to June 14 from 10:30am to 1pm and 2 to 6pm. Admission is 3.05€ ($3.95).

WHERE TO STAY & DINE NEARBY

Château de Rochegude ★★   This Relais & Châteaux member stands on 10 hectares (25 acres) of parkland. The castle is at the edge of a hill, surrounded by vineyards. The 12th-century turreted residence has been renovated by a series of distinguished owners, ranging from a pope to a dauphin. Each room is done in Provençal style, with fabrics and furniture influenced by the region's 18th- and 19th-century traditions. As befits a château, rooms come in many shapes and sizes, and some are quite spacious. All have bathrooms with tub/shower. Both the food and the service are exceptional. You can enjoy meals in the stately dining room, barbecue by the pool, and refreshments on sunny terraces. Fixed-priced lunches cost 16€ to 32€ ($21–$42), fixed-price dinners 35€ to 85€ ($46–$111).

26790 Rochegude. ℃ **04-75-97-21-10.** Fax 04-75-04-89-87. www.chateauderochegude.com. 25 units. 170€–350€ ($196–$403) double; 430€–700€ ($559–$910) suite. AE, DC, MC, V. Free parking. Closed Nov. Take D976 13km (8 miles) north of Orange, following signs toward Gap and Rochegude. **Amenities:** Restaurant; bar; outdoor pool; tennis court; limited room service; laundry service; nonsmoking rooms. *In room:* A/C, TV, dataport, minibar.

Hostellerie Le Beffroi 🏿 *Finds*   This charming hotel from 1554 boasts ocher walls and original detailing on the exterior, and flowered wallpaper, heavy ceiling beams, plaster detailing, and fireplaces in the rustic interior. The elegantly furnished rooms display 19th-century antiques. Bedrooms offer fine linen on a comfortable French bed, most often a double or two twins. Bathrooms are small but neat. In the garden you can order meals under a giant fig tree and dine with a view of town. The hotel, across from the chiseled fountain in the Haute-Ville sector, maintains a limited number of parking spaces.

The town itself is worth exploring, for it contains some fascinating reminders of its former Roman occupation, including Les Ruines Romaines, two areas that have been excavated—the Quartier Puymin and Quartier Villasse.

Rue de l'Evèché, 84110 Vaison-la-Romaine. ℃ **04-90-36-04-71.** Fax 04-90-36-24-78. www.le-beffroi.com. 22 units. 85€–130€ ($111–$169) double. AE, DC, MC, V. Parking 8€ ($10). Closed Feb to mid-Mar. From Orange, drive 34km (21 miles) northeast, following the signs to Vaison-la-Romaine. The hotel is in Vaison's medieval core (Cité Médiévale). **Amenities:** 2 restaurants; bar; outdoor pool; laundry service; dry cleaning. *In room:* TV, minibar, hair dryer.

2 Châteauneuf-du-Pape

671km (417 miles) S of Paris; 19km (12 miles) N of Avignon; 13km (8 miles) S of Orange

Near Provence's north border, the Château-du-Pape was built as the Castelgandolfo, the country seat of the French popes of Avignon, during the 14th-century reign of Pope John XXII. Now in ruins, it overlooks the vast acres of vineyards that the popes planted, the start of a regional industry that today produces some of the world's best reds as well as an excellent white.

ESSENTIALS
GETTING THERE   For **rail information,** call Rail Europe ℃ **800/387-6782.** About three buses a day arrive from both towns. Buses from Avignon are also a possibility. Bus passengers are deposited and retrieved in place de la Bascule, behind Châteauneuf's post office. The tourist office (below) is the best source for schedules and information about bus access.

If you're **driving** from Avignon, head north on A7 to the intersection with Route 17, at which point you continue northwest following the well-posted signs into Chateauneuf-du-Pape.

VISITOR INFORMATION   The **Office de Tourisme** is at place du Portail (℃ **04-90-83-71-08**). Summer hours are 9:30am to 7pm Monday to Saturday. Winter hours are 9:30am to 12:30pm and 2 to 6pm Monday to Saturday. Open Sunday during Wine Festival.

A SPECIAL EVENT   Since the Middle Ages, the annual **Fête de la Véraison** has been held in early August. See below for details.

WINE LURE & LORE
What makes the local wines distinctive is the blending of 13 varieties of grapes, grown on vines surrounded by stones that reflect heat onto them during the day and keep them warm in the cool night. As a result, the wines produced in the district's vineyards

are among the most potent in France, with an alcohol content of at least 12.5% and, in many instances, as high as 15%. The region played a central role in the initiation of the Appellation d'Origine Contrôlée, France's strict quality-control system. This was formed when the late Baron Le Roy de Boiseaumarie, the most distinguished of the local vintners, initiated geographical boundaries and minimum standards for the production of wines given the Châteauneuf-du-Pape label. In 1923, local producers won exclusive rights to market their Côtes du Rhônes under that label, and thus paved the way for other regions to identify and protect their distinctive wines. You'll see a plaque devoted to his memory in the town's place de la Renaissance.

To learn about the town's wine-related lore, there are two major *associations de vignerons*, each representing a consortium of individually owned vineyards whose owners pool their marketing, advertising, and bottling programs. Open Monday through Friday from 8am to noon and 2 to 6pm, **Prestige et Tradition,** 3 rue de la République (✆ **04-90-83-72-29**), represents 10 vintners. They offer *dégustations* and sales.

Another useful source is **La Vinothèque,** 9 rue de la République (✆ **04-90-83-74-01**). A sales and marketing outlet for Madame Carre, matriarch of the Comtes d'Argelas vineyards, it's open for wine tastings and sales daily from 10am to 7pm. On the premises is La Boutique de la Vinothèque, where wine accessories (corkscrews, racks, decanters) are sold.

TOURING & TASTING THE WINES

A map posted in the village square, place du Portail (but called place de la Fontaine by just about everyone), pinpoints 22 wineries open for touring and tasting. The best known is **Domaine de Mont-Redon,** on D68 about 5km (3 miles) north of the town center (✆ **04-90-83-72-75**). It offers samplings of recent vintages of red and white wines and sales of *eau-de-vie*, a clear grape liqueur produced in a limited batch of 2,000 bottles annually. A noteworthy competitor is **Clos des Papes,** avenue Le Bienheureux Pierre de Luxembourg, in the town center (✆ **04-90-83-70-13**), where humidified cellars produce what many connoisseurs consider the region's best wine. Both establishments prefer advance notice before your arrival.

The town's only museum devotes all its exhibition space to winemaking. The **Musée des Vieux Outils de Vignerons of the Caves du Père-Anselme,** avenue Le Bienheureux Pierre de Luxembourg (✆ **04-90-83-70-07**), contains the history and artifacts of local wine production, including a 16th-century winepress, winemakers' tools, barrel-making equipment, and a tasting cellar. It's open daily from mid-April to mid-September from 9am to 7pm, and the rest of the year from 9am to noon and 2 to 6pm. Admission and tastings are free.

A WINE FESTIVAL   During 3 days in early August, the village hosts the annual **Fête de la Véraison** ✿, a medieval fair. It includes tasting stalls set up by local winemakers, actors impersonating Provençaux troubadours, bear-baiters (who are much kinder to their animals than their medieval counterparts), falconers with their birds, lots of merchants selling locally made handicrafts, battered flea market kiosks, and food. Don't expect dancing—what you'll get is a festival where the antique fountain on place du Portail spurts out wine, and vast amounts of that beverage are consumed. If you attend, you can drink all the wine you want for the price of a *verre de la Véraison.* This souvenir glass, filled on demand at any vintner who participates, costs 3.05€ and is sold at strategically positioned kiosks around town.

WHERE TO STAY

Hostellerie du Château des Fines-Roches ⊕⊕   This medieval-inspired manor house is from late in the 19th century. Named for the smooth rocks *(fines roches)* found in the soil of the nearby vineyards, the château devotes its huge cellars to the storage of thousands of bottles of local wines. The guest rooms on the upper floors of this charming hotel are renovated and include Provençal styling with a scattering of antiques. The bathrooms are small but well organized, each with shower.

We highly recommend taking a meal in the restaurant here. Menu items, carefully crafted and full of flavor, include filets of red mullet prepared with aromatic herbs and garnished with its own liver marinated in vinaigrette, barigoule of crayfish tails with artichokes, filet of bull from the Camargue marinated in a particular vintage *(syrah)* of strong red wine, and roast rack of local lamb with a gratin of eggplant and sheep's cheese. The wine list focuses on local vintages, particularly those from the village.

Rte. d'Avignon, 84230 Châteauneuf-du-Pape. ⊘ **04-90-83-70-23.** Fax 04-90-83-78-42. www.chateaufinesroches.com. 6 units. 155€–200€ ($202–$260) double. AE, DC, MC, V. From the center of town, drive 3km (2 miles) south, following the signs to Avignon. **Amenities:** Restaurant; bar; limited room service. *In room:* A/C, TV, minibar, hair dryer.

WHERE TO DINE

La Mère Germaine ⊛ PROVENÇAL   Named after the matriarch who established this place several generations ago, La Mère Germaine contains both a restaurant gastronomique and a simple bistro. Both enjoy sweeping panoramas from terraces where tables are set out in the summer months. Cuisine in both establishments is based on the traditions of Provence. In the bistro, you're likely to find simple platters of grilled fish, stews, casseroles, and grilled meats, but in the restaurant, cuisine is more elaborate, intricate, and tuned to the seasons. Dishes in the restaurant include zucchini flowers stuffed with mushrooms and drizzled with ratatouille juice, roasted rabbit stuffed with black-olive tapenade and fresh tomatoes, filet of turbot with *barigoule* (Provençal vinaigrette), and crispy rack of lamb scented with herbs from the surrounding *garrigue* (scrubland).

Eight simple, well-scrubbed bedrooms are available on the premises. None has a phone or elaborate amenities, but for a comfortable sojourn after a meal in the restaurant, they all offer good value and a sense of comfort and efficiency.

Place de la Fontaine, 84230 Châteauneuf-du-Pape. ⊘ **04-90-83-54-37.** Fax 04-90-83-50-27. Reservations recommended. In the bistro, platters 9€–25€ ($12–$33); in the restaurant, fixed-price menus 22€–42€ ($29–$55). AE, DC, MC, V. Daily noon–2pm and 7–9pm.

Finds Wine & Chocolate

One of the newest industries in Châteauneuf is the **Chocolaterie Castelain,** whose factories and showrooms lie on the Route d'Avignon (⊘ **04-90-83-54-71**), about 3km (2 miles) south of town. They've become known for a popular type of black chocolate *(la ganache)* flavored with a distilled version *(vieu marc de Châteauneuf)* of the red wine produced in local vineyards. The brand name of their chocolates is **Palet des Pâpes.** The chocolates taste extremely good when consumed with any of the local vintages.

3 Avignon ⭐⭐⭐

684km (425 miles) S of Paris; 80km (50 miles) NW of Aix-en-Provence; 106km (66 miles) NW of Marseille

In the 14th century, Avignon was the capital of Christendom—the popes lived here instead of in Rome. The legacy left by their "court of splendor and magnificence" makes Avignon one of the most interesting and beautiful of Europe's medieval cities.

The popes are long gone, but life goes on exceedingly well. Today this walled city of some 100,000 residents reaches its peak celebration time during the famous Festival d'Avignon, a 3-week stint of music, art, and theater when bacchanalia reigns in the streets. Avignon at any time of the year is a major stopover on the route from Paris to the Mediterranean. Lately, it has become well known as a cultural center. Artists and painters in increasing numbers have been moving here. Experimental theaters, painting galleries, and art cinemas have brought diversity to the inner city, especially rue des Teinturiers.

ESSENTIALS

GETTING THERE   The fastest and easiest way to get here is to **fly** from Paris's Orly Airport to Aéroport Avignon-Caumont (✆ **04-90-81-51-51**), 8km (5 miles) southeast of Avignon (trip time: 1 hr.). Taxis from the airport to the center cost 19€ to 21€ ($25–$27). From Paris, TGV **trains** from Gare de Lyon take 2 hours and 38 minutes. The one-way fare is 114€ ($148) in first class, 83€ ($108) in second class. Trains arrive frequently from Marseille, taking 70 minutes and costing 23€ ($30); and from Arles, taking 30 minutes and costing 5.70€ ($7.40). For train information and reservations, call ✆ **08-92 35-35-39.**

Eurostar's high-speed trains now bridge the gap between London's Waterloo Station and Avignon. This route is offered every Saturday between July 20 and September 7; the journey, excluding one stop in Ashford in Kent, lasts 6 hours. For information or to purchase tickets, which must be reserved at least 14 days in advance, call **Rail Europe** at (✆ **800/387-6782** or visit www.raileurope.com.

If you're **driving** from Paris, take A6 south to Lyon, then A7 south to Avignon. If you'd like to explore the area by **bike,** go to **Cycles Peugeot,** 80 rue Guillaume-Puy (✆ **04-90-86-32-49**), which rents all sorts of bikes, including 10-speed road bikes and mountain bikes, for around 14€ ($18) per day. A deposit of 200€ ($260), in cash or a credit card imprint, is required.

VISITOR INFORMATION   The **Office de Tourisme** is at 41 cours Jean-Jaurès (✆ **04-32-74-32-74;** www.ot-avignon.fr).

SPECIAL EVENTS   The biggest celebration is the **Festival d'Avignon,** held during the last 3 weeks in July and the first week in August. The international festival focuses on avant-garde theater, dance, and music. Part of the fun is the nightly bacchanal in the streets. Prices for rooms and meals skyrocket, so make reservations far in advance. For information, contact the **Bureaux du Festival,** Espace Saint-Louis, 20 rue du Portail Boquier, 84000 Avignon (✆ **04-90-27-66-50;** www.festival-avignon.com). Tickets cost 10€ to 35€ ($13–$46).

Palais des Papes ⭐⭐⭐   Dominating Avignon from a hill is one of the most famous (or notorious, depending on your point of view) palaces in the Christian world. Headquarters of a schismatic group of cardinals who came close to toppling the authority of the popes in Rome, it is part fortress, part showplace. It all began in 1309, when Pope Clement V fled to Avignon to escape political infighting in Rome. His successor, John

XXII, chose to stay in Avignon. The third Avignon pope, Benedict XII, was the one responsible for the construction of this magnificent palace. Avignon became, for a time, the Vatican of the north. During the period, dubbed "the Babylonian Captivity" by Rome, the popes held extravagant court in the palace; art and culture flourished—and so did prostitution and vice. When Gregory XI was persuaded to return to Rome in 1376, Avignon proceeded to elect its own rival pope, and the Great Schism split the Christian world. The real struggle, of course was about the wealth and power of the papacy. The reign of Avignon's antipopes finally ended in 1417 with the election of Martin V, and the papal court here was disbanded.

Chapelle St-Jean is known for its beautiful frescoes, attributed to the school of Matteo Giovanetti and painted between 1345 and 1348. The frescoes present scenes from the life of John the Baptist and John the Evangelist. More Giovanetti frescoes can be seen above the Chapelle St-Jean in the **Chapelle St-Martial.** The frescoes here depict the miracles of St. Martial, patron saint of Limousin.

Grand Tinel (Banquet Hall) is about 41m (135 ft.) long and 9m (30 ft.) wide, and the pope's table stood on the southern side. The **pope's bedroom** is on the first floor of the Tour des Anges. Its walls are entirely decorated in tempera with foliage on which birds and squirrels perch; birdcages are painted in the recesses of the windows. In a secular vein, the **Studium (Stag Room)**—study of Clement VI—was frescoed in 1343 with hunting scenes. Added under the same Clement, who had a taste for grandeur, the **Grande Audience (Great Audience Hall)** contains frescoes of the prophets; these are also attributed to Giovanetti and were painted in 1352.

Between two and four French-language guided tours are offered every day at schedules that vary widely according to the season and day of the week. Tours usually last 50 minutes, and aside from the exceptions mentioned above, they are somewhat monotonous, since most of the rooms have been stripped of their once-legendary finery. Self-guided tours in English, using a handheld audio mechanism, are available anytime during opening hours.

Place du Palais des Papes. (℡ **04-90-27-50-00.** Admission (including tour with guide or recording) 9.50€ ($12) adults, 7.50€ ($9.75) seniors and students, free for children under 8. July daily 9am–8pm; Apr–June and Aug–Oct daily 9am–7pm; Nov–Mar daily 9:30am–5:45pm.

MORE ATTRACTIONS

Even more famous than the papal residency is the ditty *"Sur le pont d'Avignon, l'on y danse, l'on y danse."* **Pont St-Bénézet** ✦✦ (℡ **04-90-27-51-16)** was far too narrow for the *danse* of the rhyme, however. Spanning the Rhône and connecting Avignon with Villeneuve-lèz-Avignon, the bridge is now a ruin, with only four of its original 22 arches. According to legend, it was inspired by a vision that a shepherd named Bénézet had while tending his flock. The bridge was built between 1177 and 1185 and suffered various disasters. (In 1669, half of it fell into the river.) On one of the piers is the two-story **Chapelle St-Nicolas**—one story in Romanesque style, the other in Gothic. The remains of the bridge are open daily November to mid-March 9:30am to 5:45pm; mid-March to June and October 9:30am to 6pm; July 9am to 9pm; and August to September 9am to 8pm. Admission is 3.50€ ($4.55) for adults, 3€ ($3.90) for seniors and students, free for children under 8. Once you pay to walk on the bridge, the small chapel on the bridge can be visited as part of the overall admission fee.

It's worth at least an hour to walk through the **Quartier de La Balance,** where the Gypsies lived in the 1800s. Over the years, La Balance had grown seedy, but since the

Avignon

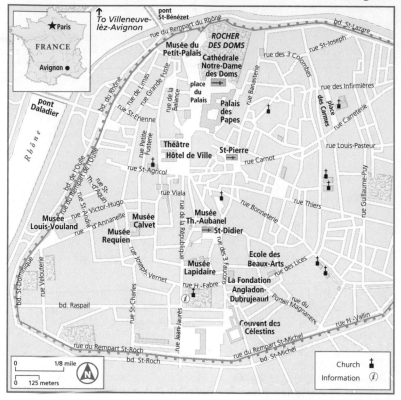

1970s, major renovations have taken place. Start at place du Palais, going along rue de La Balance, detouring, if possible, into the historically evocative rue de la Grande Fusterie and the rue des Grottes. The main interest here is the restoration of the old town houses with their renewed elegant facades, many graced with mullioned windows. In the district are some of the ramparts that used to surround Avignon, stretching for 4km (2¾ miles). Built in the 14th century by the popes, these ramparts were partially restored in the 19th century by that busy restorer of medieval monuments, Viollet-le-Duc. The most intriguing section is along rue du Rempart-du-Rhône, leading east to place Crillon. After a look, you can return to place de l'Horloge via rue St-Etienne.

Cathédrale Notre-Dame des Doms 🐾 Near the palace is the 12th-century cathedral, containing the Flamboyant Gothic tomb of some of the apostate popes. Crowning the top is a gilded statue of the Virgin from the 19th century. The cathedral's hours vary according to whatever religious ceremony is scheduled, but generally it's open during the hours noted below. From the cathedral, enter the promenade du Rocher-des-Doms to stroll through its garden and enjoy the view across the Rhône to Villeneuve-lèz-Avignon.

Place du Palais. ℂ **04-90-86-81-01.** Free admission. Daily 9am–noon and 2–6pm; hours may vary according to religious ceremonies.

La Fondation Angladon-Dubrujeaud ✿   This museum, opened in 1995, contains the magnificent art collection of Jacques Doucet, renowned Parisian haute couture designer and belle époque dandy and dilettante. Doucet cultivated a number of young artists, among them Picasso, Braque, Max Jacob, Marcel Duchamp, and Guillaume Apollinaire, and began to collect their early works. For decades, Doucet's heirs kept the treasure trove a relative secret and lived in quiet splendor amid canvases by Cézanne, Sisley, Derain, Degas, and Modigliani. Today you can wander through Doucet's former abode, which is also filled with rare antiques and art objects that include 16th-century Buddhas and Louis XVI chairs designed by Jacob. Doucet died in 1929 at the age of 76, his own fortune so diminished that his nephew paid for his funeral. But his rich legacy lives on here.

5 rue Laboureur. ☎ **04-90-82-29-03**. Admission 6€ ($7.80) adults, 4€ ($5.20) students and children 14–18, 1.50€ ($1.95) children 7–13. Wed–Sun 1–6pm.

Musée Calvet ✿   An extensive collection of ancient silver is housed in this lovely 18th-century neoclassical mansion. The museum displays works of Vernet, David, Corot, Manet, and Soutine. Our favorite oil is by Brueghel the Younger, *Le Cortège nuptial (The Bridal Procession)*.

65 rue Joseph-Vernet. ☎ **04-90-86-33-84**. Admission 6€ ($7.80) adults, 3€ ($3.90) students, free for children under 13. Wed–Mon 10am–1pm and 2–6pm.

Musée du Petit-Palais   This was the bishop's palace where the first two Avignon popes lived until Benedict XII constructed the Palais des Papes. It holds an important collection of paintings from the Italian schools of the 13th to 16th centuries, including works from Florence, Venice, Siena, and Lombardy. In addition, salons display 15th-century paintings done in Avignon, and several galleries are devoted to Roman and Gothic sculptures.

Place du Palais des Papes. ☎ **04-90-86-44-58**. Admission 6€ ($7.80) adults, 3€ ($3.90) students, free for children under 13. June–Sept Wed–Mon 10am–1pm and 2–6pm; Oct–May Wed–Mon 9:30am–1pm and 2–5:30pm.

Musée Lapidaire ✿   Behind a baroque facade, a 17th-century Jesuit church has been turned into an intriguing museum of mainly Gallo-Roman sculptures that can be viewed in less than an hour. In the museum you can trace the history of the various civilizations that have cultivated Provence. Some of the exhibitions are scary, including the statue of a man-eating monster discovered at Noves called *Tarasque*. Fascinating Greco-Roman statues are on exhibition, including a magnificent copy of Praxiteles' *Apollo the Python Killer* ✿. A large number of ancient sarcophagi and funerary art is also on show, including an unusual series of masks from Vaison.

27 rue de la République. ☎ **04-90-86-33-84**. Admission 2€ ($2.60) adults, 1€ ($1.30) students 12–18, free for children under 13. Wed–Mon 10am–1pm and 2–6pm.

Musée Louis-Vouland   In a 19th-century mansion opening onto a lovely garden, Avignon's treasure trove of lavish 17th- and 18th-century antiques and objets d'art is displayed. The collection includes Sèvres porcelain, the comtesse du Barry's tea set, great tapestries from Aubusson and Gobelins, glittering chandeliers, and commodes to equal those at Versailles. Our favorites are the Louis XV inkpots with silver rats holding the lids.

17 rue Victor-Hugo. ☎ **04-90-86-03-79**. Admission 4€ ($5.20) adults, 2.50€ ($3.25) students. May–Oct Tues–Sat 10am–noon and 2–6pm, Sun 2–6pm; Nov–Apr Tues–Sun 10am–noon and 2–6pm.

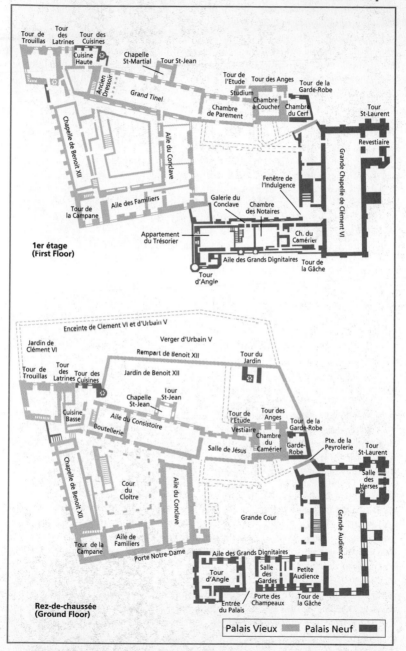

Tour de Trouillas
Tour des Latrines
Tour des Cuisines
Cuisine Haute
Chapelle St-Martial
Tour St-Jean
Ancien Dressoir
Grand Tinel
Tour de l'Etude
Tour des Anges
Tour de la Garde-Robe
Studium
Chambre à Coucher
Chambre du Cerf
Tour St-Laurent
Chambre de Parement
Revestiaire
Chapelle de Benoît XII
Aile du Conclave
Fenêtre de l'Indulgence
Grande Chapelle de Clément VI
Tour de la Campane
Aile des Familiers
Galerie du Conclave
Chambre des Notaires
Appartement du Trésorier
Ch. du Camérier
Aile des Grands Dignitaires
Tour de la Gâche
Tour d'Angle

1er étage (First Floor)

Enceinte de Clement VI et d'Urbain V
Jardin de Clément VI
Verger d'Urbain V
Rempart de Benoît XII
Tour du Jardin
Tour de Trouillas
Tour des Latrines
Tour des Cuisines
Jardin de Benoît XII
Chapelle St-Jean
Tour St-Jean
Cuisine Basse
Aile du Consistoire
Tour de l'Etude
Tour des Anges
Tour de la Garde-Robe
Boutellerie
Vestiaire
Chambre du Camérier
Garde-Robe
Pte. de la Peyrolerie
Tour St-Laurent
Salle de Jésus
Chapelle de Benoît XII
Cour du Cloître
Aile du Conclave
Grande Cour
Salle des Herses
Aile de Familiers
Grande Audience
Tour de la Campane
Porte Notre-Dame
Aile des Grands Dignitaires
Tour d'Angle
Salle des Gardes
Petite Audience
Entrée du Palais
Porte des Champeaux
Tour de la Gâche

Rez-de-chaussée (Ground Floor)

Palais Vieux   Palais Neuf

Musée Requien   For aficionados only, this offbeat museum can easily take up an hour of your time. Located next to the Musée Calvet, it was named after the naturalist Espirit Requien (1788–1851), who was largely responsible for the nucleus of the collection. The museum houses one of the most important natural history libraries in France but is most often visited for its **herbarium** ⚘, containing some 200,000 specimens gathered by botanists from around the world. To round out the collection is a parade of exhibits that trace the geology, zoology, and botany of Provence.

67 rue Joseph-Vernet. ☎ **04-90-82-43-51.** Free admission. Tues–Sat 9am–noon and 2–6pm.

SHOPPING

Since the 1960s, **Antiquités Bourret,** 5 rue Limas (☎ **04-90-86-65-02**), has earned a reputation for 18th- and 19th-century Provençal antiques. The idea behind **Mistral-Les Indiens de Nîmes,** 19 rue Joseph-Vernet (☎ **04-90-86-32-05**), is to duplicate 18th- and 19th-century Provençal fabric patterns. Fabrics are available by the meter and in the form of clothing for men, women, and children. In addition, you can buy kitchenware and furniture inspired by Provence and the steamy wetlands west of Marseille.

The clothing at **Souleiado,** 5 rue Joseph Vernet (☎ **04-90-86-47-67**), derives from traditional Provençal costumes. Most of the clothing is for women. Fabrics are for sale by the meter. The name means "first ray of sunshine after a storm."

Hervé Baume, 19 rue Petite Fusterie (☎ **04-90-86-37-66**), is for those who yearn to set a Provençal table. The place is piled high with a little bit of everything—from Directoire dinner services to French folk art to handblown crystal hurricane lamps. **Jaffier-Parsi,** 42 rue des Fourbisseurs (☎ **04-90-86-08-85**), is known for its copper saucepans from the Norman town of Villedieu-les-Poêles, which has been making them since the Middle Ages. If you're seeking a new perspective on Provençal pottery, go to **Terre è Provence,** 26 rue de la République (☎ **04-90-85-56-45**). You can pick up wonderful kitsch—perhaps terra-cotta plates decorated with three-dimensional cicadas.

Most markets in Avignon are open 6am to 1pm. The biggest covered market with 40 different merchants is **Les Halles,** place Pie, open Tuesday to Sunday. Other smaller **food markets** are on rampart St-Michel on Saturday and Sunday, and on place Crillon on Friday. The **flower market** is on place des Carmes on Saturday, and the **flea market** is in the same place on Sunday.

WHERE TO STAY
VERY EXPENSIVE

La Mirande ⚘⚘⚘   In the heart of Avignon behind the Palais des Papes, this 700-year-old town house is one of France's grand little luxuries. In 1987, Achim and Hannelore Stein transformed this place into a citadel of opulence. The hotel displays 2 centuries of decorative art, from the 1700s Salon Chinois to the Salon Rouge, with striped walls in Rothschild red. Room no. 20 is the most sought after—its lavish premises open onto the garden. All the rooms are stunning, with exquisite decor, hand-printed fabrics on the walls, antiques, bedside controls, and huge bathtubs. The restaurant, among the finest in Avignon, deserves its one Michelin star.

4 place de la Mirande, 84000 Avignon. ☎ **04-90-85-93-93.** Fax 04-90-86-26-85. www.la-mirande.fr. 20 units. 195€–475€ ($254–$618) double; 570€–720€ ($741–$936) suite. AE, DC, V. Parking 22€ ($29). **Amenities:** Restaurant; bar; limited room service; babysitting; laundry service; dry cleaning; nonsmoking rooms; limited-mobility rooms. *In room:* A/C, TV, dataport, minibar, hair dryer, safe.

EXPENSIVE

Hôtel d'Europe ✫✫✫   This deluxe hostelry, in operation since 1799, is almost the equal of the Mirande (above), though slightly cheaper. You enter the vine-covered hotel through a courtyard, which holds tables in the warmer months. The grand hall and salons contain antiques, and the good-size guest rooms have handsome decor and period furnishings. Three suites are on the roof, with views of the Palais des Papes. In some twin-bedded rooms, the beds are a bit narrow. Overall, accommodations are comfortable, with touches of Gallic charm. The spacious bathrooms are handsomely equipped, and each has a combination tub/shower. The restaurant, **La Vieille Fontaine,** which specializes in traditional French and Provençal cuisine, is one of the best in Avignon.

12 place Crillon, 84000 Avignon. ℂ **04-90-14-76-76.** Fax 04-90-14-76-71. www.heurope.com. 44 units. 135€–429€ ($176–$558) double; 617€–732€ ($802–$952) suite. AE, DC, MC, V. Parking 14€ ($16). **Amenities:** Restaurant; bar; business services; limited room service; babysitting; laundry service; dry cleaning; nonsmoking rooms. *In room:* A/C, TV, dataport, minibar, hair dryer, safe.

MODERATE

Hôtel Bristol   In the center of Avignon, on one of the principal streets leading to the landmark place de l'Horloge and the Palais des Papes, the Bristol is one of the town's better bets. A traditional hotel, it offers comfortably furnished well-maintained rooms, most recently renovated in the early 1990s. Most bedrooms contain twin beds. Bathrooms are compact and tiled. Breakfast is the only meal served. Though it's not the most atmospheric place in Avignon, it offers good, solid value in an expensive city.

44 cours Jean-Jaurès, 84000 Avignon. ℂ **04-90-16-48-48.** Fax 04-90-86-22-72. www.bristol-hotel-avignon.com. 67 units. 70€–102€ ($91–$133) double; 113€–154€ ($147–$200) suite. AE, DC, MC, V. Parking 10€ ($13). **Amenities:** Bar; limited room service; laundry service; dry cleaning; limited-mobility rooms. *In room:* A/C, TV, minibar, hair dryer, safe.

Hôtel Clarion Cloître St-Louis ✫   This hotel is in a former Jesuit school built in the 1580s. Much of the original premises remain, including the baroque facade, the wraparound arcades, and the soaring ceiling vaults. Guest rooms are more functional; in fact, they're rather dull as a result of renovations. Rooms range from medium-size to spacious, and some have sliding glass doors overlooking the patio. Each unit has modern decor without a lot of extras; all but three have tub/shower combinations.

20 rue du Portail Boquier, 84000 Avignon. ℂ **800/CLARION** in the U.S., or 04-90-27-55-55. Fax 04-90-82-24-01. www.cloitre-saint-louis.com. 80 units. 100€–250€ ($130–$325) double; 220€–315€ ($286–$410) suite. AE, MC, V. Parking 10€–12€ ($13–$16). **Amenities:** Restaurant; bar; outdoor pool; limited room service; nonsmoking rooms; limited-mobility rooms. *In room:* A/C, TV, dataport, minibar, hair dryer, safe.

Hôtel du Palais des Papes   From the twin terraces of this simple but well-established hotel, you'll enjoy views of both the clock tower (overlooking the place de l'Horloge) and the Palais des Papes. Few other hotels boast as central a location, and only a handful are able to combine construction that was completed in series between the 15th century and the 1920s. You'll access the three floors of this place via a corkscrew-shape stone staircase that, in addition to exposed stone walls, massive ceiling beams, and wrought-iron bedsteads, evokes a modern twist on the Middle Ages that, fortunately, includes neatly tiled bathrooms. There are two dining rooms in this hotel, one medieval-looking, with a big fireplace, and the other with a beamed ceiling but slightly more modern. Cuisine is Provençal and French, flavorful, and served in generous portions. The hotel and its restaurant have been operated for many previous generations by the Donche-Gay family, members of whom are almost always on hand.

1 rue Gérard Philippe, 84000 Avignon. ℭ **04-90-86-04-13.** Fax 04-90-27-91-17. www.hotel-avignon.com. 26 units. 65€–75€ ($85–$98) double; 110€–120€ ($143–$156) junior suite. AE, MC, V. Parking 8€ ($10) per night in a nearby municipal parking lot. **Amenities:** Restaurant; bar. *In room:* TV, minibar.

Hôtel Mercure Cité-des-Papes   Nearly adjacent to the Palais des Papes, this five-story modern building offers bedrooms that offer solid comfort, though they are not particularly stylish. Views from many of its windows extend over the place de l'Horloge. Although there's no restaurant, the hotel's central location makes it easy to find a nice place to dine out.

1 rue Jean-Vilar, 84000 Avignon. ℭ **04-90-80-93-00.** Fax 04-90-80-93-01. www.mercure.com. 89 units. 112€–130€ ($146–$169) double. AE, DC, MC, V. Parking 8€ ($10). **Amenities:** Laundry service; babysitting; limited-mobility rooms. *In room:* A/C, TV, dataport, minibar, hair dryer, safe.

INEXPENSIVE

Hôtel d'Angleterre   This three-story Art Deco structure in the heart of Avignon is the city's best budget hotel, with the advantage of being located inside the city ramparts. It was built in 1929 of gray stone, emulating the style that local builders imagined was characteristic of English houses. The rooms are on the small side, but they are comfortably furnished, and most have compact shower-only bathrooms. Breakfast is the only meal served.

29 bd. Raspail, 84000 Avignon. ℭ **04-90-86-34-31.** Fax 04-90-86-86-74. www.hoteldangleterre.fr. 39 units, 38 with private bathroom. 40€–43€ ($52–$56) double without bathroom; 55€–78€ ($72–$101) double with bathroom. MC, V. Free parking. Closed Dec 20–Jan 20. **Amenities:** Laundry service; lounge. *In room:* TV, dataport.

Hôtel Danieli ⋇   This hotel's Italian influence is clear in its arches, chiseled stone, tile floors, and baronial stone staircase. Built during the reign of Napoleon I, it's classified as a historic monument in its own right. Its small, informal public rooms are outfitted mostly in antiques acquired by the history-conscious owner. The guest rooms, however, have painted bamboo furnishings and acceptably comfortable mattresses. Tiled bathrooms are compact and efficiently organized and have tub/shower combos. Unless special arrangements are made for a group (and this hotel accepts many), breakfast is the only meal served.

17 rue de la République, 84000 Avignon. ℭ **04-90-86-46-82.** Fax 04-90-27-09-24. www.hoteldanieli-avignon.com. 29 units. 60€–80€ ($78–$104) double. AE, MC, V. Parking 9€ ($12). **Amenities:** Lounge; bar. *In room:* TV.

Hôtel de Blauvac ⋇ *(Finds)*   Named after its original owner and builder, the early-17th-century Marquis de Blauvac, this hotel occupies a converted two-story town house whose neoclassical facade and interior stonewalls and ceiling beams have been carefully preserved. Inside, amid Provençal fabrics and accessories, you'll find a cozy and appealing collection of public rooms and bedrooms. Each is high-ceilinged and charming, with an unpretentious decor—usually with a large old-fashioned armoire and other antique touches—that you'll almost never find in large chain-motif hotels. Bathrooms are small but tidy with tub/shower combos.

11 rue de la Bancasse, 84000 Avignon. ℭ **04-90-86-34-11.** Fax 04-90-86-27-41. www.hotel-blauvac.com. 16 units. 55€–65€ ($72–$85) double. AE, DC, MC, V. Parking 8.60€ ($11) per night in a nearby public lot. *In room:* TV, minibar.

Hôtel le Médiéval   About 3 blocks south of the Palais des Papes, this three-story town house from the late 1600s is well maintained and uncomplicated. Under beamed ceilings, the comfortable guest rooms are medium-size to spacious. Most peaceful are the units that overlook the inner courtyard, with its pots of flowers and shrubs. Those that overlook a congested medieval street corner might be noisier, but they have a rough-and-ready charm of their own. Most of the small bathrooms have tub/shower combinations.

15 rue Petite Saunerie, 84000 Avignon. ℂ **04-90-86-11-06.** Fax 04-90-82-08-64. www.hotelmedieval.com. 34 units. 53€–68€ ($69–$88) double. Extra bed 8€ ($10). MC, V. **Amenities:** Limited room service; nonsmoking rooms. *In room:* TV, dataport, hair dryer.

WHERE TO DINE
EXPENSIVE

Brunel PROVENÇAL   This flower-filled restaurant is in the heart of Avignon. Managed by the Brunel family, it offers such specialties as assorted grilled fish. The chef prepares such superb dishes as monkfish with anise-flavored butter; confit of lamb couscous; and tuna steak with coulis of capers and onions. Artichoke hearts accompany grilled John Dory, and even pigs' feet are sublime. The desserts are prepared fresh daily. You can order house wines by the carafe.

46 rue de La Balance. ℂ **04-90-85-24-83.** Reservations required. Main courses 9€–19€ ($12–$25) at lunch, 25€–30€ ($33–$39) at dinner; fixed-price menu 30€ ($39). AE, MC, V. Tues–Sat noon–2pm and 7:30–9:30pm. Closed first 2 weeks in Aug and Dec 20–Jan 6.

Christian Etienne ✦✦✦ PROVENÇAL   The stone house containing this restaurant was built in 1180, around the same time as the Palais des Papes (next door). Owner Christian Etienne reaches new culinary heights. His dining room contains early-16th-century frescoes honoring the marriage of Anne de Bretagne to the French king in 1491. Several of the fixed-price menus feature themes: Two present seasonal tomatoes, mushrooms, or other vegetables; one offers preparations of lobster; and the priciest relies on the chef's imagination *(menu confiance)* for unique combinations. In summer, look for the vegetable menu entirely based on ripe tomatoes; the main course is a mousse of lamb, eggplants, tomatoes, and herbs. The vegetable menus aren't completely vegetarian; they're flavored with meat, fish, or meat drippings. A la carte specialties include filet of perch with Châteauneuf-du-Pape, rack of lamb with fresh thyme and garlic essence, filet of venison with foie gras, and a dessert of fennel sorbet with saffron-flavored English cream sauce.

10 rue Mons. ℂ **04-90-86-16-50.** Reservations required. Main courses 28€–40€ ($36–$52); fixed-price lunch 30€–105€ ($39–$137); fixed-price dinner 55€–105€ ($72–$137). AE, DC, MC, V. Tues–Sat noon–1:30pm and 8–9:30pm. Closed first 2 weeks in Aug and Dec 20–Jan 6.

Hiély-Lucullus ✦✦ FRENCH   Before the arrival of Christian Etienne (see above), this Relais Gourmand property reigned supreme in Avignon. Today it is still formidable competition. The Belle Epoque decor enhances the grand cuisine. Market-fresh products go into innovative dishes such as crayfish-stuffed ravioli flavored with fresh sage and served with pumpkin sauce; filet of female venison with tangy honey sauce; and escalope of sautéed foie gras on toasted rye bread. Lots of fresh fish is imported daily and cooked to perfection. The pièce de résistance is *agneau des Alpilles grillé* (grilled Alpine lamb). Dessert might be vanilla-bourbon cream in puff pastry. Carafe wines include Tavel Rosé and Châteauneuf-du-Pape.

5 rue de la République. ℂ **04-90-86-17-07.** Reservations required. Main courses 15€–26€ ($20–$34); fixed-price menu 28€–45€ ($36–$59). AE, MC, V. Daily noon–2pm and 7–10pm.

MODERATE

La Fourchette *Value* FRENCH   This bistro offers creative cooking at a moderate price, although it shuts down on the weekends. It has two airy dining rooms with large bay windows that flood the inside with light. You might begin with fresh sardines flavored with citrus, ravioli filled with haddock, or parfait of chicken livers with spinach flan and confit of onions. For a main course, we recommend monkfish stew with endive, or daube of beef with gratin of macaroni.

7 rue Racine. ℭ **04-90-85-20-93**. Fixed-price lunch 24€–29€ ($31–$38); fixed-price dinner 29€ ($38). MC, V. Mon–Fri 12:30–1:45pm and 7:15–9:45pm. Closed 3 weeks in Aug. Bus: 11.

Piedoie ℛ *Finds* MODERN FRENCH   In an intimate yellow-and-ocher-colored dining room behind the city ramparts, this place is the creative statement of its namesake, Thierry Piedoie, a chef who takes his food seriously. Menu items change with the seasons and availability of ingredients, but are likely to include a warm tartlet of asparagus tips and Serrano ham; a platter with smoked Scottish salmon, black Provençal olives, and herb salad; sweetbreads with glazed ginger and a confit of lemons; and filet of sole served with sesame seeds and grapefruit segments.

26 rue des Trois-Faucons. ℭ **04-90-86-51-53**. Reservations recommended. Main courses 13€–38€ ($17–$49); fixed-price menus 18€–30€ ($23–$39) lunch, 26€–52€ ($34–$68) dinner. MC, V. Thurs–Tues noon–1:30pm and 7:15–9:30pm. Closed 2 weeks in Feb and 2 weeks in Nov.

NEARBY ACCOMMODATIONS & DINING

Auberge de Cassagne ℛℛ   This could be your best bet for food and lodging in the greater Avignon area. The hotel, set in a park, is an enchanting little Provençal inn with country-style rooms. Rooms, most of which are connected by the pleasant, tree-studded inner courtyard, have been recently renovated and boast fine Provençal linens and tile flooring. The roomy bathrooms are handsomely maintained, with generous shelf space and deluxe toiletries. The cuisine is exceptionally good, much of it in the style of Paul Bocuse. You can enjoy your meals in an elegantly rustic dining room or at a table in the garden. The kitchens feature dishes like a duo of turbot and salmon served with a ragout of mushrooms, foie gras braised in port wine, and tagliatelle with a confit of tomatoes and olive oil.

450 allée de Cassagne, Rte. de Vèdene (D62), Le Pontet, 84130 Avignon. ℭ **04-90-31-04-18**. Fax 04-90-32-25-09. www.aubergedecassagne.com. 40 units. 160€–377€ ($208–$490) double; 378€–420€ ($491–$546) junior suite. AE, DC, MC, V. Free parking. Take N7 and D62 for 6km (4 miles) northeast. **Amenities:** Restaurant; outdoor pool; nearby golf course; tennis court; health club; Jacuzzi (in some); sauna; limited room service; babysitting; laundry service; dry cleaning. *In room:* A/C, TV, dataport, minibar, hair dryer, safe.

Hostellerie de l'Abbaye de la Celle ℛℛ   One of France's most famous chefs, Alain Ducasse, whose five-star Michelin ratings have been the source of endless jealously and competition, is the owner of this idyllic Provençal inn. It lies in the hamlet of La Celle, midway between Nice and Avignon, on rocky, rolling land, a short walk from an 18th-century monastery that's the architectural highlight of the village. Within its premises, Ducasse set out to create an inn that lives up to one's fantasy of Provence. The components that go into this include a dining room featuring simple and delicious cooking, and individually decorated rooms that evoke what you might have found within a distinguished Mediterranean villa. Five of them are within an annex that Ducasse commissioned in 1999; the others are within an ocher-sided manor house that was built in 1745 as one of the outbuildings of the nearby monastery. Bathrooms are roomy and luxurious.

Place du Général-de-Gaulle, 83170 La Celle. ℭ **04-98-05-14-14**. Fax 04-98-05-14-15. www.abbaye-celle.com. 10 units. 205€–345€ ($267–$449) double. AE, DC, MC, V. From Avignon, take the A8 Autoroute in the direction of Toulon, then exit at Brignoles, and follow the signs to La Celle. It's a total distance of 35km (22 miles) and takes about 40 min. each way. **Amenities:** Restaurant; bar; outdoor pool; library; babysitting; limited-mobility rooms. *In room:* A/C, TV, minibar, safe, hair dyer.

AVIGNON AFTER DARK

Near the Palais des Papes is **Le Grand Café,** La Manutention (© **04-90-86-86-77**), a restaurant-bar-cafe that just might become your favorite watering hole. Behind the Palais des Papes, it lies in an entertainment complex in a former military supply warehouse. The dance-club standby is **Les Ambassadeurs,** 27 rue Bancasse (© **04-90-86-31-55**); it's more animated than its competitor, **Piano Bar Le Blues,** 25 rue Carnot (© **04-90-85-79-71**). Nearby is a restaurant, **Red Zone,** 27 rue Carnot (© **04-90-27-02-44**), that books live performances in the bar area by whatever band happens to be in town.

Winning the award for most unpronounceable name is **Le Woolloomoolloo** (it means "black kangaroo" in an Australian Aboriginal dialect), 16 bis rue des Teinturiers (© **04-90-85-28-44**). The bar and cafe complement a separate room devoted to the cuisine of France and a changing roster of cuisines from Asia, Africa, and South America. An alternative is **Bokao's Café,** 9 quai St-Lazare (© **04-90-82-47-95**), a restaurant and disco. The most viable option for lesbians and gays is **L'Esclav,** 12 rue de Limas (© **04-90-85-14-91**), a bar and disco that are the focal point of the city's gay community.

VISITING VILLENEUVE-LEZ-AVIGNON ⚑

The modern world is impinging on Avignon, but across the Rhône, the Middle Ages slumber on. When the popes lived in exile at Avignon, cardinals built palaces *(livrées)* across the river. Many visitors prefer to stay or dine here rather than in Avignon. Villeneuve-lèz-Avignon lies just across the Rhône from Avignon, and is easiest to reach on bus no. 11, which crosses the larger of the two relatively modern bridges, the **pont Daladier.** For information about the town, contact the **Office de Tourisme,** 1 place Charles David (© **04-90-25-61-33**).

Cardinal Arnaud de Via founded the **Eglise Notre-Dame,** place Meissonier (© **04-90-25-46-24**), in 1333. Other than its architecture, the church's most popular attraction is an antique copy (by an unknown sculptor) of Enguerrand Charonton's *Pietà,* the original of which is in the Louvre. The church is open April to September, daily from 10am to 12:30pm and 2 to 6:30pm; October to March daily 10am to noon and 2 to 5pm (closed Feb). Admission is free.

Chartreuse du Val-de-Bénédiction   Inside France's largest Carthusian monastery, built in 1352, you'll find a church, three cloisters, rows of cells that housed the medieval monks, and rooms depicting aspects of their daily lives. Part of the complex is devoted to a workshop (the Centre National d'Ecritures et du Spectacle) for painters and writers, who live in the cells rent-free for up to a year to pursue their craft. Photo and art exhibits take place throughout the year.

Pope Innocent VI (whose tomb you can view) founded this charterhouse, which became the country's most powerful. The 12th-century graveyard cloister is lined with cells where the fathers prayed and meditated.

Rue de la République. © 04-90-15-24-24. Admission 6.10€ ($7.95) adults, 4.10€ ($5.35) students, free for children under 18. Apr–Sept daily 9am–6:30pm; Oct–Mar daily 9:30am–5:30pm.

Tour Philippe le Bel   Philippe the Fair constructed this tower in the 13th century, when Villeneuve became a French possession; it served as a gateway to the kingdom. If you have the stamina, you can climb to the top for a view of Avignon and the Rhône Valley.

Rue Montée-de-la-Tour. ℂ **04-32-70-08-57**. Admission 1.60€ ($2.10) adults, .90€ ($1.15) students and children 12–17. Apr–Sept daily 10am–12:30pm and 2–7:30pm; Mar and Oct–Nov Tues–Sun 10am–12:30pm and 3–7pm. Closed Dec–Feb.

WHERE TO STAY & DINE IN VILLENEUVE-LEZ-AVIGNON

Best Western La Magnaneraie ★★ One of the most charming accommodations in the region is this 15th-century country house on a hectare of gardens, under the direction of Gérard and Eliane Prayal. Tastefully renovated, the place is furnished with antiques and good reproductions. Bathrooms are neatly arranged. Many guests who arrive for only a night remain for many days to enjoy the good food and atmosphere, garden, tennis court, and landscaped pool. Madame Prayal's cuisine is excellent: Menu items might include zucchini flowers stuffed with mushroom-and-cream purée, feuilleté of foie gras and truffles, croustillant of red snapper with basil and olive oil, and rack of lamb with thyme. Dessert might be gratin of seasonal fruits with sabayon of lavender-flavored honey.

37 rue Camp-Bataille, 30400 Villeneuve-lèz-Avignon. ℂ **04-90-25-11-11**. Fax 04-90-25-46-37. www.bestwestern. com. 32 units. 118€–230€ ($153–$299) double; 310€ ($403) suite. AE, DC, MC, V. Free parking. **Amenities:** Restaurant; bar; outdoor pool; tennis court; 24-hr. room service; babysitting; laundry service/dry cleaning; nonsmoking rooms; limited-mobility rooms. *In room:* A/C, TV, dataport, minibar, beverage maker, hair dryer, safe.

Hôtel de l'Atelier *(Value)* Villeneuve's budget offering is this 16th-century village house that has preserved much of its original style. Inside is a tiny duplex lounge with a large stone fireplace. Outside, a sun-filled rear garden, with potted orange and fig trees, provides fruit for breakfast. The immaculate accommodations are comfortable and informal, though a bit dowdy. Bathrooms are small but nicely arranged. In the old bourgeois dining room, a continental breakfast is the only meal served.

5 rue de la Foire, 30400 Villeneuve-lèz-Avignon. ℂ **04-90-25-01-84**. Fax 04-90-25-80-06. www.hoteldelatelier.com. 23 units. 46€–91€ ($60–$118) double. AE, DC, MC, V. Parking 8€ ($10) in nearby garage, free on street. **Amenities:** Breakfast room; lounge. *In room:* TV.

Le Prieuré ★★★ This small, charming, well-managed property was converted from a 1322 cardinal's residence. Roger Mille purchased it in 1943, and three generations of his family have been running it. Adjacent to the village church, it has an ivy-covered stone exterior, along with green shutters, a tiled roof, and a series of rustic but plush public rooms. There is a choice of bedrooms. Those in the main house, the actual old priory, are a bit smallish but filled with antique charm. Those in the modern annex by the swimming pool are much more spacious and offer better views. Whatever your assignment, you'll be rewarded with grand style and luxe living. One of the finest Relais & Châteaux properties in the south of France, "The Priory" remains the first choice for those with traditional taste who demand the very best wherever they travel.

Tables at the in-house restaurant are eagerly booked, as Le Prieure has long been known for the excellence of its cuisine and the charm of its setting. June through September, lunches, which feature an array of dishes, especially freshly made salads, are served on a luxurious terrace adjacent to the pool.

7 place du Chapitre, 30400 Villeneuve-lèz-Avignon. ℂ **04-90-15-90-15**. Fax 04-90-25-45-39. www.leprieure.fr. 36 units. 128€–228€ ($166–$296) double. AE, DC, MC, V. Free parking. Closed Nov–Mar. **Amenities:** Restaurant; bar; outdoor pool; 2 tennis courts. *In room:* A/C, TV, minibar, hair dryer, safe.

4 Uzès ⓚ

682km (424 miles) S of Paris; 39km (24 miles) W of Avignon; 51km (32 miles) NW of Arles

This scenically beautiful village is set on a limestone plateau that straddles the line between Provence and the Garrigues region, the severe though charming countryside along the foot of the ancient Massif Central. It is famous for the long-standing House of Uzès, home of France's highest-ranking ducal family, who still live in the ducal palace of Le Duché that dominates the town.

Jean Racine lived here in 1661, sent by his family to stay with an uncle, the vicar general of Uzès, in hopes that his dramatic ambitions might be dispelled. They weren't, and he went on to claim his place as one of France's great dramatists/poets. More recently, Uzès was the setting of Jean-Paul Rappeneau's version of *Cyrano de Bergerac,* in which Gérard Depardieu played the part of the soldier-poet.

In 1962, the village was named one of France's 500 *villes d'art* and has since taken good advantage of preservation funds set aside for restoration of its historic district. However, the designation has been viewed as a mixed blessing since many visitors, notably Parisians taking a break from city life, have since discovered the charms of the village.

ESSENTIALS

GETTING THERE   There's no rail station in Uzès. **Train** passengers must get off at Avignon or Nîmes (both are a 1-hr. bus ride away). For rail information and schedules, call Rail Europe ⓒ **800/387-6782.** There are about eight **buses** a day from both places. For bus information, contact the **Gare Routière d'Uzès,** avenue de la Libération, through the tourist office ((ⓒ **04-66-22-68-88**). By **car** from Avignon, take N100 west to the intersection with D981, following the road signs northwest into Uzès.

VISITOR INFORMATION   The **Office de Tourisme** is on place Albert-1er (ⓒ **04-66-22-68-88**).

SPECIAL EVENTS   The well-attended **Nuits Musicales d'Uzès** draws musicians of many stripes and talents from all over the world to a series of musical concerts performed at various venues throughout the town. The event takes place during the second half of July, with tickets costing from 8€ to 35€ ($10–$46) per performance, depending on seating arrangements. Tickets for these events along with announcements of concerts are available at the tourist office.

SEEING THE SIGHTS

In the old part of town, every building is worth a moment or two of consideration. A pleasant square for a stroll, the asymmetrical **place aux Herbes** is defined by the medieval homes and sheltered walkways along its edges. The **Cathédrale St-Théodorit,** place de l'Evêché (ⓒ **04-66-22-13-26**), still utilizes its original 17th-century organ, a remarkable instrument composed of 2,772 pipes. The cathedral is open daily from 8am to 7pm. If you're lucky enough to be here during the last 2 weeks of July, you can attend one of the organ concerts that highlight the Nuits Musicales d'Uzès festival (see above). Adjacent is the circular six-story **Tour Fenestrelle,** all that remains of the original 12th-century cathedral that was burnt down by the Huguenots. It's closed to the public.

Le Duché ⓚ   The palace is a massive conglomeration of styles, the result of nearly continuous expansion of the residence in direct correlation to the rising wealth and power of the duke and duchess. The Renaissance facade blends Doric, Ionic, and

Corinthian elements. Easily seen from below is the Tour de la Vicomté, a 14th-century watchtower recognizable by its octagonal turret.

Large segments of the compound, most notably its sprawling annex, are occupied by the Duc and Duchesse de Crussol d'Uzès and cannot be visited. You can climb the winding staircase in the square 11th-century Tour Bermonde for a sweeping view over the countryside from its elevated terrace. The 11th-century cellar, noted for its huge dimensions and vaulted ceilings, contains casks of wine from the surrounding vineyards. Tours of the site end with a *dégustation* of the reds and rosés of the Cuvée Ducale. The building's showcase apartments include a dining room with Louis XIII and Renaissance furnishings, a great hall (Le Grand Hall) done in the style of Louis XV, a large library that includes family memoirs, and the 15th-century Chapelle Gothique. Visits are usually part of an obligatory French-language tour, but you can follow the commentary with an English-language pamphlet.

Place du Duché. ⓒ **04-66-22-18-96.** Admission 11€ ($14) adults, 8€ ($10) students and teens 12–16, 4€ ($5.20) children 8–11, free for children 7 and under. Mid-Sept to late June daily 9am–noon and 2–6pm; late June to mid-Sept daily 9–6pm.

WHERE TO STAY

Hôtel du Général Entraigues ⍟ *(Value* The core of this hotel is a 15th-century manor house, expanded into two separate buildings, and much of it still looks as it did 300 years ago. It's nestled in a Mediterranean garden adjacent to the cathedral. Room furnishings vary from comfortably old-fashioned to modern contemporary. Like Marie d'Agoult, d'Entraigues is imbued with the charm of yesterday, but the comfort isn't as lavish here; Marie d'Agoult also has far greater amenities such as a pool and tennis courts. D'Entraigues's strongest selling point is in its remarkable price.

8 rue de la Calade, 30700 Uzès. ⓒ **04-66-22-32-68.** Fax 04-66-22-57-01. www.leshotelsparticuliers.com. 34 units. 55€–98€ ($72–$127) double. AE, DC, MC, V. Parking 10€. **Amenities:** Restaurant; bar; limited room service. *In room:* A/C, TV, minibar, hair dryer, safe.

Hôtel Marie d'Agoult (Château d'Arpaillargues) ⍟⍟ The foundations of this place are believed to date from a 3rd-century fortress, making it as old as the Gallo-Roman occupation of Provence. The combination of rough and chiseled stone construction you see today is from the late 1600s and early 1700s, and was a site where silkworms were raised when this area was a silk-making center. The hotel is named for a former occupant, Marie d'Agoult, mistress of Franz Liszt and mother of Richard Wagner's wife, Cosima. The place offers a sleepy insight into a way of life of long ago. The rooms, on the ground floor, have vaulted ceilings with exposed brick, and bathrooms are small but tidy.

Arpaillargues, 30700 Uzès. ⓒ **04-66-22-14-48.** Fax 04-66-22-56-10. www.leshotelsparticuliers.com. 27 units. 90€–210€ ($117–$273) double; 225€–250€ ($293–$325) suite. AE, MC, V. Closed Oct–Mar. Drive 4km (2½ miles) west of Uzès, following the signs to Andouze-Arpaillargues. **Amenities:** Restaurant; bar; outdoor pool; tennis court; limited room service. *In room:* A/C in most units, TV, minibar, hair dryer, safe.

WHERE TO DINE

If you'd like to dine in town, consider the **Jardins de Castille,** the restaurant of the Hôtel du Général Entraigues (see above). However, the area's best place to dine is in the hamlet of **St-Maximin,** 6km (3½ miles) southeast of Uzès. To reach it from Uzès, follow the signs to St-Maximin.

Les Fontaines MEDITERRANEAN In a 12th-century building in the heart of Uzès, you can enjoy thoughtful service and a well-seasoned roster of mostly Mediterranean dishes. Menu items include roasted breast of duckling with cherry sauce; a brochette of scallops served with braised leeks and cinnamon sauce; thin sliced chicken cutlets cooked in a salt crust flavored with cocoa; and roasted monkfish served with a fennel flan. The selection of cheeses offered from the trolley is wide and comprehensive, and a particularly succulent dessert is a frozen white-chocolate soufflé served with a whiskey-flavored cream sauce. The courtyard contains a scattering of summertime tables and a pair of verdant fig trees.

6 rue Entre les Tours. ℭ **04-66-22-41-20.** Reservations recommended. Main courses 19€–33€ ($25–$43); set menus 20€–24€ ($26–$31). AE, MC, V. Mar–June and Sept–Jan Tues–Sun noon–2pm and 7:30–10pm; July–Aug daily.

5 Arles ★★★

724km (450 miles) S of Paris; 35km (22 miles) SW of Avignon; 89km (55 miles) NW of Marseille

Often called the soul of Provence, this town on the Rhône attracts art lovers, archaeologists, and historians. To the delight of visitors, many of the vistas van Gogh painted so luminously remain. The painter left Paris for Arles in 1888, the same year he cut off part of his left ear. He painted some of his most celebrated works here, including *Starry Night, The Bridge at Arles, Sunflowers,* and *L'Arlésienne.*

The Greeks are said to have founded Arles in the 6th century B.C. Julius Caesar established a Roman colony here. Constantine the Great named it the second capital of his empire in 306 A.D., when it was known as "the little Rome of the Gauls." Arles was incorporated into France in 1481.

Though Arles doesn't possess as much charm as Aix-en-Provence, it's still rewarding to visit, with first-rate museums, excellent restaurants, and summer festivals. The city today, with a population of 55,000, isn't quite as lovely as it was when Picasso lived here, but it has enough of the antique charm of Provence to keep its appeal alive.

ESSENTIALS

GETTING THERE   **Trains** from Paris's Gare de Lyon arrive at Arles's Gare SNCF, avenue Paulin-Talabot, a short walk from the town center. One high-speed direct TGV travels from Paris to Arles each day (4½ hr.; 120€/$156 first class, 72€/$83 second class). For other trains, you must change in Avignon. There are hourly connections between Arles and Avignon (15 min.; 8€–10€/$10–$13), Marseille (1 hr.; 15€–17€/$20–$22), and Aix-en-Provence via Marseille (1¾ hr.; 15€–21€/$20–$27). For rail schedules and information, call ℭ **08-92-35-35-35.** There are about four **buses** per day from Aix-en-Provence (trip time: 1¾ hr.). For bus information, call ℭ **08-10-00-08-16.** If you're **driving,** head south along D570 from Avignon.

VISITOR INFORMATION   The **Office de Tourisme** is on esplanade Charles-de-Gaulle (ℭ **04-90-18-41-20;** www.tourisme.ville-arles.fr). Here you can buy a *billet global,* a pass that admits you to the town's museums, Roman monuments, and major attractions for 14€ ($18) for adults, 12€ ($16) for students and children under 19.

GETTING AROUND   If you'd like to get around by bicycle, head for a kiosk ten minutes south of the city center, **Europbike,** kiosk à Journaux Le Provençal, esplanade Charles de Gaulle (ℭ **04-90-49-54-69**). A six-speed road bike, the only kind they have, rents for 14€ ($18) per day and requires a deposit of 260€ ($338).

EXPLORING THE TOWN

Arles is full of Roman monuments. **Place du Forum,** shaded by plane trees, is around the old Roman forum. The Café de Nuit, immortalized by van Gogh, once stood on this square. You can see two Corinthian columns and fragments from a temple at the corner of the Hôtel Nord-Pinus. Three blocks south of here is **place de la République,** dominated by a 15m-tall (50-ft.) blue porphyry obelisk. On the north is the **Hôtel de Ville** (town hall) from 1673, built to Mansart's plans and surmounted by a Renaissance belfry.

Eglise St-Trophime ⟡ On the east side of the square, this church's 12th-century portal is one of the finest achievements of the southern Romanesque style. In the pediment, Christ is surrounded by the symbols of the Evangelists. Frederick Barbarossa was crowned king of Arles on this site in 1178. The cloister, in both the Gothic and Romanesque styles, is noted for its medieval carvings. Be warned that the hours listed below are sometimes unpredictable; they can change at the whim of the custodial staff.

East side of place de la République. ℂ **04-90-49-33-53.** Free admission to church; cloister 3.50€ ($4.55) adults, 2.60€ ($3.40) students and children 12–18, free for children under 12. Church daily 8:30am–6:30pm. Cloister Nov 11–Feb 28 daily 10am–5pm; Mar 1–Apr 30 and Oct 1–Oct 30 daily 9am–6pm; May 2–Sept 30 daily 9am–6:30pm. Closed Jan 1, May 1, Nov 1, and Dec 25.

Les Alyscamps ⟡ This is one of the most famous necropolises of the western world. Its fame began when Genesius, a Roman civil servant, refused to write down an edict calling for persecution of Christians. For this, he was beheaded in 250; later he was made a saint when it was said that miracles began to happen on this site. In time, the fame of Les Alyscamps spread throughout the Christian world; more of the faithful wanted to be buried here, and coffins were shipped down the Rhône for burial. By the 10th century, the legend spread that the heroes of Roncevaux—Roland and Olivier—were also entombed here, which brought the place even more fame. Dante even mentioned it in his *Inferno.*

In the Middle Ages, there were 19 churches and chapels on the site. After the Renaissance, the graveyard was desecrated: Tombs were removed and stones were taken to construct other buildings. For an evocative experience, walk down L'Allée des Sarcophages, where 80 generations have been buried over 2,000 years. The lane is lined with sarcophagi under tall poplar trees.

Rue Pierre-Renaudel. ℂ **04-90-49-36-87.** Admission 3.50€ ($4.55) adults, 2.60€ ($3.40) children 12–18, free for children 11 and under. Nov 2–Feb 28 daily 10am–5pm; Mar 1–Apr 30 and Oct 1–Oct 30 daily 9–6pm; May 2–Sept 30 daily 9am–6:30pm. Closed Jan 1, May 1, Nov 1, and Dec 25.

Musée de l'Arles Antique ⟡⟡ Opened in 1995, the museum holds one of the world's most famous collections of Roman Christian sarcophagi as well as a rich ensemble of sculptures, mosaics, and inscriptions from the Augustinian period to the 6th century A.D. Eleven detailed models show ancient monuments of the region as they existed in the past. Allow 1 hour to view the museum's holdings.

Presqu'île du Cirque Romain. ℂ **04-90-18-88-88.** Admission 5.50€ ($7.15) adults, 4€ ($5.20) students and children under 18. Mar 1–Oct 31 daily 9am–7pm; Nov 11–Feb 28 daily 10am–5pm. Closed Jan 1, May 1, Nov 1, and Dec 25.

Museon Arlaten ⟡ The museum was founded by Frédéric Mistral, the Provençal poet who led a movement to establish modern Provençal as a literary language, using the money from his Nobel Prize for Literature in 1904. This is really a folklore museum, with regional costumes, portraits, furniture, dolls, a music salon, and a room devoted to mementos of Mistral. Among its curiosities is a letter (in French) from President Theodore Roosevelt to Mistral, bearing the letterhead of the Maison Blanche in Washington, D.C.

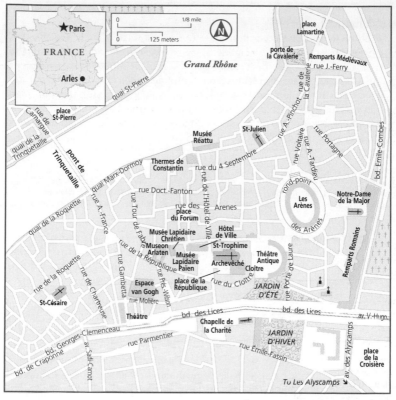

29 rue de la République. ℂ **04-90-93-58-11.** Admission 4€ ($5.20) adults, 3€ ($3.90) students and children under 18. June–Aug daily 9:30am–noon and 2–6:30pm; Sept daily 9:30am–noon; Apr–May Tues–Sun 9:30am–noon and 2–6pm; Oct–Mar Tues–Sun 9:30am–12:30pm and 2–5pm.

Théâtre Antique/Amphitheatre (Les Arènes) ⭐⭐ These are the city's two great classical monuments. The Roman theater, begun by Augustus in the 1st century, was mostly destroyed and only two Corinthian columns remain. Here the famous *Venus of Arles* was discovered in 1651. A copy of a masterpiece of Hellenistic statuary, it was broken into three pieces and armless when discovered. Arles offered it to Louis XIV, who had it restored, and today it is in the Louvre. To reach the theater, take rue de la Calade from the city hall.

Nearby, also built in the 1st century, the Amphitheater seats almost 25,000 and still hosts bullfights in summer. The government warns you to visit the old monument at your own risk, since the stone steps are uneven and much of the masonry is worn down to the point where it might be a problem for older travelers or for those with disabilities. For a good view, you can climb the three towers that remain from medieval times when the amphitheater was turned into a fortress. Note that the theater and Les Arènes maintain the same hours and the same fluid scheduling as Eglise St-Trophime.

Finds **Les Olivades**

In a somewhat isolated position 12km (7½ miles) north of Arles, **Les Olivades Factory Store,** chemin des Indienneurs, St-Etienne-du-Grès (*©* **04-90-49-19-19**), stands beside the road that's signposted to Tarascon and Avignon. Because of the wide array of art objects and fabrics inspired by the traditions of Provence, it's worth your while to make a trek out here. Fabrics, dresses, shirts for men and women, table linens, and fabric by the yard are all available at retail outlets of the Olivades chain throughout Provence, but here the selection is a bit cheaper and more diverse.

Théâtre Antique: Rue du Cloître. *©* **04-90-49-36-25**. Admission 3€ ($3.90) adults, 2.20€ ($2.85) students and children 12–18, free for children under 12. Amphitheatre: Rond-pont des Arènes. *©* **04-90-49-36-86**. 4€ ($5.20) adults, 3€ ($3.90) students and children under 19. Daily May–Sept 9am–7pm; Mar–Apr and Oct daily 9am–6pm; Nov–Feb 10am–4:30pm.

Thermes de Constantin   Near the banks of the Rhône is the entrance to some 4th-century Roman baths, which have been partially restored with characteristic bands of brickwork. The baths or thermae are all that remain of a once grand imperial palace that stood here, Palais Constantin. These baths are the largest that remain in Provence. Dating from Constantine's era, the ruins of the baths measure 98×45m (322×148 ft.). You enter by the tepidarium, going through the caldarium, with its remaining hypocaust. Allow about half an hour to inspect the ruins.

Rue Dominique-Maisto. *©* **04-90-49-35-40**. 3€ ($3.90) adults, 2.20€ ($2.85) children. Daily 9am–7pm.

Musée Réattu *𝒜*   The town's museum is named for the rather mediocre local painter Jacques Réattu, but it contains more important works—etchings and drawings by Picasso, and paintings by Alechinsky, Dufy, Léger, Henri Rousseau, and Zadkine. Note the Arras tapestries from the 16th century.

10 rue du Grand-Prieuré. *©* **04-90-49-37-58**. Admission 4€ ($5.20) adults, 3€ ($3.90) students and children 12–18, free for children under 12. May–Sept daily 10am–noon and 2–6:30pm; Mar–Apr and Oct daily 10am–noon and 2–5pm; Nov–Feb daily 1–5:30pm.

WHERE TO STAY
EXPENSIVE

Grand Hôtel Nord-Pinus *𝒜*   Few other hotels in town evoke Provence's charm as well as this one, which originated as a bakery at the turn of the 20th century. Occupying a town house on a tree-lined square in the heart of Arles, it has public rooms filled with antiques, an ornate staircase with wrought-iron balustrades, and many of the trappings you'd expect in an upscale private home. Guest rooms are glamorous, even theatrical; they come in a range of shapes, sizes and decors, and are filled with rich upholsteries and draperies arranged artfully beside oversize French doors. Bathrooms contain combination tub/showers. Many bullfighters and artists have stayed here—their photographs, as well as a collection of safari photos by Peter Beard, decorate the public areas.

14 place du Forum, 13200 Arles. *©* **04-90-93-44-44**. Fax 04-90-93-34-00. www.nord-pinus.com. 25 units. 137€–275€ ($178–$358) double; 412€ ($536) suite. AE, MC, V. Parking 15€ ($20). **Amenities:** Restaurant; bar; limited room service; laundry service; dry cleaning; nonsmoking rooms. *In room:* TV, dataport.

Hôtel Jules César ✦✦✦   This 17th-century Carmelite convent is now a stately country hotel with one of the best restaurants in town. Although it's in a noisy neighborhood, most rooms face the unspoiled cloister. You'll wake to the scent of roses and the sounds of birds singing. Throughout, you'll find a blend of neoclassic architecture and modern amenities. The decor is luxurious, with antique Provençal furnishings found at auctions in the countryside. The interior rooms are the most tranquil and the darkest, though enlivened by bright fabrics. Most of the downstairs units are spacious; the upstairs rooms are small but have a certain old-world charm. The rooms in the modern extensions are comfortable but lack character. Each bathroom comes with a combination tub/shower.

9 bd. des Lices, 13631 Arles Cedex. ⓒ 04-90-52-52-52. Fax 04-90-52-52-53. www.hotel-julescesar.fr. 58 units. 132€–225€ ($172–$293) double; 300€–385€ ($390–$501) suite. AE, DC, MC, V. Parking 14€ ($18). Closed Nov 10–Dec 24. **Amenities:** Restaurant; bar; limited room service; babysitting; laundry service; dry cleaning; nonsmoking rooms; limited-mobility rooms. *In room:* TV, dataport, minibar, hair dryer, safe.

MODERATE

Hôtel d'Arlatan ✦✦   This hotel occupies the former residence of the comtes d'Arlatan de Beaumont, near place du Forum and has been managed by the same family since 1920. It was built in the 15th century on the ruins of an old palace begun by Constantine—in fact, there's still a wall from the 4th century. Rooms are furnished with Provençal antiques and reproductions, with the walls covered in patterned wallpaper and, in some rare instances, tapestries in the style of Louis XV and Louis XVI. The most appealing rooms overlook the garden. This was a former private residence, so accommodations range from small (on the upper floors) to more spacious on the ground floor.

26 rue du Sauvage, 13100 Arles. ⓒ 04-90-93-56-66. Fax 04-90-49-68-45. www.hotel-arlatan.fr. 48 units. 85€–153€ ($111–$199) double; 173€–243€ ($225–$316) suite. AE, MC, V. Parking 14€ ($18). Closed Jan. **Amenities:** Bar; laundry service, babysitting; limited-mobility rooms, *In room:* A/C, TV, dataport, minibar.

INEXPENSIVE

Hôtel Calendal ✦ (Value)   Because of its reasonable rates, the Calendal is a bargain hunter's favorite. On a quiet square near the arena, it offers high-ceilinged accommodations decorated in bright colors. Most rooms have views of the hotel's garden, filled with palms and palmettos. Each unit comes with a compact shower-only bathroom. The restaurant has a limited menu featuring omelets, soups, and platters.

5 rue Porte de Laure, 13200 Arles. ⓒ 04-90-96-11-89. Fax 04-90-96-05-84. www.lecalendal.com. 38 units. 45€–99€ ($59–$129) double. Parking 10€ ($13). AE, DC, MC, V. Bus: 4. **Amenities:** Restaurant; bar; limited room service; laundry service; limited-mobility rooms; nonsmoking rooms. *In room:* A/C, TV, hair dryer.

Hôtel de la Muette   A short walk from the city's ancient Roman arena, this hotel occupies an old building that has been an inn since the 1100s. Extensively renovated and restored, it presents a severe-looking stone facade to the outside world and an interior that retains the ancient ceiling beams and rough-textured masonry walls. Cheerfulness is added in the form of many coats of white paint and traditional Provençal fabrics in bright hues of maize, red, and blue. Overall, the place is comfortable, if a bit cramped, representing good value for the money. Bathrooms are small, with barely adequate shelf space.

15 rue des Suisses, 13200 Arles. ⓒ 04-90-96-15-39. Fax 04-90-49-73-16. 18 units. 55€ ($72) double. AE, MC, V. Parking 7€ ($9.10). **Amenities:** Breakfast room; lounge; 24-hr. room service (for drinks and snacks). *In room:* TV, minibar, fridge, hair dryer.

Hôtel Le Cloître *(Value)*   This hotel, between the ancient theater and the cloister, offers great value. Originally part of a 12th-century cloister, it still has its original Romanesque vaultings. Throughout, you'll find a rich Provençal atmosphere, pleasant rooms with high ceilings, and subtle references to the building's antique origins. Guest rooms are lean on amenities except for phones and small, shower-only bathrooms. Some units have TVs available for a supplement of 4.50€ ($5.85) per day. It also has a TV lounge.

16 rue du Cloître, 13200 Arles. ⓒ **04-90-96-29-50.** Fax 04-90-96-02-88. 30 units. 55€–85€ ($72–$111) double. AE, MC, V. Parking 8€ ($10). Closed mid-Nov to Mar 15. Bus: 4. **Amenities:** TV lounge.

Hôtel Mirador   Just a minute's walk north of Arles' Roman arena, this is a pleasant family-run hotel in a central location. Bedrooms are slightly cramped but well maintained and cozy, with adequate bathrooms. The rooms with tubs are slightly higher in price. Public areas are outfitted in a *faux-antique* decor of exposed wood and flower-patterned fabrics. You'll be happiest here if you don't expect grandeur, and accept small inconveniences with a sense of humor.

3 rue Voltaire, 13200 Arles. ⓒ **04-90-96-28-05.** Fax 04-90-96-59-89. www.hotel-mirador.com. 15 units. 30€–40€ ($39–$52) double. AE, DC, MC, V. Parking 7€ ($9.10). **Amenities:** Breakfast room; lounge. *In room:* TV.

WHERE TO DINE

For a truly elegant meal, consider dining at the **Restaurant Lou Marquès** at the Hôtel Jules César (see "Where to Stay," above).

MODERATE

Brasserie Nord-Pinus ITALIAN/PROVENÇAL   It has accouterments not duplicated in any other hotel: Terraces that surround it on all sides, an ancient Roman column (part of the ancient Temple of Constantine) that rises from one edge of the terrace, a collection of photos in its bar (the Corrida Bar) of the grand painters of the 1950s who made it their hangout, and a collection of valuable photos of African wildlife taken by Peter Beard, a long-ago friend of Karen Blixen, that are artistically and historically important. Some visitors compare its high-ceilinged, lush, and artfully decadent brown, gold, and white interior to a Batista-era hotel in old Havana: It's hot, artsy, sensual, a bit imperial, comfortable, and very grand. The decor of the restaurant is vaguely baroque, filled with paneling and mirrors, with a '50s-era decor that's grand and elegant and that no one wants to change. The cuisine is one of the lightest and most sophisticated in town, employing top-notch chefs to prepare dishes based on the best of seasonal shopping. The menus change frequently but are generally a delight. The food is colorful, spicy, and artfully arranged on platters.

Place du Forum. ⓒ **04-90-93-44-44.** Reservations recommended. Main courses 15€–17€ ($20–$22); fixed-price menus 21€–35€ ($27–$46). AE, DC, MC, V. Thurs–Mon 12:30–2:30pm; Wed–Mon 7:30–11pm.

Chez Gigi *(Value)* MEDITERRANEAN/MEXICAN   A few steps from the Arena, this popular neighborhood restaurant offers home cooking at reasonable prices. It was established by Madame Gigi Boucher, *une Québecoise* who emigrated from Canada. The setting is casual, charming, and affordable, with several generations of families squeezed next to young dating couples. The menu is heavy on regional and Mediterranean specialties, using Provençal herbs and prepared with care. Occasional items on the menu from Mexico spice up the brew. Noteworthy dishes are *soupe des poissons* (fish soup served with crusty breads and cheese) and authentic *dorade Provençal* (an ocean fish grilled with regional herbs). For dessert, there's a lovely *crème brûlée*.

49 rue des Arènes. ℂ 04-90-96-68-59. Reservations required for lunch, recommended for dinner. Main courses 9.50€–15€ ($12–$20). MC, V. Tues–Sun 7:30pm–midnight.

La Gueule du Loup FRENCH/PROVENÇAL   Named after its founder, who, according to local legend, grew to resemble a wolf as he aged, this cozy, well-managed restaurant occupies a stone-fronted antique house in the historic core of Arles, near the ancient Roman arena. Today it's owned by members of the Allard family, who prepare serious gourmet-style French food that's more elaborate than the cuisine at many competitors. The best examples include hearty filet of bull braised in red wine, monkfish in saffron sauce, roasted cod with green and sweet red peppers in saffron sauce, and superb duckling cooked in duck fat and served with flap mushrooms. Reservations are important—the cozy room seats only 30.

39 rue des Arènes. ℂ 04-90-96-96-69. Reservations recommended. Main courses 12€–25€ ($16–$33); fixed-price menu 25€ ($33). MC, V. Easter–Oct Tues–Sat noon–2:30pm, Mon–Sat 7–9:30pm; Nov–Easter Tues–Sat noon–2:30pm and 7–9:30pm. Closed one week in Nov and mid-Jan to mid-Feb.

Restaurant Lou Marquès ⊛⊛ PROVENÇAL   Lou Marquès, part of a Relais & Châteaux hotel, has the best reputation in town. Seating is in the formal dining room or on the terrace. The cuisine features creative twists on Provençal specialties. A first course could be *queues de langoustine en salade vinaigrette d'agrumes et Basilque* (crustaceans and salad with citrus-and-basil vinaigrette) or *risotto de homard aux truffes* (lobster risotto with truffles). As a main course, try *pavé de loup en barigoule d'artichaut et à la sauge* (a thick slice of wolf fish with sage-stuffed artichokes) or *filet mignon de veau et ragoût fin de cèpes et salsifis* (veal with a stew of mushrooms and salsify). For a light dessert, there's *biscuit glacé au miel de lavande* (a small cake glazed with lavender honey).

At the Hôtel Jules-César, 9 bd. des Lices. ℂ 04-90-52-52-52. Reservations recommended. Main courses 28€–45€ ($36–$59); fixed-price menu 29€ ($38) lunch, 40€–80€ ($52–$104) dinner. AE, DC, MC, V. Daily noon–1:30pm and 7:30–10:30pm. Closed Nov 12–Dec 24.

ARLES AFTER DARK

Because of its relatively small population (around 50,000), Arles doesn't offer as many nightlife options as Aix-en-Provence, Avignon, Nice, or Marseille. The town's most appealing choice is the bar-cafe–music hall **Le Cargo de Nuit,** 7 av. Sadi-Carnot (ℂ **04-90-49-55-99**). Open only on Friday and Saturday night, it's a supper club that later plays live music—salsa, jazz, rock 'n' roll, whatever—and then offers disco dancing until 3am. The cover ranges from 8€ to 20€ ($10–$26).

The town's most animated cafe, where most singles go, is **Le Café van Gogh,** 11 place du Forum (ℂ **04-90-96-44-56**). Overlooking an attractive plaza, it features live music and an ambience that the almost-young and the restless refer to as *super-chouette,* or "super cool."

6 Les Baux ⊛⊛⊛

715km (444 miles) S of Paris; 19km (12 miles) NE of Arles; 80km (50 miles) N of Marseille and the Mediterranean

Cardinal Richelieu called Les Baux a "nesting place for eagles." In its lonely position high on a windswept plateau overlooking the southern Alpilles, Les Baux seems to be part of the mysterious, shadowy rock formations.

Once, it was the citadel of the powerful seigneurs of Les Baux, who ruled with an iron fist and sent their conquering armies as far as Albania. In medieval times, the flourishing culture of Les Baux attracted troubadours from all over Europe to the "court of love." Later, Les Baux was ruled by the notorious "Scourge of Provence," Raymond de Turenne, who sent his men throughout the land to kidnap people. If a victim's friends and family could not pay ransom, the poor wretch was forced to walk a gangplank over the cliff's edge.

When Les Baux became a Protestant stronghold in the 17th century, Richelieu, fed up with its constant rebellion against Louis XIII, commanded his armies in 1632 to destroy the "eagle's nest." Today the castle and ramparts are a mere shell, though you can see remains of great Renaissance mansions.

Now the bad news: Because of the beauty and drama of the area, Les Baux is virtually overrun with visitors; it's not unlike Mont-St-Michel in that respect.

ESSENTIALS

GETTING THERE   Les Baux is best reached by car; there is no rail service. Most train passengers get off at Arles. Bus service has been discontinued. Taxis in Arles (© 06-80-27-60-92) will take you to Les Baux for around 30€ ($39) each way; be sure to agree upon the fare in advance.

VISITOR INFORMATION   The **Office de Tourisme** (© 04-90-54-34-39; www. lesbauxdeprovence.com) is at Maison du Roy on rue Porte Mage, near the northern entrance to the old city.

EXPLORING THE AREA

Les Baux has two aspects: the inhabited and carefully preserved medieval village and the evocative ruins of its fortress, the "dead" village. Visitors enter the city through the

---

Moments   A Drive Through Hell

Below Les Baux is a jagged and irregular gorge, *Val d'Enfer* (Valley of Hell). You can access the valley by D27 and D78G and drive through this bleak and rugged scenery. Centuries ago, caves in the gorge were inhabited by humans. The gorge is the source of many Provençal legends—witches, sprites, and fairies are said to live in the caves.

On your way to the valley, you can stop at the **Cathédrale d'Images** *€€* (© 04-90-54-38-65), off Route du Val d'Enfer (D27), a kilometer (half-mile) north of the village, in a former quarry. Photographer Albert Plecy converted this dark, cavernous space of large, square limestone columns and high-arched ceilings into a three-dimensional palette for an interactive experience with frescoes of the Italian Renaissance. Forty-eight strategically placed projectors splash images from the frescoes in all directions: You might walk across a projection of a full fresco, while on the wall next to you a close-up of an infant's face from the scene is enlarged and displayed, and above you the dueling men in the back of the fresco are plucked out and brought into focus. The moving display, in synchronization with well-chosen musical pieces from the era, is 30 minutes long, though you can stay longer and watch the loop replay. It's open daily from 10am to 7pm; closed January 2 to February 8. Admission is 7.30€ ($9.50) for adults, 3.50€ ($4.55) for children under 18.

19th-century **Port Mage,** but in medieval times, the monumental Porte Eyguières was the only entrance to the fortified city.

From place St-Vincent are sweeping views over the Vallon de la Fontaine. This is the site of the 12th-century **Eglise St-Vincent** (no phone), with its beautiful campanile, called La Lanterne des Morts (Lantern of the Dead). The stained-glass windows were a gift from Rainier of Monaco, in his capacity as the marquis des Baux. They are modern, based on designs of French artist Max Ingrand. The church is open April to October daily from 9am to 6:30pm, November to March daily 10am to 5:30pm. **Yves Brayer Museum,** at the intersection of rue de la Calade and rue de l'Eglise (© **04-90-54-36-99**), holds a retrospective collection of the works of Yves Brayer (1907–90), a figurative painter and Les Baux's most famous native son (he's buried in the village cemetery). He painted scenes of Italy, of Morocco, and, in Spain, of many bullfights, working mainly in shades of red, ocher, and black. Brayer also decorated the restored 17th-century La Chapelle des Pénitents Blancs, which stands close to the Church of St. Vincent, with frescoes of the Annunciation, the Nativity, and Christ in Majesty. The museum is open April through September daily from 10am to 12:30pm and 2 to 6:30pm; off-season hours are Wednesday to Monday from 10am to 12:30pm and 2 to 5:30pm (closed Jan to mid-Feb). Admission is 4€ ($5.20) for adults, 2€ ($2.60) for students and children under 13. The Renaissance-era **Hôtel de Manville,** rue Frédéric-Mistral, functions today as the Mairie (Town Hall). Only its courtyard can be visited. The ancient town hall on place Louis Jou now contains the **Musée des Santons** (no phone), a collection of antique crèche figures. It's open April to October, daily from 9am to 7pm; November to March, daily from 9am to 5pm. In the Renaissance-era Hôtel Jean-de-Brion, rue Frédéric-Mistral (© **04-90-69-88-03** or 04-90-54-34-17), is the **Fondation Louis Jou,** which can be visited only by special arrangement. It has engravings and serigraphs by the artist. The 1569 **Hôtel des Porcelles** contains a collection of contemporary artists who have worked in Les Baux and in Provence.

Château des Baux   The grounds of the château encompass a complex of evocative, mostly ruined buildings, which were carved out of the rocky mountain peak. Also called *la ville morte* (the "ghost village") or La Citadelle, the Château des Baux is at the upper (northern) end of Les Baux. It's accessible via the rue du Château, at the Hôtel de la Tour du Brau, which contains a small archaeological and lapidary museum. Inside the compound is the ruined château des Baux with its tower-shaped *donjon* and surrounding ramparts, and the two towers, Tour Paravel and Tour Sarascenes. The collection of replicated medieval siege engines were built from the original plans. The ruined chapel of St-Blaise houses a little museum devoted to the olive. The site of the former castle covers an area at least five times that of the present village of Les Baux. As you stand here you can look out over the *Val d'Enfer* (Valley of Hell) and even glimpse the Mediterranean in the distance.

North end of Les Baux, via the rue de Château. © **04-90-54-55-56**. Admission 7.30€ ($9.50) adults, 5.50€ ($7.15) students, 3.50€ ($4.55) ages 7–17, 22€ ($28) family. Mar daily 9am–6:30pm; July–Aug daily 9am–8:30pm; Sept–Oct daily 9am–5pm.

WHERE TO STAY

Note that **La Riboto de Taven** (see "Where to Dine," below) has rooms for rent.

VERY EXPENSIVE

Oustaù de Baumanière ✦✦✦   This Relais & Châteaux member is one of southern France's legendary hotels. Raymond Thuilier bought the 14th-century farmhouse in 1945, and by the 1950s, it was a rendezvous for the glitterati. Today, managed by its founder's grandson, it's not as glitzy, but the three stone houses draped in flowering vines are still charming. The plush rooms evoke the 16th and 17th centuries. All units contain large sitting areas, and no two are alike. If there's no vacancy in the main building, the hotel will assign you to one of the annexes. Request Le Manoir, the most appealing. The spacious bathrooms contain tub/shower combinations. In the stone-vaulted dining room, the chef serves specialties like ravioli of truffles with leeks, *rossini* (stuffed with foie gras) of veal with fresh truffles, and roast duckling with olives. The award-winning *gigot d'agneau* (lamb) *en croûte* has become this place's trademark.

Les Baux, 13520 Maussane-les-Alpilles. ⓒ **04-90-54-33-07.** Fax 04-90-54-40-46. www.oustaudebaumaniere.com. 30 units. 230€–305€ ($299–$397) double; 355€–499€ ($462–$649) suite. AE, DC, MC, V. Closed Jan 4–Feb 5. Restaurant closed Wed all day and Thurs at lunch Oct–Mar. **Amenities:** Restaurant; outdoor pool; limited room service; babysitting; laundry service; limited-mobility rooms. *In room:* A/C, TV, dataport, minibar, hair dryer, iron, safe.

EXPENSIVE

La Cabro d'Or ⍟⍟⍟ This is the less famous, less celebrated sibling of the nearby Oustaù de Beaumanière. You'll find some of the most comfortable accommodations in the region in these five low-slung stone buildings. The original building, a farmhouse, dates from the 18th century. The guest room decor evokes old-time Provence with art and antiques. Some rooms have sweeping views over the countryside, and each comes with a combination tub/shower. The dining room sits in a much-altered agrarian building from the 1800s. The massive ceiling beams are works of art in their own right. The restaurant is flanked by a vine-covered terrace with views of a pond, a garden, and a rocky and barren landscape that has been compared to the surface of the moon. The cuisine, although not on the level of Oustaù de Baumanière's, is sublime—light and flavorful, with a special emphasis on fresh produce. Specialties include a thick roasted slice of foie gras of duckling served with lemon-flavored quince sauce and red port wine; carpaccio of red mullet flavored with olive oil and sea salt; and a lasagna of scallops served with strips of Serrano ham.

13520 Les Baux de Provence. ⓒ **04-90-54-33-21.** Fax 04-90-54-45-98. www.lacabrodor.com. 31 units. 135€–230€ ($176–$299) double; 278€–412€ ($362–$536) suite. Off-season discounts (about 25%) available. Half board 76€ ($99) per person. AE, DC, MC, V. Closed mid-Nov to Dec 21. **Amenities:** Restaurant; bar; outdoor pool; 2 tennis courts; laundry service; babysitting; limited-mobility rooms. *In room:* A/C, TV, dataport, minibar, hair dryer, iron, safe.

MODERATE

Auberge de la Benvengudo ⍟ In a quiet location about 1.5km (1 mile) south of town, this auberge is a 19th-century farmhouse surrounded by sculptured shrubbery, towering trees, and parasol pines. The property has a pool, a tennis court, and a terrace filled with the scent of lavender and thyme. About half of the rooms are in the original building, above the restaurant, and the rest in an attractive stone-sided annex. All are sunny and well maintained. Each has a private terrace or balcony, and some have antique four-poster beds. Five units come with shower only; the others have a combination tub/shower.

Vallon de l'Arcoule, rte. d'Arles, 13520 Les Baux. ⓒ **04-90-54-32-54.** Fax 04-90-54-42-58. www.benvengudo.com. 20 units. 130€–165€ ($169–$215) double; 190€ ($247) suite. AE, MC, V. Closed mid-Nov to mid-Feb. Take RD78 for 1.5km (1 mile) southwest of Les Baux, following signs to Arles. **Amenities:** Restaurant; outdoor pool; tennis court; limited room service; babysitting. *In room:* A/C, TV, dataport, hair dryer.

Mas de L'Oulivié ⍟⍟ This salmon-colored complex of traditional Provençal buildings, capped with terra-cotta roofs, is 1.6km (about a mile) from town. Lounges have beamed ceilings, terra-cotta floor tiles, and comfortable provincial furnishings.

The high-ceilinged bedrooms have casement doors that open onto the garden. The units vary in size and shape—some are quite spacious—with a corresponding wide difference in price. Bathrooms are tiled and roomy. Breakfast and lunch are the only meals served.

13520 Les Baux de Provence. (C) 04-90-54-35-78. Fax 04-90-54-44-31. www.masdeloulivie.com. 27 units. 100€–245€ ($130–$319) double; 290€–410€ ($377–$533) suite. AE, DC, MC, V. Closed Nov to mid-Mar. **Amenities:** Restaurant; bar; outdoor pool; tennis court; babysitting; laundry service; dry cleaning; garden. *In room:* A/C, TV, minibar, hair dryer, safe.

INEXPENSIVE

Hostellerie de la Reine-Jeanne *Value*   In the heart of the village, this warm, well-scrubbed inn is the best bargain in Les Baux. You enter through a typical provincial French bistro. All the guest rooms are spartan but comfortable, and three have terraces. Bathrooms are cramped and relatively modest, with a shower stall only.

Grand-Rue, 13520 Les Baux. (C) 04-90-54-32-06. Fax 04-90-54-32-33. 10 units. 55€–68€ ($72–$88) double. MC, V. Closed Jan 2–31 and mid-Nov to Dec 18. **Amenities:** Restaurant; bar; limited room service. *In room:* A/C, TV.

Hôtel Bautezar   The entrance of this inn takes you down a few steps into the large medieval vaulted dining room, where you'll find Provençal furnishings and cloth tapestries hanging from the white stone walls, and a terrace with a view of the Val d'Enfer. The well-maintained guest rooms are decorated in Louis XVI style. Bathrooms are small but tidy.

Rue Frédéric-Mistral, 13520 Les Baux. (C) 04-90-54-32-09. Fax 04-90-54-51-49. 10 units. 61€–77€ ($79–$100) double. MC, V. Closed Jan–Mar 15. **Amenities:** Restaurant; bar; lounge.

WHERE TO DINE

Two cafes near place St-Vincent offer refreshments and panoramic views: the **Hostellerie de la Reine Jeanne,** rue Frédéric-Mistral ((C) **04-90-54-32-06**), and the **Café/Restaurant Bautezar,** rue Frédéric-Mistral ((C) **04-90-54-32-09**). Note also that **L'Oustaù de Beaumanière** (see above) boasts an excellent dining room.

La Riboto de Taven *★★★*   Known for its flawless cuisine and market-fresh ingredients, this is one of the great restaurants of the area, a rival of La Cabro d'Or. The 1835 farmhouse outside the medieval section of town has been owned by two generations of the Novi family. In summer, you can sit outdoors. Brawny flavors and the heady perfumes of Provençal herbs characterize chef Jean-Pierre Novi's cuisine. Menu items may include sea bass in olive oil, fricassée of mussels flavored with basil, and lamb en croûte with olives, or perhaps, in late autumn and winter, medallions of roebuck served with caramelized root vegetables, plus homemade desserts. The menu changes virtually every day, and always features an intelligent and tasteful use of local ingredients and produce.

Accommodations include a quartet of rooms within the thick walls of the main *mas* (Provençal farmhouse), and of two "cave-dweller junior suites," which have been shoe-horned into the grottos at the far end of the establishment's garden, and which look out across the ravine toward the once-fortified citadel of Les Baux. Each of the accommodations is dry, comfortable, and gracefully accessorized with Provençal-style furniture, and each contains a minibar, phone, TV, hair dryer, and bathroom with a tub/shower combo. The property has an outdoor swimming pool.

Le Val d'Enfer, 13520 Les Baux. (C) 04-90-54-34-23. Fax 04-90-54-38-88. www.riboto-de-taven.fr. Reservations required. Fixed-price menu 48€ ($62). AE, DC, MC, V. Thurs–Tues 7:30–9:30pm. Closed Jan–Mar 1. Rooms 160€–250€ ($190–$325).

7 St-Rémy-de-Provence ⊛

705km (438 miles) S of Paris; 26km (16 miles) NE of Arles; 19km (12 miles) S of Avignon; 13km (8 miles) N of Les Baux

We're not alone in our enthusiasm for St-Rémy, for we've spotted Princess Caroline here several times. Nostradamus, the famous French physician/astrologer, was born here in 1503. In 1922, Gertrude Stein and Alice B. Toklas found St-Rémy after "wandering around everywhere a bit," as Ms. Stein wrote to Cocteau. But mainly St-Rémy is associated with Vincent van Gogh: He committed himself to an asylum here in 1889 after cutting off his left ear. His "cell" was later occupied by an interned German during World War I—Albert Schweitzer. Between moods of despair, van Gogh painted such works as *Olive Trees* and *Cypresses.*

Come to sleepy St-Rémy today not only for its history and sights, but for an experience of Provençal small-town living that you won't find in Aix or Avignon. It's a market town of considerable charm and attracts the occasional celebrity who "hides out" here away from the hordes.

ESSENTIALS
GETTING THERE   Local **buses** from Avignon (four to nine per day) take 40 minutes and cost around 5.50€ ($7.15) one-way. In St-Rémy, buses pull into the place de la République, in the town center. For bus information, call ✆ **04-90-82-07-35.** If you're **driving,** head south from Avignon along D571.

VISITOR INFORMATION   The **Office de Tourisme** is on place Jean-Jaurès (✆ **04-90-92-05-22**).

SEEING THE SIGHTS
The cloisters of the asylum at the 12th-century **Monastère de St-Paul-de-Mausolée** ⊛⊛, avenue Edgar-le-Roy (✆ **04-90-92-77-00**), were made famous by van Gogh's paintings. Now a psychiatric hospital, the former monastery is east of D5, a short drive north of Glanum (see below). You can't visit the cell where this genius was confined from 1889 to 1890, but it's still worth coming here to see the Romanesque chapel and the cloisters with their circular arches and columns and beautifully carved capitals. The cloisters are open Tuesday through Saturday from 9am to 7pm. Admission is 3.40€ ($4.40) adults, 2.25€ ($2.95) students and children 12 to 16. It's free for kids under 12. Adjacent to the church, you'll see a commemorative bust of van Gogh.

In the center of St-Rémy, the **Musée Archéologique,** in the Hôtel de Sade, rue du Parage (✆ **04-90-92-64-04**), displays sculptures and bronzes from the ancient Roman excavations at nearby Glanum. An outstanding collection on the ground floor includes votive altars, sarcophagi, obelisks, and fragments of columns and cornices from the temples of pagan gods. The courtyard contains the fragmented ruins of baths from the 4th century, along with ruins from a 5th-century baptistery. Upstairs are fragments from a temple dedicated to the goddess Valetudo, an evocative statue of a captured Gaul, and a beautiful low relief with the effigy of Fortuna and Hermes. A prehistoric collection of items from bones to flints is also on display. The museum is open year-round Tuesday to Sunday from 11am to 5pm (except Jan 1, May 1, Nov 1 and 11, and Dec 25). Entrance costs 3€ ($3.90) for adults; it's free for ages 17 and under.

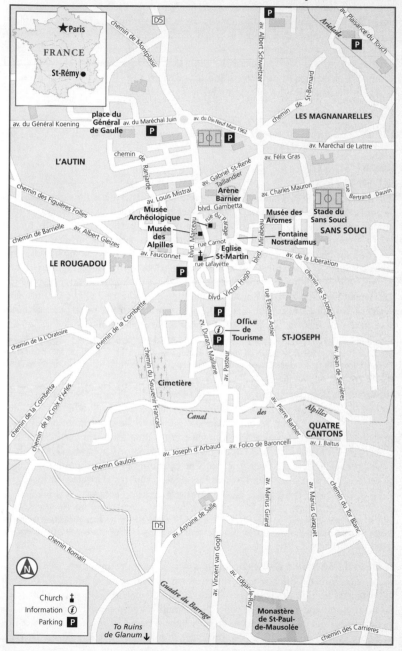

St-Rémy-de-Provence

★ Paris

FRANCE

St-Rémy ●

chemin de Montplaisir

D5

av. Plaisance du Touch

Arielade

av. Albert Schweitzer

P

P

av. du Général Koening

place du
Général
de Gaulle

P

av. du Maréchal Juin

av. du Dix-Neuf Mars 1962

P

chemin de St-Bernard

LES MAGNANARELLES

L'AUTIN

chemin de Ranjarde

av. Louis Mistral

av. Gabriel St-René
Taillandier

av. Félix Gras

av. Charles Mauron

av. Maréchal de Lattre

rue Bertrand Dauvin

chemin des Figuières Folles

Arène
Barnier

blvd. Gambetta

Stade du
Sans Souci

chemin de Barnielle

av. Albert Gleizes

Musée
Archéologique

rue du Marceau

rue du Parage

blvd. Mirabeau

Musée des
Aromes

SANS SOUCI

Musée
des
Alpilles

blvd. Marceau

rue Carnot

Fontaine
Nostradamus

LE ROUGADOU

av. Fauconnet

Eglise
St-Martin

av. de la Liberation

rue Lafayette

P

chemin de St-Joseph

blvd. Victor Hugo

rue Etienne Astier

chemin de la L'Oratoire

chemin de la Combette

P

av. Durand Maillane

Office
de
Tourisme

P

av. Pasteur

ST-JOSEPH

av. Jean de Servières

chemin de la Combette

chemin du Souvenir Francais

Cimetière

av. Pierre Barbier

Alpilles

QUATRE
CANTONS

chemin de la Croix d'Arles

Canal

des

av. J. Baltus

chemin Gaulois

av. Joseph d'Arbaud

av. Folco de Baroncelli

chemin du Tor Blanc

D5

av. Antoine de Salle

av. Vincent van Gogh

av. Marius Girard

av. Edgar-le-Roy

av. Marius Gasquet

chemin Romain

Guadre du Barrage

N

Church ♱

Information ⓘ

Parking P

To Ruins
de Glanum ↓

Monastère
de St-Paul-
de-Mausolée

chemin des Carrieres

Ruines de Glanum ⚑   A Gallo-Roman settlement thrived here during the final days of the Roman Empire. Its monuments include a triumphal arch from the time of Julius Caesar, along with a cenotaph called the Mausolée des Jules. Garlanded with sculptured fruits and flowers, the arch dates from 20 B.C. and is the oldest in Provence. The mausoleum was raised to honor the grandsons of Augustus and is the only extant monument of its type. Entire streets and foundations of private residences from the 1st-century town exist, plus some remains from a Gallo-Greek town of the 2nd-century B.C.

Av. Vincent-van-Gogh. ℭ **04-90-92-23-79.** Admission 6.10€ ($7.95) adults, 4.10€ ($5.35) students and ages 12–25, free for children under 12. Apr–Sept daily 9:30am–7pm; Oct–Mar Tues–Sun 10am–5pm. From St-Rémy, take D5 1.5km (1 mile) south, following signs to LES ANTIQUES.

WHERE TO STAY
EXPENSIVE

Château des Alpilles ⚑⚑⚑   For luxury and refinement, this is the only château in the area that can equal Vallon de Valrugues (see below). It sits in the center of a tree-studded park 2km (1¼ miles) from the center of St-Rémy. The Pichot family built it in 1827, and it housed Chateaubriand and other luminaries. When Françoise Bon converted the mansion in 1980, she wanted to create a "house for paying friends." The rooms combine an antique setting with plush upholstery, rich carpeting, and vibrant colors with a garden graced with majestic magnolias. Each guest room boasts whimsical accessories, like a pair of porcelain panthers flanking one of the mantels, and travertine-trimmed bathtubs. Units in the 19th-century annex are as comfortable as those in the main house. The midsize bathrooms have tub/showers.

Ancienne Rte. du Grès, 13210 St-Rémy-de-Provence. ℭ **04-90-92-03-33.** Fax 04-90-92-45-17. chateau.alpilles@ wanadoo.fr. 15 units. 175€–235€ ($228–$306) double; 265€–370€ ($345–$481) suite. AE, DC, MC, V. Closed Nov 15–Feb 15. **Amenities:** Restaurant; outdoor pool; 2 tennis courts; sauna; limited room service; laundry service. *In room:* TV, minibar, hair dryer, safe.

Domaine de Valmouriane ⚑⚑   This is a country-house hotel that occupies what was built at least a century ago as a farmhouse. Set on rocky, sun-flooded land, it offers charming, antiques-dotted accommodations, each with flowered upholsteries and a reference to whatever Provençal writer it was named after. Throughout, there's a sense of nostalgia for bygone eras and enormous charm. Madame Capel, the German-born owner, attends to dozens of small details. The establishment's focal point is a flowering terrace near the dining room, where Pierre Walter prepares spectacular meals.

Petite rte. Des Baux (D27), 13210 St-Rémy-de-Provence. ℭ **04-90-92-44-62.** Fax 04-90-92-37-32. www.valmouriane. com. 125€–335€ ($163–$436) double. AE, DC, MC, V. From St-Rémy, drive 5km (3 miles) from the center, following the signs to Beaucaire/Tarascon, and then, after reaching the D27, follow signs to Les Baux. **Amenities:** Restaurant; bar-cum-tearoom; outdoor pool; tennis court; Jacuzzi; babysitting; laundry service. *In room:* A/C, TV, minibar, hair dryer, safe.

Hostellerie du Vallon de Valrugues ⚑⚑⚑   Surrounded by a park, this hotel has the best accommodations and restaurant in town. Constructed in the 1970s, it resembles a fantasy version of an ancient Roman villa. Owner Jean-Michel Gallon offers beautiful rooms and suites, all of which boast marble bathrooms. The property has a putting green, and guests have access to horseback riding. The restaurant's terrace is as appealing as its cuisine, which is winning praise for innovative light dishes, such as John Dory with truffles, and frozen nougat with confit of fruit.

Chemin Canto-Cigalo, 13210 St-Rémy-de-Provence. ℭ **04-90-92-04-40.** Fax 04-90-92-44-01. www.hotelprestige-provence.com. 53 units. 160€–270€ ($208–$351) double; 390€–1,090€ ($507–$1,417) suite. AE, DC, MC, V. Closed

3 weeks in Feb. **Amenities:** Restaurant; bar; outdoor pool; 2 tennis courts; gym; sauna; babysitting; limited room service; laundry service; dry cleaning; nonsmoking rooms; limited-mobility rooms. *In room:* A/C, TV, dataport, minibar, hair dryer, safe.

MODERATE

Château de Roussan 🎯🎯 *Finds*   Although other château hotels are more stylish, this one is more evocative of another time. Its most famous resident, the psychic Nostradamus, lived in an outbuilding a few steps from the front door. Today, you'll pass beneath an archway of 300-year-old trees leading to the neoclassical facade, built in 1701. Most rooms are spacious. Expect old-fashioned plumbing with combination tub/showers. The staff can be off-putting, but the sense of mysticism and the historical importance of this place usually compensate for any crabbiness. History will envelop you as you wander the grounds, especially when you come upon the sculptures lining a basin, fed by a stream.

Rte. de Tarascon, 13210 St-Rémy-de-Provence. 📞 **04-90-92-11-63.** Fax 04-90-92-50-59. www.chateau-de-roussan. com. 21 units. 78€–100€ ($101–$129) double. AE, DC, MC, V. From the center, head in the direction of Tarascon (D99) for 2km (1¼ miles). **Amenities:** Restaurant; bar; limited room service; laundry service; limited-mobility rooms.

Mas de Cornud 🎯 *Finds*   The setting is a severely dignified, carefully renovated Provençal farmhouse, built 250 years ago and converted between 1985 and 1993 into the well-managed inn you'll see today. American-born David Carpita (formerly a banker) and his Egyptian-born wife, Nito, maintain a building that's loaded with regional memorabilia and antiques, along with artifacts from the rest of the world. Accommodations are cozy, high-ceilinged, and charming, with many yards of cheerful fabrics, a whimsical sense of nostalgia, and sometimes antique ceiling beams. The Carpitas maintain a high-caliber on-site cooking school, whose participants sometimes fill the hotel to capacity. This occurs during weeklong sojourns at 4 weeks scattered throughout the year.

Petite Rte. De Baux, 13210 St-Rémy-de-Provence. 📞 **04-90-92-39-32.** Fax 04-90-92-55-99. www.mascornud.com. 7 units. 100€–240€ ($130–$312) double. Rates include breakfast. No credit cards. Closed Nov–Mar. From St-Rémy, follow D99 to the D27 and then D31, following the signs to Mas de Cornud, driving 3km (2 miles) west of St-Rémy. **Amenities:** Restaurant; bar; outdoor pool; *pétanque* court; babysitting; laundry service. *In room:* No phone.

INEXPENSIVE

Hôtel du Soleil   In 1965, a private home was converted into this amiable, unpretentious hotel, a 4-minute walk south of the town center. The hotel is set in a garden with grand trees and a wrought-iron gazebo. Inside, the assortment of ceiling beams and Provençal accessories evoke the region around you. Guest rooms are simple but convenient, with tasteful furnishings and small, tiled bathrooms (some with both tub and shower). You'll want to spend part of your time beside the pool, ringed by chaises longues.

35 av. Pasteur, 13210 St-Rémy-de-Provence. 📞 **04-90-92-00-63.** Fax 04-90-92-61-07. www.hotelsoleil.com. 24 units. 53€–68€ ($69–$88) double. AE, DC, MC, V. Closed Nov to early Mar. **Amenities:** Bar; outdoor pool; limited room service. *In room:* TV, dataport, hair dryer, safe.

Hôtel van Gogh   Set 20m (67 ft.) east of the town's historic center, beside the highway leading to Cavaillon, this is a low-slung and pleasant hotel covered with ivy. Built in 1974 and renovated several times since then, it offers a reception area with a fireplace, parquet floors, and traditional furniture; clean bedrooms with a minimum of furniture; and small bathrooms. Breakfast, which is served on a backyard veranda with a striped canopy, is the only meal served.

1 av. Jean Moulin, 13210 St-Rémy de Provence. ⓒ **04-90-92-14-02.** Fax 04-90-92-09-05. www.hotel-vangogh.com. 21 units. 58€–72€ ($75–$94) double. AE, MC, V. Free parking. **Amenities:** Bar; lounge; outdoor pool; limited room service. *In room:* TV, hair dryer, safe (in some).

WHERE TO DINE

A great dining choice is the restaurant at **Vallon de Valrugues** (see above).

Charmeroy Maison de Gouts TEA/PASTRIES   Charming, intimate, and restful, this is a well-managed and attractive tearoom where doses of rest and relaxation are dispensed along with savory cups of some genuinely unusual teas. Operated with flair and imagination by a bilingual local resident, Madame Fabienne Charmeroy, it's a cozy environment on the boulevard that encircles the old town, near the Fountaine de la Liberté, midway between the Musée Jouenne and the Musée Floram. You'll find tea tables nestled amid displays that sell almost everything to do with the tea-drinking and tea-brewing ritual, including teapots, tea caddies, and tea cozies.

The pastries sold here are usually linked to the herbs and fruits of the region, with an emphasis on using whatever Provençal products are fresh at the time. Especially tempting are the tarts layered with slices of pear, prune, apricot, and lemon slices. But if you think the pastries are unusual, wait till you check out the teas: Many are custom-blended by Madame Charmeroy to reflect some aspect of Provence. Examples include a version named after Nostradamus, based on a 16th-century recipe, using grapes and cinnamon, that might have been consumed by the psychic himself. Other versions combine raspberries, orange blossoms, herbs from the Alpilles, edible orchids, white grapes, vanilla, figs, and apples into blends with names like Chung Hao, Fancy Oolang Black Dragon, and Gunpowder Green.

26 bd. Mirabeau. ⓒ **04-32-60-01-23.** Pots of tea 3.70€–4.10€ ($4.80–$5.35) each; pastries and ice cream 5.50€ ($7.15) each. No credit cards. Tues–Sun 10:30am–12:30pm and 3–7pm. During Jan and Feb, it's open only Fri–Sat 10:30am–12:30pm and 3–7pm.

La Maison Jaune 🌟🌟 FRENCH/PROVENÇAL   One of the most enduringly popular restaurants in St-Rémy is in the former residence of an 18th-century merchant. Today, in a pair of dining rooms occupying two floors, you'll appreciate cuisine prepared and served with flair by François and Catherine Perraud. In nice weather, additional seats are on a terrace overlooking the Hôtel de Sade. Menu items include pigeon roasted in wine from Les Baux; grilled sardines served with candied lemon and raw fennel; artichoke hearts marinated in white wine and served with tomatoes; and succulent roasted rack of lamb served with tapenade of black olives and anchovies.

15 rue Carnot. ⓒ **04-90-92-56-14.** Reservations required. Fixed-price menu 30€–55€ ($39–$72). No credit cards. Tues–Sun noon–1:30pm and 7–9:30pm. Closed Jan–Feb.

L'Assiette de Marie FRENCH/PROVENÇAL   Everything about this restaurant emulates the kind of cuisine and clutter that you'd have expected within the home of a French grandmother with roots in the Edwardian Age. It occupies a stone-fronted 200-year-old house in the center of St-Rémy, within a dining room whose walls are so densely covered with bric-à-brac (old mirrors, old paintings, old porcelain, and memorabilia from at least three of the last French governments) that, in the words of the staff, "There's not even room to hang another painting." Even the plates used at table are artfully mismatched and antique, the kind of thing you'd find within a slightly junky but endlessly fascinating antiques store.

Marie Ricco, the Corsican-Italian owner, and her polite staff offer only one dining choice: A 29€ ($38) three-course fixed-price menu whose components change with the season and the inspiration of the chef. Menu items might include *une assiette de Marie* (Marie's platter), loaded with the Provençal equivalent of antipasti (grilled and marinated peppers, tapenade of olives, and miniportions of brandade de morue) and warm cheese from local goats, resting on a bed of either mache or wild field greens. Pastas, served as main courses, are always made fresh and on-site, and might include ravioli stuffed with seasoned cod, cannelloni stuffed with ewe's cheese and fresh spinach, and an excellent version of lasagna made with magret de canard; a cassoulet of lamb; and roasted rack of rabbit. The dessert choices always include flan. If you opt to dine here, you won't be alone: Diners who preceded us have included Pamela Anderson, Princess Caroline of Monaco, and Rod Stewart.

1 rue Jaume Roux. ℭ **04-90-92-32-14.** Reservations recommended. Fixed-price menu 29€ ($38). MC, V. Wed–Mon noon–2:30pm and 7–11pm; June–Sept daily.

Le Jardin de Frédéric ⍟ TRADITIONAL FRENCH/PROVENÇAL   Charming, with a good-humored atmosphere, this restaurant occupies a green-painted villa that was built on the site of a garden where Frédéric Mistral, "national poet" of Provence, wrote part of his opus. Menu items are innovative and reflect culinary techniques from both local sources and the grand restaurants of faraway Paris. Savor the seductive, succulent soufflé of codfish, served with saffron and garlic sauce, or carpaccio of duckling with foie gras. Try the tender rack of Sisteron lamb with a creamy garlic sauce, or filet of sea bass with basil sauce. Dessert might be a chocolate mousse with vanilla sauce. In summer, the dining room expands, perhaps in a style that would have been appreciated by Mistral himself, outside into the open air.

8 bd. Gambetta. ℭ **04-90-92-27-76.** Reservations required. Main courses 15€–18€ ($20–$23); fixed-price menus 21€–29€ ($27–$38). MC, V. Thurs–Tues noon–2pm and 7:30–9:30pm. Closed Feb.

8 Gordes ⍟

713km (443 miles) SE of Paris; 35km (22 miles) E of Avignon; 16km (10 miles) NE of Cavaillon; 64km (40 miles) N of the Marseille airport

Gordes is a colorful village whose twisted narrow cobblestone streets circle a rocky bluff above the Imergue Valley. By the turn of the 20th century, as its residents migrated toward cities and factory jobs, it suffered from the kind of attrition that was affecting agrarian communities all over Europe.

The 12th-century village was saved by modern art. Cubist painter André Lhote discovered the hamlet in 1938, and renowned artists like Marc Chagall began visiting and summering here. The late Victor Vasarély, one of the founders of op art, became its most famous full-time resident.

ESSENTIALS

GETTING THERE   There's no rail station in Gordes. **Trains** arrive at nearby Cavaillon, where taxis wait at the railway station; the trip into Gordes costs around 23€ ($30). For rail information and schedules in Cavaillon, call Rail Europe ℭ **800/387-6782.** There are no local buses. By **car** from Avignon, take Route 100 east to the intersection to D2, at which point you head north following the signs into Gordes. The village itself is closed to cars, but large parking lots are along its edge.

VISITOR INFORMATION   The **Office de Tourisme** is in the Salle des Gardes du Château, place du Château (ℭ **04-90-72-02-75**).

SEEING THE SIGHTS

Dominating the skyline, the **Château de Gordes** is a fortified 12th-century structure whose dramatic silhouette contributed to the town's nickname as "the Acropolis of Provence." The château was really a fortress with crenellated bastions and round towers in each of its four corners. This is home to a museum, **Musée du Château de Gordes** (℃ **04-90-72-02-89**), site of a collection of works by Flemish-born painter Pol Mora. This collection might or might not be replaced with the *oeuvres* of other painters during the lifetime of this edition of this guide, including some by surrealist and geometric master Vasarély. It's open Wednesday through Monday from 10am to noon and 2 to 6pm. Adults pay 4€ ($5.20) admission; students and persons ages 11 to 18 pay 3.50€ ($4.55). Entrance is free for children 10 and under.

Some 4km (2½ miles) south of the village, surrounded by a rocky, arid landscape that supports only stunted olive trees and gnarled oaks (the Provençaux refer to this type of terrain as *la garrigue*), stands the **Moulin des Bouillons,** route de St-Pantaléon (℃ **04-90-72-22-11**), an olive-oil mill so ancient it was mentioned in the 1st-century writings of Pliny the Elder. It's now owned by the stained-glass artist Frédérique Duran, and its interior boasts the original Roman floors and the base of the olive press. The complex is open Wednesday through Monday from 10am to noon and 2 to 6pm. A ticket granting admission to the mill costs 4.50€ ($5.85).

Cousin to the *trullis* of Italy are the reconstructed *bories* in the **Village des Bories,** Les Savournines (℃ **04-90-72-03-48**), 3km (2 miles) southwest of town. These mysterious stone beehive structures are composed of thin layers of stone that spiral upward into a dome. The substantial buildings were constructed without mortar and are surrounded by stone boundary walls of similar construction. Their origin and use is a mystery—some sources claim they're Neolithic. What is known is that they were inhabited until the early 1800s. Their form suggests they were developed by shepherds and goat herders as shelter for themselves and their flocks. To get here, take D15, veering right beyond a fork at D2. A sign marks another right turn toward the village, where you must park and walk for about 45 minutes to visit the site. The village is open daily from 9am to dusk. Admission is 5.50€ ($7.15) for adults and 3€ ($3.90) for children.

Founded in 1148, the **Abbaye Notre-Dame de Sénanque** ✿, a Cistercian monastery 4km (2½ miles) north of Gordes on D15/D177 (℃ **04-90-72-05-72;** www.senanque.fr), sits in isolation surrounded by lavender fields. It was abandoned during the Revolution, reopened in the 19th century, closed again in 1969, and reopened yet again (by the Cistercians) in 1988. The influential 20th-century writer and Catholic theologian Thomas Merton can be counted among those who found peace here. One of Provence's most beautiful medieval monuments, it's open Monday to Saturday from 10am to noon and 2 to 6pm, and Sunday from 2 to 6pm. Admission costs 6€ ($7.80) for adults and 2.50€ ($3.25) for persons ages 6 to 18. It's free for children under 6. Be aware that this is a working monastery, not merely a tourist site. You can attend any of five Masses per day, buy religious souvenirs and texts in the gift shop, and generally marvel at a medieval setting brought back to life.

WHERE TO STAY

Hôtel La Bastide de Gordes ✿✿   This manor house dates from the 17th century. After World War II, it was enlarged to become the headquarters for the town's gendarmerie, and in 1988, it was transformed into a tasteful hotel, in a building staggered uphill near the town's summit. Some rooms have views over the valley of the Luberon. Bedrooms are luxurious and tasteful, with contemporary, antique, and reproduction furnishings and soft colors. Known for its inventive and creative cuisine, the on-site restaurant, Michel Del Burgo, is named for its chef and is a worthy choice even if you're not a guest of the hotel. Against a backdrop of old-fashioned Provençal elegance, market-fresh ingredients concocted into sublime dishes are served to an appreciative clientele with discerning palates.

Le Village, 84220 Gordes. ℂ **04-90-72-12-12.** Fax 04-90-72-05-20. www.bastide-de-gordes.com. 45 units. 140€–323€ ($182–$420) double; 363€–498€ ($472–$647) suite. AE, MC, V. Free parking. Closed Jan to mid Feb. **Amenities:** Restaurant; bar; 2 outdoor pools; health club; spa; sauna; limited room service; babysitting; laundry service; dry cleaning. *In room:* A/C, TV, minibar, hair dryer, safe.

Hôtel La Gacholle *Value*   Built in the 1960s in the form of an earth-toned Provençal *mas,* this inn combines stone walls, wooden beams, a tiled roof, brick floors, and flagstone terraces into an intimate setting. It stands in a grove of holm oak, offering a great view over the Luberon valley from its pool and dining terrace. The guest rooms are cozy, comfortable, and designed for a maximum of peace and quiet. In 2005, the hotel downsized into a three-room bed-and-breakfast.

Rte. de Murs, 84220 Gordes. ℂ **04-90-72-01-36.** Fax 04-90-72-01-81. lagacholle@caramail.com. 3 units. 107€–125€ ($139–$163) double. MC, V. Closed Jan 10–Feb 28. From town, drive 1.2km (¾ mile) northeast, following the only road with signs for Murs. **Amenities:** Outdoor pool; tennis court; babysitting. *In room:* A/C, TV, minibar, hair dryer, safe.

Hôtel Le Gordos   Set within a prosperous-looking residential neighborhood, about a kilometer (½ mile) southwest of the town center, this hotel was established in the early 1990s within the stone-sided shell of what was originally built several hundred years ago as a Provençal *mas.* Surrounded by shrubbery and capped with the kind of terra-cotta tiles you might have noticed throughout the region, it's a less expensive version of its plusher sibling, Hôtel La Bastide de Gordes. Inside you'll find a smooth and seamlessly comfortable decor that's light, airy, and traditional. Bedrooms are simple but appealing, with lots of sunlight, pale colors, and tiled bathrooms with showers in all but one room. The establishment's social center is a swimming pool that's set into the garden, where breakfast is served. There's no restaurant on-site, but many appropriate dining choices lie within a short walk or drive.

Rte. de Cavaillon, 84220 Gordes. ℂ **04-90-72-00-75.** Fax 04-90-72-07-00. www.hotel-le-gordos.com. 29 units. 104€–230€ ($135–$299) double. AE, MC, V. Free parking. From the center of Gordes, follow the signs to Cavaillon and travel 1km (½ mile) southwest. **Amenities:** Pool; tennis court; babysitting. *In room:* TV.

Hôtel Les Bories *ππ*   This is Gordes's best accommodation, a modern hotel clad in rough stone and built around the core of an old Provençal *mas.* It takes advantage of its hillside setting, offering vistas from the dining terrace, outdoor pool and terrace, glass-fronted lobby, and indoor pool. The garden ties into the valley with olive, holm oak, and lavender. The decor was inspired by high-tech Milanese design, with streamlined furniture, tile floors, and Oriental rugs in both public spaces and the spacious guest rooms. The cozy dining room is in a nook rising into a craggy stone vault, and the matching fireplace is topped by a mantle of massive rugged beams.

Rte. de l'Abbaye de Sénanque, 84220 Gordes. ℂ **04-90-72-00-51.** Fax 04-90-72-01-29. 30 units. 170€–370€ ($221–$481) double; 440€–810€ ($572–$1,053) suite. AE, DC, MC, V. Closed Jan–Feb. From town, drive 2.4km (1½ miles) north, following the signs to Abbaye de Sénanque or Venasque. **Amenities:** Restaurant; bar; 2 outdoor pools; tennis court; health club; Jacuzzi; sauna; salon; limited room service; massage; babysitting; laundry service; dry cleaning; limited-mobility rooms. *In room:* A/C, TV, minibar, hair dryer, safe.

Le Mas de Garrignon ⚜ (*Finds*)   Nine kilometers (5½ miles) east of the colorful village of Gordes, and 35km (22 miles) west of Avignon, Le Mas de Garrignon in Gordes occupies a gracious building that owner Christiane Druart custom-built in 1979, using antique building materials. (Many passersby assume, because of its attention to detail, that it's much older than it actually is.) It operates year-round as an isolated inn, offering bedrooms of charm, style, and comfort. Opening onto a view of the Luberon, each room has a different, usually monochromatic, color scheme, a rustic but elegant decor, and each is dedicated to a different artist or writer who had a history in Provence. In winter, guests check in here to enjoy the crackling fires and classical music. In summer, guests take advantage of the surrounding outdoor activities, including tennis, canoeing, mountain biking, or horseback riding. The excellent in-house restaurant serves Provençal and Mediterranean cuisine, but only to hotel residents, who pay 45€ ($59) each for a full evening meal. (It's open only for dinner.) Four of the rooms are air-conditioned, and each has a private terrace, plus a tiled bathroom with tub or shower.

Rte. de St. Saturnin d'Apt, 84220 Gordes. ℭ 04-90-05-63-22. Fax 04-90-05-70-01. www.masdegarrignon-provence.com. 9 units. 105€–135€ ($137–$176) double; 140€–170€ ($182–$221) suite. Free parking. From Gordes, follow the signs to St-Saturnin d'Apt. **Amenities:** Restaurant (for residents only); limited room service; laundry service; outdoor pool; garden. *In room:* TV, minibar.

WHERE TO DINE

The area's best cuisine is served at the **Hôtel Les Bories.**

Comptoir des Arts ⚜ PROVENÇAL   An especially appealing restaurant in Gordes occupies what was originally built in the 1850s as the town's *épicerie* (food market). Today Justine Cairel manages a kitchen staff and a limited number of seats (only 26) within a restaurant noted for its coziness and Provençal charm. Additional seating is offered on either of two outdoor terraces, set against the front and back of the restaurant, respectively. Expect furniture that's crafted from old wine cases, and a changing array of paintings by local artists, many of which are for sale. Menu items focus on regional ingredients and time-tested recipes that many local residents might remember from their childhoods. Your meal might begin with a platter of stuffed baby vegetables or a chilled slab of fresh-made foie gras. Roasted rack of lamb with Provençal herbs is an excellent choice, or perhaps a garlicky version of aioli of codfish. Desserts here are best showcased as part of an *assiette gourmande,* wherein a selection of the pastry chef's most appealing creations are artfully arranged on the same dessert platter.

Place du Château. ℭ 04-90-72-01-31. Reservations recommended. Main courses 15€–24€ ($20–$31); fixed-price menu 33€ ($42). MC, V. Daily 9am–10pm. Closed Nov to mid-Dec and mid-Jan to Easter.

Le Mas Tourteron PROVENÇAL   On the outskirts of the village of Les Imberts, this restaurant occupies an 18th-century Provençal *mas* whose cherry trees and vines still produce good fruit. It has a sun-flooded dining room, with additional seating that spills over into the verdant garden. Menu items are based on fresh ingredients and include cassoulet of asparagus and herbs with a medley of other (strictly seasonal) ingredients, charlotte of lamb with Provençal herbs, and a *tarte à l'envers* (upside-down tart) of roast rabbit with black-olive tapenade. Things here are small-scale and just a wee bit fussy, but overall, the food is very good and the staff is friendly.

Chemin de St-Blaise, Les Imberts. ℭ 04-90-72-00-16. Fixed-price lunch Wed–Fri 32€ ($42); other times, set menus 36€–52€ ($47–$68). AE, MC, V. Wed–Sun noon–2pm; Tues–Sat 7:30–9:30pm. Closed mid-Nov to mid-Feb. Take D2 for 6km (4 miles) southwest of Gordes.

9 Roussillon & Bonnieux ⟨★

These villages lie so close to each other that you can visit both in a long morning or afternoon.

ROUSSILLON

45km (28 miles) E of Avignon; 10km (6 miles) E of Gordes

Color—17 shades of ocher, to be more precise—has proven to be this village's lifeblood. From as far back as Roman times, the area's rich deposits of ocher have been valued. Beginning in the late 1700s, Roussillon's ocher powders were shipped around the world from nearby Marseille. Though the mining industry has dried up, hordes of artists and visitors still flock here to marvel and be inspired by the gorgeous ranges of the vibrant warm tones. Roussillon also served as a giant laboratory of sorts for the famous American sociologist Laurence William Wylie, who packed up his family and moved here for a year to study the village's complex life of work and play, love and family feuds, and simple day-to-day existence. He published his study as *A Village in the Vaucluse* in 1957.

ESSENTIALS
GETTING THERE   From Avignon, drive east on N7 to D973 and then to D22. Finally, turn north on D149 and follow the signs to Roussillon. The trip takes about 45 minutes. There's no train or bus service.

VISITOR INFORMATION   The **Office de Tourisme** is on place de la Poste (© **04-90-05-60-25**).

SEEING THE SIGHTS
Take time to explore the narrow, steep streets, soaking in the rusts, reds, and ochers of the stone used in the construction of the houses. From the **Castrum,** at the high point along rue de l'Eglise, you'll see a magnificent vista. Face north and gaze across the Vaucluse plateau and to Mont Ventoux. Turn south to see the Coulon valley and the Grand Luberon.

You can reach the **old ocher quarries,** with their exposed, sunburned rocks, by taking a 40-minute scenic walk east of the village. Paths to the quarries start at the tourist office (see "Essentials," above). The huge red cliffs of **Chaussée des Géants** comprise another panorama. To view them, take the path southeast of the tourist office. The walk is about 45 minutes and includes a great look back at Roussillon.

About 5km (3 miles) south of town on D149 is the **pont Julien.** Built more than 2,000 years ago, this three-arched Roman engineering feat of precisely hewn stone spans the Calavon River without the use of any mortar. It's thought to have been named in honor of the nearby Roman town of Apta Julia, known today as Apt.

WHERE TO STAY
Le Clos du Buis ⟨★ ⟨*Finds*   Set on the northern outskirts of the small town of Bonnieux, within a garden that's centered on a copse of small trees *(les buis),* this is a small-scale and intensely personalized bed and breakfast hotel that's housed within a late-18th-century stone-fronted Mediterranean-style villa. There are very few amenities within this hotel, other than a small swimming pool in the garden that functions as the single most gregarious spot on-site. Bedrooms are simple but comfortable, often with rough-hewn ceiling beams, sweeping views over the Luberon countryside, white walls, and splashes of jewel-toned color. Life here is simple, old-fashioned, and charming.

Although the hotel lacks a restaurant, guests who request it in advance can arrange an evening fixed-price meal (22€/$29 per person), whose makeup and presentation varies with the availability of raw ingredients, the season, and the number of other diners eating in that night.

Rue Victor Hugo, 84480 Bonnieux. ☎ **04-90-75-88-48.** Fax 04-90-75-88-57. www.leclosdubuis.com. 7 units. 75€–102€ ($98–$133) double. Rates include breakfast. MC, V. Free parking. Closed mid-Nov to mid-Feb. **Amenities:** Outdoor pool; laundry service; garden. *In room:* No phone.

Le Mas de la Tour   The history of this *mas* on the outskirts of town dates back some 800 years. In 1985, it was completely renovated, with all modern amenities added, including a large enticing pool. The rooms run the gamut from matchbox-size to palatial. The smaller ones have exterior entrances and are somewhat reminiscent of those found in simple motels; the larger ones have bathtubs and terraces. Each has a tiled bathroom with shower.

84400 Gargas. ☎ **04-90-74-12-10.** Fax 04-90-04-83-67. www.mas-de-la-tour.com. 31 units. 62€ ($81) double. MC, V. Closed Oct–Apr 16. From Gargas, drive 3km (2 miles) south, following the signs to Apt. **Amenities:** Restaurant; bar; pool. *In room:* TV, minibar, hair dryer.

WHERE TO DINE

David PROVENÇAL   The town's most popular restaurant, it creates a pleasurable experience with its airy dining area and panoramic views of the red cliffs and hills of the Vaucluse. In the warmer months, dining is *en plein air* on the flowered terrace. The talented chef/owner Jean David is a traditional restaurateur who takes pride in his art, which he's been practicing since the 1950s. He works alongside his wife, son, and daughter in this family-run place. Menu items include a rice casserole of scallops and spinach, grilled country lamb flank rubbed with rosemary and served with an assortment of seasonal vegetables, and a tender beef filet with dark morel sauce. The light homemade fruit sorbets are a perfect end to a satisfying meal.

Place de la Poste. ☎ **04-90-05-60-13.** Reservations recommended. Fixed-price menus 32€–45€ ($41–$59). AE, MC, V. Tues–Sun 12:30–2pm; Mon–Tues, Thurs, and Sat 7:30–9pm. Closed mid-Nov to mid-Dec.

Le Bistro de Roussillon PROVENÇAL   Here's a place where the vibrancy of a fast-paced Paris bistro collides with relaxed Provençal *savoir-vivre*. The result is a superlative ambience of hearty meals, intriguing chatter, and festive, friendly service. The bistro has one intimate dining room and two terraces—one with a vista of valley and hills and the other facing the square. Menu items vary from light salads to regional fare like *daube* (a traditional beef-and-vegetable stew often served over pasta), roast rack of pork with honey and spices, and grilled filet of hogfish.

Place de la Mairie. ☎ **04-90-05-74-45.** Reservations recommended. Main courses 10€–14€ ($13–$18); fixed-price menu 20€–25€ ($26–$33). MC, V. Tues–Sat noon–2:30pm; Tues–Sat 7–9pm.

BONNIEUX

11km (7 miles) S of Roussillon; 45km (28 miles) N of Aix-en-Provence

This romantic hill town, nestled in the heart of the Petit Luberon, commands views of nearby Roussillon, the whole Coulon Valley, and the infamous Château de Lacoste, whose ruins bear testament to the life of its disturbed owner, Donatien Alphonse François, comte de Sade (also known as the marquis de Sade), who lived there in the 1770s. The celebrated marquis, who gave us the term *sadism*, died in a lunatic asylum. Because of the danger of falling stones, the ruins of the château cannot be visited— even by the most devoted aficionados of de Sade—but merely admired from afar.

Strategically located between Spain and Italy, Bonnieux has had a bloody history of raids and battles since its beginnings in Roman times, when it stood closer to the valley floor. To better defend itself, the town was moved farther up the hill during the 1200s, when it also received sturdy ramparts and sentry towers. In the 16th century, Bonnieux grew into a Catholic stronghold and often found itself surrounded by Protestants who were suspicious and jealous of its thriving economy. Since its streets were lined with mansion after mansion belonging to prominent bishops, allegations swirled around that the town received particular "favors" to bolster its standing. Envy and zeal got the best of the Protestants, and they eventually laid siege to the town, killing approximately 3,000 of the 4,000 inhabitants. Even though Bonnieux is the largest hill town in the area, its population never truly recovered and continues to hover around 1,500.

ESSENTIALS
GETTING THERE   From Roussillon, **drive** south along D149 directly to Bonnieux. The trip takes about 15 minutes. There's no train or bus service.

VISITOR INFORMATION   The **Office de Tourisme** is at 7 place Carnot (© 04-90-75-91-90).

SEEING THE SIGHTS
You'll most likely want to work with gravity and not against it when exploring this steep village. Start at the summit with the **Vieille Eglise (Old Church)** and its cemetery. The grounds of stately cedars surrounding this Romanesque church, which dates from the 1100s, provide the best vantage point from which you can view the valley's hill towns. Hours of this church are erratic, corresponding to the whims of the priest who performs Mass here at irregular intervals. Farther down the incline is the **Musée de la Boulangerie,** 12 rue de la République (© 04-90-75-88-34), dedicated to the authentic portrayal of the art of French breadmaking. Exhibits show all stages of the process, from planting and harvesting the grain to the final mixers and ovens that turn the flour, water, salt, and yeast mixture into warm, crusty loaves. The museum is open year-round Wednesday to Monday 10am to 12:30 and 2:30 to 6pm. Admission is 3.50€ ($4.55) for adults and 1.50€ ($1.95) for children 12 and under.

At the lower extreme of town, clearly signposted from the center, is the **Eglise Neuve (New Church),** from the late 1800s. Many people find the architecture of this church to be less than inspiring. You visit it, however, to admire the four beautiful panels from the Old Church. They date from the 1500s and are painted in the brightly colored German style to show the intensity of the Passion of Christ. It's open daily from 9am to 6pm.

WHERE TO STAY
Auberge de l'Aiguebrun ℛ *Finds*   To relax in one of the most tranquil settings in Provence and soak up that special surreal sunlight, come here. Artists and lovers seek out this remarkable 19th-century manor house enclosed by the Luberon hills and a mountain river. The intimate guest rooms look out over the river or the hills. They are individually decorated in the Provençal style with tawny colors and have bathrooms with up-to-date accessories. In the public rooms, attention is lovingly paid to every detail, from the crackling fire on cooler evenings to the soft and classical music wafting from room to room. The hotel also has a superb restaurant with its own garden; it's open Wednesday to Monday (closed Wed at lunchtime).

The Libertine Trail of the Marquis de Sade

Denounced by some and a cult figure to others even today, Donatien Alphonse François, comte de Sade (1740–1814), is, of course, better known as the "marquis de Sade." The word *sadism* was coined from his name, and this "freest spirit who ever was" led a life devoted to an unleashed libido. By 1764, a police alert advised brothel madams to "refrain from providing the marquis with girls to go to any private chambers with him." Because of his prolonged sexual orgies that combined various kinds of torture (willing or unwilling), and especially because he recorded his controversial ideas for public consumption, he was often in and out of prison.

The marquis and his wife, the very plain but very wealthy Renée-Pélagie de Montreuil, hated Paris and court life and sought a secluded place in the country for their family of three. His wife, who was at first totally devoted to him, apparently overlooked his "deviant behavior," and so he was supposedly a "happily married man."

The marquis grew up in the area around Lacoste. Banished from home because of his violent rages, he spent 6 years of his childhood with his uncle, the noted cleric/scholar Abbé de Sade (who also happened to be a libertine) at the Abbé's castle at Saumane-de-Vaucluse, halfway between Lacoste and Mazan.

This crenellated fortress was a gift from the popes at Avignon, and it still stands in the hilltop village of Saumane-de-Vaucluse, to the west of Lacoste. The castle has been restored, and you can visit it. It is believed that the fictional Château de Silling, depicted in *The 120 Days of Sodom,* was based on this castle, where "all that the cruelest art and most refined barbarity could invent in the way of atrocity" was concealed for orgies and torture.

When the marquis returned to Paris, he attended the prestigious Lycée Louis Le Grand, where flagellation was the school's accepted form of punishment. He related to this on an erotic level, and the experience was the catalyst for his lifelong obsession with the exploration of the pain of pleasure and the pleasure of pain.

De Sade country really begins some 40km (25 miles) east of Avignon and not far from Ménerbes. The little village of Lacoste, surmounted by the marquis's ancestral castle, exists in a kind of time pocket, with a population that is about the same as it was back in the days of history's most articulate libertine. The château itself (not open to the public) isn't in good shape—just a moat, a few walls, some ramparts, and a scattering of rooms. More

---

Off D943, 84480 Bonnieux. ℂ **04-90-04-47-00.** Fax 04-90-04-47-01. 164€ ($213) double; 234€ ($304) suite. MC, V. Free parking. Closed Dec–Feb. From town, drive 6km (4 miles) southeast, following the signs to Lourmarin. **Amenities:** Restaurant; bar; outdoor pool; babysitting. *In room:* A/C, TV, hair dryer.

Hostellerie du Prieuré   Protected in the shadows of Bonnieux's medieval ramparts, this is an 18th-century abbey turned hotel. The bedrooms are individually furnished in a simple, dignified manner befitting the style of the building and overlook

interesting is the panoramic view—on a clear day, you can even see Bonnieux. As you stand here, it's easy to imagine the marquis's world of tortured damsels and debauched noblemen coming alive again in such a remote spot in a foreboding landscape.

Though he spent 1771 worrying about "garden, farmyard, cheeses, and firewood," in 1772 the marquis found himself deep in trouble. His manservant, Latour, had arranged for four girls to meet with the marquis. De Sade had prepared some sweets whose sugar had been soaked in extract of Spanish fly (an actual aphrodisiac); later, some of the girls complained to the police that they'd been poisoned and accused Latour and de Sade of homosexual sodomy. The marquis fled but in *absentia* was found guilty of poisoning and sodomy. The punishment under law was decapitation—de Sade and Latour were later executed in effigy at Aix-en-Provence.

In 1778, de Sade's days of indulgence came to an end. His mother-in-law, outraged at his behavior, had him legally imprisoned for life. He wrote his novels, including *Justine* and the *120 Days of Sodom,* in prison. Freed in 1790 following the onset of the Revolution, he found that his wife had finally abandoned him forever. Napoleon ordered that the marquis be placed in a mental institution, where he died in 1814 at age 74, leaving scores of unpublished manuscripts that were not to see print for more than a century.

In time, this "abominable assemblage of all crimes and obscenities" won an adoring public. Sadists looked to him as the father of their cult. Foreigners attracted to the marquis's reputation have turned Lacoste into a lively place. An American art school was founded here in the 1970s, and—surprise, surprise—many locals are proud of their hometown boy. A small theater has been built in a stone quarry just below the château, and so the marquis's long-cherished wish to make Lacoste into a mecca for thespians has come true. **Théâtre de Lacoste** now draws some 1,600 patrons at a time, equaled in size in the region only by Avignon's outdoor theater. Believe it or not, one recent production dramatized a fictional love affair between the marquis and St. Theresa of Avila. Don't expect comfort or even high-tech acoustics when you come to a production at this theater: Seats are lined up on stone ledges, and the audience is subject to the vagaries of wind and weather. For information about tickets and performances, contact the Mairie (Town Hall) of Lacoste at ⓒ **04-90-75-83-12.**

the hotel garden or the ramparts. Depending on the weather and the season, breakfast is served either inside, next to the blazing fireplace, or in the verdant, lushly landscaped garden.

Rue J.-B.-Aurard, 84480 Bonnieux. ⓒ **04-90-75-80-78.** Fax 04-90-75-96-00. 12 units. 100€–150€ ($130–$195) double; 180€ ($234) suite. V. On-street parking free, in garage 12€ ($16). Closed Nov–Mar. **Amenities:** Limited room service; laundry service; dry cleaning. *In room:* TV, hair dryer.

WHERE TO DINE

You can also consider dining at the two inns listed above.

Le Fournil PROVENÇAL/MEDITERRANEAN/REGIONAL   Charming and completely without pretension, this restaurant occupies the premises of a clean, dry, well-swept cave opening on a small-scale square graced with a 12th-century fountain. The inventive chefs, Guy Malbec and Jean-Christophe Lèche, have given recipes of long standing a new and livelier taste. The menu varies with the season and the inspiration of the chefs but might include crispy-skinned supreme of stuffed guinea fowl with baby vegetables, a confit of fruit, and parsley sauce; a platter of roasted and grilled baby goat, featuring two cooking techniques on one platter, with a confit of lemon; and filet of monkfish with sweet garlic and served with a purée of potatoes and olive oil. The wine list contains 35 to 40 selections, mainly regional choices like Côtes du Rhône and Côte de Luberon.

5 place Carnot. ⓒ **04-90-75-83-62.** Reservations recommended. Main courses 12€–21€ ($16–$27); fixed-price menus 26€–37€ ($34–$48). MC, V. Wed-Fri and Sun 12:30–1:45pm; Tues–Sun 7:30–9:45pm. Closed Nov 25–Dec 20 and Jan 10–Feb 15.

10 Apt

52km (32 miles) W of Avignon; 52km (32 miles) N of Aix-en-Provence; and 726km (451 miles) S of Paris

Known as *Colonia Apta Julia,* this was an important Gallo-Roman city and today is a large, bustling market town. Ignore the modern industrial area and head for the Vieille Ville to capture the beauty of Apt. Here you can walk long, narrow streets that wind between old houses where every nook and cranny offers something waiting to be discovered.

Apt is known for its wines—it's a region of the Rhône Valley where the grapes that go into Côte de Luberon and Côtes de Ventoux are grown. It is also known for its basket- and wickerwork and has been a producer of hats since the 17th century. Others know it as the capital of crystallized fruit or *fruit-confits,* so beloved in Provence.

The old Roman city faded into history and was eventually deserted and covered by silt from the river and the hillsides. Roman remains are still buried around 5 to 10m (16–33 ft.) below the current town.

ESSENTIALS

GETTING THERE   Apt has no railway station. From Avignon, five **buses** per day make the 75-minute trek to Apt; a one-way ticket is around 8€. Bus passengers are deposited in a parking lot beside the **Route de Digne** (ⓒ **04-90-74-20-21**), at the eastern periphery of town.

The best way to reach Apt is by **driving;** follow the N100 east from Avignon.

VISITOR INFORMATION   The **Office de Tourism** is at 20 av. Philippe-de-Girard (ⓒ **04-90-74-03-18**).

EXPLORING THE AREA

Apt, capital of Le Luberon, proclaims itself "the world capital of crystallized fruits." The town is filled with Les Confiseurs selling this treat (see "Shopping," below). The best time to visit Apt is for its Saturday-morning market centered on **place de la Bouquerie,** voted one of the 100 most appealing village markets in France. The streets are literally packed with market stalls and lined with temporary shops. Lavender growers, purveyors of goat cheese, potters, local beekeepers, and craftspeople who look like leftovers from the 1960s invade the town to peddle their wares. The Tour de l'Horloge, dating from the 1500s and straddling the rue des Marchands, is a particularly active area for the Saturday market. On market days, the town fills with jazz musicians, barrel-organ players, stand-up comics, and what one local merchant calls "assorted freaks."

Cathédrale Ste-Anne   This major monument is known for its ancient two-level crypt. According to legend, the bones of the legendary Ste-Anne, mother of the Virgin Mary, were miraculously discovered in this crypt in the 8th century, occasioning the building of the cathedral. Her life is depicted in a beautiful set of 14th-century stained-glass windows at the end of the apse. Her shroud is also displayed among the reliquaries of the treasury. Scholars speculate that Anne was not the biblical figure, but a dim memory of the primeval pan-European mother goddess sometimes known as Ana or Anna Perenna to the Romans.

In the 13th century, the present church was enlarged, and in the 18th century, the floor was raised and the broken barrel vault turned into a higher ogee vault. The oldest part of the cathedral is the tower crypt, which still has a funerary monument honoring a priest in the time of Apia Julia and Carolingian flagstones. The church and its treasury are filled with rare ecclesiastical artifacts. In the chapel of St. John the Baptist, you can see an early Christian marble sarcophagus from the Pyrenees. Among the treasures in the sacristy are 11th- and 12th-century manuscripts, elaborate vestments, and an 11th-century Arab standard brought back from the First Crusade. The nave is adorned with scenes from the life of Christ, painted by Pierre and Christophe Delpech in the 18th century.

To see the Sacristy, you must ask Claude Pion, the church caretaker. She is constantly on-site during open hours (see below) and will open it according to the schedule of daily Masses or the priorities of the priests. If she does, a donation to the maintenance of the church is appreciated.

Vieille Ville. ⓒ **04-90-74-36-60.** Free admission. Summer Mon–Sat 8:30am–6pm; winter Mon–Fri 8:30am–noon and 2–5:30pm, Sat 8:30am–noon and 3–5:30pm. Ask the caretaker for entrance to the Sacristy.

Hôtel Colin d'Albertas   The lavish 17th-century baroque interior of this building has been open for hour-long daily guided tours since 1999. It contains some of the most spectacular plaster- and stuccowork in the region and is a museum in its own right.

Rue de la République. ⓒ **04-90-74-02-40.** Tours 5.50€ ($7.15) adults, 4€ ($5.20) students. June–Sept daily 3 and 6pm.

Tips Outdoors in Luberon National Park

The information office for the **Luberon National Park** is in an 18th-century house, La Maison du Parc, 1 place Jean-Jaurès (ⓒ **04-90-04-42-00**). The office provides maps, details of hiking trails in the park, and other outdoor activities in the area. Much of the land in the Luberon area is privately owned, but trails in the park are open to the public. In summer tastings of the regional produce are held here. On-site is a small **Museum of Paleontology,** of only specialist interest. Admission is 1.50€, and it's open May through October Monday to Saturday from 8:30am to noon, and the rest of the year Monday to Friday from 1:30 to 6pm.

Musée Archéologique   The town's major museum contains Roman objects found in local excavations, including pieces of mosaics, sarcophagi, coins, and even oil lamps from the 2nd century B.C. It also displays sacred and decorative art by faïence makers from the 17th and the 19th centuries.

Place Carnot. ℂ **04-90-04-76-65.** Admission 2€ ($2.60) adults, 1€ ($1.30) students and children. June–Sept Wed–Mon 10am–noon and 2:30–5:30pm; Oct–May Wed–Mon 10am–noon and 2:30–4:30pm.

SHOPPING

The large town is filled with confiseurs selling candied fruits. The best are **Confiserie Marcel Richaud,** 112 quai de la Liberté (ℂ **04-90-74-13-56**), and **Confiseur Le Coulon/Jean Ceccon,** 24 quai de la Liberté (ℂ **04-90-74-21-90**).

WHERE TO STAY & DINE

Auberge de la Loube ☆ *Finds* PROVENÇAL   Small, personalized, and charming, this is the century-old domain of Provençal chef and entrepreneur Maurice de la Loube. Isolated on the outskirts of an agrarian hamlet known for its rolling hills and authentic Luberon flavor, it offers delicious cuisine and a look at a slower, more relaxed lifestyle that's envied by many French urbanites. The stone-fronted house has a terrace in front, with dining tables and views that sweep out over the countryside. Main courses, often focusing on local lamb that's perfectly roasted with just the right amount of Provençal seasoning, are succulent and generous, but the real culinary charm of the place might lie in the flavor and variety of Monsieur de la Loube's starters. Several of these will be carried to your table in a wicker basket and laid out with fanfare on your table. Collectively, they represent the best of traditional Provence. Depending on the configuration of your meal, they're likely to include poached asparagus in vinaigrette sauce, tapenade of local olives, brandade of codfish, braised carrots with aioli, and eggplant "caviar."

The dining room is charming, outfitted with mirrors, small lamps that cast a warm glow on the thick ocher-colored walls, and vases of flowers. Ask (either before or after your meal) to view the approximately 19 antique carriages, many of them made in the United States and imported here during the early 20th century, that are stored in a nearby outbuilding. Collecting them is the personal hobby of Monsieur de la Loube and a source of enormous personal pride.

Quartier de la Loube, Buoux. ℂ **04-90-74-19-58.** Reservations recommended. Main courses 15€–17€ ($20–$22); fixed-price menus 21€–30€ ($27–$39). No credit cards. Fri–Sun, Mon, and Wed noon–1:30pm and 8–9:30pm. Closed Jan–Feb. Located 8km (4½ miles) south of Apt; from Apt, follow signs to Buoux.

Auberge du Luberon TRADITIONAL FRENCH   Though mainly a restaurant, this place is also a hotel. It's in the heart of the city's historic center, in a century-old building. The menu reflects old-fashioned culinary virtues and style. Specialties include foie gras with a confit of fruits, in the style that Apt is famous for; a charlotte of lamb with eggplant; John Dory with artichoke hearts *barigoules;* and a trolley laden daily with 13 different desserts.

About half of the 14 bedrooms are in a nearby annex. Doubles without air-conditioning cost 52€ ($68); those with air-conditioning cost 84€ ($109).

8 place Faubourge du Ballet, 84400 Apt. ℂ **04-90-74-12-50.** Fax 04-90-04-79-49. www.auberge-luberon-peuzin.com. Reservations recommended. Main courses 27€–43€ ($35–$56); fixed-price menus 47€–62€ ($61–$81). AE, DC, MC, V. Oct–June Tues–Sun noon–1:45pm, Tues–Sat 7:30–9:30pm; July–Sept Tues–Sun noon–1:45pm, daily 7:30–9:30pm. AE, MC, V. Closed Nov 6–Dec 26.

Domaine des Andéols ★★   Established in 2003, this hyper-upscale country inn is associated, at least insofar as its marketing campaigns, with French super-chef Alain Ducasse, who "anointed" the present chef (Laurent Poulet) with a prolonged exposure to his culinary techniques, and who drops in for a (rare) site inspection. Don't expect folkloric decor or rusticity, since the place blossoms with a chic modern feel, and includes Mies van der Rohe leather lounges, Andy Warhol serigraphs, and an overall decor that's about as high-design as you're likely to find anywhere. It's set within rolling countryside that some visitors have described as "magical," to a setting that's 40km (24 miles) southeast of Avignon. Here, surrounded by lakes, gardens, and orchards, owners Olivier and Patrizia Massart have gathered paintings, furniture, and sculpture from their global travels to decorate their exotic accommodations. For rent are nine stone-sided town houses, each set end-to-end, each with between one and three elegant bedrooms and kitchenettes. Two of them boast private outdoor pools of their own. French critics have hailed this hotel as "the most progressive in southern France." The restaurant, permeated with the spirit of "Le Ducasse," has attracted clients who have included, among others, former design mogul Pierre Cardin. Adding to the flavors, the kitchen here makes its own olive oil and uses produce, including apricots and cherries, from its own gardens.

Les Andéols, 84490 Saint-Saturnin-les-Apt. ⓒ **04-90-75-50-63.** Fax 04-90-75-43-22. www.domainedesandeols.com. 9 units. 210€–650€ ($273–$845) junior suite; 280€–1,130€ ($364–$1,469) superior suite. AE, MC, V. From Avignon, drive 40km (24 miles) to the SE, following first the signs to Apt, and then the signs to St-Saturnin-les-Apt. **Amenities:** Restaurant; both outdoor and indoor pools; sauna; hammam (steam room); massage; limited room service; laundry service/dry-cleaning; garden. *In room:* TV, dataport, minibar, hair dryer.

Relais de Roquefure *(Value* Lying 6km (3½ miles) north of the center, this Logis de France country hotel in the Luberon Nature Reserve is the finest place to stay in the area. It offers good food and a good night's sleep, all at a fair price. Georges and Jeannine Rousset, the owners, are hospitable hosts. Rooms are small but comfortable, with fine, soft beds and small bathrooms. In summer, guests can sit under the shade trees. The food is some of the best in the area, emphasizing regional produce.

Along N100, 84400 Apt. ⓒ **04-90-04-88-88.** Fax 04-90-74-14-86. www.relaisderoquefure.com. 17 units. 58€–110€ ($75–$143) double. Half board 83€–104€ ($108–$135) double. MC, V. Closed Dec–Jan. **Amenities:** Restaurant; bar; outdoor pool; bike rental; laundry service; dry cleaning. *In room:* Hair dryer.

11 Salon de Provence

47km (29 miles) SE of Avignon; 37km (23 miles) NW of Aix-en-Provence; 53km (33 miles) NW of Marseille

The hometown of Nostradamus is centered between Aix-en-Provence and Avignon, and makes an excellent stopover between these towns. Today a busy modern town, it grew up as a fortified hilltop fortress centering on Château de l'Empéri. With a population of some 35,000, it has been a center of the olive oil industry since the 15th century, although it owes much of its prosperity to the French Air Force's officer training school centered here.

Salon de Provence was the birthplace of Adam de Craponne (1527–76), creator of the famous canal that irrigates the region of Crau and bears his name.

ESSENTIALS

GETTING THERE   **Train** connections, about seven a day from Avignon, are the best and most direct (40 min. each way). For information and schedules, contact the local tourist office. From Aix-en-Provence, about seven daily **buses** (trip time:

between 30 and 45 min.) make the trip to downtown Salon de Provence's place Morgan. For information on bus travel into and around Salon de Provence, call (℃ **08-91-02-40-25**). Train connections from Aix are less convenient and require a transfer in Marseille.

If you're **driving,** Salon de Provence is strategically located at the junction of highways connecting Avignon with Aix-en-Provence (N7), and Marseille with Arles and Nîmes (N113), as well as the A7 and A54 autoroutes.

VISITOR INFORMATION   The **Office de Tourisme** is at 56 cours Gimon (℃ **04-90-56-27-60**). Hours are July and August Monday to Saturday 9:30am to 6:30pm, Sunday 10am to noon. The rest of the year hours are Monday to Saturday 9:30am to 12:30pm and 2 to 6pm.

EXPLORING THE TOWN

A major attraction in the town is the **Fontaine Moussue** on the place Crousillat just outside the Porte de l'Horloge. Covered by a thick mound of moss, this much-photographed fountain dates from the 18th century. It is surrounded by plane trees planted to commemorate events over the centuries. One was planted in 1799 to mark the end of the Revolution; another was planted in 1919 to mark the end of World War I.

Château de l'Empéri   This château is surrounded by ancient circular walls. You can enter through the 17th-century Porte de l'Horloge or the Porte Bourg Neuf. The château dates from the 10th century and is one of the most beautiful in Provence, with its courtyards, towers, and walls. Once this was the residence of the archbishops of Arles, lords of Salon. Both François I, in 1516, and Marie de Médici, in 1600, visited and stayed here. From 1831, it was used as a barracks and was severely damaged in an earthquake in 1909. Over the years it, has been gradually and attractively restored.

The château houses the Musée de Art et d'Histoire Militaire, with a collection of more than 10,000 artifacts, including military uniforms, weapons, waxwork figures, and military flags. The museum covers the era from Louis XIV, the Sun King, up to France's entry into World War II.

Montée du Puech. ℃ **04-90-56-22-36**. Admission 3.05€ ($3.95) adults, 2.30€ ($3) children 7–18, free for ages 6 and under. Wed–Mon 10am–noon and 2–6pm. Closed May 1, Nov 1, Oct 12, Dec 24–25, and Jan 1.

Musée Grevin de la Provence   In this wax museum, lifelike tableaux attempt to re-create 2,600 years of the history of Provence. That history is re-created in part in the exhibition of some 15 historical paintings, one of which depicts the fabled marriage of Gyptis and Protis. Their marriage sealed the union of the Phocaeans with the Celtic-Ligurians. The exhibits go up to the 20th century, including scenes from the cinema. The museum is hardly Madame Tussaud's and it's a bit kitschy, but families with children in tow might find it worth a half-hour visit.

Place de Centuries. ℃ **04-90-56-36-30**. Admission 3.05€ ($3.95). Mid-June to mid-Sept daily 9am–noon and 2–6pm, Sat–Sun 2–6pm.

Musée Nostradamus   *Overrated*   Nostradamus (1503–66), who was born in St-Rémy-de-Provence, spent the last 19 years of his life at this little house close to the château. It's now a museum devoted to him and his famous enigmatic predictions of the future. A series of fairly unconvincing tableaux depicts scenes from his life, with a rambling commentary on portable CD players.

Nostradamus was born into a family of converted Jews and trained as a doctor in Montpellier. He treated plague victims in Lyon and Aix. He married a woman from

Salon in 1547 and settled here, where he studied astrology, publishing almanacs and inventing new recipes for cosmetics. Written in the future tense, his *Centuries* in rhyming quatrains was published in 1555, bringing him instant celebrity. Nostradamus is buried in the interesting 14th-century Eglise St-Laurent, which lies just to the north of the town center.

11 rue Nostradamus. ℂ **04-90-56-64-31.** Admission 3.05€ ($3.95). Mid-June to mid-Sept Mon–Fri 9am–noon and 3–8pm, Sat–Sun 2–6pm; rest of year Mon–Fri 9am–noon and 2–6pm.

SHOPPING

Despite the vast amounts of soap and detergent sold by large corporations in France today, Salon de Provence maintains two small-scale artisans that continue to make soap the old-fashioned way, in limited batches, by hand. They are **Rampal,** 71 rue Félix Pyat (ℂ **04-90-56-07-28**), and **Marius Fabre,** avenue Paul Bourrat (ℂ **04-90-53-24-77**). Visits to the first are conducted only by prior appointment; visits to the second are possible only on Monday and Thursday at 10:30am.

WHERE TO STAY

Abbaye de Sainte-Croix ☆☆ No hotel in the region can boast origins as authentic and charming as this ancient one-time monastery from the 1100s, 4km (2½ miles) north of the city center. A Relais & Châteaux hotel, it lies behind thick stone walls, with most of its original arches and vaults, and a severely dignified, sometimes forbidding kind of grandeur evocative of the Middle Ages. The generally spacious bedrooms feature a simple elegance: lovely old furniture, terra-cotta floors, and sometimes spectacular views over fields of lavender and rugged hills. The place is more famous as a restaurant than as a hotel—see "Where to Dine," below.

Val de Cuech, 13300 Salon de Provence. ℂ **04-90-56-24-55.** Fax 04-90-56-31-12. www.hotels-provence.com. 25 units. 170€–335€ ($221–$436) double; 422€–453€ ($549–$589) suite. AE, DC, MC, V. Free parking. Closed Nov to mid-Mar. **Amenities:** Restaurant; bar; outdoor pool; limited room service; babysitting; laundry service; dry cleaning. *In room:* A/C, TV, dataport, minibar, hair dryer, safe.

Hôtel d'Angleterre Set on the northwestern fringe of the peripheral boulevard (cours Carnot) that flanks the edge of town (a 10-min. walk from the center), this is a conservative, not particularly exciting three-story hotel with roots in British tourism during the early 1900s. Everything has been radically modernized from its original turn-of-the-20th-century charm, with touches of kitsch and an overwhelming sense of bourgeois, and somewhat tense propriety. One of the few appealing touches is the circular skylight in the breakfast room. Come here for the relatively low rates, as bedrooms are spartan and not particularly cozy. They range from small to medium and are reasonably comfortable; bathrooms are a bit cramped.

98 Cours Carnot, 13300 Salon de Provence. ℂ **04-90-56-01-10.** Fax 04-90-56-71-75. www.hoteldangleterre.fr. 26 units. 46€–64€ ($60–$83) double; 57€–74€ ($74–$96) triple. MC, V. Closed Dec 24–Jan 2. **Amenities:** Lounge. *In room:* A/C, TV, dataport, hair dryer, safe.

WHERE TO DINE

Abbaye de Sainte-Croix ☆☆☆ FRENCH/PROVENÇAL In the hotel of the same name recommended above, this restaurant serves the best food in the region. Part of its appeal comes from its architecture of medieval soaring vaults and high perpendicular lines. From its terrace is a view over the low hills of the Alpilles. Menu items change with the season and the inspiration of the chef. They include lobster salad with a walnut-oil vinaigrette; sliced sea wolf with a fondant of green and red peppers, basil, and locally produced olives and olive oil; thin-sliced roasted lamb with truffles from the Luberon in clarified butter; turbot with morels; and aiguillette of duck with a tapenade of olives.

Val de Cuech, 13300 Salon de Provence. (© **04-90-56-24-55.** Reservations recommended. Main courses 34€–42€ ($44–$55); fixed-price menus 45€ ($59) lunch, 78€–108€ ($101–$140) dinner. AE, MC, V. Closed Nov–Mar.

Mas du Soleil (Restaurant Francis Robin) ☆ FRENCH/MEDITERRANEAN
In an 1850s stone-sided farmhouse, the ocher-colored facade of this inn is a 5-minute walk from the center of town. The critically acclaimed cuisine of Francis Robin changes according to the season and the availability of the ingredients. Menu items include such treats as a rosemary-infused rack of lamb for two, filet of beef layered with escalope of foie gras, warm salad of filet of red snapper, and a medley of grilled Mediterranean fish. One tempting main course that the chef is particularly proud of is a *civet* (stew) of lobster. Dining room windows overlook a swimming pool in the garden.

An upper floor contains 10 well-maintained bedrooms outfitted with flowered wallpaper and traditional furniture. Each has a bay window overlooking the garden and terrace or a private patio. Rates are 300€ ($390) in a double.

38 chemin St-Côme, Salon de Provence. (© **04-90-56-06-53.** Reservations recommended. Main courses 13€–45€ ($17–$59); fixed-price menus 30€–87€ ($39–$113). AE, DC, MC, V. Tues–Sun noon–2pm; Tues–Sat 7:30–9pm.

12 Aix-en-Provence ★★

755km (469 miles) S of Paris; 80km (50 miles) SE of Avignon; 32km (20 miles) N of Marseille; 175km (109 miles) W of Nice

The most charming center in all Provence, this faded university town was once a seat of aristocracy, its streets walked by counts and kings. Founded in 122 B.C. by a Roman general, Caius Sextius Calvinus, who named it *Aquae Sextiae* after himself, Aix (pronounced "ex") has been, in turn, a Roman military outpost, a civilian colony, the administrative capital of a province of the later Roman Empire, the seat of an archbishop, and the official residence of the medieval comtes de Provence. After the union of Provence with France, Aix remained until the Revolution a judicial and administrative headquarters.

The celebrated son of this old capital city of Provence, Paul Cézanne immortalized the countryside nearby. Just as he painted it, Montagne Ste-Victoire looms over the town today, though a string of high-rises has now cropped up on the landscape.

The Université d'Aix has been attracting international students since 1413. Today absinthe has given way to pastis in the many cafes scattered throughout the town.

This city of some 150,000 is reasonably quiet in winter, but active and bustling when the summer hordes pour in. Summer brings frequent cultural events, ranging from opera to jazz, June through August. Increasingly, Aix is becoming a "bedroom community" for urbanites fleeing Marseille after 5pm.

ESSENTIALS
GETTING THERE   The city is easily accessible, with 21 **trains** arriving daily from Marseille. The trip takes 35 minutes and costs 8€ ($10) one-way. Eight trains arrive from Nice; the trip takes 3 to 4 hours and costs 33€ ($43) one-way. There are also eight trains per day from Cannes (3½ hr.), costing 28€ ($36) one-way. High-speed TGV trains arrive at Vitroll, 5.5km (3½ miles) west of Aix. Bus links to the center of

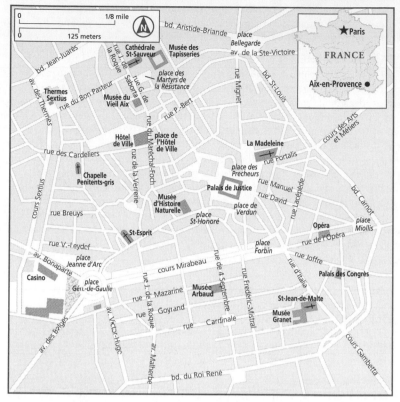

Aix cost 4.10€ ($5.35) one-way. For more information, call ℂ **08-92-35-35-35.**
Buses from Marseille arrive every 10 minutes; from Avignon, five times a day; and
twice a day from Nice. For more information, call ℂ **08-91-02-40-25.** If you're **driving** to Aix from Avignon or other points north, take A7 south to RN7 and follow it
into town. From Marseille or other points south, take A51 north into town.

To explore the region by bike, head for **Cycles Zammit,** 27 rue Mignet (ℂ **04-42-
23-19-53**), a short walk northeast of the cours Mirabeau. Here you can rent 10-speed
racing bikes or more durable mountain bikes for 13€ ($17) per day. You must leave
a deposit—your passport or driver's license, or cash or monetary objects worth the
value of the bike, usually between 350€ and 400€ ($455–$520).

VISITOR INFORMATION The **Office de Tourisme** is at 2 place du Général-de-
Gaulle (ℂ **04-42-16-11-61;** www.aixenprovencetourism.com).

SPECIAL EVENTS Aix is more geared toward the performing arts, particularly
music, than any other city in the south of France. It offers at least four summer festivals that showcase music, opera, and dance. They include the **Aix en Musique,**
ℂ **04-82-21-69-69** (June–Aug), which focuses on symphonic and chamber music,
and a **Festival International d'Art Lyrique & de Musique,** ℂ **04-82-17-34-34** (Festival d'Opera) (late July) that attracts musicians from all over the world.

Also noteworthy is the **Festival International de Danse** (3 weeks in July–Aug), attracting classical and modern dance troupes from throughout Europe and the world. For information, call © **04-42-96-05-01.**

EXPLORING THE CITY

Aix's main street, **cours Mirabeau** ʀʀ, is one of Europe's most beautiful. Plane trees stretch across the street like umbrellas, shading it from the hot Provençal sun and filtering the light into shadows that play on the rococo fountains below. Shops and sidewalk cafes line one side of the street; sandstone *hôtels particuliers* (mansions) from the 17th and 18th centuries fill the other. The street begins at the 1860 fountain on place de la Libération, which honors Mirabeau, the revolutionary and statesman. A ring of streets, including boulevard Carnot and cours Sextius, circles the heart of the old quarter (Vieille Ville, or old town). Inside this périphérique is the pedestrian zone.

After touring Aix, you might consider a side trip on D10 15km (9 miles) east to the **Château de Vauvenargues,** the privately owned site of Pablo Picasso's last home. You can't visit the château's interior, but Picasso and one of his wives, Jacqueline Roche, are buried nearby. Stop for a meal at **Au Moulin de Provence,** rue des Maquisards (© **04-42-66-02-22**), across the road from the château.

Atelier de Cézanne   Cézanne was the major forerunner of Cubism. This house, surrounded by a wall and restored by American admirers, is where he worked. Repaired in 1970, it remains much as Cézanne left it in 1906, "his coat hanging on the wall, his easel with an unfinished picture waiting for a touch of the master's brush," as Thomas R. Parker wrote.

9 av. Paul-Cézanne (outside town). © 04-42-21-06-53. Admission 5.50€ ($7.15) adults, 2€ ($2.60) students and children. Apr–Sept daily 10am–noon and 2:30–6pm; July–Aug daily 10am–6pm; Oct–Mar daily 10am–noon and 2–5pm. Closed Jan 1, May 1, and Dec 25.

Cathédrale St-Sauveur ʀ   The cathedral of Aix is dedicated to Christ under the title St-Sauveur (Holy Savior or Redeemer). Its baptistery dates from the 4th and 5th centuries, and the complex as a whole has seen many additions. It contains a 15th-century Nicolas Froment triptych, *The Burning Bush.* One side depicts the Virgin and Child; the other, Good King René and his second wife, Jeanne de Laval.

Place des Martyrs de la Résistance. © 04-42-23-45-65. Free admission. Daily 9am–noon and 2–5pm. Mass Sun 10:30am and 7pm.

Chapelle Penitents-gris (Chapelle des Bourras)   This 16th-century chapel honoring St. Joseph was built on the ancient Roman Aurelian road linking Rome and Spain. Herbert Maza, founder and former president of the Institute for American Universities, restored the chapel. M. Borricand, rector of a group of local ecclesiastics, arranges visits.

15 rue Lieutaud. © 04-42-26-26-72. Free admission; donations welcome. Visits by reservation only.

Musée des Tapisseries ʀ   Three series of tapestries from the 17th and 18th centuries line the gilded walls of this former archbishop's palace. The prelates decorated the palace with *The History of Don Quixote,* by Natoire; *The Russian Games,* by Leprince; and *The Grotesques,* by Monnoyer. The museum also exhibits rare furnishings from the 17th and 18th centuries.

28 place des Martyrs de la Résistance. © 04-42-23-09-91. Admission 2€ ($2.60) adults, free for people under 25. Wed–Mon 10am–12:30pm and 1:30–5pm. Closed Jan 1, May 1, and Dec 25.

Musée Granet (Musée des Beaux-Arts)   A former director once claimed that the walls of this museum "would never be sullied by a Cézanne." Fortunately, that's not true—the museum, closed at press time, owns eight paintings by Cézanne, none of them major. The great painter had a famously antagonistic relationship with the people of Aix. The museum is housed in the former center of the Knights of Malta and contains works by Van Dyck, Van Loo, and Rigaud; portraits by Pierre and François Puget; and an interesting *Jupiter and Thetis* by Ingres. Ingres also did an 1807 portrait of the museum's namesake, François Marius Granet. Granet's own works abound.

Place St-Jean-de-Malte (up rue Cardinale). ✆ **04-42-38-14-70.** Admission 3€ ($3.90) adults, free for ages 24 and under. Wed–Mon 10am–noon and 2:30–6pm. Closed Jan 1, May 1 and 21, July 14, Aug 15, Nov 1 and 11, and Dec 25 and 31.

SHOPPING

For the best selection of art objects and fabrics inspired by the traditions of Provence, head to **Les Olivades,** 15 rue Marius-Reinaud (✆ **04-42-38-33-66**). It sells fabrics, shirts for women and men, fashionable dresses, and table linens.

Opened more than a century ago, **Bechard,** 12 cours Mirabeau (✆ **04-42-26-06-78**), is the most famous bakery in town. It takes its work so seriously that it refers to its underground kitchens as a *laboratoire* (laboratory). Most of the pastries are made fresh every day.

Founded in 1934 on a busy boulevard just east of the center of town, **Santons Fouque,** 65 cours Gambetta, route de Nice (✆ **04-42-26-33-38**), stocks the largest assortment of santons in Aix. More than 1,900 figurines are cast in terra cotta, finished by hand, and painted according to 18th-century models. Each of the trades practiced in medieval Provence is represented, including shoemakers, barrel makers, coppersmiths, and ironsmiths, poised to welcome the newborn Jesus. Figurines range in price from 7€ to 900€ ($9.10–$1,170).

WHERE TO STAY
IN AIX
Very Expensive

Villa Gallici 🏵🏵🏵   This elegant inn is relentlessly chic. It has been stylishly decorated by its creators (architects and interior designers Messrs Dez, Montemarco, and Jouve). It was originally hailed as "divinely over the top." Each room has an individualized decor; some boast a private terrace or garden. Beds are hung with "waterfalls" of sprigged and striped cotton, mattresses are decadently comfortable, and towels are predictably plush. The villa sits in a large enclosed garden in the heart of town, close to one of the best restaurants, Le Clos de la Violette (see "Where to Dine," below), and a 5-minute walk from the town center. Despite its grand reputation as a place that requires ironbound advance reservations and where famous people bask in sybaritic anonymity, some of the staff are not as polished as they might be. But that is only a minor distraction in an otherwise well-orchestrated symphony.

Av. de la Violette (impasse des Grands Pins), 13100 Aix-en-Provence. ✆ **04-42-23-29-23.** Fax 04-42-96-30-45. www.villagallici.com. 22 units. 220€–590€ ($286–$767) double; 590€–640€ ($767–$832) suite. AE, DC, MC, V. **Amenities:** Restaurant; bar; outdoor pool; 24-hr. room service; babysitting; laundry service; dry cleaning; limited-mobility rooms. *In room:* A/C, TV, dataport, minibar, hair dryer, safe.

Expensive

Hôtel des Augustins 🏵   Converted from the 12th-century Grands Augustins Convent, this hotel has been beautifully restored, with ribbed-vault ceilings, stained-glass windows, stone walls, terra-cotta floors, and Louis XIII furnishings. The reception desk is in a chapel, and oil paintings and watercolors decorate the public rooms. Before its transformation into a hotel in 1892, this site won a place in history by sheltering an excommunicated Martin Luther on his return from Rome. The spacious soundproof guest rooms—two with terraces—all have automatic alarm-call facilities. They possess a severe kind of monastic dignity, with dark-grained wooden furniture and high ceilings. Touches of luxury, however, appear in the firm, very comfortable mattresses (a lot cozier than what was used by the monks of long ago) and big bathrooms. Breakfast is the only meal served.

3 rue de la Masse, 13100 Aix-en-Provence. © **04-42-27-28-59.** Fax 04-42-26-74-87. www.hotel-augustins.com. 95€–230€ ($124–$299) double. MC, V. **Amenities:** Laundry service. *In room:* A/C, TV, dataport, minibar.

Hôtel Paul-Cézanne ✹ *(Overrated)*   The refined interior of this place is more tasteful than you'd expect in a member of a nationwide chain. Since being sold by its former owner, however, it has lost its top position to the much more stylish and tranquil Gallici, and there have been increasing complaints about a less than cooperative staff. The lounge seems more like a private sitting room than a hotel lobby. Many of the rooms have mahogany Victorian furniture, Louis XVI chairs, marble-top chests, gilt mirrors, and oil paintings. The bathrooms have hand-painted tiles and contain a tub or shower. Breakfast is served in a small room opening onto a rear courtyard.

40 av. Victor-Hugo, 13100 Aix-en-Provence. © **04-42-91-11-11.** Fax 04-42-91-11-10. www.hotelaix.com. 55 units. 125€–140€ ($163–$182) double; 170€ ($221) suite. AE, DC, MC, V. Parking 10€ ($13). **Amenities:** Bar; lounge; babysitting; laundry service; dry cleaning. *In room:* A/C, TV, dataport, minibar, hair dryer.

Hôtel Pigonnet ✹✹   This pink-sided Provençal mansion on the edge of town is surrounded by gardens and memories of Paul Cézanne, who used to visit. The high-ceilinged bedrooms contain antique and reproduction French Provincial furnishings, elaborate curtains, and a pervasive sense of country elegance. Breakfast is served on a colonnaded veranda overlooking a reflecting pool in the courtyard. In summer, the in-house restaurant expands outward into the garden, featuring such dishes as a terrine of house-made foie gras, roasted Provençal lamb in a honey-flavored rosemary sauce, and a roulade of chicken with crayfish in shellfish sauce.

5 av. du Pigonnet, 13090 Aix-en-Provence. © **04-42-59-02-90.** Fax 04-42-59-47-77. www.hotelpigonnet.com. 49 units. 160€–270€ ($208–$351) double; 220€–550€ ($286–$715) suite. AE, DC, MC, V. Free parking. **Amenities:** Restaurant; bar; outdoor pool; fitness room; limited room service; babysitting; laundry service; dry cleaning; gardens. *In room:* A/C, TV, dataport, minibar, hair dryer, safe.

Moderate

Grand Hôtel Nègre Coste   This hotel, a former 18th-century town house, is so popular with the musicians who flock to Aix for the summer festivals that it's difficult to get a room at any price. Such popularity is understandable. Flowers cascade from jardinières, and 18th-century carvings surround the windows. Inside, there's a wide staircase, marble portrait busts, and a Provençal armoire. The medium-size soundproof rooms contain interesting antiques. The higher floors overlook cours Mirabeau or the old city. Each unit comes with a compact bathroom with shower; some have tubs as well.

33 cours Mirabeau, 13100 Aix-en-Provence. © **04-42-27-74-22.** Fax 04-42-26-80-93. 37 units. 70€–140€ ($91–$182) double. AE, DC, V. Parking 10€ ($13). **Amenities:** Limited room service; laundry service; nonsmoking rooms. *In room:* A/C, TV, minibar, hair dryer, safe.

Résidence Rotonde   A contemporary hotel in the town center, the Rotonde provides cheerful, streamlined accommodations. Occupying part of a residential building, it has an open spiral cantilevered staircase and molded-plastic and chrome furniture. The rooms have ornate wallpaper, Nordic-style beds, and adequately comfortable mattresses. Bathrooms, some with showers only and some with tubs, are a bit small but adequate for the job, with suitable shelf space. There's no restaurant, but breakfast is served.

15 av. des Belges, 13100 Aix-en-Provence. (C) **04-42-26-29-88.** Fax 04-42-26-29-98. 41 units. 75€–160€ ($98–$208) double; 180€ ($234) suite. AE, DC, MC, V. Parking 9€ ($12). **Amenities:** Breakfast room; bar; lounge. *In room:* A/C, TV, minibar.

Inexpensive

Hôtel des Quatre Dauphins   This 18th-century town house is a short walk from place des Quatre Dauphins and the cours Mirabeau. Some original motifs have survived through frequent modernizations. The medium-size guest rooms were refurbished in simplified Provençal style, some with painted ceiling beams and casement windows that overlook the street. Five units come with a compact bathroom with tub/shower, the rest with shower only. You can have breakfast in your room or in a small salon.

54 rue Roux-Alphéran, 13100 Aix-en-Provence. (C) **04-42-38-16-39.** Fax 04-42-38-60-19. 13 units. 60€–85€ ($78–$111) double. MC, V. **Amenities:** Limited room service. *In room:* TV.

Hôtel La Caravelle *Value*   Not everything in this hotel is state of the art, but because of the old-fashioned setting (an 18th-century town house loaded with personalized quirks), a collection of 18th- and 19th-century antiques, and upscale, historically appropriate upholsteries, many clients don't seem to mind. Located in the Mazarin quarter, on the side of the cours Mirabeau that's less frequently visited by foreign visitors, it has touches of nostalgia that many locals associate with old-time Provence. The annex, which lies about 7.6m (25 ft.) away, near an antique church, holds most of the suites, each of which has a simple kitchenette. Bathrooms tend to be small, usually with showers but not bathtubs.

29 bd. du Roi-René (at cours Mirabeau), 13100 Aix-en-Provence. (C) **04-42-21-53-05.** Fax 04-42-96-55-46. www.la caravelle-hotel.com. 30 units. 46€–69€ ($60–$90) double. AE, DC, MC, V. **Amenities:** Limited room service; laundry service; dry cleaning; nonsmoking rooms. *In room:* A/C, TV, dataport, minibar.

IN MEYRARGUES

Château de Meyrargues *✿✿*   This 12th-century château is one of France's oldest fortified sites, having been a Celtic outpost in 600 B.C. Once the lords of Les Baux lived here; now it's an award-winning holiday retreat. The entrance is imposing, with twin stone towers flanking a sweeping set of balustraded steps. From its terraces and rooms you can enjoy a panoramic view of the valley of the Durance. The spacious accommodations feature canopied beds, fabrics inspired by Provençal designs and colors, antiques, and tiled bathrooms with showers equipped with floods of hot water.

Meals are served in a baronial-looking dining room with a large fireplace, near a bar with a private terrace. Fixed-price menus tend to emphasize grilled fish and roasted versions of Provençal lamb. There are 4.8 hectares (12 acres) of private terrain around the château, wherein patches of verdant gardens are interspersed with a swimming pool and lots of rocky outcroppings.

13650 Meyrargues. (C) **04-42-63-49-90.** Fax 04-42-63-49-92. www.chateau-de-meyrargues.com. 11 units. 125€–200€ ($163–$260) double; 305€ ($397) suite. AE, DC, MC, V. From Aix, take A51 for 17km (11 miles) northeast, following the signs for Sisteron and Pertuis; get off at exit 14, and then follow the signs to the château. **Amenities:** Restaurant; bar; outdoor pool; limited room service; babysitting. *In room:* A/C, TV, minibar, hair dryer.

IN BEAURECUEIL
Mas de la Bertrande ♔   This charming hotel has a setting that looks like a Cézanne canvas, at the foot of Montaigne Ste-Victoire. The former stable has exposed ceiling beams, a country fireplace, and plush furniture. The hotel's staff is very attentive, and rooms are cozily outfitted with Provençal furniture. Bathrooms are well equipped and tidily maintained, with tub/shower combos.

The cuisine is one of the primary reasons for a stop here. The chef's innovative specialties are served on the terrace or in the dining room, both ringed with flowers. Specialties are herb-flavored lamb, stuffed sole, bisque of mussels, truffled chicken, rockfish soup, foie gras of the region, and an excellent *tarte tatin*. The cheese board has selections from all over France.

Chemin de la Plaine, 13100 Beaurecueil. ⓒ **04-42-66-75-75.** Fax 04-42-66-82-01. www.mas-bertrande.com. 9 units. 119€–144€ ($155–$187) double. Rates include breakfast. AE, MC, V. Closed Feb 15–Mar 15. From Aix, drive 10km (6 miles) southeast, following the signs to Trets. **Amenities:** Restaurant; bar; outdoor pool; limited room service; laundry service. *In room:* TV, minibar.

WHERE TO DINE
EXPENSIVE
Le Clos de la Violette ♔♔♔ MODERN FRENCH   This innovative restaurant is a few steps from La Villa Gallici (see "Where to Stay," above) in an elegant neighborhood that most visitors reach by taxi. The Provençal villa has an octagonal reception area and several dining rooms. The stylish, seasonal dishes highlight the flavors of Provence. A stellar example of the innovative cuisine is an appetizer of mousseline of potatoes with sea urchins and fish roe. An elegant dish is braised sea wolf with crisp fried shallots and a "cappuccino" of spicy Spanish sausages. Delightful rack of suckling lamb is stuffed with carrots and chick peas and served under an herb-flavored pastry crust. For dessert, try multilayered sugar cookies with hazelnut and vanilla-flavored cream sauce and thin slices of white chocolate. Another superb dessert is a "celebration" of Provençal figs—an artfully arranged platter containing a galette, tart, parfait, and sorbet.

10 av. de la Violette. ⓒ **04-42-23-30-71.** Reservations required. Main courses 40€–48€ ($52–$62); fixed-price lunch 54€ ($70); tasting menu 120€ ($156). AE, V. Tues–Sat noon–1:30pm and 8–9:30pm. Closed 2 weeks in Aug.

Le Passage MEDITERRANEAN   Adding feminine flair to Mediterranean cuisine, owner/manager Reine Sammut has transformed a 19th-century candy factory into a contemporary brasserie in the nucleus of Aix. Inside, you'll find two large dining rooms plus a sprawling outdoor terrace. Walls are accented with paintings, each of which is for sale. (Expositions here are coordinated by a local art gallery, with inventories that change about once a month.) The atmosphere is friendly and intimate, with lots of care behind every dish served. Menu items are linked to the seasons, and change often, but staples include *les petits farcis* (vegetables stuffed and deep-fried) served with a tomato-basil sauce; a carpaccio of John Dory with a vanilla-flavored olive sauce; marinated and grilled filet of beef with large-cut french fries and a wasabi-flavored mayonnaise; and a filet of roasted *daurade* with green asparagus. One of the best desserts in Aix is a featured specialty here: raspberry-flavored crème brûlée with a fig chutney. Also on-site are a bookshop, a tearoom, a wine boutique, and a cooking school. Note that this restaurant has two entrances.

6 bis rue Mazarine and 10 rue Villas. © **04-42-37-09-00.** Reservations recommended. Main courses 25€–48€ ($33–$62). AE, MC, V. Daily noon–2:30pm and 7:15pm–midnight.

MODERATE

Antoine Côté Cour PROVENÇAL/ITALIAN   This popular trattoria is in an 18th-century town house a few steps from place Rotonde. Regulars include Emanuel Ungaro and many film and fashion types, who mingle with old-time "Aixers." Despite its grandeur, the ambience is unpretentious, even jovial. Crusty bread and small pots of aromatic purées (anchovy and basil) arrive at your table as you sit down. A simple wine, such as Côtes-du-Rhône, goes nicely with the hearty Mediterranean fare. Examples of dishes are pasta Romano flavored with calves' liver, flap mushrooms, and tomato sauce; ravioli with goat cheese; *osso buco;* a selection of *légumes farcies* (vegetables such as eggplant and zucchini stuffed with minced meat and herbs); and at least half a dozen kinds of fresh fish.

19 cours Mirabeau. © **04-42-93-12-51.** Reservations recommended. Main courses 15€–30€ ($20–$39). DC, MC, V. Tues–Sat noon–2:30pm; Mon–Sat 7:30pm–midnight.

Chez Maxime GRILLS/PROVENÇAL   Set in the heart of Aix's pedestrian shopping zone, this likeable restaurant offers an all-Provençal ambience of Bordeaux-colored banquettes, salmon-colored walls, and tables shaded by an enormous linden tree that spill out onto the pavement during clement weather. There's a succulent array of at least a dozen kind of grills, including roasted shoulder of lamb, beefsteaks, and fresh fish, as well as a main course laced with saffron and the flavors of the sea, a *marmite* (stewpot) *de la mer.* Also appealing is house-made foie gras of duckling, a kind of pâté made from beef and Provençal herbs known as *caillette de province,* and such desserts as a *fondant au chocolat.* The wine list features dozens of vintages, many of them esoteric bottles from the region.

12 place Ramus. © **04-42-26-28-51.** Reservations recommended. Main courses 10€–25€ ($13–$33); 15€ ($20) fixed-price lunch; 23€–29€ ($30–$38) fixed-price dinner. MC, V. Tues–Sat noon–2:30pm; Mon–Sat 7:30–10:30pm.

INEXPENSIVE

Brasserie Royale TRADITIONAL FRENCH   Located on a tree-lined boulevard, the informal Brasserie Royale offers excellent, unpretentious regional cooking at reasonable prices. It's a modernized, animated, and invariably crowded place with an interior dining room and a popular glass-enclosed, canopied section on the sidewalk. You're served such hearty fare as tripe Provençal, daube Provençal (a favorite dish here), and *bourride Provençale.* The daube consists of succulent chunks of beef braised in a rich red-wine stock, enriched with various fresh vegetables, and well seasoned with herbs. The bourride is a savory fish stew richly spiced with garlic and a bouquet garni and served in a tureen on slices of fresh bread with the fish on the side. Gigot of tender alpine lamb is another specialty; the meat is perfumed with the fresh herbs of Provence. The chef is known for his *plats du jour,* which on our last visit included *lapin* (rabbit) chasseur, paella, *osso buco,* and couscous. If you're dining light, you might enjoy one of the omelets. Wines of Provence come by the half or full bottle. The brasserie is also a *glacier* during the afternoon, serving several different ice-cream specialties, milk shakes, and Irish coffee.

17 cours Mirabeau. © **04-42-26-01-63.** Main courses 11€–26€ ($14–$34); fixed-price menus 12€–25€ ($16–$32). MC, V. Daily noon–2pm and 7pm–1am.

Le Bistro Latin ★ *Value* PROVENÇAL   The best little bistro in Aix-en-Provence (for the price) is run by Bruno Ungaro and his partner, Gilles Holtz, who pride themselves on their fixed-price menus. They offer two intimate dining rooms, a street-level room and another in the cellar decorated in Greco-Latin style. The staff is young and enthusiastic, and Provençal music plays in the background. Try chartreuse of mussels, a meat dish with spinach-and-saffron cream sauce, scampi risotto, or crepe rack of lamb in an herbed crust. We've enjoyed the classic cuisine on all our visits, particularly the scampi risotto.

18 rue de la Couronne. ℭ **04-42-38-22-88.** Reservations recommended. Main courses 14€–17€ ($16–$20); fixed-price menu 16€ ($18) lunch, 21€–32€ ($24–$37) dinner. MC, V. Tues–Sat noon–2pm; Mon–Sat 7–10:30pm.

AIX AFTER DARK

An easy-to-reach bar that manages to be convenient and hip at the same time lies almost directly across from the city's tourist office: **La Rotonde,** Place Jeanne d'Arc (ℭ **04-42-91-61-70).** Open daily from 9am until at least midnight, it functions as a bar, a cafe, and a rendezvous point for friends and business associates throughout the day and evening.

People between the ages of 20 and 30 who like animated bar scenes and loud electronic music head for **Le Mistral,** 3 rue Frédéric-Mistral (ℭ **04-42-38-16-49),** where techno and house music blares long and loud, all for a cover charge of around 15€ ($20), unless you happen to be gorgeous and female, in which you'll get in free. Depending on the mood of the staff, you might even receive a free glass or two of champagne.

For jazz that's produced by a changing roster of visiting musicians, head for the **Scat Club,** 11 rue de la Verrerie (ℭ **04-42-23-00-23),** a smoky jazz den that's the preferred venue for patrons in their late 30s and 40s. Open Tuesday to Sunday, it maintains notoriously late hours, with live music often not beginning until around midnight. **Le Cox,** 23 rue de la Verrerie (ℭ **04-42-23-49-29),** was modeled on some of the very large lounge and dance bars of Paris, where at its best, surges of nubile and sexually/emotionally available rock and rollers migrate aimlessly between the lounge bar, the restaurant, and the techno and house-driven dance floor. An entrance fee of 12€ to 16€ ($16–$21), depending on the night of the week, includes a free drink. And last but certainly not least is Aix's newest see-and-get-laid bar, **La Joia,** Route de l'Enfant, in the hamlet of Les Milles, 8km (5 miles) south of Aix (to get there, follow the signs to Marseille, ℭ **06-80-35-32-94).** If you opt to go there, expect to park in one of the region's biggest parking lots (it's genuinely vast and somewhat off-putting). On-site you'll find a restaurant, several bars (each with a different visual and musical ambience), an outdoor swimming pool (the kind where you might opt to jump in topless), a dance floor with both indoor and outdoor sections, and a venue that's more hip than it is chic. Know in advance that on Fridays and Saturdays, a long line and as much as an hour's wait before you're admitted to the *sanctum santorum* will greet you. Entrance costs between 15€ and 20€ ($20–$26), unless you're either a star or self-enchanted enough to convince the doorman that you are, in which case the velvet ropes might miraculously part, without charge, like the Red Sea before Moses.

13 Marseille ★★★

771km (479 miles) S of Paris; 187km (116 miles) SW of Nice; 31km (19 miles) S of Aix-en-Provence

Bustling Marseille, with more than a million inhabitants, is the second-largest city in France (its population surpassed that of Lyon in the early 1990s) and France's premier port. It's been called France's New Orleans. A crossroads of world traffic—Dumas

Marseille

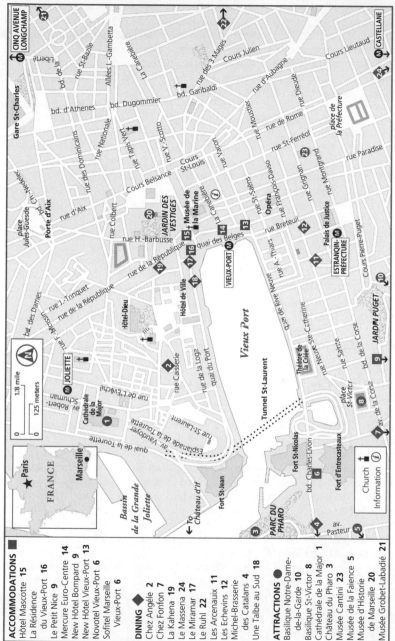

called it "the meeting place of the entire world"—the city is ancient, founded by Greeks from the city of Phocaea, near present-day Izmir, Turkey, in the 6th century B.C. Marseille is a place of unique sounds, smells, and sights. It has seen wars and much destruction, but trade has always been its raison d'être.

Perhaps its most common association is with the national anthem of France, "La Marseillaise." During the Revolution, 500 volunteers marched to Paris, singing this rousing song along the way. The rest is history.

Although in many respects Marseille is big and sprawling, dirty and slumlike in many places, there's much elegance and charm here as well. The Vieux Port, the old harbor, is especially colorful, compensating to an extent for the dreary industrial dockland nearby. Marseille has always symbolized danger and intrigue, and that reputation is somewhat justified. However, the city is experiencing somewhat of a renaissance, and because it is now so easily reached by train from Paris, there is much hope for its economic future. Since the 1970s, a great deal of Marseille's economy has revolved around thousands upon thousands of North and sub-Saharan Africans who have poured into the city, creating a lively medley of races and creeds. One-quarter of the present population of Marseille is of North African descent. These Africans have flocked here to find a better life than what they had in their own shattered lands.

Marseille today actually occupies twice the amount of land space as Paris, and its age-old problems remain, including a declining drug industry, smuggling, corruption (often at the highest levels), the Mafia, and racial tension. Unemployment, as always, is on the rise. But in spite of all these difficulties, it's a bustling, fascinating city unlike any other in France. A city official proclaimed recently that "Marseille is the unbeloved child of France. It's attached to France, but has the collective consciousness of an Italian city-state, like Genoa or Venice."

ESSENTIALS

GETTING THERE The **airport** (✆ 04-42-14-14-14), 27km (17 miles) northwest of the center of the city, receives international flights from all over Europe. From the airport, blue-and-white minivans (*navettes*) make the trip to Marseille's St-Charles rail station, near the Vieux-Port, for 8.50€ ($11). The minivans run daily from 6am every 20 minutes until the arrival of the last flight.

Marseille has **train** connections from hundreds of European cities, with especially good connections to and from Italy. The city is the terminus for the TGV bullet train, which departs daily from Paris's Gare de Lyon (trip time: 3 hr. 16 min.; one-way fare 75€/$98). Some Parisians day-trip to the Mediterranean beaches at Marseille and return to the City of Light for dinner. Local trains leave Paris almost every hour, making a number of stops before reaching Marseille. For information, call ✆ 08-92-35-35-35. **Buses** serve the Gare Routière, place Victor Hugo (✆ 04-91-08-16-40), adjacent to the St-Charles railway station.

If you're **driving** from Paris, follow A6 south to Lyon, then continue south along A7 to Marseille. The drive takes about 7 hours. From Provence, take A7 south to Marseille.

VISITOR INFORMATION The **Office de Tourisme** is at 4 la Canebière (✆ 04-91-13-89-00; www.marseille-tourisme.com; Métro: Vieux-Port).

EXPLORING THE CITY

Many visitors never bother to visit the museums, preferring to absorb the unique spirit of the city as reflected by its busy streets and at its sidewalk cafes, particularly those along the main street, **La Canebière.** Known as "can of beer" to World War II GI's,

Moments **Exploring the Massif des Calanques**

You can visit the **Massif des Calanques,** a wild and rugged terrain, from either Marseille or Cassis. This craggy coastline lies between the two ports, directly south of Marseille and to the west of Cassis. With its highest peak at 555m (1,850 ft.), the Calanques stretch for some 20km (13 miles) of dazzling limestone whiteness. This is one of France's great natural beauty areas.

Exactly what is a *calanque?* The word comes from the Provençal *cala,* meaning "steep slopes." Nature has cut steep coastal valleys into solid rock, creating steep inlets. Most of these gorges extend less than a kilometer inland from the Mediterranean. They're similar to fjords, created by glaciers, but these gorges have been created by the raging sea. The needlelike rocks and cliff faces overhanging the sea attract rock climbers and deep-sea divers.

The highlight of the Calanques is **Sormiou,** with its beach, seafood eateries, and small harbor. Sormiou is separated from another small but enchanting settlement at Morgiou by **Cap Morgiou,** which offers a panoramic belvedere with splendid views of both the Calanques and the eastern side of the massif. At **Morgiou** there are tiny inlets for swimming.

it's the spine and soul of Marseille, but the seediest main street in France. Lined with hotels, shops, and restaurants, the street is filled with sailors of every nation and a wide range of foreigners, especially Algerians, some of whom live in souklike conditions. La Canebière winds down to the **Vieux Port** 𝕬𝕬, dominated by the massive neoclassical forts of St-Jean and St-Nicholas. The port is filled with fishing craft and yachts and is ringed with seafood restaurants.

Motorists can continue along to the **corniche Président-J.-F.-Kennedy,** a promenade running for about 5km (3 miles) along the sea. You pass villas and gardens along the way and have a good view of the Mediterranean. To the north, the **Port Moderne** (also known simply as "La Joliette," or "the gateway to the East") is a man-made labyrinth of nautical engineering. Its construction began in 1844, and a century later, the Germans destroyed it. Today it's one of the busiest ports in the Mediterranean.

THE TOP ATTRACTIONS

Basilique Notre-Dame-de-la-Garde   This landmark church crowns a limestone rock overlooking the southern side of the Vieux-Port. It was built in the Romanesque-Byzantine style popular in the 19th century and topped by a 9m (30-ft.) gilded statue of the Virgin. Visitors come for the view—best at sunset—from its terrace. Spread out before you are the city, the islands, and the sea.

Rue Fort-du-Sanctuaire. © 04-91-13-40-80. Free admission. Daily 7am–7pm. Métro: Vieux-Port. Bus: 60.

Basilique St-Victor 𝕬   This semifortified basilica was built above a crypt from the 5th century, when St. Cassianus founded the church and abbey. You can visit the crypt, which also reflects work done in the 10th and 11th centuries.

Place St-Victor. © 04-96-11-22-60. Admission to crypt 2€ ($2.60). Church daily 9am–7pm. Crypt daily 10am–7pm. Head west along quai de Rive-Neuve (near the Gare du Vieux-Port). Métro: Vieux-Port.

Cathédrale de la Major This was one of the largest cathedrals (some 135m/450 ft. long) built in Europe in the 19th century. It has mosaic floors and red-and-white marble banners, and the exterior is in a bastardized Romanesque-Byzantine style. The domes and cupolas may remind you of Istanbul. This vast pile has almost swallowed its 12th-century Romanesque predecessor, built on the ruins of a Temple of Diana.

Place de la Major. ℂ **04-91-90-52-87**. Free admission. Hours vary. Métro: Vieux-Port.

Musée Cantini The temporary exhibitions of contemporary art here are often as good as the permanent collection. This museum is devoted to modern art, with masterpieces by Derain, Marquet, Ernst, Masson, Balthus, and others. It also owns a selection of works by important young international artists.

19 rue Grignan. ℂ **04-91-54-77-75**. Admission 3€ ($3.90) adults, 1.50€ ($1.95) students, free for seniors and children under 11. Oct–May Tues–Sun 10am–5pm; June–Sept Tues–Sun 11am–6pm.

Musée de la Faïence This museum contains one of the largest collections of porcelain in France. Its collections date from Neolithic times to the present. Especially numerous are the delicate and richly ornate ceramics that graced the tables of local landowners during the 18th and 19th centuries. The museum is about 5km (3 miles) south of the center of Marseille, in a stately manor house (Château Pastré) that was built by a local ship owner in 1864.

In the Château Pastré, 157 av. de Montredon. ℂ **04-91-72-43-47**. Admission 2€ ($2.60) adults, 1€ ($1.30) students and ages 11–18, free for children under 11. June–Sept Tues–Sun 11am–6pm; Oct–May Tues–Sun 10am–5pm.

Musée d'Histoire de Marseille Visitors may wander through an archaeological garden where excavations are going on, as scholars learn more about the ancient town of Massalia, founded by Greek sailors. To help you more fully realize the era, audiovisual exhibits and a free exhibition room set the scene. A medieval quarter of potters has been discovered, and is open to the public. You can also see what's left of a Roman shipwreck excavated from the site.

Centre Bourse, sq. Belsunce. ℂ **04-91-90-42-22**. Admission 2€ ($2.60) adults, 1€ ($1.15) students and children 11–18. Mon–Sat 11am–7pm. Métro: Vieux-Port.

Musée d'Histoire Naturelle If you have the time to spare and you are already visiting Palais Longchamp, consider ducking into this museum for a half-hour or so. It is usually visited jointly with a visit to the more important Musée des Beaux-Arts. The museum lies in the right wing of the Palais Longchamp and offers a parade of the fossilized remains of the animals of Provence. The museum illustrates 400 million years of the natural history of Provence in its exhibits, including a safari section that shows the diversity of animals throughout the world. Of special interest to botany lovers is a gallery showcasing regional flora and fauna. On the lowest level, a Mediterranean aquarium is devoted to fish from five oceans.

In the Palais Longchamp, place Bernex. ℂ **04-91-14-59-50**. Admission 3€ ($3.90) adults, 1.50€ ($1.95) students and ages 10–18, free for children under 10. Tues–Sun 10am–5pm.

Musée Grobet-Labadié 🏛 This collection, bequeathed to the city in 1919, includes Louis XV and Louis XVI furniture, as well as an outstanding collection of medieval Burgundian and Provençal sculpture. Other exhibits showcase 17th-century Gobelin tapestries; 15th- to 19th-century German, Italian, French, and Flemish paintings; and 16th- and 17th-century Italian and French faïence.

140 bd. Longchamp. (C) **04-91-62-21-82.** Admission 2€ ($2.60) adults, 1€ ($1.30) students and children 11–18. June–Sept Tues–Sun 11am–6pm; Oct–May Tues–Sun 10am–5pm. Closed public holidays. Métro: Cinq av. Longchamp.

PANORAMIC VIEWS

Basilique Notre-Dame-de-la-Garde, rue Fort-du-Sanctuaire ((C) **04-91-13-40-80**), crowns a limestone bluff overlooking the southern flank of the Vieux Port. Built in 1864 in the Romanesque-Byzantine style, and capped with a 9m (30-ft.) gilded statue of the Virgin, it sits atop the foundations of a fortress that was commissioned during the Renaissance by French monarch François I. Although the architecture shows France's Gilded Age at its most evocative, visitors come here not so much for the church as for the view—best appreciated at sunset—from its terrace. Spread out before you are the city, the islands, and the sea. The church is open daily from 7am to 7pm.

Another vantage point for a panoramic view is the **Parc du Pharo,** a promontory facing the entrance to the Vieux Port. Most people visit this park to escape the urban congestion of Marseille, but if you're in the mood for some history, check out the gray-stone facade of the **Château du Pharo** ((C) **04-91-14-64-95**). Built in the 1860s by Napoleon III for his empress, Eugénie (who is reputed not to have liked it and seldom visited), it's owned and maintained by the city of Marseille as a convention center and—less frequently—as a concert hall. The building has no regular hours, but if nothing is going on, you can enter the lobby and ask for a quick glance at the Salon des Génies.

BOATING TO CHATEAU D'IF ⭐⭐

From quai des Belges at the Vieux-Port, you can take a 20-minute motorboat ride to **Château d'If** for 10€ ($13) round-trip. Boats leave every 60 to 90 minutes, depending on the season. For information, contact the **Groupement des Armateurs Côtiers,** quai des Belges ((C) **04-91-55-50-09;** Métro: Vieux-Port), daily from 9am to 6:30pm. On the sparsely vegetated island of Château d'If ((C) **04-91-59-02-30** for information), François I built a fortress to defend Marseille. The site later housed a prison, where carvings by Huguenot prisoners can still be seen. Alexandre Dumas used the château as a setting for the fictional adventures of *The Count of Monte Cristo.* The château's most famous association—with the legendary Man in the Iron Mask—is also apocryphal. The château is open Tuesday through Sunday from 9am to 5:30pm (until 6:30pm Apr–Sept). Visitors pay 4€ ($5.20) to enter the island.

SHOPPING

Only Paris and Lyon can rival Marseille in breadth and diversity of merchandise. Your best bet is a trip to the Vieux Port and the streets surrounding it for a view of the folkloric objects that literally pop out of the boutiques.

ART & ANTIQUES The sunlight of Provence has always been cited by artists for its luminosity, and so Marseille has a handful of well-respected art galleries. Antiques from around Provence are sold at **Antiquités François-Décamp,** 302 rue Paradis ((C) **04-91-81-18-00**).

FASHION You don't normally think of Marseille as a place to shop for fashion, but the local fashion industry is booming. The fashion center is found along **cours Julien,** where you'll find dozens of boutiques and ateliers. Much of the clothing reflects North African influences, although there is a vast array of French styles as well.

For hats, at **Felio,** 4 place Gabriel-Péri ((C) **04-91-90-32-67**), you'll find large-brimmed numbers that would've thrilled ladies of the belle époque or guests at a stylish wedding inspired in the 1920s by Lanvin. It also carries a selection of *casquettes Marseillaises* (developed for men as protection from the *soleil du Midi*) and berets that begin at 23€ ($30).

FOLKLORE & SOUVENIRS   Especially popular are the **santons** (carved wooden crèche figurines). The best place for acquiring these artifacts is just above the Vieux Port, behind the Théâtre National de la Criée. At **Ateliers Marcel Carbonel,** 47 rue Neuve-Ste-Catherine (© **04-91-54-26-58**), more than 600 figures, available in half a dozen sizes, sell at prices beginning at 9€ ($12).

All the souvenir shops along the pedestrian **rue St-Féréol,** running perpendicular to La Canebière, sell folkloric replicas of handicrafts from Old Provence, including the cream-colored or pale-green bars of the city's local soap, **savon de Marseille.** Infused with a healthy dollop of olive oil, it's known for its kindness to skin dried out by the sun and mistral. A large selection is available at **La Savonnerie du Sérail,** 50 bd. Anatole de la Forge (© **04-91-98-28-25**).

FOOD & CHOCOLATE   At **Amandine,** 69 bd. Eugène-Pierre (© **04-91-47-00-83**), a photograph or a work of graphic art can be reproduced in various shades of chocolate on top of a delicious layer cake in any flavor you specify in advance. If you don't happen to have your scrapbook with you, you can buy a cake emblazoned with scenes of the Vieux Port or whatever. More traditional pastries and chocolates are found at **Puyricard,** 25 rue Francis-Davso (© **04-91-54-26-25**), with another location at 155 rue Jean-Mermoz (© **04-91-77-94-11**). The treats available here include chocolates stuffed with almond paste *(pâté d'amande)* or *confits de fruits,* along with a type of biscuit called *une Marseillotte.*

Since medieval times, Marseille has thrived on the legend of Les Trois Maries—three saints named Mary who, assisted by awakened-from-the-dead St. Lazarus, reportedly came ashore at a point near Marseille to Christianize ancient Provence. In commemoration of their voyage, small boat-shaped cookies called *les navettes* are flavored with secret ingredients (that include orange zest, orange-flower water, and sugar); they are forever associated with Marseille. You can find them throughout the city, notably at **Le Four des Navettes,** 136 rue Sainte (© **04-91-33-32-12**). It opened in 1791 and is dedicated to perpetuating the city's most cherished medieval myth and ferociously guarding the secret of how the pastries are made. The boat-shaped cookies are sold for 7.20€ ($9.35) per dozen.

One of the city's most sophisticated emporiums for takeout food is **La Fromagerie Marrou,** 2 bd. Baille (© **04-91-78-17-68**). Established in 1902 and known as one of the most comprehensive upscale food stores in Marseille, it sells more than just cheeses: meats, baked goods, deli items, wines, liqueurs, foie gras, and caviar. With a

---

Tips   A Day at the Beach

Bus no. 83 leaves from the Vieux-Port heading for the public beaches outside Marseille. This bus will take you to both **Plage du Prado** and **Plage de la Corniche,** the best bets for swimming and sunning. The sands are a bit gray and sometimes rocky, but the beaches are wide and the water is generally clear. These beaches are set against a scenic backdrop of the cliffs of Marseille.

main branch at 2 bd. Baille, the shop maintains secondary branches at 475 rue Paradis and 15 place Castellane.

A MARSEILLE MALL   Looking for something that approximates, with a Provençal accent, a sun-flooded mall in California? Head for the most talked-about real-estate development in the city's recent history, **L'Escale Borély,** avenue Mendès-France. Within a 25-minute transit (take the Métro to rond-point du Prado and then transfer to bus no. 19) south of Marseille, it incorporates shops, cafes, bars, and restaurants. Note the newest fad from your seat on a terrace as you sip pastis: in-line skating. For more on L'Escale Borély, see "Marseille After Dark," later in this chapter.

WHERE TO STAY
VERY EXPENSIVE
Le Petit Nice 𝓡𝓡𝓡   This is the best in Marseille, with the finest restaurant. The residence opened in 1917 when the Passédat family joined two villas. The narrow approach takes you past what looks like a row of private villas, in a secluded area below the street paralleling the beach. Rooms are decorated with tasteful fabrics and quality carpeting, and all come equipped with fine beds. Units in the main house are modern and even avant-garde—four units were inspired by Cubism and have geometric appointments and bright colors. The spacious Marina Wing across from the main building offers individually decorated rooms in the antique style, opening onto sea views. Marble bathrooms are quite sumptuous and come with deluxe toiletries.

The beautiful glass-enclosed restaurant has a view of the shore and the rocky islands off the coast. In summer, dinner is served in the garden facing the sea. It's run by Gerald Passédat, whose imaginative culinary successes include sliced sea wolf in the style of the Passédat family matriarch, Lucy; vinaigrette of *rascasse* (hogfish); and sea devil with saffron and garlic.

Corniche Président-J.-F.-Kennedy/Anse-de-Maldormé, 13007 Marseille. ⓒ **04-91-59-25-92.** Fax 04-91-59-28-08. 16 units. 190€–410€ ($247–$533) double; 610€–810€ ($793–$1,053) suite. AE, DC, MC, V. Free parking. Métro: Vieux-Port. **Amenities:** Restaurant; bar; outdoor pool; free use of bikes; limited room service; babysitting; laundry service; dry cleaning; nonsmoking rooms; limited-mobility rooms. *In room:* A/C, TV, dataport, minibar, hair dryer, safe.

EXPENSIVE
Sofitel Marseille Vieux Port 𝓡𝓡𝓡   This government-rated four-star hotel lacks the glamour and style of Le Petit Nice, but it is the highest-rated lodging in the city center. A glistening modern palace, it stands above the embankments of the old port. Some guest rooms have panoramic views of the Vieux-Port; others look out on the boulevard. Rooms are up-to-date, comfortable, and furnished in Provençal style, with a combination tub/shower. All are fairly generous in size. This hotel and its corporate sibling, the Novotel Vieux-Port (see below), are in the same building and share a staff and dining facilities.

36 bd. Charles-Livon, 13007 Marseille. ⓒ **04-91-15-59-00.** Fax 04-91-15-59-50. www.accor.com. 130 units. 200€–355€ ($260–$462) double; 555€–980€ ($722–$1,274) suite. AE, DC, MC, V. Parking 14€ ($18). Métro: Vieux-Port. **Amenities:** Restaurant; bar; 24-hr. room service; babysitting; laundry service; dry cleaning; nonsmoking rooms; limited-mobility rooms. *In room:* A/C, TV, dataport, minibar, hair dryer, safe.

MODERATE
La Résidence du Vieux-Port   This old hotel has a touch of raffish charm and an unbeatable location: directly beside the harbor. The guest rooms have loggia-style terraces opening onto the port; the rooms are simple but serviceable, each with a shower unit.

18 quai du Port, 13001 Marseille. ⓒ **04-91-91-91-22.** Fax 04-91-56-60-88. www.hotelmarseille.com. 41 units. 118€–130€ ($153–$169) double; 199€ ($259) suite. AE, DC, MC, V. Parking 6€ ($7.80). Métro: Vieux-Port. **Ameni-ties:** Cafe; bar; limited room service; laundry service; dry cleaning; nonsmoking rooms; limited-mobility rooms. *In room:* A/C, TV, dataport, minibar, hair dryer, safe.

Mercure Euro-Centre   One of the most modern hotels in town, this bronze build-ing looks out over the Greco-Roman ruins of the Jardin des Vestiges, a 2-minute walk from the Old Port and near a collection of boutiques, the Centre Bourse. The well-kept rooms are furnished in a functional chain-style format, with twin or double beds. Tiled bathrooms are compact but have adequate shelf space. The restaurant on the grounds is popular with Marseille's shoppers. Many staff members speak English.

Rue Neuve-St-Martin, 13001 Marseille. ⓒ **04-97-17-22-22.** Fax 04-91-56-24-57. 199 units. 82€–124€ double; 160€–229€ suite. AE, DC, MC, V. Parking 10€. Métro: Colbert. **Amenities:** Restaurant; bar; limited room service; laundry service. *In room:* A/C, TV, minibar, hair dryer.

New Hôtel Vieux-Port *Value*   Located close to the port, this hotel lies in a six-story turn-of-the-20th-century building. It offers comfortable rooms and a hardworking, English-speaking staff. Rooms that overlook the port are outfitted in a traditional way; the more contemporary-looking accommodations look out over the commercial neighborhood nearby. This hotel offers exceptional value for Marseille, although most of the accommodations are small. Each comes with twin or double beds; bathrooms are compact but well maintained.

3 bis rue Reine-Elisabeth, 13001 Marseille. ⓒ **04-91-99-23-23.** Fax 04-91-90-76-24. www.newhotelvieuxport.active hotels.com. 47 units. 130€–170€ ($169–$221) double. Children under 11 stay free in parent's room. AE, DC, MC, V. Parking 15€ ($20). Bus: 83. Métro: Vieux-Port. **Amenities:** Bar; lounge; health club; spa; sauna; laundry service; dry cleaning. *In room:* A/C, TV, minibar, hair dryer, safe.

Novotel Vieux-Port *Value*   In the same building as the Sofitel (see above), the Novotel broke off from its more upscale affiliate in 1987. Services are less extensive, amenities less plush, and spaces a bit more cramped than at the Sofitel, but because this is one of the most reasonably priced hotels in town, no one seems to mind. The few rooms overlooking the old port tend to fill up first. Each unit is outfitted in chain-hotel style and comes with a small, well-equipped bathroom with tub/shower.

36 bd. Charles-Livon, 13007 Marseille. ⓒ **04-96-11-42-11.** Fax 04-96-11-42-20. www.accorhotels.com. 90 units. 130€–160€ ($169–$208) double. AE, DC, MC, V. Parking 10€ ($13). Métro: Vieux-Port. **Amenities:** Restaurant; bar; outdoor pool; limited room service; babysitting; laundry service; dry cleaning; nonsmoking rooms; limited-mobility rooms. *In room:* A/C, TV, dataport, minibar, hair dryer.

INEXPENSIVE

Hôtel Mascotte   Everything about this hotel evokes the grandeur of 19th-century life in Marseille. It's less than 2 blocks from the Vieux-Port, in the heart of town. The sun and mistrals of many seasons have battered the beaux arts facade, decorated with ornate corbels and cornices. Renovations have stripped the guest rooms of some of their old-fashioned charm but have left efficient, soundproof spaces. Each unit has a compact bathroom with a shower and tub. Breakfast is the only meal served, but the neighborhood abounds with dining options.

5 la Canebière, 13001 Marseille. ⓒ **04-91-90-61-61.** Fax 04-91-90-95-61. 45 units. 84€–88€ ($109–$114) dou-ble. AE, DC, MC, V. Parking in nearby public lot 12€ ($16). **Amenities:** Limited room service; laundry service; dry cleaning; nonsmoking rooms. *In room:* A/C, TV, dataport, minibar, hair dryer.

New Hotel Bompard   This tranquil retreat, built after World War II, lies atop a cliff along the corniche, about 3km (2 miles) east of the Vieux-Port. Partly because of its garden, it might remind you of a well-appointed private home. A Provençal *mas* (farmhouse) in the garden holds four large rooms that are more luxurious and atmospheric than those in the main building. Some of the beds are baldachin-style (canopied), floors have Provençal tiles, bathrooms are relatively large, with tub/shower combos, and furnishings are romantic. Rooms in the main building are cheap, modern, and streamlined, with tub/shower combos, and not terribly romantic, although about a third were renovated in 2004.

2 rue des Flots Bleus, 13007 Marseille. © **04-91-99-22-22.** Fax 04-91-31-02-14. www.new-hotel.com. 48 units. 108€–120€ ($140–$156) standard double; 170€–220€ ($221–$286) Provençal *mas* double. AE, DC, MC, V. Free parking. Bus: 61 or 83. **Amenities:** Restaurant; bar; outdoor pool; limited room service; laundry service; nonsmoking rooms; limited-mobility rooms. *In room:* A/C, TV, dataport, minibar, hair dryer, iron, safe.

WHERE TO DINE
EXPENSIVE

Chez Fonfon ★ *Finds* PROVENÇAL/FRENCH This is one of the legendary restaurants of Marseille, with a clientele of famous actors that included John Wayne and Yves Montand in the 1950s and 1960s, and a bevy of newer, mostly French stars during the late 1990s. Its founder, a formidable but funny chef named Fonfon, died in 1998, and since then, the place has been capably handled by his great-nephew, Alexandre Pinna. Expect a location directly fronting the Port du Vallon des Auffes, a harbor for fishing boats that's within a 20-minute walk east of the more famous Vieux Port; a decor inspired by the furnishings and colors (ochers and russets) of the mid-summer Provençal landscape; and the kind of earthy, savory cuisine that many Marseillais remember from their childhoods. Examples include filet of bull braised in red wine; a savory bouillabaisse; all kinds of fish, sometimes grilled, sometimes baked in a salt crust and served on a slab of hot stone; and different variations of Provençal lamb. Appropriate starters for a meal here include fish soup, a medley of stuffed vegetables *(les petits farcis),* and fresh baby octopus, either grilled or fried.

140 rue du Vallon des Auffes, Port du Vallon des Auffes. © **04-91-52-14-38.** Reservations recommended. Main courses 22€–42€ ($29–$55); fixed-price menus 32€–50€ ($42–$65). AE, DC, MC, V. Tues–Sat noon–2pm; Mon–Sat 7–10pm. Métro: Vieux-Port.

Le Miramar ★★★ SEAFOOD Except for Le Petit Nice (see above), Le Miramar offers the grandest dining in Marseille. Since the mid-1960s, bouillabaisse aficionados have flocked here to savor a version that will surely be a culinary highlight of your trip. It's hard to imagine that this was once a rough-and-tumble recipe favored by local fisherfolk, a way of using the least desirable portion of their catch. Actually, it's traditionally two dishes, a saffron-tinted soup followed by the fish poached in the soup. It's eaten with *une rouille,* a sauce of red chiles, garlic, olive oil, egg yolk, and cayenne. The version served here involves lots of labor and just as much costly seafood. The setting is a big-windowed room with frescoes of underwater life and big windows that open onto the Vieux-Port. It's linked to a terrace that overlooks Marseille's most famous church, Notre-Dame-de-la-Garde.

12 quai du Port. © **04-91-91-10-40.** Reservations recommended. Main courses 30€–50€ ($39–$65); bouillabaisse from 50€ ($65) per person (minimum 2). AE, DC, MC, V. Tues–Sat noon–2pm and 7:15–10pm. Métro: Vieux-Port.

Michel-Brasserie des Catalans ★ SEAFOOD Although it's decorated with shel-lacked lobsters and starfish, this restaurant serves a fine bouillabaisse. Just beyond the Parc du Pharo, next to the Old Port, it's one of the best old-time restaurants in town. The cooking emphasizes the taste of the seafood rather than fancy sauces. In addition to the bouillabaisse, it offers a good *bourride* (fish stew with aioli sauce). The waiter brings you an array of fresh fish from which you make your selection. There's a kind of raffish insouciance here that you might find very appealing.

6 rue des Catalans. © **04-91-52-30-63.** Reservations recommended. Main courses 33€–55€ ($43–$72). AE, MC, V. Daily noon–4:45pm and 7:30–9:45pm. Bus: 81 or 83.

Une Table au Sud ⭑⭑ MODERN PROVENÇAL   One floor above street level, in a modern dining room with views of the Vieux-Port, this restaurant serves some of the most creative cuisine in Marseille. The historically important 19th-century building has sculpted lion heads embellishing its facade. Chef de cuisine Lionel Levy and his wife, Florence, the maître d'hotel, are the creative forces here. Their cuisine changes daily according to the ingredients available at local markets. Menu items include a creamy soup made from chestnuts and sea urchins, and a thick slice of a local saltwater fish known as *denti,* which local gastronomes compare to a daurade royale, served with flap mushrooms and chicken stock; mullet served with saffron and herb risotto; and roasted squab with Arabica coffee–flavored juices. Depending on the mood of the chef, desserts might include pineapple *dacquoise* (stacked meringue dessert) served with vanilla-flavored whipped cream.

1 quai du Port. © **04-91-90-63-53.** Reservations recommended. Main courses 25€–45€ ($33–$59); fixed-price lunches 30€–55€ ($39–$72); fixed-price dinners 43€–55€ ($56–$72). AE, MC, V. Tues–Sat noon–2pm and 7:30–10:30pm; Fri–Sat 7:30pm–midnight. Closed Aug and Dec 23–27. Métro: Vieux-Port.

MODERATE

Le Massena SEAFOOD   The venue here is rough-edged but civil at this bustling Marseille-style brasserie, where a color scheme of red and white, and big-windowed views over a fountain and the bustling square outside contribute to an experience that's exotic, savory, and carefully tuned to the rhythms of this port city. You'll pass a display of shellfish on the way inside. A fast-talking and very local staff will take orders for dishes that include a well-flavored version of *bourride* (garlic-flavored fish soup); bouillabaisse (the most expensive main course on the menu); gigot de lotte (monkfish stewed in cream sauce with fresh vegetables); platters of grilled fish served simply, perhaps with lemon sauce; and scallops cooked with morels.

19 place Castellane. © **04-91-78-18-10.** Reservations recommended. Main courses 9€–35€ ($12–$46); set-price menu 16€ ($21). MC, V. Daily noon–3pm and 7–11pm. Métro: Catellane.

Le Ruhl ⭑⭑ *(Finds* SEAFOOD   Since 1940, this restaurant has offered two versions of bouillabaisse that have wowed gastronomes with their flavor. Set about 3km (2 miles) east of the Vieux-Port, across the boulevard from a rocky stretch of seacoast, it offers two blue-and-white dining rooms, lots of varnished mahogany and polished brass, and seats that never come without some kind of sea view. Alex Galligani, the owner, recently drafted the *Charte de la Bouillabaisse Marseillaise,* which stipulates that a proper bouillabaisse must contain at least four types of fish, which may include guarnard, John Dory, anglerfish, chapon, conger, and scorpion fish. All of these are present within the standard-issue "bouillabaisse de pecheur" served here, and within the "bouillabaisse homard" you'll get chunks of lobster meat as well. The other distinctive specialty of this place is grilled fish, almost every kind that lives in the Mediterranean, a display of whose raw ingredients greets you near the restaurant's entrance.

269 Corniche Président-J.-F.-Kennedy. © **04-91-52-01-77.** Reservations recommended. Main courses 18€–25€ ($23–$33); bouillabaisse 40€–50€ ($51–$65). AE, MC, V. Daily noon–2:30pm and 8–10pm. Métro: Vieux-Port, then take bus for 3km (2 miles) east.

Les Arcenaulx ⭐ *(Finds)* PROVENÇAL   This is an architectural oddity that serves memorable cuisine. The navies of Louis XIV built these stone warehouses near the Vieux-Port; they now contain this restaurant and two bookstores, run by the charming sisters Simone and Jeanne Laffitte. Look for Provençal cuisine with a Marseillais accent in such dishes as roasted pigeon or duckling with caramelized quince; roasted scallops with hearts of violet artichokes; *daurade* (bream) roasted whole "on its skin"; and filet of beef Rossini, layered with foie gras. Equally tempting are artichokes *barigoule* (loaded with aromatic spices and olive oil) and a worthy assortment of *petites légumes farcies* (Provençal vegetables stuffed with chopped meat and herbs).

25 cours d'Estienne d'Orves. ℂ **04-91-59-80-30.** Reservations recommended. Main courses 18€–31€ ($23–$40); fixed-price menu 29€–50€ ($38–$65). AE, DC, MC, V. Mon–Sat noon–2pm and 8–11pm. Closed Aug 15–22 and Dec 27–Jan 3. Métro: Vieux-Port.

Les Echevins PROVENÇAL/SOUTHWESTERN FRENCH   On the opposite side of the building from Les Arcenaulx (see above), this restaurant occupies a former dorm for prisoners who were forced to row the ornamental barges of Louis XIV during his inspections of Marseille's harbor. Today, it contains chandeliers, plush carpets, antiques, and massive rocks and thick beams. You'll get a lot for your money—prices are relatively reasonable and ingredients very fresh. Provençal dishes include succulent baked sea wolf prepared as simply as possible—with herbs and olive oil. Particularly noteworthy is bouillabaisse (which, at 42€/$55 per person is the most expensive main course on the menu), and a delicious combination of saltwater crayfish with foie gras. Desserts usually include roasted figs served with sweet dessert wine.

44 rue Sainte. ℂ **04-96-11-03-11.** Reservations recommended. Main courses 19€–42€ ($25–$55); fixed-price menu 20€–48€ ($26–$62). AE, DC, MC, V. Mon–Fri noon–2:30pm; Mon–Sat 7:30–10:30pm. Closed mid-July to mid-Aug. Métro: Vieux-Port.

INEXPENSIVE

Chez Angèle PROVENÇAL/PIZZA   A local friend guided us here, and though most of Marseille's cheap eating places aren't recommendable, this one is worthwhile if you're watching your euros. Small and unpretentious, with a raffish kind of amiability on the part of the owner, it's a pizzeria-restaurant, with a menu more comprehensive than usual. Pizzas (the best are pistou, fresh seafood, or cèpes), well-prepared ravioli, tagliatelle, and grilled shrimp, squid, and daurade Provençal style are available. For something really ethnic, ask for Francis's version of *pieds et paquets,* a country recipe savored by locals—equal portions of grilled sheep's foot and sheep's intestines stuffed with garlic-flavored bread crumbs, herbs, and chopped vegetables. Note that this place lies on the route between Marseille and Aix.

50 rue Caisserie. ℂ **04-91-90-63-35.** Reservations recommended. Pizzas, pastas, and salads 9.50€–23€ ($12–$30); fixed-price menu 17€–22€ ($22–$29). AE, DC, MC, V. Mon–Fri noon–2pm; daily 7:30–11:30pm. Closed July 20–Aug 20. Métro: Vieux-Port.

La Kahena TUNISIAN   This is one of the busiest and most-respected Tunisian restaurants in a city that's loaded with worthy competitors. Established in 1976 and set close to the Old Port, it's a two-room enclave of savory North African aromas: minced or grilled lamb, tomatoes, eggplant, herbs, and couscous, so beloved by Tunisian expatriates. The menu lists 10 varieties of couscous, including versions with lamb, chicken, fish, the savory sausages known as *merguez,* and a "complete" version that includes a little bit of each of those ingredients. Also look for *méchoui,* a succulent version of roasted lamb. The restaurant's name, incidentally, derives from a 6th-century-B.C. Tunisian princess who was legendary for uniting all the Berber tribes of North Africa.

2 rue de la République. ℰ **04-91-90-61-93.** Reservations recommended. Main courses 11€–15€ ($14–$20). MC, V. Daily noon–2:30pm and 7:30–11pm. Métro: Vieux-Port.

NEARBY ACCOMMODATIONS & DINING

Relais de la Magdeleine ✦ *Finds* In a stone-sided, early-18th-century country mansion at the foot of the Ste-Baume mountain range, this hotel is surrounded by large homes, open fields, and woodlands, yet still near the beach. It's not far from the venerated spot where, according to medieval legend, Mary Magdalene is believed to have died. The inn has striking architectural details; note a carving of St. Roch, with his dog above the entrance. The decor is upscale, and features antiques and worthy reproductions. Guest rooms are individually furnished, in Directoire, Provençal, and Louis styles. Bathrooms are neatly kept.

The relais also serves savory and well-prepared meals. Specialties include lamb cooked with Provençal honey and thyme, and filet of sole Beau with red-wine butter and a fondue of leeks.

Rte. d'Aix, 13420 Gemenos. ℰ **04-42-32-20-16.** Fax 04-42-32-02-26. www.relais-magdeleine.com. 28 units. 95€–185€ ($124–$241) double; 190€–215€ ($247–$280) suite. AE, MC, V. Free parking. Closed Nov 15–Mar 15. Head east of Marseille for 24km (15 miles) along A50. **Amenities:** Restaurant; bar; lounge; outdoor pool; nearby golf course; nearby tennis courts; laundry service. *In room:* A/C, TV, hair dryer.

MARSEILLE AFTER DARK

For an amusing and relatively harmless exposure to the town's saltiness, walk around the **Vieux-Port,** where cafes and restaurants angle their sightlines for the best view of the harbor.

L'Escale Borély, avenue Mendès-France, is a modern-day equivalent of the Vieux-Port. It's a waterfront development south of the town center, only 20 minutes away (take bus no. 83 or 19). About a dozen cafes, as well as restaurants of every possible ilk, serve many cuisines. They offer views of in-line skaters on the promenade and the potential for conversation with friendly strangers, with less likelihood of street crime.

Unless the air-conditioning is powerful, Marseille's dance clubs produce a lot of sweat. The best is the **Café de la Plage,** in L'Escale Borély (ℰ **04-91-71-21-76**), which attracts a 35-and-under crowd to a safer part of town than many of its competitors. To get there, you can take the metro to Rond-Point du Prado, then transfer to bus no. 19; or from the center of Marseille, take bus no. 83, then walk .4km (about ¼ mile). Closer to the Vieux-Port, you can dance and drink at the **Metal Café,** 20 rue Fortia (ℰ **04-91-54-03-03**), where 20- to 50-year-olds listen to R & B, house, and the latest techno from London and Los Angeles. Or try the nearby **Trolley Bus,** 24 quai de Rive-Neuve (ℰ **04-91-54-30-45**), best known for its techno, house, hip-hop, jazz, and salsa.

If you miss free-form modern jazz and don't mind taking your chances in the less-than-savory neighborhood adjacent to the city's rail station (La Gare St-Charles—take a taxi there and back), consider dropping into **La Cité de la Musique** (also known as **La Cave à Jazz**), 4 rue Bernard-du-Bois (ℰ **04-91-39-28-28**). Other nightlife venues in Marseille evoke Paris, but with lots of extra *méridional* spice thrown in for extra flavor. Three Marseillais bars that we found particularly intriguing include **Le Pharaon,** Place de l'Opéra (ℰ **04-91-54-09-89;** Métro: Vieux-Port); a cozy enclave of deep sofas and armchairs, soft lighting, and—usually—a sense of well-being. Somewhat more bustling and animated is **l'Exit,** 12 quai de Riveneuve (ⓒ **04-91-54-09-89;** Métro: Vieux-Port), a bar with a terrace that profits from Marseille's sultry nights, and two floors of seething nocturnal energy. And for a bar that prides itself on its wide array of complicated cocktails and tapas, as well as a lot of attractive 30-somethings, consider **l'Interdit,** 9 rue Molière (ⓒ **06-22-99-51-25;** Métro: Vieux-Port). A place loaded with razzmatazz, and appealing for both its dance floor and its cabaret acts, is **Le Circus,** 5 rue du Chantier (ⓒ **04-91-33-77-22;** Métro: Vieux-Port). A fee of 15€ ($20) wins you entrance into the overall compound, after which you can visit any part of the place (cabaret vs. dance floor) that appeals to you at the time.

The gay scene is Marseille isn't as crowded, or as intriguing as the one in Nice, but its premier gay bar, **The MP Bar,** 10 rue Beauveau (ⓒ **04-91-33-64-79**), benefits from a long history of being the town's gay bar of record. It's open nightly from 6pm to sunrise. An equally valid, and equally gay, option is **The New Can Can,** 3–5 rue Sénac (ⓒ **04-91-48-59-76**), a broad and sprawling bar-and-disco venue that, at least in Marseille, seems to be everybody's favorite dance club venue. Technically, the place identifies as a mostly gay venue, but frankly, it gets so many heterosexuals that the gender-specific definitions that dominate many of the town's other nightclubs are—at least here—practically moot. One or another of its subdivisions tends to open nightly at around 8:30pm, with other components of the place going online one by one, until by the weekend, it blossoms into full electronic bloom. It closes around 5am. Cover charge, depending on the night of the week, is between 8€ and 15€ ($10–$20). If you're fond of cabaret, and if your French is extremely fluent, consider a few hours within the all-comic ambience of **Le Chocolat Théâtre,** 59 cours Julien (ⓒ **04-91-42-19-29;** Métro: Cours Julien). Shows begin at 9pm every night, last 1 hour and 45 minutes, and, depending on the night of the week, cost from 14€ to 18€ ($18–$23) with one drink included, and from 34€ to 38€ ($44–$49) per person if you want dinner as well as the show.

14 Toulon

835km (519 miles) S of Paris; 127km (79 miles) SW of Cannes; 68km (42 miles) E of Marseille

This fortress and modern town is the principal naval base of France: the headquarters of the Mediterranean fleet, with hundreds of sailors wandering the streets. With its beautiful harbor, it's surrounded by hills crowned by forts. A large breakwater protects it on the east, and the great peninsula of Cap Sicié is on the west. Separated by the breakwater, the outer roads are known as the Grande Rade, and the inner roads are the Petite Rade. On the outskirts is a winter resort colony. Like Marseille, the population of Toulon has grown because of the large influx of people from North Africa, especially French-speaking Algeria, which was once a part of France.

Note that racial tension here has worsened by the closing of the shipbuilding yards. There are no particular dangers to tourists that one wouldn't find in any Mediterranean port, be it Barcelona or Genoa. However, caution at night is always advised, especially in the immediate port area.

Park your vehicle underground at place de la Liberté; then go along boulevard des Strasbourg, turning right onto rue Berthelot. This will take you into the pedestrian zone in the core of the old city, centered on the rue d'Alger. This area is filled with shops, hotels, restaurants, and cobblestone streets but can be dangerous at night. The best beach, Plage du Mourillon, is 2km (1¼ miles) east of the heart of town.

ESSENTIALS

GETTING THERE & GETTING AROUND   **Trains** arrive from Marseille about every 30 minutes (trip time: 1 hr.); the one-way fare is 10€ ($13). If you're on the Riviera, trains arrive frequently from Nice (trip time: 2 hr.) and Cannes (trip time: 80 min.). For rail information and schedules, call © **08-92-35-35-35.**

Three **buses** per day arrive from Aix-en-Provence (trip time: 75 min.); the fare is about 10€ ($13) one-way. For information, call **Sodetrav** (© **08-25-00-06-50**). If you're **driving** from Marseille, take A50 east to Toulon. When you arrive, park your car and get around on foot—the Vieille Ville (old town) and most attractions are easy to reach. A municipal **bus** system serves the town as well. A bus map is available at the tourist office. For information, call **Le Réseau Mistral** at © **04-94-03-87-03.**

VISITOR INFORMATION   The **Office de Tourisme** is at place Raimu (© **04-94-18-53-00;** www.toulontourisme.com).

EXPLORING THE TOWN

In **Vieux Toulon,** between the harbor and boulevard de Strasbourg (the main axis of town), are many remains of the port's former days. The site where the city's raffish and gutsy style might best be appreciated is the open-air fruit and vegetable market, **Le Marché,** which spills over onto the narrow, plantain-lined streets around cours Lafayette every morning from 7:30am till around 2:30pm. Also in Old Toulon is the **Cathédrale Ste-Marie-Majeure (St. Mary Major),** rue Emile Zola (© **04-92-92-28-91**), which was built in the Romanesque style in the 11th and 12th centuries and then much expanded in the 17th century. Its badly lit nave is Gothic, and the belfry and facade are from the 18th century. It's open daily from 8:30am to 7pm.

In contrast to the cathedral, tall modern buildings line **quai Stalingrad,** opening onto Vieille d'Arse. On **place Puget,** look for the atlantes (caryatids), figures of men used as columns. These interesting figures support a balcony at the Hôtel de Ville (city hall) and are also included in the facade of the naval museum.

The **Musée de la Marine,** place du Ingénieur-Général-Monsenergue (© **04-94-02-02-01**), contains many figureheads and ship models. It's open Wednesday to Monday July and August from 10am to 6pm, and September to June from 9:30am to noon and 2 to 6pm. Admission is 4.60€ ($6) for adults and 3€ ($3.90) for students. The **Musée de Toulon,** 113 bd. du Général-Maréchal-Leclerc (© **04-94-36-81-00**), shows works from the 16th century to the present. It maintains a particularly good collection of Provençal and Italian paintings, as well as religious works. The latest acquisitions include New Realism pieces and minimalist art. It's open Wednesday to Monday from 10am to noon and 2 to 6pm. Admission is 4.60€ ($6) for adults, 3€ ($3.90) for students, free for ages under 18.

Somewhat less interesting is the **Musée du Vieux Toulon,** 69 cours Lafayette (© **04-94-62-11-07**), which is not to be confused with the above-mentioned Musée de Toulon. Its exhibits pertain to the role of commerce, shipbuilding, and the French military during the development of Toulon, with a tableau of the historic figures who either protected it or fostered its growth from medieval times to the present. It's open Tuesday to Sunday from noon to 6pm. Entrance is free.

PANORAMAS & VIEWS

We suggest taking a drive, an hour or two before sunset, along the **corniche du Mont-Faron.** It's a scenic boulevard along the lower slopes of Mont Faron, providing views of the busy port, the town, the cliffs, and, in the distance, the Mediterranean.

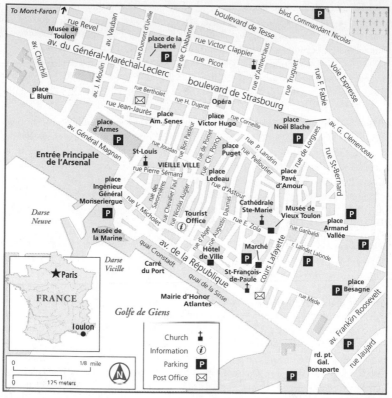

For a panoramic view over the dry, sun-flooded landscapes, consider boarding a **funicular** (℃ **04-94-92-68-25** for information), which departs from a point on the boulevard l'Amiral Vence near the Hôtel La Tour Blanche. The *télépherique* (cable car) operates Tuesday to Sunday from 9:30 to 11:45am and 2:15 to 6:30pm; the round-trip costs 5.80€ ($7.55) for adults, 4€ ($5.20) for children 4 to 10 years old. It is not in service from November 5 to February 3. At the top, enjoy the view and then visit the **Memorial du Débarquement en Provence,** Mont Faron (℃ **04-94-88-08-09**), which documents the Allied landings in Provence in 1944, among other events. It's open in summer daily from 9:45 to 11:45am and 1:45 to 4:30pm; from October to March, it's open Tuesday to Sunday from 9:15 to 11:45am and 2 to 4:45pm. Admission is 3.80€ ($4.95) for adults, 1.55€ ($2) for children 8 to 16.

WHERE TO STAY

Hôtel La Corniche An attractive hotel near the town's beaches, with an interior garden, La Corniche offers a pleasant staff, two restaurants, and comfortable accommodations. Those at the front have sea views and loggias, and are more expensive. Room decoration is in Provençal style. The more formal of the two restaurants is the Bistro; it features a trio of pine trees growing upward through the roof and a large bay window overlooking the port. The simpler restaurant is the cramped but cozy Rôtisserie, which is under different management. Both emphasize fish among their offerings. A fairly good but limited wine list complements the food, which is perfectly adequate and much improved in recent years. You'll find this place in the neighborhood known as Le Mourillon, a 15-minute walk from the congested commercial center of Toulon.

17 Littoral Frédéric-Mistral (at Le Mourillon), 83000 Toulon. ℂ 800/528-1234 in the U.S., or 04-94-41-35-12. Fax 04-94-41-24-58. www.hotel-corniche.com. 23 units. 85€–125€ ($111–$163) double; 150€–190€ ($195–$247) junior suite. AE, DC, MC, V. Parking 9€. Amenities: 2 restaurants; bar; limited room service; laundry service. In room: A/C, TV, dataport, minibar, hair dryer.

Hôtel Maritima   The most decent bargain hotel in Toulon stands near the railway station and Jardin Alexandre-1er. Built in the late 1800s, it has been frequently renovated and altered over the years. Furnishings are blandly traditional but serviceable; it's modest but well maintained. Bathrooms are small and short on shelf space, and have rather thin towels but are tidily maintained. The hotel doesn't have a restaurant, although several lie right outside the door. Breakfast is served on-site.

9 rue Gimelli, 83000 Toulon. ℂ 04-94-92-39-33. 35 units, 5 with shared bathroom. 32€ ($42) double with bathroom. No credit cards. Amenities: Lounge. In room: TV.

New Hôtel La Tour Blanche   With excellent accommodations, terraced gardens, and a pool, this 1970s hotel is one of the best in Toulon. It lies in the hills about 1.5km (1 mile) north of the center of town, which gives it sweeping views of the port and sea even from the lower floors. Many rooms, especially those overlooking the bay, have balconies. All are comfortably and simply outfitted in international modern style. The compact bathrooms have showers, but only half have tub/shower combinations. Some units have dataports. The restaurant, Les Terrasses, has a panoramic view. Fixed-price menus of traditional Provençal cuisine cost 20€ ($26).

Bd. de l'Amiral-Vence, Mont Faron, 83000 Toulon. ℂ 04-94-24-41-57. Fax 04-94-22-42-25. www.new-hotel.com. 91 units. 84€–108€ ($109–$140) double. AE, DC, MC, V. Free parking. Bus: 40. From the town center, follow signs to the Mont Faron téléphérique and you'll pass the hotel en route. Amenities: Restaurant; bar; outdoor pool; gym; limited room service; babysitting; laundry service; limited-mobility rooms. In room: A/C, TV, minibar, hair dryer, iron.

WHERE TO DINE

La Chamade ⋆ SOUTHERN FRENCH   The cuisine here is memorable, and the restaurant is the finest for miles. It's in the town center, in a nondescript building whose thick walls hint at its age. Menu items change with the seasons but might include foie gras of duckling with salty caramel sauce; eggplant with roasted lamb served with coriander sauce; and a dessert confection consisting of semi-baked, ultra-moist chocolate cake with mint-flavored cream sauce. The fixed-price menu includes a choice of three appetizers, three main courses, and three desserts.

25 rue Denfert-Rochereau. ℂ 04-94-92-28-58. Reservations recommended. Main courses 18€–26€ ($23–$35); fixed-price menu 32€ ($42). AE, MC, V. Mon–Sat noon–2:30pm and 7:15–9:30pm. Closed Aug 1–25. Bus: 1 or 21.

TOULON AFTER DARK

The temporary home of thousands of sailors is bound to have a nightlife scene that's earthier, and a bit raunchier, than those of equivalent-size towns elsewhere. A rough-and-ready bar that offers stiff drinks, live music, and a complete lack of pretension is **Le Bar 113,** 113 av. de Infanterie de la Marine (ℂ 04-94-03-42-41). At **Bar à Thym,** 32 bd. Cuneo (ℂ 04-94-41-90-10), everybody seems to drink beer, gossip, and listen to live music. Toulon is also home to one of the region's best-known gay discos, **Boy's Paradise,** 1 bd. Pierre-Toesca (ℂ 04-94-09-35-90), near the train station.

Adjacent to the port is the gay **Bar La Lampa,** Port de Toulon (*©* **04-94-03-06-09**), where tapas and live music accompany lots of beer and wine or whiskey.

If you want more resorty nightlife, you might be happy at Hyère, about 26km (16 miles) east of Toulon, where there's an upscale disco frequented by young people usually under 28 years old, **Le Fou du Roy,** in the Casino des Palmiers (*©* **04-94-12-80-80**). About 15km (9 miles) west of Toulon, in the port town of Sanary, **Mai-Tai,** route de Bandol (*©* **04-94-74-23-92**), appeals to dancers under age 30.

15 Hyères (★

852km (529 miles) S of Paris; 100km (62 miles) SE of Aix-en-Provence; 122km (76 miles) SW of Cannes; 18km (11 miles) E of Toulon

The broad avenues of Hyères, shaded by date palms, still evoke the lazy belle époque. The full name of the town is Hyères-les-Palmier, as it is known for its production of palm trees. Believe it or not, many of these trees are exported to the Middle East.

Hyères is the oldest resort along the Côte d'Azur, having once been frequented by the likes of Queen Victoria, Napoleon, Leo Tolstoy, and Robert Louis Stevenson. It was particularly popular with the British before 1939. It has changed so little from its heyday that many French film directors, including Jean-Luc Godard (*Pierrot le Fou*) and François Truffaut, who shot his last film here (*Vivement Dimanche,* released as *Confidentially Yours* in the United States), have used it as locations for period pieces. Today it lives off its past glory and its memories.

As a visitor, you'll find the most interesting section of Hyères to be the Vieille Ville, which lies 5km (3 miles) inland from the sea on a hill. Try to arrive early to attend a bustling morning market around place Massillon. The more modern town and the nucleus of the 19th-century resort stretch toward the sea.

ESSENTIALS

GETTING THERE   **Flights** from Paris arrive at the Toulon-Hyères airport, which lies between the town center and the beach. For flights, call *©* **04-42-14-14-14.** Rail connections are fairly easy, as Hyères lies on the main Nice-Lyon-Paris line. Nine local **trains** a day connect Hyères with Toulon; a one-way ticket costs 8.50€ ($11). Two **buses** per day arrive from Toulon, Cannes, and Nice. For information about bus schedules, call Phocéens Car, 2 place Massena in Nice at *©* **04-93-85-66-61.**

If you're **driving,** A5 goes through Toulon to Marseille and points north and west; A57 goes northeast to join A8, the autoroute between Nice and Aix-en-Provence.

VISITOR INFORMATION   Other than temporary, summer-only kiosks without phones that distribute brochures and advice near the ferry docks in Porquerolles and Port-Cros, there are no tourist bureaus on the islands. The offices in Hyères and Toulon try to fill in the gaps. Contact the **Office de Tourisme,** 3 av. Ambroise Thomas, Hyères (*©* **04-94-01-84-50**), or the **Office de Tourisme,** place Raimu, Toulon (*©* **04-94-18-53-00**).

EXPLORING THE AREA

The land lying between the city and the sea is unattractive, and the beaches are a bit polluted, but there are some swimming possibilities here, notably at **Hyères-Plage.** There is also a yacht marina at **Port d'Hyères.** We find the parks and old town of Hyères more interesting than its beachfront.

Heading into town from the beach, go along the wide **avenue Gambetta** shaded by double rows of palms. At the end of Gambetta, continue along rue Rabaton to **place Massillon,** the beginning of the old town and the site of many good terrace cafe-restaurants. The daily market also takes place here. The 12th-century **Tour St-Blaise,** which stands on the square, was once a command post of the Knights Templar.

Above place Massillon is a warren of intriguing old streets climbing the hillside. Many are cobblestoned and bordered by stone walls, with an abundance of flowers in summer. Look for the medieval arched *portes.* Most of the Vieille Ville houses have been restored, often painted in lovely Mediterranean pastels with contrasting shutters and doors.

Part of the ramparts have survived, although most of them have been torn down; they date from the 12th century. All that remains of the south "curtain wall" are **Porte-St-Paul,** next to the Collegiate Church, and **Porte Baruc.** A trio of lovely old towers has survived from the north curtain wall.

Steep narrow streets lead up behind Tour St-Blaise to the 18th-century **Le Collegiale St-Paul,** place St-Paul (✆ **04-94-65-83-30**). In the Romanesque narthex are 400 fragments from the Church of Notre-Dame-de-Consolation, destroyed in bombing raids in 1944. The Gothic nave dates from the 15th and 16th centuries. The church is flanked by an elegant turreted Renaissance house constructed above one of the medieval city gates. The church is open Wednesday to Saturday April to October from 10am to noon and 3:30 to 6pm. November to March, it is open Wednesday to Saturday from 3 to 5pm.

Artifacts left behind by the Greeks and Romans can be examined at the **Musée Municipal,** place Lefebvre (✆ **04-94-00-78-80**). The museum is often the venue for special exhibitions. Entrance is free, and it is open Monday, Wednesday, Thursday, and Friday from 10am to noon and 3 to 6pm. If a special exhibition is running, it is also open Saturday and Sunday from 3 to 6pm.

The main attraction of the town is **Parc St-Bernard,** 20km (13 miles) east of Toulon by N98, on the hill above Hyères. It is open year-round daily from 8am to 6:30pm. To reach the park, go up rue Saint Esprit to where it becomes rue Barbacane. Charles and Marie-Laure de Noailles, great patrons of the arts, commissioned a modern Cubist-style villa here in 1924 and brought in garden designer Gabriel Guevrekian, who created an extensive garden in the shape of an isosceles triangle, pointing away from the end of the villa. The Noailles played a role in nurturing the avant-garde artists of the Jazz Age, including F. Scott Fitzgerald. Edith Wharton was a devoted friend of the family. The villa is currently being restored, but you can visit the terraced gardens and relax on benches shaded by olives and pines. Above in the villa, in a separate compound of its own, are the ruins of **Château d'Hyères,** above the medieval old town. Signposts and arrows lead visitors on a self-guided walk through the ruins, which have unrestricted access.

WHERE TO STAY

Hôtel du Soleil   The foundations of this hotel date from the 11th century, when they were lodgings for the guards who defended the once-formidable fortress of Hyères. What you'll see, however, dates from around 1900—a boxy-looking *bastide* (masonry building) atop the old foundations. Over the years, a sheathing of ivy has softened the angles a bit, and the interior has been kept up-to-date with frequent modernizations. Bedrooms are cozy, if somewhat small, with Provençal furniture and casement windows; from the back are views of the sea, and in front are views of upscale villas on a nearby hill. Breakfast is the only meal served, although there are several places to eat (including the Bistrot de Marius, below) within a 3-minute walk.

Rue du Rempart (place Clemenceau), 83400 Hyères. © 04-94-65-16-26. Fax 04-94-35-46-00. www.hoteldu soleil.com. 27 units. 32€–80€ ($42–$104) double. AE, DC, MC, V. **Amenities:** Breakfast room. *In room:* TV.

Ibis Thalasse   This hotel is located between the coastal road and the beach, on the eastern edge of the land bridge that stretches between the French mainland and the Gien peninsula. Designed in a horseshoe shape, with the open end of the U facing the beach, the hotel places emphasis on resort life. Guest rooms are decent-size and decorated in a standardized format that includes one double bed and one single bed, a writing table, and a soothing color scheme of blue-gray. Bathrooms are motel standard, with tidy maintenance. Another Ibis hotel is located downtown.

Allée de la Mer, La Capte, 83400 Hyères-Plage. © 04-94-58-00-94. Fax: 04-94-58-09-35. 95 units. 60€–125€ ($78–$163) double. AE, DC, MC, V. **Amenities:** Restaurant; bar; outdoor pool; health club; spa. *In room:* A/C, TV, hair dryer.

WHERE TO DINE

Bistrot de Marius PROVENÇAL/SEAFOOD   Set almost adjacent to the Tour des Templiers, this restaurant dates from 1906, when it was established in a building whose foundations date from the 13th century. Its trio of dining rooms (one is upstairs) has exposed stone and paneling, and a sense of historic charm. Fish, especially grilled sea bass, monkfish, dorado, and tuna, are specialties here, along with mussels and oysters. Sauce choices include *marchand de vin* (a red wine–based sauce), and lemon-butter and basil-flavored vinaigrette. A succulent version of *bouillabaisse,* priced at 34€ ($44), is a meal in itself, and there is a limited selection of chicken, veal, and beef.

1 place Massillon. © 04-94-35-88-38. Reservations recommended. Main courses 9.50€–34€ ($12–$44); fixed-price menus 17€–30€ ($22–$39). AE, DC, MC, V. Wed–Sun noon–2:30pm and 7–11pm. Also open on Tues in Aug. Closed Nov 15–Dec 15.

Le Jardin MODERN MEDITERRANEAN   Set directly across the street from the Town Hall *(Mairie)* of Hyère, this restaurant takes gardening, and its name, seriously. During most of the year, the retractable roof, a motorized contraption of folding plastic panels, remains open to night breezes, as doors and windows and outdoor tables showcase the venerable plantings of a mature garden ringed with crabapple, orange, and palm trees. The London-trained owner, Mr. Cheval, who speaks perfect English, welcomes a young and young-at-heart crowd who keep the place amusing and convivial. Menu items derive from both the northern and southern edges of the Mediterranean, and include a salad of grilled scallops with ginger; a platter of *crudités* accessorized with both anchovy paste and a tapenade of olives; a genuinely wonderful version of octopus stew cooked in red wine *(daube de pulpe)* a tagine of the day (during our visit, it featured roasted lamb with prunes, slow-cooked in a clay pot in the Moroccan style); and a grilled filet of bluefin tuna served with wasabi-flavored mashed potatoes.

19 av. Joseph Clotis. © 04-94-35-24-12. Reservations recommended. Main courses 8€–16€ ($10–$20). AE, MC, V. Daily noon–midnight. Closed Dec. 22–Jan 24.

16 Iles d'Hyères (★)

39km (24 miles) SE of Toulon; 119km (74 miles) SW of Cannes

Off the Riviera in the Mediterranean is a little group of islands enclosing the southern boundary of the Hyères anchorage. During the Renaissance they were called the Iles d'Or, from a golden glow sometimes given off by the rocks in the sunlight. Nothing in the islands today will remind you of the turbulent time when they were attacked by pirates and Turkish galleys, or even of the Allied landings here in World War II.

Mass tourism has arrived on these sun-baked islands, with some of the tackiness that goes with it. Cars are forbidden on all three major islands, and they cannot be transported on any of the ferryboats. Expect a summer holiday spirit not unlike a Gallic version of Nantucket, with thousands of midsummer day-trippers arriving, often with children, for a day of sun, sand, and people-watching.

Which island is the most appealing? Ile des Porquerolles is the most beautiful. Thinking of heading to Le Levant? You might want to steer clear—only 25% of the island is accessible to visitors, as three-quarters of it belongs to the French army, and it is used frequently for testing missiles.

Note: Héliopolis, a section of Ile du Levant, is home to the oldest nudity colony in Europe. Islanders and visitors go *au naturel* on the beaches. Many of the more daring visitors also don't wear a lot of clothing in the village.

ESSENTIALS

GETTING THERE   Ile de Porquerolles   Ferryboats leave from several points along the Côte d'Azur. The most frequent, most convenient, and shortest trip is from the harbor of La Tour Fondue on the peninsula of Gien, a 32km (20-mile) drive east of Toulon. Depending on the season, there are 4 to 20 departures a day. The round-trip fare for the 15-minute crossing is 16€ ($21). For information, call the **Transports Maritimes et Terrestres du Littoral Varois,** La Tour Fondue, 83400 Giens (© **04-94-58-21-81**). The next-best option is the ferryboat from Toulon but only between June and September. Other options, each of them available only between June and September, involve taking one of the ferryboats maintained by the **Compagnie Maritime des Vedettes Ile d'Or & Le Corsaire** (© **04-94-71-01-02**). Their ferryboats offer crossings from Toulon's quai d'Embarquement for the Ile de Porquerolles, as well as slightly longer crossings from either of *Les Gares Maritimes* in Le Lavandou and Cavalaire.

On any of the venues noted above, round trip fares to the Ile de Porquerolles from Toulon cost 22€ ($29) for adults, and 18€ ($23) for children 4 to 11. Round-trip fares to the island from Le Lavandou or from Cavalaire cost around 5€ ($6.50) more, per category.

VISITOR INFORMATION   Other than summer-only kiosks without phones that distribute brochures and advice near the ferry docks in Porquerolles and Port-Cros, the islands have no tourist bureaus. The offices in Hyères and Toulon try to fill in the gaps. Contact the **Office de Tourisme,** 3 av. Ambroise Thomas, Hyères (© **04-94-01-84-50**), or the **Office de Tourisme,** place Raimu, Toulon (© **04-94-18-53-00**).

ILE DE PORQUEROLLES ⓡ

This is the largest and westernmost of the Iles d'Hyères. It has a rugged south coast, but the north strand, facing the mainland, is made up of sandy beaches bordered by heather, scented myrtles, and pine trees. The island is about 8km (5 miles) long and 2km (1¼ miles) wide, and is 5km (3 miles) from the mainland.

The population is only 400. The island is said to receive 275 days of sunshine annually. It's a land of rocky capes, pine forests twisted by the mistral, sun-drenched vineyards, and pale ocher houses. The "hot spots," if there are any, are the cafes around **place d'Armes** where everybody gathers.

The island has had a violent history of raids, attacks, and occupation by everybody from the Dutch, English, and Turks to the Spaniards. Ten forts, some in ruins, testify to a violent past. The most ancient is **Fort Ste-Agathe,** built in 1531 by François I. In time it was a penal colony and a retirement center for soldiers of the colonial wars.

The French government in 1971 purchased the largest hunk of the island and turned it into a national park and botanical garden.

WHERE TO STAY & DINE

Le Relais de la Poste   On a small square in the heart of the island's main settlement, this pleasant and unpretentious hotel is the oldest on the island—it opened "sometime in the 19th century" and is managed by the good-natured sixth generation of its founding family. It offers Provençal-style rooms with loggias. Most rooms are small to medium in size, and each comes with fine linen on a twin or double bed. In-room amenities are lean except for a phone. Bathrooms are compact and well organized, with shower stalls. The hotel has a billiard table and a crêperie that sells only snack-style dessert crepes and fresh fruit juice.

Place d'Armes, 83540 Porquerolles. (©) 04-98-04-62-62. Fax 04-94-58-33-57. www.lerelaisdelaposte.com. 30 units. 80€–114€ ($104–$148) double. No credit cards. Closed late Oct to Easter. **Amenities:** Bar; lounge; bike rental.

Mas du Langoustier 🐾🐾   In a large park on the island's western tip, this tranquil resort hotel is an old *mas* (farmhouse) with a view of a lovely pine-ringed bay. Employees greet guests in a covered wagon by the jetty. Guest rooms, in antique Provençal style, are the most elegantly decorated on the island. Bathrooms are roomy, and most have tub/shower combinations. Should you visit only for a meal, the menu is the finest in the Hyère islands, offering mainly seafood in a light nouvelle style. Try *loup* (wolf fish) with Noilly Prat in puff pastry, or tender kid with dried tomatoes roasted in casserole. The house wine is an agreeable rosé. You can drink and dine on the terraces.

83400 Porquerolles. (©) 04-94-58-30-09. Fax 04-94-58-36-02. www.langoustier.com. 50 units. 177€–248€ ($230–$322) double; 263€–297€ ($342–$386) suite. Rates include half board. AE, DC, MC, V. **Amenities:** 2 restaurants; bar; limited room service; babysitting; laundry service; limited-mobility rooms. *In room:* A/C, TV, dataport, minibar, safe. Closed late Sept to mid-Apr.

ILE DE PORT-CROS 🐾

Lush subtropical vegetation reminiscent of a Caribbean island makes this a green paradise, 5km (3 miles) long and 2km (1¼ miles) wide. The most mountainous of the archipelago, Port-Cros has been a French national park since 1963. A fire in 1892 devastated the island, which now abounds with pine forests and ilexes. Birders flock here to observe nearly 100 different species. Day-trippers can explore some of the many marked trails. The most popular and scenic is *sentier botanique;* the more adventurous and athletic take the 10km (6-mile) *circuit historique* (you'll need a packed lunch for this one). Divers follow a 274m (900 ft.) trail from Plage de la Palud to the islet of Rascas, where a plastic guide sheet identifies the underwater flora. Thousands of pleasure craft call here annually, which does little to help the island's fragile environment.

WHERE TO STAY & DINE

Le Manoir 🐾   This is the only bona-fide hotel on the island, but despite lack of competition, its owners work hard to make their guests as comfortable as possible. Originally, it functioned as the grandiose home of the family that owned the entire island. Today, the hotel consists of an 18th-century architectural core, plus an annex that contains most of the guest accommodations, which are simple, with bathrooms equipped with tub/shower combinations. Some rooms have air-conditioning. The restaurant serves lobster-and-fish terrine, several seasoned meats, and fresh local fish with baby vegetables, as well as regional goat cheese and velvety mousses.

83400 Ile de Port-Cros. (℃ **04-94-05-90-52.** Fax 04-94-05-90-89. lemanoir.portcros@wanadoo.fr. 23 units. 145€–185€ ($189–$241) double; 180€–210€ ($234–$273) suite. MC, V. Closed Oct–Apr. **Amenities:** Restaurant; bar; outdoor pool; limited room service; laundry service. *In room:* Dataport, hair dryer.

17 Grand Canyon du Verdon ⟨★⟩

Trigance: 72km (45 miles) S of Digne-les-Baines; 20km (13 miles) W of Castellane; 43km (27 miles) NW of Draguignan; 85km (53 miles) E of Manosque

La-Palud-sur-Verdon: 64km (40 miles) S of Digne-les-Bains; 25km (16 miles) W of Castellane; 60km (37 miles) NW of Draguignan; 66km (41 miles) E of Manosque

Over the centuries, the Verdon River, a tributary of the Durance, has cut Europe's biggest canyon into the surrounding limestone plateau. The canyon runs from pont de Soleils to Lac Ste-Croix, a distance of 21km (13 miles) east to west. The upper section of the gorge, to the east, is between 210m and 1,605m (700 ft. and 5,350 ft.) wide; the lower section narrows to between 6m and 105m (20 ft. and 350 ft.). All along its length, the cliffs rise and fall. The gorge's depth varies from 263m (875 ft.) at one point to 750m (2,500 ft.).

Vertiginous roads wind along both rims of the canyon, giving you the opportunity to pull over at any of several scenic belvederes. Among the best of these is the Balcon de la Mescla, the first stop traveling west from Trigance on the canyon's south side, where the sheer cliffs drop 270m (900 ft.) to the river. A short distance away is Falaise de Cavaliers (Horseman's Cliff), dropping 323m (1,075 ft.) and signaling the beginning of the Corniche Sublime, where the gorge plunges to 428m (1,425 ft.) along a stretch running west to Aiguines. In between these scenic stops, you can actually drive across the canyon on the dramatic pont de l'Artuby, a single-arched, 120m (400-ft.) long span, 638m (2,125 ft.) above the river.

Ancient villages cling to rocky outcroppings along the two rim roads. At Aiguines, a private castle flanked by four turrets and covered in polished variegated tiles dominates the skyline. On Route 19, 9km (5½ miles) north of the canyon on its western end, sits Moustiers-Ste-Marie, a medieval village of potters who sell their wares—but beware, prices here are celestial, especially in July and August, when tourist dollars are easy to come by.

ESSENTIALS

GETTING THERE   From the Riviera, follow A85 for 84km (52 miles) northwest from Cannes to Castellane; then take Route 952 west to the intersection with Route 955 and proceed along 955 south to Trigance, about 20km (13 miles). From here, continue south to Route 71, 3km distant, and take a left to travel west along the southern edge of the canyon. At Les-Salles-sur-Verdon, on the banks of Lac St-Croix, turn right on D957 and drive north, crossing the Verdon where it flows into Lac St-Croix; then, just south of Moustiers-Ste-Marie, turn right again on Route 952 to trace the north side of the canyon back to the east.

VISITOR INFORMATION   Information about accommodations, activities, and events is available from the tourist offices of the three largest settlements in the canyon, any of which is loaded with information about how best to take advantage of the regions natural beauty and sporting options. They include the Office de Tourisme de Castellane, 04120 Castellane (© **04-92-83-61-14**); or the Office de Tourisme de Moustiers Ste-Marie, 04360 Moustiers-Ste-Marie (© **04-92-74-67-84**). Smaller than either of the other two, and open mostly in midsummer, is the Office de Tourisme dEsparron, 04800 Esparron (© **04-92-77-15-97**).

EXPLORING THE CANYON

Activities available in the canyon include guided hikes from the Bureau des Guides, 04120 La-Palud-sur-Verdon (© **04-92-77-30-50**). Canoeing and kayaking are available through the Aqua Vivae Est, La Piscine, 04120 Castellane (© **04-92-83-75-74**), and the Club Nautique, 04800 Esparron (© **04-92-77-15-25**). Rafting trips are conducted by Acti Raft, 04120 Castellane (© **04-92-83-76-64**). All three of the organizations noted above operate in full swing between May and early September. The rest of the year, they operate with skeleton staffs, usually via answering machine and fax.

A deservedly popular walk that showcases some of the area's scenery is a 2-hour round-trip trek launched at the parking lot at Samson Corridor. The route is clearly marked as it bends its way to a tunnel after Point Sublime. Continue your trek to a footbridge spanning the Baou River. After crossing it, go straight ahead through another two tunnels until you reach a belvedere with a panoramic sweep of the Trescare Chaos. For transit through the tunnels, carry along a flashlight.

A more strenuous 6- to 8-hour hike starts at the Chalet de la Maline on the Crest Road and goes for about 15km (9½ miles) to Point Sublime. The footpath is marked with arrows. Again, you'll need a flashlight, but this trek is so long that food and water are also recommended. Before heading out, you can call © **04-92-93-61-62** to make arrangements with the most reliable of the local taxi dispatchers (Taxis Vincent) to arrange for a taxi to pick you up at a designated time after you reach Point Sublime. The cost of such transport by taxi from Port Sublime back to, say, Castellane, is around 11€ ($14) per person. Be warned in advance that arrangements like this with the local taxi operators are easiest between late May and September. The rest of the year, taxis (and virtually everything else in the region) operates at very low gear.

WHERE TO STAY

Auberge Point-Sublime   This hotel offers simple, unpretentious rooms, each with congenially battered, old-fashioned (but not antique) furniture. Bedrooms are small and without particular style, although each has a comfortable mattress, plus a somewhat cramped bathroom. You do get views over the gorge and a convenient location, 2km (1¼ miles) south of the Couloir Samson, the point where many trekkers exit from hikes in the nearby gorge. The restaurant serves all-Provençal fixed-price meals. Specialties are civets of both rabbit and lamb, a truffle-studded omelet, and crayfish with truffles. Staff here is unusually bossy, insisting that residents consume at least one meal a day on-site.

04120 Point Sublime, Rougon. © **04-92-83-60-35**. Fax 04-92-83-74-31. 15 units. 55€ ($72) double. MC, V. Closed Nov 3–Mar. From Castellane, drive 19km (12 miles) north toward Moustiers-Ste-Marie; it's beside the road on the distant outskirts of Rougon. **Amenities:** Restaurant; bar; lounge. *In room:* TV. Closed Nov–Mar.

Bastide de Moustiers 🏶🏶🏶   Very near the Gorges du Verdon, in this village of pottery makers, Alain Ducasse, arguably hailed as the world's greatest chef, has opened an informal inn of charm and grace. The property once belonged to a master potter, and the country house is filled with the celebrated Moustiers earthenware. The inn is surrounded by tree-studded grounds covering 4 hectares (10 acres). Aided by local artisans, the inn has been beautifully restored, each room individually designed. Accommodations are filled with the rewards of Ducasse's antique-hunting expeditions, and each unit is named for an aroma, color, or image of Provence—lavender, sunflowers, almonds, poppies, or even pumpkins. Bathrooms are extremely luxurious with showers and tubs—one bathroom, for example, was designed by the famous Philippe Starck. Even if you're not staying here, consider calling for a reservation for a meal here in a romantic setting. The aroma of the flavors of Provence and the Mediterranean emerge from the kitchen, and much home-grown produce is used, including from the inn's own vegetable garden. Fixed-price menus begin at 57€ ($74).

Chemin de Quinson, 04360 Moustiers Sainte-Marie. ℂ **04-92-70-47-47**. Fax 04-92-70-47-48. www.bastide-moustiers.com. 12 suites. 155€–325€ ($202–$423) double. AE, DC, MC, V. **Amenities:** Restaurant; bar; limited room service; outdoor pool. *In room:* A/C, TV, dataport, minibar, hair dryer, safe.

Château de Trigance ⓐ

This Relais & Châteaux property is the district's best hotel, rising on a rocky spur above a hamlet of fewer than 120 full-time inhabitants; it occupies the core of a 9th- and 10th-century fortress. There's no room for a garden, but virtually every window has views over the Provençal plain. The rooms contain strong hints of their medieval origins including baldachin-style beds. Modern extras include tiled bathrooms.

The dining room is unusual; originally used to store weapons, it has a vaulted ceiling that was, in accordance with the era's techniques, built without groins or a central key. A wooden form was constructed and carefully chiseled stones were fitted into position on top. When complete, the form was burnt away and the vaulting remained—somewhat precariously until it was shored up with additional mortar. The fare is intensely cultivated: "marbled" foie gras of duckling with artichoke hearts; pressed leeks with smoked salmon, crayfish, and sweet-and-sour sauce; and roasted leg of lamb "en surprise" with a "spaghetti" of zucchini and cream of garlic *en confit*. A parking lot near the entrance of the hotel saves you the arduous hike up the medieval-looking steps that were once the only route of access.

83840 Trigance, Var. ℂ **04-94-76-91-18**. Fax 04-94-85-68-99. www.chateau-de-trigance.fr. 10 units. 115€–185€ ($150–$241) double. AE, DC, MC, V. Free parking. Closed Nov 1–Mar 20. **Amenities:** Restaurant; bar; limited room service. *In room:* TV, safe.

Hôtel du Grand Canyon de Verdon ⓕinds

This is the most charming and interesting hotel along the south bank of the Verdon canyon. It's on a rocky outcropping above the precipice, vertiginously close to the edge, and exists only because of the foresight of the grandfather of the present owner. In 1946, on holiday in Provence from his home in the foggy northern French province of Pas de Calais, he fell in love with the site, opened a brasserie, and secured permission to build a hotel here. In 1982, his grandson, Georges Fortini, erected the present two-story hotel. Rooms are simple, small, but comfortable, with light-grained wood and off-white walls. Set on a 4-hectare (10-acre) tract on the Corniche Sublime, the hotel features a glassed-in restaurant overlooking a 322m (1,075-ft.) drop to the canyon bottom.

Falaise des Cavaliers, 83630 Aiguines. ℂ **04-94-76-91-31**. Fax 04-94-76-92-29. g.fortini@wanadoo.fr. 15 units. 110€–120€ ($143–$156) double. Rates include half board. AE, DC, MC, V. Closed Oct–Apr. **Amenities:** Restaurant; bar. *In room:* TV, minibar, hair dryer.

Hôtel Les Gorges du Verdon

This hotel is inspired by an earth-toned Provençal *mas*. It's in the heart of La-Palud-sur-Verdon (pop. 250, alt. 914m/3,000 ft.), about

6km (4 miles) west of the canyon edge. Though you won't be able to see the canyon from the windows, views over the rugged countryside stretch out on virtually every side. The rooms were upgraded in 2004, with elaborate curtains added that soften their modern angularity. Tiles were installed in many of the bathrooms, adding a glossy kind of modern comfort. Overall, the rooms aren't exactly plush, but they have good mattresses, and since most guests opt to spend their days in the great outdoors, no one really seems to care. Most have a private terrace or balcony overlooking a scenic landscape. Some are entered from a landing with a staircase leading down into the room, creating a mezzanine effect.

Half board is obligatory in midsummer. Nonresidents often stop for meals here. Well-prepared menu items include duck thigh stuffed with mushrooms, grilled whole sea bass with anise-flavored butter, and Provençal lamb chops with tarragon-flavored butter sauce.

04120 La-Palud-sur-Verdon. © **04-92-77-38-26.** Fax 04-92-77-35-00. www.hotel-des-gorges-de-verdon.fr. 31 units. 91€–150€ ($118–$195) double. MC, V. Free parking. Closed late Oct to Easter. **Amenities:** Restaurant; bar; covered heated pool; tennis court; limited room service; babysitting; laundry service; dry cleaning. *In room:* TV, hair dryer, safe.

Hôtel Le Vieil Amandier   At the edge of town, this hotel offers clean, uncomplicated guest rooms and a dining room with straightforward but thoughtfully prepared cuisine. Half the rooms face the pool and get southern light; the remainder are just as comfortable but without views. The largest is the rustic and woodsy no. 6; nos. 3 and 4 are more Provençal, and the others are blandly international. Your hosts are Cécile and Bernard Clap (Bernard is the hamlet's mayor). They maintain a pleasant, unpretentious restaurant where lunch and dinner are served daily. Cuisine is artful and flavorful, featuring good value for the money. Menu items include profiteroles of goat cheese with chives and olive oil, duckling with myrtle leaves and garlic, and rack of lamb in puff pastry served with fine-textured ratatouille.

83840 Trigance, Var. © **04-94-76-92-92.** Fax 04-94-85-68-65. 12 units. 52€–82€ ($68–$107) double. AE, DC, MC, V. Free parking. Closed Nov 3–Apr 1. **Amenities:** Restaurant; bar; pool; laundry service; dry cleaning. *In room:* TV, hair dryer.

WHERE TO DINE

Many of the inns recommended under "Where to Stay," above, are also the finest places to dine—notably the **Château de Trigance.**

Les Santons   FRENCH/PROVENÇAL   One of the region's most charming restaurants occupies a stone-sided 12th-century house adjacent to the village church. You'll find a cozy dining room filled with 19th-century paintings and antique pottery, reminders of Old Provence, and fewer than 20 seats. A terrace, lined with flowering plants, doubles the seating space during clement weather. These include truffles and honey. Examples are homemade noodles studded with truffles and chunks of foie gras, chicken roasted with lavender-scented honey and Provençal spices, and Sisteron lamb roasted with honey and spices and served with an herb-scented ratatouille and *gratin dauphinoise* (potatoes with grated cheese).

Place de l'Eglise, 04360 Moustiers-Ste-Marie, Alpes-de-Haut-Provence. © **04-92-74-66-48.** Reservations recommended. Main courses 28€–35€ ($36–$46); fixed-price menus 28€–55€ ($36–$72). AE, MC, V. Mon noon–2pm; Wed–Sun noon–2pm and 7:30–9:30pm. Closed mid-Nov to mid-Dec and mid-Jan to mid-Feb.

6

The Western Riviera: From St-Tropez to Cannes to Cap d'Antibes

The western part of the **Côte d'Azur** begins at glittering St-Tropez and ends at the even more elegant Cap d'Antibes. In between are mostly middle-class resort towns, like St-Raphaël, scattered along a coast that also features the wild and desolate landscape of the Massif de l'Estérel.

Ste-Maxime and Fréjus offer some of the area's best budget accommodations, having been taken over by French families in search of a holiday getaway on the once-exclusive coast.

The area does, of course, embrace Cannes, the most famous resort in the region because of the glitz and glamour surrounding its film festival, which overflows into the upscale La Napoule-Plage, home of the Clews Museum.

Inland, the terrain climbs away from the coast to the hillside communities of Grasse, with its perfume distilleries, and Mougins, a charming old village and culinary center that makes for a romantic retreat. Food also lures gastronomes to Golfe-Juan, which features one of the region's best restaurants, Chez Tétou, a stop for a rich bowl of bouillabaisse.

Nightlife is the focus of neighboring Juan-les-Pins, attracting spirited adventurers to its all-night jazz clubs and discos. Nearby Vaullaris hosts Galerie Madoura, a pottery firm with exclusive rights to reproduce Picasso's earthenware designs. Antibes also profits from its association with Picasso by the museum dedicated to his life and work. This largely middle-class resort gives way to Cap d'Antibes, the peninsular resort that's as tony today as when F. Scott Fitzgerald used it as the setting for his novel *Tender Is the Night*.

1 St-Tropez ★★

874km (543 miles) S of Paris; 76km (47 miles) SW of Cannes

Sun-kissed lasciviousness is rampant in this carnival town, but the true Tropezian resents the fact that the port has such a bad reputation. "We can be classy, too," one native has insisted. Creative people in the lively arts along with ordinary folk create a volatile mixture. One observer said that St-Tropez "has replaced Naples for those who accept the principle of dying after seeing it. It's a unique fate for a place to have made its reputation on the certainty of happiness."

St-Tropez—this palimpsest of nostalgia—was popularized by sex symbol Brigitte Bardot in *And God Created Woman*, but it had attracted the famous for a long time. Colette lived here for many years. Even the late diarist Anaïs Nin, confidante of Henry

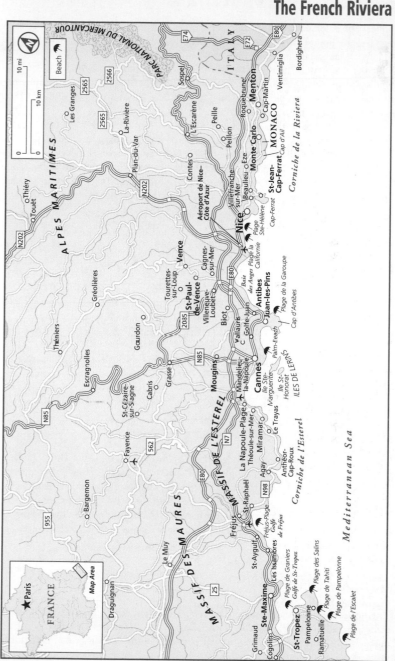

Miller, posed for a little cheesecake on the beach here in 1939 in a Dorothy Lamour–style bathing suit. Earlier, St-Tropez was visited by Matisse, Signac, and Bonnard, and even Maupassant before he died of syphilis.

Artists, composers, novelists, and the film colony come to St-Tropez in summer. Trailing them is a line of humanity unmatched anywhere else on the Riviera for sheer flamboyance. Chic people anchor their yachts here in summer but disappear long before the dreaded mistral of winter.

In 1995, Bardot pronounced St-Tropez dead—"squatted by a lot of no-goods, drugheads, and villains"—and swore she'd never go back, at least in summer. But 1997 saw her return, as headlines in France flashed the news that St-Tropez was "hot once again." Not only Bardot, but other celebrities have been showing up, including Oprah Winfrey, Don Johnson, Quincy Jones, Barbra Streisand, Jack Nicholson, Robert DeNiro, Sean "P. Diddy" Combs, and even Elton and Sly (not together!).

ESSENTIALS

GETTING THERE   The nearest rail station is in St-Raphaël, a neighboring resort. At St-Raphaël's Vieux Port, **boats** leave the Gare Maritime de St-Raphaël, rue Pierre-Auble (① **04-94-95-17-46**), for St-Tropez (trip time: 50 min.) four or five times a day from April to October. The one-way fare is 11€ ($14). Year-round, 10 to 15 Sodetrav **buses** per day leave from the Gare Routière in St-Raphaël (① **04-94-97-88-51** or 04-94-97-88-51) for St-Tropez. The trip takes 1½ to 2¼ hours, depending on the bus and the traffic, which during midsummer is usually horrendous. A one-way ticket costs 11€ ($14). Buses run directly to St-Tropez from Toulon and Hyères and from the nearest airport, at Toulon-Hyères, 56km (35 miles) away.

If you **drive,** note that parking in St-Tropez is very difficult, especially in summer. You can park in the **Parking des Lices** (① **04-94-97-34-46**), beneath place des Lices; enter on avenue Paul-Roussel. Designed for 471 cars, this lot is free for the first hour, the second hour costs 1€ ($1.30), third hour costs an additional 1€ ($1.30), and the 4th through the 24th hour charges .50€ (65¢). A 24-hour sojourn will cost 15€ ($20) in summer and in winter there is a slight reduction—around 13€ ($17). Many visitors with expensive cars prefer it, because it's more secure than any other lot. Charging the same rates, a new garage, **Parking du Nouveau Port,** avenue Charles de Gaulle (① **94-94-97-23-84**), stands at the waterfront. Every municipal engineer in St-Tropez has worked hard to funnel incoming traffic toward either of these two underground garages. A car can't enter the resort without seeing prominent signs directing traffic to either location. To get here from **Cannes,** drive southwest along the coastal highway (RD98), turning east when you see signs pointing to St-Tropez.

VISITOR INFORMATION   The **Office de Tourisme** is on quai Jean-Jaurès (① **04-94-97-45-21;** www.saint-tropez.st).

OUTDOOR PURSUITS
A DAY AT THE BEACH
The hottest Riviera beaches are at St-Tropez. The best for families are closest to the center, including the **Plage de la Bouillabaisse** and **Plage des Graniers.** More daring are the 9.5km (6-mile) crescents at **Plage des Salins** and **Plage de Pampelonne,** some 3km (2 miles) from the town center. At Pampelonne about 35 businesses occupy a 4.8km (3-mile) stretch, located about 10km (6 miles) from St-Tropez. The concessionaire that's noted as an all-gay venue is the **Aqua Club,** Plage de Pamplonne (① **04-94-79-84-35**). You'll need a car, bike, or scooter to get from town to the beach.

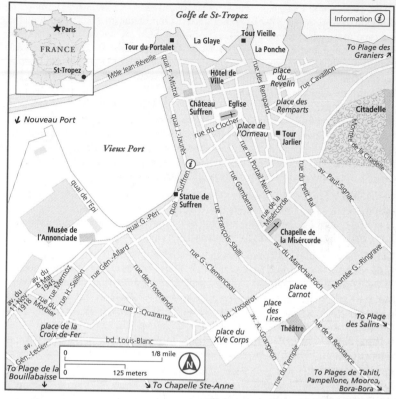

Parking is about 3.80€ ($4.95) for the day. Famous hedonistic spots along Pampelonne include the cash-only club **La Voile Rouge** (© 04-94-79-84-34), which features bawdy spring-break-style entertainment. This is the most outrageous, the sexiest, and the most exhibitionist (not for children) of the beaches of St-Tropez. Also thriving are **Le Club,** 55 bd. Patch, Plage de Pampelonne (© 04-94-55-55-55), and **Nikki Beach,** Plage de Pampelonne (© 04-94-79-82-04). Maintained by an American from Miami, Nikki Beach is wild, frenetic, uninhibited, and about as Floridian a venue as you're likely to find in the south of France. **Plage des Jumeaux** (© 04-94-55-21-80) is another active beach; it draws many families with young kids because it has playground equipment. **Sun Force Sports** (© 04-94-97-89-19, or cell 06-07-22-43-91) rents boats; **Team Water Sports** (© 04-94-79-90-11) rents jet skis, scooters, waterskiing equipment, and boats.

Notoriously decadent **Plage de Tahiti** occupies the north end of the 5.5km-long (3½-mile) Pampelonne, lined with concessions, cafes, and restaurants. It's a strip of golden sand long favored by exhibitionists wearing next to nothing (or nothing) and cruising shamelessly. If you ever wanted to go topless, this is the place to do it. Gay men tend to gravitate to **Coco Beach** in Ramatuelle, about 6.5km (4 miles) from the center of St-Tropez.

STAYING ACTIVE

BICYCLING & MOTOR-SCOOTERING   One of the town's largest renters of bicycles and motor scooters is **Mas Location** (also known as Jean-Louis Mas, S.A.R.L.), 5 rue Josef-Quaranta (℃ **04-94-97-00-60**), which operates between Easter and mid-October from premises very close to the place des Lices. Depending on the vehicle you rent, you'll be required to leave between 150€ and 1,200€ ($195–$1,560), as a deposit (cash, checks, and credit card deposits are accepted), and then pay a rental charge of between 10€ and 12€ ($13–$16) for pedal bikes (a wide range of models are available), and between 20€ and 50€ ($26–$65) per day for rental of a motorscooter, depending on the model you select. Some of the larger motorized scooters rented here require the presentation of a valid driver's license (valid foreign licenses are acceptable). Others, depending on their size, require a minimum age of either 14 (with the consent of parents or guardians) or 18.

BOATING   The highly recommended **Suncap Company,** 15 quai de Suffren (℃ **04-94-97-11-23**), rents boats 5.5m to 12m (18 ft.–40 ft.) long. The smallest can be rented to qualified sailors without a captain; larger ones come with a captain at the helm. Prices begin at 1,200€ ($1,380) per day.

GOLF   The nearest golf course, at the edge of Ste-Maxime, across the bay, is the **Golf Club de Beauvallon,** boulevard des Collines (℃ **04-94-96-16-98**), a popular 18-hole course. Sprawling over a rocky, vertiginous landscape that requires a golf cart and a lot of exertion is the Don Harradine–designed **Golf de Ste-Maxime-Plaza,** route du Débarquement, Ste-Maxime (℃ **04-94-55-02-02**). It welcomes nonguests; phone to reserve tee times. Greens fees at both golf courses range from 54€ to 60€ ($70–$78) for 18 holes per person, depending on the season. Rental of an electric golf cart, suitable for two passengers, costs around 30€ ($39) for 18 holes, year-round.

SCUBA DIVING   A team of dive enthusiasts will show you the azure-colored depths off the coast of St-Tropez from the *Octopussy I* and *II.* Both are aluminum-sided, yellow-painted dive boats. They're based year-round in St-Tropez's Nouveau Port. Experienced divers pay 35€ to 48€ ($46–$62) for a one-tank "exploration" dive, depending on how much of their own equipment they use. Novices pay 50€ ($65) for a *baptême* that includes one-on-one supervision and descent to a depth of around 5m (15 ft.). For the *baptême,* you must show strong swimming skills in advance; you must have a license to participate in the conventional dives. For reservations and information, contact *Les Octopussys,* quartier de Bertaud, Gassin, 83900 St-Tropez (℃ **04-94-56-53-10;** fax 04-94-56-46-59). For a look at the boats, head down to the Nouveau Port, where they usually tie up when not out to sea.

TENNIS   Anyone who phones in advance can use the eight courts (artificial grass or "Quick," a form of concrete) at the **Tennis-Club de St-Tropez,** route des Plages, St-Claude (℃ **04-94-97-36-39**), about half a mile from the resort's center. Open year-round, the courts rent for 17€ ($22) per hour for green set, 24€ ($31) per hour for clay set, from 8am to 9pm.

SEEING THE SIGHTS

Château Suffren is east of the port at the top end of quai Jean-Jaurès. Home to occasional art exhibits, it was built in A.D. 980 by Comte Guillaume I of Provence.

Near the junction of quai Suffren and quai Jean-Jaurès stands the bronze **Statue de Suffren,** paying tribute to Vice-Admiral Pierre André de Suffren. This St-Tropez native became one of the greatest sailors of 18th-century France, though he's largely forgotten today. In the Vieille Ville, one of the most interesting streets is **rue de la Misércorde.** It's lined with stone houses with boutiques. This street evokes medieval St-Tropez better than any other in town. At the corner of rue Gambetta is the **Chapelle de la Misércorde,** with a blue, green, and gold tile roof.

Three kilometers (2 miles) east of St-Tropez, **Port Grimaud** ⚓ makes an interesting outing. From St-Tropez, drive 4km (3 miles) west on A98 to Route 98, and then 1.5km (1 mile) north to the Port Grimaud exit. If you approach the village at dusk, when it's bathed in Riviera pastels, it looks like a hamlet from the 16th century. But this is a mirage. Port Grimaud is the dream of its promoter, François Spoerry, who carved it out of marshland and dug canals. Flanking these canals, fingers of land extend from the square to the sea. The homes are Provençal style, many with Italianate window arches. Boat owners can anchor at their doorsteps. One newspaper called the port "the most magnificent fake since Disneyland." Most shops and restaurants in Port Grimaud are closed between October and March.

Musée de l'Annonciade (Musée St-Tropez) ⚓⚓   Near the harbor, this museum occupies the former chapel of the Annonciade. It boasts one of the Riviera's finest modern art collections of post-Impressionist masters. Many of the artists, including Paul Signac, depicted the port of St-Tropez. The collection includes such works as Van Dongen's *Women of the Balustrade* and paintings and sculpture by Bonnard, Matisse, Braque, Dufy, Utrillo, Seurat, Derain, and Maillol.

Place Grammont. ℭ 04-94-97-04-01. Admission 4.60€ ($6) adults, 2.30€ ($3) children under 12. June–Sept Wed–Mon 10am–noon and 3–7pm; Oct and Dec–May Wed–Mon 10am–noon and 2–6pm. Closed Nov.

SHOPPING

St-Tropez is dense with stylish shops, but has no specific shopping street. Most shops are tucked in out-of-the-way corners of the old town. Big names include Hermès, Sonia Rykiel, and Dior. **Galeries Tropéziennes,** 56 rue Gambetta (ℭ **04-94-97-02-21**), crowds hundreds of gift items—some worthwhile, some silly—into its showrooms near place des Lices. The merchandise is Mediterranean, breezy, and sophisticated.

In a resort that's increasingly loaded with purveyors of suntan lotion, touristy souvenirs, and T-shirts, **Jacqueline Thienot,** 12 rue Georges-Clemenceau (ℭ **04-94-97-05-70**), maintains an inventory of Provençal antiques prized by dealers from as far away as Paris. The one-room shop is in an 18th-century building that shows the 18th- and 19th-century antiques to their best advantage.

Olives and wood from the trees that produce them have always been prized in Provence. For carvings made from the wood, head to **Autour des Oliviers,** 2 place de l'Ormeau (ℭ **04-94-97-64-31**), which stocks large inventories of kitchen utensils, bread boards, carved crucifixes, pottery, trays, platters, ornaments, and gift items carved from the yellow-and-brown wood. It also stocks salt for the Camargue and a wide array of French olive oils.

And even chic St-Tropez has **Le Dépôt,** boulevard Louis-Blanc (ℭ **04-94-97-80-10**), which sells secondhand designer clothes by the likes of Hermès, Moschino, Gaultier, and Chanel. Some of the merchandise even has its original tags.

On Tuesday and Saturday mornings an **outdoor market** with food, clothes, and *brocante* (flea-market finds) blooms on place des Lices. This is one of the best Provençal markets in the south of France, with more than 100 vendors selling everything from tableware to homemade bread. The fish, vegetable, and flower market is down a tiled alley (place aux Herbes) behind the tourist office. It operates daily 8am to noon in summer and Tuesday to Sunday 8am to noon in winter.

WHERE TO STAY
VERY EXPENSIVE

Hôtel Byblos ✰✰✰   The builder said he created "an anti-hotel, a place like home." That's true if your home resembles a palace in Beirut and has salons decorated with Phoenician gold statues from 3000 B.C. On a hill above the harbor, this complex encompasses intimate patios and courtyards. It's filled with antiques and rare objects like polychrome carved woodwork, marquetry floors, and a Persian-rug ceiling. Every room is unique, and all have elegant beds. Unusual features might include a fireplace on a raised hearth or a bed recessed on a dais. The rooms range in size from medium to spacious, often with high ceilings and antiques or reproductions. Some units have such special features as four-poster beds with furry spreads, or sunken whirlpool outdoors. Le Hameau, a stylish annex, contains 10 duplex suites built around a small courtyard with an outdoor spa. Some rooms have balconies overlooking an inner courtyard; others open onto a flowery terrace. Deluxe bathrooms hold tub/shower combinations.

Av. Paul Signac, 83990 St-Tropez. ✆ **04-94-56-68-00.** Fax 04-94-56-68-01. www.byblos.com. 98 units, 10 duplex suites. 370€–740€ ($481–$962) double; 590€–1,400€ ($767–$1,820) suite. AE, DC, MC, V. Parking 30€ ($39). Closed Oct 15 to mid-Apr. **Amenities:** 2 restaurants (see "Where to Dine," below); 2 bars; nightclub (see "St-Tropez After Dark," below); outdoor pool; gym; spa; sauna; salon; limited room service; massage; babysitting; laundry service; dry cleaning; nonsmoking rooms. In room: A/C, TV, dataport, minibar, hair dryer, safe.

Hôtel Le Yaca ✰   Life here is *la dolce vita.* Built in 1722 off a narrow street in the old part of town, this was the first hotel in St-Tropez. Colette lived here for a few weeks in 1927, and before that it was the temporary address of pre-Impressionists like Paul Signac. The high-ceilinged reception area overlooks an inner courtyard filled with flowers. Many rooms also have views of this courtyard; all were renovated in the early part of the millennium. Some are on the upper level, with terra-cotta floor tiles and massive ceiling timbers. Each has a comfortable bed, utilitarian furniture, and high ceilings, and most have a roomy bathroom with tub and shower.

1 bd. d'Aumale, 83900 St-Tropez. ✆ **04-94-55-81-00.** Fax 04-94-97-58-50. www.hotel-le-yaca.fr. 28 units. 255€–525€ ($332–$683) double; 775€–1,005€ ($1,008–$1,307) suite. AE, DC, MC, V. Parking 20€ ($26). Closed mid-Oct to mid-Apr. **Amenities:** Restaurant; bar; outdoor pool; limited room service; massage; babysitting; laundry service; dry cleaning; nonsmoking rooms. In room: A/C, TV, dataport, minibar, hair dryer, safe.

Hôtel Villa Belrose ✰✰ *Finds*   Small-scale and *luxe,* this pocket of posh is set within a sloping garden in Gassin, an upscale residential neighborhood that's within a 10-minute drive northwest of downtown St-Tropez. It was built in 1997 in an ocher-and-white-walled replica of a rambling private villa, with views that sweep from most of the bedrooms out over the gulf of St-Tropez. Much of the establishment's identity derives from its elegant restaurant, open daily for lunch and dinner to nonresidents who reserve a table in advance. Chef Thierry Thiercelin prepares fixed-price menus that focus on Mediterranean cuisine that's as chic as St-Tropez itself. Bedrooms in this hideaway are lavishly and opulently accessorized with fine linens and lots of upscale toiletries in the bathrooms, but there's no disguising the fact that they fall midway along the spectrum of being either cozy or cramped, depending on your point of view. In many cases, glass doors open onto private terraces, a well-landscaped garden with plenty of botanical surprises and charm, and those magnificently ethereal views.

Gassin, St-Tropez. © **04-94-55-97-97.** Fax 04-94-55-97-98. www.villabelrose.com. 38 units. 230€–710€ ($299–$923) double; 700€–2,450€ ($910–$3,185) suite. Half board 100€ ($130) extra per person per day. AE, DC, MC, V. Outdoor parking free; indoor parking 20€ ($26). Closed Nov to mid-Mar. **Amenities:** Restaurant; outdoor poolside grill; outdoor pool; exercise room; spa; 24-hr. room service; babysitting; laundry service; dry cleaning. *In room:* A/C, TV, minibar, hair dryer, safe.

La Bastide de St-Tropez ✸✸✸   Near the landmark place des Lices, this tile-roofed replica of a Provençal manor house looks deliberately severe, but the interior is opulent. It contains a monumental staircase leading from a sun-filled living room to the upper floors. The guest rooms are named according to their individual decor: Rose of Bengal, Fuchsia, or Tangerine Dawn. Each has a terrace or private garden, and some have Jacuzzis. Several, however, are quite small. The soft beds under fine quilting with matching draperies are among the most luxurious in St-Tropez. The well-appointed bathrooms have deluxe toiletries. The hotel is noted for its restaurant, L'Olivier.

Rte. des Carles, 83990 St-Tropez. © **04-94-55-82-55.** Fax 04-94-97-21-71. www.bastide-saint-tropez.com. 26 units. 190€–450€ ($247–$585) double; 275€–680€ ($358–$884) suite. AE, DC, MC, V. Closed Jan. **Amenities:** Restaurant; bar; outdoor pool; 24-hr. room service; babysitting; laundry service; dry cleaning. *In room:* A/C, TV, minibar, hair dryer, safe.

Résidence de la Pinède ✸✸✸   This deluxe palace is just a grade below Byblos but, to compensate, offers even finer cuisine. This Relais & Châteaux hotel was built in the 1950s around a rustic stone-sided tower once used to store olives. Jean-Claude and Nicole Delion are the owners of this luxurious place on the seaside. The airy, spacious rooms open onto balconies or terraces with a view over the bay of St-Tropez. The stylish but offhand staff seems constantly overburdened. The hotel is St-Tropez's only rival to the Byblos, and, though just as luxurious, it tends to have a more serious and staid clientele. Rooms are stylish and plush, accompanied by neatly kept bathrooms.

Plage de la Bouillabaisse, 83990 St-Tropez. © **04-94-55-91-00.** Fax 04-94-97-73-64. www.relaischateaux.fr/pinede. 40 units. 255€–820€ ($332–$1,066) double; 680€–1,640€ ($884–$2,132) suite. AE, DC, MC, V. Free parking. Closed mid-Oct to Mar. **Amenities:** Restaurant; bar; outdoor pool; 24-hr. room service; babysitting; laundry service; dry cleaning. *In room:* A/C, TV, minibar, hair dryer, safe.

EXPENSIVE

Hôtel La Mandarine ✸   La Mandarine is built in the Provençal style with strong angles, thick stucco walls, a tile roof, and patios. Rooms are luxuriously furnished and open onto one or more terraces; some of the suites offer as many as three terraces. Fine linens and elegant fabrics grace the comfortable beds. Beautifully maintained bathrooms are tiled and equipped with luxury toiletries. You definitely get glamour here.

Rte. de Tahiti, 83990 St-Tropez. © **04-94-79-06-66.** Fax 04-94-97-33-67. www.hotellamandarine.com. 43 units. 225€–405€ ($293–$527) double; suites from 560€ ($728). AE, MC, V. Closed Oct 15–Mar 15. Take the road leading to Plage de Tahiti; it's just off the road, 1km (½ mile) southeast of the center. **Amenities:** Restaurant; bar; outdoor pool; limited room service; massage; babysitting; laundry service; dry cleaning. *In room:* A/C, TV, minibar, safe.

Hôtel La Maison Blanche ✸   Originally designed as a private villa late in the 19th century, this small and elegant government-rated four-star hotel enjoys a superbly convenient location directly astride the most visible square in St-Tropez, the place des Lices. Much expanded and altered since its original construction, it exudes an air of whitewashed elegance that's hard to find in St-Tropez. Attesting to its charm is the in-house bar that serves only champagne by the glassful or bottle, and an 18th-century fountain that was found on-site. La Maison Blanche is in close proximity to the Port of St-Tropez, and is a 3-minute walk from the sea and beach. As such, very few of its clients feel compelled to rent a car. The rooms are comfortable and stylish, but contain very few mainstream amenities. In light of the resources of St-Tropez that lie in virtually every direction, no one seems to mind. Each of the tiled bathrooms comes with tub or shower.

Place des Lices, 83990 St-Tropez. ℂ 04-94-97-52-66. Fax 04-94-97-89-23. www.hotellamaisonblanche.com. 39 units. 168€–374€ ($218–$486) double; 350€–748€ ($455–$972) suite; 38€ ($49) extra bed. AE, DC, MC, V. Amenities: Champagne bar; laundry service/dry cleaning. In room: A/C, TV, hair dryer, safe.

Hôtel La Mistralée ❧ 𝘍𝘪𝘯𝘥𝘴 Dating to 1850 and previously the residence of a French hairdresser, this charming hotel resides in the heart of St-Tropez, 2 minutes from the Vieux Port. The decor exudes baroque sophistication, especially in the gold-and-bronze drawing room where high ceilings, Corinthian columns, and stained glass dominate. Outside, the Oriental-themed garden is no less elegant, boasting palm, lemon, and orange trees as well as bamboo and papyrus plants. All 10 rooms are individually and personally decorated, with themes ranging from "La Chanel," where a plush combination of pinks and grays complements a small balcony, to "La Chinoise," where a black marble fireplace and Chippendale armchairs in dark bamboo and black leather reign. The restaurant further develops Mistralée's slight obsession with Asia: Chef Pascale Bouissie offers Provençal cooking with a Chinese flair.

1 av. du Général Léclerc, 83990 St-Tropez. ℂ 04-98-12-91-12. Fax 04-94-43-48-43. www.hotel-mistralee.com. 10 units. 220€–590€ ($286–$767) double; 370€–760€ ($481–$988) suite; 70€ ($91) extra bed. AE, MC, V. Parking 20€ ($26). Amenities: Restaurant; 3 lounges; outdoor pool; sauna; garden. In room: A/C, TV, dataport, minibar, safe.

Hôtel La Ponche ❧❧ The same family has run this hotel overlooking the port for more than half a century. This cozy nest has long been a favorite of ours, as it's the most discreet, most charming, and least celebrity-flashy establishment in town, making Byblos look nouveau riche and a bit strident. It's filled with the original airy paintings of Jacques Cordier who died in 1978, which adds to the atmosphere. The redecorated rooms are well equipped and open onto sea views. Each floor holds two or three rooms. Sun-colored walls with subtle lighting lend a homey feeling. The beds are elegantly appointed with linen and quality mattresses, and the midsize to large bathrooms have tub/shower combinations or shower only.

Port des Pécheurs, 83990 St-Tropez. ℂ 04-94-97-02-53. Fax 04-94-97-78-61. www.laponche.com. 18 units. 140€–405€ ($182–$527) double; 180€–525€ ($234–$683) suite. AE, MC, V. Parking 21€ ($27). Closed Nov to mid-Feb. Amenities: Restaurant; bar; limited room service; babysitting; laundry service; dry cleaning. In room: A/C, TV, dataport, minibar, hair dryer, safe.

L'Hôtel des Lices ❧ One consistently reliable bet for lodgings in St-Tropez is this modern hotel in its own small garden, close to place des Lices. The tastefully furnished rooms are tranquil, overlooking either the outdoor pool or the garden; their rates vary widely according to season, size, and view. Each unit is designed for comfort, from the quality mattresses to the well-appointed bathrooms. Breakfast is the only meal served, although afternoon snacks are provided beside the pool.

135 av. Augustin-Grangeon, 83993 St-Tropez. ℂ 04-94-97-28-28. Fax 04-94-97-59-52. www.hoteldeslices.com. 42 units. 140€–335€ ($182–$436) double; 240€–525€ ($312–$683) suite. AE, V. Free parking. Closed Nov 3–Feb. Amenities: Restaurant; bar; outdoor pool; Jacuzzi; 24-hr. room service; babysitting; laundry service; dry cleaning. In room: A/C, TV, safe.

MODERATE

Hôtel Ermitage ❧ 𝘝𝘢𝘭𝘶𝘦 This hotel is attractively isolated amid the rocky heights of St-Tropez. It was built in the 19th century as a private villa. Today its red-tile roof and green shutters shelter a plush hideaway. A walled garden is illuminated at night, and a cozy corner bar near a wood-burning fireplace takes the chill off blustery evenings. The guest rooms offer good value for St-Tropez. They are pleasantly but simply furnished, with efficiently organized and well-maintained bathrooms.

Av. Paul-Signac, 83990 St-Tropez. ℂ 04-94-97-52-33. Fax 04-94-97-10-43. 27 units. 66€–164€ ($86–$213) double. AE, DC, MC, V. Amenities: Bar; limited room service; babysitting; laundry service; dry cleaning. In room: TV, hair dryer.

Hôtel La Tartane ⚗ This small hotel lies between the center of St-Tropez and the Plage des Salins, about a 3-minute drive from each. After a comprehensive upgrade, its government rating jumped from three stars to four, accompanied by a big hike in prices. It has a heated stone-rimmed outdoor pool in the garden, attractively furnished public rooms with terra-cotta floors, and attentive, hardworking management. The midsize guest rooms are bungalows surrounding the outdoor pool. Each holds a small tiled bathroom with a shower stall or tub/shower combo. Breakfasts are elaborate.

Rte. des Salins, 83990 St-Tropez. ℂ 04-94-97-21-23. Fax 04-94-97-09-16. www.latartane.com. 27 units. 180€– 650€ ($234–$845) double; 445€–900€ ($579–$1,170) suite. AE, DC, V. Closed Oct–Mar 15. Amenities: 2 restaurants; bar; outdoor pool; free shuttle to beach; spa; steam bath; salon; massage; laundry service; dry cleaning. In room: A/C, TV, dataport, minibar, hair dryer, safe.

Hôtel Le Levant On the road leading from the old town of St-Tropez to the beach at Les Salins, this hotel stands behind a screen of cypresses and palmettos. Designed like a low-slung Provençal *mas* (farmhouse), it has thick stucco walls and a tile roof. The recently redecorated rooms, in Provençal motifs, have big windows and white walls, as well as private entrances overlooking the garden and its outdoor pool. Each has comfortable double or twin beds. Tiled bathrooms are small but efficiently organized.

Rte. des Salins, 83990 St-Tropez. ℂ 04-94-97-33-33. Fax 04-94-97-76-13. www.hotelleriedusoleil.com. 28 units. 125€–145€ ($163–$189) double. AE, MC, V. Closed mid-Oct to Mar 15. Amenities: Bar; outdoor pool; limited room service; babysitting. In room: A/C, TV, minibar.

Hôtel Sube If you want to be right on the port, in a location that's perfect for ship- and celebrity-watching, this might be your first choice. It's directly over the Café de Paris bar, in the center of a shopping arcade. The two-story lounge has a beamed ceiling and a glass front, allowing a great view of the harbor. The rooms aren't large but are comfortable and decorated in French provincial style. Each was renovated in 2004. The more expensive units have scenic views of the port. Each comes with a private bathroom with a shower and tub.

15 quai Suffren, 83900 St-Tropez. ℂ 04-94-97-30-04. Fax 04-94-54-89-08. www.hotel-sube.com. 28 units. 90€–290€ ($117–$377) double. AE, MC, V. Parking nearby 30€ ($39). Amenities: Cafe; bar. In room: A/C, TV.

INEXPENSIVE

Hôtel Lou Cagnard ⚗ *Value* This pleasant roadside inn, with a tile roof and green shutters, offers quiet rooms in the rear overlooking the garden. Monsieur and Madame Yvon are the hardworking owners, explaining to newcomers the translation of the name of their hotel (*Lou Cagnard,* in Provençal dialect, means "The hot, burning Sun"). They extend a warm welcome to their guests. Although there is nothing grand about the bedrooms, they are comfortable, with fine mattresses and well-maintained bathrooms with adequate shelf space. This hotel is a bargain in pricey St-Trop.

18 Av. Paul-Roussel, 83990 St-Tropez. ℂ 04-94-97-04-24. Fax 04-94-97-09-44. 19 units. 58€–110€ ($75–$143) double. MC, V. Closed Nov 4–Dec 26. Amenities: Lounge. In room: TV, safe.

WHERE TO DINE

The restaurant at the **Résidence de la Pinède** (p. 225) serves flavor-filled Provençal dishes.

EXPENSIVE

Colors GRILLS   Relatively new on the St-Tropez dining scene, this restaurant offers a verdant garden setting and one of the town's very few wood-burning ovens, on which a succulent array of fresh meat and fish are slowly cooked. Here, amid a decor of— you guessed it—strong colors, mostly greens and violets, you can enjoy grilled filet steaks, rib eyes, and such fresh fish as sea bass. Most are accompanied with creamy house-style mashed potatoes and fresh vegetables.

3 rue du Temple. (Ⓒ **04-94-97-00-15.** Reservations required July–Aug. Main courses 20€–30€ ($26–$39). AE, DC, MC, V. Daily 8pm–midnight. Closed late Oct to late Mar.

Le Girelier PROVENÇAL   The Rouets own this portside restaurant whose blue-and-white color scheme has become a trademark. They serve grilled fish in many versions, as well as bouillabaisse (only for two). Also on the menu are brochette of monkfish, a kettle of spicy mussels, and *pipérade* (a Basque omelet with pimentos, garlic, and tomatoes). Most dishes are moderately priced.

Quai Jean-Jaurès. (Ⓒ **04-94-97-03-87.** Main courses 28€–82€ ($36–$107); fixed-price menu 42€ ($55). AE, DC, MC, V. Daily noon–2pm and 7–11pm. Closed Nov–Feb 15.

Les Mouscardins 𝔊𝔊𝔊 FRENCH/PROVENÇAL   At the end of St-Tropez's harbor, this restaurant wins awards for culinary perfection. The dining room is in formal Provençal style with an adjoining sunroom under a canopy. The menu includes classic Mediterranean dishes; as an appetizer, we recommend an unusual version of olive and almond soup, and John Dory dredged in bread crumbs, fried, and served with a purée of celery. The two celebrated fish stews of the Côte d'Azur are offered: bourride Provençale and bouillabaisse. The fish dishes are excellent, particularly the sauté of monkfish, wild mushrooms, and green beans. The dessert specialties are soufflés made with Grand Marnier or Cointreau. Hours listed below might be the posted times, but the chefs don't always follow the schedule. For example, during July and August they might not be open for lunch if "everybody is at the beach."

1 rue Portalet. (Ⓒ **04-94-97-29-00.** Reservations required. Main courses 42€–58€ ($55–$75); fixed-price menu 58€–98€ ($75–$127) at lunch and dinner; bouillabaisse 52€ ($68). AE, DC, MC, V. June–Sept Mon–Sat noon–2pm and 7:30–10pm; Oct–May Tues–Sat noon–2pm and 7:30–9:30pm.

Spoon Byblos 𝔊𝔊 FRENCH/INTERNATIONAL   This is one of the many entrepreneurial statements by Alain Ducasse, considered by some the world's greatest chef—or at least the most acclaimed. Originally launched in Paris, Spoon has traveled everywhere from London to the Riviera. Here it serves the cuisines of many cultures with produce mainly from the Mediterranean. It draws special inspiration from the food of Catalonia, Andalusia, and Morocco, and offers more than 300 wines from around the world. Background music ranges from hip-hop to the hits of the '70s. It's terribly fashionable, although you might grow a bit weary of its self-conscious sense of chic after an hour or two within its ultra-designed premises.

The restaurant opens onto a circular bar made of blue-tinted glass and polished stainless steel. The menu will have you salivating before you even take a bite. Dig into shrimp and squid consommé with a hint of jasmine and orange, or spicy king prawns on a skewer. Then try delectable lamb couscous or spit-roasted John Dory. You might top off a meal with the chef's favorite cheesecake or a slice of Neapolitan with the taste of strawberry, vanilla, and pistachio.

In the Hôtel Byblos, av. Paul-Signac. ℂ 04-94-56-68-00. Reservations required. Main courses 28€–40€ ($36–$52). AE, DC, DISC, MC, V.July–Aug daily 8pm–12:30am; otherwise daily 8–11pm. Closed mid-Oct to mid-Apr.

MODERATE

Auberge des Maures *Value* PROVENÇAL   One of our favorite cost-conscious restaurants in an otherwise very expensive town lies close to one end of the all-pedestrian rue Allard, within a stone-sided building whose roof rolls away during clement weather for a view of the moon and stars. The space within the dining room is more than doubled with the tables that members of the Salinesi family (Evelyn and Phillippe) set up during clement weather in the garden, within sight of splashing fountains and ornamental shrubbery. Adding to the drama is the dining room's view over a hardworking kitchen, where the staff wears black and churns out tempting platters that are completely based on fresh, seasonal ingredients. Menu items include grilled versions of many kinds of fresh fish and meat, and often taste best when preceded with a starter known as a *panache Provençal*, on which are piled deep-fried zucchini blossoms; hearts of artichoke *barigoule;* and a medley of *petits farcis*. Murals that highlight the stone walls of the place include such Provence-specific frescoes as fields of lavender, artfully rendered in oil colors.

4 rue du Docteur Boutin. ℂ 04-94-97-01-50. Reservations recommended. Main courses 10€–25€ ($13–$33). Set-price menu 42€ ($55). AE, DC, MC, V. Daily 7:30pm–1am. Closed Dec–Mar.

Chez Joseph TRADITIONAL FRENCH   Chic, yet casual and friendly, this restaurant has become a permanent fixture on the St-Tropez restaurant scene. The crowd is heavily gay and fashionable, and might include mini-episodes across the bar of champagne cocktails being ordered and consumed, all in a way that's breezy, airy, and usually with some degree of style. At least during high season, the crowd here tends to remain in place until as late as 6am. Adjacent to the bar is a mostly red-toned, vaguely retro-loooking restaurant with about 35 tables, giving you lots of options for people-watching. Menu items are consciously artful: A favorite salad contains wild mixed greens, mesclun, artichoke hearts, and parmesan shavings. The best main courses feature lasagna studded with chunks of lobster; brochettes of fresh-grilled fish; grilled scallops in a white wine and butter sauce; and a very unusual version of tournedos Rossini (filet steak layered with foie gras) and served with a shellfish sauce.

Place de la Mairie. ℂ 04-94-97-01-66. Reservations recommended. Set-price buffet-style lunch 25€ ($33); main courses lunch and dinner 20€–50€ ($26–$65). AE, MC, V. May–Sept daily 1–3pm and 8pm–midnight; Oct and Apr Tues–Sat 1–3pm and 8pm–midnight. Bar closes between 3 and 6am. Closed Nov–Apr.

Chez Maggi 👬👬 PROVENÇAL/ITALIAN   St-Tropez's most flamboyant gay restaurant and bar also draws straight diners and drinkers. At least half its floor space is devoted to a bar, where patrons range in age from 20 to 60. The lack of tables in front makes cruising at Chez Maggi, in the words of loyal patrons, *très crazée* and seems to extend for blocks in every direction. Meals are served in an adjoining dining room. Menu items include chicken salad with ginger, goat-cheese salad, *petits farcis provençaux* (vegetables stuffed with minced meat and herbs), brochettes of sea bass with lemon sauce, and chicken curry with coconut milk, capers, and cucumbers.

7 rue Sibille. ℂ 04-94-97-16-12. Reservations recommended. Main courses 14€–28€ ($18–$36); fixed-price menu 33€ ($43). MC, V. Restaurant daily 7pm–midnight; bar daily 7pm–3am. Closed Oct to mid-Mar.

ST-TROPEZ AFTER DARK

On the lobby level of the Hôtel Byblos, **Les Caves du Roy,** avenue Paul-Signac (© 04-94-97-16-02), is the most self-consciously chic nightclub in St-Tropez and the most famous in France. Entrance is free, but drink prices begin at a whopping 18€ ($23). It's open nightly from May to late September from 11:30pm till dawn. **Le Papagayo,** in the Résidence du Nouveau-Port, rue Gambetta (© 04-94-97-76-70), is one of the largest nightclubs in town. The decor was inspired by the psychedelic 1960s. Entrance is between 15€ and 18€ ($20–$23) and includes one drink.

Adjacent to Le Papagayo is a club whose upscale male and female patrons might be equally at home in Les Caves du Roy: **Le VIP Room,** in the Résidence du Nouveau-Port (© 04-94-97-14-70); they pay from 14€ to 15€ ($18–$20) per cocktail for the chance to (demurely or not) whoop it up. The club is all steel, chrome, mirrors, and glass. Expect an active bar area, dance floor, and the kind of social posturing and preening that can be amusing—or not.

Le Pigeonnier, 13 rue de la Ponche (© 04-94-97-84-26), rocks, rolls, and welcomes a crowd that's mostly gay or lesbian, and between 20 and 50. Most of the socializing revolves around the long, narrow bar, where patrons from all over Europe seem to enjoy chitchat. There's also a dance floor. For another gay hot spot, check out the action at **Chez Maggi** (see "Where to Dine," above).

Below the Hôtel Sube, the **Café de Paris,** sur le Port (© 04-94-97-00-56), is one of the most popular hangouts. The utilitarian room has early-1900s globe lights, an occasional 19th-century bronze artifact, masses of artificial flowers, and a long zinc bar. The crowd is irreverent and animated. The reporter Leslie Maitland aptly captured the crowd attracted to **Café Sénéquier,** sur le Port (© 04-94-97-00-90): "What else can one do but gawk at a tall, well-dressed young woman who appears *comme il faut* at Sénéquier's with a large white rat perched upon her shoulder, with which she occasionally exchanges little kisses, while casually chatting with her friends." The cafe is historic, venerable, and snobbish, and, at its worst, off-puttingly stylish.

Le Bar du Port, quai Suffren, adjacent to the Café de Paris (© 04-94-97-00-54), is breezy, airy, and almost obsessively hip and self-consciously trendy. This cafe-bar attracts a consistently young clientele. Expect lots of table-hopping, stylishly skimpy clothing, recorded music that might make you want to get up and dance, and insights into what's really going on in the minds of French 20-somethings.

If your idea of a night out is sitting in a cafe drinking wine, you can "hang out" at such joints as **Kelly's Irish Pub,** quai F. Mistral, at the bottom end of the Vieux Port (© 04-94-54-89-11), which draws a mostly foreign crowd. The tavern is casual, not chic. If you're nostalgic for St-Germain-des-Prés, head for the old-fashioned **Le Café,** place des Lices (© 04-94-97-02-25), with its famous zinc bar. Its glory lies in its location and not because of any innate value as a warm and cozy cafe—actually, it's both a bistro-restaurant and cafe today.

2 Ste-Maxime

24km (15 miles) SW of St-Raphaël; 61km (38 miles) SW of Cannes

Ste-Maxime is just across the gulf from glitzy St-Tropez, but its atmosphere is much more sedate. Young families are the major vacationers here, though an occasional refugee from across the water will come over to escape the see-and-be-seen crowd. The town is surrounded by the red cliffs of the Massif des Maures, protecting it from harsh

Tips **Wheeling around Ste-Maxime**

A great way to explore Ste-Maxime is on two wheels with some wind in your hair. Consider visiting **Rent Bike**, 13 rue Magali (© **04-94-43-98-07**), which rents bikes and mopeds. Mountain bikes are 12€ ($16) per day, with a 175€ ($228) deposit; mopeds are 17€ ($22), with a 400€ ($520) deposit.

weather. However, the wide stretches of sand and the cafe-lined promenades lure travelers to spend their days basking in the sun. More active vacationers might want to try windsurfing or water-skiing in the calm waters, or even golfing. A 16th-century fort, built by the monks of Lérins (who also named the port), houses a museum. The best thing about Ste-Maxime is the price—though the town isn't as in vogue as St-Tropez, it's fun and affordable and according to locals, a lot less decadent.

ESSENTIALS
GETTING THERE   Access to the nearest railway station is at St-Raphaël. For information about the buses that run frequently between St-Raphael and Ste-Maxime, and from Ste-Maxime on to St-Tropez, call **Sodetrav** (© **04-94-54-62-36**). One-way passage between Ste-Maxime and either St-Raphael or St-Tropez costs between 5€ and 6€ ($6.50–$7.80) per person. If you're headed to Ste-Maxime from St-Tropez anytime between February and December, there's frequent ferryboat service (transit time: 20 minutes) for a cost of 6€ ($7.80) per person, each way. For information about these boats, contact **Les Bâteaux Verts**, quai L.-Condroyer (© **04-94-49-29-39**).

VISITOR INFORMATION   The **Office de Tourisme** is on 1 promenade Simon-Lorière (© **04-94-55-75-55**).

A DAY AT THE BEACH
Beaches are the main attraction here. There are at least four nearby. Two are an easy walk from the town center: Across the road from the casino is **Plage du Casino**—we advise avoiding it because of the fumes from the nearby roadway, the narrow sands, and the hordes of sunbathers. A better bet is **Plage de la Croisette,** a wider, nominally less-congested expanse that's a 2-minute walk west of Plage du Casino. The most appealing are **Plage de la Nartelle** and the adjacent **Plage des Eléphants,** broad expanses of clean, fine-textured light-beige sand about 2km (1¼ miles) west of town. To reach them, follow signs along the coastal road pointing to St-Tropez. Here you can rent a mattress for sunbathing from any of several concessionaires for around 15€ to 20€ ($20–$26) depending on the beach.

SEEING THE SIGHTS
Start with the 16th-century **La Tour Carrée des Dames (Dames Tower)** at place des Aliziers. It was originally a defensive structure; today it's home to the **Musée des Traditions Locales,** place de l'Eglise (© **04-94-96-70-30**), with exhibits on the area's history and tradition. The museum is open Wednesday to Sunday during July and August from 10am to noon and 3 to 7pm, and September to June from 10am to noon and 3 to 6pm only. Admission is 2.30€ ($3) for adults and .75€ ($1) for children 11 and under.

Facing the tower is the **Eglise Ste-Maxime,** place des Aliziers (© **04-94-49-06-67**), with a green marble altar from the former Carthusian monastery of La Verne in the Massif des Maures. The choir stalls date from the 15th century.

St-Maxime hosts various markets, including a daily **flower-and-food market** on rue Fernand-Bessy every Tuesday to Saturday 8am to 3pm (during July and Aug, it's open daily 8am–1pm and 4–8pm). On Thursday, a **crafts market** is held on and around place du Marché; on Friday morning (8am–noon), vendors sell a variety of **knickknacks** on place Jean-Mermoz. In the pedestrian streets of the old town, an **arts-and-crafts fair** takes place daily in summer from 7pm to midnight.

Outside town are several worthy sights. About 10km (6 miles) north on the road to Muy (Route de Muy) is the **Musée du Phonographe et de la Musique Méchanique** (© 04-94-96-50-52). This extensive display of audio equipment is the result of one woman's 40-year obsession. Sometimes she gives personal tours. In the museum is one of Edison's original "talking machines" and an audiovisual pathegraphe used to teach foreign languages in 1913. The museum is open Easter through October only, Wednesday through Sunday from 10am to noon and 3:30 to 6pm. During July and August, it's open from 10am to noon, and from 4 to 6:30pm. Admission is 3€ ($3.90) for adults and 1.50€ ($1.95) for children 5 to 12 years.

If you're a nature lover, follow the signs along boulevard Bellevue for 1.5km (1 mile) north of town to the little town of **Sémaphore.** Here you'll find a panoramic view of the mountains and oceans from an altitude of 120m (400 ft.). There are also many hiking trails that wind along the coast or into the mountains. The tourist office has maps, or you can head for the Sentier du Littoral (Chemin des Douaniers), a trail that meanders along the coast toward St-Tropez and has access to the sea at almost all points along the way.

WHERE TO STAY

Although hotels are less expensive here than in the neighboring towns, you might find that you must pay for half board in July and August. Most places are closed in winter, but May, June, and September are great times to find a good deal.

VERY EXPENSIVE

Hôtel Le Beauvallon ⋆⋆⋆   At long last, Ste-Maxime offers a *luxe* palace as worthy as some of the plush joints of its rival, St-Tropez. Overlooking the St-Tropez Bay and enclosed by landscaped gardens, Le Beauvallon is a plush choice with palatial elegance and a grand cuisine. Bedrooms are spacious and sumptuously furnished in grand comfort, and modern bathrooms contain luxurious toiletries, deep tubs, and powerful showers. An ideal choice for a romantic escape, it shelters you from the tacky world of the heavily built-up waterfront, with its apartments, condos, and hotels. The resort is so all-encompassing that you might find it tempting not to leave the grounds. Guests dine at three venues, including on the fine white sands of the hotel's private beach. Golfers can play on the adjacent 18-hole course.

Baie de St-Tropez, Beauvallon Grimaud 83120 Ste-Maxime. © 04-94-55-78-88. Fax 04-94-55-78-78. www.lebeauvallon.com. 69 units. 205€–540€ ($267–$702) double; 495€–2,320€ ($644–$3,016) suite. AE, DC, MC, V. **Amenities:** 3 restaurants; 2 bars; golf; private spas; 24-hr. room service; babysitting; laundry service; dry cleaning. *In room:* A/C, TV, minibar, hair dryer, safe.

EXPENSIVE

Hôtel La Belle Aurore ⋆⋆   La Belle Aurore is on its own private beach and is one of the finest addresses in the area for the cost. If it has a serious challenger, it's Les Santolines (see below). Though the well-furnished guest rooms aren't air-conditioned, each has a terrace overlooking the sea; the breezes keep the inside temperature comfortable. Tiled bathrooms are small and tidy.

5 bd. Jean-Moulin, 83120 Ste-Maxime. ℂ **04-94-96-02-45.** Fax 04-94-96-63-87. www.belleaurore.com. 17 units. 130€–314€ ($169–$408) double; 350€–550€ ($455–$715) suite. AE, DC, MC, V. Closed Oct 15–Mar 15. **Amenities:** Restaurant; lounge; outdoor pool; limited room service; babysitting; laundry service; dry cleaning. *In room:* A/C, TV, minibar, hair dryer, safe.

MODERATE

Best Western Hôtel Montfleuri ⚗ *(Finds*   This hotel on a hillside in a quiet residential neighborhood opens onto a superb view of the Gulf of St-Tropez. The large guest rooms come with balconies. Each has fine linen, twin or double beds, and a small bathroom. The hotel restaurant serves "family cooking" Provençal style in a pleasant garden.

3 av. Montfleuri, 83120 Ste-Maxime. ℂ **800/528-1234** in the U.S. and Canada, or 04-94-55-75-10. Fax 04-94-49-25-07. www.montfleuri.com. 30 units. 70€–185€ ($91–$241) double; 150€–230€ ($195–$299) suite. AE, DC, MC, V. Closed Nov 5–Dec 23 and Jan 5–Mar 1. **Amenities:** Restaurant; bar; outdoor pool; laundry service; dry cleaning. *In room:* A/C, TV, minibar, hair dryer, safe.

Hôtel La Croisette ⚗   This charming hotel is surrounded by its own lush garden and has an intimate aura, lying 200m (656 ft.) from the beach. Room rates vary according to view—those with a balcony and sea view are most expensive; those that open onto the garden are less. Homey and cozy, they are decorated in a provincial southern style; the tiled bathrooms are tidy. Maintenance here is high quality.

2 bd. des Romarins, 83120 Ste-Maxime. ℂ **04-94-96-17-75.** Fax 04-94-96-52-40. www.hotel-la-croisette.com. 19 units. 99€–170€ ($129–$221) double; 242€–290€ ($315–$377) suite. AE, MC, V. Closed Nov–Mar 15. **Amenities:** Bar; limited room service; babysitting; laundry service; dry cleaning. *In room:* A/C, TV, minibar, hair dryer, safe.

Hôtel Les Santolines ⚗⚗   This is an excellent choice for those who want to remove themselves from the crowds. Les Santolines is 10 minutes from the busy center area but still close to the beach. The building is arranged around a grassy courtyard that has an outdoor pool and the town's most inviting *jardin fleuri* (flower garden). Rooms are comfortable and private; most have balconies. The look is very French provincial. Some bathrooms are rather dramatically tiled in sea blue; all have double basins.

Quartier de la Croisette, 83120 Ste-Maxime. ℂ **04-94-96-31-34.** Fax 04-94-49-22-12. www.hotel-les-santolines.com. 13 units. 70€–140€ ($91–$182) double. AE, MC, V. Closed Jan 3–Feb 3. **Amenities:** Bar; outdoor pool; babysitting. *In room:* A/C, TV, minibar, hair dryer.

INEXPENSIVE

Hôtel de la Poste   This modern hotel's location in the town center, convenient to the beach and shopping, makes up for what it lacks in personality. With a head-to-toe renovation in spring 2000, and membership in the well-respected Logis de France group, the inside is cool and comfortable, with a quiet lounge and a pleasant bar. Guest rooms are clean, well maintained, and comfortably furnished. Bathrooms are small but well maintained. The staff is friendly and always happy to help you decide how to spend your day.

11 bd. Frédéric-Mistral, 83120 Ste-Maxime. ℂ **04-94-96-18-33.** Fax 04-94-55-58-63. www.hotelleriedusoleil.com. 28 units. 75€–115€ ($98–$150) double. AE, DC, MC, V. **Amenities:** Lounge; bar; outdoor pool; limited room service; babysitting; laundry service; dry cleaning. *In room:* A/C, TV, minibar, hair dryer, safe.

Hôtel Le Chardon Bleu   Situated 10m (33 ft.) from the beach, Le Chardon Bleu is also close to the pedestrian area and the casino. The hotel has a garden where you can enjoy the aroma of the flowers. The well-maintained rooms are comfortable and inviting, though the furnishings are standard; all have small balconies. Bathrooms are tiled and compact.

29 rue de Verdun, 83120 Ste-Maxime. ℂ **04-94-55-52-22.** Fax 04-94-43-90-89. www.aubergeduchardonbleu.fr. 25 units. 47€–75€ ($61–$98) double. AE, DC, MC, V. **Amenities:** Lounge. *In room:* A/C, TV, minibar, safe.

WHERE TO DINE

La Gruppi FRENCH/PROVENÇAL　Earthy and amusing, this restaurant thrives on the promenade adjacent to the sea and has done so ever since the Lindermanns opened it in the 1960s. La Gruppi is the Provençal word for a miniature trough used to feed barnyard animals, here used affectionately and nostalgically. Bay windows illuminate dining rooms on two floors, decorated with rattan furnishings. The deluxe version of the establishment's savory bouillabaisse must be ordered a day in advance; otherwise, you get a simplified version, which the chefs refer to as a *soupe de poisson.* Other menu items are seafood platters; herbed and roasted lamb from Sisteron; and veal, chicken, and all the vegetarian bounty of Provence. If you opt for fish, a staff member will carry a basket filled with the best of the day's catch for your inspection and advise you on their respective merits. One particularly succulent example is braised sea wolf in champagne sauce.

82 av. Charles-de-Gaulle. ℂ **04-94-96-03-61.** Reservations recommended. Main courses 25€–30€ ($33–$39); fixed-price menus 23€–32€ ($30–$42); bouillabaisse 40€ ($52); soupe de poisson 12€ ($16). AE, MC, V. Apr–Sept daily noon–2:30pm and 7–10pm; Oct–Mar Tues noon–2:30pm, Thurs–Mon noon–2:30pm and 7–10pm. Closed 2 weeks in Dec.

Restaurant Sans Souci FRENCH/PROVENÇAL　Philippe Sibilia's Italian-born grandfather opened this place in 1953, and since then it's always been reliable. In a turn-of-the-20th-century building next to the church, it has a Provence-inspired decor with ceiling beams and old-time accessories. Menu items prepared by the good-humored owner are concocted from fresh ingredients and years of practice. Examples are pan-fried Provençal veal, sea wolf with fennel, octopus salad, filet of hake with basil, and one of our favorite dishes anywhere, noisettes of lamb with a tapenade of olives that's enhanced with pulverized anchovies and a hint of fresh cream.

58 rue Paul-Bert. ℂ **04-94-96-18-26.** Reservations recommended. Main courses 14€–18€ ($18–$23); fixed-price menus 19€–24€ ($24–$31). V. Feb–Oct daily noon–2pm and 7–10:30pm.

3 Fréjus ⟨★

3km (2 miles) W of St-Raphaël; 14km (9 miles) NE of St-Tropez

Fréjus was founded by Julius Caesar in 49 B.C. as Forum Julii; later, under Augustus's rule, it became a key naval base. The warships with which Augustus defeated Antony and Cleopatra at the battle at Actium were built here in 31 B.C. By the Middle Ages, however, the port had declined. It began to silt up from disuse and was eventually filled in. Today the port lies more than 3km (2 miles) inland.

The Vieille Ville still boasts remnants from Roman times, including parts of an arena and a theater. An interesting section also dates to medieval times called the "Cité Episcopale." The baptistery is one of France's oldest ecclesiastical buildings.

In more recent times, Fréjus has again expanded toward the water. The beach area, Fréjus Plage, tends to blend into St-Raphaël. The two towns are often considered a single holiday destination, though serious beachgoers often opt to stay in St-Raphaël, where the hotels are closer to the water and cheaper.

ESSENTIALS

GETTING THERE　From the main station at St-Raphaël, several **trains** a day arrive at a small train station in Fréjus on rue Martin-Bidoure (ℂ **08-36-35-35-35**).

The beach is a shorter walk (about 15 min.) from the St-Raphaël station than from the Fréjus station.

Aglobus (© **04-94-95-16-71**), which functions in cooperation with **Estérel Bus** (© **04-94-53-78-46**), operates routes throughout Provence and the Riviera, including a bus service into Fréjus from St-Raphaël every 30 minutes. Buses arrive at the **Fréjus Gare Routière,** place Paul-Vernet (© **04-94-83-87-63**), at the east end of the town center. One-way tickets cost 3.25€ ($4.25). **Sodetrav** buses (© **04-94-97-88-51**) en route to St-Tropez from St-Raphaël, stop along the coast in Fréjus.

GETTING AROUND   You can rent mopeds at **Action 2 Roues,** 18 av. Des Portes-du-Soleil (© **04-94-44-48-34**). Prices range from 25€ to 40€ ($33–$52) depending on the model, and credit card deposits are required. **Cycles Patrick Beraud,** 337 rue de Triberg (© **04-94-51-20-20**), rents the pedal-powered version of two-wheeled transportation. Expect to pay 9€ to 22€ ($12–$29), plus a security deposit.

VISITOR INFORMATION   The **Office de Tourisme** is at 325 rue Jean-Jaurès (© **04-94-51-83-83**).

SPECIAL EVENTS   The **Fête des Plantes** is held annually in the park of the Villa Aurélienne (see below), during a 3-day period in late March and April. For information, call © **04-94-51-83-83** or contact the local tourist office.

EXPLORING THE TOWN
THE TOP SIGHTS

The best preserved of the ruins is the **Amphithéâtre (Les Arènes)** ☆, rue Henri-Vadon (© **04-94-51-34-31**). In Roman times, it held up to 10,000 spectators. The upper levels of the galleries have been reconstructed with the same greenish stone used to the original building. Today it's used as a venue for rock concerts and the city's two annual Spanish-style *corridas* (bullfights). Ask the tourist office for dates and details. It's open November to April, Tuesday to Sunday 9:30am to 12:30pm and 2 to 5pm; and May to October, Tuesday to Sunday 9:30am to 12:30pm and 2 to 6pm. Admission is 2€ ($2.60) for all ages.

A half-kilometer (⅓ mile) north of town on rue du Théâtre-Romain, the **Théâtre Romain** (© **04-94-51-34-31**), not to be confused with the amphitheater, has been largely destroyed. However, one wall and a few of the lower sections remain and are used as a backdrop for occasional summer concerts. The site is open 24 hours, and visits, which aren't monitored, are free. Northwest of the theater, you can see a few soaring arches as they follow the road leading to Cannes. These are the remaining pieces of the 40km (25-mile) aqueduct that once brought fresh water to Fréjus's water tower.

Cité Episcopale ☆☆   The town's most frequently visited site is its fortified cathedral in the heart of the Vieille Ville. At its center is the **Cathédrale St-Léonce,** completed in the 16th century after many generations of laborers had worked on it. It was begun in the 10th century, and parts of it date from the 12th and 13th centuries. Its most striking features are Renaissance—ornately carved walnut doors depicting scenes from the Virgin's life and tableaux inspired by Saracen invasions. The 5th-century **baptistery** ☆☆ is one of the oldest in France. Octagonal like many paleo-Christian baptisteries, it features eight black granite columns with white capitals. Most interesting are the two doors, which are different sizes. Catechumens would enter by the smaller of the two; inside, a bishop would wash their feet and baptize them in the center outdoor pool. The baptized would then leave through the larger door; this signified their enlarged spiritual stature.

The most beautiful of all the structures in the Episcopal quarter is the 12th-century **cloister** 𝕽𝕽. The colonnade's two slender marble pillars are typical of the Provençal style. Inside, the wooden ceiling is divided into 1,200 small panels decorated with animals, portraits, and grotesques by 15th-century artists. A bell tower rises above the cloister, its steeple covered with colored tiles.

Place Formigé. ① 04-94-51-26-30. Admission includes entrance to all sites, the museum, and (optional) guided tour of cloister and baptistery: 4.60€ ($6) adults, 3.10€ ($4.05) students under 25 and children. Apr–Sept daily 9am–7:30pm; Oct–Mar daily 9am–noon and 2–7pm.

MORE SIGHTS

The small, round **Chapelle Cocteau,** avenue Nicola (① 04-94-53-27-06), was designed by the artist, film director, social gadfly, and *prince des poètes* Jean Cocteau. It was built between 1961 and 1965, and was decorated by Cocteau himself. Its octagonal shape, low-slung with small windows, might remind you of an African thatch-covered hut. It's open Wednesday to Monday April to September from 2 to 6pm, and October to March from 2 to 5pm. Admission is free.

Just outside Fréjus are two curiosities that reflect the cultural mixture of France's early-20th-century empire. The **Pagode Hong-Hien** (① 04-94-53-25-29), still used as a Buddhist temple, is about 2km (1¼ miles) northeast on R.N. 7. It was built in 1919 by soldiers conscripted from Indochina as a shrine to their fallen comrades. It's open daily from 9am to noon and 2 to 7pm; admission is 1.50€ ($1.95) for all ages. Off D4, leading to Bagnols, you can see the purple-red exterior of the **Mosquée Soudanaise** (no phone), built by Muslim soldiers conscripted from the French colony of Mali. It's controlled by the French Ministry of Defense and is off-limits to casual visitors.

The grand neoclassical **Villa Aurélienne,** avenue du Général-d'Armée Calliès (① 04-94-53-11-30), was originally a holiday home for an English industrialist in the 1880s. It's the venue of a widely varied series of temporary art exhibitions. Admission prices vary according to the venue. Call for information. The park surrounding the villa hosts occasional festivals (see "Special Events," above).

Parc Zoologique, Le Capitou (① 04-98-11-37-37), is off A8 about 5.5km (3½ miles) north of the center of Fréjus. The zoo is home to more than 250 species of animals and is open daily May to September 10am to 6pm, and October to April from 10am to 5pm. Admission is 12€ ($16) for adults and 8€ ($10) for children 3 to 10.

WHERE TO STAY

Hôtel L'Aréna 𝕽𝕽   This hotel in the center of the Vieille Ville is created from a former bank. Beautifully restored in bright Provençal colors, L'Aréna is an appropriately informal beach-town retreat. Each of the small but comfortable rooms opens onto a garden area where tropical plants give the air a sweet smell. Furnishings and mattresses are comfortable and simple, but not at all plush. Likewise, bathrooms are tidy and small. The staff is friendly, and the hotel is a good value for the area.

145 rue du Général-de-Gaulle, 83600 Fréjus. ① 04-94-17-09-40. Fax 04-94-52-01-52. www.arena-hotel.com. 36 units. 90€–145€ ($117–$189) double. AE, DC, MC, V. Closed Dec 15–Jan 16. **Amenities:** Restaurant; bar; outdoor pool; 24-hr. room service; babysitting; laundry service; dry cleaning. *In room:* A/C, TV, hair dryer.

WHERE TO DINE

Les Potiers 𝕽 *Finds* FRENCH/PROVENÇAL   The town's smallest and most charming restaurant lies midway between the town hall and the ancient arena. Spearheaded by Richard François and his charming wife, Marilou Fortunato (who supervises the dining room), it occupies a century-old stone house and has only 15 seats. Menu items change with the seasons but usually include such highly successful dishes as fried slabs of foie gras of duckling; ravioli of crayfish with ricotta cheese and hazelnut oil; daurade "royale" with wild rice and a parmesan-flavored cream sauce; crisp-roasted rack of lamb cooked in a salt crust; and cannelloni stuffed with strips of rabbit served with a saffron-flavored medley of vegetables. A dessert with undeniable charm is a platter with five small portions of crème brûlée, each differently flavored. Their "perfumes" include versions flavored with licorice, pistachios, orange, vanilla, and chicory.

135 rue des Potiers. ℂ 04-94-51-33-74. Reservations required. Main courses 14€–17€ ($18–$22); fixed-price menus 23€–33€ ($30–$43). MC, V. Mon–Sat noon–1:45pm 7–9pm.

4 St-Raphaël

3km (2 miles) E of Fréjus; 43km (27 miles) SW of Cannes

Between the red lava peaks of the Massif de l'Estérel and the densely forested hills of the Massif des Maures, St-Raphaël was first popular during Roman times, when rich families came to the large resort here. Barbaric hordes and Saracen invasions characterized the Middle Ages; it wasn't until 1799, when a proud Napoleon landed at the small harbor beach on his return from Egypt, that the city once again drew attention.

Fifteen years later, that same spot in the harbor was the point of embarkation for the fallen emperor's journey to exile on Elba. In 1864, Alphonse Karr, a journalist and ex-editor of *Le Figaro*, helped reintroduce St-Raphaël as a resort. Dumas, Maupassant, and Berlioz came here from Paris on his recommendation. Gounod also came; he composed *Romeo et Juliet* here in 1866. Unfortunately, most of the belle époque villas and grand hotels were destroyed during World War II when St-Raphaël served as a key landing point for Allied soldiers.

Today some of the mansions have been rebuilt and others have been replaced by modern resorts and buildings. However, the city still offers the wide beaches, good restaurants and hotels, and coastal ambience of other Côte d'Azur resorts—at a fraction of the price. This is why St-Raphaël, one of the richest towns on the coast, draws more families than couture-clad Parisians.

ESSENTIALS

GETTING THERE Reaching St-Raphaël is easier than ever. The town sits directly on the rail lines running parallel to the coast between Marseille in the west and the Italian border town of Ventimiglia in the east. Within some 3 hours you can take a fast **TGV train** from Paris to Marseille. For rail information and schedules, call ℂ 877/2TGVMED or check www.raileurope.com. Once at Marseille, it is another 1¾ hours by train to St-Raphaël. Trains leave Marseille every hour during the day, costing 23€ ($30) one-way. Trains from Cannes head east to St-Raphaël every 30 minutes during the day (25-min. trip); one-way fare costs 8€ ($10).

The bus station behind the train station provides both local and regional service. **Aglobus** (ℂ 04-94-93-87-63) links directly with Fréjus, charging around 2.25€ ($2.95) each way for buses that run at 30-minute intervals, and around 6.50€ for service from Nice, a 60-minute transit. **Sodetrav** (ℂ 04-94-97-88-51) links St-Raphaël with St-Tropez (trip time: 70–90 min.); fares are around 9€ ($12) each way. Buses from Nice arrive every hour until 1am. Another option for local bus service into nearby hills and hamlets is provided by **Beltrame** (ℂ 04-94-95-95-16).

Between April and October, **Les Bateaux Bleus** (✆ 04-94-95-17-46) provides waterborne transit—about a half-dozen boats per day—between a point near the railway station of St-Raphaël and St-Tropez for around 11€ ($14) each way. **By car** from St-Tropez in the west, take D98A northwest to N98, at which point you drive east toward St-Raphaël. From Cannes, head west along N98.

GETTING AROUND   Normally, taxis line up at the bus station; if you can't find one, call ✆ 04-94-95-04-25. You can rent bikes and scooters from **Patrick Moto,** 260 av. du Général-Leclerc (✆ 04-94-53-87-11). Bikes rent for 9€ ($12), with a 130€ ($169) deposit; mountain bikes rent for 15€ ($20), with a 300€ ($390) deposit; and scooters go for 20€ ($26), with a 400€ ($520) deposit. MasterCard and Visa can be used for the deposit.

VISITOR INFORMATION   The **Office de Tourisme** faces the train station on rue Waldeck-Rousseau (✆ 04-94-19-52-52; www.saint-raphael.com).

SPECIAL EVENTS   The **Competition Internationale de Jazz de New Orleans** is held during 3 days in early July, when Dixieland-style musicians from around the world congregate to display their talent. Call ✆ 04-94-19-88-47, or contact the tourist office, for exact dates and musical venues. In mid-August, the **Festival St-Pierre des Pêcheurs** is conducted in and around the town center. Honoring the fishers who helped feed the town throughout most of its existence, it features a night of fireworks, a brief medieval-style procession to and from the village church, music, dancing on platforms built beside the port, and a series of jutes (mock naval battles between competing boat teams) where everyone gets soaking wet.

A DAY AT THE BEACH

Of course, most visitors come here to have fun on the beaches. The best ones (some rock, some sand) are between the Vieux Port and Santa Lucia; stands rent equipment for watersports on each beach.

The closest to the town center is the **Plage du Veillat,** a long stretch of sand that's crowded and family friendly. Within a 5-minute walk east of the town center is **Plage Beau Rivage,** whose name is misleading because it's covered with a smooth and even coating of light-gray pebbles that might be uncomfortable to lie on without a towel. History buffs will enjoy a 7km (4½-mile) excursion east of town to the **Plage du Débarquement,** a partly pebble and partly sand stretch that was hurled into world headlines on August 15, 1944, when Allied forces overran the southern tier of occupied France, bringing World War II to a more rapid conclusion. Today expect relatively uncrowded conditions, except during the midsummer crush.

St-Raphaël's answer to the decadence of nearby St-Tropez is most visible in the municipality's official nude beach, the **Plage de St-Ayguls,** 10km (6 miles) west of the town center. Surrounded by thick screens of reeds that thrive along the marshy seafront, it's a short, clearly signposted walk from the heart of the simple fishing village of St-Ayguls.

SEEING THE SIGHTS

St-Raphaël is divided in half by railroad tracks. The historically interesting **Vieille Ville** (old city) lies inland from the tracks. Here you'll find St-Raphaël's only intact ancient structure, the **Eglise des Templiers,** place de la Vieille Eglise, Quartier des Templiers (✆ 04-94-19-25-75). The 12th-century church is the third to stand on this site; two Carolingian churches underneath the current structure have been revealed during digs. A Templar watchtower sits atop one of the chapels, and at one time, watchers were posted to look out over the sea for ships that might pose a threat. The church served as a fortress and refuge in case of pirate attack. In the courtyard are fragments of a Roman aqueduct that once brought water from Fréjus. You can visit the church June to September every Tuesday to Saturday from 10am to noon and 2 to 5:30pm. Ironically, no Masses are conducted in this church on Sunday—it's a consecrated church, but one that's been relegated to something akin to an archaeological rather than religious monument.

St-Raphaël's other major church, **Notre-Dame-de-la-Victoire,** boulevard Félix-Martin (℡ **04-94-19-81-29**), was completed in 1887, an ostentatious monument to the gilded age of commerce that helped finance its construction. May to September, it's open daily from 7:30am to 10pm; October to April, it's open daily from 7am to 8pm. Entrance is free.

Near the Eglise des Templiers, the **Musée d'Archéologie Sous-Marine (Museum of Underwater Archaeology),** rue des Templiers (℡ **04-94-19-25-75**), displays amphorae, ships' anchors, ancient diving equipment, and other interesting items recovered from the ocean's depths. At one time, rumors circulated about a "lost city" off the coast of St-Raphaël. Jacques Cousteau came to investigate; instead of a sunken city, he discovered a Roman ship that had sunk while carrying a full load of building supplies. October to May, the museum is open Tuesday to Saturday from 10am to noon and 2 to 5:30pm. June to September, it's open Tuesday through Saturday from 9am to noon and 3 to 6:30pm. Admission costs 3.50€ ($4.55) for adults and 2€ ($2.60) for students and children 17 and under.

You'll also find **flower and fruit markets** in the old city. Stall owners open every morning. Every Tuesday from 9am to 6pm, vendors selling a variety of odds and ends, La Marché au Brocante, also appear. Also check out the **Marché Alimentaire de St-Raphaël,** where carloads of produce, fish, meat, wines, and cheeses are sold Tuesday to Sunday from 8am to 1pm at two sites—place Victor-Hugo and place de la République—a 5-minute walk apart.

The seafront's broad **promenades,** dotted with statues dedicated to Félix Martin (a 19th-c. mayor and tireless promoter of the resort) and Alphonse Karr (a 19th-c. artist and local luminary), wind between the beaches and hotels. Near the old port, a **pyramid** commemorating Napoleon's return to France from Egypt stands on avenue du Commandant-Guilbaud.

WHERE TO STAY

There are plenty of accommodations in St-Raphaël, but during summer even the less-than-desirable places fill up fast. Reserve well in advance.

Best Western Hôtel La Marina   Overlooking the yacht-basin harbor at Santa Lucia, this hotel provides comfortable accommodations in a setting a bit removed from the crowded beaches. Most of the well-furnished rooms, each renovated and upgraded in 2005, have private balconies; the tiled bathrooms are tidily organized. The restaurant boasts well-prepared regional food, which can be served on a sunny terrace that overlooks the sailboats and yachts.

Nouveau Port Santa Lucia, 83700 St-Raphaël. ℡ 800/528-1234 in the U.S. and Canada, or 04-94-95-31-31. Fax 04-94-82-21-46. www.lamarina-sr-fr. 100 units. 65€–156€ ($85–$203) double; 115€–180€ ($150–$234) suite. AE, DC, V. Parking 9€ ($12). **Amenities:** Restaurant; bar; outdoor pool; health club; limited room service; massage; babysitting; laundry service; dry cleaning. *In room:* A/C, TV, minibar, hair dryer, safe.

Hôtel Continental *Value*   The Continental is a good choice for a cost-conscious beach vacation. Rooms come in a wide variety, ranging from compact (relatively cramped) to spacious, with rates charged according to view (seascape or urban). All have well-maintained tiled bathrooms and each was renovated in 2004. No meals are served other than breakfast, but many well-recommended restaurants lie within a short walk.

100 promenade du Président-René-Coty, 83700 St-Raphaël. © 04-94-83-87-87. Fax 04-94-19-20-24. www.hotel continental.fr. 44 units. 70€–205€ ($91–$267) double. AE, MC, V. Parking 11€ ($14). **Amenities:** Lounge; babysitting; laundry service; dry cleaning. *In room:* A/C, TV, minibar, hair dryer, safe.

Hôtel Excelsior   This hotel, on the beachfront promenade, is a charming family-run place—the best address at St-Raphaël. The small to medium-size guest rooms are comfortably appointed, with tidy bathrooms; most have views of the ocean. A sand beach is directly across the street.

193 promenade du Président-René-Coty, 83700 St-Raphaël. © 04-94-95-02-42. Fax 04-94-95-33-82. www. excelsior-hotel.com. 40 units. 120€–170€ ($156–$221) double. AE, DC, MC, V. **Amenities:** Restaurant; pub; lounge; limited room service; laundry service; dry cleaning. *In room:* A/C, TV, minibar, hair dryer, safe.

WHERE TO DINE

L'Arbousier ✿   FRENCH/PROVENÇAL   Thanks to the charm and humor of Christien Troncy, director of the dining room, and the cuisine of her husband, Philippe, this restaurant is a success story that deserves to be better known than it already is. In their own words, the architecture of the building "isn't particularly pretty," although lots of money was spent making it cozier and more Provençal-looking. But there's something innately stylish and even fun about this place that keeps clients coming back again and again. Flavors are rich, sunny, and sometimes earthy; typical dishes are green asparagus and lobster served with lemon-flavored butter; cannelloni-shaped filets of red snapper and squid served with hearts of artichokes, chopped onions and peppers, and white wine; and a sophisticated version of roasted pigeon in a stewpot, accompanied by pigeon-stuffed ravioli, served with sherry sauce and pepper. Hearty appetites usually appreciate the roasted rabbit with dried plums and garnished with foie gras of duckling. Dessert might be a delectable crystallized version of local strawberries served with a pepper-flavored mint sauce.

6 av. de Valescure. © 04-94-95-25-00. Reservations recommended. Main courses 25€–35€ ($33–$46); fixed-price lunches 27€–58€ ($35–$75); fixed-price dinners 35€–58€ ($46–$75). AE, DC, MC, V. Tues–Sun noon–2:30pm; Tues–Sat 7:30–10:30pm.

ST-RAPHAEL AFTER DARK

Because this is a family vacation spot, the after-dark scene is a little sparse. Nights at the **Grand Casino,** square de Grand (© 04-98-11-17-77), feature slot machines and gambling, plus a nightly dance party in summer with an upbeat orchestra. The slot machines are open daily from 11am to 4am; gambling begins at 8pm, and the dance club opens at 10pm. In summer, the entire place stays open to 4am.

One of our favorite bars is **Le Coco Club,** Port Santa Lucia (© 04-94-95-95-56), open Wednesday to Sunday only, where live music and stiff drinks contribute to a kind of gregarious, often flirtatious conviviality. Alternative choices include **La Réserve** (© 04-94-95-02-02), a popular disco with a punk-rock crowd between 16 and 25, and **Le Cristal,** rue Jules-Barbier (© 04-94-95-29-20) a disco with less emphasis on youth culture. Gay people, both men and women, tend to congregate at **Le Pipeline,** 16 rue Charabois (© 04-94-95-93-98), where disco music and a long-standing reputation as a dance palace can be animated and fun for everyone. For more information, contact the town's tourist office.

5 Massif de l'Estérel (★(★(★

3km (2 miles) NE of Fréjus; 8km (5 miles) SE of Cannes

Stretching for 39km (24 miles) of coast from La Napoule to St-Raphaël, this mass of twisted red volcanic rock is a surreal landscape of dramatic panoramas. Forest fires have devastated all but a small section of cork oak, adding barrenness to an already otherworldly place. This was once the stamping ground of a colorful 19th-century highwayman, Gaspard de Besse, who hid in the region's many caves and terrorized local travelers until, at age 25, he was hanged and then decapitated by military authorities in the main square at Aix-en-Provence.

Following the path of the ancient Roman Aurelian Way, N7 traces the area's northern edge, running through the Estérel Gap between Fréjus and Cannes. To get to the massif's summit, **Mont Vinaigre** (elevation 589m/1,962 ft.), turn right at the Testannier crossroads 11km (7 miles) northeast of Fréjus. A parking area allows you to leave your car and make the final 15 minutes of the ascent on foot, climbing to the observation deck of a watchtower for a view stretching from the Alps to the Massif des Maures. At La Napoule, turn around to follow the southwesterly trail of N98 back to Fréjus.

This route offers the massif's most stunning vistas, first turning inland just beyond Le Trayas at **Pointe de l'Observatoire,** where you can ascend to the **Grotte de la Ste-Baume** for the views that inspired the medieval hermit St. Honorat, who once dwelt in the cave. Farther along N98, at **Pointe de Baumette,** is a memorial to the French writer/aviator Antoine de St-Exupéry. At Agay, turn inland again to reach the rocky **Gorge du Mal-Infernet,** a twisted rut in the earth, offering a contrast to the surrounding peaks with their overview of the region. Continuing along this inland route leads you to **Pic du Cap-Roux,** at 431m (1,438 ft.), and **Pic de l'Ours,** at 488m (1,627 ft.), both offering sweeping views of land and sea. Technically, the park is administered by the **Office National des Forêts** (© 04-94-44-16-45), from an office that's open 24 hours a day, and which is located at the northeastern entrance to the park, in the Maison Forestière, on the Route des Colles/Route du Pic de l'Ours. But since the above-noted organization is more deeply concerned with maintenance and safety issues within the park, it's usually wiser, and more productive, to get touring and tourist information from the tourist offices of any of the towns and villages nearby, especially from the tourist office of nearby St-Raphaël (© **04-94-19-52-52**).

ESSENTIALS
GETTING THERE   Both of the area's twisted boundary roads run from Cannes to Fréjus, with N7 tracing the northern boundary and the southerly N98 following a route along the coast.

VISITOR INFORMATION   You can get additional information on sights, routes, and accommodations at the **Offices de Tourisme** in St-Raphaël, rue Waldeck-Rousseau (© **04-94-19-52-52**); Fréjus, 325 rue Jean-Jaurès (© **04-94-51-83-83**); Les-Adrets-de-l'Estérel, place de la Mairie (© **04-94-40-93-57**); and Agay, boulevard de la Plage (© **04-94-82-01-85**).

WHERE TO STAY

Note that the **Auberge des Adrets** (see below) also rents rooms.

L'Estirado des Andrets & Auberge Panoramique 🖈 *Finds*
In the heart of Estérel, this is a combined hotel and restaurant that's worth a detour. A stay, or even a stopover for lunch, is like a journey back in old-time Provence. Everything is traditional in style, with cozy, well-furnished bedrooms with a private bathroom or shower. On a hot summer day in Provence, guests congregate at the outdoor swimming pool or else lounge in the sun against a scenic backdrop of forested hills. The food at Auberge Panoramique is among the best in the area, highlighting a Provençal and French cuisine that changes with the seasons. Dining can be in the shade of a straw hut in summer or else close to a roaring fireplace in winter. Between sea and hills, the location is in the village of Les Andrets between Cannes and St. Raphaël.

83600 Les Andrets de l'Estérel. © 04-94-40-90-64. Fax 04-94-40-98-52. www.estirado.com. 21 units. 60€–80€ ($78–$104) double; 105€–125€ ($137–$163) suite. MC, V. **Amenities:** Restaurant; lounge; outdoor pool; limited room service; babysitting; laundry service; dry cleaning. *In room:* TV, dataport, hair dryer, safe.

WHERE TO DINE

Auberge des Adrets 🖈🖈 PROVENÇAL/FRENCH
Despite an official mailing address that places this medieval inn in Fréjus, it lies only 2km (1¼ miles) east of Les-Adrets-de-l'Estérel. Records of its existence go back to A.D. 824, when troubadours sang and horses rested here after treks across a landscape even rougher and more arid than other points nearby. In 1653, the site was designated a Relais de Poste, where travelers and their horses could find lodging. Today it focuses on upscale versions of Provence's rural dishes, as interpreted by noted chef Christian Née. He presides over an antique-filled dining room that spills out onto a large terrace overlooking arid landscapes and the faraway Baie de Cannes. Menu items are likely to include warm foie gras sautéed with roughly textured bread, magret of duckling roasted with a honey-flavored sesame sauce, a sophisticated roster of risottos (including one with lobster), and aromatic rack of lamb with an olive tapenade. Dessert might be a hot soufflé with black chocolate.

The hotel also offers 10 carefully decorated rooms, each with air-conditioning, some kind of ornate (usually baldachin) bed, and views over a garden. Doubles cost 168€ to 219€ ($218–$285) in high season; breakfast is 12€ extra.

R.N. 7, 83600 Fréjus. © 04-94-82-11-82. Fax 04-94-82-11-80. Main courses 12€–20€ ($16–$26); fixed-price menu 36€ ($47). AE, DC, MC, V. Tues–Sat noon–2pm and 7:30–10pm; Sun noon–2pm; July–Aug daily noon–2pm and 7:30–10pm. Closed Nov.

6 La Napoule-Plage 🖈

901km (560 miles) S of Paris; 8km (5 miles) W of Cannes

This secluded resort is on the sandy beaches of the Golfe de la Napoule. In 1919, the once-obscure fishing village was a paradise for the eccentric sculptor Henry Clews, son of a New York banker, and his wife, Marie, an architect. Clews fled America's "charlatans," whom he believed had profited from World War I. His house is now a museum.

ESSENTIALS

GETTING THERE La Mandelieu Napoule-Plage lies on the **bus** and **train** routes between Cannes and St-Raphaël. For information and schedules, call © **08-36-35-35-35.** If you're **driving,** take A8 west from Cannes.

VISITOR INFORMATION   The **Office de Tourisme** is on avenue de Cannes (© **04-93-49-95-31;** www.ot-mandelieu.fr).

THE MAIN ATTRACTION

Château de la Napoule/Musée Henry-Clews 🏰🏰   An inscription over the entrance to this fairy-tale-like château reads: ONCE UPON A TIME. The château, a brooding, medieval-looking fortress whose foundations begin at the edge of the sea, was rebuilt from the ruins of a real medieval château. Clews covered the capitals and lintels with his own grotesque menagerie—scorpions, pelicans, gnomes, monkeys, lizards—the revelations of a tortured mind. Women and feminism are recurring themes in the sculptor's work; an example is the distorted suffragette depicted in his *Cat Woman.* The artist was preoccupied with old age in both men and women, and admired chivalry and dignity in man as represented by Don Quixote—to whom he likened himself. Clews died in Switzerland in 1937, and his body was returned to La Napoule for burial. Marie Clews later opened the château to the public as a testimonial to the inspiration of her husband.

Bd. Henry-Clews. © **04-93-49-95-05.** Admission 4€ ($5.20), free for children under 5. Feb 7–Nov 7 daily 10am–6pm; Nov 8–Feb 6 Sat–Sun 10am–6pm. Tours in French and English Feb 7–Nov 7 daily at 11:30am, 2:30pm, 3:30pm, and 4:30pm.

WHERE TO STAY

La Calanque *(Value*   The foundations of this charming hotel date from the Roman Empire. The present hotel, run by the same family since 1942, looks like a hacienda, with salmon-colored stucco walls and shutters. Register in the bar in the rear (through the dining room). Bedrooms range from small to medium, each with a comfortable mattress. Those who take the bathless units will find the corridor bathrooms adequate and well maintained. Aside from a phone, in-room amenities in all units are a bit scarce. The hotel's restaurant spills onto a terrace and offers some of the cheapest meals in La Napoule.

Av. Henry-Clews, 06210 La Napoule. © **04-93-49-95-11.** Fax 04-93-49-67-44. 17 units. 84€–111€ ($109–$144) double. Rates include half board. AE, MC, V. Closed Nov to mid-Feb. **Amenities:** Restaurant; bar. *In room:* TV.

L'Ermitage du Riou 🏰🏰 *(Finds*   This old Provençal house, the most tranquil choice at the resort, is a seaside government-rated four-star hotel bordering the Riou River and the Cannes-Mandelieu golf club. The rooms are furnished in regional style, with authentic furniture and ancient paintings. The rooms range in size from medium to spacious, and each has an elegant bed and fine linen. The most expensive ones have safes. The good-size bathrooms have tub/shower combinations. Views are of the sea or the golf course.

Av. Henry-Clews, 06210 La Napoule. © **04-93-49-95-56.** Fax 04-92-97-69-05. www.ermitage-du-riou.fr. 41 units. 126€–301€ ($164–$391) double; 341€–529€ ($443–$688) suite. AE, DC, MC, V. **Amenities:** Restaurant; bar; outdoor pool; sauna; nonsmoking rooms; limited-mobility rooms. *In room:* A/C, TV, dataport, minibar, hair dryer, safe.

Sofitel Royal Hôtel Casino 🏰🏰   A member of the Accor group, this Las Vegas–style hotel is on the beach near a man-made harbor, about 8km (5 miles) from Cannes. It was the first French hotel with a casino and the last (before building codes changed) to have a casino directly on the beach. The hotel has one of the most contemporary designs on the Côte d'Azur. Most of the good-size rooms angle toward a sea view; those facing the street are likely to be noisy, despite soundproofing. Each has a well-kept bathroom with a tub/shower combination.

Following La Route Napoleon

On March 1, 1815, having escaped from a Senate-imposed exile on Elba that began in April 1814, Napoleon, accompanied by a small band of followers, landed at Golfe-Juan. The deposed emperor was intent on marching northward to reclaim his throne as emperor.

Though the details of his journey have been obscured by time, two versions of a local legend about one of his first mainland encounters exist. The first version claims that shortly after landing at Golfe-Juan, Napoleon and his military escort were waylaid by highwaymen unimpressed by his credentials. The other turns the story around, claiming that Napoleon's men, attempting to build a supply of money and arms, waylaid the coach of the prince de Monaco, whose principality, stripped of independence during the Revolution, had just been restored by Louis XVIII. When the prince told Napoleon that he was on his way to reclaim his throne, the exiled emperor stated that they were in the same business and bid his men to let the coach pass unhindered.

In the 1930s, the French government recognized Napoleon's positive influence on internal affairs by building Route 85, **La Route Napoleon,** to roughly trace the steps of the exiled emperor in search of a throne. It stretches from Golfe-Juan to Grenoble, but the most scenic stretch is in Provence, between Grasse and Digne-les-Bains. The route is well marked with commemorative plaques sporting an eagle in flight, though the "action" documented south of Grenoble revolves around simple stops made for food and sleep along the way.

The **Office de Tourisme** at place du Tour, St-Vallier-de-Thiey ((✆ 04-93-42-78-00), can provide you with a detailed account of the trek, a map of the three campsites where Napoleon and his men slept, and a map indicating where the road deviates from Napoleon's actual route, now maintained as a hiking trail where you can follow in his footsteps. The office is open Monday through Friday from 9am to noon and 2:30 to 5:30pm, and Saturday from 10am to noon.

After embarking from Cannes on the morning of March 2, the group passed through Grasse and halted just beyond St-Vallier-de-Thiey, spending the night. From this point to our end destination at Digne-les-Baines, the route touches only a handful of small settlements; the most notable is Castellane and the village of Barrème, where an encampment was set up on the night of March 3. The next day, the group stopped for lunch in Digne-les-Bains before leaving the region to continue north toward the showdown at Grenoble. Although the relais where he dined is long gone, you can stop at **Hostellerie de Préjoly,** avenue Gaston de Fontmichel, in St-Vallier-de-Thiey ((✆ 04-93-42-60-86). Cozy, historic, and with a staff that's consciously tied into the travails and tribulations of Napoleon during his transit through their town, it serves tasty set-price menus for between 17€ and 24€ ($21–$31). During July and August, it's open daily for lunch and dinner, but the rest of the year, it's closed Sunday night, Tuesday night, and all day on Wednesday.

605 av. du Général-de-Gaulle, 06212 La Mandelieu–La Napoule. ℭ **800/221-4542** in the U.S. and Canada, or 04-92-97-70-00. Fax 04-93-49-51-50. www.sofitel.com. 213 units. 195€–425€ ($254–$553) double; from 630€ ($819) suite. AE, DC, MC, V. Parking 12€ ($16). **Amenities:** 2 restaurants (see "Where to Dine," below); 4 bars; 2 tennis courts; exercise room; sauna; Turkish bath; 24-hr. room service; babysitting; laundry service; dry cleaning; limited-mobility rooms. *In room:* A/C, TV, dataport, minibar, hair dryer.

WHERE TO DINE

Note that the restaurant in **La Calanque** (see above) is open to nonguests.

Brocherie II SEAFOOD/TRADITIONAL FRENCH   The way this restaurant curves along the shoreline gives the impression that you're riding out to sea on a floating houseboat. You'll enter its precincts by crossing a gangplank lined with flaming torches. Specialties include virtually every fish that can be found in local waters—the freshest and best are grilled and served as simply as possible. Your choices of sauce include a rich hollandaise or béarnaise, or an herb-flavored version of white wine, butter, or vinaigrette. There's also a heady version of bouillabaisse, priced at 40€ ($52) per person, and a selection of (very expensive) lobsters from the establishment's bubbling holding tank. Meat dishes include succulent brochettes of Provençal lamb with rosemary and red wine.

Au Port. ℭ **04-93-49-80-73.** Reservations recommended. Main courses 12€–18€ ($16–$23); fixed-price menu 32€ ($42). MC, V. Daily 9am–10pm. Closed Jan.

Le Féréol ✿ MODERN FRENCH   This well-designed restaurant services most of the culinary needs of the largest hotel (and the only casino) in town, the Sofitel Royal Hôtel Casino (above). Outfitted in a nautical style that includes some of the seagoing accessories of an upscale yacht, it offers one of the most impressive lunch buffets in the neighborhood. At night the place is candlelit and elegant, and the view through bay windows over the outdoor pool is soothing. Menu items include foie gras, scampi tails fried with ginger, zucchini flowers with mousseline of lobster, mignon of veal with Parma ham and tarragon sauce, sole braised with shrimp, and an émincé of duckling baked under puff pastry with cèpes. The dessert buffet lays out a wide array of sophisticated pastries, some light and fruity summer dishes, and others designed as irresistible temptations for chocoholics.

In the Sofitel Royal Casino, 605 av. du Général-de-Gaulle. ℭ **04-92-97-70-20.** Reservations recommended. Main courses 20€–78€ ($26–$101); fixed-price menu 27€ ($35) lunch, 38€ ($49) dinner. AE, DC, MC, V. Daily 12:30–2:30pm (to 3:30pm July–Aug) and 7–10:30pm (to 11pm July–Aug).

L'Oasis ✿✿✿ FRENCH   This is one of the great dining rooms along the Western Riviera. At the entrance to the harbor of La Napoule, in a 40-year-old house with a lovely garden and an unusual re-creation of a mock-medieval cloister, this restaurant became world-famous under the now-retired Louis Outhier. Today chef Stéphane Raimbault prepares the most sophisticated cuisine in La Napoule. Presumably, Raimbault has learned everything Outhier had to teach him and charts his own culinary course. Because Raimbault cooked in Japan for 9 years, many of his dishes are of the East-meets-West variety. In summer, meals are served in the shade of the plane trees in the garden. Menu choices might include roasted saddle of monkfish and risotto of squid with an ink sauce; medallions of veal and duck in a muscat-wine and grape sauce; and a roasted Dover sole with parsley scorzonera. The wine cellar houses one of the finest collections of Provençal wines anywhere. Regrettably, there can be rocky moments here, thanks to a staff that's a lot less helpful than it could be.

Rue Honoré-Carle. ☎ **04-93-49-95-52.** Reservations required. Main courses 35€–55€ ($46–$72); fixed-price menu 45€–48€ ($59–$62) lunch, 68€–148€ ($88–$192) dinner. AE, DC, MC, V. Daily noon–2pm and 7:30–10pm. Closed mid Dec to mid-Jan, for lunch Apr–Oct, and Nov to end of Mar on Sun night and Mon.

7 Cannes ★★★

905km (562 miles) S of Paris; 164km (101 miles) E of Marseille; 26km (16 miles) SW of Nice

When Coco Chanel came here, got a suntan, and returned to Paris bronzed, she startled the milk-white ladies of society. Today the bronzed bodies—in nearly nonexistent swimsuits—that line the sandy beaches of this chic resort continue the trend started by the late fashion designer.

Cannes is at its most frenzied during the International Film Festival at the Palais des Festivals on promenade de la Croisette. On the seafront boulevards, flashbulbs pop as the stars and wannabes emerge and pose and pose and pose. For wannabes (particularly female), *outrageous* is the key word. The festival's stellar activities are closed to most visitors, who are forced to line up in front of the Palais des Festivals. Known as "the bunker," this concrete structure is the venue for premiers that draw some 5,000 spectators. International regattas, galas, *concours d'élégance,* and even a Mimosa Festival in February—something's always happening at Cannes, except in November, traditionally a dead month.

ESSENTIALS

GETTING THERE   Trains from the other Mediterranean resorts, Paris, and the rest of France arrive frequently throughout the day. By train, Cannes is 15 minutes from Antibes and 35 minutes from Nice. The TGV from Paris via Marseille reaches Cannes in about 5½ to 6 breathless hours. The one-way fare from Paris is about 95€ ($124). For rail information and schedules, call ☎ **08-92-35-35-35. Rapide Côte d'Azur,** place de l'Hôtel de Ville, Cannes (☎ **04-93-39-11-39**), offers bus service to Nice and back every 20 minutes during the day (trip time: 1½ hr.). The one-way fare is 9.50€ ($12).

The Nice **international airport** (☎ **08-20-42-33-33**) is a 30-minute drive northeast. **Buses** pick up passengers at the airport every 40 minutes during the day and drop them at the Gare Routière, place de l'Hôtel de Ville (☎ **04-93-45-20-08**). Bus service from Antibes operates every half-hour.

By **car** from Marseille, take A51 north to Aix-en-Provence, continuing along A8 east to Cannes. From Nice, follow A8 southwest to Cannes.

VISITOR INFORMATION   The **Office de Tourisme** is in the Palais des Festivals, esplanade Georges-Pompidou (☎ **04-92-99-84-22;** www.cannes.fr).

SPECIAL EVENTS   Cannes is at its most frenzied at the end of May, during the **International Film Festival** at the Palais des Festivals on promenade de la Croisette. It attracts not only film stars, but seemingly every photographer in the world. You have a better chance of being named prime minister of France than you do of attending one of the major screenings. (Hotel rooms and tables at restaurants are equally scarce during the festival.) But the people-watching is fabulous. If you find yourself here at the right time, you can join the thousands who line up in front of the Palais des Festivals, where the premiers are held. With paparazzi shouting and gendarmes holding back fans, the guests parade along the red carpet, stopping for a moment to strike a pose. *C'est Cannes!*

You may also be able to get tickets for some of the lesser films, which play 24 hours. For information, see "Provence Calendar of Events" in chapter 2 or visit **www.festival-cannes.fr.**

SEEING THE SIGHTS

For many, Cannes consists of only one street, **promenade de la Croisette** (or just La Croisette) 𝒜𝒜, curving along the coast and split by islands of palms and flowers. It's said that Edward, Prince of Wales (before he became Edward VII) contributed to its original cost. But he was a Johnny-come-lately to Cannes. In 1834, Lord Brougham, a lord chancellor of England, set out for Nice and was turned away because of an outbreak of cholera. He landed at Cannes and liked it so much that he decided to build a villa here. Returning every winter until his death in 1868, he proselytized it in London, drawing a long line of British visitors. In the 1890s, Cannes became popular with Russian grand dukes (it's said that more caviar was consumed here than in all of Moscow). One French writer claimed that when the Russians returned as refugees in the 1920s, they were given the garbage-collection franchise.

A port of call for cruise liners, the seafront of Cannes is lined with hotels, apartment houses, and chic boutiques. Many of the bigger hotels, some dating from the 19th century, claim part of the beach for the private use of their guests. But public areas also exist. Above the harbor, the old town of Cannes sits on Suquet Hill, where you'll see a 14th-century tower, the **Tour du Suquet,** which the English dubbed "the Lord's Tower."

Nearby is the **Musée de la Castre** 𝒜, in the Château de la Castre, Le Suquet (✆ **04-93-38-55-26**). It contains paintings, sculpture, and works of decorative art. The ethnography section includes objects from all over, including Peruvian and Maya pottery. It also maintains a gallery devoted to relics of Mediterranean civilizations, from the Greeks to the Romans, from the Cypriots to the Egyptians. Five rooms hold

---

Seeing Cannes from a Petit Train

One of the best ways to get your bearings in Cannes is to climb aboard a white-sided *Petit Train touristique de Cannes.* The diesel-powered vehicles roll through the streets on rubber tires. They operate every day from 9:30am to between 7 and 11pm, depending on the season (there's no service in Nov). Two itineraries are offered: For views of glittery modern Cannes, board the train at a designated spot in front of either of the town's two casinos for a ride along La Croisette and its side streets. For a ride through the narrow streets of Vieux Cannes (Le Suquet), board the train at a clearly designated site on the seaward side of La Croisette, opposite the Hôtel Majestique. Both tours depart every hour. They last around 45 minutes, depending on traffic, and cost 5€ to 6€ ($6.50–$7.80) for adults, 2.50€ to 3€ ($3.25–$3.90) for children under 10, depending on the tour. (The tour of the old town is the less expensive.) A combination ticket to both tours (good on separate days, if you prefer) costs 8€ ($10) for adults, 5€ ($6.50) for children under 10. For details, call ✆ **06-14-09-49-39.**

Cannes

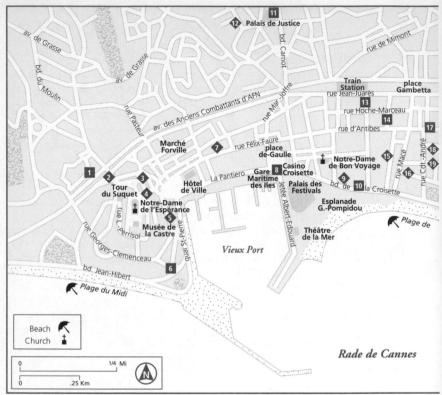

19th-century paintings. The museum is open June to August Tuesday to Sunday 10am to 1pm and 3 to 7pm; April, May, and September Tuesday to Sunday 10am to 1pm and 2 to 6pm; and October to March Tuesday to Sunday 10am to 1pm and 2 to 5pm. Admission is 3€ ($3.90). Admission is free the first Sunday of every month.

Though nobody plans a trip to Cannes to see churches, the city does contain some worthy examples. The largest and most prominent is **Notre-Dame de Bon Voyage,** square Mérimée, near the Palais des Festivals; it was built in a faux Gothic style in the late 19th century. The most historic church, **Notre-Dame de l'Espérance,** place de la Castre (*©* **04-93-99-55-07**), was built between 1521 and 1627 and combines both Gothic and Renaissance elements. The town's most unusual church is the **Eglise Orthodoxe Russe St-Michel Archange,** 36–40 bd. Alexandre-III (*©* **04-93-43-00-28**), built in 1894 through the efforts of Alexandra Skripytzine, a Russian in exile; it's capped with a cerulean-blue onion dome and a gilded triple cross. Be warned that it's usually locked, except for services on Saturday at 5pm and Sunday between 9:30am and noon.

A DAY AT THE BEACH
Beachgoing in Cannes has more to do with exhibitionism and voyeurism than with actual swimming.

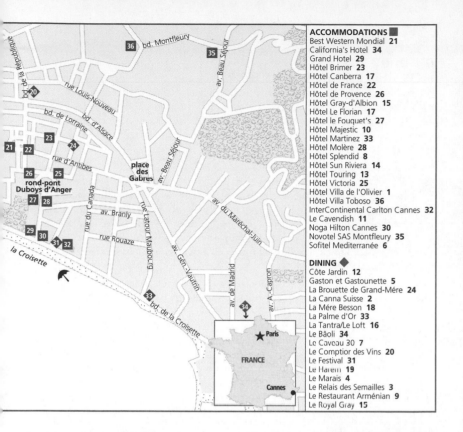

Plage de la Croisette extends between the Vieux Port and the Port Canto. Though the beaches along this billion-dollar stretch of sand aren't in the strictest sense private, they're *payante,* meaning entrance costs 15€ to 22€ ($20–$29). You don't need to be a guest of the Noga Hilton, Martinez, Carlton, or Majestic to use the beaches associated with those hotels, though if you are you'll usually get a 50% discount. A wooden barricade that stops close to the sea separates each beach from its neighbors, making it easy for you to stroll from one to another.

Why should you pay a fee at all? Well, it includes a full day's use of a mattress, a chaise longue (the seafront isn't sandy or even soft, but covered with pebbles and dark-gray shingles), and a parasol, as well as easy access to freshwater showers and kiosks selling beverages. You can also dine at outdoor restaurants where no one minds if you appear in your swimsuit.

For nostalgia's sake, our favorite beach is the one associated with the **Carlton** (see "Where to Stay," below)—it was the first beach we went to, as teenagers, in Cannes. The merits of each of the 20 or so beaches vary daily depending on the crowd. And because every beach allows topless bathing (keep your bottom covered), you're likely to find the same forms of décolletage along the entire strip.

Looking for a free public beach where you'll have to survive without renting chaises or parasols? Head for **Plage du Midi,** sometimes called Midi Plage, just west of the

Vieux Port (no phone), or **Plage Gazagnaire,** just east of the Port Canto (no phone). Here you'll find families with children and lots of caravan-type vehicles parked nearby.

OUTDOOR PURSUITS

BICYCLING & MOTOR-SCOOTERING   Despite the roaring traffic, the flat landscapes between Cannes and satellite resorts like La Napoule are well suited for riding a bike or motor scooter. At **Cycles Daniel,** 2 rue du Pont Romain (© **04-93-99-90-30**), *vélos tout terrain* (mountain bikes) cost 13€ ($17) a day. Motorized bikes and scooters cost 28€ ($36) per day; renters must be at least 14 years old. For larger scooters, you must present a valid driver's license. Another purveyor of bikes is **Mistral Location,** 4 rue Georges Clemenceau (© **04-93-99-25-25**), which charges 12€ ($16) per day.

BOATING   Several companies rent boats of any size, with or without a crew, for a day, a week, or a month. An outfit known for short-term rentals of small craft, including motorboats, sailboats, and canoes, is **Elco Marine,** 110 bd. du Midi (© **04-93-47-12-62**). For larger boats, including motor-driven and sailing yachts and craft suitable for deep-sea fishing, try **International Yacht Charter** 45 La Croisette (© **04-92-98-39-93**).

GOLF   One of the region's most challenging courses, **Country-Club de Cannes-Mougins,** 175 av. du Golf, route d'Antibes, Mougins (© **04-93-75-79-13**), 6.5km (4 miles) north of Cannes, is a 1976 reconfiguration by Dye & Ellis of a 1920s-era course. Noted for the olive trees and cypresses that adorn the flat terrain, it has many water hazards and technical challenges. Since 1981, the par-72 course has played host to the Cannes-Mougins Open, a stop on the PGA European Tour. The course is open to anyone (with proof of handicap) willing to pay greens fees of 100€ ($130) per person. An electric golf cart rents for 45€ ($59), golf clubs for 35€ ($46). Reservations are recommended.

SWIMMING   Cannes probably has more privately owned swimming outdoor pools, per capita, than anywhere else in France. If your hotel doesn't have one, consider an excursion to the **Piscine Pierre de Coubertin,** avenue P. de Coubertin (© **04-93-47-12-94**). Its length of almost 23m (75 ft.) makes this outdoor pool ideal for swimming laps. Because it's used for a variety of civic functions, including practices for local swim teams, hours are limited, so call ahead. Entrance costs 2.50€ ($3.25) for adults, 1.20€ ($1.55) for children 3 to 15.

TENNIS   Some resorts have their own courts. The city of Cannes also maintains a half-dozen courts (one made from synthetic resins, five clay-topped); you'll pay 10€ to 15€ ($13–$20) per hour, depending on the court and the time you want to play, plus 4€ ($4.60) per hour for lighting. They're at **ASLM Tennis Municipal de la Bastide,** 220 av. Francis Tonner, 06400 Cannes (© **04-93-47-29-33**). If those courts are already taken, **ASLM Tennis Municipal Aérodrome,** Aérodrome de Cannes Mandelieu, 06400 Cannes (© **04-93-47-29-33**), also maintained by the municipality, charges the same rates for its five clay-topped courts.

SHOPPING

Cannes competes more successfully than many of its neighbors in a highly commercial blend of resort-style leisure, luxury glamour, and media glitz. So you're likely to find branch outlets of virtually every stylish Paris retailer.

Ferrying to the Iles de Lérins

Across the bay from Cannes, the Lérins Islands are the major excursion from the port. Ferries depart every half-hour from 7:30am to 30 minutes before sundown. The largest of the ferry companies in Cannes is **Compagnies Estérel-Chanteclair,** 1 Port de Cannes (© **04-93-39-11-82).** Competitors include **Cie Horizon IV,** CQ (© **04-92-98-71-36); Compagnie Maritime Cannoise,** Quai St. Pierre (© **04-93-38-29-92);** and **Trans-Côte d'Azur,** quai St-Pierre (© **04-92-98-71-30).** Departures are from the Gare Maritime des Iles in Cannes. Round-trip fare is 12€ ($16) for adults, 6€ ($7.80) for children 5 to 10, and free for children under 5

Ile Ste-Marguerite   The first island is named after St. Honorat's sister, Ste. Marguerite, who lived here with a group of nuns in the 5th century. Today it is a youth center whose members (when they aren't sailing and diving) are dedicated to the restoration of the fort. From the dock where the boat lands, you can stroll along the island (signs point the way) to the **Fort de l'Ile,** built by Spanish troops from 1635 to 1637. Below the hill is the 1st-century-B.C. Roman town where the unlucky man immortalized in *The Man in the Iron Mask* was imprisoned.

One of French history's most perplexing mysteries is the identity of the man who allegedly wore the *masque du fer,* a prisoner of Louis XIV who arrived at Ste-Marguerite in 1698. Dumas popularized the legend that he was a brother of Louis XIV, and it has even been suggested that the prisoner and a mysterious woman had a son who went to Corsica and "founded" the Bonaparte family. However, the most common theory is that the prisoner was a servant of the superintendent, Fouquet, named Eustache Dauger. He might have earned his fate by aiding Fouquet in embezzling the king's treasury. At any rate, he died in the Bastille in Paris in 1703.

You can visit his cell at Ste-Marguerite, where it seems that every visitor has written his or her name. As you stand listening to the sound of the sea, you realize what a forlorn outpost this was.

Musée de la Mer, Fort Royal (© **04-93-38-55-26),** traces the history of the island, displaying artifacts of Ligurian, Roman, and Arab civilizations, plus the remains discovered by excavations, including paintings, mosaics, and ceramics. The museum is open April to September Tuesday to Sunday 10:30am to 1:15pm and 2:15 to 5:45pm; October to March Tuesday to Sunday 10:30am to 1:15pm and 2:15 to 4:45pm. Admission is 3€ ($3.90) for adults, free for students and children under 18.

Ile St-Honorat   Only a mile long, but richer in history than any of its sibling islands, the Ile St-Honorat is the site of a working monastery whose origins go back to the 5th century. Today the **Abbaye de St-Honorat,** les Iles de Lérins, 06400 Cannes (© **04-92-99-54-00),** boasts a combination of medieval ruins and early-20th-century ecclesiastical buildings, inhabited by a permanent community of about 30 Cistercian monks. If space is available, outsiders can visit, for prayer and meditation only, and spend the night. However, most visitors come to wander through the pine forests on the island's western side and sun themselves on its beaches.

Every big-name designer you can think of (Saint Laurent, Rykiel, Hermès) as well as big-name designers you've never heard of (Claude Bonucci, Basile, and Durrani) are here—but, more important, real-people shops (resale shops for gently worn star-studded castoffs, two flea markets for fun junk, and a fruit, flower, and vegetable market) thrive.

ANTIQUES   In the Palais de Festivals on La Croisette, Cannes stages one of France's most prestigious **antiques salons** in mid-July and late December or early January. Its organizers refuse to include low- or even middle-bracket merchandise. This is serious, with lots of 18th- and early-19th-century merchandise. Admission is 10€ ($13). Shipping services are available. For dates and information, contact the **Salon des Antiquaires de Cannes,** 34 Rue de L'Eglise, 75015 Paris (© **01-44-26-26-26**).

Looking for top-notch antiques dealers whose merchandise will wow you? One of the city's most noteworthy is **Hubert Herpin,** 20 rue Macé (© **04-93-39-56-18**). This store carries a wide selection of marble statues, marquetry, and 18th- and 19th-century furniture.

BOOKS   A year-round bookstore, **Ciné-Folie,** 14 rue des Frères Pradignac (© **04-93-39-22-99**), is devoted entirely to films. It's called *La Boutique du Cinema.* The outlet is the finest film bookstore in the south of France and also sells vintage film stills and movie posters.

CHOCOLATE & JELLIED FRUITS   Several famous chocolatiers keep chocolate lovers in Cannes happy. Try **Maiffret,** 31 rue d'Antibes (© **04-93-39-08-29**), but the local specialty is *fruits confits* (jellied fruits, also called crystallized fruits), which became the rage in the 1880s. Maiffret sells these, especially in summer, when the chocolates tend to melt. Pâtés and confits of fruit, some of which decorate cakes and tarts, are also sold. Look for the classic Provençal confection, *calissons,* crafted from almonds, a confit of melon, and sugar. A block away is **Chez Bruno,** 13 rue Hoche (© **04-93-39-26-63**). Opened in 1929 and maintained by a descendant of its founder, the shop is famous for *fruits confits* as well as its *marrons glacés* (glazed chestnuts), made fresh daily.

DEPARTMENT STORES   Near the train station in the heart of Cannes, **Galeries Lafayette** has a small branch at 6 rue du Maréchal-Foch (© **04-97-06-25-00**). It's noted for the upscale fashion in its carefully arranged interiors.

DESIGNER SHOPS   Most of the big names in fashion, for both men and women, line **promenade de la Croisette,** known as **La Croisette,** the main drag facing the sea. Among the most prestigious is **Dior,** 38 promenade de la Croisette (© **04-92-98-98-00**). The stores are in a row, stretching from the Hôtel Carlton almost to the Palais des Festivals, with the best names closest to the **Gray-d'Albion,** 38 rue des Ferbes (© **04-92-99-79-79**), which is both a mall and a hotel (how convenient). The stores in the Gray-d'Albion mall include **Hermès.** The two-section mall serves as a cut-through

---

⌒Fun Fact A Mammillary Tribute to a Courtesan
The twin cupolas of the InterContinental Carlton were modeled on the breasts of the most fabled local courtesan, **La Belle Otéro.** The hotel's main restaurant also carries her name.

from the primary expensive shopping street, La Croisette, to the less-expensive shopping street, **rue d'Antibes.**

FLEA MARKETS   Cannes has two regular flea markets. Casual, dusty, and increasingly filled with castaways from estate sales, the **Marché Forville,** conducted in the neighborhood of the same name, near the Palais des Festivals, is a stucco structure with a roof and a few arches but no sides. From Tuesday to Sunday, it's the fruit, vegetable, and flower market that supplies dozens of grand restaurants. Monday is *brocante* day, when the market fills with dealers selling everything from grandmère's dishes to bone-handled carving knives.

On Saturdays from 8am to 6pm, a somewhat disorganized and busy **flea market** takes place outdoors along the edges of the allée de la Liberté, across from the Palais des Festivals. Hours depend on the whims of whatever dealer happens to haul in a cache of merchandise, but it usually begins around 8am and runs out of steam by around 4:30pm. *Note:* Vendors at the two flea markets may or may not be the same.

FOOD   Of the many streets that will attract with rustic and authentic Provençal allure, the most appealing, and the one lined with the greatest density of emporiums selling wine, olives, herbs, and oils, is the **rue Meynadier.**

A charmingly old-fashioned shop, **Cannolive,** 16–20 rue Vénizelos (© **04-93-39-08-19**), is owned by the Raynaud family, which founded the place in 1880. It sells Provençal olives and their by-products—*tapenades* (purées) that connoisseurs refer to as "Provençal caviar," black "olives de Nice," and green "olives de Provence," as well as three grades of olive oil from regional producers. Oils and food products are dispensed from no. 16, but gift items (fabrics, porcelain, and Provençal souvenirs) are sold next door.

MARKETS   At the edge of the Quartier Suquet, the **Marché Forville** is the town's primary fruit, flower, and vegetable market. On Monday it's a *brocante* market. See "Flea Markets," above.

PERFUME   The best shop is **Bouteille,** 59 rue d'Antibes (© **04-93-39-05-16**), also the most expensive. Its prices are high because it stocks more brands, has a wider selection, and gives away occasional samples. A selection of other shops dots rue d'Antibes. Any might feature your favorite fragrance in a promotional deal. A final option for the reasonably priced perfumes is the boutique associated with the Hôtel Grayd'Albion.

WHERE TO STAY
VERY EXPENSIVE
Hôtel Majestic 🖈🖈🖈   At the west end of La Croisette, the Majestic stands for glamour and has done so since 1926. Like the InterContinental Carlton (see below), it is a favorite with celebs during the annual film festival. Constructed around an overscale front patio, the hotel opens directly onto the esplanade and the sea. Inside, the setting is one of marble, crystal chandeliers, Oriental carpets, Louis XV silk furniture, and potted palms. The guest rooms are furnished with more of the same. All rooms are fitted with bedside controls and luxury amenities; the most special of the lot are 16 sea-view units with private terraces. The spacious, bright corner accommodations offer the best value. Bathrooms are sumptuous, with deluxe toiletries.

14 bd. de la Croisette, 06407 Cannes. © **04-92-98-77-00.** Fax 04-92-98-77-60. 287 units. 200€–900€ ($260–$1,170) double; 800€–4,590€ ($1,040–$5,967) suite. AE, DC, MC, V. Parking 33€. **Amenities:** 2 restaurants; bar; outdoor pool; salon; 24-hr. room service; babysitting; laundry service; dry cleaning. *In room:* A/C, TV, dataport, minibar, hair dryer, safe.

Hôtel Martinez 𝒜𝒜   Although it's a bit less appealing than the Carlton, this is a popular convention hotel and a desirable property for the individual. When the Art Deco hotel was built in the 1930s, it rivaled any other lodging along the coast in sheer size. Over the years, however, it fell into disrepair. But in 1982, the Concorde chain returned the hotel and its restaurants to their former luster, and today it competes with the Noga Hilton. The aim of the decor was a Roaring Twenties style, and all units boast full marble bathrooms, wood furnishings, tasteful carpets, quality mattresses, and pastel fabrics. It has a private beach, one of the finest restaurants in Cannes (La Palme d'Or), and a water-skiing school. Called a hotel within a hotel, the penthouse floor has become the chicest place to stay at the resort, featuring 11 suites, the most sought-after in town following a massive restyling.

73 bd. de la Croisette, 06406 Cannes. ℂ **04-92-98-73-00.** Fax 04-93-39-67-82. www.hotel-martinez.com. 415 units. 260€–850€ ($338–$1,105) double; from 800€ ($1,040) suite. AE, DC, MC, V. Parking 28€ ($32). **Amenities:** 3 summer restaurants (see "Where to Dine," below); 2 winter restaurants; bar; private beach; outdoor pool; 7 tennis courts nearby; spa; fitness center; sauna; 24-hr. room service; babysitting; laundry service; dry cleaning; nonsmoking rooms; limited-mobility rooms. In room: A/C, TV, dataport, minibar, hair dryer, safe.

InterContinental Carlton Cannes 𝒜𝒜𝒜   Cynics say that one of the most amusing sights in Cannes is the view from under the grand gate of the Carlton. Here you'll see vehicles of every description dropping off huge amounts of baggage and numbers of fashionable (and sometimes not-so-fashionable) guests. It's the epitome of luxury and has become such a part of the city's heartbeat that to ignore it would be to miss the resort's spirit. The twin gray domes at either end of the facade are often the first things recognized by starlets planning their grand entrances, grand exits, and grand scenes in the hotel's public and private rooms.

Built in 1912, the Carlton once attracted the most prominent members of Europe's *haut monde.* Today the hotel is more democratic, booking lots of conventions and motor-coach tour groups; however, in summer (especially during the film festival) the public rooms still fill with all the voyeuristic and exhibitionistic fervor that seems so much a part of the Riviera. Guest rooms are plush and a bit airier than you might expect. The most spacious rooms are in the west wing, and many upper-floor rooms open onto waterfront balconies. The large bathrooms are in the grand *luxe* style.

58 bd. de la Croisette, 06400 Cannes. ℂ **04-93-06-40-06.** Fax 04-93-06-40-25. http://cannes.interconti.com. 338 units. 200€–1,000€ ($260–$1,300) double; from 800€ ($1,040) suite. AE, DC, MC, V. Parking 30€ ($39). **Amenities:** 3 summer restaurants; 1 winter restaurant; 2 bars; health club; sauna; business center; 24-hr. room service; laundry service; dry cleaning; nonsmoking rooms; limited-mobility rooms. In room: A/C, TV, dataport, minibar, hair dryer, safe.

Noga Hilton Cannes 𝒜   This hotel is far superior to most Hiltons in the States. The owners procured one of Cannes's most sought-after sites, the lot occupied by the since-demolished Palais des Festivals. The design of the six-story building, with massive amounts of exposed glass, recalls the best aspects of its older sibling, the Noga Hilton in Geneva. You register in a soaring lobby sheathed with white marble. The soundproof guest rooms are stylish, with balconies, bedside controls, luxury beds, tub/shower combinations, and various electronic accessories; rates vary with the sea view. Many of the appointments evoke the 1930s. Prestige Rooms have large beds and elegant carpeting. Less desirable units are called Cityview and Gardenview rooms.

50 bd. de la Croisette, 06414 Cannes. ℂ **800/445-8667** in the U.S. and Canada, or 04-92-99-70-00. Fax 04-92-99-70-11. www.hiltoncannes.com. 234 units. 159€–699€ ($207–$909) double; 349€–969€ ($454–$1,260) suite. AE, DC, MC, V. **Amenities:** Restaurant; bar; casino; outdoor rooftop pool; shopping arcade; 24-hr. room service; babysit-

ting; laundry service; dry cleaning; nonsmoking rooms; limited-mobility rooms. *In room:* A/C, TV, dataport, minibar, coffeemaker, hair dryer, safe.

EXPENSIVE

Grand Hôtel 𝒢 This hotel is graced with a garden with tall date palms and a lawn sweeping down to the waterfront esplanade. A renovated structure of glass and marble, it is part of a complex of adjoining apartment-house wings and encircling boutiques. Eleven floors of rooms (with wall-to-wall picture windows) open onto tile terraces. Vibrant colors are used throughout: sea blue, olive, sunburst red, and banana. The bathrooms are lined with colored checkerboard tiles and have matching towels and rows of decorative bottles. Those rooms with sea views are the most expensive; the hotel's private beach is below.

45 bd. de la Croisette, 06140 Cannes. ℂ **04-93-38-15-45.** Fax 04-93-68-97-45. www.grand-hotel-cannes.com. 78 units. 122€–267€ ($159–$347) double. AE, MC, V. Parking 12€ ($16). Closed Nov–Dec 14. **Amenities:** Restaurant; bar; outdoor pool; limited room service; babysitting; laundry service; dry cleaning. *In room:* A/C, TV, minibar, hair dryer.

Hôtel Gray-d'Albion 𝒢𝒢 The smallest of the major hotels isn't on La Croisette. It occupies a mostly contemporary, not-particularly historic premise, and enjoys a four-star rating from the French government. Although it cannot compete on many levels with the larger, better-accessorized palace hotels (the Carlton, the Majestic) with which it is often compared, it maintains a conservative, somewhat staid image as solid, dependable, and reliable. Now part of the Lucien Barrière chain, it's uncontroversial, but nonetheless completely respectable. Groups form a large part of its clientele, but it also caters to the individual. The medium-size rooms blend contemporary and traditional furnishings; the generous-size bathrooms have tub/shower combinations. Each unit has a balcony, but the views aren't notable, except from the eighth and ninth floors, which overlook the Mediterranean.

38 rue des Serbes, 06400 Cannes. ℂ **04-92-99-79-79.** Fax 04-93-99-26-10. www.lucienbarriere.com. 200 units. 160€–665€ ($208–$865) double; 645€–1,400€ ($839–$1,820) suite. AE, DC, MC, V. **Amenities:** Restaurant; bar; salon; 24-hr. room service in summer (limited in winter); babysitting; laundry service; dry cleaning; nonsmoking rooms; limited-mobility rooms. *In room:* A/C, TV, dataport, minibar, hair dryer, safe.

Novotel SAS Montfleury 𝒢𝒢 This is a classical, contemporary hotel that has carved out a good market for itself among independent travelers, although it can't compete with the big guns reviewed above. Although it seems distant from the crush of Cannes, it's actually only a short but winding drive away. The modern palace shares a 4-hectare (10-acre) park with a sports complex. The open-air curved outdoor pool is surrounded by palms. The guest rooms are stylishly filled with all the modern conveniences, including bedside controls, and well-appointed bathrooms.

25 av. Beauséjour, 06400 Cannes. ℂ **04-93-68-86-86.** Fax 04-93-68-87-87. www.accorhotels.com. 182 units. 129€–216€ ($168–$281) double. AE, DC, MC, V. From Cannes, follow the signs to Montfleury or the blue-and-white signs to the Novotel Montfleury. **Amenities:** Restaurant; bar; outdoor pool; limited room service; babysitting; laundry service; dry cleaning. *In room:* A/C, TV, minibar, hair dryer, safe.

Sofitel Méditerranée 𝒢𝒢 On the harborfront of Cannes, with views that extend over some of the most expensive private yachts in the Mediterranean, this is a seven-story chain hotel. It has surrounding balconies and an open-air lounge on its top floor. A remake of an older hotel, it has a well-designed, bright interior, offering a well-trained staff and contemporary-looking upscale bedrooms, some with views over the sea, and well-designed bathrooms.

2 bd. Jean-Hibert, 06400 Cannes. ℂ 800/221-4542 in the U.S., or 04-92-99-73-00. Fax 04-92-99-73-13. www.sofitel. com. 149 units. 150€–222€ ($195–$289) double; from 529€ ($688) suite. Rates include breakfast. AE, DC, MC, V. Parking 17€ ($22). Bus: 1. **Amenities:** Restaurant; bar, lounge; outdoor pool; 24-hr. room service; laundry service; dry cleaning. *In room:* A/C, TV, minibar, hair dryer, safe.

MODERATE

Best Western Mondial   This modern hotel on a commercial street, with stores on its lower floor, is about a 3-minute walk from the beach. Three quarters of its rooms have views of the water, and the others overlook the mountains and a street. The soft Devonshire-cream facade has a few small balconies. The attractive rooms are the draw here, with matching fabrics for the comfortable beds and draperies, and sliding mirror doors on wardrobes. Bathrooms, though small, are neatly organized.

77 rue d'Antibes and 1 rue Teïsseire, 06407 Cannes. ℂ 800/43-HOTELS or 04-93-68-70-00. Fax 04-93-99-39-11. www.bestwestern.com. 49 units. 120€–160€ ($156–$208) double; 230€–300€ ($299–$390) suite. AE, DC, MC, V. **Amenities:** Babysitting; laundry service; dry cleaning. *In room:* A/C, TV, minibar, hair dryer, safe.

California's Hôtel 🍿🍿 *Finds*   Although you may not live exactly like a movie star, you can come close at this boutique hotel, a real charmer set in a sweet-scented garden with lemon and olive trees. An outdoor pool is available if you don't want to take the free shuttle to the beach, lying only 45m (150 ft.) away. The hotel also offers boat tours of offshore islands, plus free van rides around town. Handmade furniture, paintings from a local artist, and the tasteful Pierre Frey fabrics evoke a certain kind of charm. Bathrooms are beautifully designed with tub and shower. Breakfast is served; for other meals many restaurants are nearby.

8 Traverse Alexandre-III, 06400 Cannes. ℂ 04-93-94-12-21. Fax 04-93-43-55-17. www.hotel-californias.com. 33 units. 101€–300€ ($131–$390) double. 31€ ($40) extra person. AE, DC, MC, V. Parking: 12€ ($16). **Amenities:** Breakfast room; pool; fitness center. *In room:* TV.

Hôtel Brimer   On a quiet street about 4 blocks from the seafront, this small hotel occupies the second floor of a four-story building constructed in the 1970s. In 1998, it was renovated and upgraded by owner Brice Guëlle, who runs a tight ship. Bedrooms are well maintained, are furnished unpretentiously but comfortably, and are relatively affordable in high-priced Cannes. Breakfast is the only meal served, although there are many bistros in the neighborhood.

9 rue Jean Daumas, 06400 Cannes. ℂ 04-93-38-62-81. Fax 04-93-39-49-71. www.brimer.fr. 15 units. 120€–160€ ($156–$208) double. AE, DC, MC, V. Parking free on street. **Amenities:** Laundry service; dry cleaning. *In room:* TV, minibar, hair dryer.

Hôtel Canberra *Finds*   This hotel occupies a marvelous location between the deluxe Noga Hilton and the Palais des Festivals, but it seems little known. It's often booked during the festival by independent producers hoping to hit the big time. The rooms are well maintained, a blend of traditional and modern; those with southern exposure are sunnier and cost more. Size ranges from small to medium, but each comes with a good mattress. Breakfast is the only meal served, and limited parking is available by the hotel's small garden.

120 rue d'Antibes, 06400 Cannes. ℂ 04-97-06-95-00. Fax 04-92-98-03-47. www.hotels-ocre-azur.com. 41 units. 121€–199€ ($157–$259) double; 183€–267€ ($238–$347) suite. AE, DC, MC, V. Parking 16€ ($21). **Amenities:** Bar; limited room service; babysitting; laundry service; dry cleaning. *In room:* A/C, TV, minibar.

Hôtel le Fouquet's 🍿 *Finds*   This intimate lodging draws a discreet clientele, often from Paris, who'd never think of patronizing the grand hotels. Riviera French in design and decor, it's several blocks from the beach. Each of the cozy guest rooms, renovated in 2004, is outfitted just a bit differently from its neighbor. They're decorated in bold Provençal colors of ocher and blue, and have contemporary furniture. The owner is often on-site, making the hotel feel like an intimate B&B. Bathrooms, though small, are efficiently organized, with showers and tubs.

2 rond-point Duboys-d'Angers, 06400 Cannes. ☎ **04-92-59-25-00.** Fax 04-92-98-03-39. www.le-fouquets.com. 10 units. 100€–280€ ($130–$364) double. AE, DC, MC, V. Parking 12€ ($16). Closed Nov to mid-Mar. Bus: 1. **Amenities:** Limited room service; babysitting; laundry service; dry cleaning; nonsmoking rooms. *In room:* A/C, TV, dataport, minibar, hair dryer, safe.

Hôtel Splendid 👍 *(Value* Opened in 1871, and widely renovated in 2004, this is a favorite of scholars, politicians, actors, and musicians. The ornate white building with wrought-iron accents looks out onto the sea, the old port, and a park. The rooms boast antique furniture and paintings; about 15 have kitchenettes. Each comes with a good bed and a small but efficient bathroom with a combination tub/shower. The more expensive rooms have sea views.

4–6 Rue Félix-Faure, 06400 Cannes. ☎ **04-97-06-22-22.** Fax 04-93-99-55-02. www.splendid-hotel-cannes.fr. 62 units. 124€–254€ ($161–$330) double. Rates include breakfast. AE, MC, V. Parking 15€ ($20). **Amenities:** Limited room service; babysitting; nonsmoking rooms; limited-mobility rooms. *In room:* A/C, TV, dataport, hair dryer, safe.

Hôtel Sun Riviera 👍 This genteel, polite hotel is less well known than the block-buster mega-hotels nearby. But the fact that it's a demure, less-well-known choice, with relatively reasonable prices and a limited number of amenities, almost guarantees a healthy roster of bookings throughout the summer and throughout the film festival. Cheerful, stylish, and welcoming, with an image that's deliberately set a notch or two below what you might have expected at, say, the Carlton or the Majestic, it offers a discreetly opulent decor in the public rooms, and medium-size bedrooms that are comfortably outfitted with conservative good taste. It's set in the heart of Cannes, near most of the important shops and downtown bars and restaurants.

138 rue d'Antibes, 06400 Antibes. ☎ **04-93-06-77-77.** Fax 04-93-38-31-10. 40 units. 180€–250€ ($234–$325) double; from 425€ ($553) suite. AE, DC, MC, V. **Amenities:** Bar; outdoor pool; babysitting; laundry service; dry cleaning. *In room:* A/C, TV, minibar, hair dryer.

Hôtel Victoria 👍 The Victoria, a stylish modern hotel renovated in 2005, offers accommodations with period reproductions and refrigerators. Nearly half the rooms have balconies overlooking a small park and the hotel outdoor pool. The accommodations facing the park cost a little more but are worth it. In all units, silk bedspreads, padded headboards, and quality mattresses create a boudoir feel. Each unit has a modern tiled bathroom with a shower or tub/shower combination. After a day on the beach, guests congregate in the paneled bar and sink comfortably into couches and armchairs.

Rond-point Duboys-d'Angers, 06400 Cannes. ☎ **04-92-59-40-00.** Fax 04-93-38-03-91. www.hotel-victoria-cannes.com. 25 units. 100€–250€ ($130–$325) double. AE, DC, MC, V. Parking 17€ ($22). Closed late Nov to Dec. **Amenities:** Bar; outdoor pool; babysitting; laundry service; dry cleaning; nonsmoking rooms. *In room:* A/C, TV, dataport, minibar, hair dryer, safe.

Hôtel Villa de l'Olivier *(Finds* Charming and personal, this is a hideaway with a low-key management style. In the 1930s, it was a private villa; in the 1960s it became a hotel, with a wing extending deep into its garden. Today, you'll find buildings with lots of glass overlooking a kidney-shaped outdoor pool, and decor combining the French colonial tropics with the romantic late 19th century and Provence. Rooms have upholstered walls, each in a different color and pattern, and lots of Provençal accessories. Bathrooms come in a variety of sizes, each with a combination tub/shower.

5 rue des Tambourinaires, 06400 Cannes. (C) 04-93-39-53-28. Fax 04-93-39-55-85. www.hotelolivier.com. 24 units. 90€–135€ ($117–$175) double; 250€ ($325) suite. AE, DC, MC, V. Parking 10€ ($13). Closed Nov 22–Dec 27. **Amenities:** Bar; outdoor pool; limited room service; laundry service; dry cleaning; nonsmoking rooms. *In room:* A/C, TV, dataport, hair dryer.

Le Cavendish   Originally an 1897 private residence, this self-proclaimed "boutique hotel" opened its doors in 2001 after an exhaustive renovation. The only parts of the hotel not subject to this renovation were the elevator, the marble stairways, and the facade (a historical monument), creating a feel of updated antiquity. Despite the old-fashioned decoration, this hotel feels like home, replete with a lounge that doubles as a breakfast room and a bar, a salon, and an accommodating reception desk. The rooms retain their traditional charm, but have been furnished with modern goodies such as air-conditioning and TV with pay movies. Each comes with a tiled bathroom containing tub and shower.

11 Boulevard Carnot, 06400 Cannes. (C) **04-97-06-26-00.** Fax 04-97-06-26-01. www.cavendish-cannes.com. 34 units. 160€–295€ ($208–$384) double. AE, DC, MC, V. Parking: 18€ ($23). **Amenities:** Lounge/bar; salon. *In room:* A/C, TV, dataport, minibar, safe.

INEXPENSIVE

Hôtel de France ⭐ *(Value)*   This centrally located hotel is 2 blocks from the sea. This is one of the best of the affordable hotels in Cannes. The rooms are functional but well maintained and reasonably comfortable, with good beds. You can sunbathe on the rooftop.

85 rue d'Antibes, 06400 Cannes. (C) **04-93-06-54-54.** Fax 04-93-68-53-43. www.h-de-france.com. 33 units. 84€–143€ ($109–$186) double; 107€–195€ ($139–$254) suite. AE, DC, MC, V. Closed Nov 20–Dec 25. **Amenities:** Bar; lounge; babysitting; laundry service; dry cleaning. *In room:* A/C, TV, dataport, hair dryer, minibar (in some), safe.

Hôtel de Provence *(Value)*   Built in the 1930s, this hotel is small and unpretentious— a contrast to the intensely stylish, larger hotels with which it competes. Most of the rooms have private balconies, and many overlook the shrubs and palms of the hotel's walled garden. Guest rooms show their age but are still comfortable, and for Cannes this is a remarkable bargain. Most of the bathrooms are roomy, and many have tub/shower combinations. In warm weather, breakfast is served under the flowers of an arbor.

9 rue Molière, 06400 Cannes. (C) **04-93-38-44-35.** Fax 04-93-39-63-14. www.hotel-de-provence.com. 30 units. 71€–101€ ($92–$131) double. AE, MC, V. Parking 13€ ($17). Closed mid-Nov to mid-Dec. **Amenities:** Bar; limited room service; laundry service; dry cleaning. *In room:* A/C, TV, dataport, minibar, hair dryer, safe.

Hôtel Le Florian   This hotel is on a busy but narrow, densely commercial street that leads directly into La Croisette, near the beach. Three generations of the Giordano family have maintained it since the 1950s. Basic but comfortable, most rooms are rather small, Provençal in their styling and decors that date from 2004, but have renovated plumbing. Bathrooms are compact, with showers. Breakfast is the only meal available.

8 rue Commandant-André, 06400 Cannes. (C) **04-93-39-24-82.** Fax 04-92-99-18-30. 32 units. 48€–75€ ($62–$98) double. AE, MC, V. Parking 15€ ($20) nearby. Closed Dec to mid-Jan. Bus: 1. *In room:* A/C, TV, hair dryer.

Hôtel Molière ⭐ *(Finds)*   Although it dates from around 1990, this hotel gives the distinct impression that it's one of the solidly established old-timers in a town loaded with venerable competitors. The hotel lies just 100m (328 ft.) from the Croisette; your approach will be through a long, verdant garden studded with cypresses and flowering shrubs, in which tables and chairs are set out for gossip and contemplation. The neighborhood it occupies is quieter than you expect, just behind both the Noga Hilton and the Carlton. Bedrooms are outfitted with lots of fabric, in tones of champagne, pink, and, in some cases, teal blue, giving an overall impression of well-upholstered comfort without a lot of decorative flair. Staff works hard and is generally polite and cooperative.

5–7 rue Molière, 06400 Cannes. ℂ **04-93-38-16-16.** Fax 04-93-68-29-57. www.hotel-moliere.com. 24 units. 80€–124€ ($104–$161) double; 116€–150€ ($151–$195) suite. Rates include breakfast. AE, MC, V. Closed Nov. **Amenities:** Limited room service. *In room:* A/C, TV, hair dryer, safe.

Hôtel Touring   Simple, sparsely decorated, and uncomplicated, this hotel occupies the premises of what was built around 1900 as a beaux arts–style villa, within about a minute's walk from the railway station and a 5-minute walk from the beach. Inside you'll find a wide assortment of rooms and room sizes, with the biggest having soaring ceilings and a sense of monumental spaciousness, and the smallest being cramped but with serviceable beds. This is the type of place where you'll do little more than sleep. Around seven of the rooms have tiny balconies overlooking the street. Expect a polite staff and a clientele that includes about 40% gay men and—to a lesser extent— women, many of whom are involved, in one way or the other, with aspects of the film industry.

11 rue Hoche, 06400 Cannes. ℂ **04-93-38-34-40.** Fax 04-93-38-73-34. 26 units. 61€–75€ ($79–$98) double. AE, MC, V. Closed 2 weeks in Nov–Dec. **Amenities:** Limited room service. *In room:* TV, fridge, hair dryer, safe.

Hôtel Villa Toboso   Adjacent to the largest sports center in Cannes, this former private villa is now a small, homey hotel. (In a romantic outburst, the former owner named it after the city in Spain where Cervantes's Don Quixote is said to have met Dulcinea.) The main lounge has a concert piano, and dancers from the neighboring Rosella Hightower School often frequent the place. Most of the personalized bedrooms have windows facing the garden, and some have terraces and kitchens. Bathrooms are well kept, each with tub or shower.

7 allée des Olivers (bd. Montfleury), 06400 Cannes. ℂ **04-93-38-20-05.** Fax 04-93-68-09-32. 15 units. 65€–135€ ($85–$176) double. AE, DC, V. Free parking. **Amenities:** Outdoor pool; limited room service; babysitting; laundry service; dry cleaning. *In room:* A/C, TV, hair dryer.

ON THE OUTSKIRTS

Four Seasons Provence at Terre Blanche ★★★ *Kids*   Inaugurated in May 2004, and set almost directly atop the dividing line between Provence and the Côte d'Azur, this is one of the newest and plushest resorts to open in southern France's recent history. The location is 32km (20 miles) north of the Cannes-Mandelieu airport. It's also the only resort in the region with two 18-hole golf courses, each designed by big-name golf designer, Wales-born Dave Thomas. Great efforts were made during its design to emulate one of the "perched villages" of medieval Provence. The site is owned by the "Bill Gates" of Germany, software mogul Dietmar Hopp, and managed by the top-notch luxury group Four Seasons. Service is superb and in 2005, after only 1 year in business, the most upscale of the resort's many restaurants earned its first Michelin star. The layout evokes an isolated cluster of masonry-sided villas, each painted ocher, each capped with a terra-cotta roof, and each interconnected across manicured lawns and gardens with undulating brick walkways. Villas are artfully decorated with airy postmodern furnishings vaguely influenced by the traditions of Provence, and each comes with a luxurious private bathroom with tub or shower. Even the smallest of the accommodations here is a suite suitable for up to four occupants. The largest is a full-blown private villa suitable for up to eight occupants. Come here for golf and all manner of outdoor sports, and/or use it as a jumping-off point for visits to the touristic and historic highlights of the surrounding region.

Domaine de Terre Blanche, 83440 Tourrettes. ② **04-94-39-36-00.** Fax 04-94-39-36-01. www.fourseasons.com/province. 115 suites. Suite for 2 200€–750€ ($260–$975); villas for occupancy by between 4 and 6 650€–9,900€ ($845–$12,870). AE, DC, MC, V. **Amenities:** 4 restaurants and bars; outdoor pools; 2 par-72 18-hole golf courses; spa and fitness villa; activity programs for children ages 6–12; 24-hr. room service; laundry service; dry cleaning. *In room:* A/C, TV, dataport, kitchenettes in some, minibar.

WHERE TO DINE
VERY EXPENSIVE
La Palme d'Or ⭐⭐⭐ MODERN FRENCH   Movie stars on the see-and-be-seen circuit head here during the film festival. It's a sophisticated rendezvous that serves some of the Riviera's finest hotel cuisine. The Taittinger family (of champagne fame) set out to establish a restaurant that could rival the competition—and succeeded. The result is this tawny-colored Art Deco marvel with bay windows, a winter-garden theme, and outdoor and enclosed terraces overlooking the outdoor pool, the sea, and La Croisette. Menu items change with the seasons but are likely to include warm foie gras with fondue of rhubarb; filets of fried red mullet with a beignet of potatoes, zucchini, and olive-cream sauce; or crayfish, clams, and squid marinated in peppered citrus sauce. A modernized version of a Niçoise staple includes three parts of a rabbit with rosemary sauce, fresh vegetables, and chick-pea rosettes. The most appealing dessert is wild strawberries from Carros with Grand Marnier–flavored *nage* and "cream sauce of frozen milk." The service is worldly without being stiff.

In the Hôtel Martinez, 73 bd. de la Croisette. ② **04-92-98-74-14.** Reservations required. Main courses 50€–90€ ($65–$117); fixed-price menu 55€–145€ ($72–$189) lunch Wed–Sat, 70€–145€ ($91–$189) dinner. AE, DC, MC, V. Tues–Sat 12:30–2pm and 8–10pm. Closed Apr 17–May 2 and Nov 5–Dec 5.

EXPENSIVE
Gaston et Gastounette ⭐ TRADITIONAL FRENCH   For views of the marina, this is your best bet. Located in the old port, it has a stucco exterior with oak moldings and big windows, and a sidewalk terrace surrounded by flowers. It serves two different bouillabaisses—a full-blown authentic stewpot prepared only for two diners at a time and a less daunting individualized version designed as an appetizer. Other choices include baby turbot with hollandaise sauce; John Dory filets with wild mushrooms; and an unusual Japanese-style broth flavored with monkfish, saltwater salmon, and chives. Profiteroles with hot chocolate sauce make a memorable dessert.

7 quai St-Pierre. ② **04-93-39-47-92.** Reservations required. Main courses 25€–50€ ($32–$65); fixed-price menu 24€–36€ ($31–$47) lunch, 36€ ($47) dinner. AE, DC, MC, V. Daily noon–2pm and 7–10:30pm. Closed Dec 15–24 and Jan 3–Jan 20.

Le Bâoli FRENCH/JAPANESE   One of the ultimate hipster joints in Cannes occupies a waterfront site outfitted like a temple garden in Thailand, complete with lavishly carved doorways, potted and in-ground palms, and hints of the Spice Trade scattered artfully in the out-of-the way corners. There's room here, either indoors or on a terrace overlooking the twinkling lights of La Croisette, for up to 350 diners at a time, and plenty of room after the end of the dinner service for a dance club venue where at least some of the clients might be dancing frenetically, in scantily clad giddiness, on the tables. Menu items include Japanese-inspired *teppanyaki* dishes prepared tableside by a samurai-style chef, as well as French dishes that feature tartare of tuna spread on toasts, crisp ravioli stuffed with shrimp, lobster in citrus sauce with a confit of tomatoes, filet of sea wolf with fennel, and a particularly elegant version of macaroni that's "perfumed" with an essence of lobster. Vegetarians appreciate the availability of such dishes as risotto with green asparagus, broccoli, and fava beans. The name of the restaurant, incidentally, derives from a well in Indonesia with reputed mystical powers.

Port Canto, bd. de la Croisette. ℂ **04-93-43-03-43.** Reservations recommended. Main courses 20€–45€ ($26–$59). AE, MC, V. Daily 8pm–midnight; disco (no cover charge) nightly midnight–4am. Closed Nov–Mar.

Le Festival ⚐ TRADITIONAL FRENCH   Screen idols and sex symbols flood the front terrace during the film festival. Almost every chair is emblazoned with the name of a movie star (who may or may not have occupied it), and tables are among the most sought-after in town. You can choose from the restaurant or the less formal grill room. Meals in the restaurant may include rack of lamb; *soupe des poissons* (fish soup) with *rouille;* simply grilled fresh fish (perhaps with aioli); bouillabaisse with lobster; pepper steak; and sea bass flambéed with fennel. Items in the grill are more in the style of an elegant brasserie, served a bit more rapidly and without as much fuss but at more or less the same prices. An appropriate finish in either section might be smooth peach melba.

52 bd. de la Croisette. ℂ **04-93-38-04-81.** Reservations required. Main courses 23€–29€ ($30–$38); fixed-price menu 35€–40€ ($46–$52). AE, DC, MC, V. July–Aug daily 9am–midnight; Sept–June daily 9am–11pm (until midnight during film festival). Closed Nov 18–Dec 28.

Le Royal Gray ⚐⚐ MODERN FRENCH   This restaurant manages to be both cozy and grand, replete with leather chairs, late-19th-century colors of brown and Bordeaux, and warm lighting. Alain Roy's cuisine is subtle and sometimes surprisingly simple, not aiming for the cutting-edge cerebrality of the place's more innovative competitors. Examples are terrines of foie gras, roasted filets of John Dory with olives and baby mushrooms, grilled filet of beef with béarnaise sauce, and roasted lobster with truffle-studded risotto. Dishes developed specifically by Mr. Roy, and unique to this comfortable and upscale restaurant include marinated strips of swordfish, each grilled with sesame oil; and freshwater *sander* cooked in a sheathin of pulverized olives. Dessert might be an old-fashioned and delicious version of crêpes Suzette.

In the Hôtel Gray-d'Albion, 38 rue des Serbes. ℂ **04-92-99-79-79.** Reservations required. Main courses 19€–33€ ($25–$43); fixed-price menus 42€ ($55). AE, DC, MC, V. Tues–Sat 12:30–2pm and 8–10:30pm.

Le Tantra/Le Loft FRENCH/ASIAN   An enduring favorite on the city's dine-and-then-dance circuit is this duplex-designed restaurant and disco on a side street that runs directly into La Croisette. On the street level, you'll find a Tao-inspired dining room, artfully simple and outfitted in a way that, if it wasn't filled with chattering and gossiping diners, might inspire meditation or a yoga class. Menu items focus on a French adaptation of Asian cuisine, with lots of sushi, tempura that includes a succulent combination of deep-fried banana slices, zucchini flowers, shrimp, and lobster; a Japanese-style steak of Kobe beef marinated in teriyaki, soy, and garlic; and deep-fried noodles dotted with chunks of shrimp and lobster. Be warned in advance that the 9pm seating is relatively calm; the 11pm seating is more linked to the disco madness going on upstairs. There, in a venue lined with plush sofas and exposed stone, you'll witness all the gyrations and mating games of a scantily clad crowd of all kinds of hipsters, from across the wide, wide range of social types inhabiting Cannes.

13 rue du Dr. Monod. ⓒ 04-93-39-40-39. Reservations recommended. Main courses 25€–45€ ($33–$59). AE, DC, MC, V. Daily 9–11pm; dance club (no cover charge) nightly 11pm–4am.

MODERATE

Côté Jardin ⚘ (*Value* FRENCH/PROVENÇAL   Set near the courthouse (*Palais de Justice*) in the heart of commercial, workaday Cannes, this restaurant attracts a loyal local crowd because of its unpretentious ambience and its reasonably priced and generous portions. You'll be offered three different choices as seating options: on the street level glassed-in veranda; at a table amid the flowering shrubs of the garden terrace; or upstairs within the cozy Provençal dining room. The best menu items include open-face ravioli filled with minced beef jowls; filets of red mullet with butter-flavored parsley sauce; a range of grilled and roasted meats and fish; and a dessert specialty of praline and pineapple tart with vanilla-flavored cream sauce.

12 av. St-Louis. ⓒ 04-93-38-60-28. Reservations required, especially in summer. Set-price menus 22€–36€ ($29–$47). AE, DC, MC, V. Mon–Sat noon–2pm and 7:30–10pm. Closed 2 weeks in early Jan.

La Brouette de Grand-Mère (*Finds* TRADITIONAL FRENCH   Few other restaurants in Cannes work so successfully at establishing a cozy testimonial to the culinary skills of old-fashioned French cooking. Owner Christian Bruno has revitalized the recipes that many of the chic and trendy residents of Cannes remember from their childhoods (or from an idealized version of their childhoods). Memories are evoked, in a way that Proust might have appreciated, through dishes that include a savory meat-and-potato stew known as *pot-au-feu*, roasted quail served with cream sauce, and chicken casserole cooked with beer. Traditional starters might include sausage links, terrines, and baked potatoes stuffed with smoked fish roe and served with a small glass of vodka. Set in the heart of town just behind the Noga Hilton and the InterContinental Carlton, the place offers two dining rooms, each outfitted in Art Deco style in tones of deep red and soft violet, and an outdoor terrace.

9 bis rue d'Oran. ⓒ 04-93-39-12-10. Reservations recommended. Fixed-price menu, including aperitif and unlimited wine, 33€ ($43). MC, V. Mon–Sat 7:30–11pm. Closed June 25–July 10 and Nov to mid-Dec.

La Canna Suisse ⚘ (*Finds* SWISS   Two sisters own this small 30-year-old restaurant in Vieux Cannes. Decked out like a Swiss chalet, it specializes in the cheese-based cuisine of Switzerland's high Alps. Because its cuisine is so suitable to cold weather dining, the restaurant wisely opts to close during the crush of Cannes' midsummer tourist season. It does great business the rest of the year. The menu features two kinds of fondue—a traditional version concocted from six kinds of cheese and served in a bubbling pot with chunks of bread on skewers, and another that adds mushrooms (morels or cèpes) to the blend. The only other dining options here include raclette and equally savory *tartiflette* (an age-old recipe that combines boiled potatoes with fatback, onions, cream, herbs, and reblochon cheese). The long list of (mostly white) French and Swiss wines pairs wonderfully with these ultra-traditional dishes.

23 rue Forville, Le Suquet. ⓒ 04-93-99-01-27. Main courses 15€–22€ ($20–$29); set-price menu 25€ ($33). AE, MC, V. Mon–Sat 7:30–10:30pm. Closed June–Aug.

La Mère Besson ⚘ TRADITIONAL FRENCH   The culinary traditions of the late Mère Besson, who opened her restaurant in the 1930s, endure in one of Cannes's favorite places. The specialties are prepared with respect for Provençal traditions. Most delectable is *estouffade Provençal* (beef braised with red wine and rich stock flavored with garlic, onions, herbs, and mushrooms). Every Friday, you can sample a platter with codfish, fresh vegetables, and dollops of the famous garlic mayonnaise *(aïoli)* of Provence. Other specialties are fish soup, *bourride Provençale* (thick fish-and-vegetable stew), and roasted rack of lamb with mint.

13 rue des Frères-Pradignac. ☎ 04-93-39-59-24. Reservations required. Main courses 19€–30€ ($25–$39); fixed-price menu 27€–32€ ($35–$42) dinner. AE, MC, V. Mon–Sat 7–10:30pm. Bus: 1.

Le Caveau 30 FRENCH/SEAFOOD   The emphasis in this place, specializing in fine cuisine, is fresh seafood. Begin with a seafood platter and follow with one of the chef's classic dishes, pot-au-feu "from the sea" or shellfish paella. Bouillabaisse is the most popular dish, of course, but you might prefer a *filet au poivre* (pepper steak) or even fresh pasta. The 1930s decor, air-conditioning, and terrace all make dining a pleasant experience.

45 rue Félix-Faure. ☎ 04-93-39-06-33. Reservations required. Main courses 18€–32€ ($23–$42); fixed-price menus 22€–30€ ($29–$39). AE, DC, MC, V. Daily noon–2:15pm and 7–11pm.

Le Comptoir des Vins TRADITIONAL FRENCH   The origins of this place are from 1995, when its owners established a wine shop with bottles from between 450 and 500 wine producers from throughout France, some of them very obscure. Soon afterward, a restaurant was established in the back of the store that quickly caught on as a dining attraction in its own right. Part of its allure derives from white marble tables, bistro-style chairs, and sunlight flooding in from an overhead skylight. You can order any of 10 kinds of wine by the glass, but if you're really intrigued by anything you see in the store, the restaurant will uncork it for you for a surcharge of 10€ ($13) more than what you paid for the bottle, retail, in the shop. Menu items include an extensive selection of *charcuteries* and cheeses, piled high upon olive-wood planks, as well as a savory collection of meats, fish, and vegetarian dishes. All of these are designed to go well with wines, and with a vast inventory of vintages to choose from, the composition of a savory meal here is ripe with gastronomic possibilities.

13 bd. de la République. ☎ 04-93-68-13-26. Reservations recommended. Main courses 9€–15€ ($12–$20); fixed-price menu 12€ ($16). MC, V. Mon–Thurs 9am–3pm and 5:30–9:30pm; Fri–Sat 9am–3pm and 5:30–11pm.

Le Harem 🌟 *Finds* MEDITERRANEAN   Set in the heart of Cannes, midway between la rue d'Antibes and La Croisette, this is the hippest, most popular, and most sought-after "North African" restaurant in Cannes. It contains a trio of dining rooms, each lavishly outfitted *à la Marocaine,* with chastened brass coffeepots, tribal carpets from the sub-Saharan desert, geometrically carved panels, and leatherwork.

The menu acknowledges the cuisines of Morocco, Tunisia, and Algeria. It features at least a half-dozen *tagines* (clay pots in which chicken, lamb, fish, and vegetables are spiced, slow-cooked, and made savory) and at least three different versions of couscous (a traditional version with only lamb; a *royale* version containing merguez sausage, chicken, lamb, and beef; and a super-deluxe seafood version, priced at 70€/$91 per person, that's loaded with lobster and shellfish).

15 rue des Frères Pradignac. ☎ 04-93-39-62-70. Reservations recommended. Main courses 20€–70€ ($26–$91); set menu 30€ ($39). AE, DC, MC, V. Daily 8pm–midnight.

Le Marais FRENCH   This is the most successful gay restaurant in Cannes, with a crowd of mostly gay men from the worlds of fashion and entertainment, sometimes with their entourages. The setting is a warm and appealing mix of Parisian and

Provençal, with paneled walls and a bustling terrace that is one of the most sought-after outdoor venues in town. Menu items include sea bream filet with olive-based tapenade sauce, and a "triptych" of meats that includes magret of duck, beef filet, and shoulder of lamb with mint sauce. Know in advance that this is primarily a restaurant and doesn't cater to a crowd of folk coming in just to drink.

9 rue du Suquet. ℂ **04-93-38-39-19.** Reservations recommended. Main courses 17€–30€ ($22–$39); fixed-price menu 24€ ($31). MC, V. Tues–Sun 7–11pm (and Mon during film festival).

Le Relais des Semailles TRADITIONAL FRENCH   This long-enduring favorite is reason enough to visit Le Suquet, Cannes's old town. The casual atmosphere is complemented by the food, based on available local ingredients. Zucchini flowers stuffed with crab, and breast of duck pan-fried with herbs and spices are always beautifully prepared. Try, if featured, the salad of wild greens *(mâche)* with truffles—sublime. The grilled sea bass is perfectly fresh and aromatically seasoned with herbs. Depending on what looked good at the market that day, the chef might be inspired to, say, whip up a rabbit salad with tarragon jus. The setting is intimate, offering casual dining out on the terrace or in air-conditioned comfort.

9 rue St-Antoine. ℂ **04-93-39-22-32.** Reservations required. Main courses 27€–32€ ($35–$42); fixed-price menus 51€ ($66). AE, DC, MC, V. Tues–Fri noon–2:30pm; daily 7:30–11:30pm. Closed Dec.

Le Restaurant Arménien ★ *Finds* ARMENIAN/TURKISH/GREEK   Cannes has always been one of the most cosmopolitan cities along the Riviera, and the success of this Armenian culinary outpost seems to prove it. It has no menu, although once your experience here is finished, you'll know a lot more about the cuisines of Armenia, Turkey, and Greece than you did before. For a set price, you'll experience an abundant medley of dishes that will be brought to your table in quantities you might find staggering. Expect about 20 cold plates, at least a dozen warm plates, enough vegetables to warm the heart of the most fanatical vegetarian, and at least five different desserts. There are lots of braised eggplants, tomatoes (both stewed and raw), an emphasis on cracked wheat in the form of such dishes as *kechgeg* (stewed beef served on a bed of cracked wheat), cabbage stuffed with mint, grilled meatballs with fresh herbs, and many others. According to owners Christian and Lucie Panossian, about 80% of the dishes served here are steamed rather than fried, establishing this place as one of the most health-conscious eateries in town. You'll find this place directly on the coastal boulevard, a short walk from the Hôtel Martinez.

82 La Croisette. ℂ **04-93-94-00-58.** Reservations recommended. Fixed-price menu 40€ ($52). DC, MC, V. Sun noon–1:30pm (reservations required); Tues–Sun 7–10:30pm; July–Aug daily noon–1:30pm; 7–10:30pm.

CANNES AFTER DARK

Cannes is invariably associated with permissiveness, filmmakers celebrating filmmaking, and gambling. If gambling is your thing, Cannes has some of world-class casinos, each loaded with addicts, voyeurs, and everyone in between. The better established is the **Casino Croisette,** in the Palais des Festivals, 1 jetée Albert-Edouard (ℂ **04-92-98-78-00**). Run by the Lucien Barrière group, and a well-respected fixture in town since the 1950s, it's a competitor of the newer **Palm Beach Casino,** place F-D–Roosevelt, Pointe de la Croisette (ℂ **04-97-06-36-90**), on the southeast edge of La Croisette. Inaugurated in 1933 and rebuilt in 2002, it features three restaurants and Art Deco decor. It's glossier, newer, and a bit hungrier for new business. Both casinos maintain slot machines that operate daily from 11am to 5am. Suites of rooms devoted to *les grands jeux* (blackjack, roulette, and chemin de fer) open nightly from 8pm to 5am. Both casinos charge 11€ ($13) and require a passport or ID card for access to *les grands jeux*.

Yet a third gambling den, **Casino des Princes,** is more intimate than either of its more flamboyant competitors, occupying the subterranean levels of the Noga Hilton Cannes, 50 bd. de la Croisette (© **04-92-99-70-00**). Outfitted in tones of gold and ocher, it is open nightly from 7pm to 4am, charging an admission of 25€ ($33). A government-issued photo ID is also necessary, and jackets for men are requested. Adjoining the casino is the hotel's most upscale restaurant, Restaurant/Bar des Princes, open for dinner nightly from 8pm to 2:45am.

In the cellar of the Hôtel Gray-d'Albion, 38 rue des Serbes, is a nightlife staple, the disco **Jane's** (© **04-92-99-79-79**). It isn't ultra-hip or even particularly cutting edge, but you can have a lot of fun here. It charges a 15€ ($20) cover on Saturday and admits women for free Friday and Saturday before midnight. At the Casino Croisette is the nightclub **Jimmy's** (© **04-92-98-78-00**).

The hippest club is **Le Life,** 22 rue Macé (© **04-93-39-31-31**), where a multicultural crowd of night owls, most under 35, come to dance, drink, talk, and flirt. It opens every night from 11:30pm till 4am, and charges 16€ ($18) for admission.

The aptly named **Bar des Stars,** in the Restaurant Fouquet's in the Hôtel Majestic Barrière, 14 La Croisette (© **04-92-98-77-00**), is where deals go down during the film festival. Directors, producers, stars, press agents, screenwriters, and wannabes crowd in here at festival time. Even when there's no festival, it's a lively place for a drink; its scarlet decor evokes an Art Deco Asian fantasy.

Gays and lesbians will feel comfortable at **Le Vogue,** 20 rue du Suquet (© **04-93-39-99-18**), a mixed bar open Tuesday to Sunday from 7:30pm till 2:30am. Another gay option is **Disco Le Sept,** 7 rue Rouguière (© **04-93-39-10-36**), where drag shows appear nightly at 1:30am. Entrance is free, except on weekends when it's 16€ ($21) (includes a drink). A lot of straights go here, too.

One of the most visible gay clienteles in Cannes tend to gravitate toward **Le Hype,** 52 bd. Jean-Jaurès (© **04-93-39-20-50**), which was re-outfitted late in 2004 in a 1950s-retro venue that includes red vinyl banquettes, white walls, a busy bar, occasional drag shows, and lots of randomly scheduled and somewhat flippant theme parties. Open for drinks and dining every Wednesday to Monday from 6 to 2:30pm, with set-price meals priced at 28€ ($36), it's a popular and convivial spot for same-sex socializing. A lot rougher, darker, and more shadowy is a gay male disco, **Le Divan,** 3 rue Rouguière (© **04-93-68-73-70**), that's located within a vaulted cellar that's designed to look a lot older than it really is. This place is not for the timid: If you opt for a visit here, leave your valuables in your hotel safe and remain alert. It's open Tuesday to Sunday from around 6pm till around 4am, depending on the crowds.

A discreet ambience prevails at **Zanzibar,** 85 rue Félix-Faure (© **04-93-39-30-75**). A bartender confided to us, "If a gay man wants to meet a French version of Brad Pitt, especially at festival time, this is the place." The bar is open all night and caters to people of all sexual persuasions. At dawn the doors open and the last of the drag queens stagger out.

The popular nightclub **Whatnut's Bal-Room,** 7 rue Marceau (© **04-93-68-60-58**), in the commercial center of Cannes, got a face-lift. It has a bar area near the entrance and two dance floors that feature radically different music: One is for 1980s-style disco; the other for house, garage, and modern forms of electronic sounds.

Patrons are on the young side (18–35), admission is free, and drinks cost 5€ to 10€ ($6.50–$13). Open May to September daily 10:30pm to 5am; October to June Friday to Sunday 10:30pm to 5am.

8 Grasse (★(★

906km (563 miles) S of Paris; 18km (11 miles) N of Cannes; 10km (6 miles) NW of Mougins

Grasse, a 20-minute drive from Cannes, is the most fragrant town on the Riviera, though it *looks* tacky modern. Surrounded by jasmine and roses, it has been the capital of the perfume industry since the days of the Renaissance. It was once a famous resort, attracting such royalty as Queen Victoria and Princess Pauline Borghese, Napoleon's promiscuous sister. Today some three-quarters of the world's essences are produced here from foliage that includes violets, daffodils, wild lavender, and jasmine.

ESSENTIALS

GETTING THERE   **Buses** pull into town every 30 to 60 minutes daily from Cannes (trip time: 45 min.). The one-way fare is 4€ ($5.20). There are also about 30 buses every day from Nice (1 hr.). The one-way fare is around 6.30€ ($8.20). They arrive at the Gare Routière, place de Buanderie, avenue Thiers (© **04-93-36-37-37**), a 10-minute walk north of the town center. Visitors arriving by **car** take A8, which funnels in traffic from Monaco, Aix-en-Provence, and Marseille.

VISITOR INFORMATION   The **Office de Tourisme** is in the Palais des Congrès, place Honoré Crese (© **04-93-36-66-66;** www.grasse-riviera.com).

SEEING THE SIGHTS

A market for fruits and vegetables from the surrounding hills, **Marché aux Aires,** is conducted in the place aux Aires every Tuesday through Sunday from 8am to noon.

PERFUME FACTORIES

Parfumerie Fragonard (★   One of the best-known perfume factories is named after an 18th-century French painter. This factory has the best villa, the best museum, and the best tour. An English-speaking guide will show you how "the soul of the flower" is extracted. After the tour, you can explore the museum, which displays bottles and vases that trace the industry back to ancient times. If you're shopping for perfume and want to skip the tour, that's okay.

20 bd. Fragonard. © **04-93-36-44-65.** Free admission. Feb–Oct daily 9am–6:30pm; Nov–Jan daily 9am–12:30pm and 2–6:30pm.

Parfumerie Molinard   The firm is well known in the United States, where its products are sold at Saks, Neiman Marcus, and Bloomingdale's. In the factory you can witness the extraction of the essence of the flowers. You'll also learn all the details of the process of converting flowers into essential oils. You can admire a collection of antique perfume-bottle labels and see a rare collection of perfume *flaçons* (bottles) by Baccarat and Lalique.

60 bd. Victor-Hugo. © **04-93-36-01-62.** Free admission. May–Sept daily 9am–6pm; Oct–Apr Mon–Sat 9am–12:30pm and 2–6pm.

MUSEUMS

Musée d'Art et d'Histoire de Provence (★   This museum is in the Hôtel de Clapiers-Cabris, built in 1771 by Louise de Mirabeau, the marquise de Cabris and sister

> **_Fun Fact_ Pricey Petals**
>
> It takes 10,000 flowers to produce 2.2 pounds of jasmine petals; almost a ton of petals is needed to distill 1½ quarts of essence. These figures are important to keep in mind when looking at that high price tag on a bottle of perfume.

of Mirabeau. Its collections include paintings, four-poster beds, marquetry, ceramics, brasses, kitchenware, pottery, urns, and archaeological finds.

2 rue Mirabeau. © 04-93-36-01-61. Admission 3€ ($3.90) adults, 1.50€ ($1.95) children 10–16, free for children under 10. June–Sept daily 10am–7pm; Oct–May Wed–Mon 10am–12:30pm and 2–5:30pm.

Musée International de la Parfumerie   This museum will teach you even more than you might want to know about perfume—for example, you learn that it takes a metric ton of flowers to make 1 gram of fragrance. You can also see interesting, often bizarre exhibits relating to the perfume industry. One of the most fascinating on the second floor displays a 3,000-year-old mummy's perfumed hand and foot. Apparently, the flesh stayed preserved over the centuries because of the perfuming process. In the fourth-floor greenery, you can smell some of the base elements that go into the creation of celebrated perfumes. Was that Elizabeth Taylor we saw whiffing and sniffing, perhaps trying to come up with some new exotic fragrance?

8 place de Cours. © 04-93-36-80-20. Admission 4€ ($5.20) adults, 2€ ($2.60) children. Oct–May Wed–Mon 10am–12:30pm and 2–5:30pm; June–Sept daily 10am–7pm.

Villa Musée Fragonard   The setting is an 18th-century aristocrat's town house with a magnificent garden in back. The collection displayed here includes the paintings of Jean-Honoré Fragonard; his sister-in-law, Marguerite Gérard; his son, Alexandre; and his grandson, Théophile. Jean-Honoré Fragonard was born in Grasse in 1732. Alexandre decorated the grand staircase.

23 bd. Fragonard. © 04-93-36-01-61. Admission 3€ ($3.90) adults, 1.50€ ($1.95) children 10–16, free for children under 8. June–Sept daily 10am–7pm; Oct–May Wed–Mon 10am–12:30pm and 2–5:30pm.

WHERE TO STAY

Bastide Saint-Mathieu ★★   This is an exclusive country house and the best place to stay in the Grasse area. Lying just to the southeast of Grasse, this is a beautifully restored 18th-century country house that is elegantly furnished, a pocket of discreet luxury and personal service. Each of the spacious suites is individually decorated and furnished to a high standard, with luxurious bathrooms with tub and shower. Thoughtful touches abound, as evoked by such extras as cashmere blankets and Ralph Lauren bathrobes. The staff will guide you to the area's finest restaurants.

3 Chemin de Blumenthal, 06130 St. Mathieu (Grasse). © 04-97-01-10-00. Fax 04-97-01-10-99. 5 units. 230€–340€ ($299–$442) double. Rates include breakfast. AE, V. **Amenities:** Outdoor pool; laundry service. *In room:* A/C, TV, dataport.

Hôtel La Bellaudière *Value*   Part of the respected Logis de France chain, this unpretentious family-run hotel is 3km (2 miles) east of the town center in the hills above Grasse. The stone-sided farmhouse was built in stages beginning 400 years ago with most of what you see today built in the 1700s. Guest rooms are simple but dignified and outfitted with Provençal motifs. There's a view of the sea from many of the rooms, a garden terrace lined with flowering shrubs, and a sense of friendly cooperation from the hosts. Set price meals in the dining room cost 20€ ($26) each.

78 rte. de Nice, 06130 Grasse. ℂ 04-93-36-02-57. Fax 04-93-36-40-03. 17 units. 55€–85€ ($72–$111) double. AE, DC, MC, V. Free parking. **Amenities:** Restaurant; limited room service. *In room:* TV, dataport.

Hôtel Panorama   Built in 1984 in the commercial center, this hotel lies behind a facade in a sienna hue that its owners call "Garibaldi red." The more expensive rooms have balconies, southern exposures, and views of the sea. Furnishings are basic and simple, although all the mattresses are reasonably comfortable. Tiled bathrooms are small and well kept. It lacks a bar or restaurant, but the staff is cooperative and hard-working.

2 place du Cours, 06130 Grasse. ℂ 04-93-36-80-80. Fax 04-93-3692-04. www.hotelpanorama-grasse.com. 36 units. 54€–107€ ($70–$139) double. Children stay free in parent's room. AE, DC, MC, V. **Amenities:** Limited room service; laundry service; dry cleaning. *In room:* A/C, TV, nonalcoholic minibar.

WHERE TO DINE

For inexpensive dining, you can head for **Hôtel La Bellaudière** (see above).

La Bastide St-Antoine (Restaurant Chibois) ☆☆☆ FRENCH/PROVENÇAL
La Bastide St-Antoine offers one of the grandest culinary experiences along the Riviera. Jacques Chibois and his restaurant have attracted national attention since 1996. In a 200-year-old Provençal farmhouse surrounded by 2.8 hectares (7 acres) of trees and shrubbery, the restaurant serves a sophisticated array of dishes. The best examples are oysters flavored with yucca leaves; a terrine of foie gras with celery; roasted suckling lamb with a fricassée of fresh vegetables and basil; and fresh crayfish with sautéed flap mushrooms. Desserts might include strawberry soup with spice wine or ice cream made with olives and a hint of olive oil. The chef also does wonders with wild duck.

You can stay in one of nine rooms and seven suites, decorated in Provençal style with upscale furnishings and comfortable beds. They have air-conditioning, safes, hair dryers minibars, and TVs. Doubles cost 182€ to 318€ ($237–$413); suites 335€ to 459€ ($436–$597).

48 av. Henri-Dunant. ℂ 04-93-70-94-94. Reservations required. Main courses 32€–60€ ($42–$78); fixed-price menu 53€–170€ ($69–$221) lunch Mon–Sat, 130€–170€ ($169–$221) dinner. AE, DC, MC, V. Daily noon–2pm and 8–9:30pm.

9 Mougins ⭑

903km (561 miles) S of Paris; 11km (7 miles) S of Grasse; 8km (5 miles) N of Cannes

This once-fortified town on the crest of a hill provides an alternative for those who want to be near the excitement of Cannes but not in the midst of it. Picasso and other artists appreciated these rugged, sun-drenched hills covered with gnarled olive trees. Picasso arrived in 1936 and, in time, was followed by Jean Cocteau, Paul Eluard, and Man Ray. Picasso decided to move here permanently, choosing as his refuge an ideal site overlooking the Bay of Cannes near the Chapelle Notre-Dame de Vie, which Winston Churchill once painted. Here he continued to work and spent the latter part of his life with his wife, Jacqueline. Fernand Léger, René Clair, Isadora Duncan, and even Christian Dior have lived at Mougins.

Mougins is the perfect haven for those who feel that the Riviera is overrun, spoiled, and overbuilt. It preserves the quiet life very close to the international resorts. The wealthy come from Cannes to golf here. Though Mougins looks serene and tranquil, it's actually part of the industrial park of Sophia Antipolis, a technological center where more than 1,000 national and international companies have offices.

ESSENTIALS

GETTING THERE   The best way to get to Mougins is to **drive**. From Nice, follow E80/A8 west, then cut north on route 85 into Mougins. From Cannes, head north of the city along N85. From La Napoule–Plage, head east toward Cannes on N7, then north at the turnoff to Mougins up in the hills.

In 2005, the French railways, **SNCF**, reactivated an antique rail line stretching between Grasse (the perfume capital) and Cannes, linking the hamlet of Mouans-Sartoux en route. The village of Mouans-Sartoux lies only 457m (1,500 ft.) from the center of Mougins. Rail service costs 4€ ($5.20) one-way from either Cannes or Grasse to Mouans-Sartoux. Several trains run per day. Among buses, **Société Tam (© 08-00-06-01-06)** runs buses between Cannes and Grasse. Bus no. 600 stops in Val-de-Mougins, a 10-minute walk from the center of Mougins. One-way fares from either Cannes or Grasse cost 3.70€ ($4.80). Given the complexities of a bus transfer from Cannes, it's a lot easier just to pay about 22€ ($29) for a **taxi** to haul you and your possessions northward from Cannes.

VISITOR INFORMATION   The **Office de Tourisme** is at 15 av. Jean-Charles-Mallet (© **04-93-75-87-67**; www.mougins-coteazur.org).

SEEING THE SIGHTS

For a look at the history of the area, visit the **Espace Cultural,** place du Commandant Lamy (© **04-92-92-50-42**), in the St. Bernardin Chapel. It was built in 1618 and traces area history from 1553 to the 1950s. It's open December through October, Monday through Friday from 9am to noon and 2 to 5pm (closed Nov). Admission is free.

You can also visit the **Chapelle Notre-Dame de Vie,** chemin de la Chapelle, 1.5km (1 mile) southeast of Mougins. The chapel, once painted by Churchill, is best known for the priory next door, where Picasso spent his last 12 years. It was built in the 12th century and reconstructed in 1646; it was an old custom to bring stillborn babies to the chapel to have them baptized. The priory is still a private home occupied intermittently by the Picasso heirs. Alas, because of a series of break-ins and because of ongoing renovations, the chapel is open only during Sunday Mass from 9 to 10am.

Musée de l'Automobiliste ★★ (Kids)   This is one of the top attractions on the Riviera. Founded in 1984 by Adrien Maeght, it's a modern concrete-and-glass structure. It houses exhibitions and one of Europe's most magnificent collections of prestigious automobiles, which includes more than 100 vehicles dating from 1908 to the present. Within two steps of the sea, the museum explores the use of the automobile in both civil and military contexts. Individual cars are on display for historic, aesthetic, technical, or sentimental reasons. Children appreciate the antique toys and antique model cars collected over many generations, and any teenager who has seen pimpmobiles on TV will appreciate the cool quotient of such rare luxury rides as the 1925 Hispano-Suiza H6B and its even more opulent J12 counterpart from 1933.

Aire des Bréguières or 772 Chemin de Font de Currault. © **04-93-69-27-80**. Admission 7€ ($9.10) adults, 5€ ($6.50) children 13–18, free for children 12 and under. June–Sept daily 10am–6pm; Oct and Dec–May Tues–Sun 10am–1pm and 2–6pm. Closed Nov.

WHERE TO STAY

Note that **Le Moulin de Mougins** (see "Where to Dine," below) offers charming rooms and suites.

Le Manoir de l'Etang 🌟🌟   You'll get a strong sense of life in rural Provence within the thick, ivy-covered stone walls of this artfully renovated 19th-century manor house, located within a verdant 4-hectare (10-acre) park a short drive east from the center of Mougins. A mass of nearby olive trees and cypresses seem to showcase a small pond covered with lotuses and water lilies. New owners massively renovated and upgraded it in 2004, creating a stylish and urban-style renovation, some of it very contemporary in style, with airy bedrooms that benefited from some sophisticated decorating. The interior, including the bedrooms, is bright and modern, the perfect place for a hideaway, off-the-record weekend. The in-house restaurant serves artfully conceived food, some of the platters arranged in ways that qualify them as sculptural statements in their own right. Despite its modernity, and its airy and contemporary decorative style, the place still captivates the romance of the old, Romantic Riviera of long ago.

Aux Bois de Font-Merle, allée du Manoir, 06250 Mougins. ℂ **04-92-28-36-00.** Fax 04-92-28-36-10. www.manoir-de-letang.com. 21 units. 160€–280€ ($208–$364) double; 325€–400€ ($423–$520) suite; from 360€ ($468) apt for 4. AE, MC, V. Closed late Oct to Mar. **Amenities:** Restaurant; bar; outdoor pool; limited room service; laundry service; dry cleaning; nonsmoking rooms. *In room:* A/C, TV, dataport, minibar.

Le Mas Candille 🌟🌟   With a staff that at times might be just a bit too easygoing, this 200-year-old Provençal *mas* (farmhouse) was renovated in 2005 and gained a well-designed annex in 2001. The public rooms contain many 19th-century furnishings, and some open onto the gardens. Rooms are individually decorated in different styles, including Japanese, medieval, French colonial (Indochina), and Provençal regional. Bathrooms are of good size, with tub/shower combinations. The dining room, with stone detailing and a massive fireplace with a timbered mantel, serves exceptional food. Fresh salads and light meals are available throughout the day. In clement weather, lunch is served on the terrace; dinner is served on the terrace in summer only.

Bd. Clément Rebuffel, 06250 Mougins. ℂ **04-92-28-43-43.** Fax 04-92-28-43-40. www.lemascandille.com. 40 units. 275€–495€ ($358–$644) double; 625€–745€ ($813–$969) suite. AE, DC, MC, V. **Amenities:** 2 restaurants; bar; 2 outdoor pools; 3-hole golf course; gym; spa; 24-hr. room service; laundry service; dry cleaning; nonsmoking rooms; limited-mobility rooms. *In room:* A/C, TV, dataport, minibar, hair dryer, safe.

WHERE TO DINE

Brasserie de la Méditerranée FRENCH/PROVENÇAL   This outfit adds a much-needed informality to the restaurant scene of a town noted for hyper-upscale gastronomy. Set within a modern building overlooking the village's main square, and outfitted in tones of white and off-white, it specializes in the kind of cuisine you'd expect in a bustling brasserie in Lyons, but with a Provençal accent. Menu items include scallops with a balsamic vinaigrette; superb lobster served with a *barigoule* of artichoke hearts; sliced turbot in a white-butter sauce; and veal saltimbocca (with ham).

Place de la Mairie. ℂ **04-93-90-03-47.** Reservations recommended. Main courses 11€–31€ ($14–$40); set menus 22€–43€ ($28–$56) lunch, 31€–43€ ($40–$56) dinner. AE, DC, MC, V. Daily noon–2:30pm and 7–10:30pm. Closed Jan 10–Feb 10.

L'Amandier de Mougins Café-Restaurant 🌟 *(Value* NIÇOISE/PROVENÇAL   The illustrious founder of this relatively inexpensive bistro was the world-famous Roger Vergé, whose much more expensive Moulin de Mougins is described below. Originally conceived as a mass-market satellite to its exclusive neighbor, and now owned by another entrepreneur, Pierre Houe, this restaurant serves relatively simple platters in an airy stone house. The specialties are usually based on traditional recipes and might include a terrine of the elusive Mediterranean hogfish with lemon; a tartare of fresh salmon and a seviche of tuna with hot spices; grilled jumbo shrimp with artichokes; magrêt of grilled duckling with honey sauce and lemons, served with deliberately undercooked polenta; rack of lamb served with a risotto of zucchini flowers; and filets of farm-raised sea bass on a Moroccan-inspired ragoût of vegetables and saffron-flavored potatoes.

Place des Patriotes. ℂ 04-93-90-00-91. Reservations recommended. Main courses 28€–45€ ($36–$59); fixed-price menu 25€ ($33) lunch, 33€–50€ ($43–$65) dinner. AE, DC, MC, V. Daily noon–2pm and 7–9:30pm.

Le Feu Follet _Value_ FRENCH/PROVENÇAL   Beside the square in the old village, this restaurant offers two roughly plastered rooms that always seem cramped and overcrowded, but the quality of the cuisine (and the affordable prices) make it a worthy choice. Only top-quality ingredients, the best in the market, go into the cooking. One longtime habitué, describing the Provençal vegetables served here, claimed they were "filled with the sun." Fancy sauces and overpreparation of dishes are never a factor, and the fresh herbs of Provence are used effectively. Typical dishes are baked filet of beef in red wine and butter, crayfish in lemon juice, and snails in garlic cream.

Place de la Mairie. ℂ 04-93-90-15-78. Reservations required. Main courses 22€–30€ ($29–$39); fixed-price menu 35€ ($45). AE, MC, V. Tues–Sat noon–2pm and 7–10pm; Sun 2:30–7pm.

Le Moulin de Mougins ✿✿✿ FRENCH   The new chef here has a big toque to fill. In 2004 Alain Llorca took over the celebrated inn, until recently the kingdom of Roger Vergé, a _maître cuisinier de France_ and one of the country's top three chefs. After 7 years as chef of the fabled Negresco Hôtel in Nice, Llorca was just the man to succeed Vergé. He employs market-fresh ingredients in his "cuisine of the sun," a reference to Provence's light-drenched countryside.

Cuisine here is earthy but upscale, often with modern twists on old culinary traditions both from Provence and other parts of the French-speaking world. Examples include hearts of artichoke stuffed with marinated seafood; an _accras de morue_ (codfish fritters) like you might have expected in Martinique; spaghetti with shellfish; roasted Provençal goat with herbs; sweetbreads with mushrooms fried in grease; and a succulent version of _magret_ of duckling with honey sauce, lemons, and polenta.

The inn also rents four suites and three rooms with air-conditioning, minibars, and TVs. Rooms cost 140€ to 190€ ($182–$247) double, suites 300€ to 330€ ($390–$429).

Notre-Dame de Vie, 06250 Mougins. ℂ 04-93-75-78-24. Fax 04-93-90-18-55. Reservations required. Main courses 40€–105€ ($52–$137); fixed-price menu 48€–115€ ($62–$150) lunch, 95€–115€ ($124–$150) dinner. AE, DC, MC, V. Tues–Sun noon–2pm and 7:30–10pm.

10 Golfe-Juan ✦ & Vallauris

913km (567 miles) S of Paris; 6km (4 miles) E of Cannes

Napoleon and 800 men landed at Golfe-Juan in 1815 to begin his Hundred Days. Protected by hills, Golfe-Juan was also the favored port for the American navy, though today it's primarily a family resort known for its beaches. It contains one notable restaurant: Chez Tétou.

The 2km (1¼-mile) R.N. 135 leads inland from Golfe-Juan to Vallauris. Once merely a stopover along the Riviera, Vallauris (now noted for its pottery) owes its reputation to Picasso, who "discovered" it. The master came to Vallauris after World War II and occupied a villa known as "The Woman from Wales."

ESSENTIALS

GETTING THERE   You can **drive** to Golfe-Juan or Vallauris on any of the Riviera's three east-west highways. Although route numbers are not always indicated, city names are clear once you're on the highway. From Cannes or Antibes, N7 east is the fastest route. From Nice or Biot, take A8/E80 west.

There's a sleepy-looking rail station in Golfe-Juan, on avenue de la Gare. To get here, you'll have to transfer from a **train** in Cannes. The train from Cannes costs 2.50€ ($3.25) each way. For railway information, call ✆ **08-92-35-35-35.** A flotilla of **buses** operated by Envibus (✆ **04-93-64-18-37**) makes frequent trips from Cannes; the 20-minute trip costs 2.40€ ($3.10) each way; from Nice, the 90-minute trip costs 6€ ($7.80) each way.

VISITOR INFORMATION   The **Office de Tourisme** is on av. des Frères-Roustan, Golfe-Juan (✆ **04-93-63-73-12**), and another is on square du 8-Mai, 1945 Vallauris (✆ **04-93-63-82-58;** www.vallauris-golfe-juan.fr).

SEEING THE SIGHTS

Landlocked Vallauris depends on the sale of tourist items and ceramics. Merchants selling the colorful wares line both sides of **avenue Georges-Clemenceau,** which begins at a point adjacent to the Musée Picasso and slopes downhill and southward to the edge of town. Some of the pieces displayed in these shops are in poor taste. In recent years, the almost-universal emphasis on the traditional rich burgundy color has been replaced with a wider variety geared to modern tastes.

On the place du Marché in Vallauris, near the site where Aly Khan and Rita Hayworth were married, you'll see Picasso's **Homme et Mouton (Man and Sheep).** The town council of Vallauris had intended to ensconce this statue in a museum, but Picasso insisted that it remain on the square "where the children could climb over it and the dogs water it unhindered."

Bordering place de la Liberation is a chapel of rough-hewn stone, shaped like a Quonset hut, containing the **Musée Picasso La Guerre et La Paix** (✆ **04-93-64-16-05**), and also the entrance to the 16th-century **Château de Vallauris** (same phone). Inside the château is a two-in-one museum, **Musée Alberto Magnelli** and the **Musée de la Céramique Moderne.** This trio of museums developed after Picasso decorated the chapel with two paintings: La Paix (Peace) and La Guerre (War), offering contrasting images of love and peace on the one hand, and violence and conflict on the other. In 1970, a house painter gained illegal entrance to the museum one night and, after whitewashing a portion of the original, substituted one of his own designs. When the aging master inspected the damage, he said, "Not bad at all." In July 1996, the site was enhanced with a permanent exposition devoted to the works of the Florentine-born Alberto Magnelli, a pioneer of abstract art whose first successes were acclaimed in 1915 and who died in 1971, 2 years before Picasso. The third section showcases ceramics, both traditional and innovative, from potters throughout the region. All three museums are open June to August Wednesday to Monday 10am to 6pm; September to May Wednesday to Monday 10am to noon and 2 to 5pm. Admission costs 3€ ($3.90) for adults and 1.50€ ($1.95) for students and children 15 and under.

A DAY AT THE BEACH

Because of its position beside the sea, Golfe-Juan developed long ago into a warm-weather resort. The town's twin strips of beach are **Plages du Soleil** (east of the Vieux Port and the newer Port Camille-Rayon) and **Plages du Midi** (west of those two). Each stretches 1km (½ mile) and charges no entry fee, with the exception of small areas administered by concessions that rent mattresses and chaises and offer access to kiosks dispensing snacks and cold drinks. Regardless of which concession you select (on Plage du Midi, they sport names like Au Vieux Rocher, Palma Beach, and Corail Plage; on Plage du Soleil, they're Plage Nounou and Plage Tétou), you'll pay 13€ ($17) for a day's use of a mattress. Plage Tétou is associated with the upscale Chez Tétou (see "Where to Dine," below). If you don't want to rent a mattress, you can cavort unhindered anywhere along the sands, moving freely from one area to another. Golfe-Juan indulges bathers who remove their bikini tops, but, in theory, it forbids nude sunbathing.

SHOPPING IN VALLAURIS

Galerie Madoura, avenue de Georges et Suzanne Ramié, Vallauris (© **04-93-64-66-39**), is the only shop licensed to sell Picasso reproductions. It's open Monday through Friday from 10am to 12:30pm and 3 to 6pm. Some of the reproductions are limited to 25 to 500 copies. Another gallery to seek out is the **Galerie Sassi-Milici,** 65 bis av. Georges-Clemenceau (© **04-93-64-65-71**), which displays works by contemporary artists.

Market days in Vallauris are Tuesday to Sunday from 7am to 12:30pm, at **place de l'Homme au Mouton,** with its flower stalls and local produce. For a souvenir, you may want to visit a farming cooperative, the **Cooperative Nérolium,** 12 av. Georges-Clemenceau (© **04-93-64-27-54**). It produces such foods as bitter-orange marmalade and quince jam, olive oils, and scented products like orange-flower water. Another unusual outlet for local products is the **Parfumerie Bouis,** 50 av. Georges-Clemenceau (© **04-93-64-38-27**).

La Boutique de l'Olivier, 46 av. Georges-Clemenceau (© **04-93-64-66-45**), specializes in olive-wood objects. They include pepper mills, salad servers, cheese boards, free-form bowls, and bread-slicing boxes. **Terres à Terre,** 58 av. Georges-Clemenceau (© **04-93-63-16-80**), is known for its culinary pottery, made of local clay. This is an excellent outlet for terra-cotta pottery. Gratin dishes and casseroles have long been big sellers.

WHERE TO STAY

Hôtel Beau-Soleil   Set on a quiet cul-de-sac, within a 5-minute walk from the center of the town or the beach, this pink-and-white, boxy-looking hotel was built in 1973. The angles of the architecture might remind you of a modern-day adaptation by a 1920s-era cubist painter. Bedrooms are outfitted in Provence-inspired colors, with small-scale crystal chandeliers, big windows overlooking either the hotel's shaded terrace or the faraway hills, a writing table, and neat bathrooms with showers. The social center is the shaded terrace, dotted with potted plants.

Impasse Beau-Soleil, 06220 Golfe-San-Juan (Vallauris). © **04-93-63-63-63.** Fax 04-93-63-02-89. www.hotel-beau-soleil.com. 30 units. 59€–125€ ($77–$163) double. MC, V. Free parking. **Amenities:** Restaurant; bar; outdoor pool; nearby golf courses; tennis court. *In room:* A/C, TV, hair dryer, minibar, safe.

WHERE TO DINE

Chez Tétou 🏶🏶🏶 SEAFOOD   In its own amusing way, this is one of the Côte d'Azur's most famous restaurants, capitalizing on the beau monde that came here in the 1950s and 1960s. Retaining its Provençal earthiness despite its high prices, it has thrived in a white-sided beach cottage for more than 65 years. Appetizers are limited to platters of *charcuterie* (cold cuts) or several almost-perfect slices of fresh melon. Most diners order the house specialty, bouillabaisse. Also on the limited menu are grilled sea bass with tomatoes Provençal, sole meunière, and several preparations of lobster—the most famous is grilled and served with lemon-butter sauce, fresh parsley, and basmati rice. Dessert might be a powdered croissant with grandmother's jams (winter) or raspberry-and-strawberry tart (summer).

Av. des Frères-Roustan, sur la Plage, Golfe-Juan. ⓒ **04-93-63-71-16.** Reservations required. Main courses 53€–65€ ($69–$85); bouillabaisse 70€–90€ ($91–$117). No credit cards. Thurs–Tues noon–2:30pm and 8–10:30pm. Closed Nov to early Mar.

11 Juan-les-Pins ⭐⭐

913km (567 miles) S of Paris; 10km (6 miles) S of Cannes

This suburb of Antibes is a resort that was developed in the 1920s by Frank Jay Gould. At that time, people flocked to "John of the Pines" to escape the "crassness" of nearby Cannes. In the 1930s, Juan-les-Pins drew a chic crowd during winter. Today it attracts young Europeans from many economic backgrounds in pursuit of sex, sun, and sea, in that order.

Juan-les-Pins is often called a honky-tonk town or the "Coney Island of the Riviera," but anyone who calls it that hasn't seen Coney Island in a long time. One newspaper writer called it "a pop-art Monte Carlo, with burlesque shows and nude beaches"—a description much too provocative for such a middle-class resort. Another newspaper writer said that Juan-les-Pins is "for the young and noisy." Even F. Scott Fitzgerald decried it as a "constant carnival." If he could see it now, he'd know that he was a prophet.

ESSENTIALS

GETTING THERE   Juan-les-Pins is connected by **rail** and bus to most other Mediterranean coastal resorts, especially Nice (trip time: 30 min.; one-way fare: 4€/$5.20). For rail information and schedules, call ⓒ **08-92-35-35-35. Buses** arrive from Nice and its airport at 40-minute intervals throughout the day. A bus leaves for Juan-les-Pins from Antibes at place Guynemer (ⓒ **04-93-34-37-60**) daily every 20 minutes and costs 1.45€ ($1.90) one-way (trip time: 10–15 min.). To **drive** to Juan-les-Pins from Nice, travel along N7 south. Juan-les-Pins is just outside of Cannes; follow the road signs.

VISITOR INFORMATION   The **Office de Tourisme** is at 51 bd. Charles-Guillaumont (ⓒ **04-92-90-53-05;** www.antibesjuanlespins.com).

SPECIAL EVENTS   The town offers some of the best nightlife on the Riviera, and the action reaches its height during the annual jazz festival. The 10- to 12-day **Festival International de Jazz,** in mid-July, attracts jazz masters and their fans. Concerts are in a temporary stadium, custom-built for the event in Le Parc de la Pinède. Tickets cost 30€ to 60€ ($39–$78) and can be purchased at the Office de Tourisme in both Antibes and Juan-les-Pins.

A DAY AT THE BEACH

Part of the reason people flock here is that the town's beaches have sand, unlike many of the other resorts along this coast, which have pebbly beaches. **Plage de Juan-les-Pins** is the most central beach. Its subdivisions, all public, include **Plage de la Salis** and **Plage de la Garoupe.** If you don't have a beach chair, go to the concessions operated by each of the major beachfront hotels. Even if you're not a guest, you can rent a chaise and mattress for around 15€ to 18€ ($20–$23). The most chic is the area maintained by the Hôtel des Belles-Rives. Competitors more or less in the same category are La Jetée and La Voile Blanche, both opposite the tourist information office. Topless sunbathing is permitted, but total nudity isn't.

WATERSPORTS

If you're interested in scuba diving, check with your hotel staff, **Club de la Mer,** Port Gallice (✆ **04-93-61-26-07**), or **EPAJ,** embarcadère Courbet (✆ **04-93-67-52-59**). A one-tank dive costs 42€ ($55), including all equipment. **Water-skiing** is available at virtually every beach in Juan-les-Pins. Concessionaires include one outfit that's more or less permanently located on the beach of the Hôtel des Belles-Rives. Ask any beach attendant or bartender, and he or she will guide you to the water-skiing representatives who station themselves on the sands. A 10-minute session costs about 24€ ($31).

WHERE TO STAY
EXPENSIVE

Hôtel des Belles-Rives 🐸🐸🐸 This is one of the Riviera's fabled addresses, on a par with the equally famous Juana (see below), though the Juana boasts superior cuisine. Once it was a holiday villa occupied by Zelda and F. Scott Fitzgerald, and the scene of many a drunken brawl. It later played host to the illustrious, like the duke and duchess of Windsor, Josephine Baker, and Edith Piaf. A 1930s aura lingers through recent renovations. Double glazing and air-conditioning help a lot. As befits a hotel of this age, rooms come in a variety of shapes and sizes, from small to spacious; each has a luxurious bathroom with a combination tub/shower. The lower terraces hold garden dining rooms, a waterside aquatic club with a snack bar and lounge, and a jetty. There's also a private beach and a dock.

33 bd. Edouard Baudoin, 06160 Juan-les-Pins. ✆ **04-93-61-02-79.** Fax 04-93-67-43-51. www.bellesrives.com. 44 units. 200€–700€ ($260–$910) double; 400€–1,400€ ($520–$1,820) suite. AE, DC, MC, V. Free parking. Closed Jan to mid-Feb. **Amenities:** 2 summer restaurants; 1 winter restaurant; 2 bars; courtesy car; limited room service; babysitting; laundry service; dry cleaning; nonsmoking rooms. *In room:* A/C, TV, dataport, minibar, hair dryer, safe.

Hôtel Juana 🐸🐸🐸 This balconied Art Deco hotel, beloved by F. Scott Fitzgerald, is separated from the sea by the park of pines that gave Juan-les-Pins its name. The hotel is constantly being refurbished, as reflected in the attractive rooms with mahogany pieces, well-chosen fabrics, tasteful carpets, and large bathrooms (tub and shower) in marble or tile. The rooms often have such extras as balconies. The hotel has a private swimming club where you can rent a "parasol and pad" on the sandy beach at reduced rates. Nearby is a park with umbrella-shaded tables and palms.

La Pinède, av. Gallice, 06160 Juan-les-Pins. ✆ **04-93-61-08-70.** Fax 04-93-61-76-60. www.hotel-juana.com. 50 units. 235€–635€ ($306–$826) double; 455€–750€ ($592–$975) suite. AE, MC, V. Parking 15€ ($17). Closed Nov 10–Dec 26. **Amenities:** Restaurant; 2 bars; heated outdoor pool; gym; bike rentals; secretarial services; limited room service; massage; babysitting; laundry service; dry cleaning; nonsmoking rooms. *In room:* A/C, TV, dataport, minibar, hair dryer, iron, safe.

MODERATE
Hôtel des Mimosas This elegant 1870s-style villa sprawls in a tropical garden on a hilltop. The decor is a mix of high-tech and Italian-style comfort, with antique and modern furniture. Guest rooms come in a variety of shapes and sizes—some quite small—each with a compact tub/shower bathroom. The rooms open onto balconies.

An outdoor pool sits amid huge palm trees. The hotel is fully booked in summer, so reserve far in advance.

Rue Pauline, 06160 Juan-les-Pins. ✆ **04-93-61-04-16.** Fax 04-92-93-06-46. www.hotelmimosas.com. 34 units. 80€–120€ ($104–$156) double. AE, MC, V. Free parking. Closed Sept 30–Apr. From the town center, drive .4km (¼ mile) west, following N7 toward Cannes. **Amenities:** Bar; outdoor pool; limited room service; laundry service; dry cleaning; nonsmoking rooms. *In room:* A/C, TV, minibar, hair dryer, iron, safe.

Hôtel Le Pré Catelan   In a residential area near the town park, 200m (654 ft.) from a sandy beach, this year-round Provençal villa (built ca. 1900) features a garden with rock terraces, towering palms, lemon and orange trees, large pots of pink geraniums, and outdoor furniture. The atmosphere is casual, the setting uncomplicated and unstuffy. Furnishings are durable and basic. As is typical of such old villas, guest rooms come in a variety of shapes and sizes. Some have kitchenettes, and more expensive units have terraces. Despite the setting in the heart of town, the garden lends a sense of isolation. Breakfast is the only meal served.

27 av. des Palmiers, 06160 Juan-les-Pins. ✆ **04-93-61-05-11.** Fax 04-93-67-83-11. www.precatelan.com. 24 units. 86€–155€ ($112–$202) double; 174€–215€ ($226–$280) suite. AE, MC, V. Parking 6€ ($7.80). **Amenities:** Bar; outdoor pool; babysitting; laundry service; dry cleaning; nonsmoking rooms. *In room:* TV, dataport, minibar, hair dryer, safe.

INEXPENSIVE

Hôtel Cecil ⟨Value⟩   A stone's throw from the beach, this well-kept small hotel is one of the best bargains in Juan-les-Pins. It originated in 1929 when a 19th-century villa was radically enlarged with another story and transformed into a hotel. The traditionally furnished rooms are worn yet well kept, ranging from small to midsize, each with a compact tiled bathroom with shower only. The owners provide a courteous welcome and good meals.

Rue Jonnard, 06160 Juan-les-Pins. ✆ **04-93-61-05-12.** Fax 04-93-67-09-14. www.hotelcecilfrance.com. 21 units. Feb–Oct 52€–82€ ($68–$107) double. AE, DC, MC, V. Parking 8€ ($9.20). Closed Nov 7–Jan 14. **Amenities:** Restaurant; limited room service; babysitting; nonsmoking rooms. *In room:* A/C, TV, dataport, hair dryer.

Hôtel Le Passy   Centrally located and blandly modern, Le Passy opens onto a wide flagstone terrace. The other side faces the sea and coastal boulevard. The furnishings are Nordic modern, and the newer rooms have little balconies. Those that overlook the sea carry the higher price tag. Most rooms are small but have comfortable beds; each bathroom is compact and tidily maintained. In high-priced Juan-les-Pins, this is considered one of the more affordable choices, even though it's a bit sterile.

15 av. Louis-Gallet, 06160 Juan-les-Pins. ✆ **04-93-61-11-09.** Fax 04-93-67-91-78. www.hotels-lepassy-cyrano.com. 35 units. 58€–99€ ($75–$129) double. AE, DC, MC, V. Parking 8€ ($10). **Amenities:** Lounge; limited room service; babysitting. *In room:* A/C, TV, safe.

WHERE TO DINE
EXPENSIVE

Le Bijou Plage ⟨Value⟩ FRENCH/PROVENÇAL   This upscale brasserie has flourished beside the seafront promenade since 1923. The marine-style decor includes lots of varnished wood and bouquets of blue and white flowers in a mostly blue-and-white interior. Windows overlook a private beach that's much less crowded than the public beaches nearby. Menu items are sophisticated and less expensive than you'd expect. Examples are excellent bouillabaisse, grilled sardines, risotto with John Dory and truffled butter, steamed mussels with *sauce poulette* (frothy cream sauce with herbs and butter), grilled John Dory with a vinaigrette enriched by tapenade of olives and fresh basil, and a super-size *plateau des coquillages et fruits de mer* (shellfish). Don't confuse this informally elegant place with its beachfront terrace, open April 15 to September 15 daily noon to 4pm.

Bd. du Littoral. ℂ 04-93-61-39-07. Reservations recommended. Main courses 18€–51€ ($23–$66); fixed-price menu 20€–45€ ($26–$59). AE, DC, MC, V. Daily noon–2:30pm and 7:30–10:30pm.

MODERATE

Le Perroquet PROVENÇAL   The cuisine is well presented and prepared, and the restaurant's ambience is carefully synchronized to the resort's casual and carnival-like summer aura. It's across from the Parc de la Pinède and is decorated with depictions of every imaginable form of parakeet, the restaurant's namesake. Look for savory versions of fish, at its best when grilled simply with olive oil and basil, and served with lemons. A worthwhile appetizer is the *assortiment Provençale*, which includes tapenade of olives, marinated peppers, grilled sardines, and stuffed and grilled vegetables. Steaks might be served with green peppercorns or béarnaise sauce, and desserts include three types of pastries on the same platter.

Av. Georges-Gallice. ℂ 04-93-61-02-20. Reservations recommended. Main courses 16€–28€ ($21–$36); fixed-price menus 28€–34€ ($36–$44). MC, V. Daily noon–2pm and 7–11pm. Closed Nov–Dec 26.

JUAN-LES-PINS AFTER DARK

For starters, visit the **Eden Casino,** boulevard Baudoin in the heart of Juan-les-Pins (ℂ **04-92-93-71-71**), and try your luck at the roulette wheel or at one of the slot machines. The area containing slot machines doesn't charge admission. It's open every day from 10am to 5pm. The area containing *les grands jeux* (blackjack, roulette, and chemin de fer) is open daily from 9:30pm to 5am and charges 11€ ($14) per person. A photo ID is required, preferably in the form of a passport.

For a faux-tropical experience, head to **Le Pam Pam,** route Wilson (ℂ **04-93-61-11-05**), where you can sip rum drinks in an atmosphere that celebrates reggae, Brazilian, and African performances of music and dance.

If you prefer high-energy reveling, check out the town's many discos. **Whisky à Gogo,** boulevard de la Pinède (ℂ **04-93-61-26-40**), attracts young trendsetters with its rock beat. In summer it fills up with the young, restless, and horny. Between October and Easter, it's open only on Friday and Saturday night. **Le Village,** 1 bd. de la Pinède (ℂ **04-93-61-18-71**), boasts an action-packed dance floor and DJs spinning the latest sounds from the international music scene. The cover charge is 15€ ($20).

For a more relaxed evening, go to the British pub **Le Ten's Bar,** 25 av. du Dr.-Hochet (ℂ **04-93-67-20-67**), where you'll find 50 brands of beer and a sociable crowd of young and old merrymakers.

12 Antibes ✶✶ & Cap d'Antibes ✶✶

913km (567 miles) S of Paris; 21km (13 miles) SW of Nice; 11km (7 miles) NE of Cannes

On the other side of the Baie des Anges (Bay of Angels), across from Nice, is the port of Antibes. This old Mediterranean town has a quiet charm unique on the Côte d'Azur. Its little harbor is filled with fishing boats and pleasure yachts, and in recent years it has emerged as a new "hot spot." The marketplaces are full of flowers, mostly roses and carnations. If you're in Antibes in the evening, you can watch fishermen playing the traditional Riviera game of boules.

Spiritually, Antibes is totally divorced from Cap d'Antibes, which is a peninsula studded with the villas and outdoor pools of the super-rich. In *Tender Is the Night,*

F. Scott Fitzgerald described it as a place where "old villas rotted like water lilies among the massed pines." Photos of film and rock stars lounging at the Eden Roc have appeared in countless magazines.

ESSENTIALS
GETTING THERE   **Trains** from Cannes arrive at the rail station, place Pierre-Semard, every 20 minutes (trip time: 10 min.); the one-way fare is 3€ ($3.90). Trains from Nice arrive every 30 minutes (trip time: 18 min.); the one-way fare is around 4€ ($5.20). For rail information, call ⓒ **08-92-35-35-35.** The **bus** station, La Gare Routière, place Guynemer (ⓒ **04-93-34-37-60**), receives buses from throughout Provence.

If you're **driving,** follow E1 east from Cannes and take the turnoff to the south for Antibes, which will lead to the historic core of the old city. From Nice, take E1 west until you come to the turnoff for Antibes. From the center of Antibes, follow the coastal road, boulevard Leclerc, south to Cap d'Antibes.

VISITOR INFORMATION   The **Office de Tourisme** is at 11 place du Général-de-Gaulle (ⓒ **04-92-90-53-00;** fax 04-92-90-53-01; www.antibesjuanlespins.com).

SEEING THE SIGHTS
Musée Picasso 𝄞𝄞   On the ramparts above the port is the Château Grimaldi, once the home of the princes of Antibes of the Grimaldi family, who ruled the city from 1385 to 1608. Today it houses one of the world's great Picasso collections. Picasso came to town after the war and stayed in a small hotel at Golfe-Juan until the museum director at Antibes invited him to work and live at the museum. Picasso spent 1946 painting here. When he departed, he gave the museum all the work he'd done: 24 paintings, 80 pieces of ceramics, 44 drawings, 32 lithographs, 11 oils on paper, 2 sculptures, and 5 tapestries. In addition, a gallery of contemporary art exhibits Léger, Miró, Ernst, and Calder, among others.

Place du Mariejol. ⓒ **04-92-90-54-20.** Admission 3€ ($3.90) adults, 1.50€ ($1.95) children 12–18, free for children under 12. June–Sept Tues–Sun 10am–6pm; Oct–May Tues–Sun 10am–noon and 2–6pm.

Musée Naval et Napoléonien 𝒦𝒾𝒹𝓈   In this stone-sided fort and tower, built in stages in the 17th and 18th centuries, you'll find an interesting collection of Napoleonic memorabilia, naval models, and paintings, many of which were donated by at least two world-class collectors. A toy soldier collection depicts various uniforms, including one used by Napoleon in the Marengo campaign. A wall painting on wood shows Napoleon's entrance into Grenoble; another shows him disembarking at Golfe-Juan on March 1, 1815. In contrast to Canova's Greek-god image of Napoleon, a miniature pendant by Barrault reveals the general as he really looked, with pudgy cheeks and a receding hairline. In the rear rotunda is one of the many hats worn by the emperor. You can climb to the top of the tower for a view of the coast that's worth the admission price.

Batterie du Grillon, bd. J.-F.-Kennedy. ⓒ **04-93-61-45-32.** Admission 3€ ($3.90) adults; 1.50€ ($1.95) seniors, students, and ages 12–25; free for children under 12. Mon–Sat 9:30–noon; Mon–Fri 2:15–6pm.

WHERE TO STAY
VERY EXPENSIVE
Hôtel du Cap–Eden Roc 𝄞𝄞𝄞   Legendary for the glamour of its setting and its clientele, this Second Empire hotel, opened in 1870, is surrounded by masses of gardens.

It's like a country estate, with spacious public rooms, marble fireplaces, paneling, chandeliers, and upholstered armchairs. The guest rooms are among the most sumptuous on the Riviera, with deluxe beds. Bathrooms are spacious, with brass fittings and tub/ shower combinations. Even though the guests snoozing by the outdoor pool—blasted out of the cliff side at enormous expense—appear artfully undraped during the day, evenings are upscale, with lots of emphasis on clothing and style. The world-famous Pavillon Eden Roc, near a rock garden apart from the hotel, has a panoramic sea view. Venetian chandeliers, Louis XV chairs, and elegant draperies add to the drama. Lunch is served on a terrace, under umbrellas and an arbor.

Bd. J.-F.-Kennedy, 06600 Cap d'Antibes. ✆ 04-93-61-39-01. Fax 04-93-67-13-83. www.edenroc-hotel.fr. 140 units. 420€–550€ ($546–$715) double; 1,030€–1,200€ ($1,339–$1,560) suite. No credit cards. Closed mid-Oct to Apr. Bus: A2. **Amenities:** Restaurant; 2 bars; outdoor pool; gym; sauna; secretarial services; limited room service; massage; babysitting; laundry service; dry cleaning; nonsmoking rooms; limited-mobility rooms. *In room:* A/C, TV (on request), hair dryer, safe.

Hôtel Impérial Garoupe 🛇🛇   Within steps of the beach, this hotel is the centerpiece of a small park with rows of pines that block some of the sea views. The heiress to the Moulinex housewares fortune built it in 1993. Gilbert Irondelle, son of the director of Antibes's Grand Hôtel du Cap-Ferrat, has transformed it into a pocket of posh that's less intimidating than his father's more monumental hotel. The luxurious rooms contain contemporary furnishings, luxury beds, and deluxe bathrooms with tub/shower combinations. The in-house restaurant serves continental fare.

60–74 chemin de la Garoupe, 06600 Cap d'Antibes. ✆ 800/525-4800 in the U.S., or 04-92-93-31-61. Fax 04-92-93-31-62. www.imperial-garoupe.com. 34 units. 300€–550€ ($390 $715) double; 400€–750€ ($520–$905) suite. AE, DC, MC, V. Bus: A2. **Amenities:** Restaurant; bar; heated outdoor pool; 24-hr. room service; babysitting; laundry service; dry cleaning; nonsmoking rooms; limited-mobility rooms. *In room:* A/C, TV, dataport, minibar, hair dryer.

EXPENSIVE

Hôtel Royal   Built 90 years ago, this is the oldest hotel in Antibes. The famous guests of yesterday, like novelist Graham Greene, have long since checked out, and celebrities now go elsewhere. But the Royal has done a good job of staying abreast of changing times. All of its bedrooms have been modernized. The furniture is undistinguished, but the good mattresses are firm. The hotel also has a private stretch of beach for guest enjoyment. Even if you're not staying at the hotel, you can enjoy a meal at Le Dauphin, one of the hotel's two restaurants.

16–19 bd. du Maréchal-Leclerc, 06600 Antibes. ✆ 04-93-34-03-09. Fax 04-93-34-23-31. www.activehotels.com. 37 units. 90€–190€ ($117–$247) double. AE, DC, MC, V. Parking 8€. Closed Nov 2–Dec 18. Bus: A2. **Amenities:** Restaurant; bar; 24-hr. room service. *In room:* A/C, TV, hair dryer.

La Baie Dorée   Set between the sea and the coastal road, this hotel appears to rise from the water like a series of boxy, interlocked rectangles, each capped with a terracotta roof and ringed with strategically positioned balconies and terraces. From its base, a pier jutting out to sea allows guests to swim and boat, despite the lack of a sandy beach nearby. Public areas are dignified modern spaces with high ceilings; rectilinear lines; simple, summery furnishings; and big windows that seem to flood the interior with views of the nearby sea, almost as if you were aboard a yacht. Each room has a private terrace and a neatly kept bathroom. The upper-tier rooms have Jacuzzis.

579 bd. de la Garoupe, 06160 Cap d'Antibes. ✆ 04-93-67-30-67. Fax 04-92-93-76-39. www.baiedoree.com. 17 units. 200€–300€ ($260–$390) double; 400€–680€ ($520–$884) suite or duplex. Extra bed 40€ ($52). AE, MC, V. Closed Nov to mid-Dec. **Amenities:** Restaurant; 2 bars; 24-hr. room service; babysitting; laundry service; dry cleaning. *In room:* A/C, TV, minibar, hair dryer, safe.

MODERATE

Castel Garoupe *(Value* We highly recommend this Mediterranean villa, which was built in 1968 on a private lane in the center of the cape. It offers tastefully furnished, spacious rooms with fine beds and compact bathrooms with showers and tubs. Many rooms have private balconies, and each has shuttered windows. Some units have air-conditioning, and some have TVs. A tranquil garden flourishes on the premises.

959 bd. de la Garoupe, 06160 Cap d'Antibes. ℂ **04-93-61-36-51.** Fax 04-93-67-74-88. www.castel-garoupe.com. 28 units. 117€–150€ ($152–$195) double; 139€–245€ ($181–$319) studio apt with kitchenette. Rates include breakfast. AE, MC, V. Closed Nov to mid-Mar. Bus: A2. **Amenities:** 2 bars; outdoor pool; exercise room; limited room service; babysitting; laundry service; dry cleaning; nonsmoking rooms. *In room:* Dataport, kitchenette, minibar, hair dryer, safe.

Hôtel Beau Site   This white stucco villa with a tile roof and heavy shutters is surrounded by eucalyptus trees, pines, and palms. Located off the main road, a 7-minute walk from the beach, it has a low wall of flower turns and wrought-iron gates. The interior is like a country inn, with oak beams and antiques. The guest rooms are comfortable and well maintained, and bathrooms are small.

141 bd. J.-F.-Kennedy, 06150 Cap d'Antibes. ℂ **04-93-61-53-43.** Fax 04-93-67-78-16. www.hotelbeausite.net. 30 units. 85€–137€ ($111–$178) double. AE, DC, MC, V. Bus: A2. Closed Oct 21–Feb 17. **Amenities:** Bar; outdoor pool; 24-hr. room service; babysitting; laundry service; dry cleaning. *In room:* A/C, TV, hair dryer.

INEXPENSIVE

Le Cameo   On a historic square, this 19th-century Provençal villa is in the center of town. The rooms are old-fashioned and admittedly not for everyone—perhaps they are typical of the kind of place where Picasso might have stayed when he first hit town. Mattresses are well worn but still have comfort in them. Locals gather in the home-style dining room, with its bouquets of flowers and crowded tables. Look for a simple setting here and a goodwilled welcome from the accommodating staff.

Place Nationale, 06600 Antibes. ℂ **04-93-34-24-17.** Fax 04-93-34-35-80. 9 units, 5 with bathroom, 4 with shower only. 60€ ($78) double with shower; 65€ ($85) double with bathroom. DC, MC, V. Parking 5.30€ ($6.90). Closed Jan–Feb. Bus: A2. **Amenities:** Restaurant; bar, lounge. *In room:* TV.

WHERE TO DINE

Le Taverne du Saffranier *(Value* PROVENÇAL   Earthy and irreverent, this brasserie in a century-old building serves a changing roster of savory local specialties. Portions are generous. Examples are a platter of *petits farcis* (stuffed vegetables); a mini-bouillabaisse for single diners; savory fish soup; and an assortment of grilled fish (including sardines) that's served only with a dash of fresh lemon.

Place du Saffranier. ℂ **04-93-34-80-50.** Reservations recommended. Main courses 15€–30€ ($20–$39); fixed-price lunch menu 13€ ($17). No credit cards. Tues–Sun noon–2:30pm; Tues–Sat 7–10:30pm. Closed Jan.

Le Vieux Murs FRENCH/SEAFOOD   This charming Provençal tavern is inside the 17th-century ramparts that used to fortify the old seaport, not far from the Musée Picasso. White paint complements soaring stone vaults, and a glassed-in front terrace overlooks the water. The owner, Philippe Bensimon, and his chef, Thierry Gratarolla, run a warm, welcoming place. They use market-fresh ingredients, especially seafood, which is prepared with flavor and served with style. Daily offerings depend on what was best at the market. Provençal meat and poultry dishes are menu staples.

Promenade de l'Amiral-de-Grasse. ℂ **04-93-34-06-73.** Reservations recommended. Main courses 28€–35€ ($36–$46); fixed-price menu 39€–60€ ($51–$78). AE, MC, V. Daily 7:30–10:30pm.

Restaurant de Bacon ⭐⭐⭐ SEAFOOD   The Eden Roc restaurant at the Hôtel du Cap is more elegant, but Bacon serves the best seafood around. Surrounded by ultra-expensive residences, this restaurant on a rocky peninsula offers a panoramic coast view. Bouillabaisse aficionados claim that Bacon offers the best in France. In its deluxe version, saltwater crayfish float atop the savory brew; we prefer the simple version—a waiter adds the finishing touches at your table. If bouillabaisse isn't to your liking, try fish soup with garlic-laden *rouille* sauce, fish terrine, sea bass, or John Dory.

Bd. de Bacon. ⓒ **04-93-61-50-02**. Reservations required. Main courses 19€–118€ ($25–$153); fixed-price menu 48€–70€ ($62–$91). AE, MC, V. Wed–Sun noon–2pm; Tues–Sun 8–10pm. Closed Oct to mid-Feb.

7

The Eastern Riviera: From Biot to Monaco to Menton

At Biot, the Riviera continues east through a string of upscale resorts that embody the glamour of the **Côte d'Azur.** Several have been home to the 20th century's great writers and artists. Biot is no exception, with its museum dedicated to the art and life of long-time resident Fernand Léger. Set back from the coast, nearby Villeneuve-Loubet pays tribute to another art in the haute cuisine of Auguste Escoffier, the greatest chef ever to man a kitchen in a nation with a rich culinary heritage.

Farther into the foothills, many artisans live and work in Tourrettes-sur-Loup, where they sell their wares in small shops. Nearby Vence boasts Matisse's Chapelle du Rosaire, adorned by the masterful painter in his twilight years. The great artist is represented side by side with his contemporaries in St-Paul-de-Vence's Fondation Maeght, a museum as modern as the art it houses. Along the coast, Cagnes-sur-Mer continues the region's list of who's who in the 20th century—it was once home to Simone de Beauvoir, and it contains Les Collettes, Renoir's final home.

Nice, the Riviera's capital and largest city, is one of the few budget-oriented resorts on the coast, making it a good base for exploring the region. It features no less than five worthy museums and is filled with noteworthy architecture. Its residents have included Matisse, Stendhal, Nietzsche, George Sand, and Flaubert.

East of Nice is Villefranche-sur-Mer, a fishing village and naval port where small houses climb the hillside; these were once the residences of notables like Aldous Huxley, Katherine Mansfield, and Jean Cocteau. If you can't afford to stay in ultrachic St-Jean-Cap-Ferrat, you can at least sample the lifestyle at the Musée Ile-de-France, former home of a Rothschild heir, Baronne Ephrussi. Beaulieu is another pocket of posh, featuring a replica of an ancient Greek residence. Eze attracts with its garden of exotic plants, and the Roman ruins at La Turbie ensure a never-ending stream of visitors. Peillon is a scenic foothill village, seated 300m (1,000 ft.) above the nearby shore.

The tiny principality of Monaco is awash with rumors of royal romance and indiscretion, glamorous nightlife, and gambling. Just inland, northeast of Monaco, is the tranquil medieval mountain village of Roquebrune. Cap-Martin is another spot associated with the rich and famous ever since Empress Eugénie wintered here in the 19th century. And sleepy Menton, 8km (5 miles) east of Monaco, is more Italianate than French as it stands right at the border with Italy at the far eastern extremity of the Côte d'Azur.

The cornices of the Riviera, depicted in countless films, stretch from Nice to Menton. The Alps drop into the Mediterranean here, and roads were carved along the way. The lower road, 32km (20 miles) long, is the **Corniche Inférieure.** Along this road are the ports of Villefranche, Cap-Ferrat, Beaulieu, and Cap-Martin. The 31km (19-mile) **Moyenne Corniche (Middle Road)** ⍟⍟, built between World War I and World War II, runs from Nice to Menton, winding in and out of tunnels and through mountains. Napoleon built the **Grande Corniche** ⍟⍟⍟—the most panoramic—in 1806. La Turbie and Le Vistaero are the principal towns along the 32km (20-mile) stretch, which reaches more than 480km (1,600 ft.) high at Col d'Eze.

1 Biot ⍟

917km (570 miles) S of Paris; 10km (6 miles) E of Cagnes-sur-Mer; 6km (4 miles) NW of Antibes

Biot has been famous for its pottery ever since merchants began to ship earthenware jars to Phoenicia and destinations throughout the Mediterranean. Biot was first settled by Gallo-Romans and has had a long, war-torn history. The potters and other artists still work at their ancient crafts today. Biot is also the place Fernand Léger chose to paint until the day he died.

ESSENTIALS

GETTING THERE   Biot's **train** station is 3km (2 miles) east of the town center. There's frequent service from Nice and Antibes. For rail information and schedules, call ℂ **08-92-35-35-35.** The **bus** from Antibes is even more convenient than the train. For bus information and schedules, call ℂ **04-93-34-37-60** in Antibes. To **drive** to Biot from Nice, take N7 west. From Antibes, follow N7 east.

VISITOR INFORMATION   The **Office de Tourisme** is at 46 rue St-Sebastien (ℂ **04-93-65-78-00;** www.biot.fr).

EXPLORING THE TOWN

To explore the village, begin at the much-photographed **place des Arcades,** where you can see the 16th-century gates and the remains of the town's former ramparts. The **Eglise de Biot,** place des Arcades (ℂ **04-93-65-00-85**), dates from the 15th century, when it was built by Italian immigrants who arrived to resettle the town after its population was decimated by the "black death." The church is known for two stunning 15th-century retables: the red-and-gold *Retable du Rosaire* by Ludovico Bréa, and the recently restored *Christ aux Plaies* by Canavesio. The church is open daily from 8am to 7pm between May and June. And usually, but not always, on Friday or Saturday at 9pm, it's the site of Les Heures Musicales, wherein a series of classical concerts makes the ceiling vaults resonate with the sounds of classical music.

Musée d'Histoire Locale et de Céramique Biotoise   This museum displays the historical and contemporary work of local glassblowing artists, potters, ceramists, painters, and goldsmiths of the area. The museum, which can be visited in less than an hour, is mainly of interest to the serious collector. At least it helps you understand why Biot is the capital of glassblowing on the Riviera. You learn that the local soils provide the best sand for glassblowing. Since 1956 the old methods of making oil lamps and carafes have been revived. Look for the narrow-spouted *pontons* from which a jet of liquid such as wine can be poured straight into one's mouth.

Place de la Chapelle. ℂ **04-93-65-54-54.** Admission 2€ ($2.60) adults, 1€ ($1.30) children 6–16, free for children under 6. Wed–Sun 10am–6pm.

Musée National Fernand-Léger ⭐⭐   The artist's widow, Nadia Léger, assembled this collection and donated it to the French government after the artist's death, in 1955. Léger's mosaic-and-ceramic mural enhances the stone-and-marble facade. On the grounds is a polychrome ceramic sculpture, *Le Jardin d'enfant;* inside are two floors of geometrical forms in pure, flat colors. The collection includes paintings, ceramics, tapestries, and sculptures showing the artist's development from 1905 until his death. His paintings abound with cranes, acrobats, scaffolding, railroad signals, buxom nudes, casings, and crankshafts. The most unusual work depicts a Léger Mona Lisa *(La Giaconde aux Clés)* contemplating a set of keys, a wide-mouthed fish dangling over her head.

Chemin du Val-de-Pome (on the eastern edge of town, beside the road to the rail station). ℂ 04-92-91-50-30. Admission 4€ ($5.20), free for children under 7. July–Sept Wed–Mon 10:30am–6pm; Apr–June Wed–Mon 10am–12:30pm and 2–6pm; Oct–Mar Wed–Mon 10am–12:30pm and 2–5:30pm.

SHOPPING

Glass, pottery, and other crafts are what to look for in Biot. In the late 1940s, glassmakers created a bubble-flecked glass known as *verre rustique.* It comes in brilliant colors like cobalt and emerald and is displayed in many store windows on the main shopping street, **rue St-Sebastien.** Many interesting stores are also found in the pedestrian zone in Biot's historic center. Stroll along some of the oldest streets, like the **rue des Tines** and the **place des Arcades.** Most of the glassworks, and many shops selling glass, are at the lower (southern) side of town, beside the **Route de la Mer.**

The best place to watch the glassblowers and buy glass is **Verreries de Biot,** 5 chemin des Combes (ℂ **04-93-65-03-00**), at the edge of town. Established in 1956, it was the first, and remains the largest, of the many glassblowing establishments. Have a look at one-of-a-kind collector pieces at the Galerie International du Verre, where the beautifully displayed glass is for sale, often at exorbitant prices. Hours are Monday through Saturday from 9am to 6:30pm. You can also visit the showroom on Sunday from 10:30am to 1pm and 2:30 to 6:30pm (until 8pm in July and Aug).

The namesake of the **Galerie Jean-Claude Novaro** (also known as Galerie de la Patrimoine), place des Arcades (ℂ **04-93-65-60-23**), is known as the "Picasso of glass artists." His works are pretty and colorful, though sometimes lacking the diversity and intellectual flair of the artists displayed at the Galerie International du Verre.

La Poterie Provençale, 1689 rte. de la Mer (ℂ **04-93-65-63-30**), almost adjacent to the Musée Fernand-Léger, about 3km (2 miles) southeast of town, is one of the last potteries in Provence to specialize in the tall, amphora-like containers known as *jarres.* The place refers to itself as *une jarrière* because of its emphasis on the containers.

WHERE TO STAY

Domaine du Jas   Set at the base of the hill on which sits medieval Biot, this well-managed and intimate inn was built in the early 1990s in the form of three villa-inspired low-rise buildings clustered within a palm-studded garden around a rectangular swimming pool. Each unit has its own terrace or balcony, views of the pool or garden, and, in some cases, panoramas of medieval Biot rising dramatically on the slopes above. Color schemes, both around the pool and within the bedrooms, reflect the ochers, strong yellows, and verdant greens of Provence; throughout, floors are sheathed with slabs of flagstones. The Mascella-Torgoman family (Cherif and Christine) maintain this place much like a private home where friends of the family happen to drop in for extended stays. There's no reception desk, per se, but rather, an informal ambience that might remind you of a private house party.

No formalized restaurant or bar (that is, with a full-time waitstaff or bartender) is on the premises, but drinks and light luncheon platters and salads are served informally around the pool.

625 rte. de la Mer, 06410 Biot. ℂ 04-93-65-50-50. Fax 04-93-65-02-01. www.domainedujas.com. 19 units. 100€–235€ ($130–$306) double. AE, MC, V. Free parking. Closed Nov 15–Mar 15. **Amenities:** Outdoor pool; solarium; limited room service; babysitting; laundry service. *In room:* A/C, TV, dataport, hair dryer, safe.

WHERE TO DINE

Les Terraillers ✿✿✿ MEDITERRANEAN   This stone-sided restaurant is .8km (about ½ mile) south of Biot, in a 16th-century studio for the production of clay pots and ceramics. The cuisine of chef Claude Jacques, Michael Fulci, and their staff changes with the seasons and is more sophisticated and appetizing than that at many competitors. Examples are a platter containing two preparations of pigeon (thigh and breast cooked in different ways), served with a corn galette and the pigeon's own drippings; fish of the day in saffron sauce; roasted scallops with saffron and mussel-flavored cream sauce and leek confit; a tart with artichoke hearts and tomatoes en confit with lobster salad; braised John Dory Provençal style, with olive oil and a fricassée of zucchini, artichokes, tomatoes, and olives; and ravioli filled with pan-fried foie gras and served with essence of morels and mushroom duxelles.

11 rte. du Chemin-Neuf. ℂ 04-93-65-01-59. Reservations required as far in advance as possible. Main courses 32€–37€ ($42–$48); fixed-price menu 35€–40€ ($46–$52) lunch, 49€–70€ ($64–$91) dinner. AE, MC, V. June–Sept Fri–Wed noon–2pm and 7–10pm; Oct and Dec–May Fri–Tues noon–2pm and 7–10pm. Closed late Oct to Nov. Take rte. du Chemin-Neuf, following signs to Antibes.

2 Tourrettes-sur-Loup ✦

929km (577 miles) SE of Paris; 29km (18 miles) W of Nice; 6km (4 miles) W of Vence; 21km (13 miles) NE of Grasse

Often called the "City of Violets" because of the small purple flowers cultivated in abundance beneath the olive trees, Tourrettes-sur-Loup sits atop a sheer cliff overlooking the Loup valley. Though violets are big business for the town (they're sent to the perfume factories in Grasse, made into candy, and celebrated during a festival held each March), you'll probably find the many shops lining the streets much more interesting. These small businesses are often owned by artisans who sell their own art—most notably hand-woven fabrics and unique pottery. Even if you're not interested in buying, walking through the old town is worth the trip up the hill.

The unusual city was built so that the walls of the outermost buildings form a rampart; three towers rising above the village give it its name. A rocky horseshoe-shape path leads from the main square and then loops back again; follow it for a pleasant tour of the medieval village. Along the way, you'll pass the Chapelle St-Jean, with naïve frescoes that tell biblical stories, weaving in the traditions of local life. Also in the village is a 12th-century church that has paintings by the school of Brea. Immediately adjacent is a ruined 1st-century pagan shrine in honor of the Roman god Mercury. Access to these monuments is erratic and whimsical, depending on a local representative of the nearby **town hall** (ℂ 04-93-59-30-11). In theory, the sites can be visited Monday through Friday from 9am to 6pm, but to make sure, consult the town hall.

ESSENTIALS

GETTING THERE   The nearest rail junction (ℂ 04-97-03-80-80 for rail info) is at Cagnes-sur-Mer; buses run about every 45 minutes from Cagnes to Vence, where you must change to another bus to arrive in Tourettes (about six a day; trip time: 10

min.). The town has no bus station; the bus disembarks in the place du Village, in front of the Café des Sports. For **bus schedules** and information, call Ⓒ **04-93-42-40-79.** To go from Cagnes to Tourrettes takes about an hour—it's more convenient to take a taxi **R.A.I.S.** (Ⓒ **04-93-59-32-87** or 06-07-10-65-38) from Cagnes (they line up at the train station), around 22€ ($29) each way.

VISITOR INFORMATION   The **Office de Tourisme** is at 2 place de la Libération (Ⓒ **04-93-24-18-93**).

SHOPPING

Tourrettes-sur-Loup boasts more crafts studios than any other town its size in Provence. Nearly 30 artisans, including a handful of noted ones from as far away as Paris, have set up their studios and outlets, often in stone-sided buildings facing the town's main street, **Grand'Rue.** The best way to sample their offerings is to wander and window shop (the town's small size makes this feasible). Here's a list of recommendable artisans:

You'll find jewelry, in designs ranging from old-fashioned to contemporary, at **La Paësine,** 14 Grand'Rue (Ⓒ **04-93-24-14-55**). Original clothing—sometimes in silk—for men and women, as well as draperies, bed linens, and tablecloths, usually in creative patterns, is available at the **Atelier Arachnée,** 8 Grand'Rue (Ⓒ **04-93-24-11-42**). Ceramics crafted from local clay in patterns inspired by the many civilizations that have pillaged or prospered in Provence are sold at **Poterie Tournesol,** 7 Grand'Rue (Ⓒ **04-93-59-35-62**). **Isette L'Amoureux Fonderie d'Art,** 73 Grand'Rue (Ⓒ **04-93-24-11-74**), sells very unusual bronzes, some authorized by well-known masters of the modernist movement. For a view of canvases by painters inspired by the colors and traditions of Provence, head for **Galerie Eponyme,** 65 Grand'Rue (Ⓒ **04-93-24-39-72**), where the featured artist and owner is someone named Macha, a situation that could easily change by the time of your visit.

Looking for a pick-me-up after a day of shopping? Head for one of the region's best candy shops, **Confiserie des Gorges du Loup,** rue Pont St. Loup (Ⓒ **04-93-59-32-91**), where age-old techniques are used to layer fresh fruit with sugar. The result is an ultrachewy, ultrasweet confection that gradually melts as it explodes flavor into your mouth—the taste has been called "angelic." Sample chocolate-covered orange peel, rose-petal jam, and sugar-permeated sliced apricots, tangerines, plums, cherries, and grapes. Even the local violets are transformed into edible, sugary treats.

WHERE TO STAY

Auberge Belles Terrasses   This hotel offers views of the faraway peninsula of Antibes and the sea beyond. Its boxy shape and terra-cotta roof were inspired by an architect's fantasy of an old Provençal manor house, and it was named after the terraces that are angled for maximum exposure to the view. The rooms are simple, traditional, and comfortable, but not particularly stimulating. Bathrooms are small. Much of the allure of this place is its restaurant. Menu items include civet of roast suckling pig, young hen with freshwater crayfish, roast wild hare with mustard sauce, Provençal frogs' legs with garlic-and-butter sauce, and assorted game dishes.

1315 rte. de Vence, 06140 Tourrettes-sur-Loup. Ⓒ **04-93-59-30-03.** Fax 04-93-59-31-27. 15 units. 50€–73€ ($65–$95) double. MC, V. Closed mid-Nov to mid-Dec. From town, drive about a kilometer (a half-mile), following the signs toward Vence. **Amenities:** Restaurant. *In room:* TV.

WHERE TO DINE

Auberge Belles Terrasses (see "Where to Stay," above) is also recommended for its cuisine, except on Monday, when it's closed to nonguests.

If you're looking for a head-on view of everyday Provençal life, consider either a *plat du jour,* a glass of pastis, or *un petit café* at the most colorful and animated pub in town, **Le Café des Sports,** 1 Rte. de Vence/place de la Libération (© **04-93-59-30-26**). Its paneled interior is representative of old-fashioned Provence. It's open for drinks and coffee every day from 6:30am to 11pm, although the generous *plats du jour,* priced at 10€ ($13) (no credit cards), are trotted out only between noon and 2:45pm. Recorded music, gossip, chitchat, and the sounds of local scandal-mongering permeate the place every day after around 7pm, when it's everybody's favorite hangout.

Le Baccanale TRADITIONAL FRENCH   Uncomplicated and old-fashioned, and set on the street level of a 17th-century building on an all-pedestrian street in the heart of the town's historic zone, this restaurant serves traditional French dishes with an occasional modern twist. Your meal might begin with a platter of cured ham with bread and butter; steaming bowlfuls of leek and potato soup; foie gras of duckling with acacia-scented honey; and roasted lamb with rosemary and thyme.

21 Grand'Rue, Tourrettes-sur-Loup. © **04-93-24-19-19.** Reservations recommended. Main courses 12€–25€ ($16–$33); fixed-price menus 18€–42€ ($23–$55). AE, MC, V. Thurs–Mon noon–2pm and 7:30–10pm.

3 St-Paul-de-Vence ★★

925km (575 miles) S of Paris; 23km (14 miles) E of Grasse; 27km (17 miles) E of Cannes; 31km (19 miles) N of Nice

ESSENTIALS

GETTING THERE   The nearest **rail** station is in Cagnes-sur-Mer. Some 20 **buses** per day leave from Nice's Gare Routière, dropping passengers off in St-Paul-de-Vence (one-way fare: 4.10€/$4.70), then in Vence. For information, call the **Compagnie SAP** (© **04-93-58-37-60**). If you're **driving** from Nice, take the coastal A8 highway east, turn inland at Cagnes-sur-Mer, and follow signs north to St-Paul-de-Vence.

VISITOR INFORMATION   The **Office de Tourisme** is at 2 rue Grande (© **04-93-32-86-95;** www.saint-pauldevence.com).

EXPLORING THE TOWN

Except for local residents and service-related deliveries (such as dropping your luggage off at your hotel), driving a car within the center of St-Paul's old town is prohibited. The pedestrian-only **rue Grande** is the most interesting street, running the entire length of St-Paul. Most of the stone houses along it are from the 16th and 17th centuries, many still bearing the coats-of-arms placed here by the original builders. Today most of them are antiques shops, art-and-crafts galleries, and souvenir and gift shops—some are still artists' studios.

Near the church is the **Musée d'Histoire de St-Paul,** place de l'Eglise (© **04-93-32-41-13**), a museum in a village house that dates to the 1500s. It was restored and refurnished in 16th-century style, with artifacts illustrating the history of the village. It's open daily from 10am to 12:30pm and 1:30 to 5:30pm. Admission is 3€ ($3.90) adults, 2€ ($2.60) students and children 5 to 11, free for children under 5.

Fondation Maeght ★★★   This avant-garde building houses one of the most modern art museums in Europe. On a hill in pine-studded woods, the Fondation Maeght is like Shangri-La. Nature and the creations of men and women blend harmoniously in this unique achievement of the architect José Luis Sert. Its white concrete arcs give the impression of a giant pagoda.

A stark Calder rises like some futuristic monster on the lawn. In a courtyard, the bronze works of Giacometti and marble statues by Miró and mosaics by Chagall form a surrealistic garden. Sculpture is displayed inside, but the museum is at its best in a natural setting of terraces and gardens. Built on several levels, its many glass walls provide an indoor-outdoor vista. The foundation, a gift "to the people" from Aimé and Marguerite Maeght, also provides a showcase for new talent. Everywhere you look, you see 20th-century art: mosaics by Chagall and Braque, Miró ceramics in the "labyrinth," and Ubac and Braque stained glass in the chapel. Bonnard, Kandinsky, Léger, Matisse, Barbara Hepworth, and many other artists are well represented. On the property are a library, a cinema, and a cafeteria. In one showroom you can buy original lithographs by artists like Chagall and Giacometti, and limited-edition prints.

Outside the town walls. ℂ 04-93-32-81-63. Admission 11€ ($14) adults, 9€ ($12) students and ages 10–25, free for children under 10. July–Sept daily 10am–7pm; Oct–June daily 10am–12:30pm and 2:30–6pm.

La Collégiale de la Conversion de St-Paul   The church was constructed in the 12th and 13th centuries, though it was much altered over the years. The Romanesque choir is the oldest part, containing some remarkable stalls carved in walnut in the 17th century. The bell tower was built in 1740, but the vaulting was reconstructed in the 1800s. Although the facade today isn't alluring, the church is filled with art, notably a painting of Ste-Catherine d'Alexandrie, attributed to Tintoretto and hanging to the left as you enter. The Trésor de l'Eglise is one of the most beautiful in the Alpes-Maritimes, with a spectacular ciborium. Look also for a low relief of the Martyrdom of St-Clément on the last altar on the right. In the baptismal chapter is a 15th-century alabaster Madonna.

Place de l'Eglise. No phone. Free admission. Daily 9am–6pm (till 7pm July–Aug).

SHOPPING

Climb down some steep steps to a 14th-century wine cellar to visit **La Petite Cave de St-Paul,** 7 rue de l'Etoile (ℂ **04-93-32-59-54**), which stocks an excellent selection of regional wine. Among the shop's most prized wines are bottles from Le Mas Bernard, the winery owned by the Fondation Maeght, which owns only 3 hectares (7 acres) of vineyards west of St-Paul. The wine from Le Mas Bernard is very good and unavailable in the United States because of the small production. Other inventories within this shop include upscale and often esoteric wines from Provence, Les Alpes-Maritimes, and even the vineyards of the Ile St-Honorat, off the coast of Cannes, where an extremely limited production of wine derives from a local monastery there.

The village streets are chock-full of expensive boutiques and galleries. Some top galleries include Atelier/Boutique Christian Choisy, 5 rue de la Tour/Ramparts Ouest (ℂ **04-93-32-01-80**); and the small and less well-funded Galerie Lilo Marti, à la Placette (ℂ **04-93-32-91-22**). Focusing on sculpture and paintings, sometimes from Japan, jewelry lovers will want to check out Nicola's Tahitian Pearl, 47 rue Grande (ℂ **04-93-32-67-05**).

WHERE TO STAY

La Colombe d'Or (p. 290) also rents deluxe rooms.

VERY EXPENSIVE

Le Mas d'Artigny ✶✶✶ This hotel, one of the Riviera's grandest, evokes a sprawling Provençal homestead set in an acre of pine forests. In the lobby is a constantly changing art exhibit. Each of the comfortably large rooms has its own terrace or balcony, and suites have a private pool with hedges. Bathrooms are deluxe, with tub/shower combinations. The swimming situation is remarkable—guests in the 60 conventional rooms share a large pool, each of the suites has its own 2×6m (6×20 ft.) pool, and each of the four villas has an even bigger pool. The restaurant has magnificent views of the sea. The chef employs the flavors of Provence in his French, international, and Provençal specialties, using quality ingredients to shape his harmonious cuisine. The wine cellar deserves a star for its vintage collection, but watch those prices!

Rte. des Salettes, 06480 La Colle sur Loup. ℂ **04-93-32-84-54.** Fax 04-93-32-95-36. www.mas-artigny.com. 68 units. 150€–450€ ($195–$585) double; 650€–990€ ($845–$1,287) suite. Off-season discounts (about 30%) available. AE, DC, MC, V. From the town center, follow signs west about 2km (1¼ miles). **Amenities:** Restaurant; bar; 27 outdoor pools; tennis court; exercise room; sauna; mountain bikes; limited room service; babysitting; laundry service; dry cleaning. *In room:* A/C, TV, dataport, minibar, hair dryer.

EXPENSIVE

Hôtel Le St-Paul ✶✶✶ Converted from a 16th-century Renaissance residence and retaining many original features, this Relais & Châteaux member is in the heart of the village. The guest rooms, decorated in sophisticated Provençal style, have sumptuous beds and midsize bathrooms with tub/shower combinations. One woman wrote us that while sitting on the balcony of room no. 30, she understood why Renoir, Léger, Matisse, and Picasso were inspired by Provence. Many rooms enjoy a view of the valley with the Mediterranean in the distance. The restaurant has a flower-bedecked terrace sheltered by the 16th-century ramparts and a superb dining room with vaulted ceilings.

86 rue Grande, 06570 St-Paul-de-Vence. ℂ **04-93-32-65-25.** Fax 04-93-32-52-94. www.lesaintpaul.com. 19 units. 190€–300€ ($247–$390) double; 270€–560€ ($351–$728) suite. AE, DC, MC, V. Closed Dec to mid-Jan. **Amenities:** Restaurant; bar; 3 tennis courts; limited room service; babysitting; laundry service; limited-mobility rooms. *In room:* A/C, TV, minibar, hair dryer, safe.

Hôtel Les Vergers de Saint-Paul ✶ *(Finds* This is a small *hôtel de charme,* as the French say, lying just outside this medieval walled village. Completely renovated in 2002, the hotel lies only 900m (2,952 ft.) from the center of the village in an idyllic setting surrounded by greenery. Near the famous Fondation Maeght, the hotel is beautifully modern, opening onto a large pool. Bedrooms are tasteful, comfortable, and elegantly refined. All the accommodations come with a balcony or a terrace overlooking the pool.

940 rte. de la Colle, 06570 St-Paul-de-Vence. ℂ **04-93-32-94-24.** Fax 04-93-32-91-07. www.stpaulweb.net. 17 units. 135€–185€ ($176–$241) double; 225€–260€ ($293–$338) suite. AE, MC, V. **Amenities:** Bar; lounge; outdoor pool; limited room service; babysitting. *In room:* A/C, TV, hair dryer.

Villa St. Maxime ✶✶ *(Finds* An elegant discovery, this is one of the most charming of the small boutique hotels along the Riviera. Set on beautifully landscaped grounds, the hotel boasts a large panoramic terrace, a beautiful garden, and an Olympic-size pool. The location is beneath the ramparts of this old fortified town. Antiquity is combined with modern luxuries here. The town is ancient, but the villa is like a work of contemporary art, built with Provençal stone sculpted in bold lines, with a retractable and glass-enclosed reception atrium. Vaulted and pillared halls are architectural grace notes, as is the sleek marble flooring. Views extend from almost every window, even of the faraway Mediterranean. The best room is the largest suite with a trip of separate rooms; it contains the most luxurious bathroom in the hills of Nice. Other rooms are also a delight. Accommodations open onto private balconies or terraces.

390 rte. de la Colle, 06570 St-Paul-de-Vence. ⓒ **04-93-32-76-00.** Fax 04-93-32-93-00. www.villa-st-maxime.com. 6 units. 140€–190€ ($182–$247) double; 170€–350€ ($221–$455) suite. AE, MC, V. **Amenities:** Bar; outdoor pool; babysitting; gardens. *In room:* A/C, TV, minibar, hair dryer.

MODERATE
Auberge Le Hameau ⚘ *Value*　This romantic Mediterranean villa is on a hilltop on the outskirts of St-Paul-de-Vence, on the road to Colle at Hauts-de-St-Paul. Built as a farmhouse in the 1920s and enlarged and transformed into a hotel in 1967, it contains high-ceilinged rooms, each with a compact tub/shower bathroom. You'll have a remarkable view of the surrounding hills and valleys. There's also a vineyard and a sunny terrace with fruit trees, flowers, and a pool.

528 rte. de la Colle (D107), 06570 St-Paul-de-Vence. ⓒ **04-93-32-80-24.** Fax 04-93-32-55-75. 16 units. 94€–159€ ($122–$207) double; from 159€ ($207) suite. MC, V. Closed Jan 6–Feb 15 and Nov 16–Dec 22. From the town, take D107 about 1km (a half-mile), following the signs south of town toward Colle. **Amenities:** Bar; outdoor pool; laundry service. *In room:* TV, dataport.

Auberge Les Orangers ⚘ *Finds*　M. Franklin has created a "living oasis" in his villa which is configured like a highly personalized bed-and-breakfast. The scents of roses, oranges, and lemons waft through the air. The main lounge is decorated with original oils and furnished in a provincial style. Expect to be treated like a guest in a private home. The rooms, with antiques and Oriental carpets, have panoramic views; the small bathrooms have tub/shower combinations. Banana trees and climbing geraniums surround the sun terrace.

Quartier les Fumerates, rte. de la Colle (D107), 06570 St-Paul-de-Vence. ⓒ **04-93-32-80-95.** Fax 04-93-32-00-32. www.stpaulweb.com/hlo. 5 units. 120€–185€ ($156–$241) double. Rates include breakfast. MC, V. Free parking. From the town center, follow the signs to Cagnes-sur-Mer for 1km (½ mile) south. **Amenities:** Limited room service; babysitting. *In room:* Dataport, hair dryer.

INEXPENSIVE
Les Bastides St-Paul　This hotel is in the hills outside town, 1.5km (1 mile) south of St-Paul and 4km (2½ miles) south of Vence. Spread over two buildings, it offers comfortable carpeted rooms, each accented with regional artifacts and opening onto a terrace and garden. The compact bathrooms hold tub/shower combinations. On the premises is a pool shaped like a cloverleaf. Long-time hoteliers Marie José and Maurice Giraudet head the responsive management staff. Breakfast is served anytime you want it.

880 rte. des Blaquières (rte. Cagnes-Vence), 06570 St-Paul-de-Vence. ⓒ **04-92-02-08-07.** Fax 04-93-20-50-41. 20 units. 84€–125€ ($109–$163) double. AE, DC, MC, V. From the town center, follow signs toward Cagnes-sur-Mer for 1.5km (1 mile) south. **Amenities:** Outdoor pool; limited room service; babysitting; nonsmoking rooms; limited-mobility rooms. *In room:* A/C, TV, dataport, minibar, safe.

WHERE TO DINE
La Colombe d'Or ⚘ PROVENCAL　"The Golden Dove" is St-Paul's most celebrated restaurant—not for cutting-edge cuisine or exotic experiments, but for its remarkable art collection. You can dine amid Mirós, Picassos, Klees, Dufys, Utrillos, and Calders. In fair weather everyone tries for a seat on the terrace. You may begin your meal with smoked salmon or foie gras from Landes if you've recently won at the

casino. If not, you can count on a soup made with fresh seasonal vegetables. The best fish dishes are poached sea bass with mousseline sauce, and sea wolf baked with fennel. Tender beef comes with *gratin dauphinois* (potatoes), or you may prefer lamb from Sisteron. A classic finish to any meal is a *soufflé flambé au Grand-Marnier.*

The guest rooms (16 doubles, 10 suites) contain French antiques and Provençal accessories. Rooms are housed within the original 16th-century stone house and in two wings added in the 1950s, one of which stretches into the garden next to the pool. Some units have exposed stone and ceiling beams; all are comfortable, with air-conditioning, minibars, and TVs. Prices are 200€ to 320€ ($260–$416) for a double, from 320€ ($416) for a suite.

1 place du Général-de-Gaulle, 06570 St-Paul-de-Vence. (C) **04-93-32-80-02.** Fax 04-93-32-77-78. Reservations required. Main courses 14€–38€ ($18–$49). AE, DC, MC, V. Daily noon–2pm and 7:30–10pm. Closed Nov–Dec.

4 Vence ⋆

925km (575 miles) S of Paris; 31km (19 miles) N of Cannes; 24km (15 miles) NW of Nice

Travel up into the hills northwest of Nice—across country studded with cypresses, olive trees, and pines, where carnations, roses, and oleanders grow in profusion—and Vence comes into view. Outside the town, along boulevard Paul-André, two olive presses carry on with their age-old duties. But the charm lies in the Vieille Ville. Visitors invariably have themselves photographed on place du Peyra in front of the urnshape Vieille Fontaine, a background shot in several motion pictures. The 15th-century square tower is also a curiosity.

ESSENTIALS

GETTING THERE Frequent **buses** (no. 400 or 94) originating in Nice take about an hour to reach Vence; the one-way fare is 4.70€ ($6.10). For information, contact the **Compagnie SAP** ((C) **04-93-58-37-60).** The nearest **rail** station is in Cagnes sur Mer, about 10km (6 miles) southwest from Vence. From there, about 20 buses per day priced at 2.60€ ($3.40) make the trip to Vence. For train information, call (C) **08-92-35-35-35.** To **drive** to Vence from Nice, take N7 west to Cagnes-sur-Mer, then D236 north to Vence.

VISITOR INFORMATION The **Office de Tourisme** is on place Grand-Jardin ((C) **04-93-58-06-38;** www.ville-vence.fr).

EXPLORING THE TOWN

If you're wearing the right kind of shoes, the narrow, steep streets of the Old Town are worth exploring. Dating from the 10th century, the cathedral on place Godeau is unremarkable except for some 15th-century Gothic choir stalls. But if it's the right day of the week, most visitors quickly pass through the narrow gates of this once-fortified walled town to where the sun shines more brightly.

Chapelle du Rosaire ⋆⋆ It was a beautiful golden autumn along the Côte d'Azur. The great Henri Matisse was 77, and after a turbulent time he set out to design and decorate his masterpiece—"the culmination of a whole life dedicated to the search for truth," he said. Outside Vence, Matisse created the Chapelle du Rosaire for the Dominican nuns of Monteils. (Sister Jacques-Marie, a member of the order, had nursed him back to health after a serious illness.) From the front you might find it unremarkable and pass it by—until you spot a 12m (40-ft.) crescent-adorned cross rising from a blue-tile roof.

Exploring the Gorges du Loup

After paying your respects to Matisse at the Chapelle du Rosaire in Vence, you can take D2210 through some of the Riviera's most luxuriant countryside. The **Gorges du Loup** isn't as dramatic as the Grand Canyon du Verdon (see chapter 5) but still features a scenic 13km (8-mile) drive that loops along the gorge's eastern and western edges. This drive showcases waterfalls, most notably the **Cascades des Demoiselles,** with its partially fossilized plant life, and the 39m (130-ft.) **Cascade de Courmes.** There are also jagged glacial holes best exemplified by the **Saut du Loup** at the valley's northeastern end.

Gourdon, the only village along the gorge's western rim, has a year-round population of only 60 (100 if you include the population of the region immediately nearby), but in summer, its population swells into something approaching a honky-tonk tourist trap. If you stop here, ignore the dozens of souvenir shops and visit the immense and foreboding 13th-century **Château de Gourdon** (✆ **04-93-09-68-02**). The château houses two completely separate museums: **Musée Historique** features a collection of arms, furniture, sculpture (including *The Martyrdom of San Sebastian* by El Greco), and paintings (including *Descent from the Cross* by Rubens). Entrance costs 4€ ($5.20) for adults, 3€ ($3.90) for students and persons 10 to 18.

The château's other museum, which, frankly, we find more intriguing, and which draws bigger crowds, is the **Musée des Arts Décoratifs et de la Modernité** (sometimes abbreviated to simply **Musée de la Modernité**). Established in 2003, its inventions focus on about 800 pieces of Art Deco furniture from the 1920s and 1930s, and include some very fine pieces by such arts pioneers as Ruhlmann, Majorelle, Charou, and Mallet-Stevens, some of whose works profoundly affected the aesthetics of the Jazz Age on either side of the Atlantic. Entrance costs 10€ ($13) for adults, and 8€ ($10) for students and persons ages 10 to 18. Children under 10 are discouraged from entering because of the fragility of some of the pieces. Note that these museums are privately owned, and not in any way associated with any national or local government entity. Both of them are open June to September, daily from 11am to 1pm and 2 to 7pm, and October to May Wednesday to Monday from 2 to 6pm. Acquiring a ticket to either museum allows access to the château's formal, topiary-studded gardens, whose layout was designed by Le Nôtre, whose other works included some of the gardens at Versailles. Visits to the gardens are allowed during opening hours of the museum only.

Matisse wrote: "What I have done in the chapel is to create a religious space . . . in an enclosed area of very reduced proportions and to give it, solely by the play of colors and lines, the dimensions of infinity." The light picks up the subtle coloring in the simply rendered leaf forms and abstract patterns: sapphire blue, aquamarine, and lemon yellow. In black-and-white ceramics, St. Dominic is depicted in only a few lines. The most remarkable design is in the black-and-white-tile Stations of the Cross,

The **Musée de Peinture Naïve** offers a small Rousseau portrait, among other works. The magnificent 17th-century formal garden is graced with topiaries often photographed by gardening magazines. The museums are open June through September daily from 11am to 1pm and 2 to 7pm, and October through May Wednesday through Monday from 2 to 6pm. A combined ticket to the garden and the museums is 3.80€ ($4.95). Tickets to one or the other aren't available.

On the southeastern edge of the gorge, at Pont-du-Loup, go to **La Confiserie des Gorges du Loup,** rue Principale (© **04-93-59-32-91**), where you can sample sweets while watching the confectioners sugarcoat tangerines or chocolate-dip orange peels. Less than a kilometer farther south, the 15th-century Gothic church at Le Bar-sur-Loup features a morbid *Danse Macabre,* a 15th-century painting of fallen and dancing humans whose souls are being wrested away by black demons and then weighed by St. Michael before being tossed into the pits of hell. Speculation links the anonymous work of art to the plague.

After taking in this sober vision, backtrack to Pont-du-Loup and travel 8km (5 miles) east to **Tourrettes-sur-Loup,** where you can find accommodations in an unspoiled medieval village on a rocky bluff high above a violet-filled valley (see earlier in this chapter).

If you're coming from Cannes, take A85 for 21km (13 miles) northwest to Grasse, and then travel east for 6km (3¾ miles) on Route 2085, where you'll turn north at Magagnosc, following D3 for 8km (5 miles) north to Gourdon, at the edge of the gorge. To come from Nice, take E80 for 3km (2 miles) west to Route 2085, and then drive 26km (16 miles) west to Magagnosc, to follow the same path north to Gourdon. Once in Gourdon, you can continue north on D3 along the western rim of the gorge; after 6km (4 miles), turn right onto D6 to return south along its eastern lip. Turn east on D2210 at Pont-du-Loup for a 8km (5-mile) drive to Tourrettes-sur-Loup, or continue on to Vence, another 3km (2 miles) along, where you can turn south on Route 36 for a 9km (5½-mile) drive back to the coast.

For information, contact the **Office de Tourisme,** 22 cours Henri-Cresp, 06130 Grasse (© **04-93-36-66-66**); place Grand-Jardin, 06140 Vence (© **04-93-58-06-38**); or 5, Route de Vence, 06140 Tourrettes-sur-Loup (© **04-93-24-18-93**).

---

with Matisse's self-styled "tormented and passionate" figures. The bishop of Nice came to bless the chapel in the late spring of 1951 when the artist's work was completed. Matisse died 3 years later.

Av. Henri-Matisse. © **04-93-58-03-26**. Admission 2€ ($2.60) adults, free for children under 12; contributions to maintain the chapel are welcome. Dec 16–Nov 14 Tues and Thurs 10–11:30am; Mon–Thurs and Sat 2–5:30pm. Sun Mass 10am, followed by visit at 10:45am. Closed Nov 15–Dec 15.

WHERE TO STAY

VERY EXPENSIVE

Le Château du Domaine St-Martin ✦✦✦   If you're heading into the hill towns above Nice and you seek luxury and refinement, this is your address. The château, in a 14-hectare (35-acre) park with terraced gardens, was built in 1936 on the grounds where the "Golden Goat" treasure was reputedly buried. The main building holds the standard units; suites are in the tile-roofed villas. You can walk through the gardens on winding paths lined with tall cypresses, past the chapel ruins and olive trees. The spacious rooms are distinctively decorated, and the large rose-colored bathrooms have tub/shower combinations. The luxurious restaurant has a view of the coast and offers superb French cuisine. In summer, many guests prefer the poolside grill.

Av. des Templiers BP102, 06142 Vence. ℂ **04-93-58-02-02.** Fax 04-93-24-08-91. www.chateau-st-martin.com. 34 units, 6 villas. 245€–830€ ($319–$1,079) double; 660€–1,550€ ($858–$2,015) suite. AE, DC, MC, V. Closed mid-Oct to Feb. From the town center, follow signs toward Coursegoules and Col-de-Vence for 1.5km (1 mile) north. **Amenities:** Restaurant; bar; outdoor pool; 2 tennis courts; salon; 24-hr. room service; massage; babysitting; laundry service; dry cleaning; limited-mobility rooms. *In room:* A/C, TV, dataport, hair dryer, safe.

MODERATE

Hôtel Relais Cantemerle ✦   One of the most appealing places in Vence is this artfully designed cluster that resembles an old-fashioned compound of Provençal buildings. Capped with rounded terra-cotta roof tiles, they stand on a lawn dotted with old trees, surrounding a pool. Public areas, stylishly outfitted with Art Deco furniture and accessories, include a paneled bar and a sun-flooded flagstone terrace where meals are served. Rooms aren't overly large but contain unusual reproductions of overscale Art Deco armchairs, louvered wooden closet doors, and balcony-style sleeping lofts with comfortable beds. Most of the good-size bathrooms hold a combination tub/shower. The restaurant serves worthwhile regional and mainstream French cuisine.

258 chemin Cantemerle, 06140 Vence. ℂ **04-93-58-08-18.** Fax 04-93-58-32-89. www.relais-cantemerle.com. 28 units. 170€–195€ ($221–$254) double; 50€ ($65) extra bed. Half board 50€ ($58). AE, MC, V. Closed late Oct to mid-Mar. **Amenities:** Restaurant; bar; indoor pool; outdoor pool; gym; sauna; limited room service; babysitting; laundry service; dry cleaning; 2 limited-mobility rooms. *In room:* A/C, TV, dataport, minibar, hair dryer, safe.

Le Floréal   On the road to Grasse is this pleasant, comfortable hotel with a view of the mountains and a refreshing lack of pretension. Many of the well-furnished rooms look out into the garden, where orange trees and mimosas add fragrance to the breezes. Most accommodations are medium-size, and each is most comfortable, with quality linens. Bathrooms are compact and tiled.

Av. Rhin-et-Danube, 06140 Vence. ℂ **04-93-58-64-40.** Fax 04-93-58-79-69. 42 units. 65€–205€ ($85–$267) double. AE, DC, MC, V. Free parking. **Amenities:** Restaurant; bar; outdoor pool; sauna; 24-hr. room service; babysitting; laundry service; dry cleaning. *In room:* A/C, TV, hair dryer.

INEXPENSIVE

Auberge des Seigneurs ✦   This 400-year-old stone hotel gives you a taste of old Provence. Decorative objects and antiques are everywhere. The guest rooms are well maintained, but the management dedicates its energy to the restaurant. Nevertheless, the Provençal-style rooms are comfortable, with lots of exposed paneling and beams. Two have nonworking fireplaces. The small, tiled bathrooms contain showers. The restaurant is in a stone building that used to be the kitchen of the Château de Villeneuve, where François I spent part of his youth. The specialty is grills prepared on the open spit in view of the dining room, which holds a long wooden table and an open fireplace with a row of hanging copper pots and pans. Set menus cost from 30€ to 40€ ($39–$52).

Place du Frêne, 06140 Vence. ⓒ 04-93-58-04-24. Fax 04-93-24-08-01. 6 units. 65€–75€ ($85–$98) double. AE, DC, MC, V. Closed Nov–Mar 15. **Amenities:** Restaurant; bar; limited room service; nonsmoking rooms. *In room:* Dataport, hair dryer.

WHERE TO DINE

Auberge des Seigneurs (see above) is an excellent place to dine at reasonable prices.

La Farigoule PROVENÇAL   In a century-old house that opens onto a rose garden, this restaurant specializes in Provençal cuisine. Menu items are conservative but flavorful; they include *bourride Provençale* (bouillabaisse with a dollop of cream and lots of garlic); shoulder of roasted lamb with a ragoût of fresh vegetables, served with fresh thyme; aioli; and such fish dishes as dorado with confit of lemons and fresh, aromatic coriander. In the summer, you can dine in the rose garden.

15 rue Henri-Isnard. ⓒ 04-93-58-01-27. Reservations recommended. Main courses 22€–27€ ($29–$35); fixed-price menu 29€–43€ ($38–$56) dinner. MC, V. Thurs–Mon noon–2pm and 7:30–10pm. Closed Dec 7–Jan 7.

La Table d'Amis Jacques Maximum 🌟🌟🌟 MODERN FRENCH   This deluxe dining room is justly hailed as one of the Riviera's grandest restaurants. The setting is an artfully rustic 19th-century manor house that was transformed in the mid-1980s into the private home of culinary superstar Jacques Maximin. Today, it's the target of pilgrimages by foodies and movie stars venturing north from the Cannes Film Festival, including Hugh Grant, Elizabeth Hurley, and Robert De Niro. You can sample a menu devoted to the seasonal produce of the surrounding countryside. Stellar examples are salads made with asparagus and truffles, Canadian lobster, or fresh scallops; line-caught sea wolf Niçoise (with stewed tomatoes and peppers); pigeon breast with cabbage and lentil cream sauce; peppered duck; and some of the best beef dishes in the region. Expect surprises from the capricious chef, whose menu changes virtually every day.

689 chemin de la Gaude. ⓒ 04-93-58-90-75. Reservations required. Main courses 25€–65€ ($33–$85); fixed-price menu 50€ ($65) including wine. AE, MC, V. Wed–Sun 12:30–2pm and 7:30–10pm. Closed Nov 12–Dec 12. From the historic core of Vence, drive southwest for 4km (2½ miles), following signs to Cagnes-sur-Mer.

5 Cagnes-sur-Mer 🌟/Le Haut-de-Cagnes 🌟

917km (570 miles) S of Paris; 21km (13 miles) NE of Cannes

Cagnes-sur-Mer, like the Roman god Janus, has two faces. Perched on a hill in the "hinterlands" of Nice, **Le Haut-de-Cagnes** is one of the most charming spots on the Riviera. Naomi Barry of the *New York Times* wrote that it "crowns the top of a blue-cypressed hill like a village in an Italian Renaissance painting." At the foot of the hill is an old fishing port and rapidly developing beach resort called **Cros-de-Cagnes,** between Nice and Antibes.

For years, Le Haut-de-Cagnes attracted the French literati, including Simone de Beauvoir, who wrote *Les Mandarins* here. A colony of painters also settled in—Renoir stated that the village was "the place where I want to paint until the last day of my life." The racecourse is one of the finest in France.

ESSENTIALS

GETTING THERE   The **train** depot, Gare SNCF, lies in Cagnes-Ville (the more commercial part of town) at avenue de la Gare. It serves trains that run along the Mediterranean coast, with arrivals every hour from both Nice (trip time: 13 min.;

one-way fare 4.70€/$6.10) and Cannes (23 min.; 5.50€/$7.15). For rail information, call ℭ 08-92-35-35-35. **Buses** from Nice and Cannes stop at Cagnes-Ville and at Béal/Les Collettes, within walking distance of Cros-de-Cagnes. For information, call **The Société de Transports de Cagnes** (ℭ 04-93-20-45-05). The climb from Cagnes-Ville to Haut-de-Cagnes is strenuous; a free minibus runs daily about every 30 minutes year-round from place du Général-de-Gaulle in the center of Cagnes-Ville to Haut-de-Cagnes. By **car** from any of the coastal cities of Provence, follow the A8 coastal highway, exiting at CAGNES-SUR-MER/CROS-DE-CAGNES.

VISITOR INFORMATION The **Office de Tourisme** is at 6 bd. Maréchal-Juin, Cagnes-Ville (ℭ 04-93-20-61-64; www.cagnes-tourisme.com).

SPECIAL EVENTS Cagnes is the site, for 2 days every August, of a **Medieval Festival** *(La Fête Médiévale de Cagnes)* that dominates the medieval core of Hauts-de-Cagnes. Highlights include equestrian tournaments, jousting exhibitions, and knights, knaves, and damsels in medieval costumes. Tickets to and information about each of the individual events comprising the festival sell for between 7€ and 15€ ($9.10–$20) each, and are available at the local tourist office.

SEEING THE SIGHTS

The orange groves and fields of carnations of the upper village provide a beautiful setting for the narrow cobblestone streets and 17th- and 18th-century homes. Drive your car to the top, where you can enjoy the view from place du Château and have lunch or a drink at a sidewalk cafe.

While in Le Haut-de-Cagnes, visit the **fortress** on place Grimaldi. It was built in 1301 by Rainier Grimaldi I, a lord of Monaco and a French admiral (see the portrait inside). Charts reveal how the defenses were organized. In the early 17th century, the dank castle was converted into a more gracious Louis XIII–style château.

The château contains two interconnected museums, the **Musée de l'Olivier (Museum of the Olive Tree)** and the **Musée d'Art Moderne Méditerranéen (Museum of Modern Mediterranean Art),** 7 place Grimaldi (ℭ 04-92-02-47-30). The modern art gallery displays works by Kisling, Carzou, Dufy, Cocteau, and Seyssaud, among others, with temporary exhibitions. In one salon is an interesting *trompe-l'oeil* fresco, *La Chute de Phaeton*. From the tower, you get a panoramic view of the Côte d'Azur. The museums are open Wednesday to Monday: May to September 10am to noon and 2 to 6pm, and October to April 10am to noon and 2 to 5pm. Admission to both museums is 3€ ($3.90) for adults and 1.50€ ($1.95) for students and children under 12.

A DAY AT THE BEACH

Cros-de-Cagnes, a part of Cagnes-Sur-Mer is known for its 4km (2½ miles) of seafront, covered with light-gray pebbles smoothed by centuries of wave action. These beaches are **Plages de Cros-de-Cagnes.** As usual, toplessness is accepted but full nudity isn't.

At least five concessions along this expanse rent beach mattresses and chaises for 15€ ($20). The most centrally located are **Tiercé Plage** (ℭ 04-93-20-13-89), **Le Cigalon** (ℭ 04-93-07-74-82), **La Gougouline** (ℭ 04-93-31-08-72) and **Le Neptune** (ℭ 04-93-20-10-59).

The orange groves and fields of carnations of the upper village provide a beautiful setting for the narrow cobblestone streets and 17th- and 18th-century homes. Drive to the top, where you can enjoy the view from **place du Château** and have lunch or a drink at a sidewalk cafe.

A NEARBY ATTRACTION

Musée Renoir & Les Collettes ⍟   Les Collettes has been restored to its appearance when Renoir lived here, from 1908 until his death in 1919. He continued to sculpt here, even though he was crippled by arthritis. He also continued to paint, with a brush tied to his hand and with the help of assistants.

The house was built in 1907 in an olive and orange grove. There's a bust of Mme Renoir in the entrance room. You can explore the drawing room and dining room on your own before going up to the artist's bedroom. In his atelier are his wheelchair, easel, and brushes. The terrace of Mme Renoir's bedroom faces a stunning view of Cap d'Antibes and Haut-de-Cagnes. On a wall hangs a photograph of one of Renoir's sons, Pierre, as he appeared in the 1932 film *Madame Bovary.* Although Renoir is best remembered for his paintings, in Cagnes he began experimenting with sculpture. The museum has 20 portrait busts and portrait medallions, most of which depict his wife and children. The curators say they represent the largest collection of Renoir sculpture in the world.

19 chemin des Collettes. ⓒ **04-93-20-61-07.** Admission 3€ ($3.90) adults, 1.50€ ($1.95) children 12–18, free for children under 12. May–Sept Wed–Mon 10am–noon and 2–6pm; Oct–Apr Wed–Mon 10am–noon and 2–5pm. Ticket sales end 30 min. before lunch and evening closing hours.

WHERE TO STAY

IN CAGNES-SUR-MER

Domaine Cocagne ⍟   This is the finest hotel in Cagnes-sur-Mer. An inviting and modern building, it strides a hilltop overlooking the Mediterranean, and 4.8 hectares (12 acres) of park and forest. Many of the medium-size and well-furnished bedrooms open onto a view of the château. Bedrooms are most comfortable, each coming with a tiled bathroom with tub or shower. The restaurant around the swimming pool serves a savory Mediterranean cuisine and has an excellent wine cellar of regional wines. You can rent standard double rooms, or, if you're willing to pay more, a fully furnished apartment.

30 Chemin du Pain de Sucre, Colline de la route de Vence. 06800 Cagnes-sur-Mer. ⓒ **04-92-13-57-77.** Fax 04-92-13-57-89. www.domainecocagne.com. 17 suites. 184€–244€ ($239–$317) double; 300€–720€ ($390–$936) apt; 268€–335€ ($348–$436) suite. AE, MC, V. **Amenities:** Restaurant; bar; outdoor pool; limited room service; babysitting; limited-mobility rooms. *In room:* A/C, TV, dataport, minibar, hair dryer.

Hôtel Le Chantilly ⟨*Value*⟩   This is the best bargain for those who prefer to stay near the beach. Built in a boxy and angular style in 1960, it won't win any architectural awards, but the owners have landscaped the property and made the interior as homey and inviting as possible, with Oriental rugs and potted plants. Most rooms are small but cozily furnished and well kept, often opening onto balconies; each has a compact tiled bathroom with shower. In fair weather you can enjoy breakfast, the only meal served, on an outdoor terrace.

31 chemin de la Minoterie, 06800 Cagnes-sur-Mer. ⓒ **04-93-20-25-50.** Fax 04-92-02-82-63. www.chdemeures.com/chantilly. 20 units. 56€–69€ ($73–$90) double; 96€–126€ ($124–$164) suite. AE, DC, MC, V. Parking 6€ ($7.80). **Amenities:** Limited room service; babysitting; nonsmoking rooms. *In room:* TV, dataport, minibar.

IN LE HAUT-DE-CAGNES

Note that **Le Grimaldi** (see "Where to Dine," below) also rents rooms.

Le Cagnard ⭐⭐⭐ Several 13th-century houses were joined in the 1960s to form this complex, a glamorous Relais & Châteaux property. The dining room is covered with frescoes, and there's a vine-draped terrace. The rooms and salons are furnished with antiques such as provincial chests, armoires, and Louis XV chairs. Each room has its own style: Some are duplexes; others have terraces and views of the countryside. The luxurious bathrooms are spacious, with tub/shower combinations.

The cuisine of chef Jean-Yves Johany is reason enough to make the trip. Fresh ingredients go into delectable dishes. Set-price menus cost 55€ to 85€ ($72–$111) at lunch, and 65€ to 85€ ($85–$111) at dinner. The hotel is open year-round; the restaurant closes from November to December 15 and on Monday, Tuesday, and Thursday at lunch.

Rue du Pontis-Long, Le Haut-de-Cagnes, 06800 Cagnes-sur-Mer. © **04-93-20-73-21**. Fax 04-93-22-06-39. www.le-cagnard.com. 25 units. 135€–255€ ($176–$332) double; 180€–485€ ($234–$631) suite. AE, DC, MC, V. Parking 8€ ($10). **Amenities:** Restaurant; bar; limited room service; babysitting; laundry service; dry cleaning; nonsmoking rooms; limited-mobility rooms. *In room:* A/C, TV, dataport, minibar, hair dryer, iron, safe.

WHERE TO DINE
IN LE HAUT-DE-CAGNES

Fleur de Sel FRENCH/PROVENÇAL Energetic owners Philippe and Pascale Loose run this charming restaurant in a 200-year-old stone-sided house in the center of the village. In two ocher-toned dining rooms outfitted with Provençal furniture and oil paintings of bouquets of culinary ingredients, you'll enjoy the kind of cuisine that Philippe learned during employment stints at some of the grandest restaurants of France, including a brief time with Marc Meneau at L'Espérance in Vezélay. Tasty recommendations include foie gras with artichoke hearts in puff pastry; cappuccino of crayfish with paprika and pistachios; scallops braised with spinach; and filet of beef braised in a hearty local red wine, Bellet.

85 Montée de la Bourgade. © **04-93-20-33-33**. Reservations recommended. Main courses 14€–23€ ($18–$30); fixed-price menu 21€–39€ ($27–$51). MC, V. Fri–Tues noon–2pm; Thurs–Tues 7:30–10pm.

Josy-Jo ⭐⭐ TRADITIONAL FRENCH Le Cagnard (see "Where to Stay," above) has a more elegant setting, but the food here is comparable. Behind a 200-year-old facade covered with vines and flowers, this restaurant was the home and studio of Modigliani and Soutine during their hungriest years. Paintings cover the walls, and the Bandecchi family runs everything smoothly. The menu features grilled meats and a variety of fish. You can enjoy brochette of gigot of lamb with kidneys; calves' liver; homemade terrine of foie gras of duckling; stuffed Provençal vegetables "in the style of Grandmother"; and an array of salads.

8 place du Planastel. © **04-93-20-68-76**. Reservations required. Main courses 25€–28€ ($33–$36). AE, MC, V. Mon–Fri 12:30–2pm; Mon–Sat 7:30–9:30pm. Closed Nov 19–Dec 22.

Le Grimaldi TRADITIONAL FRENCH Here you can dine under bright parasols on the town's main square or, if you prefer, within a room that was originally built during the Middle Ages. Taken over by new, English-speaking owners in 2004, the restaurant attracts many local diners thanks partly to a well-prepared versions of salad Niçoise, risotto laced with scallops; velvety foie gras, roasted rabbit with mushrooms and fresh vegetables, and poached turbot with butter-flavored wine sauce, fresh asparagus, and vegetable flan.

The establishment, which was radically upgraded by the owners, offers five comfortable but unfrilly bedrooms, usually with the original, rough-hewn ceiling beams and furniture inspired by traditional Provençal models. With breakfast included, doubles rent for 125€ ($163) per night, suites 165€ ($215), plus 9€ ($12) per night for overnight parking. Each unit has a private bathroom with shower.

6 place du Château. (C) 04-93-20-60-24. Reservations recommended. Fixed-price menus 32€–52€ ($42–$68). AE, DC, MC, V. Daily noon–3pm and 7:30–11pm. Closed Jan 15–Feb 15.

IN CROS-DE-CAGNES

Loulou (La Réserve) *逸逸* FRENCH   This restaurant, which like Josy-Jo and Cagnard has a Michelin star, makes the Cagnes area a gourmet enclave. It's across the boulevard from the sea and named for a famous long-departed chef. Brothers Eric and Joseph Campo prepare spectacular versions of fish soup; shrimp steamed and served with fresh ginger and cinnamon; and grilled versions of the catch of the day. These dishes are served as simply as possible, usually with just a drizzling of olive oil and balsamic vinegar. Meat dishes include flavorful veal kidneys with port sauce, and delicious grilled steaks, chops, and cutlets. Dessert might include caramelized-apple tart. The glassed-in veranda in front is a prime people-watching spot.

91 bd. de la Plage. (C) 04-93-31-00-17. Reservations recommended. Main courses 27€–85€ ($35–$111); fixed-price menu 38€ ($49). AE, MC, V. Mon–Fri noon–1:30pm and 7:30–9:30pm; Sat 7–9:30pm.

6 Nice *★★★*

929km (577 miles) S of Paris; 32km (20 miles) NE of Cannes

The Victorian upper classes and tsarist aristocrats loved Nice in the 19th century, but it's solidly middle class today, and far less glamorous and expensive than Cannes—the least expensive of any resort. It's also the best excursion center on the Riviera, especially if you're dependent on public transportation. For example, you can go to San Remo, "the queen of the Italian Riviera," and return to Nice by nightfall. From the Nice airport, the second largest in France, you can travel by bus along the entire coast to resorts like Juan-les-Pins and Cannes.

Nice is the capital of the Riviera, the largest city between Genoa and Marseille. It's also one of the most ancient, having been founded by the Greeks, who called it "Nike," or Victory. Because of its brilliant sunshine and relaxed living, it has attracted artists and writers. Among them were Dumas, Nietzsche, Apollinaire, Flaubert, Victor Hugo, George Sand, Stendhal, Chateaubriand, and Mistral. Henri Matisse, who made his home in Nice, said, "Though the light is intense, it's also soft and tender." The city has, on the average, 300 days of sunshine a year.

ESSENTIALS

GETTING THERE   **Trains** arrive at Gare Nice-Ville, avenue Thiers (© 08-92-35-35-35). From there you can take trains to Cannes, Monaco, and Antibes, with easy connections to anywhere else along the Mediterranean coast. A small tourist center is open at the train station from Monday to Saturday from 8am to 7pm and Sunday from 9am to 6pm. If you face a long delay, you can eat at the cafeteria and even shower at the station.

Buses to and from Monaco, Cannes, St-Tropez, and other parts of France and Europe serve the main bus station, or **Gare Routière**, 5 bd. Jean-Jaurès (© 04-93-85-61-81).

Transatlantic and intercontinental flights land at **Aéroport Nice–Côte d'Azur** (© 08-20-42-33-33). From there, municipal bus no. 98 departs at 20-minute intervals for the Gare Routière (see above); the one-way fare is 1.30€ ($1.70). Bus nos. 23

and 99 go to Gare SNCF. More luxurious is a yellow-sided shuttle bus *(la navette de l'aéroport)* that charges 3.50€ ($4.55) for a ride between the airport and the bus station. A **taxi** from the airport into the city center will cost at least 20€ to 25€ ($26–$33) each way. Trip time is less than 30 minutes.

VISITOR INFORMATION   Nice maintains three tourist offices, the largest and most central of which is at 5 promenade des Anglais, near place Masséna (℃ 08-92-70-74-07; fax 04-92-14-48-73; www.nicetourism.com). Additional offices are in the arrivals hall of the Aéroport Nice–Côte d'Azur and the railway station on avenue Thiers. Any office can make a hotel reservation (but only for the night of the day you show up), for a modest fee that varies according to the classification of the hotel.

GETTING AROUND   Most local buses serve the **Station Central SNCF,** 10 av. Félix-Faure (℃ 04-93-13-53-13), a very short walk from the place Masséna. Municipal buses charge 1.30€ ($1.70) for a ride within Greater Nice. To save money, consider buying a *carnet* entitling you to 14 rides for 16€ ($18). Bus nos. 2 and 12 make frequent trips to the beach.

No point within downtown Nice is more than about a 10-minute walk from the sea-fronting promenade, site of such well-known quais as the promenade des Anglais and the promenade des États-Unis. Bus nos. 2 and 12 run along its length, dropping passengers off at any of the beaches and beach-fronting concessions that front the edge of the sea.

The best place to rent bikes and mopeds is **Cycles Arnaud,** 5 rue François 1er (℃ 04-93-87-88-55), just behind the place Grimaldi. Open Monday to Friday from 9am to noon and 2 to 7pm, it charges 15€ ($20) per day for a bike or moped, and requires a deposit of at least 50€ ($65), depending on the value of the machine you rent. Somewhat less appealing, but useful when Cycles Arnaud is closed, is **Nicea Rent,** 12 rue de Belgique (℃ 04-93-82-42-71, or 06-12-44-15-37 for somewhat erratic mobile phone service). It charges about the same rates, but the staff isn't always on the premises.

SPECIAL EVENTS   The **Nice Carnaval** draws visitors from all over Europe and North America. The "Mardi Gras of the Riviera" begins sometime in February, usually 12 days before Shrove Tuesday, celebrating the return of spring with 3 weeks of parades, *corsi* (floats), *veglioni* (masked balls), confetti, and battles in which young women toss flowers. Only the most wicked throw rotten eggs instead of carnations. The climax, a fireworks display on Shrove Tuesday, lights up the Baie des Anges (Bay of Angels). King Carnival goes up in flames on his pyre but rises from the ashes the following spring. For information, contact the tourist office (see above).

The **Nice Festival du Jazz** runs for a week in mid-July, when jazz artists perform in the ancient Arène de Cimiez. For information, call ℃ **04-97-13-36-86.**

EXPLORING THE CITY

In 1822, the orange crop at Nice was bad and the workers faced a lean time, so the English residents put them to work building the **promenade des Anglais** ⚘⚘, a wide boulevard fronting the bay. Split by "islands" of palms and flowers, it stretches for about 6km (4 miles). Fronting the beach are rows of grand cafes, the **Musée Masséna,** villas, and hotels—some good, others decaying.

In the east, the promenade becomes **quai des Etats-Unis,** the original boulevard, lined with some of the best restaurants in Nice, all specializing in bouillabaisse. Rising sharply on a rock is the site known as **Le Château,** the spot where the ducs de

Nice Attractions

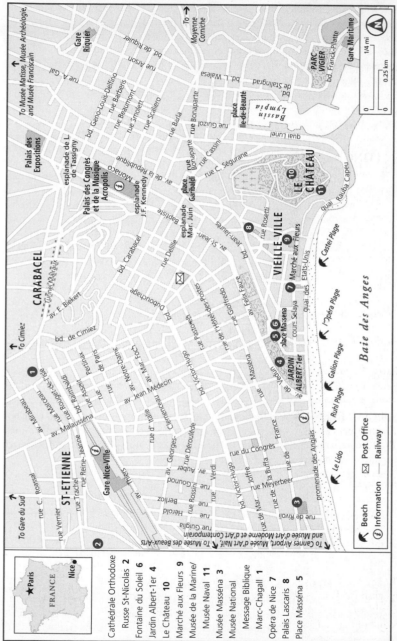

Cathédrale Orthodoxe
Russe St-Nicolas **2**
Fontaine du Soleil **6**
Jardin Albert-1er **4**
Le Château **10**
Marché aux Fleurs **9**
Musée de la Marine/
Musée Naval **11**
Musée Masséna **3**
Musée National
Message Biblique
Marc-Chagall **1**
Opéra de Nice **7**
Palais Lascaris **8**
Place Masséna **5**

🏖 Beach
ℹ Information
⊠ Post Office
— Railway

Savoie built their castle, which was torn down in 1706. All that remains are two or three stones—even the foundations have disappeared in the wake of Louis XIV's deliberate destruction of what was viewed at the time as a bulwark of Provençal resistance to his regime. The hill has been turned into a garden of pines and exotic flowers. To reach the panoramic site, you can take an elevator. The park is open daily from 8am to dusk.

At the north end of Le Château is the famous old **graveyard** of Nice, visited primarily for its lavishly sculpted monuments that make their own enduring art statement. It's the largest in France and the fourth largest in Europe.

Continuing east from "The Rock," you reach the harbor, where the restaurants are even cheaper and the bouillabaisse is just as good. While sitting here lingering over an aperitif at a sidewalk cafe, you can watch the boats depart for Corsica (or perhaps take one yourself). The port was excavated between 1750 and 1830. Since then, an outer harbor—protected by two jetties—has also been created.

The "authentic" Niçoise live in **Vieille Ville** ⚘, the old town, beginning at the foot of "The Rock" and stretching out from place Masséna. Sheltered by sienna-tiled roofs, many of the Italianate facades suggest 17th-century Genoese palaces. The old town is a maze of narrow streets, many of them teeming with local life. Some, including the rue Masséna, the rue Droite, and the rue Pairolière, are reserved exclusively for pedestrians. On these narrow streets, you'll find some of the least expensive restaurants in Nice. Buy *la pissaladière* (an onion pizza) from one of the local vendors. Many of the old buildings are painted a faded Roman gold, and banners of multicolored laundry flaps in the sea breezes.

While here, try to visit the **Marché aux Fleurs,** the flower market at cours Saleya. The vendors start setting up their stalls Tuesday through Sunday from 8am to 6pm in summer, and from 8am till between 2 and 4pm in winter. A flamboyant array of carnations, violets, jonquils, roses, and birds of paradise is hauled in by vans or trucks and then displayed in the most fragrant market in town.

Nice's commercial centerpiece is **place Masséna,** with pink buildings in the 17th-century Genoese style and the **Fontaine du Soleil (Fountain of the Sun)** by Janoit, from 1956. Stretching from the main square to the promenade is the **Jardin Albert-1er,** with an open-air terrace and a Triton Fountain. With palms and exotic flowers, it's the most relaxing oasis at the resort.

MUSEUMS

Nice has a higher density of museums than in many comparable French cities. If you decide to forgo the beach and devote your time to some of the best-respected museums in the south of France, buy a **Carte Passe-Musée,** which admits you to seven of the city's largest municipal museums. A 7-day pass, available from the tourist office or any of the municipal museums, costs 6€ ($7.80). There are no discounts for students or children. For more information, call ⓒ **04-93-62-61-62.**

Musée d'Art Moderne et d'Art Contemporain ⚘⚘   French and American
avant-garde art from the 1960s until the 21st century is displayed here in a museum composed of a quartet of square towers with rooftop terraces. Each section is linked by a glass passageway. We know of no other museum that so dramatically reveals the growth of parallel art movements in two countries, evolving at the same time. In the '60s it was called American pop art, whereas on the Riviera it was known as Nouveau Réalisme, but the results are very similar. Pop artists such as all the big names, including Andy Warhol, Roy Lichtenstein, and Robert Rauschenberg are featured, of course.

One entire section of the museum is devoted to the French artist Yves Klein (1928–92). His two major works, *Garden of Eden* and *Wall of Fire*, can be seen on the rooftop terraces. Some of the outstanding works displayed are by artists of the Nice School, including Sacha Sosno, Robert Malavaal, Ben Vautier, and Jean-Claude Fahri.

Promenade des Arts. ℂ **04-93-62-61-62.** Admission 4€ ($5.20) adults, 2.50€ ($3.25) students, free for ages 17 and under. Tues–Sun 10am–6pm. Bus: 1, 2, 3, 5, 6, 16, or 25.

Musée des Beaux-Arts ⚘⚘   The collection is in the former residence of the Ukrainian Princess Kotchubey. It has an important gallery devoted to the masters of the Second Empire and the belle époque, with an extensive collection of 19th-century French experts. The gallery of sculptures includes works by J. B. Carpeaux, Rude, and Rodin. Note the important collection by a dynasty of painters, the Dutch Vanloo family. One of its best-known members, Carle Vanloo, born in Nice in 1705, was Louis XV's premier *peintre*. A fine collection of 19th- and 20th-century art includes works by Ziem, Raffaelli, Boudin, Monet, Guillaumin, and Sisley.

33 av. des Baumettes. ℂ **04-92-15-28-28.** Admission 4€ ($5.20) adults, 2.50€ ($3.25) students, free for children under 18. Tues–Sun 10am–6pm. Bus: 3, 9, 12, 22, 24, 38, 60, or 62.

Musée International d'Art Naïf Anatole-Jakovsky (Museum of Naïve Art) ⚘
This museum is in the beautifully restored Château Ste-Hélène in the Fabron district. The museum's namesake, for years one of the world's leading art critics, once owned the collection. His 600 drawings and canvases were turned over to the institution and opened to the public. Artists from more than two dozen countries are represented by everything from primitive painting to 20th-century works.

Château St-Héléne, av. de Fabron. ℂ **04-93-71-78-33.** Admission 4€ ($5.20) adults, 2.50€ ($3.25) seniors and students, free for children under 19. Wed–Mon 10am–6pm. Bus: 9, 10, 12, or 23; 10-min. walk.

MORE SIGHTS

Cathédrale Orthodoxe Russe St-Nicolas à Nice ⚘   Ordered and built by none other than Tsar Nicholas II, this is the most beautiful religious edifice of the Orthodoxy outside Russia, and a perfect expression of Russian religious art abroad. It dates from the belle époque, when some of the Romanovs and their entourage turned the Riviera into a stomping ground (everyone from grand dukes to ballerinas walked the promenade). The cathedral is richly ornamented and decorated with icons. You'll spot the building from afar because of its collection of ornate onion-shaped domes. During church services on Sunday morning, the building closes to tourist visits.

Av. Nicolas-II (off bd. du Tzaréwitch). ℂ **04-93-96-88-02.** Admission 2.50€ ($3.25) adults, 2€ ($2.60) students, free for children under 12. May–Sept daily 9am–noon and 2:30–6pm; Oct–Apr daily 9:30am–noon and 2:30–5pm. From the central rail station, head west along av. Thiers to bd. Gambetta, then go north to av. Nicolas-II.

Palais Lascaris *Kids*   The baroque Palais Lascaris in the city's historic core is associated with the Lascaris-Vintimille family, whose recorded history predates the year 1261. Built in the 17th century, it contains elaborately detailed ornaments. An intensive restoration by the city of Nice in 1946 brought back its original beauty, and the palace is now classified as a historic monument. The most elaborate floor, the *étage noble*, retains many of its 18th-century panels and plaster embellishments. A pharmacy, built around 1738 and complete with many of the original Delftware accessories, is on the premises.

15 rue Droite. ℂ **04-93-62-72-40.** Free admission. Wed–Mon 10am–6pm. Bus: 1, 2, 3, 5, 6, 14, 16, or 17.

NEARBY SIGHTS IN CIMIEZ

In the once-aristocratic hilltop quarter of **Cimiez** ⍟, Queen Victoria wintered at the Hôtel Excelsior and brought half the English court with her. Founded by the Romans, who called it Cemenelum, Cimiez was the capital of the Maritime Alps province. Recent excavations have uncovered the ruins of a Roman town, and you can wander among the diggings. The arena was big enough to hold at least 5,000 spectators, who watched contests between gladiators and wild beasts shipped in from Africa. To reach this suburb, take bus no. 15 or 17 from place Masséna.

Monastère de Cimiez (Cimiez Convent) ⍟   The convent embraces a church that owns three of the most important works by the locally prominent Bréa brothers, who painted in the late 15th century. See the carved and gilded wooden main altarpiece. In a restored part of the convent where some Franciscan friars still live, the Musée Franciscain is decorated with 17th-century frescoes. Some 350 documents and works of art from the 15th to the 18th centuries are on display, and a monk's cell has been re-created in all its severe simplicity. Also visit the 17th-century chapel. From the magnificent gardens, you'll have a panoramic view of Nice and the Baie des Anges. Matisse and Dufy are buried in the cemetery.

Place du Monastère. ℂ **04-93-81-00-04.** Free admission. Museum Mon–Sat 10am–noon and 3–6pm. Church daily 9am–6pm.

Musée Matisse ⍟   This museum honors the artist, who died in Nice in 1954. Seeing his nude sketches today, you'll wonder how early critics could have denounced them as "the female animal in all her shame and horror." Most of the pieces in the museum's permanent collection were painted in Nice, and many were donated by Matisse and his heirs. These include *Nude in an Armchair with a Green Plant* (1937), *Nymph in the Forest* (1935–42), and a chronologically arranged series of paintings from 1890 to 1919. The most famous of these is *Portrait of Madame Matisse* (1905), usually displayed near a portrait of the artist's wife by Marquet, painted in 1900. There's also an assemblage of designs he prepared as practice sketches for the Matisse Chapel at Vence. Also here are *The Créole Dancer* (1951), *Blue Nude IV* (1952), and around 50 dance-related sketches he did between 1930 and 1931. The artist's last work, *Flowers and Fruit* (1953), is made of cut-out gouache.

In the Villa des Arènes-de-Cimiez, 164 av. des Arènes-de-Cimiez. ℂ **04-93-53-40-53.** Admission 4€ ($5.20) adults, 2.50€ ($3.25) students, free for children under 18. Wed–Mon 10am–6pm. Closed Jan 1, May 1, and Dec 25.

Musée National Message Biblique Marc Chagall ⍟⍟   In the hills of Cimiez, this handsome museum, surrounded by pools and a garden, is devoted to Marc Chagall's treatment of biblical themes. Born in Russia in 1887, Chagall became a French citizen in 1937. The artist and his wife donated the works—the most important Chagall collection ever assembled—to France in 1966 and 1972. On display are 450 of his oils, gouaches, drawings, pastels, lithographs, sculptures, and ceramics; a mosaic; three stained-glass windows; and a tapestry. Chagall decorated a concert room with brilliantly hued stained-glass windows. Temporary exhibits each summer feature great periods and artists of all times.

Av. du Dr.-Ménard. ℂ **04-93-53-87-20.** Admission 5.50€ ($7.15) adults, 4€ ($5.20) students, free for children under 18. July–Sept Wed–Mon 10am–6pm; Oct–June Wed–Mon 10am–5pm.

OUTDOOR PURSUITS

BEACHES   Nice's seafront offers at least seven public beaches. Beaches extend for an uninterrupted stretch of more than 7km (4 miles), going from the edge of Vieux-Port (the old port) to the international airport, with most of the best bathing spots subdivided into public beaches and private concessionaires. None has sand; they're covered with gravel (often the size of golf balls). The rocks are smooth but can be mettlesome to people with poor balance or tender feet. Tucked between the public beaches are the private beaches of hotels such as the Beau Rivage. Most of the public beaches consist of two sections: a free area and one where you can rent chaises longues, mattresses, and parasols, use changing rooms, and take freshwater showers. For that, you'll pay 10€ to 12€ ($13–$16) for a half day, 12€ to 15€ ($16–$20) for a full day. Nude sunbathing is prohibited, but toplessness is common. Take bus no. 9, 10, 12, or 23 to get to the beach.

GOLF   The oldest golf course on the Riviera is about 16km (10 miles) from Nice: **Golf Bastide du Roi** (also known as the Golf de Biot), route d'Antibes, Biot (℗ **04-93-65-08-48**). Open daily, this is a flat, not particularly challenging sea-fronting course. (Golfers must cross a highway twice before completing the full 18 holes.) Tee times are 8am to 6pm; you can play until the sun sets. Reservations aren't necessary, though on weekends you should probably expect to wait. Greens fees are 40€ ($52) Monday to Friday, 45€ ($59) Saturday and Sunday.

HORSEBACK RIDING   **Club Hippique de Nice,** 368 rte. de Grenoble (℗ **04-93-71-24-34**), rents about a dozen of its horses. About 5km (3 miles) from Nice, near the airport, it's hemmed in on virtually every side by busy roads and highways, and conducts all activities in a series of riding rinks. Riding sessions should be reserved in advance; they last about an hour and cost 16€ ($21).

SCUBA DIVING   The best outfit is the **Centre International de Plongée (CIP) de Nice,** 2 ruelle des Moulins (℗ **06-09-52-55-57** or 04-93-55-59-50), adjacent to the city's old port, between quai des Docks and boulevard Stalingrad. A *baptême* (dive for first-timers) costs 30€ ($39). A one-tank dive for experienced divers, equipment included, is 32€ ($42); appropriate diver's certification is required.

TENNIS   The oldest tennis club in Nice is the **Nice Lawn Tennis Club,** Parc Impérial, 5 av. Suzanne-Lenglen (℗ **04-92-15-58-00**). It's open daily from 9am to 8pm from mid-October to mid-April (closed winter) and charges 20€ ($26) per person for 2 hours of court time, or 50€ to 60€ ($65–$78) per person, depending on the season, for 1 week of unlimited access. The club has a cooperative staff, a loyal clientele, 13 outdoor clay courts, and 6 outdoor hard-surface courts. There are no indoor courts. Reserve the night before.

SHOPPING

You might want to begin with a stroll through the streets and alleys of Nice's historic core. The densest concentrations of boutiques are along **rue Masséna, place Magenta, avenue Jean-Médecin, rue de Verdun,** and **rue Paradis,** and on the streets around them. A shop of note is **Gigi,** 10 rue de la Liberté (℗ **04-93-87-81-78**), which sells sophisticated clothing for women.

Opened in 1949 by Joseph Fuchs, the grandfather of the present English-speaking owners, the **Confiserie Florian du Vieux-Nice,** 14 quai Papacino (℗ **04-93-55-43-50**), is near the Old Port. The specialty is glazed fruit crystallized in sugar or artfully arranged into chocolates. Look for exotic jams (rose-petal preserves, mandarin marmalade) and the free recipe leaflet as well as candied violets, verbena leaves, and rosebuds. One of the oldest chocolatiers in Nice, **Confiserie Auer,** 7 rue St-François-de-Paule, near the opera house (℗ **04-93-85-77-98**), was established in 1820. Since then, few of the original decorative accessories have changed. The shop specializes in chocolates, candies, and *fruits confits* (jellied fruits), the signature Provençal goodies.

Façonnable, 7–9 rue Paradis (℃ **04-93-87-88-80**), is the original site of a chain with several hundred branches around the world. This is one of the largest, with a wide range of men's suits, raincoats, overcoats, sportswear, and jeans. The look is youthful and conservatively stylish, for relatively slim French bodies. An outlet for women's clothing and sportswear (Façonnable Sport) and the main line of Façonnable women's wear (Façonnable Femmes) lies immediately across the street at 10 rue Paradis (℃ **04-93-88-06-97**).

If you're thinking of indulging in a Provençale *pique-nique,* **Nicolas Alziari,** 14 rue St-François-de-Paule (℃ **04-93-85-76-92**), will provide everything from olives, anchovies, and pistous to aiolis and tapenades. It's one of Nice's oldest purveyors of olive oil, with a house brand that comes in two strengths: a light version that aficionados claim is vaguely perfumed with Provence, and a stronger version suited to the earthy flavors and robust ingredients of a Provençal winter. Also for sale are objects crafted from olive wood.

For arts and crafts, head to the **Atelier Contre-Jour,** 3 rue du Pont Vieux (℃ **04-93-80-20-50**). It carries painted-wood handicrafts, including picture frames; painted furniture, and silk lampshades, as well as decorative posters showing the best of their painted work of the past 25 years. **Plat Jérôme,** 34 rue Centrale (℃ **04-93-62-17-09**), stocks varnished pottery. Many artists' studios and galleries are on side streets near the cathedral in the old town.

La Couquetou, 8 rue St-François-de-Paule (℃ **04-93-80-90-30**), sells *santons,* the traditional Provençal figurines. The best selection of Provençal fabrics is at **Le Chandelier,** 7 rue de la Boucherie (℃ **04-93-85-85-19**), where you'll see designs by two of the region's best-known producers of cloth, Les Olivades and Valdrôme.

Nice is also known for its street markets. In addition to the flower market, **Marché aux Fleurs** (see "Exploring the City," earlier in this chapter), the main flea market, **Marché à la Brocante,** also at cours Saleya, takes place Monday from 8am to 5pm. Another flea market on the port, **Les Puces de Nice,** place Robilante, is open Tuesday to Saturday 9am to 6pm.

WHERE TO STAY
VERY EXPENSIVE
Hôtel Negresco 𝄞𝄞𝄞   The Negresco, on the seafront in the heart of Nice, is one of the Riviera's super-glamorous hotels. The Victorian wedding-cake hotel is named after its founder, Henry Negresco, a Romanian who died franc-less in Paris in 1920. The country's châteaux inspired both the interior and the exterior, with its mansard roof and domed tower. The hotel's decorators scoured Europe to gather antiques, tapestries, and art. Some of the accommodations, such as the Coco Chanel room, are outfitted in homage to the personalities who stayed here. Others are modeled on literary or musical themes, such as *La Traviata.* In 1998, most of the bathrooms, which all have tubs and showers, were upgraded. Suites and public areas are even grander; they include the Louis XIV salon, reminiscent of the Sun King, and the Napoleon III suite, where swagged walls, a leopard-skin carpet, and a half-crowned pink canopy create a sense of majesty. The most expensive rooms with balconies face the Mediterranean and the private beach. The staff wears 18th-century costumes. The restaurant is one of the Riviera's greatest.

Nice Accommodations & Dining

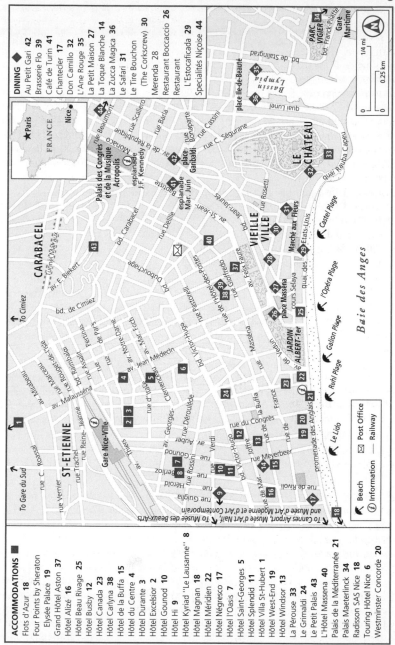

ACCOMMODATIONS ■

Flots d'Azur **18**
Four Points by Sheraton
Elysée Palace **19**
Grand Hôtel Aston **37**
Hôtel Alizé **16**
Hôtel Beau Rivage **25**
Hôtel Busby **12**
Hôtel Canada **23**
Hôtel Carlyna **38**
Hôtel de la Buffa **15**
Hôtel du Centre **4**
Hôtel Durante **3**
Hôtel Excelsior **2**
Hôtel Gounod **10**
Hôtel Hi **9**
Hôtel Kyriad "Le Lausanne" **8**
Hôtel Magnan **18**
Hôtel Méridien **22**
Hôtel Négresco **17**
Hôtel l'Oasis **7**
Hôtel Saint-Georges **5**
Hôtel Splendid **11**
Hôtel Villa St-Hubert **1**
Hôtel West-End **19**
Hôtel Windsor **13**
La Pérouse **33**
Le Grimaldi **24**
Le Petit Palais **43**
L'Hôtel Massena **40**
Palais de la Méditerranée **21**
Palais Maeterlinck **34**
Radisson SAS Nice **18**
Touring Hôtel Nice **6**
Westminster Concorde **20**

DINING ◆

Au Petit Gari **42**
Brasserie Flo **39**
Café de Turin **41**
Chantecler **17**
Don Camillo **32**
L'Ane Rouge **35**
La Petit Maison **27**
La Toque Blanche **14**
La Zucca Magica **36**
Le Safari **31**
Le Tire Bouchon
(The Corkscrew) **30**
Merenda **28**
Restaurant Boccaccio **26**
Restaurant
L'Estocaficada **29**
Specialités Niçoise **44**

■ Beach   ⊠ Post Office
ⓘ Information   — Railway

307

37 promenade des Anglais, 06007 Nice Cedex. (C) **04-93-16-64-00**. Fax 04-93-88-35-68. www.hotel-negresco-nice.com. 145 units. 250€–425€ ($325–$553) double; from 605€ ($787) suite. AE, DC, MC, V. Free parking. **Ameni-ties:** 2 restaurants (see "Where to Dine," later in this chapter); bar; fitness center; secretarial services; 24-hr. room service; massage; babysitting; laundry service; dry cleaning; nonsmoking rooms. *In room:* A/C, TV, dataport, minibar, hair dryer.

La Pérouse *★★* *Finds* Once a prison, La Pérouse has been reconstructed and is now a unique Riviera hotel. Set on a cliff, it's built right in the gardens of an ancient château-fort. No hotel affords a better view over both the old city and the Baie des Anges. In fact, many people stay here just for the view. The hotel resembles an old Provençal home, with low ceilings, white walls, and antique furnishings. The lovely, spacious rooms are beautifully furnished, often with Provençal fabrics. Most have log-gias overlooking the bay. The bathrooms are large, clad in Boticino marble, and hold tubs and showers.

11 quai Rauba-Capéu, 06300 Nice. (C) **04-93-62-34-63**. Fax 04-93-62-59-41. www.hotel-la-perouse.com. 62 units. 240€–360€ ($312–$468) double; 465€–800€ ($605–$1,040) suite. AE, DC, MC, V. Parking 24€ ($31). **Amenities:** Restaurant (mid-May to mid-Sept); bar; outdoor pool; exercise room; Jacuzzi; sauna; limited room service; babysit-ting; laundry service; nonsmoking rooms. *In room:* A/C, TV, dataport, minibar, hair dryer, safe.

Palais de la Méditerranée *★★★* She's back! Long hailed as a Queen of the Nice Riviera, this glittering seaside palace on the Promenade des Anglais reigned from 1929 to 1978 and then was shuttered. In its heyday, and in its hotel theater, everybody per-formed from Maurice Chevalier ("thank heaven for little girls") to the American chanteuse, Josephine Baker, wearing high heels, a skirt of bananas—and nothing else. Its Art Deco facade was left intact after a restoration, but the interior of this place was gutted and turned into a marble pile with glamorous touches such as plush hallways and such modern amenities as a heated outdoor swimming pool.

As an homage to yesteryear, monumental chandeliers and stained-glass windows, among other architectural features, were spared in the renovations. Bedrooms, midsize to grandly spacious, are outfitted in a tasteful modern decor, with luxurious bath-rooms with tub and shower. Ninety of the bedrooms also open onto sea views. Behind the facade, the hotel's casino has been restored to its Art Deco glamour.

13–15 promenade des Anglais, 06011 Nice. (C) **04-92-14-77-00**. Fax 04-92-14-77-14. www.lepalaisdelamediterranee. com. 182 units. 280€–665€ ($364–$865) double; from 1,100€ ($1,430) suite. AE, DC, MC, V. **Amenities:** Restaurant; bar; casino; 2 pools (indoor and outdoor); fitness center; solarium; watersports; 24-hr. room service; nonsmoking rooms; casino; Turkish bath; limited-mobility rooms. *In room:* A/C, TV, dataport, minibar, hair dryer, safe.

Palais Maeterlinck *★★★* On 3.6 hectares (9 acres) of landscape east of Nice, this deluxe hotel occupies a *fin-de-siècle* villa inhabited between the World Wars by the Bel-gian writer Maurice Maeterlinck, winner of the Nobel Prize for literature. Although many visitors find the setting sumptuous, the service and experience of the staff pale in comparison to the Negresco's. But on the plus side, it's more tranquil than the hotels in more central locations. It has verdant terraces and a large outdoor pool, set amid banana trees, olive trees, and soaring cypresses. A funicular will carry you down to the rock-strewn beach and marina. Each elegant guest room, decorated in neoclas-sical Florentine style, is outfitted in a different monochromatic color scheme. All but a few have terraces opening onto views of Cap d'Antibes and Cap-Ferrat, and deluxe bathrooms containing tubs and showers.

30 bd. Maeterlinck, 06300 Nice. (C) **04-92-00-72-00**. Fax 04-92-04-18-10. www.palais-maeterlinck.com. 40 units. 245€–580€ ($319–$754) double; from 450€ ($585) suite. AE, DC, MC, V. Free parking. Drive 6.5km (4 miles) east of Nice along the Basse Corniche. **Amenities:** Restaurant; bar; outdoor pool; fitness center; limited room service;

babysitting; laundry service; dry cleaning; nonsmoking rooms; 1 limited-mobility room. *In room:* A/C, TV, dataport, minibar, hair dryer, safe.

EXPENSIVE

Four Points by Sheraton Elysée Palace 𝄞𝄞   Views sweep out over the sea from

most of the rooms of this hotel. Decor is conservative and contemporary, and the amenities in the rooms are typical. The seafront rooms, of course, are the more desirable. Rooms on the fifth, sixth, and seventh floors overlook the Mediterranean. Bathrooms are clad in marble with bidets, but you have to request robes and hair dryers from reception. The hotel has its own private beach a short walk from its premises.

59 promenade des Anglais, 06005 Nice. © **04-93-97-90-90.** Fax 04-93-44-06-55. www.elyseepalace.com. 143 units. 210€–380€ ($273–$494) double; 300€–380€ ($390–$494) suite. AE, DC, MC, V. Parking 16€ ($21). Bus: 9, 10, or 12. **Amenities:** 2 restaurants; bar; pool; 24-hr. room service; babysitting; laundry service; dry cleaning; nonsmoking rooms. *In room:* A/C, TV, dataport, minibar, hair dryer, safe.

Grand Hôtel Aston 𝄞   This elegantly detailed 19th-century hotel is one of the

most alluring in its price bracket. After radical renovations, the rooms are now outfitted with comfortable furnishings and restored bathrooms with tub/shower combinations. Room prices vary according to the view: over the street, the splashing fountains of place Masséna, or the coastline panorama from the uppermost floor. On summer evenings, a garden-style bar on the top floor sometimes schedules dance music. It was fully renovated in 2004.

12 av. Félix-Faure, 06000 Nice. © **04-92-17-53-00.** Fax 04-93-80-40-02. www.hotel-aston.com. 155 units. 160€–290€ ($208–$377) double; 310€–450€ ($403–$585) suite. AE, DC, MC, V. Parking 20€ ($26). Bus: 12 or 98. **Amenities:** Restaurant; bar; rooftop pool; limited room service; laundry service; dry cleaning; nonsmoking rooms. *In room:* A/C, TV, dataport, minibar, hair dryer, safe.

Hôtel Beau Rivage 𝄞   This hotel across from the beach is famous for having

housed both Matisse and Chekhov during its heyday around the turn of the 20th century. It was radically renovated in the early 1980s, and today the interior has a bland but tasteful modern decor and a staff that seems to make a point of appearing overworked regardless of how few guests there might be. The soundproof rooms are vaguely Art Deco and small, with contemporary bathrooms. For dining, Le Bistrot du Rivage is relatively formal and very appealing. Its specialties are meats and fish prepared on a large grill. Between May and September, tables are set on a terrace.

24 rue St-François-de-Paule, 06300 Nice. © **04-92-47-82-83.** Fax 04-93-80-55-77. www.nicebeaurivage.com. 118 units. 145€–395€ ($189–$514) double; 290€–610€ ($377–$793) suite. Children stay free in parent's room. AE, DC, MC, V. Bus: 1, 2, 5, or 12. **Amenities:** Restaurant; bar; limited room service; babysitting; laundry service; dry cleaning. *In room:* A/C, TV, dataport, minibar, hair dryer, safe.

Hôtel Hi 𝄞 *Finds*   An architectural and decorative "statement," this hotel occupies a

former boardinghouse that dates to the 1930s. Spearheaded by Matali Crasset, a onetime colleague of Philippe Starck, a team of architects and engineers created one of the most aggressively avant-garde hotels in the south of France. The angular seven-story hotel opened in 2003. Each of the nine high-tech room "concepts" is different. They range from hospital white-on-white to birchwood veneer and acid green to cool violet and gray. The unconventional layouts might include a bathtub tucked behind a screen of potted plants or elevated to a position of theatrical prominence. Electronic gizmos include state-of-the-art CD systems. The Japanese word "hi" describes the black mottling on the back of an ornamental carp, which has traditionally been associated with good luck.

3 av. des Fleurs, 06000 Nice. ℂ **04-97-07-26-26.** Fax 04-97-07-26-27. www.hi-hotel.net. 38 units. 180€–670€ ($234–$871) double. AE, DC, MC, V. Parking 20€ ($26). Bus: 23. **Amenities:** 24-hr. bar and snack bar; rooftop swimming pool; laundry service; nonsmoking rooms; limited-mobility rooms. *In room:* A/C, TV, dataport, iron, safe.

Hôtel Méridien ⓖ   One of Nice's largest hotels, this one rises five floors above the junction of the promenade des Anglais and a small formal park, the Jardin Albert-1er. Built in the 1960s by Air France in an angular design with lots of shiny metal and glass, it was later acquired by Britain's Forte group and hosts many organized tours from Britain and northern Europe. Two escalators carry you up through a soaring, impersonal atrium to the reception area. The recently renovated guest rooms are modern and standardized, many with sea views. The seafront rooms, though desirable for the view over the hotel's private beach, are actually the smallest in the hotel; space has been sacrificed to make way for terraces or balconies. Bathrooms are well equipped. There's a zesty restaurant, Le Colonia Café, that celebrates the late-19th-century overseas conquests of France and England—the emphasis is on spicy, sometimes curried international cuisine.

1 promenade des Anglais, 06046 Nice. ℂ **04-97-03-44-44.** Fax 04-97-03-44-45. www.lemeridien.com. 318 units. 280€–420€ ($364–$546) double; 680€–1,400€ ($884–$1,820) suite. Discounts of around 15% during selected dates Oct–Apr. AE, DC, MC, V. Bus: 8, 9, 10, or 3. **Amenities:** 2 restaurants; bar; pool; health club; 24-hr. room service; massage; babysitting; laundry service; dry cleaning. *In room:* A/C, TV, minibar, hair dryer, safe.

Hôtel Splendid ⓖ   This is one of Nice's best modern hotels, on the corner of a wide boulevard lined with shade trees, 4 blocks from its private beach. Built on the site of the Hôtel Splendid (ca. 1881), it was heralded as a new era in French hotels. Frequent renovations have kept the place fresh. The rooms usually have terraces or balconies, and several floors are reserved for nonsmokers. Accommodations come in various shapes and sizes, but all have private safes, electronic locks, and soundproofing. Beds are a bit narrow, but the mattresses are first-class. Bathrooms are tiled and well equipped.

50 bd. Victor-Hugo, 06048 Nice. ℂ **04-93-16-41-00.** Fax 04-93-87-02-46. www.splendid-nice.com. 127 units. 175€–245€ ($228–$319) double; 265€–350€ ($345–$455) suite. AE, DC, MC, V. Parking 19€ ($25). Bus: 9 or 10. **Amenities:** Restaurant; bar; pool; health club; sauna; steam room; limited room service; babysitting; laundry service; dry cleaning. *In room:* A/C, TV, minibar, beverage maker (in some), hair dryer, trouser press, safe.

Hôtel West-End   A belle époque monument, originally built around 1870, whose flowering terrace overlooks the sea, this Best Western is named after London's theater district. Though the ornate facade and the stately lobby were retained in honor of the original construction, the guest rooms were streamlined during several modernizations, most recently in 2005, yet are comfortable and well furnished. The largest units are found on the fifth and sixth floors. Other rooms are more standardized and commercial, often filled with business travelers. All come with comfortable mattresses, most often on twin or double beds; many offer sea views. You can enjoy drinks on the terrace near a restaurant serving French and international cuisine. Because of the hotel's relatively large size, the staff can often appear a bit overworked, but overall it's a worthy choice.

31 promenade des Anglais, 06000 Nice. ℂ **800/528-1234** in the U.S., or 04-92-14-44-00. Fax 04-93-88-85-07. www.hotel-westend.com. 125 units. 180€–350€ ($234–$455) double; 380€–600€ ($494–$780) suite. AE, DC, MC, V. Parking 20€ ($26). Bus: 78. **Amenities:** Restaurant; bar; 24-hr. room service; laundry service; dry cleaning. *In room:* A/C, TV, minibar, hair dryer, safe.

Radisson SAS Nice ⓖ   Set alongside the major beachside thoroughfare of Nice, this streamlined and tastefully contemporary hotel has undergone more name and ownership changes than any other major hotel in town. In 1998, it was acquired by the Radisson chain, which inaugurated renovations to the public areas and bedrooms. Many business travelers come here. Standardized accommodations come with built-in furniture, double glazing, and comfortable beds. Overall, one finds a sense of bustle, with an alert staff that's hip to the goings-on in Nice and along the Côte d'Azur—a feel of Paris-on-the-beach. Visitors enjoy soft piano music in the sophisticated lobby. Les Mosaiques offers a gastronomic French cuisine.

223 promenade des Anglais, 06200 Nice. © 04-93-37-17-17. Fax 04-93-71-21-71. www.radissonsas.com. 331 units. 220€–340€ ($286–$442) double; 355€–550€ ($462–$715) suite. AE, DC, MC, V. Parking 20€ ($26). Pets allowed. Bus: 8. **Amenities:** Restaurant; bar; pool; health club; sauna; 24-hr. room service; massage; babysitting; laundry service; dry cleaning. *In room:* A/C, TV, dataport, minibar, hair dryer, safe.

Westminster Concorde 𝒜   This 1860 hotel occupies a prominent position on the famous promenade. Among many renovations, its elaborate facade has been restored to its former grandeur. The contemporary rooms are comfortable and have soundproof windows; a few open onto balconies. Most rooms have high ceilings, antique mirrors, French windows, and brass beds, and each comes with a midsize tiled bathroom with tub and shower.

27 promenade des Anglais, 06000 Nice. © 04-92-14-86-86. Fax 04-93-82-39-33. www.westminster-nice.com. 102 units. 150€–255€ ($195–$332) double; from 355€ ($462) junior suite. AE, DC, MC, V. Parking 24€ ($28) in public lot next door. Bus: 9, 10, or 11. **Amenities:** Restaurant; bar; business center; limited room service; babysitting; laundry service; dry cleaning; nonsmoking rooms; limited-mobility rooms. *In room:* A/C, TV, dataport, minibar, hair dryer, safe in some.

MODERATE

Hôtel Busby   This place should please you if you want a nostalgic hotel of faded early-20th-century grandeur. The Busby family, who were the original owners, refer to its ornate facade as "style Garibaldi" and have retained the balconies and the shutters on the tall windows. Renovated at regular intervals, yet looking a bit tired, the guest rooms are dignified; some contain mahogany twin beds and white-and-gold wardrobes. Mattresses are a bit worn, but are still comfortable. Likewise, the tiled bathrooms are a bit cramped but have adequate shelf space.

36–38 rue du Maréchal-Joffre, 06000 Nice. © 04-93-88-19-41. Fax 04-93-87-73-53. www.busby-hotel.com. 80 units. 130€–140€ ($169–$182) double. AE, DC, MC, V. Closed Nov 15–Dec 20. Bus: 9, 10, 12, or 22. **Amenities:** Bar; lounge; babysitting; laundry service; dry cleaning. *In room:* A/C, TV, dataport, hair dryer.

Hôtel Excelsior   The Excelsior's ornate corbels and stone pediments rise grandly a few steps from the railway station. This much-renovated 19th-century hotel has modern decor, most of it from the mid-1990s, and rooms each outfitted in tones of Provençal ocher, blue, and brown, that have seen a lot of wear but are still comfortable. They have small, shower-only bathrooms. Furnishings, for the most part, are functional and conservative. The hotel has a garden and the beach is a 20-minute walk through the residential and commercial heart of Nice.

19 av. Durante, 06000 Nice. © 04-93-88-18-05. Fax 04-93-88-38-69. 42 units. 90€–120€ ($117–$156) double. AE, MC, V. Parking 15€ ($20) in nearby lot. Bus: 99. **Amenities:** Nonsmoking rooms. *In room:* A/C, TV, hair dryer.

Hôtel Gounod 𝒜   A winning choice in the city center, this hotel is a 5-minute walk from the sea. It was built around 1910 in a neighborhood where the street names honor composers. The Gounod boasts ornate balconies, a domed roof, and an elaborate canopy of wrought iron and glass. The attractive lobby and adjoining lounge are festive and stylish, with old prints, copper flowerpots, and antiques. The high-ceilinged guest rooms are quiet; most overlook the gardens of private homes. The tiled bathrooms are small but efficiently organized, mainly with shower units. Guests have free unlimited use of the pool, cafe-bar, and Jacuzzi at the Hôtel Splendid, next door.

3 rue Gounod, 06000 Nice. ✆ **04-93-16-42-00.** Fax 04-93-88-23-84. www.gounod-nice.com. 46 units. 100€–140€ ($130–$182) double; 135€–200€ ($176–$260) suite. AE, DC, MC, V. Parking 12€ ($16). Closed Nov 20–Dec 20. Bus: 8. **Amenities:** Bar; outdoor pool; gym; Jacuzzi; sauna; 24-hr. room service; massage; babysitting; laundry service; dry cleaning; nonsmoking rooms. *In room:* A/C, TV, dataport, minibar, hair dryer, safes in suites.

Hôtel Kyriad "Le Lausanne"   This is a solid, middle-bracket hotel with a central location in a commercial neighborhood in the heart of Nice. It was radically renovated in the mid-1990s and does not retain very many of its original architectural embellishments. Views from the windows look out over the street, and its efficient bedroom furnishings are standard for the well-respected Clarine chain. Rooms have comfortable mattresses, tiled bathrooms, and adequate shelf space. Overall, this is a reliable, although not particularly exciting, hotel choice.

36 rue Rossini, 06000 Nice. ✆ **04-93-88-85-94.** Fax 04-93-88-15-88. www.nice-hotel-kyriad.com. 35 units. 65€–117€ ($85–$152) double. MC, V. Parking 11€ ($14). Bus: 8. **Amenities:** Lounge; babysitting. *In room:* A/C, TV, dataport, hair dryer.

Hôtel Windsor *(Value* One of the most arts-conscious hotels in Nice is in a *maison bourgeoise* built by disciples of Gustav Eiffel in 1895. It's near the Negresco and the promenade des Anglais. Each unit is a unique decorative statement by a different artist. The heir and scion of the longtime owners, the Redolfi family, commissioned manifestations of his mystical and mythical visions after years of traveling through Asia, Africa, and South America. In the "Ben" room, for example, a Provençal artist of the same name painted verses of his own poetry, in tones of blue, orange, yellow, and green, on a white background. You can take your chances or select a room based on the photos on the hotel website. Most units have a combination tub/shower. The fifth-floor superstructure holds the health club, steam room, and sauna. The garden contains scores of tropical and exotic plants, and the recorded sounds of birds singing in the jungles of the Amazon.

11 rue Dalpozzo, 06000 Nice. ✆ **04-93-88-59-35.** Fax 04-93-88-94-57. www.hotelwindsornice.com. 57 units. 75€–140€ ($98–$182) double. MC, V. Parking 10€ ($13). Bus: 9, 10, or 22. **Amenities:** Restaurant; bar; outdoor pool; health club; sauna; limited room service; babysitting; nonsmoking rooms. *In room:* A/C, TV, dataport, minibar, hair dryer, safe.

L'Hôtel Masséna *(★* Few other hotels evoke the belle époque as gracefully or as authentically as this stone-and-wrought-iron monument to the architecture of the early 20th century. The owners have upgraded the bedrooms, transforming the hotel into a well-orchestrated bastion of calm and comfort. Many of the rooms are upholstered in fabrics depicting the olive tree or olive branches. The most expensive rooms are airy, spacious, and outfitted in tones inspired by the colors of Provence, especially peach and soft green. Less expensive rooms are altogether comfortable, albeit somewhat smaller. Although all units have soundproofing, the ones that are the quietest are those overlooking the hotel's back side, or its interior courtyard.

58 rue Gioffredo, 06000 Nice. ✆ **04-92-47-88-88.** Fax 04-92-47-88-89. www.hotel-massena-nice.com. 111 units. 100€–260€ ($130–$338) double. Extra bed 30€ ($39). AE, DC, MC, V. Parking 18€ ($24). Bus: 15. **Amenities:** Bar; 24-hr. room service; babysitting; laundry. *In room:* A/C, TV, dataport, minibar, hair dryer, safe.

Le Grimaldi   Two gorgeous belle époque buildings sharing an inner courtyard comprise this hotel set in the center of Nice. Inside, however, the decor of the rooms has been modernized, using glass, wrought iron, and fabrics to convey a sophisticated, yet natural, charm. The rooms contain contemporary amenities, and those on the upper floors overlook the rooftops of Nice. Among the best features of the place are its generous breakfast offerings: homemade Provençal jams, fresh fruit, and crusty pastries made by one of the town's best bakers.

15 rue Grimaldi, 06000 Nice. © **04-93-16-00-24.** Fax 04-93-87-00-24. www.le-grimaldi.com. 46 units. 90€–230€ ($117–$299) double; 25€ ($33) extra person. AE, MC, V. **Amenities:** 2 lounges; business center. *In room:* A/C, TV, dataport, minibar, safe.

Le Petit Palais ⭐ *Finds*   This whimsical hotel occupies a mansion built around 1890; in the 1970s, it was the home of the actor/writer Sacha Guitry, a name that's instantly recognized in millions of French households. It lies about a 10-minute drive from the city center in the Carabacel residential district. Much of its architectural grace remains, as evoked by the Florentine moldings and friezes and the Art Deco/Italianate furnishings. The preferred rooms, and the most expensive, have balconies for sea views during the day and sunset watching at dusk. Accommodations are generally small to medium, each with a neatly organized bathroom with shower or tub.

17 av. Emile-Bieckert, 06000 Nice. © **04-93-62-19-11.** Fax 04-93-62-53-60. www.hotel-petit-palais.com. 25 units. 100€–130€ ($130–$169) double. AE, DC, MC, V. Parking 12€. **Amenities:** Room service; laundry service. *In room:* TV.

INEXPENSIVE

Flots d'Azur   This three-story 19th-century villa is next to the sea and a short walk from the more elaborate and costlier promenade hotels. The rooms vary in size and decor; all have good views and sea breezes. Twelve units have TVs and minibars, and each comes with a tiled bathroom with shower. Double-glazed windows cut down on noise. Continental breakfast is served on the sun terrace.

101 promenade des Anglais, 06000 Nice. © **04-93-86-51-25.** Fax 04-93-97-22-07. www.flotsdazur.com. 20 units. 50€–105€ ($65–$137) double. MC, V. Free parking. Bus: 23. **Amenities:** Laundry service; dry cleaning; nonsmoking rooms. *In room:* A/C, TV, minibar, hair dryer.

Hôtel Alizé *Value*   Right on the promenade des Anglais and boulevard Gambetta, this modest hotel, near the chic and pricey Negresco, is a real bargain. Breakfast is the only meal served, but there are many restaurants nearby. Each of the small to medium-size bedrooms comes with a good mattress; the decor features bright, inviting colors. The accommodations are much improved, as are the bathrooms with tub or shower.

65 rue Buffa, 06000 Nice. © **04-93-88-99-46.** Fax 04-93-16-88-60. www.hotel-alizee.com. 11 units. 45€–74€ ($59–$96) double. Children up to age 4 stay free in parent's room. MC, V. Parking 20€ ($26). Bus: 8. **Amenities:** Lounge. *In room:* A/C, TV, dataport, hair dryer.

Hôtel Canada *Value*   Lying 50m (164 ft.) from the sea, and just west of the landmark place Masséna, this is one of the bargains of Nice. Some two dozen marble steps lead up to the lobby, which is decorated with mirrors and paintings. Steps, no elevator, take you to the bedrooms that range from small to spacious. We won't even pretend the bedrooms are state of the art, but they are clean and comfortable, if a bit frayed here and there. The best room is no. 5, adjoining a terrace garden where breakfast is served. The best units are on the third floor with private balconies or terraces, some opening onto distant views of the water. The tiled bathrooms are small, containing shower units. No one ever complains when it comes time to pay the bill.

8 rue Halévy, 06000 Nice. © **04-93-87-98-94.** Fax 04-93-87-17-12. www.hotel-canada.fr. 17 units. 30€–75€ ($39–$98) double. AE, DC, MC, V. **Amenities:** Breakfast room. *In room:* A/C, TV, kitchenette (in some), minifridge (in some).

Hôtel Carlyna   Built "sometime before 1940," and positioned in the commercial heart of Nice, midway between two popular restaurants, this hotel offers a format of simple, well-scrubbed functionality at relatively reasonable rates. The Bouvet family has owned the place since 1998 and has made many improvements since then. Each of the bedrooms is different from its neighbors, each outfitted in soft tones of either red or blue and accessorized with cheerful fabrics. The spacious bathrooms are tiled and often equipped with hand-held Danish-style showers.

8 rue Sacha-Guitry, 06000 Nice. © 04-93-80-77-21. Fax 04-93-80-08-80. www.carlyna-hotel-nice.com. 24 units. 60€–75€ ($78–$98) double. AE, DC, MC, V. Bus: 1, 4, or 7. **Amenities:** Room service (breakfast only); laundry service. *In room:* A/C, TV.

Hôtel de la Buffa ⭐ *(Value)*   Lying only a few steps from the Promenade de Anglais and the pebbly beaches, this centrally located hotel combines charm with value. Decorated with a certain flair and style, it offers a prevailing family atmosphere. Rooms are tastefully and comfortably furnished, with the larger accommodations suitable for a family of up to four persons. If you wish, a safe and a refrigerator can be installed in your room. All the midsize bathrooms contain showers. Those units facing the streets have double glazing on their windows. If you would like to partake of discounted meals, an arrangement can be made for you to take half or full board at the adjoining restaurant under different management.

56 rue de la Buffa, 06000 Nice. © 04-93-88-77-35. Fax 04-93-88-83-39. www.hotel-buffa.com. 13 units. 66€–78€ ($86–$101) double; 86€ ($112) quad. AE, DC, V. Bus: 23. **Amenities:** Discounts at next-door restaurant. *In room:* A/C, TV, fridge in some, hair dryer, safe in some.

Hôtel du Centre   Near the train station, this simple hotel dates from 1947 and has been restored. The rooms are very close to the attractions and bars of downtown Nice. The small bathrooms are tiled and equipped with shower units. The staff is well versed in the many diversions of the city.

2 rue de Suisse, 06000 Nice. © 04-93-88-83-85. Fax 04-93-82-29-80. www.nice-hotel-centre.com. 28 units. 50€ ($65) double. MC, V. Parking 8€ ($10). Bus: 23 or 99. *In room:* A/C, TV, dataport, minibar, hair dryer, safe.

Hôtel Durante   A comfortable and much modified building dating from around the turn of the 20th century, this hotel is very popular with producers, actors, and directors during the nearby Cannes Film Festival. Many rooms face a quiet courtyard. The furnishings have known better days, but the beds are still quite comfortable. The owner dispenses both charm and information about local cinematic events.

16 av. Durante, 06000 Nice. © 04-93-88-84-40. Fax 04-93-87-77-76. www.nice-hotel-durante.com. 24 units. 69€–100€ ($90–$130) double. MC, V. **Amenities:** Bar; babysitting. *In room:* A/C, TV, kitchenette (in some), fridge, hair dryer, safe.

Hôtel l'Oasis ⭐ *(Finds)*   The strongest memories that remain with clients of this establishment involve its semitropical garden, where antique fountains were filled in long ago with verdant plants, and where you can imagine the ghosts of the influential people who stayed here during the first half of the 20th century, when the place was a boardinghouse with goodly numbers of Russians. They included Anton Chekhov, who composed part of *Three Sisters* here, and Lenin, who spent a holiday here in 1911. Although an air of old-fashioned manners remains intact, bedrooms have been modernized many times since, most recently in a contemporary, vaguely Provençal motif. Bathrooms are tiled and well scrubbed; accommodations are well maintained. The location, about a 12-minute walk from the railway station, is convenient to virtually everything in Nice.

23 rue Gounod, 06000 Nice. ℭ **04-93-88-12-29.** Fax 04-93-16-14-40. 38 units. 79€–100€ ($103–$130) double. AE, DC, MC, V. Parking 8€ ($10). **Amenities:** Bar service in garden; limited room service; babysitting. *In room:* A/C, TV, hair dryer.

Hôtel Magnan   This well-run modern hotel was built around 1945 and has been renovated frequently. It's a 10-minute bus ride from the heart of town but only a minute or so from the promenade des Anglais and the bay. Many of the simply furnished rooms have balconies facing the sea, and some contain minibars. The look is a bit functional, but for Nice this is a good price, especially considering the comfortable beds. The bathrooms are small, each with a shower stall. Owner Daniel Thérouin occupies the apartment on the top floor, guaranteeing close supervision. Breakfast can be served in your room.

Sq. du Général-Ferrié, 06200 Nice. ℭ **04-93-86-76-00.** Fax 04-93-44-48-31. www.hotelmagnan-nice.com. 25 units. 48€–58€ ($62–$75) double. AE, MC, V. Parking 7.50€ ($9.75). Bus: 23. **Amenities:** Nonsmoking rooms. *In room:* TV, dataport, minibar.

Hôtel Saint-Georges   Originally built during the grand days of Niçoise tourism, this hotel dates from around 1900 and still retains a few of its original architectural grace notes. A verdant patio and garden are the site of clusters of iron chairs and tables, where breakfast is served, and which many clients select as a spot for afternoon reading. Inside the motif is less nostalgic—angular and contemporary, it has mirrored, sometimes stark walls and efficient modern furnishings. Most bedrooms have high ceilings and casement doors that open onto tiny porches hemmed in with wrought-iron railings. The rooms are fairly small, but each comes with a firm mattress and compact tiled bathrooms. In 2005, most of the bathrooms were upgraded and renovated.

7 av. Georges Clemenceau, 06000 Nice. ℭ **04-93-88-79-21.** Fax 04-93-16-22-85. 35 units. 64€–70€ ($83–$91) double. AE, DC, MC, V. Bus: 1 or 4. **Amenities:** Lounge; garden. *In room:* A/C, TV, hair dryer.

Hôtel Villa St-Hubert ✦ *(Value*   Set 5 blocks inland from the seacoast and the beach, this hotel consists of an interconnected pair of early-20th-century town houses. Today they're the property of the Chevalier family, who maintain clean, well-appointed bedrooms, each with a different color scheme. Bedrooms are medium in size, with firm mattresses and well-maintained bathrooms. One of the hotel's most appealing corners is the ivy-covered, geranium-filled courtyard, the site of morning breakfast and afternoon teas. No meals are served other than breakfast, but in light of the many nearby restaurants, no one seems to care.

26 rue Michel-Ange, 06100 Nice. ℭ **04-93-84-66-51.** Fax 04-93-84-70-96. www.villasainthubert.com. 13 units. 65€–85€ ($85–$111) double. AE, DC, MC, V. Parking 8€ ($10). **Amenities:** Lounge; limited room service. *In room:* A/C in some, TV, kitchenette in some, minibar, hair dryer, safe.

Touring Hôtel Nice   Set within a century-old building, this hotel evokes a severely dignified town house in Tuscany. It was built during the height of France's railway-building frenzy. In 2000, the venerable building was acquired by two couples, the Jean dit Gautiers and the Einaudis, who brought years of hotel experience in some of the grandest hotels of Monaco to their new enterprise. Today this is one of the best-managed hotels in Nice in its price range, with a staff that's a lot more sophisticated and worldly than what you might have expected in such an unpretentious setting. Bedrooms are simple, durable, soundproof, and comfortable, and breakfast is served in what was originally conceived as a grand, full-scale restaurant, with many of the original architectural adornments still in place.

5 rue de Russie, 06000 Nice. © **04-93-88-70-15.** Fax 04-93-87-91-06. www.touring-hotel-nice.com. 18 units. 50€–65€ ($65–$85) double. Children under 10 stay free in parent's room. MC, V. Bus: 1, 2, or 12. **Amenities:** Alcohol-free bar. *In room:* TV.

WHERE TO DINE
VERY EXPENSIVE
Chantecler ✸✸✸ TRADITIONAL/MODERN FRENCH   This is Nice's most prestigious and best restaurant. In 1989, a redecoration sheathed its walls with panels removed from a château in Pouilly-Fuissé; a Regency-style salon was installed for before- or after-dinner drinks; and a collection of 16th-century paintings, executed on leather backgrounds in the Belgian town of Malines, was imported. A much-respected chef, Bruno Turbot, revised the menu to include the most sophisticated and creative dishes in Nice. They change almost weekly but may include turbot filet served with purée of broad beans, sun-dried tomatoes, and asparagus; roasted suckling lamb served with beignets of fresh vegetables and ricotta-stuffed ravioli; and a melt-in-your-mouth fantasy of marbled hot chocolate drenched in almond-flavored cream sauce.

In the Hôtel Negresco, 37 promenade des Anglais. © **04-93-16-64-00.** Reservations required. Main courses 35€–100€ ($46–$130); fixed-price menu 55€–90€ ($72–$117) lunch, 70€–130€ ($91–$169) dinner. AE, MC, V. Daily 12:30–2pm and 8–10pm. Closed Jan to mid-Feb. Bus: 8, 9, 10, or 11.

EXPENSIVE
Specialités Niçoise ✸ NIÇOISE   For several generations, this cozy restaurant was directed by a domineering matriarch, Mme Barale, whose autocratic behavior with her guests and staff was almost legendary. Today, much liberated from the demands of its founder (Mme Barale retired from the scene late in 2003), the venue now revolves less around her personality cult, but it can still be a lot of fun. The setting includes several interconnected dining rooms, each outfitted with gleaming copper pots, patterned fabrics, comfortable banquettes, and lots of ceramics. In a separate room, presented like objects in a museum, is a trio of Citroëns from the 1920s, each restored to its original glossiness. Menu items reflect the old-fashioned culinary traditions of Nice: pissaladière, salad Niçoise, house-made ravioli, and savory slices of spinach tart.

39 rue Beaumont. © **04-93-89-17-94.** Reservations recommended. Set-price dinner 35€ ($46), includes aperitif, wine, coffee, and after-dinner drinks. No credit cards. Sept–June Tues–Sun 8–11pm; July–Aug Wed–Sun 8pm–midnight.

MODERATE
Don Camillo ✸✸ ITALIAN/PROVENÇAL   Named in the 1950s after its founder, Camille, a Niçoise patriot (who preferred the Italian version of his name), this nine-table restaurant promises (and delivers) some of Nice's most authentic Provençal food. Off cours Saleya, the dining room is adorned with pleasant, light colors and modern paintings, many of which are for sale, and whose components change every 6 months. Menu items change with the seasons, as supervised by owner Stéphane Viano, but might include jumbo shrimp flambéed with pastis and served with deliberately under-cooked vegetables; risottos with vegetables from the vendors of the nearby cours Saleya; filet of John Dory served with a confit of tomatoes and artichokes; and standing roasted rack of lamb served with Provençal herbs and Parmesan-dusted zucchini.

5 rue des Ponchettes. © **04-93-85-67-95.** Reservations recommended. Main courses 12€–26€ ($16–$34); fixed-price menus 32€–56€ ($42–$73). AE, DC, MC, V. Mon 8–9:30pm; Tues–Sat noon–1:30pm and 8–10pm. Bus: 8.

Merenda ✸✸ *Finds* NIÇOISE   Because there's no phone, you have to go by this place twice: once to make a reservation and once to dine. It's worth the effort. Forsaking his chef's crown at Chantecler (above), Dominique Le Stanc opened this tiny bistro serving sublime cuisine. Though he was born in Alsace, his heart and soul belong to the Mediterranean, the land of black truffles, wild morels, sea bass, and asparagus. His food is a lullaby of gastronomic unity, with texture, crunch, richness, and balance. Le Stanc never knows what he's going to serve until he goes to the market. Look for specials on a chalkboard. Perhaps you'll find stuffed cabbage, fried zucchini flowers, or oxtail flavored with fresh oranges. Lamb from the Sisteron is cooked until it practically falls from the bone. Raw artichokes are paired with a salad of mâche. Service is discreet and personable. We wish we could dine here every day.

4 rue Terrasse. No phone. Reservations required. Main courses 30€–45€ ($39–$59). No credit cards. Mon–Fri seatings at 7:15 and 9:15pm. Closed Apr 26–May 2, July 31–Aug 22, and Nov 29–Dec 12. Bus: 8.

L'Ane Rouge 🎯🎯 PROVENÇAL   Facing the old port and occupying an antique building whose owners have carefully retained its ceiling beams and stone walls, this is one of the city's best-known seafood restaurants. In the two modern yet cozy dining rooms, you can enjoy traditional specialties like bouillabaisse, *bourride* (stew), filet of John Dory with roulades of stuffed lettuce leaves, mussels stuffed with breadcrumbs and herbs, and salmon in wine sauce with spinach. Service is correct and commendable.

7 quai des Deux-Emmanuels. ℰ 04-93-89-49-63. Reservations required. Main courses 25€–57€ ($33–$74); fixed-price menu 33€–70€ ($43–$91) lunch, 48€–70€ ($62–$91) dinner. AE, DC, MC, V. Fri–Tues noon–2pm; Thurs–Tues 8–10:30pm. Closed 3 weeks in Feb. Bus: 30.

La Toque Blanche *(Value* FRENCH/SEAFOOD   La Toque Blanche has only about a dozen tables amid a decor loaded with fresh flowers, big windows, and a changing array of contemporary paintings. The owners, Gilles and Diana Houbron, pay particular attention to their shopping, buying only very fresh ingredients, often from markets nearby. Cuisine is skillfully prepared: Try the filet of beef Rossini (layered with foie gras); the hake cooked in a salt crust; and sweetbreads sautéed with crayfish. The foie gras here makes a particularly good starter.

40 rue de la Buffa. ℰ 04-93-88-38-18. Main courses 14€–25€ ($18–$33); fixed-price menus 24€–30€ ($31–$39). AE, DC, MC, V. Tues–Sat 7–10:30pm; Sun noon–2:30pm and 7–10:30pm. Closed Jan 10–20 and 2 weeks in mid-Aug. Bus: 8.

Restaurant Boccaccio MEDITERRANEAN   Adjacent to place Masséna, in a pedestrian zone that enhances the desirability of its streetfront terrace, this restaurant boasts worthy cuisine and a devoted local following. Bouillabaisse is reasonably priced here, and the range of fresh fish (grilled with lemon butter or baked in a salt crust) is broad and well prepared. The paella might remind you of Spain, and desserts like cappuccino tiramisu and crêpes suzettes round out meals nicely. There's a large dining room upstairs, inspired by the interior of a yacht, if the terrace doesn't appeal to you.

7 rue Masséna. ℰ 04-93-87-71-76. Reservations recommended. Main courses 25€–40€ ($33–$52); fixed-price menu 49€–100€ ($64–$130); bouillabaisse 34€ ($44) per person. AE, DC, MC, V. Daily noon–2:30pm and 7–11pm. Bus: 4, 5, or 22.

INEXPENSIVE

Au Petit Gari TRADITIONAL FRENCH   Set beneath the arcades of the place Garibaldi, this restaurant features a hip and friendly staff and a decor and menu that are distinctly and deliberately old-fashioned. The setting evokes an early-20th-century bistrot, replete with banquettes, etched glass, and a fast-moving pace that keeps clients well fed and briskly moving in and out of the available seats. Menu items are written in chalk on blackboards, and include a gratin of scallops and shrimp served on a bed of braised leeks; a terrine of rabbit with prunes; deliberately undercooked tuna steak served with a tapenade of olives and mashed potatoes; and an old-fashioned magret (grilled breast) of duck.

2 Place Garibaldi. ⓒ **04-93-26-89-09.** Reservations recommended. Main courses 13€–22€ ($17–$29). MC, V. Mon–Fri noon–2pm; Mon–Sat 7–10pm. Closed 2 weeks in Jan.

Brasserie Flo *Kids* TRADITIONAL FRENCH   This is the town's most bustling brasserie. In 1991, the Jean-Paul Bucher group, a French chain noted for its skill at restoring historic brasseries, bought the premises of a faded early-1900s restaurant near place Masséna and injected it with new life. The original frescoes cover the high ceilings. The place (which is affiliated with Brasserie Flo in Paris) is brisk, stylish, reasonably priced, and fun. Menu items include an array of grilled fish, *choucroute* (sauerkraut) Alsatian style, steak with brandied pepper sauce, and fresh oysters and shellfish.

2–4 rue Sacha-Guitry. ⓒ **04-93-13-38-38.** Reservations recommended. Main courses 15€–22€ ($20–$29); fixed-price menu 23€–32€ ($30–$42) lunch, 30€ ($39) dinner; children's menu 13€ ($17). AE, DC, MC, V. Daily noon–2:30pm and 7pm–midnight. Bus: 1, 2, or 5.

Café de Turin *Kids* CONTINENTAL/SEAFOOD   The origins of this place began in 1900, when it served glasses and carafes of wine to local office workers and laborers. In the 1950s, it added a kitchen to its premises, and ever since, it's churned out the kinds of hearty, bistro-style platters that go well with wines and beer. Much of the energy of the place is expressed outside, under the arcades of the central plaza (place Garibaldi), where local hipsters strut their stuff, people jump to their feet to table-hop, and harassed but well-intentioned waiters do their best to keep the food and beverages flowing. The place is celebrated for its *coquillage* (raw shellfish), attracting the likes of Princess Caroline, who drives over from Monaco. Other items include whatever species of grilled fish is available that day: pâtés, terrines, salads, pastas, and a satisfying selection of ice creams and pastries.

5 place Garibaldi. ⓒ **04-93-62-29-52.** Reservations recommended weekends at night; otherwise, not necessary. Main courses 13€–30€ ($17–$39). MC, V. Daily 9am–11pm. Bus: 9 or 10.

La Petite Maison *Finds* FRENCH/PROVENÇAL   This bustling and noisy tavern is set in the heart of the old town, within what was originally conceived in the 19th century as a grocery store, beneath vaulted ceilings. Locals guard the address, hoping it won't be mobbed by tourists. Those regulars include Elton John and his longtime companion, who live in a villa a few miles away. It's usually packed with diners wanting to taste this array of Niçoise cuisine, the authenticity of which is virtually unequalled in the city. Try the town's finest zucchini blossom fritters, and finish with a dessert that will send you rushing to the phone to call *Gourmet* magazine—homemade ice cream flavored with pine nuts and candied orange blossoms. In between, you might enjoy a succulent array of grilled fish, pastas, and steaks, all prepared with the right Mediterranean touches and just enough garlic.

11 rue St.-Francoise de Paule. ⓒ **04-93-85-71-53.** Reservations recommended. Main courses 10€–35€ ($13–$46). AE, V. Mon–Sat noon–2:30pm and 7:30pm–midnight.

La Zucca Magica *Finds* VEGETARIAN/ITALIAN   The chef at this popular harborside restaurant has been named the best Italian chef in Nice. That this honor should go to a vegetarian restaurant was the most startling part of the news. Chef Marco, who opened his restaurant in 1997 after cooking for many years in Rome, certainly has a fine pedigree—he's a relative of Luciano Pavarotti. He serves refined cuisine at reasonable prices, using recipes from Italy's Piedmont region and updating them with no meat or fish. The red-and-green decor (the colors of Italy) will put you in the mood for the creative cuisine. You'll have to trust Marco, though, because everyone is served the same meal. You can count on savory cuisine using lots of herbs, Italian cheeses, beans, and pasta. Lasagna is a specialty.

4 bis quai Papacino. ℂ **04-93-56-25-27.** Reservations recommended. Fixed-price menu 17€ ($22) lunch, 27€ ($35) dinner. No credit cards. Tues–Sat noon–2pm and 7–10pm.

Le Safari ✦ PROVENÇAL/NIÇOISE   The decor couldn't be simpler: a black ceiling, white walls, and an old-fashioned terra-cotta floor. The youthful staff is relaxed, sometimes in jeans, and always alert to the latest fashion. Many diners prefer the outdoor terrace overlooking the Marché aux Fleurs, but all appreciate the reasonably priced meals that appear in generous portions. Menu items include a pungent *bagna cauda,* which calls for diners to immerse vegetables in a sizzling brew of hot oil and anchovy paste; grilled peppers bathed in olive oil; *daube* (stew) of beef; fresh pasta with basil; and an omelet with *blettes* (tough but flavorful greens). The unfortunately named *merda de can* (dog shit) is gnocchi stuffed with spinach and is a lot more appetizing than it sounds.

1 cours Saleya. ℂ **04-93-80-18-44.** Reservations recommended. Main courses 14€–30€ ($18–$39); fixed-price menu 28€–35€ ($36–$46). AE, DC, MC, V. Daily noon–3pm and 7:30–11pm. Bus: 1.

Le Tire Bouchon ("The Corkscrew") SOUTHWESTERN FRENCH   Set in the heart of the old city, this is a cozy restaurant with a Bordeaux-tinged color scheme, two dining rooms, an old-fashioned decor, and an allegiance to the rich and hearty cuisine of France's southwest. Menu items reflect the kind of conservative cuisine that hasn't changed very much since the days when its clients might have been children. The best examples include onion soup with a crusty top, cassoulet (the earth pork-and-bean stew of Toulouse—but only in winter), confit of duckling, curried crayfish and monkfish, foie gras and pâté of duck with figs and hazelnuts, and various forms of fish. The place attracts a bevy of local residents, many of whom have been coming regularly since the place was established more than a decade ago.

19 rue de la Préfecture. ℂ **04-93-92-63-64.** Reservations recommended. Main courses 17€–24€ ($22–$31); set menu 28€ ($36). MC, V. Daily 7–10:30pm. Bus: 9 or 10.

Restaurant L'Estocaficada *(Finds)* NIÇOISE   *Estocaficada* is the Provençal word for stockfish, Europe's ugliest fish. There might be a dried-out, balloon-shaped version on display in the cozy dining room. Brigitte Autier is the owner and chef, and her kitchens are visible from everywhere in the dining room. Descended from a matriarchal line (since 1958) of mother-daughter teams who've managed this place, she's devoted to the preservation of recipes prepared by her Niçoise grandmother. Examples are gnocchi, beignets, several types of *farcies* (tomatoes, peppers, or onions stuffed with herbed fillings), grilled sardines, and bouillabaisse served as a main course or in a miniversion. The place also serves pastas.

2 rue de l'Hôtel-de-Ville. ℂ **04-93-80-21-64.** Reservations recommended. Main courses 15€–38€ ($20–$49); fixed-price menu 22€ ($29) and 35€ ($46). AE, MC, V. Tues–Sat noon–2pm and 7:30–10pm. Bus: 1, 2, or 5.

NICE AFTER DARK

Nice has some of the most active nightlife along the Riviera. Evenings usually begin at a cafe. At kiosks around town you can pick up a copy of *La Semaine des Spectacles,* which outlines the week's diversions.

The major cultural center on the Riviera is the **Opéra de Nice,** 4 rue St-François-de-Paule ((C) **04-92-17-40-00**), built in 1885 by Charles Garnier, fabled architect of the Paris Opéra. It presents a full repertoire, with emphasis on serious, often large-scale operas. In one season you might see *Tosca, Les Contes de Hoffmann,* Verdi's *Macbeth,* Beethoven's *Fidelio,* and *Carmen,* as well as a *saison symphonique,* dominated by the Orchestre Philharmonique de Nice. The opera hall is also the major venue for concerts and recitals. Tickets are available (to concerts, recitals, and full-blown operas) a day or two prior to any performance. You can show up at the box office (Mon–Sat 10am–5:30pm, Sun 10am–6pm) or buy tickets in advance with a major credit card by phoning (C) **04-92-17-40-40.** Tickets run 8€ ($10) for nosebleed (and we mean it) seats to 80€ ($104) for front-and-center seats on opening night.

Near the Ambassador Hotel, **Le Before,** 18 rue des Congrès ((C) **04-93-87-85-59**), is an aperitif bar—called *apero-bar*—where a stylish all-ages crowd goes before heading off to more dance-oriented places. The decor is "New York inspired," with lots of brick like you'd find in a grotty Gotham cellar. Open daily from 6pm to 2am, with cold platters served until 10pm.

Cabaret du Casino Ruhl, in the Casino Ruhl, 1 promenade des Anglais ((C) **04-97-03-12-22**), is Nice's answer to the more ostentatious glitter of Monte Carlo and Las Vegas. It includes just enough flesh to titillate; lots of spangles, feathers, and sequins; a medley of cross-cultural jokes and nostalgia for the old days of French *chanson;* and an acrobat or juggler. The 16€ ($21) cover includes one drink; dinner and the show, complete with a bottle of wine per person, costs 65€ ($85). Shows begin Friday and Saturday at 10:30pm. No jeans or sneakers.

The casino contains an area exclusively for slot machines, open daily from noon to 4am, entrance to which is free. A more formal gaming room (jacket required, but not a tie), with blackjack, baccarat, and chemin de fer, charges 10€ ($13) admission every Monday to Thursday, and 13€ ($17) every Friday to Sunday. Presentation of a government-issued photo ID, preferably a passport, is required. It's open Monday to Friday 8pm to 4am, Saturday and Sunday from 5pm to 5am.

Le Relais, in the Hôtel Negresco, 37 promenade des Anglais ((C) **04-93-16-64-00**), is the most beautiful museum-quality bar in Nice, with an oxblood-red ceiling, Oriental carpets, English paneling, Italianate chairs, and tapestries. It was once a haunt of the actress Lillie Langtry. With its piano music and white-jacketed waiters, the bar still attracts a chic crowd. The Negresco, including its bar, is to an increasing degree appreciated as a museum of the 19th-century decorative arts.

At many bars in the old town, Americans will feel right at home. They include the **Scarlett O'Hara Irish Pub,** at the corner of rue Rosetti and rue Droite ((C) **04-93-80-43-22**); **Chez Wayne,** 15 rue de la Préfecture ((C) **04-93-13-46-99**); and **William's Pub,** 4 rue Centrale ((C) **04-93-62-99-63**), which has live music. If you'd rather hang out with French people, try **La Civette,** 29 rue de la Préfecture ((C) **04-93-62-35-51**), a popular spot for aperitifs. Two nearly adjacent sports bars with roughly equivalent decors, clienteles, and sports priorities include Chez Wayne and **Le Master Home Bar,** 11 rue de la Prefecture ((C) **04-93-80-33-82**), off place Rossetti in Vieux Nice. Both regularly sponsor live bands, both have more wide-screens telecasting sporting events than you could possibly take in at one sitting, and both offer the option of a rollicking and often raucous good time. Thursday, at Chez Wayne, is karaoke night. When live music is presented at either of these bars, it tends to begin around 9pm.

You can also make a night of it at **Latino's,** 6 rue Chauvin (© **04-93-85-01-10**); and at its roughly equivalent competitor a few buildings away, **La Bodeguita,** 14 rue Chavin (© **04-93-92-67-24**). Both serve tapas, wine by the glass, lots of beer, and both re-create some of the sun-and-salsa motifs of nightlife at its best in the Caribbean and South America.

GAY NIGHTLIFE

Near the Hôtel Negresco and promenade des Anglais, **Le Blue Boy,** 9 rue Jean-baptiste Spinetta (© **04-93-44-68-24**), is the oldest gay disco on the Riviera. With two bars and two floors, it's a vital stop for passengers aboard the all-gay cruises that call at Nice. The cover is 10€ ($13).

A more trend-conscious gay bar in Nice is **Le Klub,** 6 rue Halevy (© **04-93-16-27-56**), near the Casino Ruhl. Entrance costs 15€ ($20) and includes one free drink. Expect a hard-dancing, high-energy crowd of mostly gay men here, many of them under 35, as well as lots of straight people who come for the nonstop barrage of house music and the focus inside on dance, dance, dance.

7 Villefranche-sur-Mer ⭐

935km (581 miles) S of Paris; 6km (4 miles) E of Nice

According to legend, Hercules opened his arms and Villefranche was born. It sits on a big blue bay that looks like a gigantic bowl, large enough to accommodate U.S. Sixth Fleet cruisers and destroyers. Quietly slumbering otherwise, Villefranche takes on the appearance of an exciting Mediterranean port when the fleet is in.

Once popular with such writers as Katherine Mansfield and Aldous Huxley, it's still a haven for artists, many of whom take over the little houses—reached by narrow alleyways—that climb the hillside. Two of the more recent arrivals who have bought homes in the area are Tina Turner and Bono.

ESSENTIALS

GETTING THERE   Trains arrive from most towns on the Côte d'Azur, especially Nice (every 30 min.), but most visitors **drive** via the Corniche Inférieure (Lower Corniche). For more rail information and schedules, call © **08-92-35-35-35**. There's no formal **bus** station in Villefranche. As regards bus transits into Villefranche, the Sun Bus company (© **04-93-85-61-81**) maintains service at 15-minute intervals aboard line no. 100 from Nice and from Monte Carlo. One-way bus transit from Nice costs 2€ ($2.60); one-way bus transit from Monaco is 3€ ($3.90). Buses deposit their passengers in the heart of town, directly opposite the tourist information office.

VISITOR INFORMATION   The Office de Tourisme is on Jardin François-Binon (© **04-93-01-73-68;** www.villefranche-sur-mer.com).

EXPLORING THE TOWN

The vaulted **rue Obscure** is one of the strangest streets in France. In spirit it belongs more to a North African casbah than to a European port. People live in tiny houses, and occasionally there's an open space, allowing for a courtyard. To get there, take rue de l'Eglise.

Jean Cocteau, the painter, writer, filmmaker, and well-respected dilettante, spent a year (1956–57) painting frescoes on the 14th-century walls of the Romanesque **Chapelle St-Pierre,** quai de la Douane/rue des Marinières (© **04-93-76-90-70**). He presented it to "the fishermen of Villefranche in homage to the Prince of Apostles, the patron of fishermen." One panel pays tribute to the Gypsies of the Stes-Maries-de-la-Mer. In the apse is a depiction of the miracle of St. Peter walking on the water, not knowing that an angel supports him. Villefranche's women, in their regional costumes, are honored on the left side of the narthex. The chapel charges 2€ ($2.60) admission for everyone (adults and children). It is open June to August Tuesday to Sunday 10am to noon and 4 to 8:30pm; September to November 15 Tuesday to Sunday 9:30am to noon and 2 to 6pm; December 16 to May Tuesday to Sunday 9:30am to noon and 2 to 5pm. (It's closed Nov 16–Dec 15.)

WHERE TO STAY

Hôtel Versailles   Several blocks from the harbor and outside the main part of town, this three-story hotel gives you a perspective of the entire coast. The hotel offers comfortably furnished rooms and suites (suitable for up to three) with big windows and panoramas. Guests can order breakfast or lunch under an umbrella on the roof terrace. Rooms are clean and bright, with comfortable beds and tiled bathrooms with tub or shower.

7 av. Princesse-Grace-de-Monaco, 06230 Villefranche-sur-Mer. ℂ **04-93-76-52-52.** Fax 04-93-01-97-48. www.hotelversailles.com. 46 units. 100€–140€ ($130–$182) double; 155€–220€ ($202–$286) suite. AE, DC, MC, V. Free parking. Closed Nov–Jan. **Amenities:** Restaurant; lounge; pool; limited room service. *In room:* A/C, TV.

Hôtel Welcome ✦   This is as good as it gets in Villefranche. The Welcome was a favorite of author and filmmaker Jean Cocteau. In this six-story villa hotel, with shutters and balconies, everything has been modernized and extensively renovated. Try for a fifth-floor room overlooking the water. All the midsize to spacious rooms are comfortably furnished, each with a small bathroom, and most with a combination tub/shower. The sidewalk cafe is the focal point of town life. The on-site wine bar and the restaurant, St-Pierre, have open fireplaces and fruitwood furniture.

1 quai Amiral-Courbet, 06231 Villefranche-sur-Mer. ℂ **04-93-76-27-62.** Fax 04-93-76-27-66. www.welcome hotel.com. 36 units. 85€–189€ ($111–$246) double; 299€–343€ ($389–$446) suite. AE, DC, MC, V. Closed Nov 10–Dec 20. **Amenities:** Bar; limited room service; babysitting; laundry service. *In room:* A/C, TV, dataport, minibar, hair dryer, safe.

WHERE TO DINE

Chez Michel's FRENCH/PROVENÇAL   This bustling and animated brasserie is owned and managed by the husband-and-wife team Michel and Michelle. The setting is a cozily unpretentious dining room lined with Provençal landscapes. Well-prepared menu items made with fresh ingredients include dishes such as a filet of beef Rossini (layered with foie gras), wok-fried calamari, grilled sea bass with a tapenade of olives, rack of lamb with Provençal herbs, roasted veal with mustard sauce, and a roster of fresh chargrilled fish of the day that is usually served either with a basil-flavored vinaigrette or with lemon-flavored butter sauce. Salads, including versions with shrimp, are excellent.

Place Amélie Pollonnais. ℂ **04-93-76-73-24.** Reservations recommended. Main courses 18€–35€ ($23–$46). AE, MC, V. Wed–Mon noon–3pm and 7–11pm.

La Mère Germaine FRENCH/SEAFOOD   This is the best of the string of restaurants on the port. Plan to relax over lunch while watching fishermen repair their nets. Mère Germaine opened the place in the 1930s. These days a descendant, Remy Blouin, handles the cuisine, producing bouillabaisse celebrated across the Riviera. We recommend grilled sea bass with fennel, sole Tante Marie (stuffed with mushroom purée), lobster ravioli with shellfish sauce, and beef filet with garlic and seasonal vegetables. Perfectly roasted *carré d'agneau* (lamb) is prepared for two.

Quai Courbet. 🕐 **04-93-01-71-39.** Reservations recommended. Main courses 20€–88€ ($26–$114); fixed-price menu 34€ ($44); bouillabaisse 57€ ($74). AE, DC, MC, V. Daily noon–2:30pm and 7–10pm. Closed mid-Nov to Christmas.

La Trinquette 🔭 PROVENÇAL/SEAFOOD   Charming and traditional, in a pre-Napoleonic building a few steps from the harborfront, this restaurant prides itself on the excellence of its fish and bouillabaisse. The fish is brought out from a back room if anyone is skeptical enough to ask to see the actual fish before it's cooked. You can choose from among 15 to 20 kinds, prepared any way you specify, with a wide variety of well-flavored sauces. Bouillabaisse is an enduring favorite—much cheaper here than at many other places. A roasted version of *chapon de mer* is served with a Provençal sauce. How do the hardworking owners, Paul and Monique Osiel, assisted by their son, Rubens, recommend their fresh John Dory? Roasted as simply as possible, served only with a hint of *beurre blanc.*

Port de la Darse. 🕐 **04-93-01-71-41.** Reservations recommended. Main courses 10€–25€ ($13–$33); bouillabaisse 40€ ($52); fixed-price menus 22€–33€ ($29–$43). No credit cards. Thurs–Tues noon–2:15pm and 7–10pm. Closed Dec–Jan.

8 St-Jean-Cap-Ferrat 🔭

938km (583 miles) S of Paris; 10km (6 miles) E of Nice

This place has been called "Paradise Found"—of all the oases along the Côte d'Azur, none has quite the snob appeal of Cap Ferrat. It's a 15km (9-mile) promontory sprinkled with luxurious villas, outlined by sheltered bays, beaches, and coves. The vegetation is lush. In the port of St-Jean, the harbor accommodates yachts and fishing boats.

ESSENTIALS

GETTING THERE   Most visitors drive or take a **bus** or **taxi** from the rail station at nearby Beaulieu. Buses from the station at Beaulieu depart hourly for Cap-Ferrat; the one-way fare is 1.80€ ($2.35). There's also bus service from Nice. For bus information and schedules, call 🕐 **04-93-85-64-44.** By **car** from Nice, take N7 east.

VISITOR INFORMATION   The **Office de Tourisme** is on 59 avenue Denis-Séméria (🕐 **04-93-76-08-90**).

SEEING THE SIGHTS

One way to enjoy the scenery here is to wander on some of the public paths. The most scenic goes from **Plage de Paloma** to **Pointe St-Hospice,** where a panoramic view of the Riviera landscape unfolds.

You can also wander around the hamlet **St-Jean,** a colorful fishing village with bars, bistros, and inns.

Everyone tries to visit the **Villa Mauresque,** avenue Somerset-Maugham, but it's closed to the public. Near the cape, it's where Maugham spent his final years. When tourists tried to visit him, he proclaimed that he wasn't one of the local sights. One man did manage to crash through the gate, and when he encountered the author, Maugham snarled, "What do you think I am, a monkey in a cage?"

Once the property of King Leopold II of Belgium, the **Villa Les Cèdres** lies west of the port of St-Jean. Although you can't visit the villa, you can go to the nearby **Parc Zoologique,** boulevard du Général-de-Gaulle, northwest of the peninsula (🕐 **04-93-76-04-98**). It's open May to September daily from 9:30am to 7:30pm; April and

October daily from 9:30am to 5:30pm (closed Nov–Mar). Admission is 12€ ($16) for adults, 8€ ($10) for students, 8€ ($10) for children 3 to 10. This private zoo is in the basin of a drained lake. It houses a wide variety of reptiles, birds, and animals in outdoor cages.

Musée Ile-de-France (aka Villa Ephrussi de Rothschild) 𝓡𝓡 Built by Baronne Ephrussi de Rothschild, this is one of the Côte d'Azur's legendary villas. Born a Rothschild, the baronne married a Hungarian banker and friend of her father, about whom even the museum's curator knows little. She died in 1934, leaving the Italianate building and its gardens to the Institut de France on behalf of the Académie des Beaux-Arts. The museum preserves the wealth of her collection: 18th-century furniture; Tiepolo ceilings; Savonnerie carpets; screens and panels from the Far East; tapestries from Gobelin, Aubusson, and Beauvais; Fragonard drawings; canvases by Boucher; Sèvres porcelain; and more. The sprawling gardens contain fragments of statuary from churches, monasteries, and palaces. An entire section is planted with cacti.

Av. Denis-Séméria. ℂ 04-93-01-45-90. Admission 8.50€ ($11) adults, 6.50€ ($8.45) students and children 7–18. Mar–Oct daily 10am–6pm; Nov–Feb Mon–Fri 2–6pm, Sat–Sun 10am–6pm.

WHERE TO STAY
VERY EXPENSIVE
Grand Hôtel du Cap-Ferrat 𝓡𝓡𝓡 One of the best features of this early-1900s palace is its location: at the tip of the peninsula in the midst of a 5.6-hectare (14-acre) garden of semitropical trees and manicured lawns. It has been the retreat of the international elite since 1908 and occupies the same celestial status as the Réserve and Métropole in Beaulieu. Its cuisine even equals the Métropole's. Parts of the exterior have open loggias and big arched windows; you can also enjoy the views from the elaborately flowering terrace over the sea. Accommodations look as if the late Princess Grace might settle in comfortably at any minute. They're generally spacious and open to sea views, and most come with a sumptuous bathroom with tub and shower. Rates include admission to the pool, Club Dauphin. The beach is accessible by funicular from the main building. The hotel is open year-round.

71 bd. du Général-de-Gaulle, 06230 St-Jean-Cap-Ferrat. ℂ **04-93-76-50-52.** Fax 04-93-76-04-52. www.grand-hotel-cap-ferrat.com. 53 units. 355€–1,100€ ($462–$1,430) double; 1,070€–2,550€ ($1,391–$3,315) suite. Rates include breakfast. AE, MC, V. Indoor parking 80€ ($104); outdoor parking free. Closed Jan 3–Mar 1. **Amenities:** 2 restaurants; 2 bars; Olympic-size heated outdoor pool; 2 tennis courts; sauna; use of bicycles; 24-hr. room service; babysitting; laundry service; dry cleaning; nonsmoking rooms; limited-mobility rooms. In room: A/C, TV, dataport, minibar, hair dryer, safe.

La Voile d'Or 𝓡𝓡 Established in 1966, the "Golden Sail" is a tour de force. It offers intimate luxury in a converted 19th-century villa at the edge of the little fishing port and yacht harbor, with a panoramic coast view. It's equal to the Grand Hôtel in every feature except cuisine, which is just a notch lower. The guest rooms, lounges, and restaurant open onto terraces. Accommodations are individually decorated, with hand-painted reproductions, carved gilt headboards, baroque paneled doors, parquet floors, antique clocks, and paintings. The luxurious bathrooms have tub/shower combinations. Guests gather on the canopied outer terrace for lunch, and in a stately room with Spanish armchairs and white wrought-iron chandeliers for dinner.

31 av. Jean-Mermoz, 06230 St-Jean-Cap-Ferrat. ℂ **04-93-01-13-13.** Fax 04-93-76-11-17. www.lavoiledor.fr. 45 units. 215€–710€ ($280–$923) double; 435€–815€ ($566–$1,060) suite. Rates include continental breakfast. AE, MC, V. Parking 22€ ($25). Closed Nov to late Mar. **Amenities:** 2 restaurants; bar; 2 saltwater outdoor pools; exercise room; sauna; limited room service; babysitting; laundry service; dry cleaning. In room: A/C, TV, dataport, minibar, hair dryer, safe.

EXPENSIVE

Hôtel Royal Riviera ⭐⭐   Rising five graceful stories above the thin line that separates the quietly prestigious towns of St.-Jean and Beaulieu, this hotel evokes the Riviera's Gilded Age, having been constructed in 1904. Fans of Zelda and F. Scott Fitzgerald know they frolicked here in the '30s, creating pages that might have been torn from *Tender Is the Night.* In 1988, an unfortunate modernization destroyed much of the belle époque charm of the palace, before Grace Leo-Andrieu, one of France's most inventive hoteliers, arrived from Paris to help the hostelry regain its old reputation. She can't help the location near the train tracks, which makes some of the front rooms noisy, but she's done everything else in her power to make this a pocket of posh that's becoming increasingly chic by the minute. It occupies a .4-hectare (1-acre) tract with a beach of its own, to which tons of sand are added at regular intervals. Bedrooms are posh and plush, with big windows, private balconies, deep sofas, and fruitwood armoires. The largest and most appealing are the corner units (any room ending in "16"). Regardless, each is charming, elegant, chic, and modern. Bathrooms are fairly routine but well equipped, with robes.

3 av. Jean Monnet, 06230 Saint-Jean-Cap-Ferrat. ℭ **04-93-76-31-00.** Fax 04-93-01-23-07. www.royal-riviera.com. 93 units. 110€–140€ ($143–$182) double; 550€–1,110€ ($715–$1,443) suite. Rates include half board. AE, DC, MC, V. Free parking. **Amenities:** 2 restaurants; bar; pool; 24-hr. room service; babysitting; laundry service; dry cleaning. *In room:* A/C, TV, minibar, hair dryer, safe.

MODERATE

Hôtel Brise Marine   Built around 1878, this villa with front and rear terraces sits on a hillside. A long rose arbor, beds of subtropical flowers, palms, and pines provide an attractive setting. The atmosphere is casual and informal, and the rooms are comfortably but simply furnished. They have small, tiled bathrooms with shower and tub. You can have breakfast in the beamed lounge or under the rose trellis. The little corner bar serves afternoon drinks.

58 av. Jean-Mermoz, 06230 St-Jean-Cap-Ferrat. ℭ **04-93-76-04-36.** Fax 04-93-76-11-49. www.hotel-brise marine.com. 18 units. 130€–180€ ($169–$234) double. AE, DC, MC, V. Parking 10€ ($13). Closed Nov–Jan. **Amenities:** Bar; limited room service. *In room:* A/C, TV, dataport, minibar, hair dryer, safe.

Hôtel Clair Logis *(Value*   The grandmother of the present owners created this B&B by adding two outbuildings to the grounds of her early-1900s villa. It's on an otherwise pricey resort strip about a 10-minute walk from the beach. The pleasant rooms, each named after a flower, are scattered over three buildings in the confines of the garden. The most romantic and spacious are in the main building, a comfortably proportioned *maison bourgeoise* built in 1903; the seven rooms in the 1960s annexes are the most modern but have the least character and tend to be smaller and cheaper. The hotel's most famous guest was de Gaulle, who stayed in the Strelitzias (Bird of Paradise) room during many of his retreats from Paris.

12 av. Centrale, 06230 St-Jean-Cap-Ferrat. ℭ **04-93-76-51-81.** Fax 04-93-76-51-82. www.hotel-clair-logis.fr. 18 units. 95€–170€ ($124–$221) double. AE, DC, MC, V. Free parking. Closed Jan 10 to early Feb and Nov–Dec 15. **Amenities:** Limited room service; laundry service; nonsmoking rooms; limited-mobility rooms. *In room:* TV, dataport, minibar, hair dryer.

Hôtel Le Panoramic *(Value*   This hotel, built in 1958 with a red-tile roof and much style and glamour, is one of the more affordable choices here. You'll reach the hotel by passing over a raised bridge lined with colorful pansies. The well-furnished rooms have a sweeping view of the water and the forest leading down to it. Accommodations are a bit small, but each is fitted with fine linen, plus a compact tiled bathroom. Breakfast is the only meal served.

3 av. Albert-1er, 06230 St-Jean-Cap-Ferrat. ℂ **04-93-76-00-37.** Fax 04-93-76-15-78. www.hotel-lepanoramic.com. 20 units. 110€–150€ ($143–$195) double. AE, DC, MC, V. Free parking. Closed mid-Nov to Dec 26. **Amenities:** Limited room service; laundry service; dry cleaning. *In room:* TV.

WHERE TO DINE

Capitaine Cook ⊛ PROVENÇAL/SEAFOOD   Next door to the fancy La Voile d'Or hotel (see above), a few blocks uphill from the center of the village, this restaurant specializes in seafood served in hearty portions. Diners enjoy a panoramic view of the coast from the terrace; inside, the decor is maritime and rugged. Oysters, served simply on the half shell or in several creative ways with sauces and herbs, are a specialty. Roasted catch of the day is the mainstay, but filet mignon is also popular. The staff speaks English.

11 av. Jean-Mermoz. ℂ **04-93-76-02-66.** Main courses 18€–29€ ($23–$38); fixed-price menu 23€–28€ ($30–$36). MC, V. Fri–Tues noon–2pm; Thurs–Tues 7:15–11pm. Closed mid-Nov to Dec.

Le Provençal ⊛ FRENCH/PROVENÇAL   With the possible exception of the Grand Hôtel's dining room, this is the grandest restaurant in town. Near the top of Nice's highest peak, it has the most panoramic view, which can sweep as far as the Italian border. Many of the menu items are credited to the inspiration of "the Provençal" in the kitchens. Selections include marinated artichoke hearts beside half a lobster, *tarte fine* of potatoes with deliberately undercooked foie gras, rack of lamb with local herbs and tarragon sauce, and crayfish with asparagus and black-olive tapenade. The best way to appreciate the desserts is to order the sampler, *les cinq desserts du Provençal*—five dishes that usually include macaroons with chocolate and crème brûlée.

2 av. Denis-Séméria. ℂ **04-93-76-03-97.** Reservations required. Main courses 35€–50€ ($46–$65); fixed-price menu 72€ ($94). AE, MC, V. Apr–Sept daily noon–2:30pm and 7:30–11pm; Oct–Mar Wed–Sun noon–2:30pm and 7:30–11pm.

Le Sloop FRENCH/PROVENÇAL   Le Sloop is the most popular and most reasonably priced bistro in this expensive area. Outfitted in blue and white inside and out, it sits at the edge of the port, overlooking the yachts in the harbor. A meal might begin with a salad of flap mushrooms steeped "en cappuccino" with liquefied foie gras, or perhaps tartare of salmon with aioli and lemon crepes. You might follow with a filet of sea bass served with red-wine sauce, or a mixed fish fry of three kinds of Mediterranean fish, bound together with olive oil and truffles. Dessert might include strawberry soup with sweet white wine and apricot ice cream or any of about seven other choices, each based on "the red fruits of the region." The regional wines are reasonably priced.

Au Nouveau Port. ℂ **04-93-01-48-63.** Reservations recommended. Main courses 22€–32€ ($29–$42); fixed-price menu 28€ ($36). AE, MC, V. July–Aug Thurs–Mon noon–2pm, Wed 7–9:30pm,Thurs–Tues 7–10pm; Sept–May Wed 7–9:30pm, Thurs–Tues noon–2pm and 7–10pm. Closed mid-Nov to mid-Jan.

9 Beaulieu ⊛

938km (583 miles) S of Paris; 10km (6 miles) E of Nice; 11km (7 miles) W of Monte Carlo

Protected from the cold north winds blowing down from the Alps, Beaulieu-sur-Mer is often referred to as "La Petite Afrique" (Little Africa). Like Menton, it has the mildest climate along the Côte d'Azur and is especially popular with the wintering wealthy. Originally, English visitors staked it out. Beaulieu is graced with lush vegetation, including oranges, lemons, and bananas, as well as palms.

ESSENTIALS

GETTING THERE   Most visitors **drive** from Nice on the Moyenne Corniche or the coastal highway. **Trains** connect Beaulieu with Nice, Monaco, and the rest of the Côte d'Azur. For rail information, call ☎ **08-36-35-35-36.**

VISITOR INFORMATION   The **Office de Tourisme** is on place Georges-Clemenceau (☎ **04-93-01-02-21;** www.ot-beaulieu-sur-mer.fr).

EXPLORING THE TOWN

Villa Kérylos ✿, rue Gustave-Eiffel (☎ **04-93-76-44-09**), is a replica of an ancient Greek residence, painstakingly designed and built by the archaeologist Théodore Reinach. Inside the cabinets are filled with a collection of Greek figurines and ceramics. But most interesting is the reconstructed Greek furniture, much of which would be fashionable today. One curious mosaic depicts the slaying of the minotaur and provides its own labyrinth (if you try to trace the path, expect to stay for weeks). It's open July to August daily 10am to 7pm; February to June and September to October daily 10am to 6pm; November to January Monday to Friday 2 to 6pm, Saturday to Sunday 10am to 6pm. Admission is 7.50€ ($9.75) adults, 5.50€ ($7.15) for seniors and children 7 to 18, and free for children under 7.

    Casino de Beaulieu, avenue Fernand-Dunan (☎ **04-93-76-48-00**), was built in the Art Nouveau style in 1903. The slot machines are open daily, without charge, from 11am to 4am. The *salles des grands jeux* are open Friday and Saturday from 8pm to 4am, Sunday to Thursday 9pm to 4am. Management strongly recommends that men wear jackets, or at least appropriate clothing. Entrance to the *grands jeux* costs 11€ ($14), and patrons must present a photo ID.

    Also in the casino is a deluxe restaurant, **La Coupole** (☎ **04-93-76-48-00**), which overlooks the Mediterranean. The upscale *brasserie de luxe,* serves seasonal gourmet cuisine that might include snails in garlic butter, roast breast of duckling with citrus sauce or with figs, and a wide array of grilled fresh fish. It's open Wednesday to Sunday from noon to 2pm and 7pm to midnight.

    The town boasts an important church, the late-19th-century **Eglise de Sacré-Coeur,** a quasi-Byzantine, quasi-Gothic mishmash at 13 bd. du Maréchal-Leclerc (☎ **04-93-01-18-24**). With the same address and phone is the 12th-century Romanesque chapel of **Santa Maria de Olivo,** used mostly for temporary exhibits of painting, sculpture, and civic lore. Both sites are open daily from 8am to 7pm.

    As you walk along the **seafront promenade,** you can see many stately belle époque villas that evoke the days when Beaulieu was the very height of fashion. Although you can't go inside, you'll see signs indicating Villa Namouna, which once belonged to Gordon Bennett, the owner of the *New York Herald,* who sent Stanley to Africa to find Livingstone; and Villa Léonine, former home of the marquess of Salisbury.

MEMORABLE STROLLS

For a memorable 90-minute walk, start directly north of boulevard Edouard-VII, where a path leads up the Riviera escarpment to **Sentier du Plateau St-Michel.** A belvedere here offers panoramic views from Cap d'Ail to the Estérel. A 1-hour alternative is the stroll along **promenade Maurice-Rouvier,** beginning at a point adjacent to the sea and the Royal Riviera hotel. The promenade runs parallel to the water and stretches between Beaulieu and the old port of St-Jean de Cap Ferrat. Expect a walk of about 30 minutes each way, although you might opt to prolong the experience with a cafe or drink in Cap Ferrat once you get there. As you walk, you'll see some of the region's most elegant mansions, set within manicured gardens overlooking the blue sea and the curving shoreline of the French Riviera.

A DAY AT THE BEACH

Don't expect soft sands. Some seasons might have more sand than others, depending on tides and storms, but usually the surfaces are covered with light-gray gravel that has a finer texture than beaches at other resorts nearby. The longer of the town's two free public beaches is **Petite Afrique,** adjacent to the yacht basin; the shorter is **Baie des Fourmis,** beneath the casino. **Africa Plage** (℃ **04-93-01-11-00**) rents mattresses for 14€ to 16€ ($18–$21) per day and sells snacks and drinks.

WHERE TO STAY
VERY EXPENSIVE

La Réserve de Beaulieu 🐸🐸🐸   A Relais & Châteaux member, this pink-and-white *fin-de-siècle* palace is one of the Riviera's most famous hotels. Here you can sit, have an aperitif, and watch the sunset while a pianist plays Mozart. A number of the lounges open onto a courtyard with bamboo chairs, grass borders, and urns of flowers. The social life revolves around the main drawing room. The individually decorated guest rooms range widely in size and design; most overlook the Mediterranean, and some have a view of the mountains. They come with deluxe beds and luxurious bathrooms with tubs and showers. Some have private balconies. The dining room has a frescoed ceiling, parquet floors, chandeliers, and windows facing the Mediterranean.

5 bd. du Maréchal-Leclerc, 06310 Beaulieu-sur-Mer. ℃ **04-93-01-00-01.** Fax 04-93-01-28-99. www.reserve beaulieu.com. 39 units. 170€–590€ ($221–$767) double; 460€–1,020€ ($598–$1,326) suite. AE, DC, MC, V. Parking 33€ ($43). Closed mid-Nov to Dec 20. **Amenities:** Restaurant; bar; outdoor pool; fitness center; gym; salon; 24-hr. room service; massage; babysitting; laundry service; dry cleaning; nonsmoking rooms; billiards. *In room:* A/C, TV, dataport, minibar, hair dryer, safe.

Le Métropole 🐸🐸   This Italianate villa is as good as it gets—except for La Réserve de Beaulieu (see above). It offers some of the Riviera's most luxurious accommodations. The Relais & Châteaux member sits on .8 hectare (2 acres) of grounds discreetly shut off from the traffic of the resort. Here, you'll enter a world of French elegance, with lots of balconies opening onto sea views, marble accents, Oriental carpets, and a polite staff. The guest rooms are furnished in tasteful fabrics and wallpapers, with deluxe mattresses; the roomy bathrooms have tub/shower combinations. The restaurant has a seaside terrace and bar.

15 bd. du Maréchal-Leclerc, 06310 Beaulieu-sur-Mer. ℃ **04-93-01-00-08.** Fax 04-93-01-18-51. www.le-metropole. com. 41 units. 170€–590€ ($221–$767) double; 460€–1,020€ ($598–$1,326) suite. AE, DC, MC, V. Closed Oct 20–Dec 20. **Amenities:** Restaurant; bar; outdoor pool; 24-hr. room service; babysitting; laundry service; dry cleaning; limited-mobility rooms. *In room:* A/C, TV, dataport, minibar, hair dryer, safe.

MODERATE

Inter-Hôtel Frisia   Most of the Frisia's rooms, decorated in a modern style, open onto views of the harbor. The water-view units are the most expensive. All rooms have small bathrooms, with a combination tub/shower. Two spacious suites with kitchenettes are in free-standing villas near the hotel's main building. Public areas include a sunny garden and inviting lounges. English is widely spoken here, and the management makes foreign guests feel especially welcome. Breakfast is the only meal served, but many reasonably priced dining places are nearby.

Bd. Eugène-Gauthier, 06310 Beaulieu-sur-Mer. ℂ **04-93-01-01-04.** Fax 04-93-01-31-92. www.frisia-beaulieu.com. 32 units. 60€–135€ ($78–$176) double; 140€–205€ ($182–$267) suite. AE, MC, V. Closed Nov 12–Dec 13. Parking: 9€ ($12). **Amenities:** Bar; limited room service; babysitting; laundry service; dry cleaning. *In room:* A/C, TV, dataport, minibar, hair dryer, safe.

INEXPENSIVE

Hôtel Le Havre Bleu *(Value)*   This is a great little bargain if you don't need a lot of services and amenities. Le Havre Bleu has one of the prettiest facades of any inexpensive hotel in town. In a former Victorian villa, the hotel has arched ornate windows and a front garden dotted with flower-filled urns. The impeccable guest rooms are comfortable and functional. The in-room amenities are few, except for a phone; the compact bathrooms have showers. Breakfast is the only meal served.

29 bd. du Maréchal-Joffre, 06310 Beaulieu-sur-Mer. ℂ **04-93-01-01-40.** Fax 04-93-01-29-92. www.hotel-lehavre bleu.fr. 22 units. 57€ ($74) double; 76€ ($99) triple; 94€ ($122) quad. AE, MC, V. Free parking. **Amenities:** Bar; limited room service; babysitting; laundry service. *In room:* TV, dataport.

Hôtel Marcellin   The early-20th-century Marcellin is a good budget selection in an otherwise high-priced resort. Built around 1900 for a local family, the sprawling, much-altered villa was divided into two about 25 years ago, and half was converted into this pleasant, cost-conscious hotel (the other half remains a private home). The restored rooms come with homelike amenities and a southern exposure. They're small to midsize, but comfortably furnished. All units have a small tiled bathroom with shower. Breakfast is the only meal served, but many restaurants are nearby.

18 av. Albert-1er, 06310 Beaulieu-sur-Mer. ℂ **04-93-01-01-69.** Fax 04-93-01-37-43. www.hotel-marcellin.com. 21 units. 54€–83€ ($70–$108) double. MC, V. **Amenities:** Bar; limited room service; babysitting; limited-mobility rooms. *In room:* A/C, TV, dataport, hair dryer.

WHERE TO DINE

The African Queen INTERNATIONAL   Named by its movie-loving founders after the Hollywood classic, this hip and popular restaurant is filled with posters of Hepburn and Bogie and has a jungle-inspired decor. Much influenced by the United States, it has welcomed stars like Jack Nicholson, Raymond Burr, Robert Wagner, and Diana Ross during the nearby Cannes Film Festival. Menu specialties are a *dégustation de bouillabaisse,* African curry of lamb or beef and served like a rijstaffel with about a dozen condiments, or any of an array of steaks, fish, or shellfish. Less expensive are the seven or eight kinds of pizza, which even visiting Italians claim are very good. The African Queen serves *the dégustation de bouillabaisse* only as a special order placed in advance. It's vastly more expensive (68€/$88 per person) than the other main courses. No one will mind if you stop in for only a strawberry daiquiri or piña colada. The check is presented in a videocassette case labeled—what else?—*The African Queen.*

Port de Plaisance. ℂ **04-93-01-10-85.** Reservations recommended. Main courses 14€–30€ ($18–$39); pizzas 10€–12€ ($13–$16). MC, V. Daily noon–midnight.

La Pignatelle *(Value)* FRENCH/PROVENÇAL   Even in this expensive town, you can find an excellent, affordable Provençal bistro. After all, the locals have to eat somewhere, and not every visitor can afford the costlier places. Despite its relatively low prices, La Pignatelle prides itself on the fresh ingredients in its robust cuisine.

Specialties include mushroom-stuffed ravioli with truffled cream sauce; succulent *soupe de poissons* from which the kitchen has labored to remove the bones; cassoulet of mussels; monkfish steak garnished with olive oil and herbs; fricassée of sea bass with shrimp; and *petite friture du pays* that incorporates small fish with old Provençal cooking traditions.

10 rue de Quincenet. ℂ 04-93-01-03-37. Reservations recommended. Main courses 12€–26€ ($16–$34); fixed-price menu 24€ ($31). MC, V. Thurs–Tues noon–2pm and 7–10pm. Closed Nov.

Le Catalan *Value* FRENCH/CATALAN/INTERNATIONAL   This place is endlessly popular, and endlessly busy, thanks to relatively low prices and succulent food. You'll dine within any of three separate dining rooms or on a terrace overlooking the sea. A sought-after menu item is pizza, which comes in at least a dozen varieties here and is baked to bubbling perfection in a wood-burning beehive oven. More substantial fare involves such dishes as paella and zarzuela, pasta with shellfish, and a full roster of grilled meats and fish. Everybody from dock workers in grimy clothes to plump society matrons from Paris dine here virtually elbow to elbow in an establishment that's acclaimed for its *égalité*.

52 bd. Général Leclerc. ℂ 04-93-01-02-78. Reservations recommended. Pizzas 7€–12€ ($9.10–$16); main courses 10€–28€ ($13–$36). MC, V. Tues–Sat noon–2:30pm and 7–11pm.

Les Agaves ★★ MODERN FRENCH   One of the most stylish restaurants in Beaulieu is in an early-1900s villa across the street from the railway station. U.S.-based publications such as *Bon Appétit* have praised the cuisine. Of note are curry-enhanced scallops with garlic-flavored tomatoes and parsley, terrine of pork with confit of onions, lobster salad with mango, bouillabaisse, rockfish soup, chopped shrimp with Provençal herbs, and several preparations of foie gras. Filet of sea bass with truffles and champagne sauce is delectable.

4 av. Maréchal Foch. ℂ 04-93-01-13-12. Reservations recommended. Main courses 20€–35€ ($26–$46); fixed-price menu 32€ ($42). AE, MC, V. Daily 7:30–10pm. Closed Nov 15–Dec 15.

10 Eze & La Turbie ★

941km (585 miles) S of Paris; 11km (7 miles) NE of Nice

The hamlets of Eze and La Turbie, though 6.4km (4 miles) apart, have so many similarities that most of France's tourist officials speak of them as if they were one. Both boast fortified feudal centers high in the hills overlooking the Provençal coast, built during the early Middle Ages to stave off raids from corsairs. Clinging to the rocky hillsides around these hamlets are upscale villas, many of which were built since the 1950s by retirees. Closely linked, culturally and fiscally, to nearby Monaco, Eze, and La Turbie each has a full-time population of fewer than 3,000.

ESSENTIALS

GETTING THERE   Eze (also known as Eze-Village) is accessible via the Moyenne (Middle) Corniche road; La Turbie is accessible via the Grande (Upper) Corniche. Signs are positioned along the coastal road indicating the direction motorists should take to reach either of the hamlets.

VISITOR INFORMATION   The **Office de Tourisme** is on place du Général-de-Gaulle, Eze-Village (ℂ **04-93-41-26-00;** www.eze-riviera.com).

EXPLORING THE TOWNS

The medieval cores of both towns contain art galleries, boutiques, and artisans' shops that have been restored. Two art galleries of particular note within Eze are **Galerie Sevek,** rue du Barri (© **04-93-41-06-22**), and **Galerie Doussot,** rue Principale (© **04-93-41-01-62**).

The leading attraction in Eze is the **Jardin d'Eze** ⚘, boulevard du Jardin-Exotique (© **04-93-41-10-30**), a showcase of exotic plants in Eze-Village, at the pinnacle of the town's highest hill. Admission is 4€ ($5.20) for adults, 2€ ($2.60) for students and ages 12 to 25, 1€ ($1.30) for children under 12. In July and August, it's open daily from 9am to 8pm; the rest of the year, it opens daily at 9am and closes between 5 and 7:30pm, depending on the time of sunset.

La Turbie boasts a ruined monument erected by Roman emperor Augustus in 6 B.C., the **Trophée des Alps (Trophy of the Alps)** ⚘. It's near a rock formation known as La Tête de Chien, at the highest point along the Grand Corniche, 450m (1,500 ft.) above sea level. The Roman Senate ordered the creation of the monument, which many locals call La Trophée d'Auguste, to celebrate the subjugation of the people of the French Alps by the Roman armies.

A short distance from the monument is the **Musée du Trophée d'August,** rue Albert-1er, La Turbie (© **04-93-41-20-84**), a minimuseum containing finds from digs nearby and information about the monument's restoration. It's open daily from 9:30am to 5pm (until 6pm Apr–June, until 7pm July–Sept). Admission is 4.60€ ($6) for adults, 3.10€ ($4.05) for students and ages 12 to 25, free for children under 12. It's closed January 1, May 1, November, and December 25.

WHERE TO STAY

Auberge Le Soleil   This pale pink late-19th-century villa is a few steps from the Basse Corniche. It has a quiet rear terrace, and the decor features rattan chairs, exposed brick, and lots of brass. In 2004, it was bought, upgraded, and transformed by the congenial, Italian-born new owner, Ester Parodi, who manages to imbue many everyday situations with a welcome humor. Simply furnished doubles draw mainly a summer crowd, though the inn is open most of the year. Bedrooms are small but decently furnished. Bathrooms are tiled and compact. Half board is a good deal here—the meals are satisfying and wine is included.

44 av. de la Liberté, 06360 Eze-Bord-de-Mer. © 04-93-01-51-46. Fax 04-93-01-58-40. www.auberge-lesoleil.com. 7 units. 75€ ($98) double. Half board 75€ ($98) per person extra. AE, DC, MC, V. Closed mid-Nov to mid-Dec. **Amenities:** Restaurant; lounge. *In room:* TV, minibar, hair dryer.

Château Eza ⚘⚘⚘   This château is the former Riviera home of Prince William of Sweden. It stands at the edge of a cliff at 396m (1,300 ft.) looking out over the resort of St. Jean-Cap-Ferrat. This is one of the Riviera's great pockets of posh. Entered on a narrow cobblestone street, it offers sumptuous bedrooms, a celebrated gourmet cuisine, and service fit for royalty. The elegant bedrooms are spread over a cluster of restored buildings dating from the Middle Ages. Each of the guest rooms is reached by walking under stone passageways past cavelike shops. Although the setting is ancient, the rooms are thoroughly modernized, with private bathrooms, charming fireplaces, and private balconies opening onto panoramic views. Canopied beds, art objects, beautiful carpets, and valuable tapestries set the tone. This is as close as the Riviera gets to fantasy living.

Rue de la Pise, Eze Village, 06360. © 04-93-41-12-24. Fax 04-93-41-16-64. www.chateaueza.com. 10 units. 150€–540€ ($195–$702) double; 420€–840€ ($546–$1,092) suite. AE, DC, MC, V. Closed Dec–Mar. **Amenities:**

Restaurant; bar; lounge; limited room service; babysitting; laundry service; dry cleaning. *In room:* A/C, TV, minibar, hair dryer, safe.

Hostellerie du Château de la Chèvre d'Or ✦✦✦   This is one of the grandest resort hotels along the Eastern Riviera. The miniature-village retreat was built in the 1920s in neo-Gothic style. It's a Relais & Châteaux property in a complex of village houses, all with views of the coastline. But unlike most villages in the area, this one doesn't have a beach. The decor of the "Golden Goat" maintains its character while adding modern comfort. The spacious guest rooms are filled with quality furnishings, and the large bathrooms have excellent fixtures, including tub/shower combinations. Even if you don't spend the night, try to visit for a drink in the lounge, which has a panoramic view.

Rue du Barri, 06360 Eze-Village. ✆ **04-92-10-66-66.** Fax 04-93-41-06-72. www.chevredor.com. 33 units. 270€–780€ ($351–$1,014) double; from 1,650€ ($2,145) suite. AE, MC, DC, V. Closed mid-Nov to early Mar. **Amenities:** 3 restaurants; bar; outdoor pool; gym; sauna; limited room service; babysitting; laundry service; dry cleaning. *In room:* A/C, TV, dataport, minibar, hair dryer, safe.

WHERE TO DINE

Le Troubadour FRENCH/PROVENÇAL   The stone-fronted medieval house that contains this well-known restaurant has, since World War I, housed businesses that have included a bar, a delicatessen, and the local post office. Since its transformation into a restaurant, it has received clients who included Robert Mitchum (in the mid-1950s), lots of local athletes, and drag-race drivers from the races in nearby Monaco. Today, within three dining rooms, each accented with thick ceiling beams, you can order succulent and flavorful dishes that include braised rabbit in aspic, served with warm hearts of artichoke, foie gras, and carrots; a delightful filet of John Dory with stuffed and deep-fried zucchini blossoms; roasted rack of lamb with parsley sauce; and other dishes that each manage to showcase some aspect of the Mediterranean diet. You'll find the place close to the village church, in the upper heights of Eze Village.

4 rue du Brec, Eze Village. ✆ **04-93-41-19-03.** Reservations recommended. Main courses 20€–35€ ($26–$46); set-price menus 32€–45€ ($42–$59). MC, V. Tues–Sat 1–2:30pm and 7–10pm. Closed late Nov to Christmas, 1 week between late Feb and Mar, and 2 weeks in late June to early July.

11 Peillon ✦✦

19km (12 miles) NW of Nice

This fortified medieval town is the most spectacular "perched village" along the Côte d'Azur. At 300m (1,000 ft.) above the sea, it's also unspoiled, unlike so many other perched villages that are filled with day-trippers and souvenir shops.

The main incentive to visit Peillon is the town itself, with its semifortified architecture, which makes you feel that even today it could lock its doors, bar its windows, and keep any intruder at bay. Specific sites of interest include the town's severely dignified parish church, the **Eglise St-Sauveur,** open daily from 8am to around 6pm. Built in a simple country-baroque style, it's the site of many marriages, baptisms, and wedding ceremonies. Another site of interest is the 15th-century **Chapelle des Pénitents Blancs,** on place August-Arnuls. It's usually locked, so visits require that you first drop by the Tourist Office on la rue Centrale in Peillon-Village (✆ **04-93-91-98-34**)—if it's convenient and if he or she isn't busy, an employee will accompany you with a key and wait for you while you admire the interior. The service is free, but a gratuity is appreciated. If you plunk .20€ (25¢) into a machine near the gate, lights will illuminate the interior's noteworthy frescoes. Painted in 1491 by Jean Cannavesio, they represent the eight stages of the passion of Christ.

The narrow streets radiate outward from the town's "foyer," **place Auguste-Arnuls,** which is shaded by rows of plantain trees centered around a fountain that has splashed water from its basin since 1800. Some of the streets are enclosed with vaulting and accented with potted geraniums and strands of ivy.

If you're in the mood for walking, consider a 2-hour, 12km (7½-mile) northward hike across the dry and rocky landscape to Peillon's remote twin, Peille, a smaller version of Peillon.

ESSENTIALS

GETTING THERE   Few other towns in Provence are as easy to reach by **car** and as inconvenient to reach by public transportation. Peillon is an easy 25-minute drive (depending on traffic) northeast from Nice; take D2204 to D21.

Only two **trains** a day stop near Peillon at St-Thècle, an antiquated station connecting Nice with Coni, a town across the border in Italy. For rail information and schedules, call © **08-36-35-35-35.** You'll find lots of dilapidated local color at the railway station of St-Thècle. There are no taxis waiting and no bus service to carry you on to Peillon. If you can find a phone in St-Techle, the phone number of the best local **cab service** is © **04-93-27-00-83.** You can also contact the company's cellphone by dialing © **06-13-43-89-24.** Transit from the railway station at St-Thècle to Peillon costs about 8€ ($10) each way. Most backpackers continue into Peillon by hitchhiking.

The T.R.A.M. bus line operates four buses a day from Nice, with multiple stops en route (trip time: around 25 min.). Don't expect it to be convenient—you'll be dropped off about 3km (2 miles) from Peillon's center, at a tiny crossroads known as Le Moulin. Many hardy souls opt to continue on to the center by foot because there's no transport into Peillon. For **bus information,** call © **08-00-06-01-06.**

VISITOR INFORMATION   Peillon established its own tourist office in 2005. Located on the very short rue Centrale in Peillon-Village (© **04-93-91-98-34**), it's open for limited hours throughout the year. If the staff happens to not be open at the time of your call, the tourist office in Nice (© **04-93-79-92-04**) is usually well informed about the attractions and allures of Pellion. Barring that, you can always contact the Town Hall (La Mairie) of Peillon (© **04-93-79-91-04**), where staff members have in the past been extraordinarily helpful. Additionally, the receptionists at the town's most colorful inn, L'Auberge de la Madone (see below) are usually helpful and informative about the layout and attractions within their town.

WHERE TO STAY & DINE

Auberge de la Madone ★★   This hotel, with its well-recommended restaurant, is the leading choice and has been since it opened back in the 1930s. The oldest section of the stone-sided complex of buildings dates from the 12th century. Evocative of a sprawling *mas Provençal,* it gives you a real glimpse of a Provence from long ago. It's capped with terra-cotta tiles and draped with a small version of the hanging gardens of Babylon. On the opposite side of place Auguste-Arnuls from the rest of the village, it boasts a wide terrace offering a great view of the town's vertical, angular architecture. The guest rooms are comfortable and rustic, outfitted with Provençal themes and fabrics. In 1998, the hotel built an annex within a 5-minute walk, with seven additional rooms—the annex's accommodations are much simpler than those in the main building; rates depend on the plumbing and views. Bathrooms are generally small.

The hotel restaurant is by far the most formal in town, serving lunch and dinner every day except Wednesday and during the annual closing noted below. Menu items are based on cuisine that developed over the centuries and include unusual dishes like *tourton des pénitents,* a salty tart enriched with 17 herbs, almonds, eggs, and cream; suckling lamb with garlic mashed potatoes and a tapenade of olives; farm-raised guinea fowl with a confit of pears; and a pot au feu, a savory kettle of seafood served with aioli. A recipe that was specifically praised early in 1999 by the American edition of *Bon Appetit* for its originality and subtle flavors was a white beet tart capped with a "petal" of foie gras.

2 place Auguste Arnulf, 06440 Peillon. ⓒ **04-93-79-91-17.** Fax 04-93-79-99-36. 20 units. Main building 90€–200€ ($117–$260) double; 105€–225€ ($137–$293) suite. Annex 50€–79€ ($65–$103) double. MC, V. Free parking. Closed Jan 7–31 and Oct 20–Dec 20. **Amenities:** Restaurant (closed Wed); bar; lounge. *In room:* TV, hair dryer.

12 Monaco ⭐⭐⭐

954km (593 miles) S of Paris; 18km (11 miles) E of Nice

The outspoken Katharine Hepburn once called Monaco "a pimple on the chin of the south of France." She wasn't referring to the principality's lack of beauty, but rather to the preposterous idea of having a little country, a feudal anomaly, taking up some of the choicest coastline along the Riviera. Hemmed in by France on three sides and facing the Mediterranean, tiny Monaco staunchly maintains its independence. Even Charles de Gaulle couldn't force the late Prince Rainier to do away with his tax-free policy. As almost everybody in an overburdened world knows by now, the Monégasques do not pay taxes. Nearly all their country's revenue comes from tourism and gambling.

Monaco—or rather, its capital of Monte Carlo—has for a century been a symbol of glamour. Its legend was further enhanced by the 1956 marriage of the man who was at that time the world's most eligible bachelor, Prince Rainier III, to the American actress Grace Kelly. Ms. Kelly died in 1982, Prince Rainer in 2005. She had met the prince when she was in Cannes for the film festival to promote *To Catch a Thief,* the Hitchcock movie she made with Cary Grant. A journalist friend arranged a *Paris Match* photo shoot with the prince—and the rest is history. The Monégasques welcomed the birth of daughter Caroline in 1957 but went wild at the birth of Albert, a male heir, in 1958. According to a 1918 treaty, Monaco will become an autonomous state under French protection if the ruling dynasty becomes extinct. However, the fact that Albert is still a bachelor has the entire principality concerned. The third royal daughter, Stephanie, was born in 1965.

Though not always happy in her role, Princess Grace won the respect and adoration of her people. In 1982, a sports car she was driving, with her daughter Stephanie as a passenger (not as the driver, as was viciously rumored), plunged over a cliff, killing Grace but only injuring Stephanie. The Monégasques still mourn her death.

Monaco became a property of the Grimaldi clan, a Genoese family, as early as 1297. With shifting loyalties, it has maintained something resembling independence ever since. In a fit of impatience the French annexed it in 1793, but the ruling family recovered it in 1814; however, the prince at that time couldn't bear to tear himself away from the pleasures of Paris for "dreary old Monaco."

ESSENTIALS

GETTING THERE Monaco has rail, bus, and highway connections from other coastal cities, especially Nice. **Trains** arrive every 30 minutes from Cannes, Nice,

Monaco

ACCOMMODATIONS ■
Columbus Hotel **21**
Hôtel Alexandra **3**
Hôtel Balmoral **14**
Hôtel Cosmopolite **18**
Hôtel de France **18**
Hôtel de Paris **12**
Hôtel Hermitage **13**
Hôtel Mirabeau **8**
Hôtel Port Palace **15**
Le Métropole Palace **9**
Fairmont Hotel Monte Carlo **7**
Monte-Carlo Beach Hotel **1**

DINING ◆
Bacarat **10**
Bar et Bœuf **4**
L'Argentin **7**
Le Café de Paris **12**
Le Grill de l'Hôtel de Paris **12**
Le Louis XV **12**
Le Texan **17**
Pizzeria Monégasque **24**
Rampoldi **5**
Restaurant du Port **16**
Stars'n Bars **25**

ATTRACTIONS ●
Collection des Voitures Anciennes de
   S.A.S. le Prince de Monaco **22**
Jardin Exotique **20**
Les Grands Appartments
   du Palais **23**
Monte Carlo Casino **11**
Musée d'Anthropologie
   Préhistorique **19**
Musée de l'Oceanographie **26**
Musée National de Monaco **2**
Palais du Prince/Musée du Palais **23**
Sun Casino **6**

Menton, and Antibes. For more rail information, call ☎ **08-92-35-35-35**. Monaco's railway station (Gare SNCF) is on avenue Prince Pierre. It's a long walk uphill from the train station to Monte Carlo. If you'd rather take a **taxi** but can't find one at the station, call ☎ **93-15-01-01**. No border formalities exist when entering Monaco from mainland France.

In late 1999, Monaco opened an enormous train station .4km (¼ mile) east of the old station. This station has three exits on three levels, and if you don't know which exit to use, you might have trouble finding your hotel. Monaco is a confusing place to navigate, so you might want to pick up a free map at the station's tourist office (open daily June–Sept 8:30am–7:30pm). Arriving at the Monaco train station after 9pm is like arriving on Wall Street after 9pm—it's desolate, and there's not a soul on the street. On the bright side, Monaco restaurants serve dinner late, so you can usually get a full meal at least until 11pm.

There's frequent **bus service** (every 15 min.) to Nice, Beaulieu, and Menton on line no. 100 of the French bus company Rapides Côte d'Azur (© **04-93-85-64-44**). The trip from Nice to Monaco by bus takes a half-hour and costs 6.80€ ($8.85) round-trip or 3.90€ ($5.05) one-way. The times and prices are the same to Menton. The easiest place to catch a bus is in front of the gardens that preface the Casino, but it also stops in front of the port (on bd. Albert-1er at the Stade Nautique stop) and at several other spots around town.

If you're **driving** from Nice to Monaco, take N7 northeast. The 19km (12-mile) drive takes about 35 minutes because of heavy traffic; Cannes to Monaco requires about 55 minutes. If driving from Paris, follow A6 to Lyon. In Lyon, take A7 south to Aix-en-Provence and A6 to Monaco.

VISITOR INFORMATION   The **Direction du Tourisme et des Congrés** office is at 2A bd. des Moulins (© **92-16-61-66;** www.monaco-tourisme.com).

GETTING AROUND   The best way to get around Monaco is by **bus,** and you can buy bus cards, which cost 1.80€ ($2.35) per ride, directly on the bus. Bus stops are set up every few blocks on the main streets in town, including boulevard Albert-1er, avenue St-Martin in Monaco Ville, and boulevard des Moulins in Monte Carlo. Buses go to all the major tourist sights; just look at the front of the bus to see the destination.

For a **taxi,** call © **93-15-01-01.** Taxi stands are in front of the Casino on avenue de Monte-Carlo, at place des Moulins in Monte Carlo; at the Port de Monaco on avenue Président J. F. Kennedy; and in front of the Poste de Monte-Carlo on avenue Henry-Dunant. A **Hertz** car rental office is at 27 bd. Albert-1er (© **93-50-79-60**), and an **Avis** office at 1 av. des Guelphs (© **97-97-18-55**).

SPECIAL EVENTS   Two of the most-watched **car-racing events** in Europe are in January (Le Rallye) and May (the Grand Prix). In mid-April is one of the Riviera's most famous **tennis tournaments.** In June, Monte Carlo is home to a weeklong convention that attracts media moguls from virtually everywhere, **Le Festival International de la Télévision,** Grimaldi Forum, avenue Princess Grace (© **93-10-40-60**). Shows from all over the world are broadcast and judged on their merits.

Tips Number, Please: Monaco's Telephone System

Since 1996, Monaco's phone system has been independent of France.

To call Monaco from within France, dial 00 (the access code for all international long-distance calls from France), followed by the **country code, 377,** then the eight-digit local phone number. (Don't dial the 33 code; that's the country code for France.)

To call Monaco from North America, dial the international access code, 011, the country code, 377, then the eight-digit Monaco number.

To call any other country from within Monaco, dial 00 (the international access code), then the applicable country code, and the number. For example, to call Cannes, you would dial 00, 33 (France's country code), 4 (the city code, without the zero), and the eight-digit number.

EXPLORING THE PRINCIPALITY

The second-smallest state in Europe (Vatican City is the tiniest), Monaco consists of four parts. The old town, **Monaco-Ville,** on a promontory, "The Rock," 60m (200 ft.) high, is the seat of the royal palace and the government building, as well as the Oceanographic Museum. To the west of the bay, **La Condamine,** the home of the Monégasques, is at the foot of the old town, forming its harbor and port sector. Up from the port (walking is steep in Monaco) is **Monte Carlo,** once the playground of European royalty and still the center for the wintering wealthy, the setting for the casino and its gardens and the deluxe hotels. The fourth part, **Fontvieille,** is a neat industrial suburb.

Ironically, **Monte-Carlo Beach,** at the far frontier, is on French soil. It attracts a chic crowd, including movie stars in scanty bikinis and thongs. The resort has a fresh-water pool, an artificial beach, and a sea-bathing establishment.

No one used to go to Monaco in summer, but now that has totally changed—in fact, July and August tend to be so crowded that it's hard to get a room. Furthermore, with the decline of royalty and multimillionaires, Monaco is developing a broader base of tourism (you can stay here moderately—but it's misleading to suggest that you can stay cheaply). The Monégasques very frankly court the affluent visitor. And at the casinos here, you can also lose your shirt. "Suicide Terrace" at the casino, though not used as frequently as in the old days, is still a real temptation to many who have foolishly gambled away family fortunes.

Life still focuses on the **Monte Carlo Casino** ★, which has been the subject of countless legends and the setting for many films (remember poor Lucy Ricardo and the chip she found lying on the casino floor?). High drama is played to the fullest here. Depending on the era, you might have seen Mata Hari shooting a tsarist colonel with a jewel-encrusted revolver when he tried to slip his hand inside her bra to discover her secrets—military, not mammary. The late King Farouk, known as "The Swine," used to devour as many as eight roast guinea hens and 50 oysters before losing thousands at the table. Richard Burton presented Elizabeth Taylor with the obscenely huge Koh-i-noor diamond here. Surrounded by cultivated gardens, the casino stands on a **panoramic terrace** ★★, offering one of the grandest views along the entire Riviera.

SEEING THE SIGHTS

Collection des Voitures Anciennes de S.A.S. le Prince de Monaco *Kids*   The late Prince Rainier III opened a showcase of his private collection of more than 100 vintage autos, including the 1956 Rolls-Royce Silver Cloud that carried the prince and princess on their wedding day. Monaco shopkeepers gave it to the royal couple as a wedding present. A 1952 Austin Taxi on display was once used as the royal "family car." Other exhibits are a "woodie" (a 1937 Ford station wagon Prince Louis II used on hunting trips); a 1925 Bugatti 35B, winner of the Monaco Grand Prix in 1929; a 1903 De Dion Bouton; and a 1986 Lamborghini Countach.

Les Terrasses de Fontvieille. © **92-05-28-56.** Admission 6€ ($7.80) adults, 3€ ($3.90) students and children 8–14, free for children under 8. Daily 10am–6pm. Closed Dec 25.

Jardin Exotique ★★   Built on the side of a rock, the gardens are known for their cactus collection. They were begun by Prince Albert I, who was a naturalist and scientist. He spotted some succulents growing in the palace gardens and created this garden from them. You can also explore the grottoes here, as well as the **Musée d'Anthropologie Préhistorique** (© **93-15-80-06**). The view of the principality is splendid.

Bd. du Jardin-Exotique. ℂ **93-15-29-80.** Admission (includes museum) 6.70€ ($8.70) adults, 3.40€ ($4.40) children 6–18, free for children under 6. Mid-May to mid-Sept daily 9am–7pm; mid-Sept to Nov 14 and Dec 26 to mid-May daily 9am–6pm. Closed Nov 15–Dec 25.

Les Grands Appartements du Palais ☆ Most summer day-trippers from Nice want to see the home of Monaco's royal family, the Palais du Prince, which dominates the principality from "the Rock." Prince Albert governs Monaco from these premises. A tour of the Grands Appartements allows you a glimpse of the Throne Room and some of the art (including works by Brueghel and Holbein) as well as Princess Grace's state portrait. The palace was built in the 13th century, and part dates from the Renaissance. The ideal time to arrive is 11:55am, to watch the 10-minute **Relève de la Garde** (changing of the guard).

In a wing of the palace, the **Musée du Palais du Prince (Souvenirs Napoléoniens et Collection d'Archives)** holds a collection of mementos of Napoleon and Monaco. When the royal residence is closed, this museum is the only part of the palace the public can visit.

Place du Palais. ℂ **93-25-18-31.** Combination ticket 6€ ($7.80) adults, 3€ ($3.90) children 8–14, free for children under 8. Palace and museum June–Sept daily 9:30am–6pm; Oct daily 10–5pm. Palace closed Nov–May. Museum also Nov 1–11 daily 10am–5pm; Dec 17–May Tues–Sun 10:30am–noon and 2–4:30pm. Closed Nov 12–Dec 16.

Musée National de Monaco ☆ (Kids) In a villa designed in a style that might have been by Charles Garnier (architect of Paris's Opéra Garnier), this museum houses a magnificent collection of antique mechanical toys and dolls. See the 18th-century Neapolitan crib, which contains some 200 figures. This collection, assembled by Mme de Galea, was presented to the principality in 1972; it originated with the 18th- and 19th-century practice of displaying new fashions on doll models.

17 av. Princesse-Grace. ℂ **93-30-91-26.** Admission 6€ ($7.80) adults, 3.50€ ($4.55) students and children 6–14, free for children under 6. Easter–Sept daily 10am–6:30pm; Oct–Easter daily 10am–12:15pm and 2:30–6:30pm. Closed Jan 1, May 1, Nov 19, Dec 25, and 4 days during Grand Prix.

Musée de l'Océanographie ☆☆ (Kids) Albert I, great-grandfather of the late prince Rainier, founded this museum in 1910. In the main rotunda is a statue of Albert in his favorite costume: that of a sea captain. Displayed are specimens he collected during 30 years of expeditions. The aquarium, one of the finest in Europe, contains more than 90 tanks.

The collection is exhibited in the zoology room. Some of the exotic creatures were unknown before he captured them. You'll see models of the ships aboard which he directed his scientific cruises from 1885 to 1914. The most important part of the laboratory has been preserved and re-created as closely as possible. Skeletons of specimens, including a whale that drifted ashore at Pietra Ligure in 1896, are on the main floor. The whale skeleton is remarkable for its healed fractures sustained when a vessel struck the animal as it was drifting on the surface. An exhibition devoted to the discovery of the ocean is in the physical-oceanography room on the first floor. Underwater movies are shown in the lecture room. The shark lagoon is a perennial favorite.

Av. St-Martin. ℂ **93-15-36-00.** Admission 11€ ($14) adults, 6€ ($7.80) children 6–18, free for children under 6. July–Aug daily 9:30am–7:30pm; Apr–June and Sept daily 9:30am–7pm; Oct–Mar daily 10am–6pm.

OUTDOOR PURSUITS
A DAY AT THE BEACH
Just outside the border, on French soil, the **Monte-Carlo Beach Club** adjoins the Monte-Carlo Beach Hôtel, 22 av. Princesse-Grace (ℂ **04-93-28-66-66**). The beach

club has thrived for years; it's an integral part of Monaco's social life. Princess Grace used to come here in flowery swimsuits, greeting her friends and subjects with humor and style. The sand is replenished at regular intervals. You'll find two large pools (one for children), cabanas, a restaurant, a cafe, and a bar. As the temperature drops in late August, the beach closes for the winter. The admission charge of 50€ to 75€ ($65–$98), depending on the season, grants you access to the changing rooms, toilets, restaurants, and bar, and use of a mattress for sunbathing. A day's use of a cubicle, where you can lock up your street clothes, costs an extra 18€ to 25€ ($23–$33). A fee of 147€ ($191) will get you a day's use of a private cabana. Most socializing occurs around the pool's edges. As usual, topless is *de rigueur,* but bottomless isn't.

Monaco, the quintessential kingdom by the sea, offers swimming and sunbathing at the **Plage de Larvotto,** off avenue Princesse-Grace (✆ **93-30-63-84**). There's no charge to enter this strip of beach, whose surface is frequently replenished with sand hauled in by barge. Part of it is open; other sections are private.

OTHER OUTDOOR ACTIVITIES

GOLF   The prestigious **Monte Carlo Golf Club,** route N7, La Turbie (✆ **04-92-41-50-70**), on French soil, is a par-72 course with scenic panoramas. Certain perks (including use of electric carts) are reserved for members. In order to play, nonmembers are asked to show proof of membership in another club and provide evidence of their handicap. Greens fees for 18 holes are 90€ ($117) Monday through Friday, 110€ ($143) Saturday and Sunday. Clubs rent for 20€ ($26). The course is open daily from 8am to sunset.

SPA TREATMENTS   In 1908, the Société des Bains de Mer launched a seawater (thalassotherapy) spa in Monte Carlo, inaugurated by Prince Albert I. It was bombed during World War II and didn't reopen until 1996. **Les Thermes Marins de Monte-Carlo,** 2 av. de Monte-Carlo (✆ **92-16-40-40**), is one of the largest spas in Europe. Spread over four floors are a pool, a Turkish *hamman,* a diet restaurant, a juice bar, two tanning booths, a fitness center, a beauty center, and private treatment rooms. A day pass, giving access to the sauna, steam rooms, fitness facilities, and pools, costs 65€ ($85). Massages cost 60€ ($78) for a 30-minute session, 105€ ($137) for a 60-minute session.

SWIMMING   Overlooking the yacht-clogged harbor, the **Stade Nautique Rainier-III,** quai Albert-1er, at La Condamine (✆ **93-30-64-83**), a pool frequented by the Monégasques, was a gift from the prince to his subjects. It's open May through October daily from 9am to 6pm (until midnight July–Aug). Admission for a one-time visit costs 5.20€ ($6.75) per person; discounts are available if you plan to visit 10 times or more. Between November and April, it's an ice-skating rink. If you want to swim in winter, try the indoor **Piscine du Prince Héréditaire Albert,** in the Stade Louis II, 7 av. de Castellane (✆ **92-05-42-13**). It's open Monday, Tuesday, Thursday, and Friday from 7:30am to 2:30pm; Saturday from 2 to 6pm; and Sunday from 8am to 1pm. Admission is 3.50€ ($4.55).

TENNIS & SQUASH   The **Monte Carlo Country Club,** 155 av. Princesse-Grace, Roquebrune-St-Roman, France (✆ **04-93-41-30-15**), has 21 clay and 2 concrete tennis courts. The 36€ ($47) fee provides access to a restaurant, health club with Jacuzzi and sauna, putting green, beach, squash courts, and the well-maintained tennis courts. Guests of the hotels administered by the Société des Bains de Mer (Hôtel de Paris, Hermitage, Mirabeau, and Monte Carlo Beach Club) pay half-price. Plan to spend at

The Shaky House of Grimaldi

Monaco, according to Somerset Maugham, is 149 sunny hectares (370 acres) peopled with shady characters. According to a 1918 treaty, Monaco must maintain an ongoing stream of male heirs to retain its independence from France. The tax-free principality is the oddest fiscal and social anomaly in Europe, a blend of Las Vegas hype and aristocratic glitter whose luster has been sorely tarnished since the demise of Princess Grace ("a snow-covered volcano," said Alfred Hitchcock).

The marriage of the world's most eligible bachelor and the Hollywood golden goddess dominated headlines in April 1956. However, like Grace and Rainier themselves, the marriage did not age gracefully. Rainier's snide public assessments of his celebrity wife's accomplishments showed an unpleasant rivalry. In turn, Grace, beneath her cool veneer, was a lonely and frustrated woman who sought solace in a string of affairs.

The children of this ill-fated union have rebelled against the strictures imposed on them by their less-than-noble parents. More at home in the watering holes of big-city Paris than in the claustrophobic and judgmental homeland, they take turns being the one most likely to shock the multinational residents of their tax-free domain.

The most obviously disaffected is Stephanie, whose tantrums as a 13-year-old were duly noted by scads of journalists and whose sexual insouciance contributed, according to local wits, to the ill health of her late father. Her affairs have included the sons of both Jean-Paul Belmondo and Alain Delon, also children of second-generation fame. For a time, she moved to Los Angeles, where she tried to build a show-business career. Promising beginnings in Stephanie's fertile roster of career options were stymied by maneuvering from the Grimaldi fortress. Her ambitions have mostly collapsed, as have her attempts to become a model or pop singer. In 1995, Stephanie married a former palace guard, Alain Ducruet, by whom she bore two children; however, a year later she divorced him because he had been caught cavorting naked with Miss Bare Breasts of Belgium. In 1998, Stephanie continued to make headlines by staying mum about her new baby's dad—Camille Marie Kelly was Stephanie's third child born out of wedlock. One palace guard summed up Stephanie's affairs and babies: "In these times, it's not a question of morals. A princess can do what she likes." "From Tiaras to Trailer Parks" blares the headlines in the world press today. Princess Stephanie now spends her days traveling with the circus in Europe, with her companion, Franco Knie, owner of the caravan.

Everyone in his prospective kingdom constantly urges Albert, now the ruler, to take a bride and produce a male heir. He has publicly denied rumors of homosexuality and has cavorted with an assortment of famous faces, from Brooke Shields to Donna Rice to Claudia Schiffer. As a local commentator has said, "It's one thing for him to marry a bimbo; it's another to marry someone like his mother." At the moment (subject to change at any minute), Albert continues to play the field, finding no replacement to fill the shoes of Princess Grace.

In the summer of 2005, Prince Albert shocked his subjects when he acknowledged that he'd father a child out of wedlock. He admitted that he had fathered a child with an African-born Air France flight attendant. Little Alexandre, Albert's son with Nicole Coste, will never be eligible for the throne, however. The constitution of Monaco excludes illegitimate children from the line of succession. In another surprise on the night before assuming the throne, Albert also admitted that there may be others with paternity claims. He offered no further details.

Caroline, mother of three, has done her royal part. She would if she could, according to observers, force a power struggle with Albert for the right of succession. Her first husband, the much older businessman/boulevardier Philippe Junot, was the sort of man every mother hopes her daughter will not marry—which is probably why Caroline did. After she announced that she was divorcing womanizing Junot, the Vatican was called in to annul the marriage (which it finally did in 1992). Within a year of her mother's death, Caroline met and fell deeply in love with 27-year-old Stefano Casiraghi, son of an Italian industrialist. She was 4 months pregnant when they married in 1984, and she and Stefano had two more children (who remained "illegitimate" until 3 years after their father's death). In 1989, Stefano died in a speedboating accident and Caroline went into severe mourning, chopping off her hair and withdrawing from her duties. Eventually, she and her children moved to France and she returned to her position as "First Lady of Monaco." On January 23, 1999, her 42nd birthday, Caroline took a new husband, Prince Ernst of Hanover, who had been married to her best friend. Oddly, by marrying Ernst, she fulfilled the wishes of her late mother, who always wanted her to marry him. The couple will not be poor: Ernst is reportedly worth $800 million.

On May 31, 1997, Prince Rainier and his family marked the 700th anniversary of Grimaldi rule—6,600 Monégasques showed up for an open-air ceremony at place du Palais. With all their troubles and scandals, the clan has come a long way since January 8, 1297—that's when a political refugee from Genoa, Francesco Grimaldi, accompanied by some cronies in monks' clothing, persuaded the defenders of the local castle to give him shelter. Once he and his men penetrated the defenses, they ripped off their hoods and took the castle by force. The Principality of Monaco was born, and it's been in Grimaldi hands ever since.

At the age of 81, Prince Rainier III died in a Monaco hospital in 2005 suffering very bad health, including problems with his heart and kidneys. He had been Europe's longest-reigning monarch, having assumed the throne on May 9, 1949. Upon his death, the throne was assumed by Prince Albert, a shy, passionate sportsman often seen as a reluctant heir. Albert turned 47 on March 14, 2005. Should Albert die or fail to rule, Princess Caroline would assume the throne, according to a revised constitution in 2002 that sought to ensure the Grimaldi dynasty.

One Monégasque summed up the Grimaldi situation well: "I go to church every morning to pray for the prince and his family. I pray God will keep them safe and sane. Because that is my security. Without the Grimaldis, we would be merely hors d'oeuvres for France."

least half a day, ending a round of tennis with use of any of the other facilities. It's open daily from 8am to 8 or 9pm, depending on the season.

SHOPPING

Bijoux Marlene, Les Galeries du Métropole, 207 av. des Spélugues (✆ **93-50-17-57**), sells only imitation gemstones. They're shamelessly copied from the real McCoys sold by Cartier and Van Cleef & Arpels. Made in Italy of gold-plated silver, the jewelry (the staff refers to it as Les Bijoux Fantaisies) costs 10€ to 1,000€ ($13–$1,300) per piece.

Boutique du Rocher, 1 av. de la Madone (✆ **93-30-91-17**), is the larger of two boutiques Princess Grace opened in 1966 as the official retail outlets of her charitable foundation. The organization merchandises Monégasque and Provençal handicrafts. A short walk from place du Casino, the shop sells carved frames for pictures or mirrors; housewares; gift items crafted from porcelain, textiles, and wood; toys; and dolls. On the premises are workshops where artisans produce the goods. The second branch is at 25 rue Emile de Loth, Monaco-Ville (✆ **93-30-33-99**).

Argument, 17 bd. des Moulins (✆ **93-50-33-85**), aims at a solid middle-bracket man who simply wants to dress appropriately and look good. You can pick up a swimsuit, shorts, slacks, a blazer, and a pair of socks to replace the ones you ruined on too many walking tours, at prices that won't require that you remortgage your house.

If you insist on ultra-fancy stores, you'll find them cheek by jowl with the Hôtel de Paris and the casino, lining the streets leading to the Hôtel Hermitage, and across from the gardens at the minimall Park Palace. **Allée Serge-Diaghilev** is just that, an alley, but a very tiny one filled with designer shops.

You don't have to be Princess Caroline to shop in Monaco, especially now that **FNAC** (✆ **93-10-81-81**) has opened in the heart of town. A branch of the big French chain that sells CDs, tapes, and books, it's at the **Galeries du Métropole,** 17 av. des Spélugues, in the Jardins du Casino, next to the Hôtel Métropole and across from the casino.

The Galeries du Métropole also has a few specialty shops worth visiting. Check out **Geneviève Lethu** (✆ **93-50-09-41**) for colorful and country tabletop accessories; or **Manufacture de Monaco** (✆ **93-50-64-63**) for glorious bone china and elegant tabletop items. If the prices make you want to take to your bed, two doors away is a branch of the chic but often affordable French linen house **Yves Delorme** (✆ **93-50-08-70**). **Royal Food** (✆ **93-15-05-04**) is a gourmet grocery store down a set of curving stairs hidden in the side entrance of the mall; here you can buy food from France, Lebanon, and the United States, or stock up for *le pique-nique* or for day trips. This market is open Monday to Saturday 10am to 7:30pm.

For real-people shopping, stroll **rue Grimaldi,** the principality's most commercial street, near the fruit, flower, and food market (see below); and **boulevard des Moulins,** closer to the casino, where you'll see glamorous boutiques. There's also a pedestrian thoroughfare with shops less forbiddingly chic than those along boulevard des Moulins: **rue Princesse-Caroline** is loaded with bakeries, flower shops, and the closest thing you'll find to funkiness in Monaco. Also check out the **Formule 1** shop, 15 rue Grimaldi (✆ **93-15-92-44**), where everything from racing helmets to specialty key chains and T-shirts celebrates the roaring, high-octane racing machines.

No one comes to the Riviera for bargain shopping but, even in chic Monte Carlo, **Stock Griffe,** 5 bis av. St-Michel (✆ **93-50-86-06**) slashes prices on Prada, Pucci, Escada, and the like. A tremendous amount of merchandise is packed into these tiny precincts. The place may be small, but not the discounts, some of which add up to an astonishing 90 percent. Reductions are greater for older garments that didn't move, but you can also snap up some newer fashions.

MARKETS For a look at the heart and soul of the real Monaco, head to place des Armes for the **fruit, flower, and food market,** which starts daily at 7:30am. The indoor and outdoor market has a fountain, cafes, and hand-painted vegetable tiles beneath your feet. The outdoor market packs up at noon, and some dealers at the indoor market stay open to 2pm. If you prefer bric-a-brac, a small but funky (especially for Monaco) flea market, **Les Puces de Fontvieille,** opens on Saturday from 9:30am to 5:30pm on the Quai Jean-Charles Rey, immediately adjacent to Port de Fontvieille.

WHERE TO STAY
VERY EXPENSIVE

Hôtel de Paris ★★★   On the resort's main plaza, opposite the casino, this is one of the world's most famous hotels. The ornate facade has marble pillars, and the lounge has an Art Nouveau rose window at the peak of the dome. The decor includes marble pillars, statues, crystal chandeliers, sumptuous carpets, Louis XVI chairs, and a wall-size mural. Elegant fabrics, rich carpeting, classic accessories, and an excellent restaurant make this hotel a favorite of the world's most discerning travelers. The guest rooms come in a variety of styles, with period or contemporary furnishings. Some units are enormous. Bathrooms are large, with marble and elegant brass fittings, plus tub/shower combinations. *Note:* The rooms opening onto the sea aren't as spacious as those in the rear.

Place du Casino, 98007 Monaco. © **92-16-30-00.** Fax 92-16-26-26. www.montecarloresort.com. 191 units. 390€–790€ ($507–$1,027) double; from 2,000€ ($2,600) suite. AE, DC, MC, V. Valet parking 25€ ($33). **Amenities:** 3 restaurants (see "Where to Dine," below); bar; large indoor pool; fitness center; Thermes Marins spa offering thalassotherapy under medical supervision; 2 saunas; concierge; salon; 24-hr. room service; babysitting; laundry service; dry cleaning; nonsmoking rooms. *In room:* A/C, TV, dataport, minibar, hair dryer, safe.

Hôtel Hermitage ★★   Picture yourself sitting in a wicker armchair, enjoying a drink under an ornate stained-glass dome with an encircling wrought-iron balcony. You can do this at the cliff-top Hermitage. The "palace," with its wedding-cake facade, was the creation of Jean Marquet (who also created marquetry). Most rooms have large brass beds, and decoratively framed doors that open onto balconies. Even the smallest rooms are medium-size, and the largest one is fit for the biggest movie star with the most trunks. Large mirrors, elegant fabrics and upholstery, deluxe bathrooms with tubs and showers, and sumptuous beds make living here idyllic. In 2003, the hotel added two floors to its century-old main building. Guest rooms are modern and sleek in the styling. High-season rates apply during Christmas, New Year's, Easter, and July and August.

Sq. Beaumarchais, 98005 Monaco Cedex. © **92-16-40-00.** Fax 92-16-38-52. www.montecarloresort.com. 225 units. 355€–850€ ($462–$1,105) double; from 800€ ($1,040) suite. AE, DISC, MC, V. Parking 20€ ($26). **Amenities:** Restaurant; 2 bars; indoor pool; health club; sauna; 24-hr. room service; babysitting; laundry service; dry cleaning; nonsmoking rooms. *In room:* A/C, TV, dataport, minibar, hair dryer, safe.

EXPENSIVE

Columbus Hotel ★ *Value*   Beneficiary of a $10-million upgrade of a 10-year-old hotel in 2001, this nine-story hotel offers good value and lots of style from a location in the residential community of Fontvieille, a 5-minute drive from the glitter of Monte Carlo. Bedrooms are airy, champagne-colored, and outfitted with minimalist ("very cool") furniture. In many cases, they open onto small balconies. This is the flagship of a chain of chic, midprice hotels founded by British investor Ken McCulloch. Don't be confused by recent name changes associated with this place, including the Abela Monaco and the S.M.H. Hotel Monaco.

23 av. des Papalins, 98000 Monaco. ⓒ 92-05-90-00. Fax 92-05-91-67. www.columbushotels.com. 181 units. 245€–335€ ($319–$436) double; 350€–540€ ($455–$702) suite. AE, MC, V. Parking 25€ ($33). Amenities: Restaurant; bar; outdoor pool; fitness room; business center; 24-hr. room service; babysitting; laundry service; dry cleaning. In room: A/C, TV, minibar, hair dryer, safe.

Fairmont Hotel Monte Carlo 🕊 Although a bit down the scale from the two previous choices, this is also a deluxe palace, built by the Loews Corporation in 1998. It hugs the coast below the terraces that support the famous casino, on one of the most valuable pieces of real estate along the Côte d'Azur. Architecturally daring when built (some of its foundations were sunk into the seabed, and some of the principality's busiest highways roar beneath it), the resort is viewed as an integral enhancement of Monégasque life. It contains Monaco's highest concentration of restaurants, bars, and nightclubs—think of it as Las Vegas with a Gallic accent. The guest rooms are conservatively furnished. Each has a pastel decor that's flooded with light from big windows, and views over the town or the sea. All units contain large bathrooms with tubs and showers.

12 av. des Spélugues, 98007 Monaco. ⓒ 93-50-65-00. Fax 93-30-01-57. www.fairmont.com. 619 units. 275€–495€ ($358–$644) double; from 560€ ($728) suite. AE, DC, MC, V. Parking 25€ ($33). Amenities: 4 restaurants; 2 bars; outdoor pool; health club; sauna; 24-hr. room service; babysitting; limited-mobility rooms. In room: A/C, TV, dataport, minibar, hair dryer, safe.

Hôtel Mirabeau 🕊🕊 In the heart of Monte Carlo, next to the casino, the Mirabeau combines modern design with a refined atmosphere. Large mirrors, spacious lighted closets, and sumptuous beds with luxurious mattresses make staying here idyllic; many rooms have terraces with views overlooking the Mediterranean. Although the newest rooms are as fine as those in the main building, many guests prefer older ones for their old-fashioned French decor and street-front exposures. Bathrooms are well appointed, with tub/shower combos.

1 av. Princesse-Grace, 98000 Monaco. ⓒ 92-16-65-65. Fax 93-50-84-85. www.montecarloresort.com. 103 units. 270€–490€ ($351–$637) double; from 500€ ($650) suite. AE, DC, MC, V. Parking 25€ ($33). Amenities: Restaurant; bar; outdoor pool; gym; sauna; limited room service; babysitting; laundry service; dry cleaning; nonsmoking rooms. In room: A/C, TV, dataport, minibar, hair dryer, safe, robes.

Hôtel Port Palace 🕊🕊🕊 Although not quite as grand as the Paris or the Hermitage, this—the first boutique hotel in Monaco—also helps define luxury in the principality. Overlooking the yacht-clogged Monte Marlo Marina, it is excessively opulent and each of the accommodations is a suite. All units are spacious and elegantly furnished, with state-of-the-art private bathrooms, some of which contain a private steam room. Only first-class materials went into the suites, including rare woods, refined silks, Carrara marble, and premium leather, along with all the modern amenities such as 42-inch plasma TV screens. The hotel's restaurant, Grand Large, is one of the finest in Monaco, without offering too serious a challenge to the gourmet citadels at the Hôtel de Paris.

7 av. John F. Kennedy, 98000 Monte-Carlo. ⓒ 97-97-90-00. Fax 97-97-90-01. www.portpalace.com. 50 suites. 300€ ($390) junior suite; 350€ ($455) deluxe junior suite; 500€ ($650) corner suite; 700€ ($910) executive suite. AE, DC, MC, V. Amenities: Restaurant; bar; spa; fitness center; sauna; steam room; limo service; 24-hr. room service; car rental; yacht rental; jet ski rental; nonsmoking rooms; limited-mobility rooms. In room: A/C, TV, dataport, Jacuzzi, private bar, safe.

Le Métropole Palace ⭐   In the heart of Monaco, this hotel is rebuilt on the site of the original Métropole, on Monte Carlo's "golden square." The hotel is superb in every way and has an array of handsomely furnished and beautifully decorated rooms. Each includes a radio, hypoallergenic pillows, and a full line of toiletries. Spaces are generous and furnishings are classical, including occasional antiques; all come with double glazing and soothing pastel color schemes. Marble bathrooms have robes and often a shower with a whirlpool tub. The upscale Le Jardin serves splendid French and international cuisine.

B.P. 19, 4 av. de la Madone, 98007 Monaco. Ⓒ **93-15-15-15**. Fax 93-25-24-44. www.metropole.mc. 146 units. 340€–450€ ($442–$585) double; 495€–5,200€ ($644–$6,760) suite. AE, DC, MC, V. Parking 25€ ($33). **Amenities:** Restaurant; bar; outdoor pool; spa w/private hammams; 24-hr. room service; babysitting; laundry service; dry cleaning; nonsmoking rooms. *In room:* A/C, TV, minibar, hair dryer.

Monte-Carlo Beach Hôtel ⭐   Despite its name, this hotel is in France, not Monaco. The most beautiful accommodation is the circular unit above the lobby. Eva Peron stayed here in 1947 during her infamous Rainbow Tour of Europe. Princess Grace came here almost every day in summer to paddle around the pool, a rendezvous for the rich and beautiful. All the spacious rooms are luxurious, right down to the sea views; the beautiful bathrooms have tub/shower combinations. The greatest choice of dining venues is available between June and September, when Le Restaurant serves gourmet meals at lunch and dinner. Le Rivage offers brasserie-style lunches and dinners near the pool. La Potinière features gastronomic lunches. La Vigie, a short walk from the hotel near several piers where yachts can tie up, offers buffets inspired by the cuisine of Provence.

Av. Princesse Grace, Monte-Carlo Beach, 06190 Roquebrune–Cap-Martin. Ⓒ **04-92-16-25-25**. Fax 92-16-26-26. www.montecarloresort.com. 45 units. 255€–610€ ($332–$793) double; from 750€ ($975) suite. AE, DC, MC, V. Free parking. Closed Nov–Mar. **Amenities:** 4 restaurants; 2 bars; outdoor pool; gym; sauna; 24-hr. room service; babysitting; laundry service; dry cleaning; nonsmoking rooms. *In room:* A/C, TV, dataport, minibar, hair dryer, safe.

MODERATE

Hôtel Alexandra   This hotel is on a busy, often-noisy street corner in the center of the business district above the Casino Gardens. Its comfortably furnished guest rooms don't generate much excitement, but they're reliable and respectable. The Alexandra knows it can't compete with the giants of Monaco and doesn't even try. But it attracts those who'd like to visit the principality without spending a fortune.

35 bd. Princesse-Charlotte, 98000 Monaco. Ⓒ **93-50-63-13**. Fax 92-16-06-48. www.monaco-hotel.com/monte carlo/alexandra. 56 units. 125€–170€ ($163–$221) double. AE, DC, MC, V. Parking 6.50€ ($8.45). **Amenities:** Limited room service; babysitting. *In room:* A/C, TV, minibar, iron, hair dryer.

Hôtel Balmoral ⭐   This is one of the most solidly dependable choices in the moderately priced field. This hotel was built in 1898 by the grandfather of the present owner, Jacques Ferreyrolles. On a cliff halfway between the casino and the Palais du Prince, it boasts eight floors of rooms and lounges with sea views. The rooms are like the public rooms—homey, immaculate, and quiet. You get comfort here but not necessarily a lot of space to spread out. Mattresses are firm, and white, crisp linen is used. Bathrooms are small and tiled. The Balmoral is so inviting that guests often extend their stays.

12 av. de la Costa, 98006 Monaco. Ⓒ **93-50-62-37**. Fax 04-93-15-08-69. www.hotel-balmoral.mc. 70 units. 115€–210€ ($150–$273) double; 150€–300€ ($195–$390) suite. AE, DC, MC, V. Parking 10€ ($13). **Amenities:** Restaurant; bar; limited room service; babysitting; laundry service; dry cleaning. *In room:* A/C, TV.

INEXPENSIVE

Hôtel Cosmopolite   Bargains and Monaco rarely go together, but this hotel is an exception to the expensive rule. When it was built in the 1930s, this hotel was sited in the then-fashionable neighborhood a few steps downhill from the railway station. Today it's an appealingly dowdy Art Deco monument with three floors, no elevator, and comfortable but anonymous-looking rooms. Madame Gay Angèle, the English-speaking owner, is proud of her "Old Monaco" establishment. Her more expensive rooms have showers, but the cheapest way to stay here is to request a room without a shower—there are adequate facilities in the hallway. Mattresses are a bit thin, but are reasonably comfortable, especially for these prices.

4 rue de la Turbie, 98000 Monaco. (℡) **93-30-16-95.** Fax 93-30-23-05. 24 units, 7 with bathroom. 65€–90€ ($85–$117) double without bathroom; 75€–170€ ($98–$221) double with bathroom. No credit cards. Free parking on street. Closed Dec–Jan 3. Bus: 1 or 2. *In room:* Hair dryer.

Hôtel de France   Not all Monégasques are rich, as a stroll along this street will convince you. Here you'll find some of the cheapest accommodations and eating places in the high-priced principality. This 19th-century hotel, 3 minutes from the rail station, has modest furnishings but is well kept and comfortable. The guest rooms and bathrooms are small, and each unit has a shower.

6 rue de la Turbie, 98000 Monaco. (℡) **93-30-24-64.** Fax 92-16-13-34. www.monte-carlo.mc/france. 26 units. 78€ ($101) double. Rates include breakfast. MC, V. Parking 7.20€ ($9.35). **Amenities:** Bar; limited room service; non-smoking rooms; limited-mobility rooms. *In room:* TV, hair dryer.

WHERE TO DINE
VERY EXPENSIVE

Le Grill de l'Hôtel de Paris ★★★ MODERN FRENCH   In the flood of publicity awarded to this hotel's street-level restaurant, Le Louis XV (see below), it's been easy to overlook the equally elegant contender on the rooftop. The view alone is worth the expense, with the turrets of the fabled casino on one side and the yacht-clogged harbor of Old Monaco on the other. The decor is gracefully modern, with an ambience somewhat less intense than that in the self-consciously cutting-edge Ducasse citadel downstairs. Despite that, the place is undeniably elegant, with a two-fisted approach to cuisine that includes every imaginable sort of grilled fish (sea wolf, monkfish, sole, salmon, mullet, cod, or turbot) and meat such as Charolais beef and roasted lamb from the foothills of the nearby Alps. In fair weather and in summer, the ceiling opens to reveal the starry sky. The fine cuisine is backed up by one of the Riviera's finest wine lists, with some 600,000 bottles; the wine cellar is carved out of the rock below. Service is faultless but never intimidating or off-putting.

In the Hôtel de Paris, place du Casino. (℡) **92-16-29-66.** Reservations required. Main courses 35€–130€ ($45–$169). AE, DC, MC, V. Daily noon–2:15pm and 8–10:15pm. Closed Jan 6–31 and at lunch in summer.

Le Louis XV ★★★ FRENCH/ITALIAN   In the Hôtel de Paris, the Louis XV offers what one critic called "down-home Riviera cooking within a Fabergé egg." Star chef Alain Ducasse creates refined but not overly adorned cuisine, served by the finest staff in Monaco. Everything is light and attuned to the seasons, with intelligent, modern interpretations of Provençal and northern Italian dishes. You'll find chargrilled breast of baby pigeon with sautéed duck liver, an ongoing specialty known as "Provencal vegetables with crushed truffles," and everything from truffles and caviar to the best stewed salt cod on the coast. Ducasse divides his time between this enclave and his restaurants in Paris and New York. The hotel keeps its collection of rare fine wines in a dungeon chiseled out of the rocks.

In the Hôtel de Paris, place du Casino. ℂ 92-16-29-76. Reservations recommended. Jacket and tie required for men. Main courses 80€–92€ ($104–$120); fixed-price menu 160€–180€ ($208–$234) dinner. AE, MC, V. Thurs–Mon 12:15–1:45pm and 8–9:45pm; also June–Sept Wed 12:15–1:45pm. Closed Feb 8–23 and mid-Nov to Dec 29.

EXPENSIVE

Baccarat ⍟ ITALIAN   Baccarat is an elegant testimonial to the flavors and presentations of Italy, with an emphasis on Sicily, birthplace of owner-chef Carmelo Gulletta. The avant-garde paintings of Monégasque painter Clérissy line the walls of the vaguely Art Deco space, but the owners say the cuisine is more Italian and less "Monésgasque" than anything else in Monaco. Guletta's French-born, English-speaking wife, Patricia, supervises the dining room. The antipasti selection is the best in the principality, ranging from steamed asparagus with hollandaise to Andalusian gazpacho. The chefs turn out risottos as good as anything in Italy along with Monaco's most enticing pastas, like savory spaghetti with baby clams. In general, fish dishes such as sole meunière are better than meat and poultry offerings.

4 bd. des Moulins. ℂ 93-50-66-92. Reservations recommended. Main courses 10€–32€ ($13–$42). AE, MC, V. Daily noon–2:30pm and 7–10:30pm.

Bar et Boeuf ⍟⍟ INTERNATIONAL   This restaurant is one of the many jewels in the crown of super-chef Alain Ducasse, who is, according to many critics, both a culinary genius and the orchestrator of an upscale international assembly line. Gael Greene has referred to him as "Robo-Chef," and a small number of increasingly vocal critics complain about "franchise sprawl." You can still get a genuinely good meal here, even if none of it is prepared or even supervised by Ducasse. Bar et Boeuf is an upscale Gallic reinvention of a surf-and-turf restaurant. The only fish here is sea bass *(bar)*, and the beef is perhaps the most cosseted and fussed-over meat in France. Examples include filets of sea bass with citrus marmalade and an assortment of species of braised celery; filet steak with Sicilian herbs; beef Wellington; and beef with a sauté of *taggiasche* (Italian) olives and wine glaze, served with fried spiny artichokes. The most lavish dish is tournedos Rossini layered with foie gras and truffles, served with a *tartare* of truffled foie gras and exotic pan-fried mushrooms.

In the Sporting d'Eté Monte Carlo, av. Princesse-Grace. ℂ 92-16-60-60. Reservations recommended. Main courses 30€–54€ ($35–$62). AE, DC, MC, V. Open late May to late Sept 8pm–1am. Closed winter.

L'Argentin ⍟ STEAKS/GRILLS   Loaded with panache, and decorated like a very upscale version of what you might have found somewhere on the Argentine plains, this stylish restaurant is on the lobby level of a hotel that the Fairmont group took over in March 2005. Within an environment loaded with autumn colors, polished copper, leather banquettes, and big windows overlooking the sea, diners enjoy some of the best grilled meat dishes in town. (A limited array of fish is served, but because the same hotel also maintains a separate seafood restaurant, Le Pistou, on its seventh floor, most clients are here for the meats.) One of the specialties on which this place has built its name is a *tampiquea,* a much-marinated spicy filet of beef served with guacamole, salsa, tortillas, and a puree of string beans. An equally succulent choice is a standing hunk of roast beef presented on a wheeled trolley and carved at tableside.

In the Fairmont Hotel Monte Carlo, 12 av. des Splugues. ℂ 93-50-65-00. Reservations recommended. Main courses 25€–40€ ($33–$52). AE, DC, MC, V. Daily 7:30pm–12:30am.

Le Café de Paris ⓖ TRADITIONAL FRENCH   Its *plats du jour* are well prepared, and its location, the plaza adjacent to the casino and the Hôtel de Paris, allows a front-row view of the comings and goings of the nerve center of Monte Carlo. We find this 1985 re-creation of old-time Monaco a bit too enraptured with the devil-may-care glamour of early-1900s Monte Carlo. Despite that, the Café de Paris continues to draw patrons who appreciate the razzmatazz and all the glass and chrome. Menu items change frequently. Local office workers appreciate the platters, especially at lunchtime, because they can be served and consumed quickly. They range from fresh grilled sea bass to steak tartare with matchstick *frites*. Adjacent to the restaurant, you'll find (and hear) a jangling collection of slot machines and a predictable cluster of boutiques.

Place du Casino. ⓒ 92-16-20-20. Reservations recommended. Main courses 17€–55€ ($22–$72); breakfast 15€–20€ ($20–$26). AE, DC, MC, V. Daily 7am–1am.

Rampoldi ⓖ FRENCH/ITALIAN   More than any other restaurant in Monte Carlo, Rampoldi is linked to the charming but somewhat dated interpretation of *La Dolce Vita*. Opened in the 1950s at the edge of the Casino Gardens and staffed with a mix of old and new, it's more Italian than French in spirit. It also serves some of the best cuisine in Monte Carlo. Menu items include an array pastas, such as tortelloni with cream and white truffle sauce; sea bass roasted in a salt crust; ravioli stuffed with crayfish; and veal kidneys in Madeira sauce. Crêpes suzette makes a spectacular finish.

3 av. des Spélugues. ⓒ 93-30-70-65. Reservations required. Main courses 25€–50€ ($33–$65). AE, MC, V. Daily 12:15–2:30pm and 7:30–11:30pm. Closed Feb 6–21.

Restaurant du Port ⓖ ITALIAN/FRENCH   Set in a big-windowed restaurant directly on one of the quays overlooking the old port, this is a seafood restaurant that's a bit tough but glamorous, with a sometimes hysterically busy staff that might remind you of the dockyards of Genoa. The venue is very much macho Italian. Menu items might include a selection of elegant pastas (tagliatelle with smoked salmon and spaghetti with lobster), antipasti, and meat dishes like filet of beef aux délices, mignon of veal in orange sauce, rack of lamb with Mediterranean herbs, and a full array of Italian and French wines. Other excellent courses from across-the-border Italy include spaghetti with seafood and a superb filet of veal with porcini mushrooms. The very fresh fish of the day is grilled to perfection. Dessert? Why not a *cassata siciliana*, a Sicilian dessert made with ricotta cheese, lots of candied fruit, sponge cake, almond paste, and liqueur? In summer, the restaurant expands onto an outdoor terrace overlooking the yachts of the harbor. Interestingly, this restaurant, thanks to its location astride the route followed every year by the Grand Prix de Monaco auto race, rents tables on its veranda for 1,000€ ($1,300) each for the entire duration of the day of the race. The price includes lunch, but wine is extra.

Quai Albert-1er. ⓒ 93-50-77-21. Reservations recommended. Main courses 16€–32€ ($21–$42). DISC, MC, V. Daily noon–2:30pm and 8–10:30pm. Closed Nov 1–15.

INEXPENSIVE

Le Texan TEX-MEX/INDIAN/MOROCCAN   These incongruous specialties have entertained even the most discriminating French taste buds. Le Texan has a handful of outdoor tables, a long bar, a roughly plastered dining room with the flag of the Lone Star State, a bar whose shape was inspired by the Alamo in San Antonio, and a scattering of Mexican artifacts. You'll find it on a sloping street leading down to the harbor—a world away from the casinos and nightlife of the upper reaches. Menu items include T-bone steak, barbecued ribs, pizzas, nachos, tacos, a Dallasburger (*avec* guacamole), and the best margaritas in town. Thanks to several members of the kitchen staff who hail from India and Morocco, the restaurant also produces some great curry dishes (chicken, beef, and lamb) as well as couscous North African style.

4 rue Suffren-Reymond. ℂ **93-30-34-54**. Reservations recommended. Main courses 15€–22€ ($17–$25). AE, DC, MC, V. Daily noon–midnight.

Pizzeria Monégasque FRENCH/ITALIAN   This *pizzeria de luxe* offers four dining rooms and an outdoor terrace. Almost anyone might arrive—in a limousine or on a bicycle, in all kinds of garb that could quickly convince you that Monaco is actually a rather small and gossipy town. The owner has grown accustomed to seeing all the follies and vanities of this town pass through his door; he serves pizzas, fish, and grilled meats to whoever shows up. Specialties are *magret du canard* (duckling), grilled steaks, carpaccio, and beef tartare. Of the 10 kinds of pizza, the most popular are pizza Terrazzini (it includes cheese and pistou) and the "special" version that's served with Tunisian-style *merguez*.

4 rue Terrazzani. ℂ **93-30-16-38**. Pizzas 9€–10€ ($12–$13); main courses 10€–22€ ($13–$29). AE, MC, V. Mon–Sat noon–1:45pm and 7:30–11pm (till midnight Fri–Sat). Closed Dec 25–Jan 1.

Stars 'n' Bars *Kids* AMERICAN/PACIFIC RIM   Modeled on the sports bars popular in the U.S., this place features two dining and drinking areas devoted to American-style food, as well as a bar decorated with memorabilia of notable athletes. No one will mind if you drop in just for a drink, but if you're hungry, menu items read like an homage to the American experience. Try an Indy 500, a Triathlon salad, or the Breakfast of Champions (eggs and bacon and all the fixings). For kids under 12, order the Little Leaguer's Platter or pizza. In 2004, its owners added an all-new dining venue, **Fusion Cuisine** (same address and phone), to a space upstairs from the main dining room. Here, platters inspired by the cuisines of the Pacific Rim are featured, each within the same price range, and the same hours, as the food served on the restaurant's street level. Examples include sushis, tempuras, rice-based dishes, and fast-wok–fried dishes of meats and seafood.

6 quai Antoine-1er. ℂ **97-97-95-95**. Reservations recommended. Dinner salads and platters 12€–20€ ($16–$26); sandwiches 9€ ($12); pizzas 12€ ($16). AE, DC, MC, V. June–Sept daily 11am–midnight; Oct–May Tues–Sun 11am–midnight. Bar open till 3am.

MONACO AFTER DARK

Sun Casino, in the Monte Carlo Grand Hôtel, 12 av. des Spélugues (ℂ **93-50-65-00**), is a huge room filled with one-armed bandits. It also features blackjack, craps, and American roulette. Additional slot machines are on the roof, with a wide view of the sea. Slot machines operate daily from 11am to 4am, and gaming tables are open daily from 5pm to 4am. Admission is free.

François Blanc developed the **Monte-Carlo Casino,** place du Casino (ℂ **92-16-21-21**), into the most famous in the world, attracting the exiled aristocracy of Russia, Sarah Bernhardt, Mata Hari, King Farouk, and Aly Khan. The architect of Paris's Opéra Garnier, Charles Garnier, built the oldest part of the casino, and it remains an example of the 19th century's most opulent architecture. The building encompasses the casino and other areas for different kinds of entertainment, including a theater (see below) presenting opera and ballet. Baccarat, roulette, and chemin de fer are the most popular games, though you can play *le craps* and blackjack as well.

The casino's **Salle Américaine,** containing only slot machines, opens at noon, as do doors for roulette and *trente-quarente.* A section for roulette and chemin de fer opens at 3pm. Additional rooms open at 4pm with more roulette, craps, and blackjack. The gambling continues until very late or early, depending on the crowd. The casino classifies its "private rooms" as the more demure, nonelectronic areas without slots. To enter the casino, you must show a passport or other photo ID, be at least 18, and pay 10€ to 20€ ($13–$26), depending on where you want to go. After 9pm, the staff will insist that men wear jackets and neckties for entrance to the private rooms.

Also on the premises is a **Cabaret,** in the Casino Gardens, where a well-rehearsed orchestra plays before the show. A performance featuring feathers, glitter, jazz dance, ballet, and Riviera-style seminudity begins at 10:30pm Wednesday to Saturday mid-September through June. For reservations, call © **92-16-36-36.** Entrance to the cabaret costs 62€ ($81) and includes one drink and dinner.

Theoretically, the **Opéra de Monte-Carlo,** whose patron is Prince Albert, is headquartered in the lavish belle époque **Salle Garnier** of the casino. It is closed for renovations until sometime in 2005. Meanwhile, venues for concerts, ballets, and operas are the **Salle du Canton,** Les Terrasses, av. de Fontvieille (© **92-16-22-99** for tickets and information), and the **Grimaldi Forum,** 10 av. Princesse-Grace (© **99-99-30-00** for tickets and information). At both the Salle du Canton and the Grimaldi Forum, ballet tickets cost 8€ to 26€ ($10–$34); concert tickets cost 15€ to 30€ ($20–$39); and opera tickets cost 30€ to 115€ ($39–$150).

If tickets are hard to come by, your best bet is to ask your hotel concierge for assistance. You can also inquire at the **Atrium du Casino** (© **92-16-22-99**), a ticket kiosk and information agency open Tuesday to Sunday 10am to 5:30pm.

DANCING & DRINKING   The Legend, 3 avenue des Spélugues (© **93-50-53-13**), is a favorite of the 25- to 30-year-old crowd who like a glamorous modern setting. It's open Thursday to Sunday from 11:30pm to dawn. Entrance is free. The wildest night is Saturday, when it's mobbed. At **Le Living Room** (© **93-50-80-31**), 7 av. des Spélugues, crowds are international and dance-oriented. It's open every night from 10:30pm until dawn. Cozy and comfortable, it's a bit more formal and sedate than the Legend, attracting patrons over 35. There's no cover. Two nearly neighboring piano bars are **Le Sass-Café,** 5 av. des Spélugues (© **93-25-52-00**), and the **Zebra Square Café,** 10 av. des Spélugues (© **99-99-25-50**). Drink prices start at around 10€ ($13). Toniest of all, and under the same management as the Hôtel de Paris, is **Jimmy's,** in the Sporting d'Eté, av. Princesse-Grace (© **92-16-22-77**) open nightly 11am to 5am.

Newest on the Monte Carlo nightlife scene is **Le Karement,** in the Grimaldi Forum (© **99-99-20-20**). Sprawling, ultra-contemporary, and bigger than any nightlife venue ever before seen in Monte Carlo, it boasts two bars inside, a third bar on an outdoor terrace, a sprawling bay window that encompasses a view of the sea, and the kind of house and garage music that the young and young-at-heart clientele can really dance to. Open nightly, year-round, from 10pm till at least 4am, and often later, if business allows, it charges 20€ ($26) for entrance, including a free drink.

13 Roquebrune ⋆⋆ & Cap-Martin ⋆⋆

953km (592 miles) S of Paris; 5km (3 miles) W of Menton

Roquebrune, along the Grande Corniche, is a charming mountain village with vaulted streets. It has been restored, though some critics have found the restoration "artificial."

Today its rue Moncollet is lined with artists' workshops and boutiques with inflatedly priced merchandise.

Five kilometers (3 miles) west of Menton and 2km (1½ miles) west of Roquebrune, Cap-Martin is a satellite of the larger resort, associated with the rich and famous since Empress Eugénie wintered here in the 19th century. In time the resort was honored by the presence of Sir Winston Churchill, who came here often in his final years. Two famous men died here—William Butler Yeats in 1939 and Le Corbusier, who drowned while swimming off the cape in 1965. Don't think you'll find a wide sandy beach—you'll encounter plenty of rocks, against a backdrop of pine and olive trees.

ESSENTIALS

GETTING THERE   To **drive** to Roquebrune and Cap-Martin from Nice, follow N7 east for 26km (16 miles). Cap-Martin has **train** and bus connections from the other cities on the coast, including Nice and Menton. For **railway** information and schedules, call 𝕔 **08-92-35-35-35.** To reach Roquebrune, you'll have to take a **taxi.** There's no formal station in Roquebrune; you get off on the side of the highway. For bus information, contact the Gare Routière in Menton (𝕔 **04-93-35-93-60**).

VISITOR INFORMATION   The **Office de Tourisme** is at 218 av. Aristide-Briand, Roquebrune (𝕔 **04-93-35-62-87;** www.roquebrune-cap-martin.com). Two-hour walking tours of Roquebrune and St-Martin, each arranged with advance notice by the tourist office, cost 5€ ($6.50) for adults, and 2€ ($2.60) for students and children under 18. Each departs from the tourist office, and each encompasses a running commentary, in both French and English, on the visual and historic attractions of Roquebrune and Cap-Martin.

EXPLORING ROQUEBRUNE

It will take you about an hour to explore the site of this hill village. You can stroll through its colorful covered streets, which still retain their authentic look even though the buildings are now devoted to handicrafts, gift and souvenir shops, or art galleries. From the parking lot at place de la République, you can head for place des Deux-Frères, turning left into rue Grimaldi. Then head left to **rue Moncollet** 𝕏, the town's most interesting street dating back to the 10th century. This long, narrow street is covered with stepped passageways and filled with houses that date from the Middle Ages, most often with barred windows.

Rue Moncollet leads into rue du Château, where you might want to take time to explore the **Château de Roquebrune** 𝕏 (𝕔 **04-93-35-07-22**). The only one of its kind, the château was originally a 10th-century Carolingian castle—the present structure dates in part from the 13th century. Dominated by two square towers, it houses a museum. The towers command a panoramic view along the coast. The interior is open in July and August daily 10am to 12:30pm and 2 to 7:30pm; April to June and September daily 10am to 12:30pm and 2 to 6:30pm; February, March, and October daily 10am to 12:30pm and 2 to 6pm; November to January daily 10am to 12:30pm and 2 to 5pm. Admission is 3.50€ ($4.55) for adults, 2.50€ ($3.25) for seniors, 2.50€ ($3.25) for students and children 7 to 11, free for children under 7.

Rue du Château leads to place William-Ingram. After crossing this square, you reach rue de la Fontaine. Take a left. This will lead you to the **Olivier Millénaire** (millennary olive tree). This olive tree is said to be one of the oldest in the world, having survived for at least 1,000 years.

Back on rue du Château, you can reach the 12th-century **Eglise Ste-Marguerite** (no phone), which hides behind a relatively ordinary baroque facade. The interior is of polychrome plaster. Look for two paintings by a 17th-century local artist, Marc-Antoine Otto—a Crucifixion (the second altar) and a Pietà (above the entrance door). The church is open Monday to Saturday 3 to 5pm, Sunday from 10am to 5pm.

EXPLORING CAP-MARTIN

Cap-Martin is a rich town. At the center of the cape is a feudal tower, used today as a telecommunications relay station. At its base you can still see the ruins of the **Basilique St-Martin,** the only remains of a priory constructed here by the monks of the Lérins Islands in the 11th century. After repeated pirate raids in the 15th century, it was destroyed and abandoned. If you follow the road (by car) along the eastern shoreline of the cape, you'll be rewarded with a view of Menton set against a backdrop of mountains. In the far distance looms the coastline of the Italian Riviera, and you can see as far as the resort of Bordighera.

You can take one of the most interesting walks along the Riviera here, but be aware that it's a 3-hour trek. If you have a car, you can leave it in the parking lot at avenue Winston-Churchill. The coastal path, called **Sentier Touristique** 🞰🞰, leads from Cap-Martin to Monte-Carlo Beach. The path is marked by a sign labeled PROMENADE LE CORBUSIER. As you go along, you can take in a view of Monaco set in a natural amphitheater. In the far distance, you'll see Cap-Ferrat and even Roquebrune, with its château. The scenic path comes to an end at Monte-Carlo Beach.

You can also take a scenic 10km (6-mile) drive that takes about an hour. Leave by D23, following the signs to **Gorbio,** a perched village standing on a hill. Along the way on the narrow, winding road, you'll pass homes of the wealthy in a verdant setting of pines and silvery olives. The site of the village is wild and rocky, the buildings having been constructed as a safe haven from pirate attacks. The most interesting street is **rue Garibaldi,** which leads past an old church to a panoramic belvedere.

WHERE TO STAY

Hôtel Victoria   This rectangular low-rise building is behind a garden in front of the Cap-Martin beach. Built in the 1970s, it was renovated in the mid-1990s in a neoclassical style that weds tradition and modernity. It's the second choice in town for those who can't afford the Vista Palace. Opening onto balconies fronting the sea, each of the midsize rooms is well furnished with contemporary furniture and has a neatly tiled bathroom with shower and tub. The casual bar and lounge sets a stylishly relaxed tone. Breakfast is the only meal served.

7 promenade du Cap, 06190 Roquebrune–Cap-Martin. ℭ **04-93-35-65-90.** Fax 04-93-28-27-02. www.hotelmenton. com/hotel-victoria. 32 units. 88€–102€ ($114–$133) double. AE, DC, V. Parking free outdoors, 9€ ($12) indoors. **Amenities:** Bar; limited room service; laundry service; dry cleaning. *In room:* A/C, TV, minibar.

Hôtel Vista Palace 🞰🞰🞰   This extraordinary hotel and restaurant stands above Cap-Martin on the outer ridge of the mountains running parallel to the coast, giving it a spectacular "airplane view" of Monaco. The design of the Vista Palace is just as fantastic: Three levels are cantilevered out into space so every unit seems to float. Nearly all the rooms have balconies facing the Mediterranean. You stay in *luxe* comfort here in grandly furnished guest rooms, with first-class bathrooms containing tubs and showers.

Grande Corniche, 06190 Roquebrune–Cap-Martin. ℭ **04-92-10-40-00.** Fax 04-93-35-18-94. www.vistapalace.com. 68 units. 210€–400€ ($273–$520) double; 405€–1,200€ ($527–$1,560) suite. AE, DC, V. Parking 20€ ($26).

Amenities: 3 restaurants; bars; outdoor pool; health club; sauna; Jacuzzi; limited room service; massage; babysitting; laundry service; dry cleaning; nonsmoking rooms; limited-mobility rooms. *In room:* A/C, TV, dataport, minibar, hair dryer, safe.

WHERE TO DINE

Au Grand Inquisiteur ⚜ *(Finds* TRADITIONAL FRENCH   This 28-seat restaurant occupies a two-room vaulted cellar near the top of the medieval mountaintop village of Roquebrune. On the steep, winding road to the château, the building is made of rough-cut stone, with large oak beams. The cuisine, though not the area's most distinguished, is good, including the chef's duck special and scallops meunière. Most diners opt for one of the fresh fish choices. Other dishes include stuffed zucchini flowers with morel sauce. The wine list is exceptional—some 150 selections, most at reasonable prices.

18 rue du Château. ℂ **04-93-35-05-37.** Reservations required. Main courses 16€–24€ ($21–$31); fixed-price menu 25€–37€ ($33–$48). AE, MC, V. Wed–Sun noon–1:30pm and 7:30–10pm. Closed June 27–July 4 and mid-Nov to mid-Dec.

Hippocampe TRADITIONAL FRENCH   Opened in 1963, this fine restaurant along the seafront offers a full view of the bay and even the Italian coastline. Made safe by a thick stone wall, its terrace is shaded by five crooked pines. The "Sea Horse" is a stone-and-glass garden house with a tile roof and scarlet-and-pink potted geraniums. Specialties include filets de sole en brioche with hollandaise sauce, coq au vin (chicken cooked in wine), terrine of hogfish and salmon in basil sauce, and galantine duck.

44 av. Winston-Churchill. ℂ **04-93-35-81-91.** Reservations required. Main courses 17€–55€ ($22–$72); fixed-price menus 30€–46€ ($39–$60). AE, DC, MC, V. Tues–Wed and Fri–Sat noon–1:45pm and 7:30–9:30pm; Thurs and Sun noon–1:45pm. Closed Nov 1–Jan 15.

14 Menton ⚜⚜

959km (596 miles) S of Paris; 63km (39 miles) NE of Cannes; 8km (5 miles) E of Monaco

Menton is more Italianate than French. Right at the border of Italy, Menton marks the eastern frontier of the Côte d'Azur. Its climate is the warmest on the Mediterranean coast, and in winter it attracts a large, elderly British colony. The impact of these seniors on the population of 130,000 has earned Menton the sobriquet "the Fort Lauderdale of France."

According to a local legend, Eve was the first to experience Menton's glorious climate. When she and Adam were expelled from the Garden of Eden, she tucked a lemon in her bosom, planting it at Menton because it reminded her of her former stamping grounds. Lemons still grow in profusion here, and the fruit is given a position of honor at the Lemon Festival held over a 2-week period in February. Actually, the oldest Menton visitor might have arrived 30,000 years ago. He's still around—or, at least, his skull is—in the Musée de Préhistoire Régionale (see below).

Don't be misled by all those "palace-hotels" studding the hills. They are no longer hotels—they've been divided up and sold as private apartments. Many of these turn-of-the-20th-century structures were erected to accommodate elderly Europeans, English and German, who arrived carrying a book written by one Dr. Bennett in which he extolled the joys of living at Menton.

ESSENTIALS

GETTING THERE   Many visitors arrive by **car** on one of the corniche roads. The drive on N7 east from Nice takes 45 minutes.

Menton has good **bus** and **rail** connections. Two trains per hour pull in from Nice (trip time: 35 min.; one-way fare: 4.10€/$5.35), and two trains per hour arrive from Monte Carlo (trip time: 10 min.; 1.95€/$2.55 one-way). For rail information and schedules, call ✆ **08-36-35-35-35.** RCA (✆ **04-97-00-07-00** or 04-93-85-64-44) runs buses between Nice, Monte Carlo, and Menton, usually around two per hour; the round-trip fare from Nice is 5.20€ ($6.75).

VISITOR INFORMATION The **Office de Tourisme** is in the Palais de l'Europe, 8 av. Boyer (✆ **04-92-41-76-76;** www.villedementon.com).

SEEING THE SIGHTS

Menton is situated on the Golfe de la Paix (Gulf of Peace) on a rocky promontory that divides the bay in two. The fishing town, the older part with its narrow streets, is in the east; the tourist zone and residential belt are in the west.

The filmmaker, writer, and artist Jean Cocteau liked this resort, and in the **Musée Jean-Cocteau,** Bastion du Port, quai Napoléon-III (✆ **04-93-57-72-30**), you can see his death portrait, sketched by MacAvoy. Some of the artist's memorabilia is here—stunning charcoals and watercolors, brightly colored pastels, ceramics, and signed letters. The museum is open Wednesday through Monday from 10am to noon and 2 to 6pm. Admission is 3€ ($3.90).

At **La Salle des Mariages,** in the Hôtel de Ville (town hall), rue de la République (✆ **04-92-10-50-00**), Cocteau painted frescoes depicting the legend of Orpheus and Eurydice, also the subject of his film *Orphée.* A tape in English helps explain them. The room, with its red-leather seats and leopard-skin rugs, is used for civil marriage ceremonies. It's open Monday to Friday 8:30am to 12:30pm and 1:30 to 5pm. Admission is 1.50€ ($1.95). Advance reservations are necessary.

Musée de Préhistoire Régionale, rue Lorédan-Larchey (✆ **04-92-41-77-70**), presents human evolution on the Côte d'Azur for the past million years. It contains the 25,000-year-old head of the *Nouvel Homme de Menton* (sometimes known as "Grimaldi Man"), found in 1884 in the Baousse-Rousse caves. Audiovisual aids, dioramas, and videocassettes enhance the exhibition. The museum is open Wednesday to Monday 10am to noon and 2 to 6pm. Admission is free.

Musée des Beaux-Arts, Palais Carnoles, 3 av. de la Madone (✆ **04-93-35-49-71**), contains 14th-, 16th-, and 17th-century paintings from Italy, Flanders, Holland, and the French schools, as well as modern paintings by Dufy, Valadon, Derain, and Leprin—all acquired by a British subject, Wakefield-Mori. The museum is open Wednesday to Monday 10am to noon and 2 to 6pm. Admission is free.

A DAY AT THE BEACH

Menton's beaches stretch for 3.2km (2 miles) between the Italian border and the city limits of Roquebrune and are interrupted only by the town's old and new ports. Collectively, they're known as **La Plage de la Promenade du Soleil** and, with rare exceptions, are public and free. Don't expect soft sands or even any sand at all: The beaches are narrow, are covered with gravel (or, more charitably, big pebbles), and are notoriously uncomfortable to lie on. Don't expect big waves or tides, either. Who goes there? In the words of one nonswimming resident, mostly Parisians or residents of northern France, who are grateful for any escape from their urban milieux. Topless bathing is widespread, but complete nudity is forbidden.

Unlike Cannes, where tens of thousands of chaises pepper the beaches, there aren't many options in Menton for renting mattresses and parasols; most people bring their own. Two exceptions are **Le Splendid Plage** (© **04-93-35-60-97**) and **Les Sablettes** (© **04-93-35-44-77**); both charge around 15€ ($20) for use of a mattress. They're immediately to the east of the Vieux Port.

WHERE TO STAY

Hôtel Aiglon *(Kids)*   A nugget along the coast, this hotel is a converted villa. In a large park filled with Mediterranean vegetation, it offers a more intimate environment than any competing hotel in Menton. The rooms come in various shapes and sizes, each well upholstered and containing elegant beds, plus good-size bathrooms with tubs and showers. The magnet of the hotel is a heated pool surrounded by a veranda. The garden setting is beautifully maintained. An excellent Provençal-and-international cuisine is offered with windows opening onto the pool and garden.

7 av. de la Madone, 06500 Menton. © **04-93-57-55-55**. Fax 04-93-35-92-39. www.hotelaiglon.net. 29 units. 86€–165€ ($112–$215) double; 153€–205€ ($199–$267) suite. AE, DC, MC, V. Parking 5€ ($6.50). **Amenities:** Restaurant; bar; outdoor pool; limited room service; babysitting; laundry service; nonsmoking rooms. *In room:* A/C, TV, dataport, minibar, beverage maker, hair dryer, safe.

Hôtel Chambord   This hotel is located on the main square next to the **Casino de Menton,** 1 Avenue Félix Faure (© **04-92-10-16-16**). Built in 1977, with frequent renovations, it is well maintained, with rows of balconies and awnings. The comfortable guest rooms have generous space and are neatly organized, with streamlined modern furniture. Bathrooms are well maintained. Breakfast is the only meal served.

6 av. Boyer, 06500 Menton. © **04-93-35-94-19**. Fax 04-93-41-30-55. www.hotel-chambord.com. 40 units. 100€–115€ ($130–$150) double. AE, MC, V. Parking 10€ ($13). **Amenities:** Lounge. *In room:* A/C, TV, minibar, hair dryer, safe.

Hôtel Le Dauphin   This affable three-star hotel lies just off the beach. The double-insulated rooms are bright and uncluttered, each with a balcony opening onto the mountain range or the sea. Small to medium in size, they are tidily maintained with modern safari-inspired (mahogany) furnishings. The attentive staff is welcoming. Three meals per day are served, featuring many specialties of Provence.

28 av. du Général-de-Gaulle, 06500 Menton. © **04-93-35-76-37**. Fax 04-93-35-31-74. www.hotel-ledauphin.com. 28 units. 60€–90€ ($78–$117) double; 75€–105€ ($98–$137) triple. Rates include continental breakfast. AE, MC, V. Closed Nov 12–Dec 23. **Amenities:** Restaurant; bar; fitness center. *In room:* A/C, TV, minibar, hair dryer, safe.

Hôtel Méditerranée   This white-and-salmon hotel is 3 short blocks from the sea. A raised terrace with a view of the water, chaise longues, and potted plants are on the premises. The rooms are attractively decorated and include private balconies opening onto the sea. Each was renovated in 2005. Most are spacious, with comfortable beds (usually twins). The hotel also has a restaurant, which offers a veranda for dining in fair weather.

5 rue de la République, 06500 Menton. © **04-93-28-25-25**. Fax 04-92-41-81-82. www.hotel-med-menton.com. 89 units. 70€–99€ ($91–$129) double. Children 4 and under stay free in parent's room. AE, DC, MC, V. Parking 7€. **Amenities:** Restaurant; panoramic bar; laundry service; dry cleaning. *In room:* A/C, TV, minibar, hair dryer, safe.

Hôtel Napoléon   This government-rated hotel benefited, early in 2005, from one of the most radical renovations in Menton, a process that added three "Theme-decorated" suites, one of which is dedicated to Jean Cocteau, with many framed representations of his paintings, and amenities that include a small-scale fitness center. It sits on a palm-shaded avenue, just across from a beach, where it maintains a seasonal restaurant, open from May to September, and a scattering of parasols and chaise longues. Some of the public areas might remind you of a large living room. Guest rooms, each with contemporary furniture and vivid colors, have comfortable beds and balconies that overlook either the sea or the old town. Staff members here are particularly attentive and charming.

29 Porte de France, 06503 Menton. ⓒ **04-93-35-89-50.** Fax 04-93-35-49-22. www.napoleon-menton.com. 44 units. 84€–119€ ($109–$155) double; 179€–219€ ($233–$285) suite. AE, DC, MC, V. Free parking. **Amenities:** Bar; lounge; outdoor pool; fitness center; private beach with summer restaurant (May–Sept); babysitting; limited room service; laundry service; dry cleaning; garden. *In room:* A/C, TV, minibar, hair dryer, safe.

Hôtel Princesse et Richmond   At the edge of the sea, this hotel boasts a facade of Mediterranean colors, with a garden terrace. The building is a 1970s-style boxy structure with an angular design. The comfortable, soundproof, midsize rooms have modern and French traditional furnishings and balconies. Most of the average-size bathrooms have tubs and showers. Drinks are served on the roof terrace, where you can enjoy a view of the curving shoreline. A restaurant in the garden of the nearby Hôtel Aiglon, under the same ownership, offers lunch and dinner beside a heated pool you may use as well. The staff organizes sightseeing excursions.

617 promenade du Soleil, 06500 Menton. ⓒ **04-93-35-80-20.** Fax 04-93-57-40-20. www.princess-richmond.com. 46 units. 82€–112€ ($94–$129) double; 145€–185€ ($167–$213) suite. AE, DC, MC, V. Free parking. Closed Nov 3–Dec 16. **Amenities:** Bar; use of outdoor Jacuzzi; exercise room; limited room service; laundry service; dry cleaning; nonsmoking rooms. *In room:* A/C, TV, minibar, hair dryer, safe.

Hotel Riva   This hotel is adjacent to a verdant park, a few steps across the seafront boulevard from the beach. Its design is conservative and angular-looking. It has many of the luxuries and much of the feeling of a hotel you would find along the coast of southern Florida. Its modern design includes lots of balconies and multileveled terraces for sunbathing and drinking cocktails. Bedrooms are small to medium in size but are elegantly furnished with quality mattresses and fine linen. High-quality materials such as marble and granite are used throughout, complementing dignified beechwood furniture. Other than breakfast and brunch, no meals are served, but considering the proximity of many restaurants, no one seems to mind.

600 promenade du Soleil, 06500 Menton. ⓒ **04-92-10-92-10.** Fax 04-93-28-87-87. www.rivahotel.com. 40 units. 86€–115€ ($112–$150) double. AE, DC, MC, V. Parking 9€ ($12). **Amenities:** Bar; lounge; sauna; Jacuzzi; babysitting; laundry service; dry cleaning. *In room:* A/C, TV, minibar, hair dryer, safe.

WHERE TO DINE

Le Bruit Qui Court FRENCH/MEDITERRANEAN   It's been on-site only since 2004, but already rumors *(les bruits qui court)* about the worthiness of this place have spread throughout Menton and its suburbs. The setting is a century-old building adjacent to the sea, with two dining rooms (one on an upstairs floor with a panorama of the sea) and a seafront terrace. Amid a color scheme inspired by the soft pumpkin and ocher tones of Provence, diners can choose from fresh menu items, some of which reflect the traditions of the coastal Mediterranean. The best examples include fried slabs of foie gras served with caramelized apples; grilled scallops served on a bed of braised leeks garnished with pink peppercorns; a *marmite des pêcheurs* (seafood stew) with saffron-flavored tomato sauce; and a very unusual version of Rossini-style tuna steak, cut down the middle and garnished with a slab of foie gras.

31 quai Bonaparte. ⓒ **04-93-35-94-64.** Reservations recommended. Main courses 16€–23€ ($21–$30); set-price menus 22€–35€ ($29–$46). AE, MC, V. Tues–Sun noon–2:30pm and 7–11pm. Closed Jan 10–30.

Petit Port SEAFOOD   Small and charming, with enough Italian overtones to make you believe that you've finally crossed the border, this restaurant occupies a cozy, partially paneled dining room in a century-old house near the medieval port of Menton. Surrounded by nautical accents and oil paintings of the wide blue sea, you'll enjoy a menu that focuses almost exclusively on seafood. Tasty specialties include grilled sardines, fish soup, and many different kinds of grilled fish. The kitchen will prepare the day's catch in whatever way your taste dictates.

4 rue Jonquier, at place Fontana. © **04-93-35-82-62.** Reservations recommended. Main courses 22€–30€ ($29–$39); some shellfish platters 50€ ($65); set menu 20€–30€ ($26–$38). AE, MC, V. Sat–Wed noon–3pm; Fri–Wed 7pm–midnight. Closed Jan 10–31.

Appendix:
Glossary of Useful Terms

It is often amazing how a word or two of halting French will change your hosts' disposition in their home country. At the very least, try to learn a few numbers, basic greetings, and—above all—the life-raft phrase, *Parlez-vous anglais?* ("Do you speak English?"). As it turns out, many people do speak a passable English and will use it liberally, if you demonstrate the basic courtesy of greeting them in their language. Go out, try our glossary, and don't be bashful. *Bonne chance!*

1 Useful French Words & Phrases

English	French	Pronunciation
Yes/No	**Oui/Non**	wee/noh
Okay	**D'accord**	*dah*-core
Please	**S'il vous plaît**	seel voo *play*
Thank you	**Merci**	*mair*-see
You're welcome	**De rien**	duh ree-*ehn*
Hello (during daylight)	**Bonjour**	bohn-*jhoor*
Good evening	**Bonsoir**	bohn-*swahr*
Goodbye	**Au revoir**	o ruh-*vwahr*
What's your name?	**Comment vous appellez-vous?**	kuh-*mahn* voo za-pell-ay-voo?
My name is	**Je m'appelle**	*jhuh* ma-pell
How are you?	**Comment allez-vous?**	kuh-*mahn* tahl-ay-voo?
So-so	**Comme ci, comme ça**	kum-*see,* kum-*sah*
I'm sorry/excuse me	**Pardon**	pahr-*dohn*

GETTING AROUND & STREET SMARTS

English	French	Pronunciation
Do you speak English?	**Parlez-vous anglais?**	par-lay-voo zahn-glay?
I don't speak French	**Je ne parle pas français**	jhuh ne parl pah frahn-*say*
I don't understand	**Je ne comprends pas**	jhuh ne kohm-*prahn* pas
Could you speak more loudly/ more slowly?	**Pouvez-vous parler plus fort/plus lentement?**	Poo-*vay* voo par-lay ploo for/ ploo lan-te-*ment*?
What is it?	**Qu'est-ce que c'est?**	kess kuh *say*?

English	French	Pronunciation
What time is it?	Qu'elle heure est-il?	kel uhr eh-*teel?*
What?	Quoi?	kwah?
How? or What did you say?	Comment?	ko-*mahn?*
When?	Quand?	kahn?
Where is?	Où est?	ooh eh?
Who?	Qui?	kee?
Why?	Pourquoi?	poor-*kwah?*
here/there	ici/là	ee-*see*/lah
left/right	à gauche/à droite	a goash/a drwaht
straight ahead	tout droit	too drwah
Fill the tank (of a car), please	Le plein, s'il vous plaît	luh plan, seel-voo-*play*
I want to get off at	Je voudrais descendre à	jhe voo-*dray* day-son drah-ah
airport	l'aéroport	lair-o-*por*
bank	la banque	lah bahnk
bridge	le pont	luh pohn
bus station	la gare routière	lah gar roo-tee-*air*
bus stop	l'arrêt de bus	lah-*ray* duh boohss
cashier	la caisse	lah *kess*
cathedral	la cathedral	lah ka-tay-*dral*
church	l'église	lay-*gleez*
driver's license	permis de conduire	per-*mee* duh con-*dweer*
elevator	l'ascenseur	lah sahn *seuhr*
exit (from a building or a freeway)	une sortie	ewn sor-*tee*
gasoline	du pétrol/de l'essence	duh pay-*trol*/de lay-*sahns*
hospital	l'hôpital	low-pee-*tahl*
luggage storage	la consigne	lah kohn-*seen*-yuh
museum	le musée	luh mew-*zay*
no smoking	défense de fumer	day-*fahns* de fu-may
one-way ticket	aller simple	ah-*lay* sam-pluh
round-trip ticket	aller-retour	ah-*lay* re-*toor*
second floor	premier étage	prem-ee-*ehr* ay-*taj*
slow down	ralentir	rah-lahn-*teer*
store	le magasin	luh ma-ga-*zehn*
street	rue	roo
subway	le métro	le *máy*-tro
telephone	le téléphone	luh tay-lay-*phone*

English	French	Pronunciation
ticket	**un billet**	uh *bee*-yay
toilets	**les toilettes/les WC**	lay twa-*lets*/les vay-*say*

NECESSITIES

English	French	Pronunciation
I'd like	**Je voudrais**	jhe voo-*dray*
a room	**une chambre**	ewn *shahm*-bruh
the key	**la clé (la clef)**	la clay
How much does it cost?	**C'est combien?/Ça coûte combien?**	say comb-bee-*ehn?*/sah coot comb-bee-*ehn?*
Do you take credit cards?	**Est-ce que vous acceptez les cartes de credit?**	es-kuh voo zaksep-*tay* lay kart duh creh-*dee?*
I'd like to buy	**Je voudrais acheter**	jhe voo-dray ahsh-*tay*
aspirin	**des aspirines**	deyz ahs-peer-*een*
condoms	**des préservatifs**	day pray-ser-va-*teef*
dress	**une robe**	ewn robe
gift	**un cadeau**	uh kah-*doe*
handbag	**un sac**	uh sahk
hat	**un chapeau**	uh shah-*poh*
map of the city	**un plan de ville**	uh plahn de *veel*
newspaper	**un journal**	uh zhoor-*nahl*
phone card	**une carte téléphonique**	ewn cart tay-lay-fone-*eek*
postcard	**une carte postale**	ewn carte pos-*tahl*
road map	**une carte routière**	ewn cart roo-tee-*air*
shoes	**des chaussures**	day show-*suhr*
stamp	**un timbre**	uh *tam*-bruh

IN YOUR HOTEL

English	French	Pronunciation
Are taxes included?	**Est-ce que les taxes sont comprises?**	ess-keh lay taks son com-*preez?*
balcony	**un balcon**	uh bahl-cohn
bathtub	**une baignoire**	ewn bayn-*nwar*
hot and cold water	**l'eau chaude et froide**	low showed ay fwad
Is breakfast included?	**Petit déjeuner inclus?**	peh-*tee* day-jheun-*ay* ehn-*klu?*
room	**une chambre**	ewn *shawm*-bruh
shower	**une douche**	ewn dooch
sink	**un lavabo**	uh la-va-*bow*
suite	**une suite**	ewn sweet
We're staying for . . . days	**On reste pour . . . jours**	ohn rest poor . . . jhoor

NUMBERS & ORDINALS

English	French	Pronunciation
zero	**zéro**	*zare*-oh
one	**un**	oon
two	**deux**	duh
three	**trois**	twah
four	**quatre**	*kaht*-ruh
five	**cinq**	sank
six	**six**	seess
seven	**sept**	set
eight	**huit**	wheat
nine	**neuf**	noof
ten	**dix**	deess
eleven	**onze**	ohnz
twelve	**douze**	dooz
thirteen	**treize**	trehz
fourteen	**quatorze**	kah-*torz*
fifteen	**quinze**	kanz
sixteen	**seize**	sez
seventeen	**dix-sept**	deez-*set*
eighteen	**dix-huit**	deez-*wheat*
nineteen	**dix-neuf**	deez-*noof*
twenty	**vingt**	vehn
thirty	**trente**	trahnt
forty	**quarante**	ka-*rahnt*
fifty	**cinquante**	sang-*kahnt*
one hundred	**cent**	sahn
one thousand	**mille**	meel

THE CALENDAR

English	French	Pronunciation
Sunday	**dimanche**	dee-*mahnsh*
Monday	**lundi**	luhn-*dee*
Tuesday	**mardi**	mahr-*dee*
Wednesday	**mercredi**	mair-kruh-*dee*
Thursday	**jeudi**	jheu-*dee*
Friday	**vendredi**	vawn-druh-*dee*
Saturday	**samedi**	sahm-*dee*
yesterday	**hier**	ee-*air*
today	**aujourd'hui**	o-jhord-*dwee*
this morning/ this afternoon	**ce matin/cet après-midi**	suh ma-*tan*/set ah-preh mee-*dee*

English	French	Pronunciation
tonight	ce soir	suh *swahr*
tomorrow	demain	de-*man*

2 Food, Menu & Cooking Terms

English	French	Pronunciation
I would like to eat	Je voudrais manger	jhe voo-*dray* mahn-*jhay*
Please give me	Donnez-moi, s'il vous plaît	doe-nay-*mwah*, seel voo play
a bottle of	une bouteille de	ewn boo-*tay* duh
a cup of	une tasse de	ewn tass duh
a glass of	un verre de	uh vair duh
a plate of breakfast	une assiette de le petit-déjeuner	ewn ass-ee-*et* duh luh puh-*tee* day-zhuh-*nay*
a cocktail	un apéritif	uh ah-pay-ree-*teef*
the check/bill	l'addition/la note	la-dee-see-*ohn*/la noat
dinner	le dîner	luh dee-*nay*
a knife	un couteau	uh koo-*toe*
a napkin	une serviette	ewn sair-vee-*et*
a spoon	une cuillère	ewn kwee-*air*
Cheers!	A votre santé!	ah vo-truh sahn-*tay!*
fixed-price menu	un menu	uh may-*new*
fork	une fourchette	ewn four-*shet*
Is the tip/service included?	Est-ce que le service est compris?	ess-ke luh ser-*vees* eh com-*pree?*
Waiter!/Waitress!	Monsieur!/ Mademoiselle!	mun-*syuh*/mad-mwa-*zel*
wine list	une carte des vins	ewn cart day *van*
appetizer	une entrée	ewn en-*tray*
tip included	service compris	sehr-*vees* cohm-*pree*
sampling of the chef's best efforts	menu dégustation	may-*new* day-gus-ta-see-*on*

MEATS

English	French	Pronunciation
beef stew	du pot-au-feu	dew poht o *fhe*
marinated beef braised with red wine and served with vegetables	du boeuf à la mode	dew bewf ah lah *mhowd*
chicken	du poulet	*dew poo*-lay

English	French	Pronunciation
rolls of pounded and baked chicken, veal, or fish	des quenelles	day ke-*nelle*
chicken, stewed with mushrooms and wine	du coq au vin	dew cock o vhin
ham	du jambon	dew jahm-*bohn*
lamb	de l'agneau	duh lahn-*nyo*
rabbit	du lapin	dew lah-pan
sirloin	de l'aloyau	duh lahl-why-*yo*
steak	du bifteck	dew beef-*tek*
veal	du veau	dew *voh*

FISH

English	French	Pronunciation
Mediterranean fish soup or stew	de la bouillabaisse	duh lah booh-ya-*besse*
lobster	du homard	dew oh-*mahr*
mussels	des moules	day *moohl*
mussels in herb-flavored white wine with shallots	des moules marinières	day moohl mar-ee-nee-*air*
oysters	des huîtres	dayz hoo-*ee*-truhs
shrimp	des crevettes	day kreh-*vette*
smoked salmon	du saumon fumé	dew sow-mohn fu-*may*
tuna	du thon	dew tohn
trout	de la truite	duh lah tru-*eet*

FRUITS & VEGETABLES

English	French	Pronunciation
eggplant	de l'aubergine	duh loh-ber-*jheen*
grapes	du raisin	dew ray-*zhan*
green beans	des haricots verts	day ahr-ee-coh *vaire*
lemon/lime	du citron/du citron vert	dew cee-tron/dew cee-tron *vaire*
pineapple	de l'ananas	duh lah-na-*nas*
potatoes	des pommes de terre	day puhm duh *tehr*
potatoes au gratin	des pommes de terre dauphinois	day puhm duh tehr doh-feen-wah
french-fried potatoes	des pommes frites	day puhm *freet*

English	French	Pronunciation
spinach	des épinards	dayz ay-pin-*ards*
strawberries	des fraises	day *frez*

SOUPS & SALADS

English	French	Pronunciation
fruit salad	une salade de fruit/ une macédoine de fruits	ewn sah-lahd duh *fwee*/ewn mah-say-doine duh fwee
green salad	une salade verte	ewn sah-lahd *vairt*
lettuce salad	une salade de laitue	ewn sah-lahd duh lay-tew
onion soup	de la soupe à l'oignon	duh lah soop ah low-*nyon*
vegetable soup with basil	de la soupe au pistou	duh lah soop oh pees-tou

BEVERAGES

English	French	Pronunciation
beer	de la bière	duh lah bee-*aire*
milk	du lait	dew *lay*
orange juice	du jus d'orange	dew joo d'or-*ahn*-jhe
water	de l'eau	duh lo
red wine	du vin rouge	dew vhin *rooj*
white wine	du vin blanc	dew vhin *blahn*
coffee (black)	un café noir	uh ka-fay *nwahr*
coffee (with cream)	un café crème	uh ka-fay *krem*
coffee (with milk)	un café au lait	uh ka-fay o *lay*
coffee (decaf)	un café décaféiné (slang: un déca)	un ka-fay day-kah-fay-*nay* (uh *day*-kah)
coffee (espresso)	un café espresso (un express)	uh ka-fay e-*sprehss-o* (un ek-*sprehss*)
tea	du thé	dew *tay*
herbal tea	une tisane	ewn tee-*zahn*

Index

THE NEW TRAVELOCITY GUARANTEE

**EVERYTHING YOU BOOK WILL BE RIGHT, OR WE'LL WORK
WITH OUR TRAVEL PARTNERS TO MAKE IT RIGHT, RIGHT AWAY.**

*To drive home the point,
we're going to use the word "right" in every single sentence.*

Let's get right to it. Right to the meat! Only Travelocity guarantees everything about your booking will be right, or we'll work with our travel partners to make it right, right away. Right on!

Here's a picture taken smack dab right in the middle of Antigua, where the guarantee also covers you.

The guarantee covers all but one of the items pictured to the right.

For example, what if the ocean view you booked actually looks out at a downright ugly parking lot? You'd be right to call – we're there for you. And no one in their right mind would be pleased to learn the rental car place has closed and left them stranded. Call Travelocity and we'll help get you back on the right track.

Now, you may be thinking, "Yeah, right, I'm so sure." That's OK; you have the right to remain skeptical. That is until we mention help is always right around the corner. Call us right off the bat, knowing that our customer service reps are there for you 24/7. Righting wrongs. Left and right.

Now if you're guessing there are some things we can't control, like the weather, well you're right. But we can help you with most things – to get all the details in righting,* visit **travelocity.com/guarantee**.

*Sorry, spelling things right is one of the few things not covered under the guarantee.

I'd give my right arm for a guarantee like this, although I'm glad I don't have to.

travelocity
You'll never roam alone.

IF YOU BOOK IT, IT SHOULD BE THERE.

Only Travelocity guarantees it will be, or we'll work
with our travel partners to make it right, right away.
So if you're missing a balcony or anything else you
booked, just call us 24/7. **1-888-TRAVELOCITY.**

travelocity
You'll never roam alone.